Electronic Discovery and Records and Information Management Guide: Rules, Checklists, and Forms

2013–2014 Edition

Jay E. Grenig
Matthew J. Stippich
Kelly H. Twigger
Browning E. Marean

For Customer Assistance Call 1-800-328-4880

Mat #41295413

e-mail copyright.west@thomsonreuters.com or fax (651) 687-7551

ISBN 978-0-314-61072-0

About the Authors

Jay E. Grenig is a Professor of Law at Marquette University Law School. He has taught at Pepperdine University School of Law, Willamette University College of Law, Vermont Law School, Cornell University School of Industrial and Labor Relations, the University of Southern California Graduate School of Public Administration, Golden Gate University, and Chapman College. Prof. Grenig practiced law in the San Francisco Bay Area for several years. He received a B.A. from Willamette University and a J.D. from the University of California, Hastings College of the Law.

Prof. Grenig is the author or co-author of numerous books and articles, including *Handbook of Federal Civil Discovery and Disclosure* (with Kinsler), *Virginia Practice: Civil Discovery* (with others), *Illinois Practice: Civil Discovery* (with others), *eDiscovery and Digital Evidence* (with Gleisner), *West's Federal Jury Practice and Instructions* (with others), *Alternative Dispute Resolution*, and *West's Federal Forms: District Court*. He is managing editor of *Electronic Discovery and Records Management Quarterly*.

Prof. Grenig is Reporter for the Local Rules Committee for the U.S. District Court for the Eastern District of Wisconsin and a former member of the Wisconsin Judicial Council. He is a member of the American Law Institute, the Working Group on Electronic Document Retention and Production of the Sedona Conference, the College of Labor and Employment Lawyers, ARMA International, AIIM, and the Order of the Coif. He was selected as one of the Wisconsin Leaders in the Law in 2008.

Matthew J. Stippich is a principal, General Counsel and President of Professional Services for Digital Intelligence, Inc., an industry leader in providing digital forensic and eDiscovery equipment, training and services. He advises, implements and performs ESI strategies for clients ranging from emerging growth companies to Fortune 100 companies, law firms and government agencies with a focus on managing costs associated with the preservation, searching and production of ESI as well as internal investigations. Mr. Stippich works extensively with corporate legal and IT teams to develop proactive best-practices for managing ESI issues associated with litigation, employment and security events. Past projects have included developing and implementing ESI strategies in response to SEC and US DOJ investigations of potential FCPA violations across more than 40 countries.

Mr. Stippich Frequently writes and speaks on topics related to e-discovery and digital forensics. He is a Charter Affiliate Member of the Association of Certified E-Discovery Specialists, and is maintains a CEDS certification. He is also a partner in the Milwaukee based law firm of Stippich Selin & Cain, LLC. Mr. Stippich received his J.D. from Marquette University and his undergraduate degree from Grinnell College.

Kelly H. Twigger is the owner of ESI Attorneys, a niche law firm devoted to advising clients on issues in e-discovery, compliance and information management. As a former commercial litigator who understands technology, Kelly bridges the gap between legal, IT and information management professionals to help lawyers and businesses understand their obligations with ESI (electronically stored information) and achieve best practices.

Kelly advises businesses, law firms, lawyers and records managers on how to prepare for e-discovery, including drafting appropriate policies and procedures for implementing legal holds, managing the legal hold process, handling social media, building a data map, and advising on strategy for e-discovery issues in litigation. In addition to her practice, Kelly conducts training for in-house legal departments, records managers and outside counsel around the country in each of these areas. Kelly also serves as e-discovery counsel for her clients, working with law firms, individual lawyers and businesses to devise the most effective strategy for e-discovery in a particular matter and manage the e-discovery processes and practice for a case.

Prior to starting ESI Attorneys, Kelly was a partner in the commercial litigation group at an AmLaw 200 law firm where she managed class action and complex commercial engineering matters. While maintaining a full-time litigation practice, she established the firm's e-discovery practice and grew it to over 25 members of attorneys, litigation support and knowledge management professionals.

Kelly is a nationally recognized speaker and blogger on e-discovery, data mapping and information management issues, and a guest lecturer at Marquette University Law School. She holds a bachelors degree from Washington University in St. Louis and graduated Magna Cum Laude from Marquette University Law School.

Browning E. Marean is a partner in DLA Piper's San Diego office. He is a member of the firm's Litigation Group and is co-chair of the firm's Electronic Discovery Readiness and Response Group. Mr. Marean specializes in the areas of complex business litigation, technology matters, professional responsibility, and knowledge management. He is admitted to practice in California and Texas.

Mr. Marean joined the firm (then Gray Cary Ames & Frye) in 1969. He is a member of DLA Piper's Technology Committee, and is an emeritus member of the California State Bar Law Practice Management Committee. He is a member of the San Diego County Bar Association Ethics Committee and the Sedona Conference.

Mr. Marean is a nationally known teacher and lecturer on various topics including electronic discovery, records retention, knowledge management, and computer technology. Mr. Marean received his law degree from the University of California, Hastings College of the Law, and his undergraduate degree from Stanford University.

Preface

This book provides a comprehensive guide to all aspects of electronic discovery—from records management to spoliation. While reference is made to applicable rules of the Federal Rules of Civil Procedure, the book is intended to provide guidance for discovery in state courts, as well.

Part I examines the nature and sources of electronically stored information, and provides the reader with some background on the rapid development of the law in electronic discovery since the amendments to the Federal Rules of Civil Procedure in 2006. Rules of procedure and best practices applicable to electronically stored information are identified. Additionally, the need to protect electronically stored information and to establish policies governing use of computers are explored in Part I. Part I also includes a section on ethical issues.

The costs of electronic discovery are driving organizations and parties to identify ways to reduce the quantity of information available for discovery. The best way to control this is to manage records and information before discovery becomes an issue. Part II—Preparing for Electronic Discovery—discusses the various steps parties should take to prepare for electronic discovery to reduce costs during litigation, including developing a program on records and information management, understanding records management and its role in the organization, and why parties should consider hiring knowledgeable experts before litigation to reduce risk and save money.

Part III—Managing Electronic Discovery in Litigation—examines the issues in managing eDiscovery, including legal holds, the discovery conference, drafting and responding to written discovery and depositions. The issues relating to obtaining electronic discovery from third-parties are also addressed in Part III.

Part IV looks at electronic discovery from the perspective of the responding party. The critical issues of privilege and spoliation are discussed. Dealing with not reasonably accessible electronically stored information and cost-shifting are also addressed in Part IV, as is the expanding role of utilizing third parties in e-discovery to mitigate risk and cost.

The Guide features more than fifty checklists and over one hundred electronic discovery forms. In addition, the Guide includes the text (including Advisory Committee Notes) for the 2006 and 2007 amendments to the discovery rules of the Federal Rules of Civil Procedure. It also contains the 2007 edition of the Sedona Principles Best Practices Recommendations & Principles for Addressing Electronic Document Production, an examination of the proposed new Rule 502 of the Federal Rules of Evidence governing privilege waiver, and an essential glossary of electronic discovery terms.

The format of the book for this edition has been substantially revised to reflect the way a party approaches electronic discovery—Preparing for it and managing it within litigation. This edition includes more information on the sources of ESI.

The 2013–2014 edition includes recent court decisions. In addition, it includes an expanded discussion of search methodology, predictive coding, analytics and review procedures. It includes an expanded discussion of social media. It also includes a discussion of possible amendments to the Federal Rules of Civil Procedure. There is a helpful discussion of litigation trends, too.

Readers who have suggestions or comments are encouraged to contact the authors at Marquette University Law School, P.O. Box 1881, Milwaukee, WI 53201-1881 (jgrenig@earthlink.net).

Jay E. Grenig
Matthew J. Stippich
Kelly H. Twigger
Browning E. Marean

Milwaukee, Wisconsin
August 2013

Table of Contents

PART I. INTRODUCTION

CHAPTER 1. E-DISCOVERY

I. GUIDELINES

II. CHECKLISTS

III. FORMS

CHAPTER 2. RULES OF PROCEDURE, BEST PRACTICES AND CASE LAW UPDATE

I. GUIDELINES

II. CHECKLISTS

III. FORMS

CHAPTER 3. PROTECTING ELECTRONICALLY STORED INFORMATION

I. GUIDELINES

CHAPTER 5. DEVELOPING RECORDS AND INFORMATION MANAGEMENT PROGRAMS

I. GUIDELINES

II. CHECKLISTS

CHAPTER 6. UNDERSTANDING RECORDS MANAGEMENT

I. GUIDELINES

II. FORMS

CHAPTER 7. DESTROYING ELECTRONICALLY STORED INFORMATION AND PAPER RECORDS

I. GUIDELINES

II. CHECKLISTS

III. FORMS

PART III. E-DISCOVERY IN LITIGATION

CHAPTER 8. USING THIRD PARTIES IN E-DISCOVERY

I. GUIDELINES

II. FORMS

CHAPTER 9. PRESERVATION AND LEGAL HOLDS

I. GUIDELINES

II. CHECKLISTS

III. FORMS

CHAPTER 10. DISCOVERY AND DISCLOSURE

I. GUIDELINES

II. CHECKLISTS

III. FORMS

CHAPTER 11. DISCOVERY CONFERENCES

I. GUIDELINES

II. CHECKLISTS

III. FORMS

CHAPTER 12. DEPOSITIONS

I. GUIDELINES

II. CHECKLISTS

III. FORMS

CHAPTER 13. INTERROGATORIES

I. GUIDELINES

II. CHECKLISTS

III. FORMS

CHAPTER 14. REQUESTS FOR PRODUCTION AND INSPECTION

I. GUIDELINES

II. CHECKLISTS

III. FORMS

PART IV. MISCELLANEOUS

CHAPTER 15. REQUESTS FOR ADMISSIONS

I. GUIDELINES

II. CHECKLISTS

III. FORMS

CHAPTER 16. DISCOVERY FROM NON-PARTIES OF ELECTRONICALLY STORED INFORMATION

I. GUIDELINES

II. CHECKLISTS

III. FORMS

CHAPTER 17. PRIVILEGE AND PRIVACY

I. GUIDELINES

A. INTRODUCTION

B. STATUTES PROTECTING ELECTRONICALLY STORED INFORMATION

C. WORK PRODUCT

D. PRIVILEGES

E. LEGAL HOLD NOTICES

F. FIFTH AMENDMENT

G. INADVERTENT PRODUCTION

II. CHECKLISTS

III. FORMS

Part I

INTRODUCTION

Chapter 1

E-Discovery

I. GUIDELINES

II. CHECKLISTS

III. FORMS

Research References

A.L.R. Library

ABA Discovery Standards, http://www.abanet.org/litigation/discoverystandards/2005civildiscoverystandards.pdf Admissibility of computerized private business records, 7 A.L.R.4th 8

Treatises and Practice Aids

Grenig and Gleisner, eDiscovery & Digital Evidence §§ 6:10 to 6:12

Additional References

Grenig & Kinsler, Handbook of Federal Civil Discovery and Disclosure §§ 13.1 to 13.6 (3d ed.)
E-Discovery Institute, http://www.ediscoveryinstitute.org/founders.html
Electronic Discovery Reference Model Project, www.edrm.net
The Sedona Conference, www.thesedonaconference.org

KeyCite®: Cases and other legal materials listed in KeyCite Scope can be researched through the KeyCite service on Westlaw®. Use KeyCite to check citations for form, parallel references, prior and later history, and comprehensive citator information, including citations to other decisions and secondary materials.

I. GUIDELINES

§ 1:1 Generally

Today most information is stored electronically. The growth in electronically stored information and the variety of systems or devices for creating and storing such information has been dramatic. This creates significant issues for discovery as electronically stored information may exist in dynamic databases and other forms very different from paper documents.[1] Because nearly all information is stored electronically, this means nearly all discovery of documents—whether produced in electronic form or paper form—involves the discovery of electronically stored information.

Discovery and disclosure of electronically stored information pose many of the same problems as discovery and disclosure of paper documents, but they also pose additional problems. The volume, number of storage locations, and volatility of electronically stored information are significantly greater than those of paper documents. Electronically stored information contains nontraditional types of data including metadata, system data, and deleted data. Furthermore, the costs of locating, reviewing, and preparing electronically stored information for production may be greater than in conventional discovery proceedings.[2]

Discovery of electronically stored information also has advantages over paper-based discovery.[3] Costs of photocopying and transport can be much lower, and frequently nonexistent in e-discovery. Reviewing and organizing evidence using various forms of computer manipulation can be less expensive than in paper-based discovery. The cost of using a litigation support system is greatly reduced if the documents are in electronic form from the beginning.

This Guide takes a proactive approach to discovery of electroni-

---

[Section 1:1]

[1]See Ball, *Piecing Together the E-Discovery Plan*, Trial, June 2008 ("The problem is, e-discovery is not simple. It's complex, technical, and tricky. There are no shortcuts—no form, checklist, or script that's going to get the defendant to find the relevant information and turn it over in a reasonably usable way.").

[2]A study by the Federal Judicial Center released in March 2010 found that plaintiffs who requested and produced electronically stored information reported approximately 48 percent higher costs. For each dispute over electronically stored information, a party had approximately 10 percent higher costs. http://www.fjc.gov/public/pdf.nsf/lookup/costciv1.pdf/$file/costciv1.pdf. See also Bronstad, E-Discovery Crushing Costs, Nat'l L. J., Jan. 30, 2012, at 1; Brown, *Reining in E-Discovery,* LITIG., Summer 2011, at 18; Malloy, *Firms Report Less Litigation, Higher Costs; Express Concern Over E-Discovery Spending*, 80 U.S.L.W. 535 (Oct. 24, 2011); Degnan, *Accounting for the Costs of Electronic Discovery*, 12 MINN. J.L. SCI. & TECH. 151 (2011); Note, *Using Computer Forensics to Enhance the Discovery of Electronically Stored Information*, 7 U. ST. THOMAS L.J. 727 (2010); Note, *Discovery in the Paperless World: How Speed and Ease of Technology Has Slowed and Complicated the Process*, 14 SMU SCI. & TECH. L. REV. 159 (2010).

[3]See Mason, *"Show Me the Money . . . or Not!" How Can You Save Money on E-Discovery,* NAT'L L. J., Dec. 20, 2010, at 17; Maddox, *Effective e-Discovery on a Small-Firm Budget,* THE YOUNG LAWYER, Nov. 2010.

cally stored information—proper planning in advance of possible discovery can greatly reduce the costs and burden of complying with discovery requests. Thus, initial emphasis is given to records management. Records and information management (RIM) is important for both plaintiffs and defendants.

The Guide recognizes that issues relating to the discovery of electronically stored information arise in state and federal court, as well as in administrative proceedings. While specific references are made to the amendments to the Federal Rules of Civil Procedure, the discussion in the Guide includes e-discovery in state and federal courts.

While discovery is frequently thought of (and written about) as though it is the plaintiff that is discovering information in the possession of the defendant, in actual practice plaintiffs can also be the target of discovery requests by defendants. The Guide addresses e-discovery from the perspectives of both producing and responding parties—whether plaintiffs or defendants.

§ 1:2 Electronically stored information

"Electronically stored information" (frequently referred to as "ESI") has a very broad meaning. The Uniform Rules Relating to the Discovery of Electronically Stored Information states that "electronically stored information" is "information stored in an electronic medium and is retrievable in perceivable form." Electronically stored information comprises all current types of computer-based information, and it encompasses future changes and developments. Electronically stored information may be found in databases having no counterpart in hard copy materials.

The ordinary operation of computers—including turning a computer on and off or accessing a particular file—can alter or destroy electronically stored information. Computer systems automatically discard or overwrite as part of their routine operation. Computers can create information without the operator's direction or awareness—something that cannot be done with paper documents. Although electronically stored information may be deleted, it continues to exist, but in forms often difficult to locate, retrieve or search. Electronically stored information may be incomprehensible when it is separated from the system creating it. These distinctive features of e-discovery can often increase the expense and burden of discovery.

In *Zubulake v. UBS Warburg LLC*,[1] District Judge Scheindlin divided electronically stored information into two broad categories:

1. Data kept in an accessible format, broken down into three subcategories, listed in order from most accessible to least accessible:
   a. Active, online data, such as hard drives
   b. Near-line data, such as optical disks
   c. Offline storage/archives lacking the coordinated control of an intelligent disk subsystem
2. Electronic data that are relatively inaccessible, broken down into two subcategories, ranked in order of accessibility:
   a. Backup tapes
   b. Erased, fragmented or damaged data

§ 1:3 Locations and sources of electronically stored information

Electronically stored information can be found in a wide range of locations and sources, including individual desktop computers, laptop computers, network hard drives, removable media, servers, backup tapes or other storage media, personal digital assistants, cellular telephones, Internet websites, paging devices, GPS navigation systems, thumb drives, MP3 players, DVDs, photocopiers, audiotapes, videotapes, and voice mail.[1] Even automobiles may contain "black boxes" with electronically stored information.[2]

§ 1:4 Volume of electronically stored information

Not only is there more electronically stored information than there are paper documents, electronically stored information is

---

[Section 1:2]

[1]Zubulake v. UBS Warburg LLC, 217 F.R.D. 309, 324, 91 Fair Empl. Prac. Cas. (BNA) 1574 (S.D. N.Y. 2003).

[Section 1:3]

[1]See, e.g., Cohen v. City of New York, 255 F.R.D. 110 (S.D. N.Y. 2008) (subpoena for videotapes of plaintiff's arrest upheld); Smith v. Cafe Asia, 246 F.R.D. 19, 102 Fair Empl. Prac. Cas. (BNA) 155, 90 Empl. Prac. Dec. (CCH) ¶ 43044 (D.D.C. 2007) (ordering plaintiff to preserve graphic images stored on cell phone).

[2]See Slagle & Yee, *The Black Box*, TIPS AUTO. LAW COMMITTEE NEWSLETTER, Spring 2008, at 5; Gritzinger, *Black Box on Board*, AUTOWEEK, Sept. 22, 2008, at 22; Erfle, *Learning How to Live with Electronic Data Recorders*, THE BRIEF, Fall 2008, at 14.

created at much greater rates than paper documents. Consequently, the amount of information available for potential discovery has greatly increased with the advent of electronically stored information.

Electronically stored information is being generated constantly and at unprecedented levels.[1] This rapid growth in electronically stored information is due in part to the massive numbers of mobile and Internet-connected devices now in use.[2] In 2000, all new data created globally totaled about 2 million terabytes.[3] In 2011, 1.8 zettabytes (1.8 trillion gigabytes) was generated worldwise.[4] Obviously, records management programs are essential to dealing with this rapidly increasing volume of electronically stored information.

§ 1:5 Persistence of electronically stored information

Electronically stored information is more difficult to dispose of than paper documents. While a shredded paper document is usually irretrievably lost, disposal of electronically stored information is much different. Deleting electronically stored information normally does not actually erase the information from the computer's storage devices. When deleting, the computer simply finds the information's entry in the disk director and changes it to a "not used" status.

When electronically stored information is deleted, the computer can write over the deleted information. Until the computer writes over the deleted information, the information can be recovered by searching the disk itself rather than the disk's directory. Electronically stored information may be recoverable long after the information has been deleted.

§ 1:6 Dynamic nature of electronically stored information

Unlike paper documents, electronically stored information has

---

[Section 1:4]

[1]See Big Data & Storage: The Impact Rapidly Increasing Data Growth Has on Data Centers, PC Today, Dec. 2012, at 12. See also Ingram, Data Aren't Going to Organize Themselves, Nat'l L. J., Dec. 3, 2012, at 13.

[2]See Big Data & Storage: The Impact Rapidly Increasing Data Growth Has on Data Centers, PC Today, Dec. 2012, at 12.

[3]See Big Data & Storage: The Impact Rapidly Increasing Data Growth Has on Data Centers, PC Today, Dec. 2012, at 12.

[4]See Big Data & Storage: The Impact Rapidly Increasing Data Growth Has on Data Centers, PC Today, Dec. 2012, at 12.

dynamic content likely to change over time, even without human intervention. Workflow systems automatically update files and transfer electronically stored information from one location to another. Web pages are constantly updated with information fed from other applications. E-mail systems reorganize and remove electronically stored information automatically. Merely accessing or moving electronically stored information can change it.

§ 1:7 Electronically stored information and metadata

Unlike paper, electronically stored information contains metadata.[1] Metadata are information about the document or file recorded by the computer to assist the computer, and often the user, in storing and retrieving the document or file at a later date. Metadata may be useful for the system administration, as they provide information regarding the generation, handling, transfer, and store of the electronically stored information. However, metadata can reveal more than is apparent from the document itself.

§ 1:8 Environmental dependence and obsolescence of electronically stored information

Electronically stored information, unlike information on paper, may be incomprehensible when separated from its environment. If the raw data in a database are produced without the underlying structure, the raw data will appear as a long list of undefined numbers of characters. To make sense of the raw data, the viewer needs the context including labels, columns, report formats, and other information.

§ 1:9 Dispersal and searchability of electronically stored information

While paper documents are often kept in a relatively small number of boxes or filing cabinets, electronically stored information can reside in multiple locations, such as desktop hard drives, laptop computers, network servers, floppy disks, backup tapes, flash drives, photocopiers, the "cloud," and thumb drives. In many cases, it may be much easier and less expensive to copy electronically stored information. It may also be easier to search and orga-

---

[Section 1:7]

[1]See Bennett & Cloud, *Coping with Metadata: Ten Key Steps*, 61 MERCER L. REV. 471 (2010).

nize electronically stored information compared with the manual alternatives.[1]

§ 1:10 Cloud computing

"Cloud computing" results in further dispersal of electronically stored information. "Cloud computing" is the use of the Internet or the numerous servers around the world to store or access documents.[1] When a person says electronically stored information is stored in the cloud, the person means the file or application lives on a server or servers accessed over an Internet connection, by means of a Web browser or an application, rather than on local devices such as a computer, netbook, or smartphone.[2] While the phrase "cloud computing" is somewhat new, the concept is not. Since the inception of computer based information, users have used third-party computer systems to store information and data.

Cloud-based servers permit many users to view, comment on, and edit the same material. Cloud-based products and services store and share files, keep data on all devices synchronized, and perform tasks such as word processing or editing files.[3] Some products provide hybrid cloud and local services. For example SugarSync and Dropbox back up selected folders to the Web and synchronize them to the hard disks on the user's computer.[4]

Five reasons have been suggested why cloud-based technology should be adopted:

- Cloud-based technology provides higher standard of protection than most law firms can provide with on-premise solutions.

[Section 1:9]

[1]See, e.g., In re Bristol-Myers Squibb Securities Litigation, 205 F.R.D. 437, 51 Fed. R. Serv. 3d 1212 (D.N.J. 2002). See also MANUAL FOR COMPLEX LITIG. (Fourth) § 11.446.

[Section 1:10]

[1]See Brady, When the Cloud Turns Dark: A Tale of Data Held Hostage, 81 U.S.L.W 1197 (Feb. 2, 2013); *Private Cloud Computing*, PC TODAY, June 2013, at 8; Comment: Electronic Discovery: The Challenge of Reaching into the Cloud, 52 SANTA CLARA L. REV. 1561 (2012); Bohorquez Jr. & Rodriguez, *How to Keep the "Cloud" from Bursting in Litigation*, Nat'l L. J., Dec. 20, 2010; at 13. See also Heads in the Cloud, ABA J., May 2013, at 30 (30.7% of respondents question in 2013 said they had used Web-based software).

[2]Mossberg, *Learning About Everything Under the "Cloud,"* WALL STREET J., May 6, 2010, at D1. See, e.g., www.hotmail.com; www.yahoomail.com.

[3]See, e.g., www.google.com/google-d-s/documents/.

[4]See, e.g., www.dropbox.com; www.sugarsynch.com.

- Cloud-based technology provides a higher standard of communication privacy than e-mail.
- Cloud-based technology is more economical than maintenance, upgrades and traditional licenses.
- Cloud-based data are easily accessible yet secure.
- The cloud-based technology "less is more" approach to features so you worry less about learning it and focus more on your practice.[5]

In choosing a cloud storage system, consideration should be given to whether the cloud changes stored documents and whether documents can be retrieved and read when needed.

- Does the cloud change document systems dates when it is moved or copied into the cloud?
- What platforms (e.g., Mac or Microsoft) are supported by the cloud?
- Can documents stored in the cloud be read from a mobile device?
- Can documents be read when not connected to the Internet?
- Is the cloud secure?[6]

State and federal privacy and data security law requirements may be implicated in storing data with a cloud provider. Data owners must ensure that their third-party service providers are capable of maintaining the privacy and security of personal information entrusted to them.[7] The General Services Administration has posted a comprehensive set of security requirements designed to expedite the certification and accreditation process for federal agencies looking to take advantage of cloud computing.[8]

§ 1:11 Social Media

Social Media refers generally to cloud based "communities"

---

[5]See www.goclio.com/resources/white_papers/Why%20Go%20Cloud%20-%20Five%20Reasons%20Why%20Lawyers%20Should%20Adopt%20Cloud-based%20Technology.pdf.

[6]Comments of E. Rooke, of Denver, Colorado, on milogroup listserve. See also Barnes, *Putting a Lock on Cloud-Based Information*, INFORMATIONMGT., July/Aug. 2010, at 26; Blair, *Governance for Protecting Information in the Cloud, at* www.arma.org/HotTopic/HotTopic910.pdf. See Berson, *Safe in the Cloud? Online Service Risks Need Care and Coverage*, ABA J., Nov. 2011, at 28; Share, *Seven Cautions to Consider While Courting the Cloud*, 80 U.S.L.W. 527 (Oct. 25, 2011).

[7]See Sotto, et al., *Privacy and Data Security Risks in Cloud Computing*, U.S.L.W., 2741 (Feb. 16, 2010).

[8]See http://cio.gov/pages-nonnews.cfm/page/federal-risk-and-authorization-management-program-fedramp.

where individuals communicate and exchange information. Facebook, Twitter, LinkedIn, Google+ and Instagram are all examples of social media sites that may contain relevant ESI. While much of the communication on social media sites may be personal in nature, there is an increasing presence of corporate entities on social media. Businesses encourage their employees to establish a presence and expand their "brand" through these social media sites.

Social media generally has the following characteristics:[1] Shared, Interactive, Internet based, Personal and Informal.

Social media presents some unique preservation issues, both from a data management perspective as well as preservation in the event of a litigation hold. On many social media sites, the end user may have a limited ability to remove content that has been previously posted. This poses a real challenge of control for corporate users of social media. In some situations, this may also pose a challenge when trying to "preserve" a social media source for litigation hold purposes.

§ 1:12 Mobile Devices

Mobile devices are an ever increasing source of potentially responsive ESI that should not be overlooked. This includes smart phones, netbooks and handheld computing devices (iPad, Samsung Galaxy, etc.). It is common for users to access email and documents on these devices on a daily basis, thus causing these devices to contain the best and most reliable source of ESI.

§ 1:13 Unified communications

The integration of all communications, including voice and data, over the Internet is becoming more common. Organizations use unified communication to save costs and enhance collaboration. Unified communications result in traditional telephone service, including voice mail, being converted into wave (audio) files. Wave files can be difficult to search because they are audio files with no actual text information.

Unified communications can create e-discovery problems. For example, it can be an expensive challenge to convert audio files to text, accurately recognizing the voice on the file.

[Section 1:11]

[1]See Primer on Social Media: The Sedona Conference (October 2012), https://thesedonaconference.org/publication/Primer%20on%20Social%20Media.

§ 1:14 Stages of e-discovery

The stages of e-discovery can be summarized as follows:[1]

- *Records and Information Management ("RIM").* RIM involves controlling and managing electronically stored information from its creation through its destruction.
- *Identification.* In the identification stage, parties locate potential sources of electronically stored information and determine its scope, breadth, and depth.
- *Preservation.* Preservation ensures that electronically stored information is protected against inappropriate alteration or destruction.
- *Collection.* During the collection stage, electronically stored information is gathered for use in processing, reviewing, and analyzing.
- *Processing.* Processing involves reducing the volume of electronically stored information and converting it, if necessary, to forms suitable for review and analysis.
- *Review.* Electronically stored information is evaluated for relevance and privilege during the review stage.
- *Analysis.* In the analysis stage, electronically stored information is examined for content and context, including key patterns, topics, people, and discussion.
- *Production.* The production stage involves delivering electronically stored information to others in appropriate forms and using appropriate delivery methods.
- *Presentation.* The display of electronically stored information in native and near-native forms before audiences during such events as depositions, hearings, and trial occurs during the presentation stage. At this stage, further information may be elicited, existing facts or positions can be validated, and the appropriate audience may be persuaded.

§ 1:15 Reducing costs of e-discovery

With proper planning, it is possible to reduce the cost of e-discovery.[1] The implementation of a proper records and information management policy—including retention and destruction

---

[Section 1:14]

[1]See EDRMG.net/resources.

[Section 1:15]

[1]See Sadaka, <What> <You> <Should> <About> <Metadata>, TRIAL, Jan. 2012, at 44; Shetterly, *Five Tips for Saving Money on E-Discovery*, CORPORATE COMPLIANCE INSIGHTS, Feb. 20 & 21, 2012, at http://www.corporatecompliancein

policies is essential.[2] Enterprises should work with legal counsel and information technology staff to develop a plan for how to produce documents quickly and efficiently.[3] This may include preparation of a data map.

Building a team of information technology personnel trained in e-discovery and experienced e-discovery lawyers is essential.[4] Understand which e-discovery functions can be performed with technology and which functions require humans involvement.[5] Finally, put a person knowledgeable in the law and technology in charge of e-discovery efforts.[6]

§ 1:16 Ethics and sanctions—Generally

Attorneys and their clients have significant responsibilities for properly identifying, searching for, collecting and producing electronically stored information.[1] For the discovery system to function, attorneys and clients must work together to ensure that both understand how and where electronically stored information is maintained and to determine how best to locate, review, and

---

sights.com/?s=shetterly; Sharp, *New Trends Shape Ediscovery Protocols*, CORPORATE COMPLIANCE INSIGHTS, Dec. 20, 2011 at http://www.corporatecomplianceinsights.com/new-trends-shape-ediscovery-protocols/.

[2]Shetterly, *Five Tips for Saving Money on E-Discovery*, CORPORATE COMPLIANCE INSIGHTS, Feb. 20, 2012, at http://www.corporatecomplianceinsights.com/?s=shetterly.

[3]Shetterly, *Five Tips for Saving Money on E-Discovery*, CORPORATE COMPLIANCE INSIGHTS, Feb. 20, 2012, at http://www.corporatecomplianceinsights.com/?s=shetterly. See Brown, *Reining in E-Discovery*, LITIG., Summer 1981, at 18 ("Understanding your client's information storage and retrieval system is critical to using the federal rules effectively and to convincing a judge to rein in an unreasonable e-discovery request.").

[4]Shetterly, *Five Tips for Saving Money on E-Discovery*, CORPORATE COMPLIANCE INSIGHTS, Feb. 21, 2012, at http://www.corporatecomplianceinsights.com/?s=shetterly.

[5]Shetterly, *Five Tips for Saving Money on E-Discovery*, CORPORATE COMPLIANCE INSIGHTS, Feb. 21, 2012, at http://www.corporatecomplianceinsights.com/?s=shetterly.

[6]Shetterly, *Five Tips for Saving Money on E-Discovery*, CORPORATE COMPLIANCE INSIGHTS, Feb. 21, 2012, at http://www.corporatecomplianceinsights.com/?s=shetterly.

[Section 1:16]

[1]See generally Goehler, et al., Technology Traps for Litigators in a 24/7 Online World, Litig., Winter 2010, at 34; Bassett, E-Pitfalls: Ethics and E-Discovery, 36 N. Ky. L. Rev. 449 (2009); Note: The Ethical Dilemma of Scrubbing Metadata: The Pathway to a Better Approach, 36 N. Ky. L. Rev. 611 (2009); Bennett, The Ethics of Legal Outsourcing, 36 N. Ky. L. Rev. 479 (2009).

produce responsive documents. The courts will not accept ignorance on the part of either as an excuse.[2]

Various types of discovery abuse have resulted in sanctions imposed on parties and their attorneys.[3] Sanctions have been imposed using a number of theories, including negligence,[4] intentional deception,[5] purposeful sluggishness,[6] gross negligence,[7] and reckless disregard.[8]

Fed. R. Civ. Proc. 11, 26(g) and 37 provide for sanctions for discovery-related misconduct. Courts also have the inherent power to assess sanctions. In order to assess attorney's fees pursuant to its inherent power, a district court must find a party or attorney "acted in bad faith, vexatiously, wantonly, or for oppressive reasons."[9] There is a split among the circuits as to whether sanctions, other than attorney's fees, may be imposed against at-

---

[2]Qualcomm Inc. v. Broadcom Corp., 2008 WL 66932 (S.D. Cal. 2008), vacated in part on other grounds, 88 U.S.P.Q.2d 1169, 2008 WL 638108 (S.D. Cal. 2008); Phoenix Four, Inc. v. Strategic Resources Corp., 2006 WL 1409413 (S.D. N.Y. 2006).

[3]See, e.g., Metropolitan Opera Ass'n, Inc. v. Local 100, Hotel Employees and Restaurant Employees Intern. Union, 212 F.R.D. 178, 171 L.R.R.M. (BNA) 2897 (S.D. N.Y. 2003), adhered to on reconsideration, 175 L.R.R.M. (BNA) 2870, 2004 WL 1943099 (S.D. N.Y. 2004) (imposing sanctions for defendant's various and serious failings during discovery relating to electronic records).

[4]See, e.g., Finley v. Hartford Life and Acc. Ins. Co., 249 F.R.D. 329 (N.D. Cal. 2008) (defendant's failure to make initial disclosure of full version of surveillance video subject to sanction; sanctioning defendant's attorneys for failure to make reasonable inquiry concerning missing portion of surveillance video requested by plaintiff not warranted).

[5]See Qualcomm Inc. v. Broadcom Corp., 2008 WL 66932 (S.D. Cal. 2008), .

[6]In re Seroquel Products Liability Litigation, 244 F.R.D. 650 (M.D. Fla. 2007) (sanctions imposed on drug manufacturer for failing to meet its own commitments regarding electronic discovery in multi-district products liability suit).

[7]Phoenix Four, Inc. v. Strategic Resources Corp., 2006 WL 1409413 (S.D. N.Y. 2006) (imposing sanctions on defendants' counsel for failure to search computer workstations for relevant electronic records and for late production of documents).

[8]United Medical Supply Co., Inc. v. U.S., 77 Fed. Cl. 257 (2007) (sanctions against government were warranted where government repeatedly violated its obligation to maintain relevant records after it had knowledge of contractor's claim, and misrepresented its efforts to locate responsive documents and to prevent further spoliation).

[9]Chambers v. NASCO, Inc., 501 U.S. 32, 45–46, 111 S. Ct. 2123, 115 L. Ed. 2d 27, 19 Fed. R. Serv. 3d 817 (1991).

torneys or parties under the inherent-powers doctrine in the absence of bad faith.[10]

In *Qualcomm, Inc. v. Broadcom Corp.*,[11] a magistrate judge imposed sanctions of $8,568,633 against Qualcomm based on Qualcomm's intentional failure to produce over 46,000 responsive e-mails and other discovery misconduct, ordered certain in-house and former outside counsel to participate in a comprehensive "Case Review and Enforcement of Discovery Obligations" program to create a case management protocol that would serve as a model for future litigants, and referred investigation of possible ethical violations to the California State Bar. Rejecting a claim of inadvertence, the magistrate judge found that Qualcomm had failed to conduct basic searches for electronic documents. The court in *Qualcomm* relied on a "reckless" standard in concluding sanctions were appropriate under the court's inherent power.[12]

§ 1:17 Ethics and sanctions—Cloud computing

Ethical issues relating to lawyers storing files in the cloud have been the subject of several ethics opinions. An Alabama ethics opinion states that Alabama lawyers may outsource the storage of client files through cloud computing.[1] Recognizing a lawyer cannot guarantee confidentiality will never be breached, the Eth-

---

[10]Bad faith required: Youn v. Track, Inc., 324 F.3d 409, 55 Fed. R. Serv. 3d 611, 2003 FED App. 0087P (6th Cir. 2003); In re Mroz, 65 F.3d 1567, Bankr. L. Rep. (CCH) ¶ 76678, 32 Fed. R. Serv. 3d 1244 (11th Cir. 1995). Bad faith not required: Republic of Philippines v. Westinghouse Elec. Corp., 43 F.3d 65 (3d Cir. 1994); Harlan v. Lewis, 982 F.2d 1255 (8th Cir. 1993). See also U.S. v. Seltzer, 227 F.3d 36 (2d Cir. 2000) (distinguishing between misconduct undertaken as a zealous advocate on behalf of a client, which requires showing of bad faith before sanctions may be imposed, and misconduct undertaken merely as an officer of the court but not on behalf of client).

[11]Qualcomm Inc. v. Broadcom Corp., 2008 WL 66932 (S.D. Cal. 2008).

[12]Qualcomm Inc. v. Broadcom Corp., 2008 WL 66932 (S.D. Cal. 2008).

[Section 1:17]

[1]Ala. State Bar Disciplinary Comm'n, Op. 2010-02 (2010) (http://www.alabar.org/ogc/fopDisplay.cfm?oneId=425). Accord See also ABA Proposed Rules on Outsourcing at http://tinyurl.com/LNF11-Outso) (storing data in the cloud is permissible, but client confidences must be preserved); Arizona Ethics Op. 09-04 (2009) (http://www.myazbar.org/Ethics/opinionview.cfm?id=704); (http://ethics.calbar.ca.gov/LinkClick.aspx?fileticket=wmqECiHp7h4%3d&tabid=837); Nev. Ethics Op. 33 (2006) (http://64.77.93.72/sites/default/files/opinion_33.pdf); NY Bar Comm. on Prof. Ethics Opinion 842 (http://tinyurl.com/LNF11-NY); NC Bar 2011 Proposed Formal Ethics Opinion 6 (http://tinyurl.com/LNF11-NC) (using the Internet to transmit and store client information presents significant challenges; lawyers must protect against security weaknesses unique to the Internet including those found in their own law offices); Penn. Bar Ass'n Committee on

ics Commission said the duty of reasonable care owed to the client requires a lawyer to become knowledgeable about how the provider will handle the storage and security of the data being stored and to reasonably ensure the provider will abide by a confidentiality agreement in handling the data.

§ 1:18 Ethics and sanctions—ABA model rules of professional Conduct

The American Bar Association's Commission on Ethics 20/20 is examining technology's impact on the legal profession, including confidentiality-related concerns that arise from lawyers' increasing transmission and storage of electronic information.[1] One of the Commission's objectives is to determine what guidance to offer to lawyers who want to ensure that their use of technology complies with their ethical obligations to protect clients' confidential information.

The Commission has proposed revisions to comments in existing rules in the ABA Model Rules of Professional Conduct identifying factors lawyers need to consider when retaining outside lawyers to work on client matters, and affirming that a client's informed consent should be obtained before outside lawyers are retained. The Commission has also proposed revisions to the Model Rules recognizing that electronically stored information, including metadata, is material subject to confidentiality rules. It also proposed revisions directing lawyers to make reasonable efforts to prevent inadvertent disclosure of information relating to representation of a client.

§ 1:19 Stages in responding to e-discovery requests—Generally

A response to an e-discovery request is not that different from a response to a standard document request. The responding party

---

Legal Ethics and Prof. Responsibility, Formal Op. 2011.200 (http://www.padisciplinaryboard.org/newsletters/2012/pdfs/2011-200-Cloud-Computing.pdf) (establishing guidelines for using cloud to store client information); Vermont Bar Ass'n Committee on Prof. Responsibility, Op. 2010-6 (https://www.vtbar.org/FOR%20ATTORNEYS/2011%20Advisory%20Ethics%20Opinions.aspx) (lawyers may use cloud computing service with reasonable precautions). Cf. Calif. State Bar Standing Comm. on Prof. Resp. & Conduct, Formal Op. 2010-179 (2010).

[Section 1:18]

[1]See http://www.americanbar.org/groups/professional_responsibility/aba_commission_on_ethics_20_20.html. See also Podgers, *Come the Evolution: Ethics 20/20 Proposals Seek to Adapt Existing Professional Conduct Rules*, ABA J., July 2012, at 26.

must identify key internal personnel who may have relevant information, the types of documents or information that may be relevant, and the potentially relevant time period. Fed. R. Civ. P. 34(a) allows the responding party to search its records to produce the required, relevant data. Fed. R. Civ. P. 34(a) does not give the requesting party the right to conduct the actual search.[1]

In most productions of electronically stored information, the process of gathering and producing the information can be broken down into nine basic procedural steps. The nine steps are as follows:[2]

1. **Information management.** Document retention policies are fundamental business tools addressing the creation, retention and disposition of records.
2. **Identifying.** Identify potentially relevant sources of electronically stored information, as well as legal, technical, or practical issues (including time and cost) that might impact the production.
3. **Preserving.** Preserve source media containing responsive electronically stored information.
4. **Collecting**
5. **Processing.** Process the electronically stored information from the preserved media to collect potentially responsive files, separate them from the "grossly" irrelevant and privileged materials, and otherwise prepare the electronically stored information for an organized, efficient review by counsel.
6. **Reviewing.** Review the electronically stored information resulting from the processing to determine the electronically stored information responsive material to the discovery request.
7. **Analyzing.**

[Section 1:19]

[1]See, e.g., Palgut v. City of Colorado Springs, 2007 WL 4277564 (D. Colo. 2007); In re Ford Motor Co., 345 F.3d 1315, 56 Fed. R. Serv. 3d 438 (11th Cir. 2003).

[2]See Electronic Discovery Reference Model prepared by the Electronic Discovery Reference Model Project (http://www.edrm.net). Content is available free under the GNU Free Documentation License 1.2. Launched in May 2005, the Electronic Discovery Reference Model (EDRM) Project was created to address the lack of standards and guidelines in the electronic discovery market—a problem identified in the 2003 and 2004 Socha-Gelbmann Electronic Discovery surveys as a major concern for vendors and consumers alike. The completed reference model provides a common, flexible and extensible framework for the development, selection, evaluation and use of electronic discovery products and services. The completed model was placed in the public domain in May 2006.

8. **Producing.** Produce responsive electronically stored information and privilege logs.
9. **Presenting.**

§ 1:20 Stages in responding to e-discovery requests—Identification

The identification phase is used to determine the scope, breadth, and depth of electronically stored information that can be pursued during discovery. Identification takes into consideration any claims and defenses, preservation demands, disclosure requirements, and discovery demands.

Identification involves a series of inquiries to assist in determining not only sources of potentially responsive records, but also to identify legal, technical, and practical issues that might impact the production of records—such things as nondisclosure agreements, or problems associated with electronically stored information that is not reasonably accessible. Finally, identification involves making an early determination of costs, which can be instrumental in limiting the scope of discovery or supporting efforts to share or shift costs of discovery.

§ 1:21 Stages in responding to e-discovery requests—Preservation

Preservation refers to taking protective custody of electronically stored information for potential evidentiary purposes. Preservation ensures that electronically stored information is protected from destruction or alteration. It is a complicated, multi-faceted concept. It begins with the determination of when the duty to preserve arises and continues into the litigation hold process. Assessment of the preservation task involves identification of those groups of potentially relevant materials that will be most critical or most difficult to preserve or collect. Those will be driven by the issues and priorities of the individual case.

Preservation can take many forms, from evidentiary copies prepared by a forensic professional to simply taking custody of a laptop or backup tapes. Typically preservation should focus on preserving media—hard drives, floppy disks, and backup tapes, for example—rather than particular files, folders, or other forms of electronically stored information. Preserving media, as opposed to preserving just the electronically stored information that appears responsive initially, preserves not only the potentially responsive electronically stored information, but also files and other information that could become important as discovery progresses. Preserving media also preserves other data, such as metadata or deleted material that could be used later to corroborate or authenticate the electronically stored information produced.

§ 1:22 Stages in preparing response—Collection

Collection involves gathering potentially relevant electronically stored information from various sources, such as tapes, drives, portable storage devices, and networks before reviewing the information. The preserving and collecting phases can sometimes overlap. In addition, the collecting of electronically stored information will provide feedback for the identification function that may effect and expand identified content.

Electronically stored information should be collected in a manner that is comprehensive, maintains its content integrity, and preserves its form. Metadata should be collected and maintained during the collection process. In addition, information regarding chain of custody and authentication is frequently required.

§ 1:23 Stages in preparing response—Processing

The processing of electronically stored information involves the accommodation of a wide variety of unstructured data. It must handle each form in a manner appropriate to its file type, and generate output that is structured in accordance with review requirements often varying with client needs and review technology specifications. The principal objective is preparing relevant files for efficient and expedient review, production, and subsequent use.

Processing reduces the overall set of data collected by setting aside files that are duplicates or not relevant. Processing involves culling the potentially relevant electronically stored information that may be on a hard drive or backup tape from the vast amount of irrelevant information, such as the thousands of files that make up modern operating systems and applications. The purpose of processing is to reduce the amount of information that will have to be reviewed for privilege or responsiveness. Typically processing pays for itself many times over in reducing the amount of electronically stored information reviewers will have to look at before producing the information.

Processing also includes identifying duplicate files, creating records of MD5 Hash values, which are unique numerical values calculated for each record and can be used to quickly determine whether files are exactly identical or whether a particular file has changed over time. Finally, processing includes segregating files based on categories of type—such as documents, e-mail, presentation, accounting data, as well as eliminating all file types known to be irrelevant, such as executables, or music files.

By inserting Bates numbers or hash values, files can be more easily tracked over time and movement—it is not unusual for files to have similar, if not identical, names but different content. Using digital Bates numbers or hash values helps guarantee that the numbered files can be accurately identified not only as they move through processing, facilitating auditing, but also as they are produced in discovery and later used in pretrial proceedings and in trial.

It may be help to convert electronically stored information from the form in which it is found to one allowing a more effective and efficient review to be conducted. An organization may retain electronic evidence or forensics computing consultants to conduct the processing. However, unlike the preservation stage, the processing phase can be done by competent technical staff using commercially available software.

Quality control must occur throughout the entire processing phase. To ensure both technical correct result as well as deliver the review teams expected results, it is best to employ a combination of automated and manual quality controls.

Automated controls provide a consistently applied methodology to check for many important aspects of electronic discovery. Automation tools can be used to flag files containing a disproportionately high number of binary characters or size thresholds. Once the files are flagged, they can be subject to visual inspection as the remainder of the collection is processed, then integrated back into the collection. Automation can also be used for file count checks at each stage of the process to account for all data, and to check that fielded information is in conformity with field types.

Manual controls are important to ensure a review team receives an appropriate result. Visual inspection is an example of a manual control. Other manual controls include exception handling. Because source data is unstructured data and not all electronic files run through an automated process, there is some level of exception handling. Exception handling includes password cracking or manipulation of the file to ensure proper rendering of the file as an image. In data collections with a larger percentage of corrupted data, more visual inspection may be needed to ensure that the imaged data is a faithful representation of the original data.

§ 1:24 Stages in preparing response—Review

Document review involves segregating responsive documents to be produced from privileged documents to be withheld. The quantity of electronically stored information makes reviewing printouts of the information largely impractical. Organizations can save time and achieve greater accuracy by using software to review electronically stored information. Unfortunately, relying on the computer is not without problems—the most frequently encountered problem is the lack of programs to open electronically stored information.

This problem is often easily addressed by installing what is known as viewing software—software allowing one to open a large number of data files from most of the common applications. Improving on the simple file viewing approach, an indexing search utility application can be added. A number of vendors are marketing products combining the viewer and index search tools, and including a database to maintain information regarding the reviewers' notes and decisions about whether to produce or withhold particular records.

§ 1:25 Stages in preparing response—Analysis

Analysis involves evaluation of collected electronically stored information to determine relevant summary information, such as key topics, important people, specific vocabulary and jargon, and important individual documents. The information may be useful before a detailed review is conducted to help with important early decisions and to improve the productivity of all remaining e-discovery activities. Analysis is performed throughout the process as new information is uncovered and issues of the case evolve.

§ 1:26 Stages in preparing response—Production

Production can occur in a number of situations:

- Delivering electronically stored information to various recipients, such as law firms, corporate legal departments, and service providers.
- Delivering electronically stored information for use in other systems, such as automated litigation support systems, and Web-based repositories.
- Delivering electronically stored information on various media, such as CDs, DVDs, tape, hard drives, portable storage devices, and paper.

Bates numbering is used to place identifying numbers on images and documents as they are scanned or processed. Manual Bates stamping uses a self-inking stamp with numbered wheels that automatically increment each time the stamp is pressed down on a page. Electronic document discovery software can electronically stamp documents stored as computer files by superimposing numbers onto them.

At one time it was common for the producing party to print and Bates number all electronically stored information—thus producing the records on printout forms. A number of factors now make this a less acceptable procedure. Most notably, one faces the challenge of the sheer quantity of electronically stored information. It simply is not economical to print out millions upon millions of pages.

The use of hash values to identify electronic documents is becoming more common.[1] Hash is an encryption algorithm that generates a unique alphanumeric value to identify a particular computer file, group of files, or even an entire hard drive. The unique alphanumeric value of a computer file is called its "hash value." The hash value guarantees the authenticity of data, and protects it against alteration. Hash also permits the identification of particular files, and the easy filtration of duplicate documents.

Another factor that weighs against the printed-out production is that electronically stored information may not print out satisfactorily. E-mail is a good example: while it is quite easy to print out a message, it becomes more problematic to print out an e-mail with attachments. On the other hand, the producing party may prefer to produce in a mode that does not disclose metadata.

In general, it is far more economical to produce electronically stored information in digital form. In some instances, parties may prefer to convert the electronically stored information to a common format, such as TIFF or PDF. The alternative, and usually more cost effective, as well as accurate, mode of production is to produce in native format. Producing electronically stored information digitally may give the producing party a technical, rather than legal, basis to share costs with the party seeking discovery.

§ 1:27 Stages in preparing response—Presentation

Presentation involves consideration of how an organization can present most effectively the electronically stored information at depositions, hearings, and trials. While this phase is last on the list, it should be thought of as the first step in making appropri-

---

[Section 1:26]

[1]See Losey, *Hash: The New Bates Stamp*, 12 J. Tech. L. & Policy 1 (2007).

ate decisions. In presenting e-mails, it is important not to separate the attachments from the e-mails.[1]

II. CHECKLISTS

§ 1:28 Checklist for cost-effective discovery

- ☐ Take a broad view of discovery and pinpoint discovery needs.
  - ☐ What is really needed to win case?
  - ☐ Will electronically stored information help your case?
  - ☐ Can you get the same result using less expensive traditional discovery?
  - ☐ Is it cost-effective to have a computer forensics expert collect electronically stored information and perform labor intensive procedures to obtain information?
- ☐ Become educated on the various methods and formats of electronically stored information.
  - ☐ How is the information stored?
  - ☐ In what format is the information stored?
  - ☐ What methods are available for searching the electronically stored information?
  - ☐ How is the information backed up? Archived?
- ☐ Find a local, affordable computer expert. A local person, such as an academic, a graduate student, or a freelance IT person may share his or her practical knowledge and expertise to assist you in obtaining the information needed. Use the IT person to evaluate the opposing party's computer system.
- ☐ Hire a computer systems forensics expert. after you understand the information systems involved, a competent computer forensic expert can save time and money. The complexity of e-discovery requires retention of an expert at the early stages of litigation. The forensic expert can be helpful in crafting requests for production with the requisite specificity.
- ☐ Early in the case determine what you need to win the case

---

[Section 1:27]

[1]See PSEG Power N.Y., Inc. v. Alberici Constructors, Inc., 2007 WL 2687670 (N.D. N.Y. 2007) (defendant entitled to receive e-mails with related attachments, plaintiff ordered to re-produce e-mails at its expense—over $200,000—with attachments); CP Solutions PTE, Ltd. v. General Elec. Co., 2006 WL 1272615 (D. Conn. 2006) (where thousands of e-mails were produced commingled and separated from their attachments, court ordered producing party to provide requesting party with information necessary for matching e-mails and attachments).

and avoid chasing unnecessary electronically stored information. Consultation with the computer forensics expert can be very helpful at this stage.

- ☐ Use the meet and confer process to narrow issues and learn about the opposing party's position on discovery of electronically stored information. The discussion should include the opponent's preservation of evidence, description of backup systems, types of computer systems, and production formats.
- ☐ Specify the production format that will give the best results for your case.
- ☐ When a responding party designates a source of information as not reasonably accessible, it may take limited discovery, including sampling, to determine whether the sources are not reasonably accessible. Sampling may provide knowledge that can help you decide whether the sources contain useful information. The limited discovery may include:
  - ☐ Sampling information contained on sources identified as not reasonably accessible
  - ☐ Inspection of sources
  - ☐ Depositions of witnesses knowledgeable about the responding party's information system

NOTES

Commentary

This checklist is adapted from *Gonzalez & Montoya, Ten Tips Leading to Efficient and Effective eDiscovery for the Small Law Firm*, GP/Solo, April 2007.

§ 1:29 Critical decisions

Collection Choices

- ☐ **Are e-mail files part of the anticipated or requested discovery? If so, do any key people maintain Internet e-mail accounts in addition to their organization account?** Large e-mail providers frequently retain their e-mail logs for no longer than 30 days. If a case potentially requires exploration of e-mail from Internet accounts, the discovery team must promptly request the records before they are lost. Normally this requires a subpoena.
- ☐ **Is it possible illegal activity may be uncovered?** Cases involving electronically stored information may uncover wrongdoing involving a member of the IT department. Terminating the responsible employee is not necessarily the best course of action. The employee

may be the only person who knows how to access the files, find the problem, or fix it. The employee may also have the ability to access the files remotely. Unless remote access is eliminated before the employee's termination, the employee could access the network and damage it. It may be more prudent to restrict an employee's complete access privileges. The employee can then be notified of management's knowledge of the situation and given an opportunity to cooperate to mitigate the damage. If the situation involves possible criminal activity, law enforcement should be involved as early as possible.

☐ **May deleted or hidden files play a significant role in the case?** Electronic files can be collected using three methods: (1) forensically (capturing all the information contained on a specific electronic device by using either a forensic copy technique or by making an image of all or part of the device), (2) semi-forensically (using nonvalidated methods and applications to capture files), or (3) Non-forensically (using cut-and-paste copy methods to move copies of files from one location to another). Determining whether contextual information or only the content of electronic documents must be produced must be done before any data are captured. Once semi- or non-forensic methods are used, the records cannot be returned to their original state.

☐ **Are backup tapes involved?** Where backup tapes may be part of the information required to be produced, it is necessary to stop any rotation schedule.

Processing Choices

☐ **Who are the key people?** It is essential to identify people important to the case. Key individuals may include executives as well as assistants and support personnel from technology, accounting, sales and marketing, operations, and human resources.

☐ **Where are the files?** Electronically stored information can be in numerous locations. All potential locations of electronically stored information must be identified, including home computers, laptops, smart phones, MP3 players, and thumbdrives.

☐ **How can the number of files collected be limited?** Methods for limiting the number of files (and the cost of collection) include collecting only those in a certain date range, or only those containing selected key words.

☐ **How should protected files be handled?** Encrypted files or files with passwords may not be easily or quickly accessed. It may be necessary to access a subpoena to obtain a password.

☐ **How should duplicate documents be handled?** Electronically stored information almost always includes duplicate files. For example, numerous individuals may have received the same e-mail with the same attachments. Key documents may have been reviewed by several people who saved them on their hard drives. In collecting documents, it is possible to identify exact duplicate documents, limiting the number of documents requiring review. De-duping involves identifying files that are exact duplicates and eliminating them. If anything has changed in a document such as formatting, it is not an exact duplicate and is not de-duped. It is important that all parties agree on what is meant by "de-duping" Some e-discovery tools delete duplicate files so they are gone from the collection, while others do not delete the duplicates but merely identify them for future use if needed.

☐ **How should near-duplicate documents be handled?** Near duplicates are files that have been significantly altered or contain only a portion of the main document. The volume of documents may require that near duplicates be identified and reviewed as a group to reduce review time and costs. Identifying near duplicates requires comparing each document to every other document or using sophisticated software applications requiring additional processing time.

☐ **What should be the form of the collection?** The Federal Rules of Civil Procedure require the parties to meet and determine the format in which they wish to receive electronically stored information. If there is no agreement, the format is that in which the documents are ordinarily maintained or a reasonably usable format. The form requested may depend upon the litigation review system used. Native files with extracted metadata reflect the exact original file, but cannot be Bates numbered and are subject to inadvertent change. Converting native files to TIF or PDF is time consuming and expensive. Frequently, files are processed in native format, reviewed for relevancy, and choosing only those that may be produced or used extensively for conversion.

NOTES

Commentary

This checklist is adapted from Unger, *10 Critical Decisions for Successful e-Discovery*, INFORMATIONMANAGEMENT, Sept./Oct. 2007, at 70.

§ 1:30 Checklist for review process

☐ Determine the relevancy of the information or documents collected or produced.

☐ Bibliographically code database fields to facilitate improved search and retrieval of the documents collected or produced.

☐ Determine whether or not any privilege applies to the documents subject to be produced.

☐ Determine which requests for production the documents are responsive to.

☐ Identify documents that should be marked as "confidential" or have portions redacted.

☐ Relate key documents to alleged facts or legal issues previously outlined in the case.

☐ Relate key documents to key players who may testify about the documents.

☐ Identify other subjective information.

§ 1:31 Processing checklist

☐ Capture and preserve the body of electronically stored information.

☐ Associate document collections with particular users.

☐ Capture and preserve metadata associated with the electronically stored information.

☐ Establish relationship between various source data files.

☐ Automate identification and elimination of redundant duplicate data with the given data set.

☐ Provide a means to suppress programmatically material that is irrelevant to review based on criteria such as keywords, date ranges, or other available metadata.

☐ Unprotect and reveal information within files.

☐ Accomplish all process goals in a manner that is both defensible with respect to organization's legal obligations and appropriately cost effective and expedient.

III. FORMS

§ 1:32 Discovery project management template

E-DISCOVERY PROJECT MANAGEMENT TEMPLATE

Case Name *[name]*

Client Matter Number *[number]*

Item	Task	Status	As Of	Notes
1	**Initial discussions with Client**			
2	Establish responsibility for maintaining discovery audit trail			
3	Determine date range for the matter			
4	Obtain organization charts for relevant periods			
5	Identify corporate contacts			
6	Identify key corporate IT personnel			
7	Identify key records managers			
8	Identify key witnesses/custodians			
9	Identify other witnesses/custodians			
10	Obtain copy of document retention policy			
11	Determine if policy has been followed			
12	Identify and address any imminent spoliation issues			
13	Gain detailed understanding of e-mail systems			
14	Determine which e-mail systems are involved			
15	Determine how long e-mail remains on system			
16	Determine how e-mail is backed up			

Item	Task	Status	As Of	Notes
17	Determine if there is a disaster recovery plan			
18	Determine how other data backed up			
19	Determine if there are legacy systems involved			
20	Determine which voice mail system(s) and instant messaging systems involved			
21	Locate or create data map			
22	Identify sources of privileged information			
23	Develop list of all inside and outside counsel			
24	Determine if client has preferred vendors			
25	Develop outline of legal and factual issues			
26	Identify and prepare appropriate 30B6 witness			
27	**Litigation Hold/ Document Preservation Issues**			
28	Confirm that destruction policies have been suspended			
29	Conduct litigation hold strategy meeting			
30	Determine scope of hold			
31	Determine recipients of hold			
32	Coordinate with HR re incoming/departing employees subject to hold			

Item	Task	Status	As Of	Notes
33	Determine if third parties have relevant data			
34	Consider preservation notice to third parties			
35	Determine where and how to hold data			
36	Issue litigation hold communication			
37	Schedule periodic follow-up reminders re litigation hold			
38	Receive confirmation of hold instructions from recipients			
39	Inventory data sources			
40	Determine reasonable/unreasonable accessibility of data sets. [FRCP 26(b)(2)(B)]			
41	Determine if back-up tapes are implicated			
42	Consider setting aside system snapshot			
43	Determine if data exists in the cloud; develop strategy for preserving same			
44	Determine if home computers or personal e-mail accounts are implicated			
45	Determine if Instant Messaging implicated			
46	Send opposition appropriate preservation demand			
47	**Collection Issues**			
48	Develop data collection plan			

Item	Task	Status	As Of	Notes
49	Identify and retain collection vendor if required			
50	Identify sources of data			
51	Determine who will collect the data			
52	Prepare and interview IT staff re systems, back-ups, etc.			
53	Estimate amount of data			
54	Determine data formats			
55	Identify data base issues			
56	Determine if any data is encrypted			
57	Determine if there are unique software applications			
58	Anticipate which data may require native production			
59	Determine if computer forensics implicated			
60	Identify and interview key custodians			
61	Develop plan for hard copy data collection			
62	Determine OCR strategy for paper			
63	Determine extent of coding required for paper			
64	Maintain chain of custody for data gathered			
65	**Preparing for Meet and Confer**			
66	What are the issues in the case?			

Item	Task	Status	As Of	Notes
67	Who are the key players in the case?			
68	Who are the persons most knowledgeable about ESI systems?			
69	What events and intervals are relevant?			
70	When did preservation duties and privileges attach?			
71	What data are at greatest risk of alteration or destruction?			
72	Are systems slated for replacement or disposal?			
73	What steps have been or will be taken to preserve ESI?			
74	What third parties hold information that must be preserved, and who will notify them?			
75	What data require forensically sound preservation?			
76	Are there unique chain-of-custody needs to be met?			
77	What metadata are relevant, and how will it be preserved, extracted and produced?			
78	What are the data retention policies and practices?			
79	What are the backup practices, and what tape archives exist?			
80	Are there legacy systems to be addressed?			

Item	Task	Status	As Of	Notes
81	How will the parties handle voice mail, instant messaging and other challenging ESI?			
82	Is there a preservation duty going forward, and how will it be met?			
83	Is a preservation or protective order needed?			
84	What e-mail applications are used currently and in the relevant past?			
85	Are personal e-mail accounts and computer systems involved?			
86	What principal applications are used in the business, now and in the past?			
87	What electronic formats are common, and in what anticipated volumes?			
88	Is there a document or messaging archival system?			
89	What relevant databases exist?			
90	Will paper documents be scanned, and if so, at what resolution and with what OCR and metadata?			
91	What search techniques will be used to identify responsive or privileged ESI?			

Item	Task	Status	As Of	Notes
92	If keyword searching is contemplated, can the parties agree on keywords?			
93	Can supplementary keyword searches be pursued?			
94	How will the contents of databases be discovered? Queries? Export? Copies? Access?			
95	How will de-duplication be handled, and will data be re-populated for production?			
96	What forms of production are offered or sought?			
97	Will single- or multipage. tiffs, PDFs or other image formats be produced?			
98	Will load files accompany document images, and how will they be populated?			
99	How will the parties approach file naming, unique identification and Bates numbering?			
100	Will there be a need for native file production? Quasi-native production?			
101	On what media will ESI be delivered? Optical disks? External drives? FTP?			
102	How will we handle inadvertent production of privileged ESI?			

Item	Task	Status	As Of	Notes
103	How will we protect trade secrets and other confidential information in the ESI?			
104	Do regulatory prohibitions on disclosure, foreign privacy laws or export restrictions apply?			
105	How do we resolve questions about printouts before their use in deposition or at trial?			
106	How will we handle authentication of native ESI used in deposition or trial?			
107	What ESI will be claimed as not reasonably accessible, and on what bases?			
108	Who will serve as liaisons or coordinators for each side on ESI issues?			
109	Will technical assistants be permitted to communicate directly?			
110	Is there a need for an e-discovery special master?			
111	Can any costs be shared or shifted by agreement?			
112	Can cost savings be realized using shared vendors, repositories or neutral experts?			

Item	Task	Status	As Of	Notes
113	How much time is required to identify, collect, process, review, redact and produce ESI?			
114	How can production be structured to accommodate depositions and deadlines?			
115	When is the next Rule 26(f) conference (because we need to do this more than once)?			
116	**Processing Issues**			
117	Determine culling software and strategies; keyword list; date range limitations, etc.			
118	Select processing vendor(s)			
119	Obtain cost estimates for processing			
120	Obtain time estimates for processing			
121	Insure chain of custody for data			
122	Determine which metadata fields should be extracted			
123	Determine procedures for dealing with exceptions			
124	Confirm load file formats			
125	**Review issues**			
126	Determine review platform and process			
127	Formulate and test keyword search terms; test with key custodian(s)			

Item	Task	Status	As Of	Notes
128	Determine review team composition			
129	Determine if second review required/warranted			
130	Train review team			
131	Conduct intensive review of key custodian(s) data			
132	Develop budget estimate for review			
133	Develop time estimate for review			
134	Load data for review			
135	Review data for relevance and privilege			
136	Develop protocol for redaction			
137	Create privilege log			
138	**Production issues**			
139	Determine priority of data to be produced; consider rolling productions.			
140	Negotiate and obtain appropriate protective order re data including clawback agreement			
141	Determine desired production format(s)			
142	Negotiate production format(s) with opposition			
143	Negotiate timetable for production(s)			
144	Negotiate timetable for receiving production(s)			
	Roles			
	IT = Client IT staff			

Item	Task	Status	As Of	Notes
	IC = Inside Counsel			
	OC = Outside Counsel			
	LS = Outside Counsel's Litigation Support Team			
	V = Outside Vendor			

§ 1:33 Sample electronic budgeting tool

Document Review Budget Estimate				
Matter Name:				
Date:				
Total Cost Estimate		$7,796,741	$3,503,070	$1,182,802
		Large	Medium	Small
E-File Collection		*Scenario 1*	*Senario 2*	*Scenario 3*
Key Custodians		10	6	2
GB/Key Custodian		10	10	10
Tier 2 Custodians		25	9	3
GB/Tier 2 Custodians		7.5	7.5	7.5
GB Shared Server Data		15	7.5	2
Estimated GB Collected		302.5	135	44.5
Estimated Pages/GB		75,000	75,000	75,000
Page equivalent		22,687,500	10,125,000	3,337,500
Yield after Pre-Processing as %		0.3	0.3	0.3
Yield after Pre-Processing GB		90.75	40.5	13.35
Estimated # pages		6,806,250	3,037,500	1,001,250
Box Equivalent (2,500pp/box)		2,723	1,215	401
Estimated % Responsive		0.25	0.25	0.25
Estimated # Responsive Pages		1,701,563	759,375	250,313
Collection Costs				
Collection Costs (1 hour/custodian @ $300/hr)		$10,500	$4,500	$1,500
DeDup and Cull Cost/GB		1,250	1,250	1250
Estimate GB Collected		302.5	135	44.5

Total Collection, DeDup and Cull Costs		$388,625	$173,250	$57,125
EDD Processing Costs				
EDD Processing Cost/GB		$1,750	$1,750	$1,750
Total GB to be Processed		90.75	40.5	13.35
Total EDD Processing Costs		**$158,813**	**$70,875**	**$23,363**
Paper Collection and Processing				
Pages/Key Custodians (Assume 5000 pages/custodian)		50,000	30,000	10,000
Pages Tier 2 Custodians (Assume 2500 pages/custodian)		62,500	22,500	7,500
Total Pages		112,500	52,500	17,500
Scan/OCR/page		0.2	0.2	0.2
Processing costs		$22,500	$10,500	$3,500
Vendor Load Fee/page		0	0	0
Load Fees		$5,625	$2,625	$875
Total Paper Processing Costs		**$28,125**	**$13,125**	**$4,375**
Total Pre-Review Costs		**$575,563**	**$257,250**	**$84,863**
Phase 1 Review				
GB to be reviewed		90.75	40.5	13.35
Pages to be reviewed		6,806,250	3,037,500	1,001,250
Attorney review rate (pp/hour)		175	175	175
Attorney hours needed to complete review		38893	17357	5721
Cost per hour of attorney review		$65	$65	$65
Review attorney cost of Phase 1 review		$2,528,036	$1,128,214	$371,893
Supervisory billable time for training, project management, etc. (~10% Rev Atty Cost)		$252,804	$112,821	$37,189
Total Cost of Phase 1 Review		**$2,780,839**	**$1,241,036**	**$409,082**
Phase 2 Review				
Yield from Phase 1 Review		0.4	0.4	0.4

Pages to be Reviewed in Phase 2		2,722,500	1,215,000	400,500
Attorney review rate (pp/hr)		200	200	200
Attorney hours needed to complete review		13,613	6,075	2,003
Cost per hour of attorney review		$250	$250	$250
Review attorney cost of Phase 2 review		$3,403,125	$1,518,750	$500,625
Supervisory billable time for training, project management, etc. (10% Rev Atty Cost)		$340,313	$151,875	$50,063
Total Cost of Phase 2 Review		**$3,743,438**	**$1,670,625**	**$550,688**
Review of Materials Received from Opposition				
Assume Equal Amount of Data Received as Produced		0	0	0
Attorney review rate (pp/hr)		200	200	200
Attorney hours needed to complete review		0	0	0
Cost per hour of attorney review		$250	$250	$250
Review attorney cost of Phase 2 review		$0	$0	$0
Supervisory billable time for training, project management, etc. (~10% Rev Atty Cost)		$0	$0	$0
Total Cost of Reviewing Opposition Production		**$0**	**$0**	**$0**
Production				
Responsive Pages		1,701,563	759,375	250,313
Production Costs/ Page @ $0.10		$170,156	$75,938	$25,031
Total Costs of Production		**$170,156**	**$75,938**	**$25,031**
Privilege Log				
Privileged Pages (Assume 10% of Responsive Documents are Privileged)		170,156	75,938	25,031

Privileged Documents (Assume 5pp/doc)		34,031	15,188	5,006
Percent Reduced during Phase 2 Review		0.6	0.6	0.6
Privileged Documents to be Logged		13,613	6,075	2,003
Logging Pace docs/hr		8	8	8
Logging Hours Needed		1,702	759	250
Hours/day		8	8	8
Logging days needed		213	95	31
Loggers (Staff attorneys)		5	5	5
Project Days needed		43	19	6
Avg Hourly Billing Rate		$275	$275	$275
Personnel Costs		$467,930	$208,828	$68,836
Export cost/page @ $0.10		$17,016	$7,594	$2,503
Total Privilege Log Costs		**$484,945**	**$216,422**	**$71,339**
ASP Costs				
Database Set-Up Fees (Includes Initial Upload)		$1,000	$1,000	$1,000
User Set Up Fees (Assume $100/User; 20 Users)		$2,000	$2,000	$2,000
Monthly Mainentance (Assume $200/Mo; 24 Month Life of Case)		$4,800	$4,800	$4,800
Image Storage (TBD)				
Log In/Month (Assume 20 Users @ $100/user/month/24 months)		$24,000	$24,000	$24,000
Additional Uploads (TBD)				
Project Management (Assume 50 hours @ $200/hour)		$10,000	$10,000	$10,000
Total ASP Costs		**$41,800**	**$41,800**	**$41,800**
Total Cost Estimate		**$7,796,741**	**$3,503,070**	**$1,182,802**

NOTES TO FORM

Commentary

The form can be used for internal budgeting purposes and it can also be used to support a motion shifting costs. The numbers and categories are examples of the costs of e-discovery and will vary from case to case.

Chapter 2

Rules of Procedure, Best Practices and Case Law Update

I. GUIDELINES

II. CHECKLISTS

III. FORMS

Research References

Treatises and Practice Aids

eDiscovery & Digital Evidence §§ 6:10 to 6:12

Additional References

Grenig and Kinsler, Handbook of Federal Civil Discovery and Disclosure §§ 13.1 to 13.6 (3d ed.)
ABA Discovery Standards, http://www.abanet.org/litigation/discoverystandards/2005civildiscoverystandards.pdf
The Sedona Conference, http://www.thesedonaconference.org

I. GUIDELINES

§ 2:1 Generally

The discovery of electronically stored information has changed the face of litigation. As 99% of the information created today is electronic, cases of all types in state and federal court involve electronically stored information.

Because of the rapidly growing importance of discovery of electronically stored information, in 2006 the Federal Rules of Civil Procedure were amended to address the discovery of electronically stored information. Those amendments, and the committee notes that accompanied them, provided a specific framework to address the issues surrounding the volumes of electronically stored information, waiver of privilege due to inadvertent production, form of production, and the responsibilities of requesting vs. responding parties.

States, federal regulatory agencies, and U.S. district courts have also adopted rules regarding eDiscovery since the amendments to provide a framework for those jurisdictions. Individual judges have created their own case management orders and scheduling reports to include or address the discovery of electronically stored information and parties need to be aware of and review those documents prior to any meet and confer or scheduling conference—preferably before meeting with their clients for the first time to discuss identifying and preserving electronically stored information.

At least six jurisdictions[1] have implemented pilot projects in state and federal courts to develop procedures that "provide fairness and justice to all parties while reducing the cost and burden

---

[Section 2:1]

[1]Colorado, Massachusetts, New Hampshire, New York, Seventh Circuit Court of Appeals, and the Southern District of New York each have a pilot project. All pilot projects and their materials are included in the eDiscovery Assistant iPad app.

of e-discovery."[2] Thirty-seven states have implemented rules addressing the discovery of electronically stored information. Of those, thirty-one largely track the 2006 amendments to the Federal Rules of Civil Procedure, and with six following the beat of their own drummer.[3]

Uniform Rules Relating to the Discovery of Electronically Stored Information for use in state courts were approved in 2007. The National Conference of Commissioners on Uniform State Laws also approved the Uniform Interstate Depositions and Discovery Act in 2007, detailing which state's laws of evidence and procedure apply when a subpoena from one state is served on a party in another state.

Of the 94 U.S. District Courts in the states and territories, 66 have addressed the discovery of electronically stored information either through local rules, case management orders or forms for the parties to utilize, guidelines for parties to follow or local rules.[4]

Regulatory agencies have also promulgated rules, and many now have their own e-discovery counsel that negotiates directly with parties. The Department of Justice, Securities Exchange Commission and the Financial Industry Regulatory Authority have created their own guidelines for parties producing electronically stored information.[5]

§ 2:2 Federal Rules of Civil Procedure—Generally

In 2006 significant amendments relating to discovery of electronic information were made to the Federal Rules of Civil Procedure. The amended rules explicitly recognize that electronically stored information is discoverable.

Amended Fed. R. Civ. P. 26(b)(2) provides that a party is not

[2]Seventh Circuit Electronic Discovery Pilot Project, Report on Phase 1, available at http://www.discoverypilot.com/.

[3]The following states implemented rules that are not based on the Federal Rules of Civil Procedure: Idaho, Illinois, Mississippi, New Hampshire, Pennsylvania, Texas.

[4]See, e.g., the Northern District of Californa, which provides Guidelines, a Checklist for use during the meet and confer, a Model Stipulated Order for the parties, and a Joint Case Management Statement and Proposed Order, effective November 27, 2012. The materials are available online at http://www.cand.uscourts.gov/eDiscoveryGuidelines and in the eDiscovery Assistant™ iPad app.

[5]See, e.g., changes to FINRA's eDiscovery Guide for arbitrators, detailed at http://www.catalystsecure.com/blog/2013/07/finra-proposes-e-discovery-changes-to-its-discovery-guide-for-customer-cases/?goback=%2Egde_3004904_member_261085594.

required to produce electronically stored information that is not "reasonably accessible" because of "undue burden or cost." Where the producing party shows the requested information is not reasonably accessible, the requesting party has the burden of going to court and showing why it is entitled to the information. Amended Fed. R. Civ. P. 26(b)(2) attempts to codify *Zubulake v. UBS Warburg LLC*,[1] with respect to a court's limiting the frequency or extent of discovery otherwise allowed by these rules or by local rule.

Amended Fed. R. Civ. P. 26(b)(5) contains a "clawback" provision, allowing a party that has produced evidence it claims is protected by the attorney-client privilege or the work-product doctrine to notify the receiving party of its claim and provide a basis for the claim. After receiving notification, the receiving party must return, sequester, or destroy the information and may not disclose it to third parties. In the alternative, the receiving party has the option of submitting the information to the court for a decision on whether the information is protected and whether a waiver has taken place. The clawback provision can be superseded by the parties' agreement.

Under amended Fed. R. Civ. P. 16(b), a pretrial conference may include a discussion of issues relating to electronically stored information, including the form of producing electronically stored information, preservation of data, and approaches to asserting claims of privilege or work-product protection after inadvertent production in discovery.

Amended Fed. R. Civ. P. 33(d) allows a party to produce electronically stored information in response to interrogatories. Amended Fed. R. Civ. P. 34(a) provides a definition of electronically stored information. This definition clearly indicates electronically stored information is subject to production and discovery. Amended Rule 34(b) provides that, when a production format is not specified, a responding party should produce documents in the format in which the information is "ordinarily maintained" or in a form that is reasonably usable. Under Fed. R. Civ. P. 34(b)(2)(E)(iii), a party need not produce the same electronically stored information in more than one form.

Amended Fed. R. Civ. P. 37(f) provides a safe harbor, stating that "a party shall not be sanctioned for loss of electronically stored information if the loss occurs, absent exceptional

[Section 2:2]

[1]Zubulake v. UBS Warburg LLC, 217 F.R.D. 309, 322, 91 Fair Empl. Prac. Cas. (BNA) 1574 (S.D. N.Y. 2003).

circumstances. A court may not impose sanctions under these rules on a party for failing to provide electronically stored information lost as a result of the routine, good faith operation of an electronic information system." Parties are cautioned to consider case law evaluating this "safe harbor" before attempting to rely on the provision for failure to preserve.

Amended Fed. R. Civ. P. 45 provides for the discovery of electronically stored information upon subpoena of a third party (section (d)(1), as well as the ability of the responding party to object based on undue burden or sanctions. Fed. R. Civ. P. 45 (c)(1). Rule 45 (d)(1) provides for the same limits and procedures as Fed. R. Civ. P. 34—documents should be produced in the ordinary course of business, in a reasonably useable form (if not specified by the requesting party), only in one form (so make your requests carefully), and inaccessible information need only be produced upon a showing of good cause where it subjects the responding party to undue burden.[2]

Following the amendments, many issues arose with the implementation of subsection Fed. R. Civ. P. 26(b)(5) and the question of waiver following the inadvertent production of electronically stored information. In short, the procedure set out in that section—that required the producing party to request the information be returned—was unworkable. In 2008, the Federal Rules Commission enacted Federal Rule of Evidence 502 to correct that issue. Fed. R. Evid. 502 provides a framework for evaluating whether waiver has occurred, and giving the parties the option to have a court order determining how the disclosure of inadvertently produced privileged information would be handled.

§ 2:3 Federal Rules of Civil Procedure—Proposed changes

Since the 2006 amendments, courts and litigants have bemoaned the discovery process as being too expensive and barring the courthouse to parties who would otherwise pursue claims, as well as increasing the cost of doing business for large organizations (and government entities) with vast volumes of electronically stored information and no systems in place to capture and

[2]Many states that enacted rules several years after the Federal Rules of Civil Procedure did away with or did not include the distinction between accessible and inaccessible information. While those states still carry the "undue burden" language that provides for a similar analysis for the responding party, advancements in technology mean that less and less information is "inaccessible" as the Federal Judicial Commission first envisioned that term.

produce that information without great expense. As a result, since 2011, the Discovery Subcommittee on Civil Rules of the Advisory Committee on Federal Rules of Civil Procedure has been developing possible recommendations for rule changes regarding discovery.[1]

On May 8, 2013, following much debate and the widely discussed "Duke Conference,"[2] the Civil Rules Advisory Committee has proposed numerous changes to the current Rules.[3] The changes sought to address the concept of proportionality—included in the Rules since 1983, but rarely invoked. The most significant changes proposed include revisions to Rules 26(b)(1) and Rule 34(b), but also include modifications to cost-shifting considerations of Rule 26 and reducing the number of depositions and written discovery requests that can be propounded.

The report proposes that the permissible scope of discovery under Rule 26(b)(1) be modified to highlight the proportionality considerations, that although included in Rule 26(b)(2)(C), are not widely acknowledged or used:

> Parties may obtain discovery regarding any non-privileged matter that is relevant to any party's claim or defense and proportional to the needs of the case considering the amount in controversy, the importance of the issues at stake in the action, the parties' resources, the importance of the discovery in resolving the issues, and whether the burden or expense of the proposed discovery outweighs it's likely benefit.[4]

The report also reinforces the notion that discovery be confined to what is relevant for the claims at issue in the litigation. Although this provision has been included in the Rules for many years, the Report addresses that the "reasonably calculated" provision of Rule 26 was swallowing the relevancy requirement. To limit that from happening, the Committee removed the "reasonably calculated" language and replaced it with "Information

---

[Section 2:3]

[1]See http://www.uscourts.gov/uscourts/RulesAndPolicies/rules/Agenda%%20Books/Civil/CV2011-04.pdf.

[2]See Kessler & Johnson, "No Consensus Reached on Preservation: Discovery Subcommittee Holds Mini-Conference on September 9, 2011," http://www.fulbright.com/index.cfm?fuseaction=publications.detail&site_id=494&pub_id=5101.

[3]Judical Conference of the United States, Report of the Advisory Committee on Civil Rules 4 (May 8, 2013). A copy of the Report is available at http://www.uscourts.gov/uscourts/RulesAndPolicies/rules/Reports/CV05-2013.pdf.

[4]Report at 19–20.

within the scope of discovery need not be admissible in evidence to be discoverable."[5]

The Committee has also recommended eliminating the provision in Rule 26(b)(1) that presently allows the court—on a showing of good cause—to order "discovery of any matter relevant to the subject matter." In its proposed "Committee Note," the Committee justified this suggested change by reiterating its mantra about the proper scope of discovery: "Proportional discovery relevant to any party's claim or defense suffices."[6]

The Committee proposed three changes to Rule 34 to eliminate "gamesmanship" in written discovery responses—largely in response to the lack of cooperation between counsel. First, the Committee revised 34(b)(2)(B) to eliminate general objections and require that any objection be stated with specificity. Second, the Committee proposed adding the following provision to Rule 34(b)(2)(C): "An objection must state whether any responsive materials are being withheld on the basis of that objection" in an attempt to make Rule 34 responses less evasive and allow a receiving party to know what has been responded to versus not.[7]

Third, the Committee sought to clarify the date for actual production of documents—not currently addressed by Rule 34. To address this, the Committee proposed requiring the responding party to complete its production "no later than the time for inspection state in the request or [at] a later reasonable time stated in the response."[8] For rolling productions, the responding party must "specify the beginning and end dates of the production."[9]

Proposed changes would also expressly enable courts to allocate the costs of discovery among the parties, ostensibly to deal with the issues of cost-shifting only being available under the current Rules where data is "inaccessible."[10] Proposed revisions from the Committee include reductions in the number of depositions, interrogatories, and requests for admission.[11]

§ 2:4 Uniform Rules Relating to the Discovery of Electronically Stored Information

In 2006, a committee of the National Conference of Commis-

[5]Report at 11.

[6]Report, at 10–11.

[7]Report at 15–16.

[8]Report at 26.

[9]Report at 26.

[10]Report at 12, 20–21, 23.

[11]Report at 12–15.

sioners on Uniform State Laws held its initial meeting to discuss Uniform Rules Relating to Discovery of Electronically Stored Information. The drafting committee determined the significant issues relating to the discovery of information in electronic form had been vetted during the Federal Rules amendment process. It drafted uniform rules mirroring the spirit and direction of the amendments to the Federal Rules of Civil Procedure. The committee adopted, often verbatim, language from both the Federal Rules and comments that it deemed valuable. The rules were modified, where necessary, to accommodate the varying state procedures. The National Conference of Commissioners adopted the rules in 2007. To date, only one state, Connecticut, has enacted the Uniform Rules.

§ 2:5 State rules of civil procedure

Although considerable attention has been directed toward the changes in the Federal Rules of Civil Procedure, states have adopted court rules addressing discovery of electronically stored information.[1] Thirty states follow the approach of the Federal Rules of Civil Procedure in whole or in part.[2] One state, Connecticut, has adopted rules based on the Uniform Rules Relating to the Discovery of Electronically Stored Information.

§ 2:6 The Sedona Principles

The Sedona Conference Working Group on Best Practices for Electronic Document Retention & Production has promulgated fourteen principles regarding discovery of electronically stored information, entitled The Sedona Principles (Second) Best Practices Recommendations & Principles for Addressing Electronic Document Production Sedona Principles.[1] While not law, the principles are definitely persuasive authority.

[Section 2:5]

[1]See, e.g., Alabama, Alaska, Arizona, Arkansas, California, Colorado, Connecticut, Delaware, Florida, Idaho, Illinois, Indiana, Iowa, Kansas, Louisiana, Maine, Maryland, Michigan, Minnesota, Mississippi, Missouri, Montana, Nebraska, New Hampshire, New Jersey, New Mexico, New York, North Carolina, North Dakota, Ohio, Oklahoma, Oregon, South Carolina, Tennessee, Texas, Utah, Vermont, Virginia, Washington, and Wisconsin.

[2]See Canfield, An Overview of State e-Discovery Rules, www.insidecounsel.com/2012/03/15/.

[Section 2:6]

[1]http://www.thesedonaconference.org/; The Sedona Principles (Second) Best Practices Recommendations & Principles for Addressing Electronic Document Production is the product of the Sedona Conference Working Group on

The Sedona Conference has recognized that the costs associated with adversarial conduct in pretrial discovery have become a serious burden. This burden rises significantly in discovery of electronically stored information. According to the Sedona Conference, e-discovery has resulted in escalating motion practice, overreaching, obstruction, and extensive, but unproductive, discovery disputes. In response to this problem, the Sedona Conference has launched a drive to promote open and forthright information sharing, dialogue (internal and external), training, and the development of practical tools to facilitate cooperative, collaborative, transparent discovery. The Sedona Conference suggests that methods to accomplish this cooperation may include:

1. Utilizing internal ESI discovery "point persons" to assist counsel in preparing requests and responses;
2. Exchanging information on relevant data sources, including those not being searched, or scheduling early disclosures on the topic of Electronically Stored Information;
3. Jointly developing automated search and retrieval methodologies to cull relevant information;
4. Promoting early identification of form or forms of production;
5. Developing case long discovery budgets based on proportionality principles; and
6. Considering court appointed experts, volunteer mediators, or formal ADR programs to resolve discovery disputes.

The Sedona Conference acknowledges it is unrealistic to expect an outbreak of pretrial discovery cooperation. However, the Sedona Conference suggests a three-part process to increase cooperation:

Part I: Awareness. Promoting awareness of the need and advantages of cooperation, coupled with a call to action.

Part II: Commitment. Developing a detailed understanding and full articulation of the issues and changes needed to obtain cooperative fact finding.

Part III: Tools. Developing and distributing practical "toolkits" to train and support lawyers, judges, other professionals, and students in techniques of discovery cooperation, collaboration, and transparency.

Asserting that the project is not "utopian," the Sedona Conference contends the project is a tailored effort to effectuate the mandate of court rules calling for a "just, speedy, and inexpen-

---

sive determination of every action" and the fundamental ethical principles governing our profession.

Whether advocates, such as those representing employees with limited discoverable electronically stored information, will embrace this cooperative approach remains to be seen.[2] Nonetheless, it is a significant attempt to do something about the rapidly escalating costs of civil litigation—in particular the costs of discovery of electronically stored information. The alternative to this cooperative approach could be a rapid escalation in the burdensome costs of civil discovery.

§ 2:7 Electronic Discovery Reference Model Project (EDRM)

Launched in May 2005, the Electronic Discovery Reference Model (EDRM) Project was created to address the lack of standards and guidelines in the e-discovery market—a problem identified in the 2003 and 2004 Socha-Gelbmann Electronic Discovery Surveys as a major concern for vendors and consumers alike. The completed reference model provides a common, flexible and extensible framework for the development, selection, evaluation and use of e-discovery products and services. The reference model was placed in the public domain in May 2006 and updated in 2009.[1]

§ 2:8 ABA eDiscovery Standards

In August 2004, the American Bar Association added e-discovery to the ABA's Civil Discovery Standards.[1] The ABA Standards include five specific standards relating to e-discovery. The first standard addresses preserving and producing electronic information, and includes a list of the places electronic documents can be found. It also contains a list of factors courts should consider when deciding how to allocate the costs of discovery.

---

[2]See descriptions of the pitfalls of overaggressive approaches to e-discovery, in Sterle v. Elizabeth Arden, Inc., 2008 WL 961216 (D. Conn. 2008); Treppel v. Biovail Corp., 249 F.R.D. 111 (S.D. N.Y. 2008); Perfect Barrier LLC v. Woodsmart Solutions Inc., 2008 WL 2230192 (N.D. Ind. 2008). See also Manlowe, et al., *Paradigm Shifts in E-Discovery Litigation: Cooperate or Continue to Pay Dearly*, 78 DEF. COUNS. J. 170 (2011); Tadler & Withers, *Towards a Less Hostile Discovery Process*, TRIAL, Mar. 2010, at 30.

[Section 2:7]

[1]The reference model can be found at www.edrm.net.

[Section 2:8]

[1]The Standards can be downloaded from www.abanet.org/litigation/discoverystandards/2004civildiscoverystandards.pdf.

The second standard provides that, in appropriate cases, some or all discovery materials should be converted to electronic format. The third standard describes the need to confer about e-discovery at the initial discovery conference. The fourth standard examines how attorney-client privilege and attorney work product material can be protected. The fifth standard acknowledges that in the future new storage media may not be electronic and suggests that existing discovery standards be consulted when data is stored in a new form.

§ 2:9 Managing Discovery of Electronic Information: A Pocket Guide for Judges

The Federal Judicial Center has published a pocket guide for federal judges suggesting how the discovery of electronically stored information should be managed. The Pocket Guide encourages judges to actively manage cases involving electronically stored information, raising points for the parties' consideration rather than awaiting the parties' identification and argument of the points.[1]

§ 2:10 Guidelines for State Trial Courts Regarding Discovery of Electronically-Stored Information

The Conference of Chief Justices has issued guidelines for state trial courts to use in dealing with discovery of electronically stored information. They have been drafted to offer guidance to judges faced with addressing practical problems created by the discovery of electronically stored information.[1]

§ 2:11 Case law update

Since the Federal Rules of Civil Procedure were amended in 2006, there has been a proliferation of case law across the country, in both federal and state courts, and have evolved as new technologies hit the scene. In 2006, the issues were more straightforward—when to use an expert (almost always) to assist with the e-discovery process, spoliation, the scope of the duty to preserve, the standards for sanctions. As the first half of 2013 comes to a close, we continue to see some of those issues (most

---

[Section 2:9]

[1]The Guide can be downloaded at www.fjc.gov/library/fjc_catalog.nsf.

[Section 2:10]

[1]The Guidelines can be downloaded at http://www.ncsconline.org/images/EDiscCCJGuidelinesFinal.pdf.

notably the standard for imposing specific sanctions), but new ones have emerged with the full fledged frontal impact of social media on everyday life, the move towards technology assisted legal review, and courts' lack of patience with parties who still refuse to cooperate and move the e-discovery process forward efficiently and effectively on their own—instead choosing to involve the courts because they are either not educated enough, or simply have not taken the time to be—by using the provisions carefully set out in the federal and now more than often, state rules.

E-discovery has become an area of the law that cannot be ignored any longer. In 2006—even though the Rules were not operative until December 1 of that year—we saw 266 reported decisions across the country on e-discovery. 2007 brought 318; in 2008 we saw 347. 2009 picked up the pace with 431 cases, and 2010 followed with another 400. 2011 added another 322, we saw 210 in 2012 and so far in 2013, current databases have at least 67 decisions.

Key issues for 2012 and 2013 include the discovery and admissibility of social media, cost recovery for e-discovery expenses and the use of technology assisted review also referred to as predictive coding actually includes a larger set of technology than just predictive coding, but the two are often used interchangeably. The *Publicis Groupe* case in February 2012 represented the first time a judge sanctioned the use of predictive coding in a case.[1]

In assisting the parties to an agreement on how predictive coding would be used, Judge Peck touted transparency in the discovery process as a key aspect of the type of cooperation advocated by the Sedona Conference. The court drew several lessons from this case for future litigants considering computer-assisted review. First, computer-assisted review is by no means a magical "Staples Easy-Button"; it remains appropriate only in certain large-data-volume cases. Allowing computer-assisted review in this case was an easy decision since both parties agreed to it. When the requesting party does not consent to predictive coding, the question for courts becomes whether the alternative methodologies the requesting party suggests would be better. Contrary to the belief that linear manual review is still the "gold standard" for accurate discovery, studies show that computerized searches can be just as good or even better.

While technology assisted legal review may be useful in certain

---

[Section 2:11]

[1]Moore v. Publicis Groupe, 287 F.R.D. 182, 18 Wage & Hour Cas. 2d (BNA) 1479 (S.D. N.Y. 2012), adopted, 2012 WL 1446534 (S.D. N.Y. 2012).

matters, it is by no means required. Writing for the Northern District of Indiana, Judge Robert Miller held in *In re Biomet M2a Magnum Hip Implant Products Liability Litigation*[2] that the defendant's use of keyword searches instead of predictive coding was sufficient for compliance with Fed. R. Civ. P. 26(d).

Cost recovery for e-discovery related costs in federal courts under 28 U.S.C. § 1940 was also a hot topic and one that courts disagreed on what, if anything, should be covered in a Bill of Costs under Rule 54 until the Third Circuit Court of Appeal's decision in *Race Tires America. Inc. v. Hoosier Racing Tire Corp.* in March 2012. The question before the Court was "whether § 1920(4), authorizes the taxation of an electronic discovery consultant's charges for data collection, preservation, searching, culling, conversion, and production as either the 'exemplification [or] the . . . making [of] copies of any materials where the copies are necessarily obtained for use in the case.'" [emphasis added]

Fed. R. Civ. P. 54(d)(1) states that "unless a federal statute, these rules, or court order provides otherwise, costs—other than attorney's fees—should be allowed to the prevailing party." Congress specified the litigation expenses that qualify as "taxable costs" in 20 U.S.C. § 1920. Because the vendor's work in this case did not produce illustrative evidence or the authentication of public records, the charges did not qualify as "exemplification" to be allowed under § 1920(4).

The court then undertook a detailed analysis of the "making copies of any materials" language of § 1920(4) and found that the addition of "any materials" language to the statute "plainly" signified that copying costs are not limited to paper copies. Following that review and the analysis of the existing charges, the court held that the three items listed above qualified as "making copies." In reviewing decisions that had allowed a much broader view of taxable costs, the court stated:

> The decisions that allow taxation of all, or essentially all, electronic discovery consultant charges, such as the district court's ruling in this case, are untethered from the statutory mooring. Section 1920(4) does not state that all steps that lead up to the production of copies of materials are taxable. It does not authorize taxation merely because today's technology requires technical expertise nor ordinarily possessed by the typical legal professional. It does not say that activities that encourage cost savings may be taxed. Section 1920(4) authorizes awarding only the cost of making copies.

Of note is the fact Race Tires attempted to argue on appeal

---

[2]In re Biomet M2a Magnum Hip Implant Products Liability Litigation, 2013 WL 1729682 (N.D. Ind. 2013).

that the defendants had made no showing that the resulting copies (of either electronically stored information or the DVDs) were obtained for use in the case per the language of 28 U.S.C.A. § 1920(4). The Third Circuit held that both the question of whether the copies were used for the case was reviewed only under an abuse of discretion standard, and it had no basis to find any such abuse by the District court.

The court also noted that "we do not think it is significant that the Federal Rules of Civil Procedure provide for the discovery of ESI or that the parties agree to 'exchange responsive and discoverable ESI' " and reiterated the presumption that the responding party bears the expense of complying with discovery requests. According to the Court, if a party is faced with an undue burden or cost in responding, it needs to seek the protections of Rule 26(c) to attempt to reduce or shift the costs of complying. Neither of the defendants obtained such an order, and they were each required to bear their costs as provided under the Rules.

Social media—both discoverability and authentication—have been prominent in case law in 2012 and 2013. Well over 20 decisions have addressed either the discovery of social media from multiple sites or the admissibility of social media at trial. Of those, Judge Hegarty's decision in *EEOC v. Original Honeybaked Ham Co.*[3] represented one of the first and most reasoned cases on the discovery of social media. The EEOC brought claims on behalf of 20 or so female employees alleging sexual harassment, retaliation following complaints they made, and civil rights violations. On a motion to compel, defendant sought information from plaintiffs' social media profiles, and the court allowed discovery following a well thought out process balancing the privacy concerns and potential privilege of plaintiffs' information with defendant's right to the ESI.

Defendant sought "numerous categories of documents designed to examine the class members' damages—emotional and financial—as well as documents going to the credibility and bias of the class members" including content posted on Facebook. In support of its motion, defendant presented information from Facebook it had already obtained showing that many of the class members communicated via social media, specifically Facebook, about "their employment with/separation from Defendant HBH, this lawsuit, their contemporaneous emotional state, and other topics."

---

[3]E.E.O.C. v. Original Honeybaked Ham Co. of Georgia, Inc., 116 Fair Empl. Prac. Cas. (BNA) 743, 96 Empl. Prac. Dec. (CCH) ¶ 44675, 2012 WL 5430974 (D. Colo. 2012).

First addressing where the content is stored—i.e. on social media sites in the cloud—the judge viewed the content:

> [A]s logically as though each class member had a file folder titled "Everything About Me" which they have voluntarily shared with others. If there are documents in this folder that contain information that is relevant or may lead to the discovery of admissible evidence in this lawsuit, the presumption is that it should be produced. The fact that it exists in cyberspace on an electronic device is a logistical, and perhaps, financial problem, but not a circumstance that removes the information from accessibility by a party opponent in litigation.
>
> . . .
>
> If all of this information was contained on pages filed in the "Everything About Me" folder, it would need to be produced. Should the outcome be different because it is on one's Facebook account? There is a strong argument that storing such information on Facebook and making it accessible to others presents an even stronger case for production, at least as it concerns any privacy objection. It was the claimants (or at least some of them) who, by their own volition, created relevant communications and shared them with others.

Finding that the defendant had established that the Facebook information sought contains discoverable information, the court went on to outline a plan for reviewing the ESI in camera so that it could be provided to defendant:

- The court would retain a special master/forensic expert to assist it in gathering the information;
- Plaintiffs were to provide cell phones used, access to social media profiles, and access to email accounts for the relevant period;
- The parties had to work together to create a questionnaire to be given to the plaintiffs to identify the potential sources of electronically stored information and to draft instructions to be given to the Special Master defining the parameters of the information to be collected;
- The court would review the data in camera, identify relevant information and provide it to plaintiffs to review for privilege; and
- Plaintiffs would review the relevant data, provide objections to the court, create a privilege log and provide relevant, non-privileged data to defendant.

As to costs, interestingly, the court considered requiring defendant to pay for the entire process, but had the parties split the cost after finding that was not in keeping with the Federal Rules of Civil Procedure. The court found it would re-review having defendant pay for the entire costs of the Special Master if there was very little relevant information revealed by the process. Judge Hegarty's decision in this case set the stage for discovering social media—parties need to ensure that any request is narrowly tailored and has a basis for the request before it will be permitted.

Other issues that continue to plague the courts in e-discovery opinions include cooperation of counsel,[4] use of a Fed. R. Evid. 502(d) order to protect against inadvertent disclosure of privileged information[5] (hint: you should use one), cost-shifting[6] and the use of the adverse inference instruction as a sanction for failure to preserve and spoliation.[7]

II. CHECKLISTS

§ 2:12 Checklist of common e-discovery mistakes

- ☐ Failing to have a discovery plan ready to implement at the first sign of impending litigation
- ☐ Neglecting to implement a backup policy or a document retention policy
- ☐ Declining to cease document destruction practices once there is a preservation duty
- ☐ Conducting do-it-yourself collection of electronically stored information rather than using individuals properly trained in handling digital data
- ☐ Ignoring key locations of electronically stored information and important file types
- ☐ Overlooking metadata preservation
- ☐ Failing to recognize that delete does not mean delete
- ☐ Assuming the information technology department can shoulder the e-discovery burden alone
- ☐ Neglecting to chose carefully an electronic evidence expert
- ☐ Failing to use an online repository tool for paper and electronic document review

---

[4]Kleen Products LLC v. Packaging Corp. of America, 2012 WL 4498465 (N.D. Ill. 2012), objections overruled, 2013-1 Trade Cas. (CCH) ¶ 78213, 2013 WL 120240 (N.D. Ill. 2013).

[5]Rajala v. McGuire Woods, LLP, 90 Fed. R. Evid. Serv. 393 (D. Kan. 2013).

[6]See, e.g., W Holding Co., Inc. v. Chartis Ins. Co. of Puerto Rico, 2013 WL 1352426 (D.P.R. 2013).

[7]See, e.g., Sekisui America Corp. v. Hart, 2013 WL 2951924 (S.D. N.Y. 2013); Pillay v. Millard Refrigerated Services, Inc., 27 A.D. Cas. (BNA) 1716, 2013 WL 2251727 (N.D. Ill. 2013).

NOTES

Commentary

This checklist is adapted from a paper prepared by Jonathan Sachs, Legal Consultant for Kroll Ontrack.

III. FORMS

§ 2:13 Seventh Circuit standing order relating to the discovery of electronically stored information

[Caption]

STANDING ORDER RELATING TO THE DISCOVERY OF ELECTRONICALLY STORED INFORMATION

This court is participating in the Pilot Program initiated by the Seventh Circuit Electronic Discovery Committee. Parties and counsel in the Pilot Program with civil cases pending in this Court shall familiarize themselves with, and comport themselves consistent with, that committee's Principles Relating to the Discovery of Electronically Stored Information. For more information about the Pilot Program please see the Web site of The Seventh Circuit Bar Association, www.7thcircuitbar.org. If any party believes that there is good cause why a particular case should be exempted, in whole or in part, from the Principles Relating to the Discovery of Electronically Stored Information, then that party may raise such reason with the Court.

General Principles

Principle 1.01 (Purpose)

The purpose of these Principles is to assist courts in the administration of Federal Rule of Civil Procedure 1, to secure the just, speedy, and inexpensive determination of every civil case, and to promote, whenever possible, the early resolution of disputes regarding the discovery of electronically stored information ("ESI") without Court intervention. Understanding of the feasibility, reasonableness, costs, and benefits of various aspects of e-discovery will inevitably evolve as judges, attorneys and parties to litigation gain more experience with ESI and as technology advances.

Principle 1.02 (Cooperation)

An attorney's zealous representation of a client is not compromised by conducting discovery in a cooperative manner. The failure of counsel or the parties to litigation to cooperate in facilitating and reasonably limiting discovery requests and responses raises litigation costs and contributes to the risk of sanctions.

Principle 1.03 (Discovery Proportionality)

The proportionality standard set forth in Fed. R. Civ. P. 26(b)(2)(C) should be applied in each case when formulating a discovery plan. To further the application of the proportionality standard in discovery, requests for production of ESI and related responses should be reasonably targeted, clear, and as specific as practicable.

Early Case Assessment Principles

Principle 2.01 (Duty to Meet and Confer on Discovery and to Identify Disputes for Early Resolution)

(a) Prior to the initial status conference with the Court, counsel shall meet and discuss the application of the discovery process set forth in the Federal Rules of Civil Procedure and these Principles to their specific case. Among the issues to be discussed are:

(1) the identification of relevant and discoverable ESI and documents, including methods for identifying an initial subset of sources of ESI and documents that are most likely to contain the relevant and discoverable information as well as methodologies for culling the relevant and discoverable ESI and documents from that initial subset (see Principle 2.05);

(2) the scope of discoverable ESI and documents to be preserved by the parties;

(3) the formats for preservation and production of ESI and documents;

(4) the potential for conducting discovery in phases or stages as a method for reducing costs and burden; and

(5) the potential need for a protective order and any procedures to which the parties might agree for handling inadvertent production of privileged information and other privilege waiver issues pursuant to Rule 502(d) or (e) of the Federal Rules of Evidence.

(b) Disputes regarding ESI that counsel for the parties are unable to resolve shall be presented to the Court at the initial status conference, Fed. R. Civ. P. Rule 16(b) Scheduling Conference, or as soon as possible thereafter.

(c) The attorneys for each party shall review and understand how their client's data is stored and retrieved before the meet and confer discussions in order to determine what issues must be addressed during the meet and confer discussions.

(d) If the Court determines that any counsel or party in a case has failed to cooperate and participate in good faith in the meet and confer process or is impeding the purpose of these Principles, the Court may require additional discussions prior to the commencement of discovery, and may impose sanctions, if appropriate.

Principle 2.02 (E-Discovery Liaison(s))

In most cases, the meet and confer process will be aided by participation of an e-discovery liaison(s) as defined in this Principle. In the event of a dispute concerning the preservation or production of ESI, each party shall designate an individual(s) to act as e-discovery liaison(s) for purposes of meeting, conferring, and attending court hearings on the subject. Regardless of whether the e-discovery liaison(s) is an attorney (in-house or outside counsel), a third party consultant, or an employee of the party, the e-discovery liaison(s) must:

(a) be prepared to participate in e-discovery dispute resolution;

(b) be knowledgeable about the party's e-discovery efforts;

(c) be, or have reasonable access to those who are, familiar with the party's electronic systems and capabilities in order to explain those systems and answer relevant questions; and

(d) be, or have reasonable access to those who are, knowledgeable about the technical aspects of e-discovery, including electronic document storage, organization, and format issues, and relevant information retrieval technology, including search methodology.

Principle 2.03 (Preservation Requests and Orders)

(a) Appropriate preservation requests and preservation orders further the goals of these Principles. Vague and overly broad preservation requests do not further the goals of these Principles and are therefore disfavored. Vague and overly broad preservation orders should not be sought or entered. The information sought to be preserved through the use of a preservation letter request or order should be reasonable in scope and mindful of the factors set forth in Rule 26(b)(2)(C).

(b) To the extent counsel or a party requests preservation of ESI through the use of a preservation letter, such requests should attempt to ensure the preservation of relevant and discoverable information and to facilitate cooperation between requesting and receiving counsel and parties by transmitting specific and useful information. Examples of such specific and useful information include, but are not limited to:

(1) names of the parties;

(2) factual background of the potential legal claim(s) and identification of potential cause(s) of action;

(3) names of potential witnesses and other people reasonably anticipated to have relevant evidence;

(4) relevant time period; and

(5) other information that may assist the responding party in assessing what information to preserve.

(c) If the recipient of a preservation request chooses to respond, that response should provide the requesting counsel or party with useful information regarding the preservation efforts undertaken by the responding party. Examples of such useful and specific information include, but are not limited to, information that:

(1) identifies what information the responding party is willing to preserve and the steps being taken in response to the preservation letter;

(2) identifies any disagreement(s) with the request to preserve; and

(3) identifies any further preservation issues that were not raised.

(d) Nothing in these Principles shall be construed as requiring the sending of a preservation request or requiring the sending of a response to such a request.

Principle 2.04 (Scope of Preservation)

(a) Every party to litigation and its counsel are responsible for taking reasonable and proportionate steps to preserve relevant and discoverable ESI within its possession, custody or control. Determining which steps are reasonable and proportionate in particular litigation is a fact specific inquiry that will vary from case to case. The parties and counsel should address preservation issues at the outset of a case, and should continue to address them as the case progresses and their understanding of the issues and the facts improves.

(b) Discovery concerning the preservation and collection efforts of another party may be appropriate but, if used unadvisedly, can also contribute to the unnecessary expense and delay and may inappropriately implicate work product and attorney-client privileged matter. Accordingly, prior to initiating such discovery a party shall confer with the party from whom the information is sought concerning: (i) the specific need for such discovery, including its relevance to issues likely to arise in the litigation; and (ii) the suitability of alternative means for obtaining the information. Nothing herein exempts deponents on merits issues from answering questions concerning the preservation and collection of their documents, ESI, and tangible things.

(c) The parties and counsel should come to the meet and confer conference prepared to discuss the claims and defenses in the case including specific issues, time frame, potential damages, and targeted discovery that each anticipates requesting. In addition, the parties and counsel should be prepared to discuss reasonably foreseeable preservation issues that relate directly to the information that the other party is seeking. The parties and counsel need not raise every conceivable issue that may arise concerning their preservation efforts; however, the identification of any such preservation issues should be specific.

(d) The following categories of ESI generally are not discoverable in most cases, and if any party intends to request the preservation or production of these categories, then that intention should be discussed at the meet and confer or as soon thereafter as practicable:

(1) "deleted," "slack," "fragmented," or "unallocated" data on hard drives;
(2) random access memory (RAM) or other ephemeral data;
(3) on-line access data such as temporary internet files, history, cache, cookies, etc.;
(4) data in metadata fields that are frequently updated automatically, such as last-opened dates;
(5) backup data that is substantially duplicative of data that is more accessible elsewhere; and
(6) other forms of ESI whose preservation requires extraordinary affirmative measures that are not utilized in the ordinary course of business.

(e) If there is a dispute concerning the scope of a party's preservation efforts, the parties or their counsel must meet and confer and fully explain their reasons for believing that additional efforts are, or are not, reasonable and proportionate, pursuant to Rule 26(b)(2)(C). If the parties are unable to resolve a preservation issue, then the issue should be raised promptly with the Court.

Principle 2.05 (Identification of Electronically Stored Information)

(a) At the Rule 26(f) conference or as soon thereafter as possible, counsel or the parties shall discuss potential methodologies for identifying ESI for production.

(b) Topics for discussion may include, but are not limited to, any plans to:

(1) eliminate duplicative ESI and whether such elimination will occur only within each particular custodian's data set or whether it will occur across all custodians;

(2) filter data based on file type, date ranges, sender, receiver, custodian, search terms, or other similar parameters; and

(3) use keyword searching, mathematical or thesaurus-based topic or concept clustering, or other advanced culling technologies.

Principle 2.06 (Production Format)

(a) At the Rule 26(f) conference, counsel and the parties should make a good faith effort to agree on the format(s) for production of ESI (whether native or some other reasonably usable form). If counsel or the parties are unable to resolve a production format issue, then the issue should be raised promptly with the Court.

(b) The parties should confer on whether ESI stored in a database or a database management system can be produced by querying the database for discoverable information, resulting in a report or a reasonably usable and exportable electronic file for review by the requesting counsel or party.

(c) ESI and other tangible or hard copy documents that are not text-searchable need not be made text-searchable.

(d) Generally, the requesting party is responsible for the incremental cost of creating its copy of requested information. Counsel or the parties are encouraged to discuss cost sharing for optical character recognition (OCR) or other upgrades of paper documents or nontext-searchable electronic images that may be contemplated by each party.

Education Principles

Principle 3.01 (Judicial Expectations of Counsel)

Because discovery of ESI is being sought more frequently in civil litigation and the production and review of ESI can involve greater expense than discovery of paper documents, it is in the interest of justice that all judges, counsel and parties to litigation become familiar with the fundamentals of discovery of ESI. It is expected by the judges adopting these Principles that all counsel will have done the following in connection with each litigation matter in which they file an appearance:

(1) Familiarize themselves with the e-discovery provisions of Federal Rules of Civil Procedure, including Rules 26, 33, 34, 37, and 45, as well as any applicable State Rules of Procedure;

(2) Familiarize themselves with the Advisory Committee Report on the 2006 Amendments to the Federal Rules of Civil Procedure, available at http://www.uscourts.gov/rules/EDiscovery_w_Notes.pdf; and

(3) Familiarize themselves with these Principles.

Principle 3.02 (Duty of Continuing Education)

Judges, attorneys and parties to litigation should continue to educate themselves on e-discovery by consulting applicable case law, pertinent statutes, the Federal Rules of Civil Procedure, the Federal Rules of Evidence, The Sedona Conference® publications relating to e-discovery,[1] additional materials available on Web sites of the courts,[2] and of other organizations[3] providing educational information regarding the discovery of ESI.[4]

____

[typed name]
United States *[District/Bankruptcy/Magistrate]* Judge

[Section 2:13]

[1]http://www.thesedonaconference.org/content/miscFiles/publications_html?grp=wgs110.

[2]E.g. http://www.ilnd.uscourts.gov/home/.

[3]E.g. http://www.7thcircuitbar.org,www.fjc.gov (under Educational Programs and Materials).

[4]E.g. http://www.du.edu/legalinstitute.

Chapter 3

Protecting Electronically Stored Information

I. GUIDELINES

II. CHECKLISTS

III. FORMS

Research References

Treatises and Practice Aids

Grenig & Gleisner, eDiscovery & Digital Evidence §§ 10:1 to 10:20

Trial Strategy

Computer Technology in Civil Litigation, 71 Am. Jur. Trials 111

Additional References

Grenig and Kinsler, Handbook of Federal Civil Discovery and Disclosure §§ 13.1 to 13.6 (3d ed.)

Preservation and Migration of Electronic Records: The State of the Issue, U.S. National Archives & Records Administration, http://www.archives.gov/era/papers/preservation.html?template=print

I. GUIDELINES

§ 3:1 Generally

Computer use policies are an important part of a records and information management program. Because an unprotected computer can quickly be infected or hacked after connecting to the Internet, it is essential to protect electronically stored information. The use of computers and the Internet by members or employees can open an organization to liability for infringement of intellectual property rights, copyright violations, unfair competition, defamation, sexual harassment, wrongful termination, fraud, and invasion of privacy. In addition, connection to the Internet means exposure to computer hackers, data theft, viruses, and industrial espionage.

Organizations allowing employee use of computers, particularly use of the Internet, should have a computer use policy in place to limit exposure to liability and to protect electronically stored information. A computer-use policy should set forth an objective standard for employees to apply when using electronic media and services. It should describe appropriate uses of the Internet and make clear that employees are using the organization's equipment. Users should understand that there is no privacy expectation in the use of computers and that e-mail and Internet usage may be monitored. In-house counsel should be proactive in educating employees on the best practices regarding e-mail and other digital information.

Employers must take steps to protect laptops from misuse—warning employees what is and is not acceptable.[1] Employees should be urged not to use employer laptops for personal use. Employees should be informed in writing that whatever they input on the laptop belongs to the employer and there is no right of privacy.

§ 3:2 Shadow information technology—Generally

Shadow information technology (sometimes referred to as rogue IT or consumer IT) may operate outside an organization's information technology department. While shadow IT may be an important source for innovation, shadow IT is often in conflict with an organization's requirements for security, control, documentation, and reliability.[1]

Because shadow IT is not under the control of and not supported by an organization's information technology department, the use of shadow IT creates "unofficial" and "uncontrolled data flows." The use of shadow IT makes it difficult for an organization to comply with record-keeping laws such as Sarbanes-Oxley. Security risks may be created when data or applications are moved outside protected systems.

There are three categories of shadow IT: storage of convenience, tools of convenience, and applications of convenience. Organizations that do not limit shadow IT may create a number of problems, including serious problems in ensuring that all potentially relevant sources of data are located in response to discovery requests.

§ 3:3 Shadow information technology—Storage of convenience

Storage of convenience includes thumb drives, jump drives, and Internet-based storage.

[Section 3:1]

[1]See Ackerman, *Company Computer Policies Risk Becoming Obsolete*, Nat'l L. J, April 2, 2012, at 47; Baldas, *Suing Former Employees Over Laptop Theft*, Nat'l L. J., May 11, 2009, at 16.

[Section 3:2]

[1]See study reported at http://www.rsa.com/company/news/releases/pdfs/RSA-insider-confessions.pdf, finding that 35% of employees feel the need to work around security measures or protocols to be able to do their work efficiently, and 63% send documents to their home e-mail address to continue work from home, even when aware this is probably not allowed.

§ 3:4 Shadow information technology—Tools of convenience

Tools of convenience include communication platforms, utilities, hardware and software applications, MySpace, Facebook, Voice over Internet Protocol (VOIP), and Internet service provider mail such as Yahoo! and Gmail. An application of convenience is based on a corporate standard but is used in an unconventional way or instead of existing enterprise programs. Organizations that do not limit shadow IT may create a number of problems, including serious problems in ensuring that all potentially relevant sources of data are located in response to discovery requests.

§ 3:5 Shadow information technology—Applications of convenience

An application of convenience is based on a corporate standard but is used in an unconventional way or instead of existing enterprise programs. Over time, the use of applications of convenience can result in the creation of inconsistencies arising from the accumulation of small differences from one version to another.

§ 3:6 Updates

It is normally prudent to install the latest updates of applications in order to reduce security vulnerabilities. Because the installation of updates can interfere with the operation of the computer or peripherals, it is important to back up data before installing updates.

§ 3:7 Passwords

It is essential to use passwords and to keep them safe. If it is necessary to write down a password, it should be written in a code so that only the password owner can figure out the password. No one should be told a password. Any compromised password should be changed immediately. The same password should not be used for everything. One should not allow Websites to remember a password and one should not let the Web browser remember Website passwords. A password should be at least eight characters long, contain at least one upper case letter, one lower case letter, one number, and one symbol. A password should be significantly different than previously used passwords.

Because laptops, smartphones, and personal data assistants are easily lost or stolen, the built-in password protection on these devices should be enabled. However, this will probably not prevent someone with specialized knowledge from bypassing this protection. Employees and staff should also be warned about the danger of accessing the Internet on public computers. Employees accessing the Internet on public computers may be leaving behind passwords, surfing history, data in temporary files, cookies, and other personal information.

§ 3:8 Computer viruses

A computer virus is a normally undetectable program within a program that causes a computer to function in an abnormal manner. There is no excuse for not regularly using antivirus software, keeping it up to date, and using it properly. An antivirus scan should be run on the entire hard disk at least once a week and preferably daily.[1]

Even where antivirus software has been installed, employees and staff should be instructed that e-mail attachments should be opened cautiously. No one should open an attachment that is unexpected, even if the message appears to be from a known source. For example, e-mail spoofing is e-mail activity in which the sender address and other parts of the e-mail header are altered to appear as though the e-mail originated from a different source.

Consideration should be given to prohibiting the connection of MP3 players such as iPods to computers. MP3 players can accidentally put a virus on a network. In addition, MP3 players, which are nothing more than external storage with a music player built in, can be used to take information off a computer network.

Employees and staff should also be instructed not to download programs without first checking with the information systems administrator. Unauthorized downloads can compromise a computer system.

§ 3:9 Spyware and firewalls

Because information can flow both ways when connected to the Internet, a firewall is necessary to prevent unauthorized access to computers and networks. Hardware firewalls are also available to protect networks. Spyware and adware can be limited by using an anti-spyware or anti-adware programs. These programs should be run weekly and updated regularly.

[Section 3:8]

[1]But see Wiener & Celeita, *Computer Infections Are Bad Enough, But the Cure Can Kill: Anti-Virus Software Can Contaminate Evidence, Even When the Intent Is Innocent,* Nat'l L. J. 17, Aug. 24, 2009, at 17.

§ 3:10 Backup storage

It is important to have a computer backup storage system. At a minimum, data should be backed up daily. Hardware and software are available for automatic backups. A specific individual should be assigned responsibility for overseeing backups. Backup logs should reviewed on a regular basis to determine whether backups are being made as required. In addition, the backup system should be tested periodically to ensure the backup system is working.

§ 3:11 Technology use policy—Generally

Every organization should have a technology use policy, informing all persons using computers of what they can and cannot do when using e-mail, surfing the Internet, and using computers and other digital systems.[1] It is also important that a technology policy be enforced and monitored for compliance.[2] Employees must be educated about the necessity of protecting sensitive or confidential information.[3] An organization should set forth explicitly what is forbidden through a compliance policy, employee handbooks, or employee agreements.[4]

§ 3:12 Technology use policy—Access to information technology

Access to servers, routers, phone switches, and individual

[Section 3:11]

[1]See Akerman, *Time to Review Corporate Computer Policies*, Nat'l L. J., Feb. 1, 2010, at 17.

[2]See City of Ontario, Cal. v. Quon, 130 S. Ct. 2619, 177 L. Ed. 2d 216, 30 I.E.R. Cas. (BNA) 1345, 93 Empl. Prac. Dec. (CCH) ¶ 43907, 159 Lab. Cas. (CCH) ¶ 61011 (2010).

[3]See, e.g., LVRC Holdings LLC v. Brekka, 581 F.3d 1127, 29 I.E.R. Cas. (BNA) 1153 (9th Cir. 2009) (employee did not access a computer "without authorization" or "exceed authorized access," in violation Computer Fraud and Abuse Act, when he e-mailed documents from his work computer to himself and to his wife while he was still employed by employer, where his employer gave permission to use his work computer while employed, and employee entitled to obtain documents at time). But see International Airport Centers, L.L.C. v. Citrin, 440 F.3d 418, 24 I.E.R. Cas. (BNA) 129 (7th Cir. 2006) (rejected by, U.S. v. Nosal, 642 F.3d 781, 32 I.E.R. Cas. (BNA) 271 (9th Cir. 2011), reh'g en banc granted, 661 F.3d 1180 (9th Cir. 2011) and on reh'g en banc, 676 F.3d 854 (9th Cir. 2012)) (employee's authorization to use company computers is predicated on employee's agency relationship with employer).

[4]See Continental Group, Inc. v. KW Property Management, LLC, 622 F. Supp. 2d 1357 (S.D. Fla. 2009), order clarified, 2009 WL 3644475 (S.D. Fla. 2009); EF Cultural Travel BV v. Explorica, Inc., 274 F.3d 577 (1st Cir. 2001).

computers should be restricted. Something as simple as putting a password on a screensaver can prevent unauthorized users from using a computer that has been inadvertently left on. Because high-capacity USB drives or thumb drives are compact, easy to use, and can store huge amounts of information, they can be used to quickly steal data. It may be appropriate to disable USB ports on computers. Consideration should be given to using technology to control anything connecting to a USB port including thumb drives and iPods. Employees should be instructed to avoid using a home computer for work purposes if the home computer is used by others.

§ 3:13 Technology use policy—File sharing networks

Peer-to-peer file sharing networks allowing music and movies to be shared can also be used to share company secrets and personal data. Steps should be taken to prevent sharing of enterprise information on peer-to-peer file sharing networks.

§ 3:14 Technology use policy—Internet and e-mails

A technology use policy should describe the extent of usage of the Internet allowed, specifically stating the restrictions on the use of e-mail and the Internet. The policy should inform employees that the organization's computer, technology, and communications system, including e-mail and the Internet, are the sole property of the organization.[1]

It is important to inform employees that no e-mail message is considered private, and that employees should not expect their messages will remain private.[2] The policy should state that the

---

[Section 3:14]

[1]Cf. City of Ontario, Cal. v. Quon, 130 S. Ct. 2619, 177 L. Ed. 2d 216, 30 I.E.R. Cas. (BNA) 1345, 93 Empl. Prac. Dec. (CCH) ¶ 43907, 159 Lab. Cas. (CCH) ¶ 61011 (2010) (assuming police officer had reasonable expectation of privacy in text messages sent on pager provided him by city, search of text messages was reasonable where search was motivated by legitimate work-related purpose of determining whether character limit on city's contract with wireless communications provider was sufficient to meet city's needs, and search was not excessively intrusive in light of that justification)

[2]See Alamar Ranch, LLC v. County of Boise, 2009 WL 3669741 (D. Idaho 2009) (client waived attorney-client privilege for e-mails sent to her attorney from her work computer, using her work e-mail address; employer put all employees, including client, on notice that e-mails sent from work e-mail addresses were property of the employer, would be monitored and stored by the employer, and should not be assumed to be confidential); In re Application Pursuant to 28

organization reserves the right to monitor usage of e-mail and the Internet in the ordinary course of business.[3]

A technology policy should prohibit the use of e-mail or the Internet to communicate harassing, offensive, defamatory, or sensitive messages, including, but not limited to messages inappropriate under the organization's sexual harassment policy. The policy should prohibit soliciting or proselytizing for charitable, religious, political, or other nonbusiness purposes. It should also prohibit the transmission of trade secrets, confidential or privileged communications; unauthorized copying and distributing of copyrighted material; and uses such as chain mail that degrade system performance.

Employees and staff should be warned about e-mails appearing to come from legitimate companies. (This is referred to as

---

U.S.C. Section 1782 for an Order Permitting Christen Sveaas to Take Discovery from Dominique Levy, L & M Galleries and other non-participants for use in Actions Pending in the Norway, 249 F.R.D. 96 (S.D. N.Y. 2008) (attorney-client privilege waived with respect to e-mails and attachments reflecting legal advice by law firm representing buyer of sculpture when e-mails disclosed to art broker); Rhoads Industries, Inc. v. Building Materials Corp. of America, 254 F.R.D. 238 (E.D. Pa. 2008) (person receiving privileged communication in form e-mail may waive privilege by sending e-mail to third party); Business Integration Services, Inc. v. AT & T Corp., 2008 WL 5159781 (S.D. N.Y. 2008) (defendant waived attorney-client privilege by ratifying employee's disclosure to plaintiff of substantial part of substance of corporate counsel's communications); Scott v. Beth Israel Medical Center Inc., 17 Misc. 3d 934, 847 N.Y.S.2d 436 (Sup 2007) (e-mails physician sent to his personal attorney by computer system owned by physician's employer were not protected by attorney-client privilege where hospital had e-mail policy mandating that computer and e-mail systems could be used solely for business purposes and warning that employees had no expectation of privacy in any communication created, received, saved, or sent using hospital's computers). See also In re Asia Global Crossing, Ltd., 322 B.R. 247 (Bankr. S.D. N.Y. 2005); Long v. Marubeni America Corp., 2006 WL 2998671 (S.D. N.Y. 2006). But see Roth v. Aon Corp., 254 F.R.D. 538, Fed. Sec. L. Rep. (CCH) ¶ 95035 (N.D. Ill. 2009) (receipt of by nonlawyers of e-mail between corporate officer and counsel containing draft of "Compensation for Services" section of Form 10-K to be filed with SEC did not destroy attorney-client privilege attached to document where nonlawyers were corporate employees directly responsible for drafting and editing Form 10-K); Sims v. Lakeside School, 2007 WL 2745367 (W.D. Wash. 2007) (policy dictates that communications to one's spouse or lawyer be protected to preserve sanctity of communications made in confidence); Curto v. Medical World Communications, Inc., 99 Fair Empl. Prac. Cas. (BNA) 298, 2006 WL 1318387 (E.D. N.Y. 2006) (inconsistent or sporadic enforcement of computer policy insufficient to destroy employee's reasonable expectation of privacy as to e-mails at issue).

[3]But see U.S. v. Ziegler, 474 F.3d 1184, 153 Lab. Cas. (CCH) ¶ 60340 (9th Cir. 2007) (government search had to comply with Fourth Amendment where employee had reasonable expectation of privacy over personal items saved on workplace computer when computer terminal was in private, locked office).

"phishing.") These fake e-mails attempt to trick people into revealing confidential information, thinking they are replying to their bank, credit card company, or Internet service provider. Legitimate companies should not send e-mails asking that personal information be updated. The Web links in e-mails should be used with great care. It is safer to access the Website of an e-mail sender through the browser rather than the hyperlink.

§ 3:15 Technology use policy—Social media policy

Organizations should also include a simple, one page policy on the use of Social Media for both business and personal uses. Information regarding a company, individuals or a brand can be created and spread across the world in a matter of minutes. Some organizations encourage its employees to use social media to create interest in the projects they are working on, and some organizations create or use internal social media for employees to interact on during working hours. All of these scenarios mean that the need to educate employees on the risks associated with social media has increased and organizations need to provide their employees with basic tenets of how to act online.

What an employee can communicate about the workplace on social-networking sites should be addressed in a policy.[1] Although a company has an interest in preventing employees from disparaging it or releasing to the public confidential information, the company cannot deny employees rights protected by the National Labor Relations Board.[2]

§ 3:16 Theft of data

Federal and state laws require organizations to take steps to prevent data theft, notify consumers of the theft, and create new remedies for companies to sue data thieves.[1] For example, Massachusetts law requires companies maintaining personal data

---

[Section 3:15]

[1]See Allen & Wylie, *Managing and Collecting Social Media for Discovery*, INFORMATIONMANAGEMENT, May/June 2013, at 22; Radhakant & Diskin, How Social Media Are Transforming Litigation, Litig., Spring 2013, at 17; Kennedy Ackerman, *Company Computer Policies Risk Becoming Obsolete*, Nat'l L. J., Apr. 2, 2012, at 47.

[2]See Ackerman, *Company Computer Policies Risk Becoming Obsolete*, Nat'l L. J., Apr. 2, 2012, at 47.

[Section 3:16]

[1]See Ackerman, *Company Computer Policies Risk Becoming Obsolete*, Nat'l L. J., Apr. 2, 2012, at 47.

belonging to Massachusetts residents, whether or not the company does business in Massachusetts, to institute a data-compliance program including security policies that must be enforced through technology such as encryption.[2]

In 2004, the Sarbanes-Oxley Act required the New York Stock Exchange to mandate its members to promulgate policies as part of a comprehensive compliance program to protect both personal and competitively sensitive data.[3] Forty-five states have enacted statutes requiring business to notify consumers of a breach of their personal data.[4]

The Computer Fraud and Abuse Act[5] provides a civil remedy for a company that "suffers damage or loss" by reason of a violation of the Act.[6] Liability for data theft is based on whether the access to the company's computers was unauthorized or exceeded authorized access.[7]

§ 3:17 Employee-owned devices

The growing trend of employees bringing their own mobile devices to work (frequently referred to as BYOD) has increased employer concerns with respect to privacy and security while at the same time having the potential to increase productivity.[1] A individual's personal devices may provide access to the individ-

---

[2]201 CMR Sec. 17.03–17.05. Since 2003,

[3]See Ackerman, *Company Computer Policies Risk Becoming Obsolete*, Nat'l L. J., Apr. 2, 2012, at 47. See also NYSE's Listed Company Manual § 303A, ¶ 10.

[4]See, e.g., Cal. Civ. Code § 1798.82(a); Wis. Stat. § 134.98.

[5]See 18 U.S.C.A. § 1030.

[6]18 U.S.C.A. § 1030(g).

[7]See, e.g., EF Cultural Travel BV v. Zefer Corp., 318 F.3d 58 (1st Cir. 2003).

[Section 3:17]

[1]See Kozubek, *The Privacy and Security Concerns of BYOD*, INSIDECOUNSEL, Oct. 2012; Gatewood, *The Nuts and Bolts of Making BYOD Work*, INFORMATIONMANAGEMENT, Nov./Dec. 2012, at 26; Acohido, *Using Personal Devices at Work Gets More Secure*, USA TODAY, Jan. 8, 2013, at 1B. According to Fulbright's 8th Annual Litigation Trends Survey Report, 91% of the U.S. companies responding stated they allowed employees to use mobile hand-held devices to conduct company business. On the other hand, 45% of the United Kingdom companies responding said they did not allow employees to use mobile hand-held devices to conduct company business. Only 34% of the companies responding said they were concerned about any litigation or investigations arising from their employees' use of mobile devices.

ual's work email and attached files.[2] Such a personal device and the files it contains may be subject to discovery because the device was also used for the employer's business.

Some employer require employees to install mobile device management (MDM) software on their personally owned devices, giving employers control over the device—including the ability to wipe all data from device if it is lost or stolen.[3]

Employers should state their right to access and protect devices in carefully drafted stand-alone agreements written in plain English.[4] An employee mobile device policy should address the following:

- Specify which mobile communications carriers employers may use.
- Require employees to sign a waiver or release form.
- Determine who employer policies will be audited, assessed, and enforced in relation to the devices.
- Consider whether employees will be reimbursed for employer-specific use of a personal device.
- Restrict or limit software applications that employees may download.
- Determine the types of employer-related resources employees may access on their devices.
- Instruct employees on appropriate security procedures and enable them to separate the employer's information from personal information on the device.
- Require employees to load approved security-related software for access to the employer's systems and servers.
- Determine the IT support the organization will provide for the device or its applications.
- Create a procedure for retrieval of the employer's data when a personally owned device user's employment is terminated or the device is lost or stolen.
- Create a procedure for the retrieval of the device if it is

[2]See Ross, "Bring Your Own Device" Has Its Dark Side, NAT'L L. J., March 18, 2013, at 18.

[3]See Kozubek, *The Privacy and Security Concerns of BYOD*, INSIDECOUNSEL, Oct. 2012.

[4]See Kozubek, *The Privacy and Security Concerns of BYOD*, INSIDECOUNSEL, Oct. 2012.

needed for data collection and preservation in association with a legal hold order.[5]

Mobile devices should have the following minimum protections:

- The device must be protected by a passcode that automatically erases the data after a predefined number of failed attempts to access it.
- The device must be able to be locked remotely, disabling all features except allowing an emergency call to be dialed or allowing an incoming call that would be helpful in effecting the return of the device.
- The device must have a remote-wipe capability.[6]

Employer should have a clearly defined protocol for the individual and the organization to follow in the event a device is lost or stolen. The protocol should provide:

- Who to contact if the device has system access.
- What applications on the device interact with what employer systems.
- How to remotely lock or wipe the device.
- What system passwords must be changed or access temporarily removed.[7]

II. CHECKLISTS

§ 3:18 Computer use policy checklist

- ☐ **Compliance with Intellectual Property Laws**
    - ☐ Shareware properly licensed.
    - ☐ Software licenses.
    - ☐ Copyrighted material.
    - ☐ Proper use of trademarks and service marks.
    - ☐ Determine reasonable efforts to be made to avoid disclosure and consequent loss of trade secret status.
- ☐ **Authorized Computer Use**
    - ☐ Business communications.
    - ☐ Limited personal use.
- ☐ **Unauthorized Computer Use; Types of Prohibited Material**

---

[5]Gatewood, *The Nuts and Bolts of Making BYOD Work*, INFORMATION-MANAGEMENT, Nov./Dec. 2012, at 26.

[6]Gatewood, *The Nuts and Bolts of Making BYOD Work*, INFORMATION-MANAGEMENT, Nov./Dec. 2012, at 26.

[7]Gatewood, The Nuts and Bolts of Making BYOD Work, INFORMATION-MANAGEMENT, Nov./Dec. 2012, at 26.

- ☐ Fraudulent.
- ☐ Harassing.
- ☐ Intimidating.
- ☐ Sexually explicit.
- ☐ Political.
- ☐ Commercial.

☐ **Uses in Violation of U.S. Export Restrictions**

☐ **Installation of Unauthorized Software Including Encryption Software**

☐ **Maintaining confidentiality of attorney-client communications**

☐ **Virus detection and avoidance**

☐ **Identify individual(s) authorized to install and use encryption software**

☐ **Employee privacy**

- ☐ Require written employee consent to management review of material created, stored, and disseminated using company's computers and networks.
- ☐ Acknowledgment of no expectation of privacy.

☐ **Passwords**

- ☐ Employees must maintain secrecy of their passwords
- ☐ Employees must understand they will be held liable for all transactions conducted with their passwords

III. FORMS

§ 3:19 Computer use policy—Personal use prohibited

COMPUTER USE POLICY

Section One Purpose

This document describes the policies and guidelines for use of the computer and telecommunications resources of [*[name of organization]*/*[owner of computer system]*] ("Employer"). All computer users employed by Employer have the responsibility to use these resources in a professional, ethical, and lawful manner. The computers and computer accounts provided to employees by Employer are to assist them in the performance of their jobs. The computer and telecommunications system belong to Employer and may only be used for authorized business purposes.

Section Two Waiver of Privacy

Employees waive their right of privacy in anything they create, store, send, or receive on Employer's computer or telecommunications system. Employees consent to management or supervisory personnel of Employer accessing and reviewing all material employees create, store, send, or receive on the computer or telecommunications system.

Section Three Prohibited Use

Use of Employer's computer or telecommunications system for any of the following activities is strictly prohibited:

1. Sending, receiving, displaying, printing, or otherwise disseminating material that is fraudulent, harassing, embarrassing, sexually explicit, obscene, intimidating, or defamatory;
2. Sending, receiving, displaying, printing, or otherwise disseminating confidential, proprietary business information or trade secrets in violation of Employer policy or proprietary agreements;
3. Transmitting, storing, or otherwise disseminating commercial or personal advertisements, solicitations, promotions, destructive programs (for example, viruses or self-replicating code), or political material;
4. Violating any state, federal, or international law governing intellectual property (for example, copyright, trademark, and patent laws) and online activities; and
5. Violating any license governing the use of software.

Section Four Violations

Violations of this policy may result in disciplinary action, including possible termination of employment, legal action, and criminal liability.

Section Five Employee Acknowledgment

I have read, understand, and agree to comply with the foregoing policies, rules, and conditions governing the use of Employer's computer and telecommunications equipment and services.

Dated: *[Date of signing]*

Signature: *[signature, etc.]*
[printed name]
[Computer account of employee]

NOTES TO FORM

Commentary

This is basic computer-use policy restricting the use of computer and telecommunications equipment to official purposes only. Personal use by employees is prohibited. Many employers may be reluctant to adopt such a policy for fear of an employee backlash, and if personal uses are permitted, or even encouraged, then the need for appropriate policies to be in place is even more paramount. This is a particular concern in the educational environment where students and faculty generally oppose restrictions on computer use. In such cases, a simple, one-page policy can address most of the major concerns surrounding the use of computer and telecommunications equipment and resources. This form is a useful starting point for developing a more streamlined policy. Any computer use policy should require that employees acknowledge in writing that they understand the policy. Organizations that use an annual affirmation process for their code of business conduct should consider have employees review the computer use policy as well as the records management policy as a part of that process. Depending on the age of your employee population, the use of short video training to explain and demonstrate the importance of such a policy can also be a very effective communication tool.

§ 3:20 Computer use policy—Personal use restricted

COMPUTER USE POLICY

Section One Purpose

A. To remain competitive, better serve our customers and provide our employees with the best tools to do their jobs, [*[Name of business]*/*[Owner of computer system]*] makes available to our workforce access to one or more forms of electronic media and services, including computers, e-mail, telephones, voice-mail, fax machines, external electronic bulletin boards, wire services, online services, intranet, Internet, and the World Wide Web.

B. [*[name of business]*/*[owner of computer system]*] encourages the use of these media and associated services because they can make communication more efficient and effective and because they are valuable sources of information about vendors, customers, technology, and new products and services. However, all employees and everyone connected with the organization should remember that electronic media and services provided by the company are company property and their purpose is to facilitate and support company business. All computer users have the responsibility to use these resources in a professional, ethical, and lawful manner.

C. To ensure that all employees are responsible, the following guidelines have been established for using e-mail and the Internet. No policy can lay down rules to cover every possible situation. Instead, it is designed to express [*[name of business]*/

[owner of computer system]] philosophy and set forth general principles when using electronic media and services.

Section Two Prohibited Communications

Digital or electronic media cannot be used for knowingly transmitting, retrieving, or storing any communication that is:

1. Discriminatory or harassing;
2. Derogatory to any individual or group;
3. Obscene, sexually explicit or pornographic;
4. Defamatory or threatening;
5. In violation of any license governing the use of software; or
6. Engaged in for any purpose that is illegal or contrary to [*[name of business]*][*[owner of computer system]*] policy or business interests.

Section Three Personal Use

The computers, digital or electronic media and services provided by [*[name of business]*][*[owner of computer system]*] are primarily for business use to assist employees in the performance of their jobs. Limited, occasional, or incidental use of digital or electronic media (sending or receiving) for personal, nonbusiness purposes is understandable and acceptable, and all such use should be done in a manner that does not negatively affect the systems' use for their business purposes. However, employees are expected to demonstrate a sense of responsibility and not abuse this privilege.

Section Four Access to Employee Communications

A. Generally, digital or electronic information created and/or communicated by an employee using e-mail, word processing, utility programs, spreadsheets, voice-mail, telephones, Internet and bulletin board system access, and similar electronic media is not reviewed by the company. However, the following conditions should be noted. [*[Name of business]*][*[Owner of computer system]*] routinely gathers logs for most digital or electronic activities or monitors employee communications directly, for example, telephone numbers dialed, sites accessed, call length, and time at which calls are made, for the following purposes:

1. Cost analysis;
2. Resource allocation;
3. Optimum technical management of information resources; and
4. Detecting patterns of use that indicate employees are violating company policies or engaging in illegal activity.

B. *[Name of business]*/*[Owner of computer system]* reserves the right, at its discretion, to review any employee's digital or electronic files and messages to the extent necessary to ensure electronic media and services are being used in compliance with the law, this policy and other company policies.

C. Employees should not assume digital or electronic communications are completely private. Accordingly, if they have sensitive information to transmit, they should use other means.

Section Five Software

To prevent computer viruses from being transmitted through the company's computer system, unauthorized downloading of any unauthorized software is strictly prohibited. Only software registered through *[name of business]*/*[owner of computer system]* may be downloaded. Employees should contact the system administrator if they have any questions.

Section Six Security/Appropriate Use

A. Employees must respect the confidentiality of other individuals' digital or electronic communications. Except in cases in which explicit authorization has been granted by company management, employees are prohibited from engaging in, or attempting to engage in:

1. Monitoring or intercepting the files or electronic communications of other employees or third parties;
2. Hacking or obtaining access to systems or accounts they are not authorized to use;
3. Using other people's log-ins or passwords; and
4. Breaching, testing, or monitoring computer or network security measures.

B. No e-mail or other digital or electronic communications can be sent that attempt to hide the identity of the sender or represent the sender as someone else.

C. Digital or electronic media and services should not be used in a manner likely to cause network congestion or significantly hamper the ability of other people to access and use the system.

D. Anyone obtaining digital or electronic access to other companies' or individuals' materials must respect all copyrights and cannot copy, retrieve, modify, or forward copyrighted materials except as permitted by the copyright owner.

Section Seven Encryption

Employees can use encryption software supplied to them by

the systems administrator for purposes of safeguarding sensitive or confidential business information. Employees who use encryption on files stored on a company computer must provide their supervisor with a sealed hard copy record (to be retained in a secure location) of all of the passwords and/or encryption keys necessary to access the files.

Section Eight Participation in Online Forums

A. Employees should remember that any messages or information sent on company-provided facilities to one or more individuals via an electronic or digital network—for example, Internet mailing lists, bulletin boards, and online services—are statements identifiable and attributable to [*[name of business]/ [owner of computer system]*].

B. [*[Name of business]/[Owner of computer system]*] recognizes that participation in some forums might be important to the performance of an employee's job. For instance, an employee might find the answer to a technical problem by consulting members of a news group devoted to the technical area.

Section Nine Violations

Any employee who abuses the privilege of their access to e-mail or the Internet in violation of this policy will be subject to corrective action, including possible termination of employment, legal action, and criminal liability.

Section Ten Employee Agreement on Use of E-mail and the Internet

I have read, understand, and agree to comply with the foregoing policies, rules, and conditions governing the use of the Company's computer and telecommunications equipment and services. I understand that I have no expectation of privacy when I use any of the telecommunication equipment or services. I am aware that violations of this guideline on appropriate use of the e-mail and Internet systems may subject me to disciplinary action, including termination from employment, legal action and criminal liability. I further understand that my use of the e-mail and Internet may reflect on the image of [*[name of business]/ [owner of computer system]*] to our customers, competitors and suppliers and that I have responsibility to maintain a positive representation of the company. Furthermore, I understand that this policy can be amended at any time.

Dated: *[Date of signing]*

Signature: *[signature]*
[printed name]
[Computer account of employee]

NOTES TO FORM

Commentary

A written computer use policy adopted by a business should include statements that:

(1) excessive personal use could subject an employee to disciplinary actions;

(2) that there is no expectation of privacy in anything created or stored using the office computer systems; and

(3) that management may review files and e-mail.

The policy should also require employees to acknowledge in writing that they understand the policy.

§ 3:21 Computer use policy—Educational institution

COMPUTER NETWORK AND INTERNET ACCESS AND USE

Faculty, staff and student access to the *[name of institution]* ("School") Network and/or Internet is consistent with and beneficial to the educational mission of School. The Network/Internet refers to the global network of computers created by the interfacing of smaller contributing networks. Its services are intended to support curriculum, instruction, and open educational inquiry and research.

In this document, "Network/Internet Access" refers to all information accessed through the use of School equipment and resources for connection to and use of the Network/Internet online services, e-mail, bulletin board, network system, etc. Access to the Network/Internet serves as a natural extension of the educational lessons learned within the classroom by providing access to educational resources and reference materials. Such access reinforces the specific subject matter taught by requiring the use of critical thinking skills, by promoting tolerance for diverse views, and by teaching socially appropriate forms of civil discourse and expression. Therefore, faculty, staff and students shall be allowed access to both School Computer Network and the Internet consistent with School's curriculum, educational mission, and this Policy and implementing procedures.

Nevertheless, School has a duty to insure that the manner in which the Network/Internet is used does not conflict with the basic educational mission of School. Use of the Network and/or Internet may be restricted in light of the maturity level of students involved and the special characteristics of the school environment. Therefore, School will not permit student use of the Network/Internet which: (a) causes substantial disruption of the proper and orderly operation of School or School activities; (b) violates the rights of others; (c) is socially inappropriate or inappropriate due to the maturity level of the students; (d) is primarily intended as an immediate solicitation of funds; or (e) constitutes gross disobedience or misconduct.

NOTES TO FORM

Commentary

Organizations and businesses allowing use of the Internet by their members and employees should have a computer use policy in place to limit exposure to liability. The use of computers and the Internet by members or employees can open an organization to liability for infringement of intellectual property rights, copyright violations, unfair competition, defamation, sexual harassment, wrongful termination, fraud, and invasion of privacy. In addition, connection to the Internet means exposure to computer hackers, viruses, and industrial espionage.

The policy should set forth an objective standard for members and employees to apply when using electronic media and services. It should set out appropriate use of the Internet and make clear that members and employees are using the organization's equipment. Users should understand that there is no privacy expectation in the use of computers and that e-mail and Internet usage may be monitored.

Part II

PREPARING FOR E-DISCOVERY

Chapter 4

Understanding the Locations, Sources and Types of Electronically Stored Information

I. GUIDELINES

II. CHECKLISTS

Research References

Treatises and Practice Aids

Grenig and Gleisner, eDiscovery & Digital Evidence § 5:15

Trial Strategy

Computer Technology in Civil Litigation, 71 Am. Jur. Trials 111

Additional References

Grenig and Kinsler, Federal Civil Discovery and Disclosure §§ 13.1 to 13.6 (3d ed.)

ABA Discovery Standards, http://www.abanet.org/litigation/discoverystandards/2005civildiscoverystandards.pdf

ARMA, http://www.arma.org

Electronic Discovery Reference Model Project, http://www.edrm.net

The Sedona Conference, http://www.thesedonaconference.org

KeyCite®: Cases and other legal materials listed in KeyCite Scope can be researched through the KeyCite service on Westlaw®. Use KeyCite to check citations for form, parallel references, prior and later history, and comprehensive citator information, including citations to other decisions and secondary materials.

I. GUIDELINES

§ 4:1 Generally

Lawyers, paralegals, records managers and professionals without a technology background think of e-discovery and shudder. The idea that one should now have to understand the complexities of an information technology infrastructure seems too far out, and too difficult to master.

Consider two things. First, mastery is not the goal; "reasonable efforts" can be accomplished with only a general understanding of the client's information technology systems and a good relationship with those who do know information technology well—such as e-discovery counsel, a trusted vendor, or the organizaiton's own information technology staff. Second, because virtually all information is created electronically, lawyers and legal professionals who do not start thinking about the available information in digital terms will not be able to represent their clients zealously.

Virtually every electronic system keeps some type of log of activity—stoplights at intersections, parking meters, databases of calls and text messages at communications service providers. All kinds of information pertinent to disputes exists in electronic form. Thinking about what information might exist, who has it and how you can get it is now crucial to the practice of law—whether in commercial litigation, family law, due diligence in mergers and acquisitions or intellectual property matters.

This chapter describes how to think about electronically stored information by first identifying the types of information you need, then the source that generates the information and finally, the location of the information.

§ 4:2 Difference between information and records

Much of the writing about e-discovery starts with a discussion of records or information management. Those terms are often confused, so before addressing types, sources and locations of electronically stored information, it is necessary to first understand the difference between "information" and "records."

Records are a subset of the big picture of information, and e-discovery (i.e. the relevant information) for a particular case represents a smaller subset of information that may include some records. To understand how records, information and e-discovery fit together: think of a large dinner plate. That dinner plate constitutes all of the information contained in an organization—for example, e-mail, word processing documents, databases, spreadsheets, photos, marketing plans, instant messaging, accounts payable, accounts receivable, record logs, incident reports, tax records. Some of the information remains in paper, most of it is electronic, and all of it is information.

Now set a drinking glass in the middle of the dinner plate. The circumference of the glass represents the portion of the information in the organization that is records. Records are information of regular business activities that generally have legal requirements for retention. Records usually constitute roughly 10% of the information in an organization; that number goes up in highly regulated industries like financial services and banking.

By way of example, federal and most state regulations require that personnel files for employees be kept for as long as the employee is an active employee with the organization, and then for specified number of years afterwards. Those personnel files are information, but they are also records.

Each time new litigation arises, and a legal hold must be put into place for information pertaining to that case, imagine a shot glass on the plate—a shot glass of e-discovery for that case. The shot glass contains everything that might be relevant or responsive for the case and must be preserved. The e-discovery shot glass may overlap slightly with records, but predominately consists of information. A good records and information management program helps you understand what is on the plate, what is in the drinking glass, and how to figure out what is in the shot glass quickly and inexpensively. The more of the plate that must be dealt with, the more expensive e-discovery becomes.

The rest of the plate is made of such matter as e-mails between employees planning this week's status meeting, instant messages about the new policy that just came out—transitory information with no business function, but that is created and stored on the organization's information technology infrastructure. That transitory information is what drives up the cost of e-discovery.

Users create the information, lawyers ask information technology to preserve and collect it for their lawyers to review, and those review costs represent the bulk of e-discovery costs. A successful records and information management program can substantially reduce the amount of transitory information available within the organization, ensure the timely purging of business records after the retention period has expired, and identify areas to reduce the age of stored data. All three steps can substantially reduce the costs associated with e-discovery but starting with the management of the information created.

Records and information management achieves three goals:

- Reducing costs associated with storage and management of information as well as e-discovery,
- Mitigating the risk of spoliation by establishing a process for implementing and tracking legal holds and knowing where information is located on the infrastructure
- Allowing the organization to better organize and utilize the information it creates to advance the business.

§ 4:3 Determining needs

It is essential to understand the specific needs of your program. Before implementing a document records and information management program, the records and information management team should undertake an inventory of threatened and pending litigation or government investigations. The team must take steps, in consultation with counsel, to ensure that all potentially responsive information is preserved.

Rather than mastering all of the concepts of e-discovery and knowing the ins and outs of every back up tape made, what a legal professional needs to know is tied completely to what the professional deals with on a daily basis. A paralegal in an organization or law firm that manages employment litigation would need to understand generally the types of information the employees create, and the types of systems used by human resources to understand what was available and who to talk to about it. The information relevant to distributor litigation, small claims work, family law, or personal injury cases, as examples—would be different.

Before commencing e-discovery, the lawyer must identify what the lawyer needs to know, then brainstorm what those sources of information should be, talk to information technology and the right persons in the organization about where the information is, and then determine how to get the information efficiently and at low cost. Thinking all those issues through before litigation arises will save time and money, and create a shorter path to getting the information.

For organizations managing a broad spectrum of e-discovery issues, it is important to identify with the records and information team what the challenges are and make a determination of what must be known based on the challenges faced. If the organization produces largely quantitative data vs. e-mail, efforts would be better spent on understanding those databases, how reports can be generated, and what you can do in-house to save money when producing them or when opportunities may exist to shift the cost burden to the requesting party.

If e-mail is the primary type of electronically stored information produced, consideration should be given to evaluating tools to help cull information before processing to save money. Knowing the rules and some basics about the information dealt with the most is half the battle in controlling the costs of e-discovery.

§ 4:4 Records management

Records management is a program or process for managing the lifecycle of a business record within an organization. For example, a person should retain a personal income tax return for seven years after the date it was filed. Seven years after it is filed, the tax return can be deleted, shredded or thrown because it is no longer needed. In essence, that is records management.

E-discovery catapulted records management from a back basement organizational function to one of much greater prominence in organizations that regularly encounter e-discovery requests. A good records management program identifies the types of records in the organization, trains its employees on how to maintain them, and ensures compliance (i.e. purging) of those records once they have lived out their lifecycle. A good records and information management program provides many benefits for e-discovery: employees who regularly identify and purge records according to a retention schedule are thinking about the management of information and will understand the need to preserve it for litigation purposes, less outdated information will be available for discovery, and the costs of storage for paper and ESI will be reduced.

A solid records and information management program is key to preparing for e-discovery. Putting a program in place takes years, so it is essential to embark on one well in advance of when it must be relied upon. Creating a records retention schedule for each function can take three months to a year—bringing the organization into compliance with the schedule takes three to four times as long.

Many lawyers make the mistake of giving records and information management short shrift when it comes to resources and attention within an organization, believing it to be a very simple undertaking. Records and information management is not simple. It requires the attention of professionals experienced in thinking about the importance of records and information to the organization and balancing that importance with other risks—including e-discovery.

§ 4:5 Locating and understanding paper information

Although more than 99% of information is created electronically,[1] most organizations still have paper records that are managed both on and off-site. Organizations contract with off-site storage facilities to maintain an inventory of the boxes and contents (as coded by the client) containing the documents, and a date for destruction.[2] At any point in time, the facility should be able to provide an inventory of what is located in the facility and pull back a box of needed documents for review.

Coding documents sent off-site for storage is a key component to a successful records management program to allow for easier compliance with a retention schedule. For example, a box coded as personnel records for departed employees from 1993 to 2000 would be easy to find and pull back when records are needed for a former employee at the company during that time. Counsel should consider the time needed to identify, pull back and locate those records before agreeing to production dates. Paper records cannot be searched like electronically stored information.

Some organizations may also have custodians who have maintained or continue to keep paper files. It is not unusual to find a custodian who does not trust electronic systems and feels safer printing everything out. Part of the attorney's obligation is to ask specifically about paper information during the initial interviews of the legal hold process and then to locate and consider the paper records in preservation, collection and production.

§ 4:6 Websites

A Website may be a simple, static page listing the hours of operation and a contact phone number for an organization, or a

---

[Section 4:5]

[1]See, e.g., *How Much Information?* 2003, http://www.sims.berkeley.edu/research/projects/ (refer to the Executive Summary section of the How Much Information? 2003 research project).

[2]See, e.g., http://www.ironmountain.com/Services/Records-Management-And-Storage.aspx.

Website may be complex with multiple pages and interactive databases allowing remote users to change the site. Some Websites are used for conducting business transactions and storing sensitive data such as credit card numbers or personal identification information.

Content on Websites must be preserved if relevant or responsive, but this depends on factors, such as the type of information found on the site, and whether or not it exists in another place. Organizations should evaluate their Websites and develop a strategy for documenting the site as information changes. This assessment is based on the type and amount of information found on the Website and the level of risk to the organization (legal, fiscal, or administrative) if that information is lost or unavailable. This may mean that the organization retains periodic "snapshots" of the entire site, or captures individual pages or records on the site.

Materials provided on organization Websites must be managed the same way that other organization records are managed. Documents qualifying as records with permanent or long-term value should be captured and retained (either in hard copy or electronically). This may apply to individual parts of the organization Website or it may apply to the entire Website. For example, if an organization places a publication on its Website, and the publication is not available in any other form, then that publication is a record and should be captured and retained in some way.

If the organization publishes a report on its Website and has paper copies or the computer file that was used to create the report, then the copy on the Website is a duplicate copy and probably does not need to be captured. Additionally, if a Website is being used to conduct a business transaction the Web pages associated with the activity are considered part of that transaction's legal documentation and must be retained in order to establish what the user saw when the order was placed.

Attorneys seeking information from a website should consider the Wayback Machine,[1] or other sites archiving pages of Websites. Preservation letters to the opposing party should contemplate specifically naming the website and pages to be preserved. In many cases, taking screen shots of the Website existing immediately before the other party is put on notice of pending litigation can be key to not only preserving the information for use

---

[Section 4:6]

[1]See http://archive.org/web/web.php.

in the litigation, but as evidence that the other party failed to do so.

§ 4:7 Metadata

"Metadata" are generally defined as the information about the information. For example, Microsoft Word includes 30 different built-in document properties. It allows administrators to create custom properties applying to each document created on the application.[1] A general understanding of these fields can lead counsel to information that may be critical to a case. For example, employment litigation can turn on the creation date of a document as well as when the document was altered, and who altered it.

Dates are one of the most often sought forms of metadata and can be used with existing e-discovery tools to allow counsel to create timelines by filtering by date on the review tools. A process that is usually very manual and time intensive can now be done in seconds using ESI and the right tools.

The types of metadata existing depend entirely on the application used to create the electronically stored information. The key for counsel is to think about and establish a list of metadata fields to be asked for in discovery so the resource is available during litigation.

According to a Wisconsin Formal Ethics Opinion[2] the duties of confidentiality and competence require lawyers to stay reasonably informed about the types of metadata included in electronic documents they generate and take steps, when necessary, to remove metadata. The committee noted that not all metadata must be removed; in some situations, lawyers may intend to include metadata or be required by law to refrain from scrubbing documents.

The opinion explains that that lawyers must be cognizant of when metadata contained in a document is of such importance that the lawyer is ethically obliged to prevent disclosure. Metadata should be removed whenever it is reasonably foreseeable the metadata in a document may be relevant and detrimental to the client. The opinion suggests that attorneys can avoid transmitting detrimental metadata by deleting it through scrub-

---

[Section 4:7]

[1]10 Proven Tips to Minimize Document Metadata in Microsoft Word, Randall Farrar, available at http://esqinc.com/Content/WhitePapers/10-Proven-Tips-Minimizing-Document-Metadata.php#_Toc168770075.

[2]Wisconsin Formal Ethics Opinion EF-12-01.

bing programs, converting documents to Portal Document Format (PDF), or sending scanned or faxed versions.

With respect to mining for metadata, a minority of the committee believed the Wisconsin Rules of Professional Conduct either prohibit searching for metadata, or, at a minimum, do not clearly permit it. A majority of the committee did not believe the Rules prohibit Wisconsin lawyers from searching for metadata in documents received from opposing counsel or third parties. The committee found that if an electronic document contains information that was inadvertently sent, the receiving lawyer's only duty is to inform the sender.

II. CHECKLISTS

§ 4:8 Checklist of types of electronically stored information

- ☐ E-mail and e-mail attachments
- ☐ Word processing documents such as those produced in MS Word or in WordPerfect
- ☐ Spreadsheets including Excel
- ☐ Presentation documents such as PowerPoint
- ☐ Graphics
- ☐ Animations
- ☐ Images
- ☐ Audio, video and audiovisual recordings
- ☐ Voice mail
- ☐ Electronic calendars or scheduling systems
- ☐ Proprietary software files
- ☐ Internet browsing applications, including bookmarks, cookies, and history logs
- ☐ Computer programs evincing a particular process, incorporating specific information, or demonstrating the use of proprietary methodologies
- ☐ Computer operation logs containing usage information
- ☐ Logs and text of electronic messages or e-mails, including trashed or deleted messages, message drafts, or mailing lists
- ☐ Electronic messaging records for messages within a specific company's network or across a wider network, such as the Internet
- ☐ Manufacturer's specifications for a computer
- ☐ Source codes for computer programs

§ 4:9 Checklist of locations of electronically stored information

- ☐ Individual desktop or laptop computers (both work and home)
- ☐ Mainframe computer systems
- ☐ Servers including email servers, file servers and application servers
- ☐ Archival data on backup tapes or other storage media onsite and offsite
- ☐ Handheld devices including mobile phones, smart phones and touch pads
- ☐ Internet data, including instant messaging
- ☐ Paging devices
- ☐ Audio systems, including voice mail
- ☐ GPS navigation systems
- ☐ MP3 players
- ☐ Removable storage devices including discs, tapes, USB drives and flash drives
- ☐ Copiers and printers containing internal storage
- ☐ Third-party hosted data including cloud storage and applications (Dropbox, GoogleApps, iCloud, SaaS applications, etc.)
- ☐ Online social media sites (FaceBook, Twitter, Flickr, etc.)

Chapter 5

Developing Records and Information Management Programs

I. GUIDELINES

II. CHECKLISTS

Research References

Treatises and Practice Aids

Grenig and Gleisner, eDiscovery & Digital Evidence § 5:15

Trial Strategy

Computer Technology in Civil Litigation, 71 Am. Jur. Trials 111

Additional References

ABA Discovery Standards, http://www.abanet.org/litigation/discoverystandards/2005civildiscoverystandards.pdf
Electronic Discovery Reference Model Project, http://www.edrm.net
The Sedona Conference, http://www.thesedonaconference.org

> **KeyCite®:** Cases and other legal materials listed in KeyCite Scope can be researched through the KeyCite service on Westlaw®. Use KeyCite to check citations for form, parallel references, prior and later history, and comprehensive citator information, including citations to other decisions and secondary materials.

I. GUIDELINES

§ 5:1 Generally

A records and information management ("RIM") program is a multi-faceted program addressing the creation, retention and disposition of information within an organization—including electronically stored information. The vast quantities of electronically stored information created daily and the number of places electronically stored information can reside in an organization's information technology infrastructure create the perfect storm when that organization receives a request to produce electronically stored information. A successful RIM program examining the information created by the organization and establishing protocols and procedures for responding to those requests can control the costs of e-discovery, increase efficiency and limit harm to the organization's public image.

A successful RIM program enables an organization to manage the lifecycle of information and to purge records and information it is not legally required to keep and no longer serve a business purpose. In short, it gives an organization the green light to destroy information no longer needed. A successful RIM program ensures that legally required records are preserved and protected, while systematically continuing to purge electronically stored information and paper information from the organization.

The Federal Rules of Civil Procedure and courts interpreting those rules have acknowledged that organizations cannot come to a complete stand still when litigation is filed and a litigation hold must be put into place.[1] An established RIM program providing for the destruction of electronically stored information typically does not result in sanctions or raise an adverse inference of spoliation if the destruction is done in accordance with a policy (records retention, e-mail management or otherwise) without knowl-

---

[Section 5:1]

[1]See Advisory's Committee's Notes to 2006 Amendment to Fed. R. Civ. P. 26 and 37. See e.g. Convolve, Inc. v. Compaq Computer Corp., 223 F.R.D. 162 (S.D. N.Y. 2004), order clarified, 2005 WL 1514284 (S.D. N.Y. 2005).

edge the information was relevant to any party in litigation.[2] The expense of responding to government investigations or civil discovery has created incentives for organizations to establish RIM programs disposing of records or information that no longer must be maintained for legal or other purposes.

An appropriate RIM program has two additional potential advantages in e-discovery. First, understanding the availability of information or the cost to retrieve it can assist in establishing information is not reasonably accessible because of undue burden or cost.[3] Second, an organization with a successful RIM program and, more specifically, an appropriate legal hold protocol, may be able to take advantage of the "safe harbor" provision in Fed. R. Civ. P. 37(f): "Absent exceptional circumstances, a court may not impose sanctions under these rules for failing to provide electronically stored information lost as a result of the routine good-faith operation of an electronic information system." As Fed. R. Civ. P. 37(f) has played out in practice, organizations must be aware that this provision has been interpreted narrowly and is not a "warm blanket" for those with no strategies in place for implementing legal holds or RIM.[4]

The most important aspect of a RIM program is that it fit with the organization's values and vision on information. An organization's information is one of its most valuable assets, and the business' need for that information and commitment to a RIM program must be considered thoroughly at the outset of any program. Failure to consider those variables will undermine a RIM program before it starts.

While the needs of each organization for information management will vary, there are several components consistently included in successful RIM programs:

- A data map
- Policies and procedures
- E-mail management
- Retention schedule for records
- An e-discovery guide.

---

[2]See Fed. R. Civ. P. 37(f).

[3]See Fed. R. Civ. P. 26(b)(2)(B).

[4]See, e.g., Doe v. Norwalk Community College, 248 F.R.D. 372, 231 Ed. Law Rep. 292 (D. Conn. 2007) (community college and its board of trustees did not take affirmative act in good faith to prevent destruction of electronic files relevant to student's action against them pursuant to routine operation of their information system, so as to avoid imposition of sanctions, where they did not implement a litigation hold to prevent the system from destroying or altering the files).

§ 5:2 Attorney-client privilege

Because much of the work done in under the umbrella of a records and information ("RIM") program is done in anticipation of litigation now that federal and state rules require the preservation and production of e-discovery, the question comes up regularly—if I work with a lawyer to put my program in place, will it be privileged? The answer lies in the same analysis of all privilege questions—is the work covered by the attorney-client privilege or the attorney work-product doctrine?

The attorney-client privilege covers communications between the client and lawyer seeking legal advice. That privilege is narrow, and will apply to specific aspects of the program. The better umbrella is the attorney work-product doctrine: where work is done by the attorney in anticipation of litigation and that includes the mental impressions, conclusions or legal opinions of counsel, the work should be protected.[1]

Should the appropriateness of a RIM program come into question, a court may determine there has been a subject-matter waiver of the attorney-client privilege with respect to any advice counsel gave in implementing the program.[2] The attorney-client privilege can be lost when the client desires to obtain legal advice, not in relation to a possible prior wrongdoing, but to plan or facilitate future wrongdoing.[3] The crime-fraud exception assures that the "seal of secrecy" between a lawyer and client does not extend to those otherwise confidential communications "made for the purpose of getting advice for the commission of a fraud or crime."[4] Retaining and consulting a lawyer to develop a RIM program, if

---

[Section 5:2]

[1]See Hickman v. Taylor, 329 U.S. 495, 67 S. Ct. 385, 91 L. Ed. 451, 1947 A.M.C. 1 (1947) (recognizing work-product doctrine which provides that information obtained or produced by or for attorneys in anticipation of litigation may be protected from discovery).

[2]Cf. Zubulake v. UBS Warburg LLC, 220 F.R.D. 212, 216, 92 Fair Empl. Prac. Cas. (BNA) 1539 (S.D. N.Y. 2003) (referring to attorney's directive regarding litigation hold).

[3]See U.S. v. Zolin, 491 U.S. 554, 563–64, 109 S. Ct. 2619, 105 L. Ed. 2d 469, 89-1 U.S. Tax Cas. (CCH) ¶ 9380, 27 Fed. R. Evid. Serv. 833, 63 A.F.T.R.2d 89-1483 (1989). See, e.g., Highland Tank & Mfg. Co. v. PS Intern., Inc., 246 F.R.D. 239 (W.D. Pa. 2007) (under crime-fraud exception, documents are protected under attorney-client privilege unless: (1) holder of documents was committing or intending to commit a fraud or crime; and (2) their attorney-client communications were in furtherance of that alleged crime or fraud).

[4]See U.S. v. Zolin, 491 U.S. 554, 563–64, 109 S. Ct. 2619, 105 L. Ed. 2d 469, 89-1 U.S. Tax Cas. (CCH) ¶ 9380, 27 Fed. R. Evid. Serv. 833, 63 A.F.T.R.2d 89-1483 (1989).

done in anticipation of litigation, may, in some situations, invoke the crime-fraud exception to the attorney-client privilege.[5]

§ 5:3 The records and information management team

Developing and implementing an effective records and information management "RIM" program is a complicated, time-consuming task requiring collaboration between individuals with knowledge of several business functions:

- Records
- Information technology
- Legal

These persons must fully understand the organization and the types of records created by the organization. Although the persons involved will vary depending upon the size and nature of the organization, senior management from business units must be involved and provide support for the program as well as identify the key individuals within their unit best suited to assist the RIM program.

The team should include records retention specialists with the necessary skill sets for managing the process, information technology personnel familiar with the types and locations of electronically stored information the organization creates and receives, and lawyers and regulatory specialists familiar with the legal requirements for document retention. Because of the complexity and depth of a RIM initiative, organizations should consider adding an outside expert to their team with experience helping organizations navigate through RIM programs.

Perhaps the most important aspect of the RIM team for an organization is rethinking the relationship between legal and information technology. RIM requires a much more collaborative relationship between legal and information technology than presently exists in most organizations. Historically, legal has been a client of information technology, much like human resources, marketing, and the other business functions within an organization. Legal called information technology when it needed a technologi-

---

[5]See Antidote Intern. Films, Inc. v. Bloomsbury Publishing, PLC, 242 F.R.D. 248, 250 (S.D. N.Y. 2007) (e-mail fell within crime-fraud exception); Rambus, Inc. v. Infineon Technologies AG, 220 F.R.D. 264 (E.D. Va. 2004), subsequent determination, 222 F.R.D. 280 (E.D. Va. 2004) (crime-fraud exception to attorney-client privilege and work-product doctrine applies when client was engaged in or planning a fraudulent or criminal scheme when it sought advice of counsel and documents involved bear close relationship to the fraudulent or criminal scheme). See Grenig & Kinsler, Handbook of Federal Civil Discovery and Disclosure § 1:40 (3d ed.).

cal solution or a fix for a problem, and information technology handled the request from its client by identifying the appropriate solution or fix and implementing it. Very little to any input from legal was sought once the initial parameters for the solution were discussed.

RIM and specifically e-discovery require legal and information technology to work as partners to identify the risks to the organization inherent in electronically stored information. They must address those risks together through technological solutions or the elimination of multiple storage locations for electronically stored information. That partnership means sitting down together, identifying the goals for a RIM program (e.g., storage cost reduction, e-discovery cost reduction, better utilizing information) and collaborating on virtually every step of the RIM program.

§ 5:4 Creating a data map

A data map provides an overview of the systems and locations of electronically stored information within an organization's information technology infrastructure.[1] The goal of a data map is to provide the basis for an organization's decisions on where information resides that needs to be preserved once the duty to preserve is triggered. Each organization's data map will look different, as it should be tailored to the specific needs of the organization. For example, a healthcare company producing largely quantitative information from legacy database systems to state and government entities will have a data map with an entirely different focus than a manufacturing organization that largely provides e-mail and supporting contract documentation in breach of contract disputes.

When considering what systems and the level of detail to be included in a data map, an organization should evaluate its litigation portfolio, as well as all investigations and audits (internal and external), subpoenas and other inquiries for electronically stored information the organization has seen in the previous five years, or anticipates. Current assessment of the legal risks of electronically stored information within the organization is also

[Section 5:4]

[1]See Wetmore & Clary, *To Map or Not to Map: Strategies for Classifying Sources of ESI*, INFORMATIONMANAGEMENT, Sept./Oct. 2009, at 33; Balachandran, *5 Steps to Compliance Building an Automated Data Map*, INFORMATION-MANAGEMENT, Nov./Dec. 2009, at 40; Vednere, *The Quest for Ediscovery: Creating a Data Map*, INFONOMICS, Nov./Dec. 2009, at 28.

of tremendous value when determining the scope of a data map. Those risks may include privacy, security, cloud computing, e-discovery, social media and regulatory concerns.

Notwithstanding the focus of the data map (specific systems, manufacturing facilities, etc.), every data map should contain the following information:

- Sources of electronically stored information available in the organization (e-mail, instant messaging, electronic resource planning systems, file servers, proprietary databases, Sharepoint, etc.)
- Age of available electronically stored information—how far back does your data go for each source of information?
- Physical location of data—where is it? On the user's hard drive in California, on a server farm in Virginia? In the cloud? Physical location should also consider the implication of European Union privacy laws if the company has users that create or store information in the European Union.
- Type of storage electronically stored information is maintained on—tapes, disk, servers—what degree of safety does the current storage provide?
- Backup system and program for each data source—what is used to backup each system (e.g., e-mail, electronic resource planning), and how long are the data maintained on the backup system?
- Contact person who manages the data source
- Retention attached to the source, if any—may need to drill down to individual fields in the case of quantitative data. Retention in the electronically stored information system will also need to be considered when putting together the records retention schedule.

The level of inquiry for each source of electronically stored information on the data map should be different. For some systems, specific configuration settings will be needed and for others, a general overview of the system and other factors will be sufficient.

A well-thought out and planned data map can act as the core of a solid information retention program. Paired with or done jointly with an e-discovery guide identifying all the issues to be considered when negotiating e-discovery on behalf of an organization, these tools will save enormous expenses for an organization by allowing them to get to pertinent e-discovery information very quickly.

§ 5:5 Policies and procedures

Policies and procedures within an organization govern how

both users and the organization create, manage and store their information. For purposes of records and information management ("RIM"), there are three to four main policies and procedures natural to any RIM program:

- A legal hold protocol
- The RIM policy
- The social media usage policy
- An acceptable use policy.

The use of different types or names of policies or procedures will vary in organizations, but the principles should remain the same.

§ 5:6 Legal hold protocol

The routine destruction of electronically stored information may lead to severe sanctions once an organization is on notice of potential litigation. Among the most important of the policies and procedures of a records and information management ("RIM") program is the legal hold protocol. The legal hold protocol is a step-by-step process, developed and owned by legal. It lays out the actions to be taken and the individuals responsible for each step to put a legal hold in place once the duty to preserve has been triggered.

The protocol, which is generally kept in the legal department and not distributed throughout the organization, authorizes the suspension of records and information destruction and the preservation of records in the case of foreseeable, pending, or actual litigation or government investigation. Once the duty to preserve has been triggered, records destruction must cease immediately. The legal hold protocol should provide that any employee who receives any information regarding potential litigation or government investigation immediately inform the legal counsel responsible for the matter.

In conjunction with a legal hold protocol, organizations should create a legal hold template that serves as the basis for written legal holds. The template should then be modified both for the type of litigation (employment, products liability, class action) and the case itself. The hold notice should contain a brief description of the case to identify it to the users (in English, not legalese), instruct them of their responsibilities and the types of information they should preserve and provide contact information for questions. Because courts have often called upon parties to provide documentation of the legal hold process when a party has been alleged to have spoliated evidence, tracking each event in the legal hold process is key to being able to defend the organization's actions in implementing the hold.

In some jurisdictions, the failure to issue a written legal hold may constitute negligence per se. In other jurisdictions, courts have acknowledged that, where parties are notified of a hold in the normal course of business, a written legal hold may not be necessary. What is crucial is that individuals identified as having information relevant to the matter are notified in a timely manner so that information can be preserved.[2]

Commercial software exists to assist organizations with tracking legal holds, although vetting software is essential. Organizations should ask for a demonstration of the product, and even a trial period to test the product before purchasing. Given the increase in vendors in the last five years, soliciting feedback from existing clients about their satisfaction with the product is also very important.

§ 5:7 Records and information management policy

The records and information management ("RIM") policy generally makes a broader statement than its baby brother, the records retention Policy. Many organizations have moved from a records retention policy to a RIM policy and defined records vs. information within the policy. The RIM policy calls out both the legal hold protocol and the records retention schedule and advises users they are subject to both and must comply. The RIM policy also provides the definition of information and of records within the organization and lists the names of individuals responsible for answering any questions about RIM in the organization.

Many organizations are now creating RIM Websites on their intranets laying out resources for employees to utilize including frequently asked questions, retention schedules, names of records coordinators for individual business functions with contact information, and status of various projects related to RIM. Use of the intranet also allows records to have more visibility within the organization and to utilize organization communications to send out announcements of new developments, including audit and clean out days.

§ 5:8 Social media usage policy

With the explosion of the use of social media by employees both personally and on behalf of the organization, providing either

---

[Section 5:6]

[2]See, e.g., Rimkus Consulting Group, Inc. v. Cammarata, 688 F. Supp. 2d 598 (S.D. Tex. 2010).

policy or guidelines for employees to follow when posting has become paramount. Some organizations encourage their employees to engage in social media about their employment and experiences at the company, while others set up firewalls to block social media sites from their employees' use on company systems. However the company approaches social media, the policy or guidelines must be consistent with that approach. Many companies have posted their social media policies online to be publicly available. One Website, www.socialmediagovernance.com, provides policies for free.

Social media policies or guidelines should advise users how to engage appropriately online. A standard policy encourages users to identify themselves and their employment, not to post confidential or copyrighted information, not to post material that is defamatory, offensive, harassing or illegal, and not to make representations about the organization's financial performance. Although some organizations choose to imbed social media guidelines in an acceptable use policy, given the audience for social media policies, they are better set out on their own.

§ 5:9 Acceptable use policy

Acceptable use policies inform employees how to manage and use the organization's asset, primarily technology. E-mail management, use of mobile devices, use, and ownership of the computers provided by the organization and other issues are encompassed within an acceptable use policy. Typically, the acceptable use policy is owned by information technology and is enforced through information technology security.

§ 5:10 Building a retention schedule

Developing a records retention schedule is the key to managing the organization's records; it is the core of records management within an organization. ARMA International defines "official record" as a record that is legally recognized or that establishes some fact.[1] Official records reflect the intent of the organization. These records reflect the information or position the organization believes is true and complete, relies upon to conduct its affairs, and hopes others will also rely upon. Official records of the organization are generally those records found on a records retention schedule.

[Section 5:10]

[1] www.arma.org/pdf/WhatisRIM.pdf.

In determining records retention periods, the organization must first determine which electronically stored information is deemed to be a record. Next, it must determine what retention periods are required by state or federal law, or by organizational needs. The default retention period for many public records is permanent, and only a schedule can authorize its destruction. Determining the retention schedule for public records requires careful review of applicable statutes, regulations, and ordinances.

The records management needs of different parts of an organization vary and must be taken into account when creating a records and information management program. Different parties create and use records in different ways; in order to be effective, the records management program must accommodate different uses and needs.

Organizations without knowledge of records management should consider hiring a consultant with experience in evaluating an organization's need for records management and in building an appropriate schedule for that organization. Organizations should evaluate the various approaches taken by consultants to building a schedule and understand the implications of each type of schedule in terms of practical day-to-day use by employees before selecting a schedule type. Understanding the internal resources that will be devoted to compliance and auditing of the schedule will be key to choosing the right type of schedule for an organization.

The records retention schedule must be reviewed and approved in writing by the manager responsible for records management, legal counsel, a senior executive for the individual business function (e.g., human resources, marketing), and, where appropriate, the tax manager. In addition, the entire records program must be approved in writing by the organization's chief executive officer. These written approvals demonstrate the program was developed in the ordinary course of business instead of in anticipation of litigation or a government investigation. Copies of the written approvals should be maintained indefinitely.

In determining the legal retention requirements for records categories, thorough research of the law should be conducted. If a nonlawyer does the research, the research should be reviewed by a lawyer. The researcher should determine which regulatory agencies should be consulted to determine retention requirements. Relevant statutes, regulations, and guidelines should be reviewed and documented. After the records retention schedule is prepared, the proposed schedule, list of legal requirements, and copies of applicable statutes, regulations, and cases should be presented to counsel for review.

§ 5:11 E-mail management

Today, e-mail is the number one requested form of electronically stored information in e-discovery. Lawyers who know very little about technology and cannot ask specific questions about various systems within an information technology system know enough to request e-mail. Because 95% of the e-mail exchanged today is merely transitory or spam (What time should we go to lunch? Can you make a meeting at 1:00 p.m.? Thanks for your message, but I am out of the office on vacation until Monday.), producing e-mail for even five to ten custodians over a two-year time period can cost thousands of dollars.

A few statistics about e-mail illustrate the importance of the need for e-mail management to avoid the costs associated with increased storage and e-discovery:

- Over 294 billion e-mails were sent daily in 2010.
- In 2010, there were 1.9 billion users of e-mail; that number is projected to increase to 2.4 billion by 2012.
- The average user sends 43 e-mails a day and receives 130 e-mails a day (not including spam).
- 74% of adults ages 30 to 55 prefer to communicate by e-mail.
- The average employee spends one hour and 47 minutes a day on e-mail.
- 90% of e-mail is spam.[1]

E-mail is by far the most abundant source of electronically stored information within an organization. The fact it resides in so many locations on an information technology system makes it one of the most challenging sources of electronically stored information to preserve, collect and produce cost-effectively. An organization that gives mobile devices to its employees, allows employees to access the company system on home computers, allows data to be removed from the system on thumb drives or DVDs, and that encourages users to store e-mail to be archived on their hard drives creates abundance of locations where e-mail can be housed. Most organizations do all of those things. When the duty to preserve arises, counsel must be able to quickly understand the locations where pertinent e-mail exists and the age of the e-mail so counsel can make decisions about what preservation steps to take.

[Section 5:11]

[1]See http://email.about.com/gi/o.htm?zi=1/XJ&zTi=1&sdn=email&cdn=compute&tm=394&f=00&su=p284.13.342.ip__&tt=12&bt=1&bts=1&zu=http%3A//www.radicati.com/; http://news.cnet.com/8301-1009__3-10249172-83.html.

Effective e-mail management varies according to the organization's needs and its information technology infrastructure. Understanding the steps to be taken to preserve e-mail for identified custodians is key to mitigating the risk of spoliation and to reducing costs associated with e-discovery. E-mail management solutions can involve instituting retention periods on the e-mail servers or cloud, eliminating the ability of users to store e-mail on their hard drives, or any combination of strategies creating one uniform retention period for e-mail within the organization that can be relied on in e-discovery.

A common feature of e-mail management programs is a limit on the storage space available to individual e-mail users. Users are typically given a warning before e-mail is deleted. An e-mail management program may also provide for automatic deletion of user mailbox contents. Some organizations do not limit the size or duration of individual mailboxes, but focus on providing extended capacity for certain classes of employees. Some classifications, such as executives and accountants, may have all their e-mail saved for substantial periods of time as their information will probably be subject to litigation or regulatory inquiry. Information on the differences in e-mail storage solutions should be included in the e-discovery guide made available to counsel at the outset of any litigation, as the dates of available e-mail will be key to negotiating the scope of discovery.

With respect to the cloud, negotiating indemnification clauses with cloud-based e-mail providers is a nonstarter. Providers will not agree to cover any more than the cost of doing business with them in the event your data are lost. Standard contracts for these providers include standard limitations of liability, leaving the organization on the hook if a data loss occurs that subjects it to sanctions for spoliation. Providers claim that providing indemnification to their clients would leave their other clients out in the cold if a lawsuit for loss of data put them out of business, and that potential risk would preclude them from attracting additional clients to their platforms. Organizations should be aware that any risk of data loss will likely fall on them—making the undertaking of a comprehensive e-mail management strategy as part of a records information management ("RIM") initiative that much more important, and evaluation of a vendor's backup and security environments crucial to the vetting process.

Designing an e-mail management strategy for an organization is the same as designing an overall (RIM) initiative—the strategy must be the best for the organization to allow it to continue to grow and thrive, and to manage risk and the potential costs of e-discovery at the same time. There is no magic formula to apply for e-mail management, and it is a constant moving target that should be reassessed regularly by an organization, especially one that regularly is required to provide e-mail in e-discovery.

§ 5:12 E-mail management software

E-mail archiving solutions are the most common tools available on the marketplace today to assist organizations in centralizing their e-mail for e-discovery purposes. These tools have pros and cons, and each proposed tool should be evaluated carefully based on the user's requirements, both for e-discovery and on an every day basis as a search engine for an employee e-mail.

On the plus side, an e-mail archive can provide one-stop shopping for counsel to search, pull and produce e-mail in litigation. That one-stop shopping comes with a rather significant caveat—users are not permitted to store e-mail older than what is in the archive in any other locations. If that is not the case, counsel will be required to preserve all e-mail for an identified key custodian from multiple locations.

While a centralized repository like an archive can be useful for pulling information, organizations must recognize the pull of information from an e-mail archive is only as good as the search parameters that can be set, and the speed and sophistication of the search engine inside the tool. This means that getting advice from an attorney or consultant who regularly creates these searches will reduce the amount of extra information or noise (i.e. extra data) that is picked up in the search.

An archive tool with an effective search culling function allowing a user to pull a more targeted collection will reduce costs in e-discovery better than a tool that requires a user to pull a full date range of all data for key custodians and cull it down later. The first approach results in a smaller, more targeted subset to start with, while the second requires additional cost to handle, and will likely lead to much greater review costs for largely irrelevant information. If the organization has an archiving tool with an unreliable search function requiring pulling a larger initial set, consideration should be given to using more sophisticated tools to cull the data before processing to reduce costs. Culling of the data pulled from the archive, with or without a good search tool, will be required to get to the e-discovery for the matter.

E-mail archives come in both locally hosted and cloud-based versions, and cover a wide range of functionality and cost. Understanding the pros and cons of both will be key to the selection process of a tool for an organization. Although selection of such a tool is normally the province of information technology, organizations should carefully consider having an attorney or consultant well versed in these issues advise them on the selection process, so that the tool will meet information technology, business and legal requirements.

The addition of an e-mail archive tool to an organization is a significant expenditure that is borne by information technology, but the tool must meet legal requirements (as that is its primary purpose) and should also be a value add to the end user's e-mail use. Oftentimes, information technology makes these tool selections without seeking the input of legal and the organization in an attempt to conduct business as usual—the client needs a solution, and the client attempts to provide it via the selected solution. In e-discovery, that can backfire quickly and leave the organization with a contract for a tool that does not meet its needs. Selection of any tools to manage or better improve e-discovery within an organization must be a part of the team-based process.

II. CHECKLISTS

§ 5:13 Checklist for establishing records and information management program

- ☐ Senior management must support the policy.
- ☐ The team for the program should be established, and include representatives from information technology, records, legal and the appropriate business units.
- ☐ Organization specific goals should be defined for the program.
- ☐ Budgetary issues should be addressed and understood at the outset of the program and a business case established that can be revisited when management support waivers.
- ☐ Employees should be required to notify the records information management team whenever important or significant amounts of electronically stored information are transferred away from the normal storage places for any reason.
- ☐ Electronically stored information must be identified and classified.
- ☐ A records and information management program may set a time after which employees should not retain individual types of electronically stored information.
- ☐ The records and management policy should be in writing.
- ☐ Each employee should sign a receipt acknowledging the employee's reading of the policy.
- ☐ Appropriate technology should be used to manage and monitor the retention program.

- ☐ Specific persons should be assigned to monitor and audit the records and management program on a regular basis.
- ☐ Development of the policy should be done in coordination with information technology personnel.
- ☐ The records management program must embrace the entire organization.
- ☐ The records management program must ensure that all needed electronically stored information is retained.
- ☐ The records management program must ensure that all electronically stored information required to be retained are retained for the appropriate period of time.
- ☐ The records management program must provide that all authorized users can access the electronically stored information records efficiently and economically.
- ☐ The records management program must ensure that all electronically stored information can be read and used.
- ☐ The records management program must ensure that all electronically stored information will be regarded as authentic once located and retrieved.
- ☐ The records management program should provide for litigation hold procedures to ensure that potentially responsive electronically stored information is not destroyed once litigation or a government investigation is reasonably anticipated.
- ☐ The records management program should establish procedures for the timely destruction of appropriate documents as their respective retention periods expire.

NOTES

Commentary

See Melnitzer, *Keeping Track of the Invisible Paper Trail: What Legal Departments Can Learn from Boeing's Experience*, CORPORATE LEGAL TIMES, Feb. 2003, at 15.

§ 5:14 Checklist for establishing collaborative records and information management system

- ☐ Build a collaborative foundation for the records and information management system, involving customers, clients, employees, and suppliers.
- ☐ Create business process workflows—knowing where the "knowledge" resides and how it gets there, including identifying duplicate information or redundant processes.
- ☐ Choose easily improvable processes and teams with the flexibility to try new things.
- ☐ Change the view of systems from vertical to horizontal, al-

lowing entry or retrieval from multiple applications on one screen or in multiple portals.

- ☐ Understand the current portals include not only web applications, but the ability to enter and retrieve information in word processing documents, e-mail applications, and other places.

NOTES

Commentary

This form is adapted from Grote, *Five Things You're Doing Right*, at http://www.edirectimpact.com.

§ 5:15 Checklist for e-mail retention policy

- ☐ Effective date of policy
- ☐ Last change date and changes made
- ☐ Person or department responsible for policy
- ☐ Scope or coverage of policy
- ☐ Purpose of policy
- ☐ Policy statement
- ☐ Reasons for complying with policy
- ☐ Importance of complying with policy
- ☐ Definitions
- ☐ Responsibilities
- ☐ Procedures
- ☐ Other retention policy guidelines
- ☐ Duplicate copies
- ☐ Convenience copies
- ☐ Litigation hold policy
- ☐ Consequences if policy not followed

NOTES

Commentary

This checklist is adapted from Tolson, *E-mail Retention Policy: A Step-by-Step Approach*, http://searchdatabackup.techtarget.com/answer/Email-retention-policy-A-step-by-step-approach.

Chapter 6

Understanding Records Management

I. GUIDELINES

II. FORMS

Research References

Treatises and Practice Aids

Grenig and Gleisner, eDiscovery & Digital Evidence §§ 8:9, 8:10

Trial Strategy

Recovery and Reconstruction of Electronic Mail as Evidence, 41 Am. Jur. Proof of Facts 3d 1

Computer Technology in Civil Litigation, 71 Am. Jur. Trials 111

Additional References

Grenig and Kinsler, Federal Civil Discovery and Disclosure §§ 13.1 to 13.6 (3d ed.)

ABA Discovery Standards, http://www.abanet.org/litigation/discoverystandards/2005civildiscoverystandards.pdf

ARMA, http://www.arma.org

Electronic Discovery Reference Model Project, http://www.edrm.net

The Sedona Conference, http://www.thesedonaconference.org

KeyCite®: Cases and other legal materials listed in KeyCite Scope can be researched through the KeyCite service on Westlaw®. Use KeyCite to check citations for form, parallel references, prior and later history, and comprehensive citator information, including citations to other decisions and secondary materials.

I. GUIDELINES

§ 6:1 Generally

Records management is the component of records and information management ("RIM") putting structure around a process for the creation, use, and destruction of official organization records. A good records management program encompasses the identification of records within the organization, development of a schedule (called a records retention schedule) for maintaining and destroying those records once they have completed their life cycle and are not subject to a litigation or tax hold, a process for managing and monitoring compliance with the existing schedules, and training for users and those tasked with compliance for each business function.

A records management program must address more issues than the preservation of records for the amount of time required by state or federal law. It should address the retention and destruction of all records regardless of the media, destruction schedules, program controls, procedures for suspending records destruction in case of foreseeable, pending, or actual litigation or governmental investigation, and records management program record keeping. The program should not distinguish between paper or electronically stored information, and should recognize the various locations where ESI can be stored. Because some organizations microfilm original records and then destroy the original records, it is especially important that the records management component of RIM include microfilm records if they exist.

Similarly, a records management program must cover all records, including reproductions or copies. Records programs that apply only to originals or record copies are inadequate. Under the Uniform Photographic Copies of Business and Public Records as

Evidence Act,[1] reproductions or photocopies of records have the same legal significance as the original and may be used in place of the original for all purposes.

Where a records program does not cover copies, such as information copies or personal copies of records, those copies may be discovered or subpoenaed although the original records were properly destroyed under the records program. Practically speaking, organizations should identify the original creator of the record and manage that record while advising other custodians of copies to destroy them once the information has been digested.

After information is produced, employees must determine whether the information should be considered and retained as a "record" for purposes of the records management program. Each employee should be familiar with the definition of records from their records management training. The training should explain how records should be retained.

Employees should be trained to ask whether the electronically stored information reflects an activity by the organization. Does the electronically stored information reflect fiscal, operational, administrative, legal, vital, or historical value? If the information does, the information is a record, and proper steps must be taken to retain the information and its associated metadata.[2]

§ 6:2 Definition of record

ISO 15489[1] defines a record as follows:

> A "record" is information created, received, and maintained as evidence by an organization or person in the transaction of business, or in the pursuance of legal obligations, "regardless of media."

[Section 6:1]

[1]http://www.law.upenn.edu/bll/archives/ulc/fnact99/1920_69/upcbpr49.pdf.

[2]See Aguilar v. Immigration and Customs Enforcement Div. of U.S. Dept. of Homeland Sec., 255 F.R.D. 350 (S.D. N.Y. 2008) (metadata associated with e-mails and electronic files must be preserved, maintained, and produced in course of legal discovery). But see Lake v. City of Phoenix, 220 Ariz. 472, 207 P.3d 725, 28 I.E.R. Cas. (BNA) 1186 (Ct. App. Div. 1 2009), vacated in part on other grounds, 222 Ariz. 547, 218 P.3d 1004, 107 Fair Empl. Prac. Cas. (BNA) 1142, 29 I.E.R. Cas. (BNA) 1682, 37 Media L. Rep. (BNA) 2451, 54 A.L.R.6th 813 (2009) (metadata are not a public record under Arizona law and not subject to disclosure under freedom of information request).

[Section 6:2]

[1]The international standard for records management of the International Organization for Standardization. See http://www.iso.org/iso/catalogue_detail?csnumber=31908.

A record includes information holding operational, legal, fiscal, vital or historical value. Examples of records are:

- A final draft of a contract
- Evaluation report of a current employee
- Insurance-related documents
- Company charter

Information without operational, legal, fiscal, vital, or historical value is not a record. Additionally, duplicates and copies of existing records are not records. Examples include:

- Personal messages
- E-mail inviting staff to a party
- Routine notices

Duplicates and copies should be disposed of as soon as they are no longer of use or value. Retaining duplicates or copies beyond their use can increase the cost of discovery.

§ 6:3 Definition of vital records

Vital records are any records, regardless of archival value, essential to the functions of an organization during and after an emergency. Vital records include records essential to the protection of the rights and interests of that organization and of the individuals for whose rights and interests it has responsibility. The loss of vital records during a disaster could result in the disruption of essential services, exposure to unplanned expenses, loss of revenue, increased vulnerability to litigation, or loss of productivity due to gaps in information. The length of retention of vital records may be mandated by internal company policy as well as by statute or regulation.

If an organization is anticipating or engaged in a legal or regulatory discovery request, or internal investigation, then records and documents associated with the matter become vital records. Documents deemed vital to discovery may include custodian files, e-mail, and instant messages stored on servers, desktop computers, laptops, smart phones, and thumb drives. These documents must be identified and declared records for discovery purposes. They become vital records to the matter and should be managed as such. An existing vital record may be identified as relevant to a legal matter or internal investigation. In this case, the retention date for the record may have to be changed to meet the overriding requirement of the legal matter.

§ 6:4 Record identification and metadata

When a document is a record, the document and its existing

metadata must be captured. At this time, a new piece of metadata will be added—the records management classification of the record. The records management program might physically move the record into a separate repository, move it into a repository with all of the enterprise data (with slightly different metadata, like "Read Only" and the records management classification) or keep the document where it is, but record the metadata into the records management program.

There are several considerations to take into account within the confines of the records management program:

- How the record is going to be captured.
- When the record will be captured.
- What metadata will be captured.
- How the document declaration will be made.

The records management program will also need to account for different categories of electronic documents, like e-mail and Word or Excel files and databases.

A final consideration is what metadata must be captured by a records management system. The records management team might desire little other than the date, author and classification of a document. On the other hand, discovery users will need a great deal more.

§ 6:5 Document declaration

Document declaration requires an employee to decide which documents and communications are "records" and indicate that to the records management system. A document declaration step that is too intrusive risks not only hindering employee productivity, but might even result in records not being declared as employees avoid the burdens of the declaration process. On the other hand, a document declaration process is ineffective.

The timing of the declaration is important. Some file and e-mail systems allow for metadata modification, meaning that a declaration made after the document is sent or initially saved might include altered metadata. This may raise concerns during discovery. A records management program should prompt e-mail users to declare whether a message and its attachments are a record and determine where to file it when the message is sent or received. The records management program should define what qualifies as a record.

Computer applications, such as Word, Excel, PowerPoint, or Visio may be integrated with a records management program so the user is prompted, whenever a "Save" or "Close" operation is executed, to declare whether the file is a record and, if so, where to store it. The user should have a standard set of files, defined and set up by the records management team at server levels, in which to store the document or message.

Voice mail, being brief, informal messages, presents similar issues as e-mails. The records management program should provide that voice mail, including backups, is automatically erased after a brief period such as 30 days. It is probably unnecessary to allow for the formalization of voice mail records.

The Internal Revenue Service considers computer records as recordkeeping under the Internal Revenue Code. The records management program must provide that records with tax implications be maintained for the requisite period and must make the records available on a current computer system.[1]

Databases create special problems as they may contain a number of files and fields of data used for a variety of purposes. The records management program may consider retaining a database as an official record until superseded. Only the current version of the database must be maintained.

A records management program may consider drafts of documents as nonrecords for retention purposes. The records management program could permit the drafts and original notes of many documents to be destroyed in a relatively short period of time after the final draft has been accepted. The records management program should consider the final draft to be a record. Some word processing files could be saved for longer periods to facilitate the revision of drafts.

§ 6:6 Managing and monitoring compliance

A records management program must include steps for monitoring compliance and auditing the process. Employees must be trained and educated about the program and the consequences to the organization of not following the program. The program must be easy to follow, periodically reviewed, and regularly audited.

At least one person in the organization must be designated to manage and monitor the records management program. That person is responsible for ensuring that the program is up-to-date and that retention and destruction is being conducted in accordance with the records management program. The responsible person should be familiar enough with the records management

---

[Section 6:5]

[1] www.irs.gov/taxtopic/TC305.html.

program and its operation to be able to testify in court about the program.

Monitoring and managing a records management program can be difficult because of the number of records controlled by employees. A program that is not easy to understand and implement can also be a serious problem, an issue that should be considered at the outset.

The routine destruction of electronically stored information may lead to severe sanctions once an organization is on notice of potential litigation. A records management program must provide for the suspension of records destruction and the preservation of records in the case of foreseeable, pending, or actual litigation or government investigation. In such event, records destruction must cease immediately. The records program should provide that any employee who receives any information regarding potential litigation or government investigation immediately inform the legal counsel or chief executive officer.

§ 6:7 Training and publicizing the retention schedule

After taking steps to ensure the program meets all legal requirements, an organization should prove all employees with training. The program should be well publicized within the organization, and the organization should advise employees where to direct questions.

Employee compliance is essential for a records and information management program to succeed. The wide variety of employees an organization has should be considered in planning and implementing a records and information management program. Consultants, contract personnel, and vendors all require clear instruction regarding records and information.

§ 6:8 Disposition of records

With respect to backup systems, a records and information management ("RIM") program should indicate the purpose of backing up records, including e-mails, is for disaster recovery. Backup tapes created for disaster recovery may not be subject to a litigation hold unless they are accessible.[1]

Backup for purposes of disaster recovery should be distin-

[Section 6:8]

[1]See Zubulake v. UBS Warburg LLC, 220 F.R.D. 212, 218, 92 Fair Empl. Prac. Cas. (BNA) 1539 (S.D. N.Y. 2003) (while e-mail backup tapes created for disaster recovery not subject to litigation hold unless they are accessible, if a

guished from off-line storage of long-term, low access information. Off-line storage, such as annual accounting records, should be treated separately from backup. Backup of information with short-term retention, such as e-mails, should be segregated from other records.

After a RIM program is approved, records and information should be destroyed in accordance with the program's retention schedule. Where electronically stored information is inconsistently destroyed, a court may find this inconsistency to be evidence that the destruction was done in bad faith.[2]

Some RIM programs specify that the records and information manager will provide legal counsel, department managers, and the tax manager with a list of records that can be destroyed. After review, records, other than those relating to litigation or government investigation, or that are still needed by the organization, can be destroyed at the designated time.

The key to defending a RIM program in court when or if records that may be relevant to the matter no longer exist, is to be able to say the organization has a program and schedule in place, the schedule is complied with, and compliance is audited regularly. Reasonableness is the standard for considering whether an organization has preserved information relevant for litigation, and that standard is how programs and compliance with those programs are measured in the analysis by a court.

Destruction of records and information in a selective manner, even if permitted by the retention schedule, may create the impression that the RIM program has not been properly implemented. Improper destruction of records and information may be considered as suggesting guilt or liability. Improper destruction may also be found to be obstruction of justice.

§ 6:9 Software

Software that can systematically control the management of records according to a schedule is commercially available. Whether and what software might be appropriate for an organization depends on such factors as the size and complexity of the organization, knowing what the organization needs and how the

---

company can locate the information of "key players," that information should be preserved even if it exists in the form of disaster recovery backup tapes).

[2]See, e.g., In re Prudential Ins. Co. of America Sales Practices Litigation, 169 F.R.D. 598, 615, 36 Fed. R. Serv. 3d 767 (D.N.J. 1997) (adverse inference from destruction of relevant computer records because document retention policy was haphazard and uncoordinated).

software will be used, and the cost of acquiring and maintaining the software.

The first step in selecting records management software is conduct an inventory to identify records management needs. An inventory will determine the quantity of records, their physical and environmental condition, how often they are referenced, and where they are located. An inventory provides a survey of the existing records situation, determines storage needs, identifies vital and archival records, improves recordkeeping habits, and provides a foundation for a records management plan.

After the inventory is completed, an organization should determine records management software needs by investigating what records management functions the software will support, what general functions the software must possess, and what performance criteria the software must meet. Records management functions include destruction notification, destruction of electronically stored information, request processing, file and box tracking, file management, and document management. General functions include help features, menus and commands, speed and accuracy, generation of standard reports, ease of use, ability to manage records in all formats, and security classification and access privileges. Minimum performance criteria to look for include the ability to perform on a current computer system and the inclusion of vendor-supplied support, maintenance, and training.

There are many types of software products available to meet particular needs, such as indexing and searching products, document management software, and records management applications. There are commercial off-the-shelf software products immediately available providing such benefits as proven reliability, lower cost, availability of user manuals and online tutorials. Some organizations develop applications using commercially available database management software packages such as Microsoft Access or Lotus Approach. Others have a customized application written tailored to the organization's particular needs.

It is essential to carefully evaluate and test available records management software packages, as well as investigate vendors before purchasing records management software. Knowledge of what is included in the price of the software can create a more productive and efficient records management program.

§ 6:10 Documentation

The organization must keep and maintain documentation relating to the development and implementation of the records management program, including legal research, program approvals, retention schedules, and program modifications. These records and information can be of critical importance in establishing that the records and information management program was developed and implemented in the ordinary course of business. Legal research records can also be helpful in showing the organization has used its best efforts to comply with any records and information retention requirements.

II. FORMS

§ 6:11 Records management policy statement

Policy Purpose: To provide guidelines for properly establishing a records management program and assisting those departments that require long-term records retention and procedures for implementing an effective RIM program. Records management includes areas such as inactive records, vital records, microfilming, and records retention.

Policy

1. Records management is the systematic control of all records, regardless of media, from their creation or receipt, through their processing, distribution, organization, storage, and retrieval to their disposition. Information flows through the organization in the form of paper and electronic records such as word processing documents, spreadsheets, e-mail, graphical images, and voice or data transmissions. Information can be stored on a variety of storage media, such as microfilm, microfiche, diskette, optical disk, CD-ROM, videotape, and paper.
2. This policy details the requirements and responsibilities to initiate a well-defined records management program. The records management program applies to those departments that require a long-term records-retention, -storage, and -destruction program.
   a. Ensure only essential records of continuing value are preserved. Records should be retained in the active office areas as long as they serve the immediate administrative, legal, or fiscal purpose for which they were created.
   b. Establish safeguards against the illegal removal, loss, or destruction of records. Records either should be disposed of in accordance with an approved records-retention schedule or transferred to the records-retention center until the prescribed retention period has expired.
   c. Management of records is the responsibility of the owner, or

creator, of the record. The department director or the director's designated representative should contact the records manager to discuss initiating a records-management program or reviewing an existing records-management program to handle records properly from their creation through their destruction. Departments can be provided guidance on how records should be organized and stored to ensure timely and efficient retrieval.

d. The records retention schedule is the key tool for departments to use to manage their records effectively. Information is a valuable asset; however, if records that contain information cannot be retrieved efficiently or are retained beyond their legal, regulatory, or administrative retention period, they lose their value and may impose a liability to the organization.

3. The benefits of an effective records management program include:
   a. Greater assurance of legal compliance to minimize liability and discovery impacts;
   b. Improved customer service with higher quality of service and faster retrieval of documents;
   c. Improved staff productivity with effective records-management systems;
   d. Reduced storage costs through elimination of unnecessary and duplicate documents;
   e. Ensured safety of vital organizational records; and
   f. Efficient, cost-effective records-retention and -disposal system.
4. The components of an effective records management program that may be activated by the records manager include:
   a. Records-retention program;
   b. Vital records program;
   c. Inactive records-management program;
   d. Electronic records management program;
   e. Records management handbook/records liaisons' training;
   f. Micrographics (microfilming) program;
   g. Forms-management program (corporate communications);
   h. Active records management program; and
   i. Copy and reprography program (purchasing).
5. Significant recurring activities initiated by the records manager include:
   a. Annual inventory of the records center: The records manager will annually inventory all records in the records center to confirm information in the records-retention tracking system.

b. Annual review of the records retention schedule: The records manager will have the records retention schedule reviewed and validated annually for accuracy.

c. Annual files purge program: The records manager will advertise and initiate an annual files purge by all departments. The purpose is to have individuals review personal active file systems, as well as electronic document folders, and to purge documents no longer required. No original documents are to be destroyed.

Proponent

1. The vice president for information systems or designee is the proponent for the RIM program.
2. All questions concerning compliance with this policy should be directed to the records manager unless otherwise indicated.

Roles and Responsibilities

1. The vice president of finance, vice president of legal affairs, and the chief information officer, as needed, will be requested to identify to the records manager the individual who can perform the following tasks:
   a. Review and provide functional approval of an updated or changed records retention schedule, as required, for all departments.
   b. Become familiar with the purpose of the records retention schedule.
2. Department directors who need to implement a records management program should contact the records manager for guidance and assistance and will need to:
   a. Identify a records liaison and inform the records liaison of the duties of the records liaison;
   b. Review and update records-retention schedules annually;
   c. Review the records-management handbook, as needed; and
   d. Coordinate departmental activities that may impact records and information management with the records manager to include office consolidation, office closures, and approval of new or replacement, records storage, and file equipment as requested.
3. Departmental records liaisons are responsible for:
   a. Obtaining records liaisons' overview training from the records manager;

b. Becoming familiar with and maintaining the records management handbook;
c. Assisting in developing and enforcing the records retention schedule for their department;
d. Managing the department's records; and
e. Attending quarterly or as otherwise required records liaisons' meetings.

4. Records manager is responsible for:
a. Assisting in the design, development, implementation, and/or review of records management programs to include the programs listed in paragraph 2, Policy, above;
b. Managing the records retention center for all departments to ensure safe storage, quick retrieval, records confidentiality, and appropriate records disposition;
c. Developing and maintaining the records retention schedule;
d. Managing the microfilming or digitizing of records and information as required;
e. Issuing and updating the records management handbook;
f. Educating and training records liaisons;
g. Approving records storage and retrieval equipment for departmental purchase as requested;
h. Participating actively as a member of the following committees:
i. Information Management Committee on an as-needed basis for retention issues;
ii. Forms Approval Committee as a member on an as-needed basis;
i. Presenting records and information management issues, as required, to the Information Systems Steering Committee or other appropriate forum; and
j. Chairing quarterly Information Management Committee meeting with records liaison.

Procedures

Detailed procedures can be found in the records and management handbook. For the most frequent requirements, procedures are summarized below.

1. Records Retention Schedules
a. Each department is responsible for determining retention periods for records created. A record may be kept beyond the legal or regulatory retention period if it satisfies an administrative need based on business necessity, which is stated on the records-retention schedule. To create or update

a records retention schedule:

i. Contact the records manager to assist you;

ii. Inventory all current records maintained, including all media types;

iii. Create a master list of records and record types and draft preliminary retention schedule;

iv. Determine retention periods based on legal, administrative, and historical value;

v. Obtain approval for retention schedule from Information Services, Finance, and Legal;

vi. Publish and implement the retention schedule; and

vii. Review annually

b. State, federal, and/or regulatory requirements prescribe minimum records-retention periods.

c. Once the specific retention period for any paper or electronically stored information has been reached, the record will be destroyed consistent with appropriate procedures.

d. Notwithstanding minimum retention periods, all records must be maintained until all required audits are completed and must be kept beyond the listed retention period if litigation is pending or in progress. Records manager must be notified of any litigation that would require retention of records beyond normal disposition.

e. Destruction of records is permitted in accordance with the law only after expiration of the retention periods stated on the approved departmental retention schedules.

2. Files Transferred to Records Center

a. Files will be accepted throughout the year once the department has coordinated set patterns for retention with the records manager.

b. The departmental records liaison will contact records manager via e-mail of a files transfer requirement.

c. Storage boxes and Records Center Control Card Form must be obtained from records manager.

d. Files must be packed in approved storage boxes.

e. A Records Center Control Card Form must accompany the boxes.

f. Records manager will provide instructions for proper packing and labeling of boxes in the records management handbook.

g. Pickup will be coordinated with records manager.

3. Request for Retrieving Records

a. Office wishing to retrieve records will contact the records retention center.

b. The departmental records liaison will provide information for locating the file from the Records Center Control Card.
c. Telephone request should not exceed five records per call. For more than five records, a written request should be mailed or e-mailed to records management.
d. Retrieved records will be tagged with a Records Center Reference Request form. This form *must* be returned to allow prompt and accurate refiling.
e. Notify records management if file is to be reactivated.

4. Assistance in the Selection of Records Filing System Equipment
   a. All new records management and filing equipment should be reviewed by the records manager, as requested, prior to purchase to ensure they are efficient and cost-effective in storage space.
   b. Existing file systems can be reviewed and recommendations provided for improvement.
5. Records Retention Requirements for Automated Systems
   a. Systems and programming managers will contact the records manager who will assist the department that owns the data in determining records and information retention requirements for the electronically stored information on new and existing systems.
   b. A valid retention schedule will be prepared for electronically stored information.
6. Vital Records Program

The implementation of a vital records program to protect and preserve records that contain information vital to the conduct of business in the event of a major disaster is crucial. These documents contain the information necessary to recreate the organization's legal and financial position. Vital records generally represent only a small portion of all records and information maintained by the organization. The records manager will review the vital records program annually. Areas of importance are financial records, employee records, insurance policy information, ownership records, major contracts and agreements, corporate records, and negotiable instruments.

Electronic Records Policy Statement

Each organization's e-mail policy should reflect its own culture and the legal and regulatory framework within which it operates. Developers of the policy must consider factors such as legal issues, records-management retention policies, and information management administration of the e-mail system, along with financial and regulatory issues.

Sample 1: The e-mail system is owned by the company. It is to be used for company business. Occasional use of the system for messages of a personal nature will be treated like any other message. The company desires to respect the right to privacy of its employees and does not monitor e-mail messages as a routine matter. It does, however, reserve the right to access all e-mail messages, view their contents, and track traffic patterns.

Sample 2: When using e-mail, the message created or used may or may not be a record. E-mail messages are subject to the records and information policies of the company. Within the company, each person is responsible for controlling records and information according to the records and information management policies.

Sample 3: Before selecting e-mail as a means for communication or document transmission, users should consider the need for immediacy, formality, accountability, access, security, and permanence. E-mail differs from other forms of communication. It is immediate and informal, similar to a telephone conversation, yet it is more permanent. It is as irrevocable as a hard-copy document, yet easy to duplicate, alter, and distribute.

The Company (organization, company, etc.) reserves the right to monitor employee use of e-mail by systems administrators or departmental supervisors. Employees are reminded that e-mail use is provided *primarily* for business purposes and not for personal purposes and that employees cannot expect protection of their personal or business-related e-mail correspondence under privacy laws and regulations.

The Company will not monitor e-mail messages as a routine matter. The Company will, however, respond to legal processes and fulfill its obligations to third parties. The Company will inspect the contents of e-mail messages in the course of an investigation triggered by indications of impropriety or as necessary to locate substantive information that is not more readily available by other means.

Electronic Records Guideline

Retention periods are established for records according to departmental, fiscal, and legal requirements. Each record listed on a records-retention schedule specifies a specific period of time that the record is retained. *This retention applies whether the record is on paper or residing on magnetic or optical media (such as hard disks, tapes, thumb drives, external hard drives).* Once records have reached their designated time for destruction, they should be destroyed or eliminated from all storage media.

Backup media should be stored in a different location than the computer equipment that is used to create them. Electronic records retained in a backup system follow the same retention as similar paper records listed on a retention schedule.

Drafts generally are not retained and should never be retained longer than the finalized version that becomes the record.

Databases are modified over time through the addition, deletion, or revision of information. Reports may be periodically generated to capture or record the information at a point in time. Records that are in databases may use a retention period until they are superseded. Once information has been superseded, it is generally lost unless provision is made to save it as a report. Historical data should be archived or deleted according to the department's retention schedule.

NOTES TO FORM

Commentary

This form is adapted from a form provided by ARMA.

§ 6:12 Records management program

_ Company

RECORDS MANAGEMENT PROGRAM

1.0. Records

The records of *[name]* Company ("Company") include essentially all records produced by employees, whether in paper or electronic form. Records include, but are not limited to, e-mails, memoranda, calendars, appointment books, and expense records. All employees are expected to comply fully with all records retention or records destruction policies and schedules.

2.0. Legal Requirements

The law requires Company to maintain certain types of records for specified periods of time. Failure to retain records for the statutory periods may subject Company and employees to penalties and fines.

3.0. Destruction Schedules

Company has established retention or destruction schedules for specific categories of records. The minimum retention periods for the following categories of records are set forth below.

3.1. Board and Board Committee Materials. Company should keep permanent copies of all Board of Director and Board committee meeting minutes in Company's minute book. Company should keep a copy of all Board and Board committee materials for no less than three years.

3.2. Legal Files. The Company Legal Department Legal counsel should be consulted to determine the retention period of particular legal files. Generally, Company should keep legal documents for ten years.

3.3. Tax Records. Tax records include, but are not limited to, documents relating to expenses, deductions, accounting procedures, payroll, and other documents concerning Company's revenues and expenses. Tax records should be retained for at least six years from the date of filing the applicable return.

3.4. Employment and Personnel Records. State and federal law requires Company to keep certain employment and personnel information, including employment applications. Company should keep personnel files reflecting performance reviews and any complaints brought against Company or individual employees under applicable state and federal statutes. Company should keep all final memoranda and correspondence reflecting performance reviews and actions taken by or against personnel in the employee's personnel file. Employment and personnel records should be retained for six years.

3.5. Intellectual Property. Company should keep permanently documents relating to intellectual property and development of intellectual property, such as copyrights or patents

3.6. Trade Secrets. Company should keep all documents designated as containing trade secret information for at least the life of the trade secret. Documents detailing the development process are often also of value to Company and are protected as a trade secret where Company derives independent economic value from the secrecy of the information, and Company has taken affirmative steps to keep the information confidential.

3.7. Public Filings. Company should retain permanent copies of all publicly filed documents.

3.8. Marketing and Sales Documents. Company should keep final copies of marketing and sales documents for the same period of time it keeps other corporate files—generally three years. Company should keep sales invoices, contracts, leases, licenses, and other legal documentation for at least three years beyond the life of the relevant agreement.

3.9. Contracts. Company should retain executed copies of all contracts entered into by Company should be retained for at least three years beyond the life of the agreement, and longer in the case of publicly filed contracts.

3.10. E-mail. E-mail that needs to be saved should be either printed in hard copy and kept in the appropriate file, or downloaded to a computer file and kept electronically or on disk as a separate file. The retention period for e-mail depends upon the subject matter of the e-mail, as covered elsewhere in this policy.

3.11. Press Releases. Company should retain permanent copies of all press releases.

4.0. Litigation or Potential Litigation

If an employee believes, or is informed by Company, that certain records or information are relevant to litigation, or potential litigation, the employee must preserve those records and information until the Company Legal Department determines the records and information are no longer needed.

4.1. Duty to Preserve. This duty to preserve supersedes any established destruction schedule for those records and information.

4.2. Questions Regarding Duty to Preserve. If an employee believe the duty to preserve may apply, or has any question regarding the possible applicability of the duty to preserve, the employee should contact the Company Legal Department.

5.0. Failure to Comply

An employee's failure to comply with this Records Policy may result in disciplinary action, including suspension or termination. An employee should refer questions about this policy to *[name]*, at *[telephone number]* or *[e-mail address]*.

6.0. Acknowledgment

I have read and understand the Records Policy.

Dated: *[date]*

[signature of employee]

[typed name]

NOTES TO FORM

Commentary

This basic retention policy can be modified depending upon the size of the organization, and whether the organization is required by state or federal law to keep documents for particular lengths of time.

§ 6:13 Electronically stored information guidelines for access, retention, destruction

Electronically Stored Information Guidelines for Access, Retention, Destruction

1. Introduction
2. Employee Responsibility
3. Word Processing Files
4. Administrative Databases
5. Electronic Spreadsheets
6. Schedules of Daily Activities
7. Tracking and Control Records
8. WWW Materials
9. E-mail
10. Optical Imaging
11. Migration
12. Records Destruction
13. Security
14. Changes to These Guidelines
15. For More Information

INTRODUCTION

Most employees at the University create and use electronic records every day. If you send or receive e-mail, exchange notices of meetings, or create word processing documents, then you are using electronic records. The informational content of electronic record systems constitutes an important part of the University's corporate memory and must be managed as a valuable University asset documenting functions and accountability.

[State] law defines "records" as *[quote]*. *[Citation.]* The *[state]* Open Records Act mandates that "public records shall be open for inspection by any person, except as otherwise provided by *[statute]*. *[Citation.]*

Electronically stored information is subject to retention, destruction, and inspection under these laws just as if the record were stored on paper. Records management standards and principles apply to all forms of recorded information, from creation to final disposition. Guidance on records management issues, including electronically stored information, may be obtained from the University Archives and Records Center, which administers state and university policy concerning the management of university records. Feel free to call us at *[telephone number]*, e-mail us, or visit our Website at *[URL]*.

EMPLOYEE RESPONSIBILITY

University policy for management of University records is administered by the University Archives and Records Center. The Center's Director serves as the University's records manager. The Director works with departments to help them deal with records problems. However, the departments themselves—their administrators, staff, and faculty—are accountable for the day-to-day administration, control, preservation, access, and security of records within their custody in accordance with state and federal laws. It is ultimately the responsibility of the creators and users of electronically stored information to ensure that it is properly cared for.

In other words:

> University employees are responsible for maintaining the integrity of records whether stored electronically or in hard copy. Information in records systems must be maintained until the legal, fiscal, and administrative retention periods have been met.
>
> All employees must ensure that electronically stored information is maintained so that it is readily available for appropriate use, and so that established records management procedures, including disposition and/or destruction, can be carried out.
>
> Under no circumstances will employees permit the destruction or loss of records or records, in electronic or hard copy, if the employee has any reason to believe the records are related to any current open records request, subpoena, litigation, investigation, audit, or other governmental proceeding.

Offices should use electronic information systems that maintain appropriate controls when creating records and that will support them in the context of their business purpose or the activity performed. Records that are vital in supporting the core activities of the University must be identified and scheduled for routine backup. However, while simply backing up a record is crucial, it is not the same as archiving a file. Hard copies, microfilm copies, or magnetic tapes of information systems or records systems, as appropriate, will provide preservation for documents requiring long term or permanent retention.

Consistent with the University Model Schedule, most University records have a limited retention period. If an office retains records for the required length of time, on whatever medium it chooses, it is meeting legal requirements. Records required for audit purposes must be made available in hard copy or on a current computer system according to Internal Revenue procedures.

WORD PROCESSING FILES

Offices should take measures to protect permanent records produced by word processing software, either by printing the documents or preserving them in electronic form separately from materials of a non-permanent nature. This is to prevent accidental deletion or destruction with non-permanent records when the retention period for non-permanent records has expired. Non-permanent word processing files may be stored with other non-permanent electronic records and deleted with them at the end of their retention period.

Once a printed record copy is distributed, the electronic version may be deleted. If the official record copy is kept electronically, however, it must be retained for the retention period listed in the University Model Schedule.

Documents such as letters, messages, memoranda, reports, handbooks, policies and procedures, and manuals written on hard drives or diskettes are considered works in progress or drafts until the final draft is accepted as the official version. Creators may delete drafts and revisions once the record copy has been produced. The working copies should be retained only if they are used to document how decisions were reached in developing programs and policies of the office or unit, or aid in the interpretation or purpose of the final document (e.g. to explain why certain changes were made or to clarify intent.)

Some records are now created only in electronic form, whereas in years past they might have been hard copies. In these cases, the Model University Schedule that applied to the hard copy is still applicable to the current electronic version. If the retention period has been met and a hard copy would be destroyed, the electronic version may be deleted.

ADMINISTRATIVE DATABASES

Many offices use databases containing information fields arranged and secured so that the information can be maintained or removed for use for various purposes. Much of the utility of a database lies in its flexibility and dynamic character. They change often as information is added, deleted, or modified. Ultimately, from this body of raw information, many different distinct queries can produce different results.

Documents generated from selected information in databases are often produced in hard copy and distributed; however, the databases themselves are retained primarily in electronic format. Few records generated from databases are to be retained permanently. Record copies of reports and other documents generated from databases that document official policies should be printed for permanent retention. Records that are non-policy in nature and are used for informational purposes, or do not set official guidelines or procedures, may be deleted in accordance with the Model University Schedule.

If hard copy documents produced from a database are maintained in the office files, and these hard copies have a limited retention period, the electronic files may be deleted when the information is superseded or no longer useful.

ELECTRONIC SPREADSHEETS

Spreadsheets in electronic format such as hard disks or diskettes and used to produce a hard copy that is maintained in established files may be deleted when no longer useful. If the spreadsheet is kept electronically, it can be deleted when the authorized retention period is reached. If the electronic system contains several spreadsheets with different retention periods, and if the software does not easily allow deletion of individual records, delete the records after the longest retention period has been met.

SCHEDULES OF DAILY ACTIVITIES

Calendars, appointment books, and schedules documenting meetings, appointments, telephone calls, and other activities by university personnel are increasingly kept in electronic format. Calendars relating to the official activities of the president, provost, vice presidents, and deans must be retained permanently. These should be printed periodically and filed in the official records. Otherwise, calendars may be deleted at the discretion of the employee.

TRACKING AND CONTROL RECORDS

Logs, registers, and other records in electronic format used to track and document the status of correspondence, reports, or other records that are approved for destruction under the guidelines of the Model University Schedule may be deleted when no longer needed.

WEBSITE MATERIALS

University departments and schools are increasingly using the World Wide Web instead of or in conjunction with paper documents to publish information about their programs. Materials provided on University Websites must be managed as other university records are. Documents that in hard copy format would qualify as official university records with permanent or long-term value should be printed and retained. Website documents that do not set or document official policies or procedures and are of a transitory nature may be deleted once their usefulness has ended.

E-MAIL

E-mail is a major factor in University offices since correspondence, memos, and reports are increasingly sent and stored electronically. E-mail does fall under the statutory definition of public records, and as such, *the e-mail issued by and received by University employees is subject to open records requests and can be discoverable under legal actions brought against the university.* Senders and recipients of e-mail must be aware that the legal standards for the retention and disposition of University records also apply to e-mail. E-mail categories include official and general, the same as that of hard copy office correspondence.

Official is defined as documenting the major functions, activities and programs of the university and important events in its history. E-mail that falls under this definition must be retained under the guidelines in the University Model Schedule. Employees should print and retain in department files or store in an accepted, retrievable electronic format e-mail that reflects the official position of the university or that documents the administrative, legal, and fiscal requirements of the institution. The University Archives and Records Center recommends printing these e-mails as the most reliable form of long-term preservation.

General e-mail correspondence that is non-policy in nature and not critical to administrative, fiscal, or legal requirements can be deleted in accordance with guidelines in the University Model Records Retention Schedule. Form letters, notices of meetings, duplicates and forwarded messages from other offices, spam, and other e-mail messages of a transient nature can be considered reference or information-only material and can be deleted at the discretion of the user. Disposition of electronic mail should take place on a regular and systematic basis in accordance with approved records retention guidelines.

Information Technology has developed default settings for the archiving capabilities of the University's GroupWise e-mail applications. However, it is important to understand that the GroupWise client cannot determine the relative significance of individual pieces of e-mail. Responsible management of e-mail, including determining which e-mails constitute important university records and which do not, *must* be the responsibility of the account user. The University Records Manager will provide advice and support on how to make these decisions, but *it is the department and its employees that are responsible in the event of a record's being inappropriately retained or prematurely destroyed.*

As employees leave University employment, e-mail accounts remain active for one month after the termination date before being deleted. Before a staff member leaves a unit, a supervisor should confer with the staff member to determine what e-mail must be retained, who within the unit should keep it, and to ensure that the e-mail is forwarded to the proper recipient for appropriate retention. Likewise, any other electronic files maintained on a departing staff member's hard drive should be given a similar assessment. If that person also manages an e-mail service account, arrangements should be made to transfer control of the account to another person within the unit. If there are questions about what records should be retained and what may be deleted, please contact the University Archives. If there are other questions concerning the management of e-mail accounts or other electronic resources, please contact Information Technology.

OPTICAL IMAGING

Many offices now use scanners to render paper documents into computer-readable form, frequently utilizing optical storage media such as CD-ROMs or DVDs. However, as of this writing, there are no nationally recognized information management standards concerning the longevity of any digital storage media. Considering that such formats as DVDs have existed less than twenty-five years, it is difficult to make definite claims on their longevity over the many decades during which some university records must be preserved.

MIGRATION

Migration is a name for the conversion of files in obsolete formats and/or upon obsolete media into formats that may be more easily read by contemporary computers and software. (An example would be migrating old files from WordPerfect format on floppy disks to Microsoft Word format on thumb drives.)

If records are migrated to new versions of software and/or new hardware or are otherwise altered when new hardware and/or software are implemented, an audit trail of any migrations and changes must be maintained. The new system must be able to read the records that the University Model Schedule requires the University to maintain.

University offices must develop procedures for system and data migration that identify which records will be migrated and the schedule for data backups and recopying, maintaining an audit trail of any migrations that are actually completed. The full migration plan should include backward compatibility in the new electronic records system or software. This means that change to a new system or software should include the conversion of records from the previous system for access in the new one, or it should provide a mechanism such that the records from the previous system can still be accessed. If not, it will be necessary to print the inactive electronic records to paper if the records have not reached the legal destruction period.

RECORDS DESTRUCTION

Although many of the same practices apply in the application of records schedules for both hard copy and electronic copies, the destruction of these records is different. Hard copy records are destroyed in labor intensive methods such as shredding or by sending them to the landfill. Although electronically stored information may be erased or written over, records containing confidential information can sometimes be recovered even if they have been erased or the media reformatted. Software that deletes records from a drive is available and destruction of confidential records using these programs is recommended. In some cases the hard drive should also be reformatted to protect the confidentiality of the records. This precaution should be taken if a computer is sent to the Inventory Control Warehouse as surplus property. It is also important that personnel responsible for electronic records maintain a record of destruction of records that are deleted from office systems. The audit trail will include information on disposition status of records and whether the records were destroyed or transferred to hard copy.

The Office of Technology has published a set of best practices for the destruction of electronic records and sanitization of electronic media. This set of best practices can be found at *[URL]*.

For advice on how University employees can best comply with these best practices, please contact the University Information Technology Help Desk at *[URL]*.

SECURITY

Many university records contain confidential data. Unauthorized access to or disclosure of these records by university employees is prohibited. For further information on policies and procedures for computer security and computer accounts, contact Information Technology. If you have questions about privacy or confidentially, please contact the University Archives. University Archives will consult with University Counsel and/or the appropriate university office that executed the agreement regarding confidentiality restrictions as needed. If you have questions about the matter of open records requests, contact *[name]*, University's open records officer, by e-mail.

CHANGES TO THESE GUIDELINES

Because electronic technology changes quickly, the University Archives anticipates these electronic records guidelines will require revision. We welcome any suggestions on the subject of the management and preservation of electronic records from university personnel. Contact *[name]*, University Records Manager.

FOR MORE INFORMATION

To learn more about the state's policies and best practices for electronic systems and records, see *[URL]*.

For University-specific inquiries, contact the University Archives by phone at *[number]*, or by e-mail, or visit our Website at *[URL]*.

NOTES TO FORM

Commentary

This form is adapted from one used by the University of Louisville. It can easily be adapted for use by other types of public entities. By deleting the provisions regarding public records, it can also be adapted for use by private organizations.

§ 6:14 Public records management policy

University of *[name]*

Public Records Management Policy

1.0. POLICY

The policy of the University of *[name]* ("University") is to ensure that public records and information are properly managed in compliance with relevant state and federal laws.

2.0. SCOPE

This public records management policy applies to all University institutions and departments.

3.0. PURPOSE

The purpose of this policy is to facilitate the transaction of business, ensure public accountability, and preserve the history of University institutions by fulfilling state and federal legal requirements for public records management.

4.0. PUBLIC RECORDS MANAGEMENT

4.1. Definition and Ownership of Public Records. Public records include all materials, regardless of physical form or characteristics, that employees create or receive in connection with the transaction of public business on behalf of the University. All public records employees create, receive, or retain are owned by the University and the State of *[state]*.

4.2. Duties of the *[title]*. The *[title]* shall designate a public records officer.

4.3. Duties of the Public Records Officers. The public records officer shall

(1) develop and maintain a public records management program fulfilling state and federal legal requirements;

(2) provide records management training and assistance to University employees;

(3) upon request, provide special assistance to University legal counsel, legal custodians for public records requests, auditors, and archivists; and

(4) collaborate with University technology professionals in developing and maintaining information and digitization systems that create, receive, store, destroy, and archive electronic public records in compliance with state and federal legal requirements.

4.4. Characteristics of Public Records Management Programs. Public records management programs facilitate ongoing business activities, ensure public accountability, and preserve the history of the University. In order to successfully perform these vital functions, public records management programs should be developed and maintained using a collaborative decision-making process involving University institutions and departments: records and forms officers, information technology professionals, legal counsel, legal custodians, auditors, and archivists. In some instances, this collaborative decision-making process should involve University employees from other professional fields, including but not limited to: business officers, administrators, faculty, staff, students, human resource managers, and registrars.

Public records management programs shall:

(1) ensure that public records are created, received, and retained in compliance with this policy and state and federal legal requirements;

(2) properly classify public records, so as to support University functions and ensure appropriate disposition of these records;

(3) obtain approval for disposition of public records from the State of *[state] [name of agency]*;

(4) ensure secure storage of public records throughout the life cycle of these records;

(5) ensure that expired public records are destroyed, paying special attention to the additional steps necessary to destroy expired electronically stored information; and

(6) preserve the history of the University by implementing archival processes ensuring the security, accessibility, accuracy, authenticity, readability, and reliability of public records notwithstanding the passage of time.

4.5. Treatment of Electronically Stored Information. Public records management programs shall ensure that throughout their life cycle, electronic public records are secure, accessible, accurate, authentic, legible, readable, and reliable. These programs shall also ensure that upon disposition, electronic public records are either properly destroyed or archived. Because some information technology systems may retain portions of deleted electronically stored information, public records management programs must ensure that expired electronically stored information is actually destroyed.

4.6. Information and Digitization Systems and Business Tools. University employees must not purchase, support, or utilize information and digitization systems, or business tools that fail to comply with this policy and state and federal legal requirements for public records management. The procurement, development, and maintenance of information and digitization systems should include public records management functions.

4.7. Electronically-Stored Information. Information and digitization systems routinely create electronically stored information that, in many instances, comprise a public record. Therefore, University employees and the technology professionals who provide, support, and manage information and digitization systems must ensure that electronically stored information is only created, received, or retained if it supports UW System institution business functions.

4.8. Review of Public Records Management Programs. The State of *[name]* Department of has authority to periodically audit the public records management programs at University in order to evaluate legal compliance. In order to ensure the success of such an audit or to ensure compliance with this policy, the Public Records and Information Officer may conduct periodic reviews of public records management programs.

5.0. PUBLIC RECORDS MANAGEMENT ROLES AND RESPONSIBILITIES

5.1. Employee Supervisors. Supervisors of University employees are responsible for ensuring that the employees under their supervision attend public records management training sessions and manage public records in compliance with this policy and state and federal legal requirements.

5.2. Employees. University employees are responsible and accountable for managing public records in compliance with this policy and state and federal legal requirements. Failure to do so may result in loss of access to University information and digitization systems and business tools, as well as appropriate disciplinary action.

5.3. Use of Business Tools. University employees must manage and retain public records using only information and digitization systems and business tools supported by the University.

5.4. Suspension of Records Retention Schedules. Records retention schedules must be suspended whenever University records are relevant to litigation, audit, or public records requests. Any suspension of retention schedules shall be carefully tailored to the scope of the litigation, audit, or public records request. Although University will suspend records retention schedules when reasonably necessary, the University is not responsible for individual employees acting outside the scope of their authority, or in a manner inconsistent with the suspension of records retention schedules.

NOTES TO FORM

Commentary

This form is adapted from a policy used by the University of Wisconsin System. It can be adapted for use by other public agencies that have public records.

§ 6:15 Records management certification

RECORDS MANAGEMENT CERTIFICATION FOR ELECTRONIC RECORDS FORM

This certifies that the records named below maintained in electronic format are usable and certifiable for the life of the electronic system. Furthermore, the electronic system managing these records, meets the following:

- the records are managed uniformly and efficiently
- the records are accurate and reliable
- the records are accessible when needed
- the records and system are protected from unauthorized access
- the records are maintained/destroyed in accordance with the records retention and disposition schedules adopted pursuant to *[statute]*
- migration strategies standards implemented
- disaster recovery and backup systems standards implemented
- all items on the Electronically Stored Information Management Checklist have been completed per the Records Management Guideline for Electronically Stored Information

1. Record Series Title(s):

2. Court/Office:

3. Address:

4. Phone: (___) _______

5. Type or Print Name

6. Authorized Signature & Title

Date: _______

7. System Format:

8. System Director/Head Representative:

9. Phone: (___) _______

10. Type or Print Name

11. Authorized Signature & Title

Date: _______

Chapter 7

Destroying Electronically Stored Information and Paper Records

I. GUIDELINES

II. CHECKLISTS

III. FORMS

Research References

Treatises and Practice Aids

Grenig and Gleisner, eDiscovery & Digital Evidence §§ 8:9, 8:10

Trial Strategy

Recovery and Reconstruction of Electronic Mail as Evidence, 41 Am. Jur. Proof of Facts 3d 1

Computer Technology in Civil Litigation, 71 Am. Jur. Trials 111

Additional References

Grenig and Kinsler, Federal Civil Discovery and Disclosure §§ 13.1 to 13.6 (3d ed.)

ABA Discovery Standards, http://www.abanet.org/litigation/discoverystandards/2005civildiscoverystandards.pdf

ARMA, http://www.arma.org
Electronic Discovery Reference Model Project, http://www.edrm.net
The Sedona Conference, http://www.thesedonaconference.org

KeyCite®: Cases and other legal materials listed in KeyCite Scope can be researched through the KeyCite service on Westlaw®. Use KeyCite to check citations for form, parallel references, prior and later history, and comprehensive citator information, including citations to other decisions and secondary materials.

I. GUIDELINES

§ 7:1 Generally

It would be unreasonable to require an organization to institute a records and information management program that in effect required it to routinely retain all possible evidence. However, if an organization routinely destroys electronically stored information that conceivably could be detrimental to the person or entity in some future litigation, this can result in an adverse court ruling.[1]

The issue often becomes whether an organization in adopting a records and information management program knew or should have known that litigation was imminent. In *Lewy v. Remington Arms Co.*,[2] the Eighth Circuit ruled:

> In cases where a document management program is instituted in order to limit damaging evidence available to potential plaintiffs, it may be proper to give an [adverse inference] instruction similar to the one requested by the Lewys. Similarly, even if the court finds the policy to be reasonable given the nature of the documents subject to the policy, the court may find that under the particular circumstances certain documents should have been retained notwithstanding the policy. For example, if the corporation knew or should have known that the documents would become material at some point in the future then such documents should have been preserved. Thus, a corporation cannot blindly destroy documents and expect to be shielded by a seemingly innocuous document records management program.

[Section 7:1]

[1]See, e.g., Carlucci v. Piper Aircraft Corp., 102 F.R.D. 472, 38 Fed. R. Serv. 2d 1654 (S.D. Fla. 1984). But see Gippetti v. United Parcel Service, Inc., 2008 WL 3264483 (N.D. Cal. 2008) (spoliation sanctions for destruction of ESI pursuant to document retention policy denied under Fed. R. Civ. P. 37(e) safe harbor provision).

[2]Lewy v. Remington Arms Co., Inc., 836 F.2d 1104, Prod. Liab. Rep. (CCH) ¶ 11662, 24 Fed. R. Evid. Serv. 516 (8th Cir. 1988).

An effective records and information management ("RIM") program requires a comprehensive records retention policy, supporting record classification and retention schedule. There is a variety of rules, regulations, and case law regarding the duty to preserve electronically stored information. In most circumstances, there are severe consequences for failing to do so.

Electronically stored information should be destroyed under a records retention program when it is no longer needed or is no longer required to be retained. Not only is it expensive to store electronically stored information when there is no need to store it, the consequences of storing electronically stored information when it no longer must be stored can be exceptionally expensive.

In the absence of a statute or regulation, it is not necessary to document disposition of electronically stored information. However, it is prudent to develop a records destruction authorization form to authorize and document records disposal. The authorization form should include series titles and dates, quantity of records, method of destruction, and authorization signatures. One or more of the following people should sign the form:

- The records management officer
- The manager of the office that "owns" the records
- The chief administrative official.

To certify destruction, the form should also include the dated signature of the witness.

§ 7:2 Statutes

Organizations subject to regulation by various governmental agencies charged with oversight often have heavy preservation obligations due to the nature of their industry. For example, those companies who have chosen to avail themselves of being licensed brokers of the sale and exchange of securities must comply with record retention requirements of SEC 17a-3 and SEC 17a-4 (requiring all communications with clients to be maintained for periods of three and six years).

A number of statutes should be considered with respect to when and how electronically stored information may be destroyed. These include:

- Health Insurance Portability and Accountability Act (HIPAA)[1]

[Section 7:2]

[1]Pub. L. No. 104-191, 110 Stat. 1936 (Aug. 21, 1996).

- USA Patriot Act[2]
- Gramm-Leach-Bililey Act (Disclosure of Nonpublic Personal Information)[3]
- Sarbanes-Oxley Act (Public Company Accounting Reform and Investor Protection Act of 2002)[4]
- Fair and Accurate Credit Transactions Act (FACTA)[5]

§ 7:3 Identification and review

The first step in the destruction of electronically stored information is identification of the information to be destroyed in accordance with the records and information management program. Responsible persons or departments should be notified of the planned destruction and given an opportunity to halt the destruction. Destruction of specific documents or categories of documents should be halted when litigation or a government investigation is foreseeable, or an audit is anticipated.

§ 7:4 Specific considerations

Creating electronic images of paper documents to store them electronically, handling duplicates, and thinking about how to deal with vast volumes of e-mail are three issues in managing information that present challenges to organizations. Software can assist, but largely, the implementing specific policies, training your employees and having dedicated staff responsible for managing compliance are the first steps to effective management.

The cost advantages and improved efficiency offered by microfilming or electronic imaging paper documents can only be realized if the original records are destroyed after microfilming or electronic imaging. When the original records are destroyed after reproduction in accordance with any applicable legal requirements, the records continue to exit. The reproduced documents preserve the information contained in the original record, but in a different form.

Records and information management programs relating to e-mail, including associated metadata, must comply with statutory, regulatory and business requires. The programs must also reflect the need to preserve and produce e-mails as a result of litigation or investigations.

---

[2]Pub. L. No. 107-56, 115 Stat. 272 (Oct. 26, 2001); Pub. L. No. 109-177, 120 Stat. 192 (Mar. 9, 2006).

[3]15 U.S.C.A. §§ 6801 to 6809.

[4]Pub. L. No. 107-204, 116 Stat. 745 (July 30, 2002).

[5]Pub. L. No. 108-159, 117 Stat. 1952 (Dec. 4, 2003).

The ease with which electronically stored information can be duplicated creates serious records and information management problems. An effective records and information management program providing procedures for destruction of duplicate records can be helpful in reducing the burden of responding to discovery requests or implementing litigation holds.

§ 7:5 Destruction of electronically stored information

In selecting a method of destruction for electronically stored information, it is essential to evaluate carefully the records to be destroyed, local environmental restrictions, and the availability of equipment and staff resources. It is then necessary to determine the available destruction alternatives.

With electronically stored information, it is important to have procedures for the deletion of electronic files. It is possible to erase and reuse magnetic media, but for the best security it is better to erase all the information on the medium before reusing. Magnetic media can also be destroyed through incineration (which melts and deforms the media) or by shredding. Destruction of electronic records, however, can be very difficult, since copies of a single file may reside in numerous locations, some not accessible even by the organization's system administrator.

§ 7:6 Disposition of electronically stored information—Generally

A records and information management program should establish a formal disposition procedure regularly disposing of records at least once a year. An established disposition procedure safeguards against the accidental destruction of records that have not attained their minimum retention periods or that have met their retention periods but are needed for some other purpose, such as litigation or investigations.

§ 7:7 Disposition of electronically stored information—After microfilming or electronic imaging

The cost advantages and improved efficiency offered by microfilming or electronic imaging paper documents can only be realized if the original records are destroyed after microfilming or electronic imaging. When the original records are destroyed after reproduction in accordance with any applicable legal requirements, the records continue to exist. The reproduced documents preserve the information contained in the original record, but in a different form.

§ 7:8 Disposition of electronically stored information—E-mail

Records and information management programs relating to e-mail, including associated metadata, must comply with statutory, regulatory and business requirements. The programs must also reflect the need to preserve and produce e-mails as a result of litigation or investigations.

§ 7:9 Disposition of electronically stored information—Duplicates

The ease with which electronically stored information can be duplicated creates serious records and information management problems. An effective records and information management program providing procedures for the destruction of duplicate records can be helpful in reducing the burden of responding to discovery requests or implementing litigation holds.

II. CHECKLISTS

§ 7:10 Records destruction checklist

☐ Are the records confidential?
☐ What is the quantity of records to be destroyed?
☐ How often will records destruction take place?
☐ What is the physical composition of the records?
☐ Do the records contain numerous fasteners, such as staples or paper clips?
☐ Are there restrictions on incineration or disposal in a landfill in your area?
☐ Do you have access to a vendor who provides bonded recycling?
☐ Do you have space and staff for an on-site destruction program?
☐ Can your equipment handle the bulk to be destroyed?
☐ Can your shredder handle non-paper records such as microfilm?
☐ Will you be able to contain the dust produced by a shredder?
☐ Is it more efficient and economical to use an outside vendor or facility?

III. FORMS

§ 7:11 Records destruction authorization form

RECORDS DESTRUCTION AUTHORIZATION FORM

Record Series	Dates of Records	Schedule Item	Retention

Destruction authorized by Records Management Officer
____
Date ________
Department Head ____________________
Date ________
Destruction certified by Witness____________________
Date ________

§ 7:12 Certificate of records destruction

Instructions for Completing Certificate of Records Destruction

The *[form]* documents that records were destroyed properly and in accordance with the *[organization]* Records and Information Program.

Before a state agency or locality can destroy public records:

- A Records Officer for your organization must be designated in writing by completing and filing a *[form]*.
- Records to be destroyed must be covered by an *[organization]*-approved general or agency-specific Records Retention and Disposition Schedule and the retention period for the records must have expired.
- All investigations, litigation, and required audits must be completed. Existing records cannot be destroyed if they are

pertinent to an investigation (including requests under the Freedom of Information Act), litigation, or where a required audit has not been undertaken.

- The organization's designated Records Officer and an Approving Official must authorize records destruction by signing each *[form]*.

After a department has destroyed public records:

- The individual or company responsible for destroying the records must sign and date *[form]*. This final signature certifies the records have **actually been destroyed**.
- A copy of the *[form]* must be retained by the organization.
- The *[form]*, with all original signatures, must be delivered to *[place]* be retained for 50 years.
  Mail forms to: *[address]*

Instructions:

1. Enter full name of agency, locality or organization.
2. Enter name of division, department, and section.
3. Enter name of individual completing the form, preferably the individual responsible for or familiar with the records.
4. Enter address of the agency or locality completing the form.
5. Enter telephone number of the person completing the form including extension, if applicable.
6. Records to be destroyed:
   a) Enter both the retention schedule and series numbers that apply to the records to be destroyed. ENTER ONLY ONE SERIES NUMBER PER LINE.
   b) Enter the exact records series title as listed on the approved retention schedule. You may add detail to this title if it is important to identifying the records.
   c) Enter the date range of the records to be destroyed, from oldest to most recent. Indicate starting month/year and ending month/year.
   d) Enter the location where the records are stored (optional).
   e) Enter the total volume or amount of records to be destroyed. Refer to the Volume Equivalency Table (available from the Archival, Records Management Services Division) to convert boxes or drawers of paper or microform records to their cubic foot equivalents. If destroying electronic records, enter the approximate size of the files by megabyte, type of media containing data, or number of files.
   f) Enter the method used to destroy the records, i.e., trash, shredding, recycling, landfill, burning, etc.

7. Printed name and signature of individual responsible for maintaining records or agency/locality head.
8. Printed name and signature of agency/locality Records Officer.
9. Enter name of individual or company that destroyed the records and the date they were destroyed.

If multiple *[forms]* are submitted, all three required signatures must be on each page.

EXAMPLES:

a) Schedule and Records Series Number	b) Records Series Title	c) Date Range (mo/yr)	d) Location	e) Volume	f) Destruction Method
	Garnishments	1/1960–12/1997	Basement	15 cu. ft.	Burned
	Payroll Records and Deduction Authorizations	7/2001–6/2002	Server 4	30 MB	Electronic Shredding
	Hospice Program Records	1/1999–12/2003	2 cu. ft.	Shredded by vendor	
	Dairy Products Inspections Records	7/1995–6/2005	Rm. 504	52 cu. ft.	Shredded in-house

NOTES TO FORM

Commentary

This form is adapted from one used by the Commonwealth of Virginia. It can be adapted for use by public or private organizations.

§ 7:13 Guidelines for sanitization of information technology equipment and electronic media

SANITIZATION OF INFORMATION TECHNOLOGY EQUIPMENT AND ELECTRONIC MEDIA

Policy: The purpose of this policy is to ensure secure and appropriate disposal of information technology (IT) equipment, devices, network components, operating systems, application software and storage media belonging to *[organization]* to prevent unauthorized use or misuse of state information. All IT equipment shall be properly sanitized prior to disposal or release and sanitization procedures shall be properly documented to prevent unauthorized release of sensitive and/or confidential information that may be stored on that equipment and other electronic media. This policy supports the Enterprise Architecture for security and privacy and outlines procedures that must be followed to protect the *[organization]*.

Policy Maintenance: The Office of the CIO has issued this

Enterprise Policy. The *[organization]* Office of Technology (OT), Office of Infrastructure Services, is responsible for the maintenance of this policy. This policy shall be adhered to by all agencies and employees within the *[organization]*. However, departments may choose to add to this policy, in order to enforce more restrictive policies as appropriate. Therefore, employees are to refer to their department's internal policy, which may have additional information or clarification of this Enterprise Policy.

Responsibility for Compliance: Each department is responsible for assuring that appropriate employees within their organizational authority have been made aware of the provisions of this policy, that compliance by the employee is expected, and that unauthorized and/or neglectful release of computer equipment and/or related media, especially that which contain sensitive and/or confidential information, may result in disciplinary action pursuant to *[citation]* up to and including dismissal.

It is also each department manager's responsibility to enforce and manage this policy. Failure to comply may result in additional shared service charges to the department for OT's efforts to remediate issues related to lack of or improper sanitization of computer equipment and related media.

Definitions:

Clearing: The process of deleting the data on the media before the media is reused. It is important to note that clearing *will* allow for the retrieval of information if certain retrieval procedures are used and is not approved for computer equipment or media that contain sensitive and/or confidential data.

Coercivity: Magnetic media is divided into three types (I, II, III) based on their coercivity. Coercivity of magnetic media defines the magnetic field necessary to reduce a magnetically saturated material's magnetization to zero. The level of magnetic media coercivity must be ascertained before executing any degaussing procedure.

Degauss: Procedure that reduces the magnetic flux on media virtually to zero by applying a reverse magnetizing field. Properly applied, degaussing renders any previously stored data on magnetic media unreadable and may be used in the sanitization process. Degaussing is more effective than overwriting magnetic media.

Degausser: Device used to remove data from magnetic storage medium.

DoD Sanitization Standard (5520.22-M): US Department of Defense standard for clearing and sanitizing data on writable media.

Dynamic Random Access Memory (DRAM): The most common kind of random access memory (RAM) for personal computers and workstations. Unlike firmware chips (ROMs, PROMs, etc.) DRAM loses its content when the power is turned off.

Electronically Alterable PROM (EAPROM): A PROM whose contents can be changed.

Electronically Erasable PROM (EEPROM): User-modifiable read-only memory (ROM) that can be erased and reprogrammed (written to) repeatedly through the application of higher than normal electrical voltage. A special form of EEPROM is flash memory.

Erasable Programmable ROM (EPROM): Programmable read-only memory (programmable ROM) that can be erased and re-used. Erasure is caused by shining an intense ultraviolet light through a window that is designed into the memory chip.

Flash EPROM (FEPROM): Non-volatile device similar to EEPROM, but where erasing can only be done in blocks or the entire chip.

Programmable ROM (PROM): Read-only memory (ROM) that can be modified once by a user.

Magnetic Bubble Memory: A non-volatile memory device for computers that uses magnetic bubbles for recording bits. The technology was used in early 1980s but is obsolete today.

Magnetic Core Memory: Random access memory (RAM) system that was developed at MIT in 1951. Magnetic core memory replaced vacuum tubes and mercury delay lines with a much more compact and reliable technology. Semiconductor memories largely replaced magnetic cores in the 1970s.

Magnetic Plated Wire: Non-volatile memory created by Honeywell in 1960s. Magnetic plated wire consists of a copper conductor covered with a thin layer of highly magnetic material, over which a polyurethane insulating film is enameled.

Nonvolatile RAM (NOVRAM): Memory that does not lose its information while its power supply is turned off.

Oersteds: The unit of magnetic field strength in the centimeter-gram-second system.

Overwriting: A software process that replaces the data previously stored on magnetic storage media with a predetermined set of meaningless data. Overwriting is an acceptable method for clearing; however, the effectiveness of the overwrite procedure may be reduced by several factors, including: ineffectiveness of the overwrite procedures, equipment failure (e.g., misalignment of read/write heads), or inability to overwrite bad sectors or tracks or information in inter-record gaps.

Overwriting Procedure: The preferred method to clear magnetic disks is to overwrite all locations three (3) times (the first time with a random character, the second time with a specified character, the third time with the complement of that specified character).

Read Only Memory (ROM): Built-in computer memory containing data that normally can only be read, not written to. The data in ROM is not lost when the computer power is turned off. The ROM is sustained by a small long-life battery in your computer.

Sanitizing: The process of removing the data on the media before the media is reused in an environment that does not provide an acceptable level of protection for the data. In general, laboratory techniques cannot retrieve data that has been sanitized/purged. Sanitizing may be accomplished by degaussing.

Static Random Access Memory (SRAM): Random access memory (RAM) that retains data bits in its memory as long as power is being supplied. SRAM is used for a computer's cache memory and as part of the random access memory digital-to-analog converter on a video card.

Procedures:

1.0 Sanitization of IT Equipment and Electronic Media

The sale, transfer, or disposal of computers, computer peripherals, and computer software or other IT devices can create information security risks for the *[organization]*. These risks are related to potential violation of software license agreements, unauthorized release of sensitive and/or confidential information, and unauthorized disclosure of trade secrets, copyrights, and other intellectual property that might be stored on the hard disks and other storage media. It should be noted that computers containing sensitive and/or confidential data must have their hard drives securely erased as specified by the US Department of Defense (DoD) standards listed in section 1.4—Recommended DoD Sanitation Procedures.

The following procedures must be followed when a computer system is sold, transferred, or disposed of. This policy does not supersede specific policies, directives or standards required by federal or state agencies pertaining to the disposal of computer equipment. The following procedures also apply to contractor-supplied computers.

- Before a computer system is sold, transferred, or otherwise disposed of, all sensitive and/or confidential program or data

files on any storage media must be completely erased or otherwise made unreadable in accordance with DoD standards (5220.22-M) unless there is specific intent to transfer the particular software or data to the purchaser/recipient.
- The computer system must be relocated to a designated, secure storage area until the data can be erased.
- Hard drives of surplus computer equipment must be securely erased within 60 days after replacement.
- Whenever licensed software is resident on any computer media being sold, transferred, or otherwise disposed of, the terms of the license agreement must be followed.

After the sanitization of the hard drive is complete, the process must be certified and a record maintained as specified by the agency's records retention schedule.

1.1 Sanitization of Hard Drives

The following section outlines the acceptable methods to expunge data from storage media. Sanitization must be performed on hard drives to ensure that information is removed from the hard drive in a matter that gives assurance that the information cannot be recovered. Before the sanitization process begins, the computer must be disconnected from any network to prevent accidental damage to the network operating system or other files on the network.

There are three acceptable methods to be used for the sanitization of hard drives:
- Overwriting
- Degaussing
- Physical Destruction

The method used for sanitization, depends upon the operability of the hard drive:
- Operable hard drives that will be reused must be overwritten prior to disposition. If the operable hard drive is to be removed from service completely, it must be physically destroyed or degaussed.
- If the hard drive is inoperable or has reached the end of its useful life, it must be physically destroyed or degaussed.

Clearing data (deleting files) removes information from storage media in a manner that renders it unreadable unless special utility software or techniques are used to recover the cleared data. However, because the clearing process does not prevent data from being recovered by technical means, it is *not* an acceptable method of sanitizing state owned hard disk storage media.

1.1.1 Overwriting Specifications

Overwriting is an approved method for sanitization of hard disk drives. Overwriting of data means replacing previously stored data on a drive or disk with a predetermined pattern of meaningless information. This effectively renders the data unrecoverable. All software products and applications used for the overwriting process must meet the following specifications:

- The data must be properly overwritten with a pattern. OT requires overwriting with a pattern, and then its complement, and finally with a random pattern of 1s and 0s.
- Sanitization is not complete until three overwrite passes and a verification pass is completed.
- The software must have the capability to overwrite the entire hard disk drive, independent of any BIOS or firmware capacity limitation that the system may have, making it impossible to recover any meaningful data.
- The software must have the capability to overwrite using a minimum of three cycles of data patterns on all sectors, blocks, tracks, and any unused disk space on the entire hard disk medium.
- The software must have a method to verify that all data has been removed.
- Sectors not overwritten must be identified.

1.1.2 Degaussing Specifications

Degaussing is a process whereby the magnetic media is erased. Hard drives seldom can be used after degaussing. The degaussing method should only be used when the hard drive is inoperable and will not be used for further service.

Please note that extreme care should be used when using degaussers since this equipment can cause extreme damage to nearby telephones, monitors, and other electronic equipment. Also, the use of a degausser does not guarantee that all data on the hard drive will be destroyed. Degaussing efforts should be audited periodically to detect equipment or procedure failures.

The following standards and procedures must be followed when hard drives are degaussed:

- Follow the product manufacturer's directions carefully. It is essential to determine the appropriate rate of coercivity for degaussing.
- Shielding materials (cabinets, mounting brackets), which may interfere with the degausser's magnetic field, must be removed from the hard drive before degaussing.

- Hard disk platters must be in a horizontal direction during the degaussing process.

1.1.3 Physical Destruction

Hard drives must be destroyed when they are defective or cannot be repaired or sanitized for reuse. Physical destruction must be accomplished to an extent that precludes any possible further use of the hard drive. This can be attained by removing the hard drive from the cabinet and removing any steel shielding materials and/or mounting brackets and cutting the electrical connection to the hard drive unit. The hard drive should then be subjected to physical force (pounding with a sledge hammer) or extreme temperatures (incineration) that will disfigure, bend, mangle or otherwise mutilate the hard drive so it cannot be reinserted into a functioning computer.

1.2 Sanitization of Other Computer Media

If there is any risk of disclosure of sensitive data on media other than computer hard drives, the appropriate sanitization methods as outlined in the DoD recommended sanitization procedures should be followed. Particular attention should be paid to floppy disks, tapes, CDs, DVDs, and optical disks.

Memory components should also be sanitized before disposal or release. Memory components reside on boards, modules, and sub-assemblies. A board can be a module, or may consist of several modules and sub-assemblies.

Unlike magnetic media sanitization, clearing may be an acceptable method of sanitizing components for release. Memory components are categorized as either volatile or nonvolatile, as described below. DoD Sanitization Procedures should be followed as specified in section 1.4

Volatile memory components *do not* retain data after removal of all electrical power sources, and when re-inserted into a similarly configured system do not contain residual data, i.e. SRAM, DRAM.

Nonvolatile memory components *do* retain data when all power sources are discontinued. Nonvolatile memory components include Read Only Memory (ROM), Programmable ROM (PROM), or Erasable PROM (EPROM) and their variants. Memory components that have been programmed at the vendor's commercial manufacturing facility and are considered unalterable in the field may be released; otherwise, DoD Sanitization Procedures must be followed.

1.3 Certification of Sanitization

Sanitization may be required in instances other than surplusing. It is recommended that a record is kept for all sanitization procedures, it is required when equipment is surplused. Prior to submitting surplus forms (B217-2: Declared Surplus) from *[department]* to the department's appropriate organizational unit, the sanitizing process must be documented on an additional form that explicitly outlines the method(s) used to expunge the data from the storage media, the type of equipment/media being sanitized, the name of the individual requesting sanitization, and the name of the person responsible for the sanitization A template for the form is attached at the end of this policy, *[organization]* Record of IT Equipment Sanitization. Its lower portion contains the elements required by the Division of Surplus Property. A completed record (including the top section) must be maintained in a central location designated by the agency. This information must be maintained as outlined by the *[organization department]* record retention schedule.

The *[organization]* requires a copy of the proof of sanitization accompany all hard drives earmarked for disposal. This proof may be a copy of the entire "Record of IT Equipment Sanitization" or of the lower portion of the form. In instances where attaching the paper form to the equipment is a poor method, a label containing the required information may be affixed to the hard drive(s), equipment case (e.g., CPU box) or appropriate surface. The label must contain the name and signature of the person performing the sanitization, equipment identification and sanitization method used as provided in the lower portion of the "Record of IT Equipment Sanitization."

For disposition other than to the *[department]*, it is highly recommended that an adhesive label be affixed to the equipment case to record the sanitization process before transfer. Questions remain about leased equipment and equipment maintained through a service agreement. Agencies must assess liability on a case by case review.

1.4 Recommended DoD Sanitization Procedures

Media	**Procedure(s)**
Magnetic Tape	
Type I*	a, b, or m
Type II**	b or m
Type III***	m

Media	Procedure(s)
Magnetic Disk	
Bernoullis	m
Floppies	m
Non-Removable Rigid Disk	a, b, d, or m
Removable Rigid Disk	a, b, d, or m
Optical Disk	
Read Many, Write Many	m
Read Only	m, n
Write Once, Read Many (WORM)	m, n
Memory	
Dynamic Random Access Memory (DRAM)	c, g, or m
Electronically Alterable PROM (EAPROM)	j or m
Electronically Erasable PROM (EEPROM)	h or m
Erasable Programmable ROM (EPROM)	l, then c or m
Flash EPROM (FEPROM)	c, then I or m
Programmable ROM (PROM)	m
Magnetic Bubble Memory	a, b, c, or m
Magnetic Core Memory	a, b, e, or m
Magnetic Plated Wire	c and f, or m
Magnetic Resistive Memory	m
Nonvolatile RAM (NOVRAM)	c, g, or m
Read Only Memory (ROM)	m
Static Random Access Memory (SRAM)	c and f, g, or m

Sanitization Procedure Key

a. Degauss with a Type I degausser.

b. Degauss with a Type II degausser.

c. Overwrite all addressable locations with a single character.

d. Overwrite all addressable locations with a character, its complement, then a random character and verify. THIS METHOD IS NOT APPROVED FOR SANITIZING MEDIA THAT CONTAINS EXTREMELY CONFIDENTIAL OR SENSITIVE INFORMATION.

e. Overwrite all addressable locations with a character, its complement, and then a random character.
f. Each overwrite must reside in memory for a period longer than the classified data resided.
g. Remove all power to include battery power.
h. Overwrite all locations with a random pattern, all locations with binary zeros, all locations with binary ones.
i. Perform a full chip erase as per manufacturer's data sheets.
j. Perform i. above, then c. above, three times.
k. Perform an ultraviolet erase according to manufacturer's recommendation.
l. Perform k above, but increase time by a factor of three.
m. Destroy—disintegrate, incinerate, pulverize, shred, or melt.
n. Destruction required only if classified information is contained.

This information was extracted from the US Department of Defense 5220.22-M Clearing and Sanitization Matrix.

*Type 1 magnetic tape includes all tapes with a coercivity factor (amount of electrical force required to reduce the recorded magnetic strength to zero) not exceeding 350 oersteds.

**Type 2 magnetic tape includes all tapes with a coercivity factor between 350 and 750 oersteds.

***Type 3 magnetic tape commonly referred to as high-energy tape (4 or 8mm tape are examples), includes all tapes with a coercivity factor between 750 and 1700.

[Organization] Record of IT Equipment Sanitization

Date Requested: ________

Department:____

Person Submitting Request: ____________________________

Equipment Serial Number: _____________________________

Equipment Inventory Number: __________________________

Equipment Manufacturer/Model:_________________________

Equipment/Media Type:

☐ Server

☐ Workstation: Assigned to (name of user): ________

☐ Magnetic Tape (Type I, II or III)

☐ Magnetic Disk (Bernoulli, floppy, non-removable rigid disk, removable rigid disk)

☐ Optical Disk (read many-write many, read only, write once-ready many (WORM)

☐ Memory (DRAM, PROM, EAPROM, EPROM, FEPROM, ROM, SRAM etc.)

☐ Cathode Ray Tube (CRT)
☐ Printer
☐ Other (describe) ______

Disposition:

☐ Transfer ☐ Surplus ☐ Donation ☐ Repair/ maintenance

☐ Return to Contractor ☐ Other (explain) ___

Decommissioning provisions:

☐ Equipment/media has been kept in continuous physical protection until sanitization
☐ Information requiring archiving as public records identified and preserved
☐ Temporary backups made (e.g., for equipment scheduled for repair)
☐ OEM operating system and other software available for reload for repurposed equipment
☐ MARS Fixed Asset documents completed
☐ Agency asset management procedures completed
☐ _ form completed (Finance & Administration: Declared Surplus)
☐ Compliant with procedures for disposal of hazardous waste if destroyed
☐ Other (describe) ______

***General* description of data residing on equipment/media to be sanitized:**

____
____
____

Department: ______________________________
Person Performing Sanitization: ______________________________
Title: ______ Date Completed: ___
Equip. Inventory #: ______ Equip. Serial #: ______
Signature: ______________

Sanitization Method Used:

☐ DoD-compliant Overwrite (list software used): _
☐ Type I Degausser

☐ Type II Degausser
☐ Full Chip Erase
☐ Ultraviolet Erase
☐ Physical Destruction (disintegrate, incinerate, pulverize, shred, melt)
☐ Other (describe) ______________________________

NOTES TO FORM

Commentary

This form is adapted from one used by the Commonwealth of Kentucky.

Part III

E-DISCOVERY IN LITIGATION

Chapter 8

Using Third Parties in E-discovery

I. GUIDELINES

II. FORMS

Research References

Additional References

ABA Discovery Standards, http://www.abanet.org/litigation/discoverystandards/2005civildiscoverystandards.pdf
Electronic Discovery Reference Model Project, http://www.edrm.net
The Sedona Conference, http://www.thesedonaconference.org

KeyCite®: Cases and other legal materials listed in KeyCite Scope can be researched through the KeyCite service on Westlaw®. Use KeyCite to check citations for form, parallel references, prior and later history, and comprehensive citator information, including citations to other decisions and secondary materials.

I. GUIDELINES

§ 8:1 Generally

It has been more than five years since the Federal Rules of Civil Procedure were amended to provide specifically for the discovery of electronically stored information. The notion, however, that e-discovery is a substantive area of the law (like income tax, anti-trust or securities) requiring lawyers who work exclusively in the area, and that a certain subset of knowledge is required to handle e-discovery issues even at a base level, has been slow to resonate with many practitioners.

Much of that lack of acknowledgement is due to a lack of understanding of technology—what systems make up an organization's information technology system, what types of data are created and stored on those systems, how many different places electronically stored information can be stored, and the form in which different types of data can be pulled out of those systems. Lawyers who do not understand the technology are in large part still avoiding e-discovery all together, only collecting e-mail and attachments, or over-collecting information, which costs their clients more money to collect, process, review and produce it.

Engaging knowledgeable third parties in e-discovery can substantially limit both the cost of e-discovery and the risk of sanctions due to spoliation. Knowledgeable attorneys, vendors, and forensic specialists can help merits counsel and clients craft case-specific strategies identify the key information that needs to be preserved or ultimately produced, and evaluate the tools available for meeting that need at a cost that is reasonable given the value of the matter. This can be done for litigation, subpoena responses, and regulatory or other government investigations (e.g., Securities and Exchange Commission, Department of Justice, Federal Trade Commission).

Choosing the right team for e-discovery needs is vital. Organizations regularly engaging in e-discovery should proactively put a process in place for implementing and tracking legal holds, collection, and production efforts. As e-discovery becomes a larger part of in-house legal budgets, understanding and controlling e-discovery costs is also vital to staying on track—keeping annual and case-specific metrics on e-discovery costs, and a solid team in place to assist with e-discovery, are key.

Engaging third party neutrals, court-appointed special masters or experts may also be of value when counsel cannot resolve e-discovery disputes. Federal and state rules provide for the role of each, and parties who utilize experienced neutrals or special masters effectively by raising e-discovery issues early will not find their cases bogged down in discovery nightmares, but rather allow counsel to focus on the merits of the dispute, leading to a speedier resolution.

§ 8:2 Choosing your team—E-discovery counsel

Engaging knowledgeable e-discovery counsel early in the process is critical to implementing an approach that is reasonable, comprehensive, and cost-effective. True e-discovery lawyers are experienced in general and complex litigation, understand the systems used to create and store information and how to retrieve information from them, and know the ins and outs of the rules related to e-discovery as well as the ever-evolving common law. During litigation, knowledgeable e-discovery counsel can:

- Make informed decisions about the scope of preservation for a particular matter given a specific set of facts and general understanding of a client's IT infrastructure;
- Create narrowly tailored requests for information to avoid being besieged with terabytes of data that must be sifted through;
- Depose a Fed. R. Civ. P. 30(b)(6) witness on the information technology system of an organization to understand where key information resides;
- Assist information technology personnel with processes to collect data and advise on the most appropriate methods under current case law and generally accepted practices;
- Speak to information technology personnel in their language and bridge the gap between legal and information technology to meet the organization's needs cost-effectively;
- Negotiate with opposing counsel, government agencies, in-house counsel and special masters to request appropriate electronically stored information or narrowly tailor what information must be produced;
- Constantly re-evaluate the e-discovery strategy based on facts that arise in discovery and any revised value of the case;
- Identify appropriate tools to collect, cull, process and produce electronically stored information for review that will be

the most cost-effective and best tool based on the types of information implicated in the matter; and
- Prevent e-discovery costs or concerns from driving the case or settlement strategy.

E-discovery counsel can play a substantial role in an organization's development of a records and information management program as well. Within that context, knowledgeable e-discovery counsel can:

- Assist information technology and legal in evaluating tools to be deployed within the organization for information management and e-discovery;
- Advise the client on issues related to roll out of new technology within the organization and the impact on the legal hold protocol or preservation strategy;
- Draft policies and procedures for the acceptable use of electronically stored information, social media, e-mail management practices, implementation and tracking of legal holds and records and information management;
- Assist in the creation of a data map to inventory the information technology systems utilized by the client and identify issues related to the production of electronically stored information from those systems for litigation;
- Develop a guide for the client to utilize in handling e-discovery issues in individual matters; and
- Develop a records retention schedule.

Courts have identified the need for having knowledgeable e-discovery counsel involved in litigation matters. Judge Shira Schiendlin discussed the specific issues inherent in e-discovery that may call for the use of e-discovery counsel, special masters, and experts in a law review article.[1]

Many law firms have formed e-discovery departments to address clients' needs in this area. Some departments act as counsel only for that firm's clients on existing litigation matters, while some act as national e-discovery counsel for clients on all of their matters. Because the model of e-discovery is so different than the normal business model of a large law firm, independent law firms working exclusively in this area have come into play offering their clients advice solely on e-discovery and information law related issues. The existence and success of those firms lends

---

[Section 8:2]

[1]Scheindlin & Redgrave, *Special Masters and E-Discovery: The Intersection of Two Recent Revisions to the Federal Rules of Civil Procedure*, 30 Cardozo L. Rev. 347 (2008).

credence to the recognition of e-discovery as a substantive area that lawyers must begin to acknowledge.

§ 8:3 E-discovery counsel—The privilege umbrella

Perhaps one of the key and often overlooked benefits of e-discovery counsel is the protection of the attorney-client and work-product privileges, as well as the e-discovery counsel's ability to offer legal advice. Vendors who sell e-discovery products often offer consulting services with the products, but are prohibited from offering legal advice. While the advice of consultants may not be protected, legal advice from e-discovery counsel will have the protection of privilege.

§ 8:4 E-discovery counsel—Rapid development of the law

The rapid development of case law in e-discovery represents another benefit to having dedicated e-discovery counsel. In the first half of 2011—from January to June—federal and state courts issued at least 158 decisions on e-discovery issues. While jurisdictions are beginning to develop a body of law in this area, knowledge of the development of issues around the country is highly relevant to parties seeking to make new arguments in a jurisdiction that has not yet addressed an issue.

§ 8:5 Choosing your team—Vendors

Getting electronically stored information from an organization's information technology infrastructure (whatever the type) or a single laptop into one file type that can be reviewed by attorneys on a web-based platform requires specific technology. Each stage of the EDRM model[1] can require a different type of technology, and vendors of those technologies play an important role as part of the e-discovery team for a matter.

Some organizations that handle large litigation portfolios purchase and deploy tools in-house that can be utilized to collect, process and provide information in a reviewable format for merits counsel. Organizations without those internal resources need to identify cost-effective tools that are best suited for a particular matter and have the desired functionality that can be used effectively by merits counsel handling the matter.

Typically, large law firms have in-house litigation support departments that handle many of the decisions about tools to be

---

[Section 8:5]

[1] http://www.edrm.net.

used for client matters. Organizations should start evaluating what technology is being used for their cases, and whether it is, in fact, the best solution.

Litigation technical support personnel are typically technology specialists, not paralegals or lawyers who understand the ins and outs of litigation and what factors need to be considered in choosing a tool. While many of them are very good and even exceptional at what they do, organizations and attorneys should make sure that the litigation strategy necessary for the case is being considered during the selection process. Oftentimes, when the attorney managing the matter is not sophisticated or even somewhat knowledgeable in e-discovery, providing the strategic pieces that play into tool selection does not happen, and clients may miss an opportunity to reduce costs or risk.

A note of caution in selecting a vendor—the well known Socha-Gelbman report of 2010 pegged e-discovery as a $1.4 billion dollar industry set for expansion of 15–20% for 2011 and 2012.[2] The market is packed with vendors offering to sell e-discovery services—over 600 at last count. Strategies for vendors in the marketplace have changed in the last two years, and vendors who offered one piece of the EDRM model before, now either partner with other providers or have purchased other providers to offer "end-to-end" solutions for clients.

The goal of those providers is to keep all of the business for a case in-house, thereby maximizing the value. Oftentimes, a vendor is very good at one piece of the EDRM, but falls short on other aspects of the "end-to-end" solution. Organizations or attorneys hiring vendors should be certain to check references for vendors and have an understanding of the strengths and weaknesses of particular tools before signing on with a vendor.

Many vendors in the e-discovery arena excel at what they do and are a highly valuable resource of information and products for their clients. It is vendors who have simply repositioned their products and sales force to take advantage of the e-discovery trend that should cause organizations and attorneys to thoroughly vet vendors at the outset.

§ 8:6 Choosing your team—Forensic expert

Computer forensics involves the identification, preservation, examination, collection, preservation and analysis of electronically stored information. In many instances, the process involves the preparation of an expert opinion regarding and may provide

[2] http://www.sochaconsulting.com/archives/2775.

expert testimony. Computer forensics experts may be engaged as a testifying or nontestifying expert to simply aid in the e-discovery process. Computer forensic experts typically have specialized training and knowledge about computer systems, data structures, file structures and network topologies. Such knowledge is combined with special computer forensic software and systems to analyze specific and focused questions about electronically stored information.

Where e-discovery is primarily interested in "active" data, computer forensics will frequently involve the analysis of data and electronically stored information that is not commonly available or used by a typical computer user. Some examples of electronically soured information that may be retrieved and analyzed by a computer forensic expert include the following:

- Deleted file information
- Unallocated space on storage devices (this may also contain deleted file information)
- System registry files to identify how a computer was configured and used, and by whom
- Encrypted or password protected files
- Analysis of user file activity (for identification of what files a user may have created, accessed, modified, printed or deleted)
- Electronic document authenticity or manipulation
- Theft of digital assets
- Unauthorized access or possession of to electronically stored information

§ 8:7 Computer forensics—Protocol

To perform a forensic analysis, a computer forensic expert will typically start by creating a forensic copy or image of the suspect computer or storage device. The unique characteristic of digital information is that an exact duplicate can be made while ensuring the integrity of the original source. This process is normally completed with the assistance of a write-blocking device (either hardware or software). By following this protocol, the computer forensic expert can conduct analysis on the forensic image without the risk of altering the original source.

Some examples of when to hire a computer forensic expert include the following:

- Provide analysis of computer systems to determine what files were accessed, when and by whom. This is especially useful in cases like theft of intellectual property, unauthorized access, possession, etc.

- Perform recover of deleted files or portions of files that may exist on a computer system.
- Review activity of destruction of electronically stored information in support, or defense, of a claim of spoliation
- Review and analysis of system activity to determine what additional sources of electronically stored information may have been used or accessed, including network devices, USB attached storage, cloud resources, etc.
- Provide detailed early case assessment about electronically stored information (user file types, data structures, keyword analysis, concept clustering, etc.) to assist in creating and fine-tuning a collection and review strategy.
- Identification of deleted files

§ 8:8 Computer forensics—Threshold

If there is a concern that the responding party's search of its computer was not thorough, and that the documents or information produced represents only a portion of the electronically stored information that actually exists, or if there is a reasonable basis to believe electronically stored information has been deleted, the requesting party should request that it be allowed to physically examine the responding party's computer system.[1]

The discovering party must be in a position to make a credible argument to the court that there may be hidden information or other metadata that can only be discovered by seeing the data in its native format. An affidavit from a computer forensic expert will be helpful in outlining to the court the need for such analysis and the way in which a detailed protocol can shield against any concerns of intrusiveness the responding party may have. A very high threshold will have to be cleared in order to conduct such discovery.[2] If the "forensic issue" is central to the case (e.g., theft of intellectual property, destruction of data) a court will be more

---

[Section 8:8]

[1]See, e.g., G.D. v. Monarch Plastic Surgery, P.A., 239 F.R.D. 641, 67 Fed. R. Serv. 3d 352 (D. Kan. 2007) (patients who sued health care providers for wrongful disclosure of their confidential medical information stored on computer hard drive in discarded computer permitted to inspect, test, and evaluate computer itself).

[2]See, e.g., Bro-Tech Corp. v. Thermax, Inc., 2008 WL 724627 (E.D. Pa. 2008) (no evidence of intentional violation of order by producers as would warrant full disclosure of forensic copies of hard drives); Scotts Co. LLC v. Liberty Mut. Ins. Co., 2007 WL 1723509 (S.D. Ohio 2007) (Federal Rules of Civil Procedure do not require forensic computer search as a matter of course); Orrell v. Motorcarparts of America, Inc., 2007 WL 4287750 (W.D. N.C. 2007) (former

likely to grant at least a limited inspection of the adverse computer.[3]

§ 8:9 Computer forensics—Other functions

In addition to traditional computer forensic functions, computer forensic experts are increasingly engaged early in the litigation process to assist in evaluating both the client and the opposing party's electronically stored information. Examples of projects where one can leverage the knowledge of a computer forensic expert include the following:

- Establish a protocol for preserving electronically stored information and ensure the proper preservation of data
- Provide detailed early case assessment about electronically stored information (user file types, data structures, keyword analysis, concept clustering, etc.) to assist in creating and fine-tuning a collection and review strategy

---

employer entitled to inspect plaintiff's home computer where plaintiff claimed she had forwarded offensive e-mails from co-workers to her home computer); Benton v. Dlorah, Inc., 2007 WL 2225946 (D. Kan. 2007) (finding that defendants did not sustain burden of showing that plaintiff had failed to comply with requests for production, plaintiff's hard drive contained any additional information subject to discovery, or that plaintiff had spoliated evidence and denying motion that plaintiff produce hard drive); Balfour Beatty Rail, Inc. v. Vaccarello, 2007 WL 169628 (M.D. Fla. 2007) (plaintiff's request for defendants' computer hard drives denied, where plaintiff did not provide any information regarding what it sought to discover from the hard drives or make any contention that defendants had failed to provide requested information contained on hard drives); Williams v. Massachusetts Mut. Life Ins. Co., 226 F.R.D. 144, 146 (D. Mass. 2005) (plaintiff in employment discrimination suit not allowed to conduct forensic study of employer's electronically stored information in attempt to locate e-mail between company officials allegedly reflecting discriminatory practice and policy, where employer had already undertaken its own search and forensic analysis and had sworn to its accuracy, and employee provided no reliable or competent information to show employer's representations were misleading or substantively inaccurate); Menke v. Broward County School Bd., 916 So. 2d 8, 205 Ed. Law Rep. 541, 23 I.E.R. Cas. (BNA) 936 (Fla. 4th DCA 2005) (school district's expert denied right to inspect computers in home of suspended teacher to look for pornographic material); Ukiah Automotive Investments v. Mitsubishi Motors of North America, Inc., 2006 WL 1348562 (N.D. Cal. 2006) (where numerous financial statements were missing from responding party's computer records, court ordered responding party to produce computer on its own using an agreed-upon neutral inspector with expenses paid by producing party unless producing party produced information on its own).

[3]See, e.g., Frees, Inc. v. McMillian, 2007 WL 184889 (W.D. La. 2007), aff'd, 2007 WL 1308388 (W.D. La. 2007) (plaintiff allowed to inspect defendant's computer in action under Computer Fraud and Abuse Act, where plaintiff sought to show that alleged proprietary electronically stored information that was removed from plaintiff's laptop may have been downloaded to defendant's).

- Provide expert opinion regarding the accessibility or inaccessibility of data including the relative burden and cost associated with restoring, analyzing, processing and reviewing from such data sources
- Evaluate search techniques and strategies. This is especially useful when dealing with electronically stored information that is not easily accessed through traditional keyword searching
- Perform "quick peek"[1] or sampling[2] to determine whether a data source should be included or excluded from the discovery process
- Identify and process "exception" or nonstandard files, including encrypted data, corrupt files and nonsearchable files.

§ 8:10 Court appointed third parties—Special masters

Special discovery masters with significant experience in e-discovery are becoming recognized as having high value in complex state and federal cases.[1] While courts often suggest the appointment of a special master (particularly high-volume courts that sometimes are not able to address multiple discovery motions expeditiously), parties often independently suggest the appointment of a special e-discovery master because of the complex nature of the data disputes at issue.

A special master well-versed in technology can often resolve disagreements regarding, for example, what data is accessible for searching, what protocols can and should to be used for searching, what data is better produced in summarized fashion, and any fee-sharing disputes. Nationally, the Sedona Conference is now training e-discovery masters, and some courts have list of approved special discovery masters on e-discovery.

In federal court, Fed. R. Civ. P. 53 governs the appointment of special masters. Pursuant to the rule, a court may appoint a master in three circumstances: (1) To perform duties consented to by the parties, (2) to hold certain nonjury trial proceedings, or

---

[Section 8:9]

[1]Fed. R. Civ. P. 26(b)(5) expressly allows "quick peek" agreements.

[2]Fed. R. Civ. P. 34(a)(1) allows the parties to request an opportunity to test or sample materials sought under the rule in addition to inspecting and copying them. As with any other form of discovery, issues of burden and intrusiveness raised by requests to test or sample can be addressed under Fed. R. Civ. P. 26(b)(2) and 26(c).

[Section 8:10]

[1]Fed. R. Civ. P. 26(b)(5).

(3) address pre- or post-trial matters. The special master's authority is governed by court order, and may include the ability to impose noncontempt sanctions and recommend contempt sanctions. Some state courts also allow the appointment of special masters (often referred to in the rules as "referees").

§ 8:11 Court appointed third parties—Experts

In addition to special masters, courts are beginning to appoint e-discovery experts to assist the court, a special master, or the parties, in e-discovery issues in their case. For example, the recent revisions to the Wisconsin rules, adopted January 1, 2011, provide for the appointment of an expert witness "to inform the court on any aspect of the discovery of electronically stored information."[1]

The Seventh Circuit E-Discovery Pilot Program also contemplates an e-discovery liaison for each party. That person—who can be a nonmerits counsel hired specifically to address e-discovery—must be prepared to participate in e-discovery dispute resolution, be knowledgeable about the party's e-discovery efforts, be able to engage in or facilitate explanations about systems and capabilities, and be able to engage in or facilitate explanations of document storage, organization, retrieval, and search methodology.[2]

II. FORMS

§ 8:12 Sample agreement for neutral forensic analysis and retrieval of electronically stored information

Background

1. We have proposed a common and well-accepted protocol that establishes a procedure for the preservation, search, review and production of electronically stored information. This process is intended to reduce any burden on both parties related to the requested discovery, minimize associated costs and mitigate concerns related to inadvertent disclosures of privileged or otherwise protected information of *[responding party]*.

Preservation of Data

[Section 8:11]

[1]Wis. Stat. § 804.01(2)(e)1.f.

[2]Principle 2.02 Standing Order Relating to the Discovery of Electronically Stored Information, Seventh Circuit E-Discovery Pilot Program, http://www.discoverypilot.com/.

2. Assuming the data that has been requested has not yet been preserved, the first step in the process is to create "forensic copies" of any sources that may contain relevant and responsive data. Creating a forensic copy of a relevant hard drives requires that the computer forensic specialist have access to the relevant computers and the hard drives contained therein for an average of one to two hours. During this period of time, the computer forensic analyst will attach a writeblocking device to the hard drive (to prevent any change to any of the data on any of the relevant hard drives), and create an exact forensic copy of each relevant hard drive. Each forensic copy is written to a hard drive supplied by the forensic examiner. After the process is completed, the relevant computer can be placed back in to service. No data on the copied computers will be altered or changed during this process.
3. Regardless of the number of relevant computers, the copying process can be accomplished very quickly because multiple relevant computers can be copied simultaneously.
4. We believe it may also be necessary to collect relevant data from certain computer servers that may be owned, controlled or otherwise used by *[responding party]*. Depending on the size of the server and the organization of the electronically stored information on the servers, we may be able to selectively copy potentially relevant data.
5. To further minimize any inconvenience to *[responding party]*, forensic copies of all relevant computer hard drives and copying of data from relevant servers can be scheduled during convenient times including evenings, after business hours, Saturdays or Sundays. Imaging can occur on-site, or at any convenient location, including the offices of counsel.
6. The forensic copies created during the preservation process are stored at *[forensic expert's]* secure facility in *[location]*. Pursuant to an agreement of the parties or a protective order, such information would only be accessible to those employees of *[forensic expert]* who would conduct the forensic and discovery operations.
7. This forensic preservation process is minimally disruptive. In fact, this process is very efficient and ensures the creation of accurate copies of relevant data allowing the identification and extraction of relevant data to be accomplished electronically with limited disruption to *[responding party's]* business operations.

Initial Search for Relevant Data

8. Once the forensic images have been created, *[forensic expert]*

would implement search techniques to identify potentially relevant data. *[Forensic expert]* would then prepare an Initial Report of Findings. This Initial Report would contain a list of all potentially relevant files and/or data identified during the search process. *[Forensic expert]* would also provide copies of all files that have been initially identified as relevant by *[forensic expert]* based upon the search methodology. *[Forensic expert]* would also file with the Court and serve on all parties a Summary of its Report of Relevant Data, containing the following information:

(1) Number of pages in Report, Number of tables, appendices, or exhibits
(2) All search terms and the number of "hits" for each term (if search terms are utilized)
(3) A summary of the type and number of files identified in the Initial Report

Privilege Review

9. Upon receiving the Initial Report, counsel for *[responding party]* would have time to review the file list and files identified by *[forensic expert]*. Such review would be to identify potentially privileged files or data. *[forensic expert]* will provide *[responding party's]* counsel with a list of the files that can be marked to identify those files for which it seeks to claim a privilege. Typically these files would be included on a privileged log that would be subject to review by the Court. Typically this review process can be completed within a week.
10. This protocol completely satisfies concerns related to privileged or other protected communications, while permitting the parties to efficiently acquire all relevant data from all relevant computers.
11. The advantages are that the data can be identified and extracted using a computer forensic protocol that is nondisruptive, economical, and very powerful.

Production of Files to Requesting Party

12. After *[forensic expert]* has received a return copy of the Initial Report from *[responding party's]* counsel that identifies those files to be removed from production, *[forensic expert]* will produce a final copy of the relevant and responsive data. Copies of all identified files will be provided to all parties along with a Final Report of Findings that contains a summary of the produced data.

Chapter 9

Preservation and Legal Holds

I. GUIDELINES

II. CHECKLISTS

III. FORMS

Research References

Treatises and Practice Aids

Grenig and Gleisner, eDiscovery & Digital Evidence §§ 8:9, 8:10

Trial Strategy

Recovery and Reconstruction of Electronic Mail as Evidence, 41 Am. Jur Proof of Facts 3d 1
Computer Technology in Civil Litigation, 71 Am. Jur. Trials 111

Additional References

Grenig and Kinsler, HANDBOOK OF FEDERAL CIVIL DISCOVERY AND DISCLOSURE §§ 13.1 to 13.6 (3d ed.)
ABA Discovery Standards, http://www.abanet.org/litigation/discoverystandards/2005civildiscoverystandards.pdf
ARMA, http://www.arma.org
Electronic Discovery Reference Model Project, http://www.edrm.net
The Sedona Conference, http://www.thesedonaconference.org

KeyCite®: Cases and other legal materials listed in KeyCite Scope can be researched through the KeyCite service on Westlaw®. Use KeyCite to check citations for form, parallel references, prior and later history, and comprehensive citator information, including citations to other decisions and secondary materials.

I. GUIDELINES

§ 9:1 Obligations of Preservation—Generally

One of the most common information-preservation mistakes is failing to cease document destruction procedures upon notice of suit or the likelihood of suit or investigation.[1] The destruction of electronically stored information during the routine implementa-

[Section 9:1]

[1]See Micron Technology, Inc. v. Rambus Inc., 645 F.3d 1311, 98 U.S.P. Q.2d 1693 (Fed. Cir. 2011); Broccoli v. Echostar Communications Corp., 229 F.R.D. 506, 62 Fed. R. Serv. 3d 817 (D. Md. 2005) (defendant had a duty to preserve employment and termination documents when its management learned of plaintiff's potential Title VII claim); Zubulake v. UBS Warburg LLC, 220 F.R.D. 212, 218, 92 Fair Empl. Prac. Cas. (BNA) 1539 (S.D. N.Y. 2003). See Sedona Principle 1 ("Electronically stored information is potentially discoverable under Fed. R. Civ. P. 34 or its state equivalents. Organizations must properly preserve electronically stored information that can reasonably be anticipated to be relevant to litigation.").

tion of a document retention policy in the usual course of business is normally acceptable.

Once an organization reasonably anticipates litigation, it must suspend its routine document retention/destruction policy and put in place a "legal hold" (also known as "litigation hold").[2] This obligation of preservation applies to both plaintiffs and defendants.[3]

Preservation involves taking reasonable protective steps to protect electronically stored information for potential discovery or evidentiary purposes. Preservation can be accomplished through many forms, from evidentiary copies prepared by a forensic professional to simply taking custody of a laptop or backup tapes.[4] Due to the multi-dimensional qualities of electronically stored information vs. paper, it is important to preserve the integrity of the contents of electronically stored information. Depending on the nature of the information to be preserved and the facts giving rise to the case, this may include preserving information about the formatting of the document, its metadata, and, where applicable, its revision history.

Often, "normal" business operations have the potential to destroy or alter critical sources of digital information. Routine operations such as archive rotation, document deletion schedules, or simple computer use will alter electronically stored

---

[2]See In re eBay Seller Antitrust Litigation, 2007 WL 2852364 (N.D. Cal. 2007) (legal hold notices may be protected by attorney-client privilege and work product doctrine, but identities of employees receiving notices are not protected); Pension Committee of University of Montreal Pension Plan v. Banc of America Securities, 685 F. Supp. 2d 456 (S.D. N.Y. 2010) (abrogated on other grounds by, Chin v. Port Authority of New York & New Jersey, 685 F.3d 135, 115 Fair Empl. Prac. Cas. (BNA) 720, 95 Empl. Prac. Dec. (CCH) ¶ 44555 (2d Cir. 2012)); Zubulake v. UBS Warburg LLC, 220 F.R.D. 212, 218, 92 Fair Empl. Prac. Cas. (BNA) 1539 (S.D. N.Y. 2003).

[3]See, e.g., Micron Technology, Inc. v. Rambus Inc., 645 F.3d 1311, 98 U.S.P.Q.2d 1693 (Fed. Cir. 2011) (duty to preserve attached when party formed intent to enforce its patents through litigation, several years before bringing its first infringement suit).

[4]See Pension Committee of University of Montreal Pension Plan v. Banc of America Securities, 685 F. Supp. 2d 456 (S.D. N.Y. 2010) (abrogated on other grounds by, Chin v. Port Authority of New York & New Jersey, 685 F.3d 135, 115 Fair Empl. Prac. Cas. (BNA) 720, 95 Empl. Prac. Dec. (CCH) ¶ 44555 (2d Cir. 2012)); Consolidated Aluminum Corp. v. Alcoa, Inc., 244 F.R.D. 335 (M.D. La. 2006) (as general rule, party's duty to place a legal hold on evidence does not apply to inaccessible backup tapes for electronic evidence—those typically maintained solely for purpose of disaster recovery, which may continue to be recycled on the schedule set forth in party's policy, but if backup tapes are accessible (actively used for information retrieval), then such tapes would likely be subject to legal hold).

information. Counsel must evaluate the extent to which retention policies must be suspended because of the impending litigation. Systematic suspension of routine document/records/information destruction is one way to protect an organization, but it is usually not the most efficient or cost-effective way to manage preservation.

Preservation obligations are often accomplished through a comprehensive plan called a "legal hold". Because it is not practical to put an entire organization on hold each time litigation ensues, counsel should work to create a narrowly tailored plan that preserves the information required for the litigation while allowing the business to continue to function normally. In depth involvement of internal and external IT staff is almost always necessary to accomplish this goal.

Although it involves time up front, the most effective way to preserve information for litigation is to identify the types of information that will be implicated in the suit as well as the custodians. Then conduct interviews of those custodians as soon as possible. Finally, negotiate the scope of the information to be produced with opposing counsel.

This is the approach advocated by the Cooperation Proclamation produced by the Sedona Conference, and signed by over 100 federal judges.[5] Such an approach reduces the risk of potential costs associated with motions and spoliation further down the line and puts the onus on both parties to identify the scope of discovery very early in the litigation—another way to reduce litigation costs.

Narrowly targeted preservation allows the producing party to understand the scope of its duty to preserve and limits the other side from so-called "fishing expeditions." Counsel who cannot agree after attempting to negotiate the scope of preservation should seek the assistance of the court or request a special master. Special masters for e-discovery can also be helpful in cases where the parties anticipate significant e-discovery issues that do not want to wait for resolution by a very busy judge.

§ 9:2 Preservation Obligations—Triggering Events

The duty to preserve potential sources of electronically stored information and paper documents arises when litigation is "rea-

[5] http://www.thesedonaconference.org/content/tsc_cooperation_proclamation.

sonably anticipated."[1] In *Zubbulake v. UBS Warburg,*[2] the court ruled that a duty to preserve begins when litigation is "pending or reasonably foreseeable."[3] Depending on the particular jurisdiction, there can be some discrepancy as to the level of foreseeability that must arise before the obligations attach. A variety of pre-filing triggers have been recognized by various courts, ranging from employee complaints,[4] threats of litigation,[5] inquiries from potential litigants.[6]

One relatively settled, yet often overlooked, principle is the fact the duty attaches to a plaintiff upon contemplation of litigation.[7] Plaintiff's counsel should assess and make sure all preservation obligations have been satisfied prior to filing a complaint when ever possible.

The need for counsel to act quickly once a client receives notice

---

[Section 9:2]

[1]See, e.g., Micron Technology, Inc. v. Rambus Inc., 645 F.3d 1311, 98 U.S.P.Q.2d 1693 (Fed. Cir. 2011) (in patent infringement case, duty to preserve potentially relevant evidence arose in patentee at time when patentee's intellectual-property executive articulated time frame and motive for implementation of patentee's litigation strategy, which involved being ready to use its patent portfolio as weapon against perceived infringers if licensing negotiations did not go well; at that time patentee knew or should have known that general implementation of its document retention/destruction policy was inappropriate).

[2]Zubulake v. UBS Warburg LLC, 220 F.R.D. 212, 218, 92 Fair Empl. Prac. Cas. (BNA) 1539 (S.D. N.Y. 2003).

[3]Zubulake v. UBS Warburg LLC, 220 F.R.D. 212, 218, 92 Fair Empl. Prac. Cas. (BNA) 1539 (S.D. N.Y. 2003).

[4]Broccoli v Echostar Comm'ns Corp., 229 F.R.D. at 510–11 (D. Md. 2005) (complaints by employee to direct supervisors placed employer on notice of potential litigation).

[5]Testa v. Wal-Mart Stores, Inc., 144 F.3d 173, 176–78 (1st Cir. 1998) (threats of litigation sufficient to trigger notice).

[6]Blinzler v. Marriott Intern., Inc., 81 F.3d 1148, 1159 (1st Cir. 1996) ("reasonable anticipation" satisfied when attorney requested information on behalf of client relating to incident or dispute).

[7]See Pension Committee of University of Montreal Pension Plan v. Banc of America Securities, 685 F. Supp. 2d 456, 466 (S.D. N.Y. 2010) (abrogated on other grounds by, Chin v. Port Authority of New York & New Jersey, 685 F.3d 135, 115 Fair Empl. Prac. Cas. (BNA) 720, 95 Empl. Prac. Dec. (CCH) ¶ 44555 (2d Cir. 2012)); See also, Innis Arden Golf Club v. Pitney Bowes, Inc., 257 F.R.D. 334, 340, 70 Env't. Rep. Cas. (BNA) 1045 (D. Conn. 2009) (duty to preserve arose when plaintiff retained counsel in connection with potential legal action); Cyntegra, Inc. v. Idexx Laboratories, Inc., 2007 WL 5193736, *3 (C.D. Cal. 2007), order aff'd, 322 Fed. Appx. 569, 2009-1 Trade Cas. (CCH) ¶ 76574 (9th Cir. 2009) (plaintiffs must necessarily anticipate litigation before the complaint is filed).

of litigation, or reasonably anticipates litigation, cannot be overstated. Even when paper was still more widely used, the practice of waiting until a potential witness was identified in a deposition to collect their files was acceptable. Now that 99% of information is created and stored electronically and users can delete information easily, the identification of custodians, sources of ESI and the implementation of a preservation plan in place must happen quickly. How fast depends on the facts of the case. Courts evaluating motions for spoliation or sanctions will look first at the date the duty to preserve was triggered and then at when the alleged spoliated information was destroyed.

§ 9:3 Scope of duty to preserve

Once the duty of preservation has attached to a party, it is imperative to assess the scope of such duty. The court in *Zubulake v. UBS Warburg LLC*,[1] described the obligation of a party who anticipates litigation to preserve electronically stored information evidence in the following terms:

> A party or anticipated party must retain all relevant documents (but not multiple identical copies) in existence at the time the duty to preserve attaches, and any relevant documents created thereafter. In recognition of the fact that there are many ways to manage electronic data, litigants are free to choose how this task is accomplished. For example, a litigant could choose to retain all then-existing backup tapes for the relevant personnel (if such tapes store data by individual or the contents can be identified in good faith and through reasonable effort), and to catalog any later-created documents in a separate electronic file. That, along with a mirror-image of the computer system taken at the time the duty to preserve attaches (to preserve documents in the state they existed at that time), creates a complete set of relevant documents. Presumably there are a multitude of other ways to achieve the same result. Once a party reasonably anticipates litigation, it must suspend its routine document retention/destruction policy and put in place a "litigation hold" to ensure the preservation of relevant documents.[2]

[Section 9:3]

[1]Zubulake v. UBS Warburg LLC, 220 F.R.D. 212, 92 Fair Empl. Prac. Cas. (BNA) 1539 (S.D. N.Y. 2003).

[2]Zubulake v. UBS Warburg LLC, 220 F.R.D. 212, 218, 92 Fair Empl. Prac. Cas. (BNA) 1539 (S.D. N.Y. 2003). See also Equity Analytics, LLC v. Lundin, 248 F.R.D. 331 (D.D.C. 2008) (mirror image is perfect duplication of hard drive and it is physically impossible for mirror image to contain anything the hard drive does not and for there to be anything on the mirror image that is not on the hard drive). See generally Crystal, Ethical Responsibility and Legal Liability

The scope of the duty was addressed in *Zubulake IV*:[3] "[w]hile a litigant is under no duty to keep or retain every document in its possession . . . it is under a duty to preserve what it knows, or reasonably should know, is relevant in the action, is reasonably calculated to lead to the discovery of admissible evidence, is reasonably likely to be requested during discovery and/or is the subject of a pending discovery request."[4]

An organization must retain all relevant documents (but not multiple identical copies) in existence at the time the duty to preserve attaches, and any relevant documents created thereafter.[5] Organizations are free to choose how this task is accomplished.[6] The duty to preserve extends to those employees likely to have relevant information (the "key players" in the litigation).[7] Whether the party is required to preserve unsearched sources of potentially responsive information it believes are not reasonably accessible depends on the circumstances of each case.[8]

Identification involves determining the scope, breadth, and depth of electronically stored information that may be sought

---

of Lawyers for Failure to Institute or Monitor Litigation Holds, 43 Akron L. Rev. 715 (2010).

[3]Zubulake v. UBS Warburg LLC, 220 F.R.D. 212, 92 Fair Empl. Prac. Cas. (BNA) 1539 (S.D. N.Y. 2003).

[4]Zubulake v. UBS Warburg LLC, 220 F.R.D. 212, 217, 92 Fair Empl. Prac. Cas. (BNA) 1539 (S.D. N.Y. 2003); Broccoli v. Echostar Communications Corp., 229 F.R.D. 506, 510, 62 Fed. R. Serv. 3d 817 (D. Md. 2005); In re Kmart Corp., 371 B.R. 823, 843, 48 Bankr. Ct. Dec. (CRR) 178 (Bankr. N.D. Ill. 2007).

[5]Zubulake v. UBS Warburg LLC, 220 F.R.D. 212, 218, 92 Fair Empl. Prac. Cas. (BNA) 1539 (S.D. N.Y. 2003). See Sedona Principle 5 ("The obligation to preserve electronically stored information requires reasonable and good faith efforts to retain information that may be relevant to pending or threatened litigation. However, it is unreasonable to expect parties to take every conceivable step to preserve all potentially relevant electronically stored information.").

[6]Zubulake v. UBS Warburg LLC, 220 F.R.D. 212, 218, 92 Fair Empl. Prac. Cas. (BNA) 1539 (S.D. N.Y. 2003). See Sedona Principle 6 ("Responding parties are best situated to evaluate the procedures, methodologies, and technologies appropriate for preserving and producing their own electronically stored information.").

[7]See Consolidated Aluminum Corp. v. Alcoa, Inc., 244 F.R.D. 335 (M.D. La. 2006). See also Nucor Corp. v. Bell, 251 F.R.D. 191 (D.S.C. 2008) (employee engaged in sanctionable spoliation by using laptop computer after litigation hold imposed); In re NTL, Inc. Securities Litigation, 244 F.R.D. 179, 68 Fed. R. Serv. 3d 1145 (S.D. N.Y. 2007), order aff'd, 2007 WL 1518632 (S.D. N.Y. 2007) (sanctions imposed for destruction of evidence including e-mails of approximately 44 of defendants' key players).

[8]Cf. Cache La Poudre Feeds, LLC v. Land O'Lakes, Inc., 244 F.R.D. 614, 68 Fed. R. Serv. 3d 1181 (D. Colo. 2007) ($5,000 sanction for defendants' failure to preserve hard drives of departed employees).

during discovery. The identification process should take into consideration any claims and defenses, preservation demands, disclosure requirements, and discovery demands. In identifying electronically stored information that might be pursued during discovery, it is helpful to start from a larger pool of potentially discoverable electronically stored information and then assess how much should be preserved and collected.

The organization and its counsel must determine if the current electronic environment is susceptible to a cost-efficient harvesting of information. There must be an analysis of where the content resides and their inclusion of responsive electronically stored information. In addition, counsel should determine whether the client organization has systems in place to identify electronically stored information that is potentially relevant.

Counsel face a number of important considerations when it comes to deciding what electronically stored information to store and how. In deciding what electronically stored information to preserve, counsel should carefully research the subject. Counsel should not rely on counsel's own understanding of what constitutes electronically stored information or how it can be preserved, but should retain counsel who are knowledgeable in e-discovery, and can provide appropriate guidance.

Like other substantive areas of the law that require expertise, e-discovery is complex and requires an intimate working knowledge of the rules and the arguments to be made under them, a deep understanding of technology used to create the ESI that is sought in discovery, as well as the litigation experience to negotiate an appropriate position on the scope of e-discovery. E-discovery counsel will also be able to advise counsel and clients on the appropriate tools available in the marketplace that may be best suited for the type and risk associated with a particular case. Counsel who wade into e-discovery without the appropriate level of knowledge and expertise may miss crucial sources of ESI or issues that may benefit their clients, thereby subjecting themselves to malpractice claims, or perhaps worse, jeopardizing a key client relationship.

Experienced e-discovery counsel are in a position to determine:

- What general systems are included in an organization's IT infrastructure. Where the most relevant types of electronically stored information may be stored.
- An appropriate plan for identifying custodians and sources of electronically stored information that may be relevant to the dispute
- What metadata exist and how the metadata ought to be preserved, if at all.

- What the distinction is between backup and disaster tape systems.
- What backup or data storage sequences, if any, should be suspended.
- What steps should be taken to image hard drives.
- What steps should be taken to segregate business e-mail from personal e-mail or otherwise protect employee privacy or trade secret privileges.
- What must be done to distinguish between unique and duplicate electronically stored information.
- What steps should be taken to preserve web pages, intranet systems, or ASP data depositories.
- The most cost-efficient and reasonable process for handling electronically stored information for production.
- What tools are the most appropriate for the dispute given the cost, risk to the organization and value of the dispute.
- How to negotiate the scope of preservation, including navigating the challenges of producing particular types of electronically stored information (e-mail, electronic resource planning system databases, spreadsheets, etc.), and form of production.

Communication between parties to a dispute can be helpful in determining the scope of a duty to preserve electronically stored information. Fed. R. Civ. P. Rule 26(f) places considerable importance on the duty to confer. Fed. R. Civ. P. 26(f) is intended to have the parties consider the nature and basis of their claims and defenses. Courts and the Sedona Conference's Working Group on Document Retention have encouraged early negotiation between the parties on the scope of preservation.

This may be helpful in determining the duty to preserve. For example, if a plaintiff in a product liability suit has already decided it will not be pursuing a defective design strategy, but will instead pursue a different strategy, the plaintiff might agree that certain electronically stored information need not be preserved, even though the legal standards might typically suggest it should be. Of course, it is ultimately the court that approves or rejects any proposed discovery plan.

Not all relevant electronically stored information will be on the organization's systems. Responsive electronically stored information may be in the possession of contractors, agents, vendors, clients, lawyers, accountants, consultants, experts, outside directors, and former employees. Nonparties over whom the organization has control or influence must be factored into the legal hold.

§ 9:4 Implementing a legal hold—Generally

The goal of a legal hold is to prevent any alteration or destruction of electronically stored information. An organization and its counsel must take all reasonable steps to locate and preserve all relevant electronically stored information and hardcopy information.[1] Best practices dictate a legal hold notice be utilized to clarify and document a party's preservation plan and efforts. In *Pension Committee v. Banc of America Securities*,[2] the court ruled that the failure to issue a "written" legal hold "constitutes gross negligence because that failure is likely to result in the destruction of relevant information."[3] The court went on to dictate the specific types of information that should be covered in the legal hold so as to avoid gross negligence, including: identification of key players (including current and former employees), suspension of automated systems that may alter or destroy information, and retention of backup media.

Not all courts agree that the failure to implement the legal hold in written form gives rise to gross negligence.[4] The determining factor tends to be whether the failure to implement a hold did, in fact, result in the failure to preserve information and a resulting destruction or alteration of responsive information.

[Section 9:4]

[1]Pension Committee of University of Montreal Pension Plan v. Banc of America Securities, 685 F. Supp. 2d 456 (S.D. N.Y. 2010) (abrogated on other grounds by, Chin v. Port Authority of New York & New Jersey, 685 F.3d 135, 115 Fair Empl. Prac. Cas. (BNA) 720, 95 Empl. Prac. Dec. (CCH) ¶ 44555 (2d Cir. 2012)). See Sedona Principle 6 ("Responding parties are best situated to evaluate the procedures, methodologies, and technologies appropriate for preserving and producing their own electronically stored information.").

[2]Pension Committee of University of Montreal Pension Plan v. Banc of America Securities, 685 F. Supp. 2d 456 (S.D. N.Y. 2010) (abrogated on other grounds by, Chin v. Port Authority of New York & New Jersey, 685 F.3d 135, 115 Fair Empl. Prac. Cas. (BNA) 720, 95 Empl. Prac. Dec. (CCH) ¶ 44555 (2d Cir. 2012)).

[3]Pension Committee of University of Montreal Pension Plan v. Banc of America Securities, 685 F. Supp. 2d 456 (S.D. N.Y. 2010) (abrogated on other grounds by, Chin v. Port Authority of New York & New Jersey, 685 F.3d 135, 115 Fair Empl. Prac. Cas. (BNA) 720, 95 Empl. Prac. Dec. (CCH) ¶ 44555 (2d Cir. 2012)).

[4]See Victor Stanley, Inc. v. Creative Pipe, Inc., 269 F.R.D. 497, 524 (D. Md. 2010) ("a litigation hold might not be necessary under certain circumstances, and reasonableness is still a consideration"); *The Sedona Conference Commentary on Legal Holds: The Trigger & The Process*, 11 Sedona Conf. J. 265, 270, 280 (2010) ("there is no per se negligence rule and if the organization otherwise preserves the information then there is no violation of the duty to preserve").

Regardless of whether a party to litigation must have a written legal hold, it is advisable to use a legal hold to demonstrate the efforts undertaken in identifying and preserving sources of information potentially relevant to the case at hand. A written legal hold is an excellent tool to memorialize a party's efforts. Furthermore, when used in connection with an overall discovery plan, it provides counsel with a framework to negotiate scope and proportionality issues at the discovery conference.

§ 9:5 Formulating a legal hold

While a legal hold may follow a common form and style, it should not simply be a recitation of boiler-plate language. Further more, the legal hold is not simply a letter that needs to be sent to a client or organization and forgotten. The legal hold is a process that starts from a written notice of legal hold and then must be managed. The *Zubulake* court ruled that the legal hold process should be subject to "active supervision" by counsel and their clients.[1]

The goal of a legal hold letter is to place key custodians of information on notice of the obligation of preservation. To properly accomplish this goal, the communication must be clear, provide enough contextual information to describe the issue, explain the process, explain the consequences for not complying and describe how the preservation will be effectuated. The following areas are typically covered by a written legal hold letter:

- **Description of the litigation.** Often counsel is reluctant to provide a detailed description of the litigation at hand. It is necessary, however, to provide enough detail so that the recipient can properly assess what information will be subject to the hold.
- **Identification of key custodians.** Depending on who is the recipient of the legal hold, it may contain a list of custodians subject to the hold. This list should be thoroughly vetted with counsel and client to determine the list of individuals that are properly subject to the hold. Notice to an IT administrator, for example, may contain a list of all custodians for which information must be preserved and maintained.
- **Identification of information subject to the hold.** Often the subject matter of the litigation will dictate the type of

---

[Section 9:5]

[1]Zubulake v. UBS Warburg LLC, 229 F.R.D. 422, 432, 94 Fair Empl. Prac. Cas. (BNA) 1, 85 Empl. Prac. Dec. (CCH) ¶ 41728 (S.D. N.Y. 2004).

information to be held. Counsel should review a data map (if available) or otherwise identify sources of potentially responsive information with the client. These sources should be clearly identified in the legal hold notice. If communications are implicated, do not forget to identify and include methods of communication such as text messaging, Twitter, blogs, FaceBook, and other social media.

- **Guidance on how the hold will be effectuated.** Clearly tell the employee how and when the information in their possession will be preserved. If the preservation is not immediate, clearly explain to the employee what to do (and not do) prior to the preservation (i.e., do not delete email, do not modify files, etc.).
- **Describe consequence for failure to comply.** Consequence must exist for the failure to comply with the legal hold notice, and these must be communicated to the employee. They must understand that the legal hold notice describes legal obligations that must be followed.
- **Provide contact information.** If the recipient has questions or concerns, they must have some method of asking questions. Provide a key point of contact to address these issues.

§ 9:6 Communicating the legal hold

The legal hold is typically distributed to any custodian of data that is potentially relevant to the litigation. This will likely include named parties, their managers, and assistants. The information technology administrators will also be included because they control or manage network information. These information technology personnel will often play a critical role in assessing and ultimately preserving information sources relevant to the case.

If a key custodian is also a named party in the litigation, consideration should be given to the need to effectuate some form of preservation before distributing the legal hold. For example, if a manager has been named in a sexual harassment suit, the distribution of the legal hold may provide warning and incentive for the manager to destroy information within the manager's custody and control. In such a situation, counsel would be better advised to preserve the manager's data before or contemporaneously with the delivery of the legal hold letter.

The legal hold (or a similar communication) should also be sent to any third-party services providers that may maintain electronically stored information on behalf of the party. This may include email providers, SaaS (Software as a Service) providers, communication providers or any other outsourced service provider.

§ 9:7 Preservation plans

Every organization should adopt a formal, written records and information management program, including a legal hold protocol. The legal hold protocol should be a reasonable, repeatable process that is routinely followed by the organization each time it receives notice of, or reasonably anticipates, litigation. Organizations making reasonable efforts to put a legal hold in place and to preserve information relevant to the dispute will fare better in front of a judge than those that do nothing. Destruction of potentially relevant information must not be done in bad faith. Bad faith may include suddenly following the destruction schedule to limit damaging evidence available to potential litigation adversaries.[1]

A written preservation plan focuses on preserving electronically stored information once litigation is foreseeable. The success of a preservation plan depends to a very large degree on counsel's intimate knowledge of the administrative controls and architecture of the client's computer system. For attorneys who do not regularly practice in the e-discovery arena, such knowledge can only be acquired by retaining experienced counsel with knowledge of the technical issues. This is especially important when it comes to devising workable preservation plans.

Typically, preservation focuses on preserving media—hard drives, floppy disks, and backup tapes, for example—rather than particular files, folders, or other forms of data. Preserving media, as opposed to preserving just the electronically stored information that appears responsive or interesting initially, preserves not only the potentially responsive data, but also files and other data that could become important as discovery progresses. Preserving media also preserves other information, such as metadata or deleted material, that could be used latter to corroborate or authenticate the produced electronically stored information.

Engaging e-discovery counsel with the knowledge to negotiate a narrow scope of preservation may preclude having to preserve the entire media, thus saving the client thousands of dollars on

---

[Section 9:7]

[1]Rambus, Inc. v. Infineon Technologies AG, 222 F.R.D. 280, 288–89 (E.D. Va. 2004) (compelling production of documents and testimony relating to plaintiff's records management program).

the culling and review of extraneous information. For example, the average user's hard drive in a laptop today is 80 GB. Of that 80 GB, for any given matter, far less than 1 GB of data is likely to be relevant to the dispute. Experienced counsel can negotiate preservation to specific types of data with specific key words or concepts on that custodian's hard drive to prevent the need for imaging, storing and managing the remainder of the data. That is key not just from a cost perspective for the specific dispute, but for longer-term management of legal holds within the organization. Many of the individuals named as custodians are typically named on multiple suits, and managing multiple images of a custodian's hard drive can become an added expense for the organization.

Counsel should give special consideration to archived media, such as backup systems. Frequently, system administrators will only maintain a limited quantity of backup media, and then reuse them on a scheduled cycle—known as tape rotation. If backup systems are implicated—meaning that the information is not available from another active source—counsel should ensure that all relevant backup media are preserved by someone who can later establish a chain of custody for authentication purposes.

§ 9:8 Preservation orders

In appropriate cases, a party may seek a preservation order from the court. Because preservation orders are burdensome and expensive, in the absence of a clear need preservation orders should not be entered without a particularized showing of a need.[1]

§ 9:9 Preservation letters—Generally

The preservation letter is a very important tool. At a minimum, it places the other party on notice with respect to its duties to avoid spoliation. It also serves as an excellent basis for seeking sanctions, if it is later discovered that spoliation did in fact occur. Both plaintiffs, defendants, and third parties from whom discovery is sought should use the preservation letter to initiate the conversation regarding the scope of the duty to preserve.

A preservation letter is not a discovery request; it is simply a request that the other party preserve the party's electronically stored information so that it is not deleted or altered through

---

[Section 9:8]

[1]Valdez v. Town of Brookhaven, 2007 WL 1988792 (E.D. N.Y. 2007); Treppel v. Biovail Corp., 233 F.R.D. 363 (S.D. N.Y. 2006).

intentional misconduct or the normal processes associated with the deletion of computer files due to the ongoing business of a party. A party can disregard the request to preserve, but once the request has formally been made and evidence disappears, a preservation letter may place the discovering party in a superior position to seek sanctions or other relief. Counsel who do not receive a preservation letter from opposing counsel should initiate the conversation by sending a letter defining the scope of information that will be preserved unless otherwise notified.

§ 9:10 Preservation letters—Timing

A preservation letter should be sent to the other party or the other party's attorney at the earliest possible moment, describing the electronically stored information to be preserved, and requesting a meeting to construct a mutually acceptable plan for the production of electronically stored information. A preservation letter should be sent before, or at the same time, as the commencement of litigation and well before any voluntary disclosures by a party under Fed. R. Civ. P. 26 and before any discovery has occurred.[1]

§ 9:11 Preservation letters—Contents

The content of a preservation letter should be carefully thought through by counsel and be grounded in a firm understanding of the types of electronically stored information the other side likely has, as well as what types and forms of information will be relevant to the dispute at issue. The letter should be narrowly tailored to reflect the scope of the dispute and avoid overly broad and burdensome requests for organizations to cease purging any information, but specifically limit it to relevant information.[1]

Counsel drafting the letter should have a general understanding of the sources of electronically stored information the party may have available. Counsel should be prepared to request a Fed. R. Civ. P. 30(b)(6) deposition of the individuals with the most knowledge of the types of electronically stored information available in the organization to answer any questions.

[Section 9:10]

[1]See Grenig & Kinsler, FEDERAL CIVIL DISCOVERY AND DISCLOSURE §§ 1.20 to 1.25 (3d ed.).

[Section 9:11]

[1]Wiginton v. Ellis, 2003 WL 22439865 (N.D. Ill. 2003) (holding preservation letter that set out specific types of documents and limited it to relevant information was sufficient to put party on notice that ESI must be preserved; the parties later agreed on the scope of information to be preserved.)

At a minimum, a letter should begin with a general statement that the discovering party expects the party to preserve electronically stored information evidence that may be relevant to the issues in a case, or may lead to the discovery of such evidence. The preservation letter should include a request that the other party suspend its regular document retention policy for relevant information pending discovery and identify all possible locations where such evidence might conceivably reside.

The letter should inform the opposing party that a mere file backup of the hard drive is not adequate preservation. The party must be instructed to image hard drives in bit-stream copies, where all areas, used and unused, of the hard drive are copied. If a file is deleted before a backup is made, the deleted file will not be copied unless it is a bit-stream copy. The letter should also request that deleted files that are reasonably recoverable be immediately undeleted.

§ 9:12 Preservation letters—Consequences

Writing a preservation letter is not an idle gesture. Although a party has the duty to protect and preserve evidence once it is on notice that it must do so, a preservation letter must be specific with respect to the matter in dispute for a court to find that it put a party on notice for preserving specific types of information. Courts have held that a party may be under a duty to prevent spoliation even if litigation is only reasonably anticipated.[1] Serious sanctions may be imposed for failure to preserve information once a party reasonably anticipates or is on notice of litigation.

§ 9:13 Consequences of preservation

Preservation does not mean that counsel must later agree to produce evidence. By preserving electronically stored information, counsel is only assuring that the electronically stored information will be available if the information is later determined to be relevant or discoverable.

§ 9:14 Consequences of failure to preserve

If it is later determined counsel should have preserved electronically stored information but did not, counsel could face

[Section 9:12]

[1]See Treppel v. Biovail Corp., 249 F.R.D. 111 (S.D. N.Y. 2008).

charges of complicity in evidence spoliation subjecting counsel and the client to serious penalties.[1]

II. CHECKLISTS

§ 9:15 Checklist of facts triggering a legal hold

- ☐ Written notice
- ☐ Preservation letter
- ☐ Service of complaint
- ☐ Investigation notice
- ☐ Discovery demands, including subpoenas
- ☐ Court orders
- ☐ Pre-litigation discussions, demands and agreements
- ☐ Facts or circumstances that would put a reasonable person notice
- ☐ Reasonably foreseeable litigation or investigation
- ☐ Related lawsuits or investigations
- ☐ Stated threats to sue
- ☐ Knowledge of the organization, its agents, servants, and employees

§ 9:16 Checklist of Legal Hold actions

- ☐ Timely suspend document retention policies.
- ☐ Comply with preservation letters.
- ☐ Turn off digital devices only by unplugging.
- ☐ Request that information be preserved in native format whenever possible to preserve metadata.
- ☐ Quarantine digital media.
- ☐ Create bit-stream backups (imaging) of digital media.
- ☐ Avoid booting up suspect machines.
- ☐ Avoid redeploying machines unless the data they contain are irrelevant to imminent or ongoing litigation.
- ☐ Forbid forensically naive network administrators or other members of the information technology department from checking out or otherwise investigating relevant devices.

[Section 9:14]

[1]See Sedona Principle 7 ("The requesting party has the burden on a motion to compel to show that the responding party's steps to preserve and produce relevant electronically stored information were inadequate.").

NOTES

Commentary

This checklist is adapted from Van Buskirk, *Practical Strategies for Digital Discovery*, THE BRIEF, Spring 2003, at 50, 54.

§ 9:17 Checklist

- ☐ Identify the custodians at your client who may have relevant or responsive information
- ☐ Identify the dates of preservation for your matter
- ☐ Have initial conversations with key custodians to identify broad categories of documents to be preserved
- ☐ To the extent possible, review data (email archive is most likely place) to determine whether proposed date range is appropriate, too broad or too narrow and adjust appropriately
- ☐ Draft a written legal hold notice to be distributed to each custodian
- ☐ Coordinate with the individual responsible for managing the legal hold process on responses received to the legal hold via voting buttons
- ☐ Contact each custodian individually (if possible, if not, start with the most important first) and discuss retention policies and plan for preserving data
- ☐ Consider implicated systems (email, servers, etc.) and talk to appropriate parties to understand retention and whether action needs to be taken to suspend retention
- ☐ Resend legal hold notice periodically as case progresses
- ☐ Document all actions taken to identify, create and distribute legal hold notice
- ☐ Identify any third party sources of data within your client's custody or control and consider strategy for preserving data in those locations

NOTES

Commentary

This checklist is adapted from eDiscovery Assistant, an app for iPads.

§ 9:18 Checklist for preservation letter

- ☐ A statement of the name, venue and basic elements of the litigation or investigation, with sufficient specificity to provide the non-party recipient an adequate understanding of its subject matter, scope, and relevant time period.
- ☐ A description of the legal or business relationship between the requesting party and the recipient creating the need for

the recipient to take steps to preserve relevant material. If the relationship is such that the needed relevant material in the recipient's custody is, in reality, owned or within the control of the requesting party, this description should state this. To the extent known by the requesting party, this relationship description should include identification of the names, titles and locations of those persons within the non-party recipient's organization who are most likely to have been involved with the needed relevant material.

- ☐ A copy of or reference to any contract or agreement in effect during the relevant time period.
- ☐ Identification of the range of different types of material to be preserved, such as:
  - ☐ Paper and electronic documents
  - ☐ Voicemail
  - ☐ E-mail
  - ☐ Databases and other data
  - ☐ Audio Files
  - ☐ Video Files
  - ☐ Photographs or image files
  - ☐ Physical samples
  - ☐ Other
- ☐ A statement that the recipient should suspend its normal retention schedule and disposition policies for all relevant material until further written notice, and that the recipient should not delete or destroy any relevant material, regardless of routine or automated practices in effect prior to the receipt of the Preservation Notice.
- ☐ A request that the recipient distribute the Preservation Notice to all persons within their organization, or within the control of their organization, who are known or suspected to have relevant material in their possession, custody or control.
- ☐ A request that the recipient track and obtain acknowledgment from all persons within their organization, or within the control of their organization, to whom the Preservation Notice was distributed, that such persons received and understood the Preservation Notice, and that such persons identify and categorize any relevant material within their possession, custody or control. Such request should also include an inquiry as to whether such persons know of others within the organization who may have relevant material, who should also receive a copy of the Preservation Notice.

- ☐ A request that the recipient direct any questions about the subject matter or scope of the Preservation Notice to a designated legal representative of the requesting party.
- ☐ A request that the recipient, and any of its employees or agents having possession, custody or control of relevant material, hold such material in suspense and safe from modification or destruction, until they are contacted by a legal representative of their own organization (or, of the requesting party's organization, if appropriate) to provide guidance on how such relevant material will be collected.
- ☐ A request that the recipient periodically reissue and refresh the Preservation Notice distributed to persons within their organization, or within the control of their organization, to remind persons having relevant material that the Preservation Notice is still in effect, until they are advised to the contrary.
- ☐ Written acknowledgement of receipt of notice; confirmation of intent to comply with preservation request.

§ 9:19 Checklist for preservation of e-mails upon dismissal of employee

- ☐ Determine how the dismissed employee's e-mail account will be handled. The messages could be stored on a secure folder on the organization's network drive, stored on a CD-ROM, etc.)
- ☐ Determine who will review the messages? This should be someone in the organization familiar with the records that could be in the employee's e-mail account, and who has the authority to make decisions about deleting records.
- ☐ Determine how long messages should be retained, taking into account such matters as the periods for appealing unemployment compensation denials, limitation periods for the employee's filing discrimination claims, and the statute of limitations for trade secret claims. Once a case has been filed, messages must be retained for the duration of any legal investigation, audit, lawsuit or administrative hearing. If no appeal is made in the appropriate time period, then the non-record messages may be deleted.

III. FORMS

§ 9:20 Sample legal hold protocol (corporate)

>Sample Legal Hold Protocol Template:

Purpose

The purpose of this protocol is to identify the internal steps to implement, manage and release a legal hold when *[insert organization name]* has notice of an obligation to preserve information for litigation or any other legal required purpose.

Employee Subject to Protocol

All *[insert company name]* in-house counsel, paralegals, staff and other individuals with responsibilities under the protocol.

Notice of Preservation Obligation/Service of Process

Service of legal process is generally made on *[insert organization name]* via the company's registered agent *[insert name]*. Upon service, *[the registered agent]* notifies *[insert individual at organization that is notified]* via *[insert form of notification, e.g., email]* that service has been affected and attaches a copy of the document served. Original documents are then forwarded to *[insert individual at organization, e.g. General Counsel]*.

In a situation in which service occurs other then through *[the registered agent], all papers should be immediately sent to both the [insert responsible individual here, e.g. paralegal]* for logging and to *[insert individual here, e.g. Assistant to the General Counsel]*.

The General Counsel will then assign the matter to an Attorney within the department, and the original documents will be forwarded to the Attorney by *[insert responsible party here]*. For purposes of this protocol, a matter is any case in which a party asserts rights it seeks to have protected or enforced. Matters include anticipated or filed litigation whether in a court of law or with the applicable government agency, government investigations and third party subpoena obligations. Garnishments are not matters for purposes of this Protocol.

Identifying Custodians and Sources of ESI

The Responsible Attorney is responsible for identifying all Custodians who may have possession or control of matter specific relevant or responsive information and the sources of ESI at the Company that may need to be preserved for the matter. This exercise may be done in cooperation with Discovery Counsel or Outside Counsel. Where entire departments are implicated in the matter, every effort should be made to narrow the preservation obligation to those Custodians who were involved in the facts giving rise to a matter. Where ESI is managed within common systems (e.g. Sharepoint) identifying the source of the ESI and the individuals with knowledge of the matter is sufficient as long as all Custodians are notified of their obligations to preserve data.

Information to Be Preserved and Relevant Time Period

Information to be preserved includes both paper documents and all sources of ESI within the Company that are potentially relevant or responsive to this matter. The Attorney should determine the appropriate date range of preservation for the matter, including a start and end date. When identifying a range, the Attorney should make a reasonable judgment about the relevant time period based on interviews with custodians, general business practices, related litigation or other information that may be important.

Legal Hold Notice

For matters that impose an obligation to preserve, the Responsible Attorney will work with the Records and Information Director ("RIM Director")to draft and issue a legal hold notice via email to all custodians as identified by the Attorney. The notice will be based on the attached template and will utilize voting buttons in Outlook for the Custodians to use to indicate that they have read and wil comply with the notice, do not have responsive information, or have questions. Upon notification of a new matter, the RIM Director will create a new matter in the legal hold software to capture information for the legal hold. The RIM Director will be responsible for coordinating responses from the Custodians, using the Company's legal hold software, including answering any questions regarding retention obligations, with the Responsible Attorney's assistance.

The Attorney will be responsible for advising the RIM Director the names of any additional custodians or sources of ESI that are added after the initial stage so that appropriate actions can be taken.

Identifying and Preserving Relevant or Responsive Information

The Attorney and RIM Director should work directly with Discovery Counsel or Outside Counsel to identify the relevant sources of ESI within *[insert organization name]* that need to be preserved and/or collected. Identification should begin by referencing the Company's own data map and eDiscovery Guide, then further narrowing the process through discussions with custodians and Discovery Counsel, as necessary. Sources of ESI should include company systems, as well as cloud based services and any third parties who may be in custody or control of data owned by *[insert organization name]*

The RIM Director will be responsible for notifying the Attorney of any non-responsive Custodians, who will then address the issue with management for the Custodian. The RIM Director will also be responsible for stopping the destruction of any routine operation of the Company's systems to prevent the inadvertent destruction of any information that should be preserved for the matter, including setting a legal hold in the Company email archive and notifying IT liaisons of any retention that needs to be suspended.

Identification of Providers

The Attorney will work with Discovery Counsel or Outside Counsel to identify appropriate Providers for preservation, collection, handling data and setting up review of the ESI for the case. Counsel will be responsible for coordinating directly with the Custodians and IT to handle the preservation, collection and handling of data.

Reissuing the Hold Notice

At the start of the case, the Attorney and the RIM Director will determine how often the legal hold notice should be reissued to the Custodians. The RIM Director will be responsible for reissuing the notice through the Company's legal hold software.

Release of Legal Hold

Upon resolution of the matter, or when sufficient time has past that the hold can be released (i.e. expiration of time to appeal), the Attorney will advise the RIM Director that the legal hold for the matter should be released. Using the Company's legal hold software, the RIM Director will send a release notice to all named custodians as well as the IT liaisons and the Attorney. The IT liaisons will be responsible for ensuring that any ESI currently being preserved is released and purged in accordance with appropriate retention schedules. The RIM Director will be responsible for ensuring that any records preserved are released and purged in accordance with the appropriate retention schedules.

The RIM Director will also be responsible for releasing the hold in the Company's email archive.

Tracking of Information

The RIM Director will be responsible for tracking the steps taken to

1. Ensure the preservation of all relevant and responsive information,
2. Process and provide the information to Discovery Counsel or Outside Counsel as needed, and
3. Begin building metrics for review and analysis of annual costs of eDiscovery at *[insert organization name here]*.

The Attorney, Discovery Counsel or Outside Counsel and IT liaisons should provide all information to the RIM Manager for tracking. Using the Company's legal hold software, the RIM Director will generate a report of the matter with the following information for the matter file:

- Name of matter
- Description of matter
- Date notice received for matter (to be provided by Responsible Attorney)
- Responsible Attorney
- Identified custodians (including additional custodians added during matter)
- Date legal hold notice issued to identified custodians
- Date responses received from each custodian
- Response received from each custodian
- Custodian interview notes with follow ups for sources of ESI
- Sources of ESI identified
- Dates information pulled
- Name of Vendor(s) and responsibilities
- Date information provided to Vendor
- Date information provided to Outside Counsel
- Review platform utilized internally and by Outside Counsel
- Reissue date(s) for legal hold notice
- Date of Release sent to custodians
- Date of Release of email archive (if applicable)

To the extent available, the RIM Director should also record any opportunities during the eDiscovery phase of the case to improve the process, avoid additional costs and increase efficiencies so that we do not continuously reinvent the wheel.

NOTES TO FORM

Commentary

A legal hold protocol lays out the steps for an organization to manage legal holds. To be successful, any protocol should be customized to fit a particular organization. Use this template as a map to creating one that's specific to your needs, process, resources and personnel. Note that a business is better off not to have a policy than to have a policy that is not enforced, followed and audited. A protocol that fits within your existing business structure for how tasks are accomplished will have a much better chance of being followed than one that requires many changes in how things need to be done. Those responsible for the process should know and understand the potential legal implications for not following the protocol.

This form is adapted from eDiscovery Assistant, an app for iPads.

§ 9:21 Preservation letter—To party

[date]

[name]
[address]

Subject: Preservation of electronically stored information

Pursuant to the Federal Rules of Civil Procedure *[or state equivalent]*, *[party name]* has an obligation to preserve any and all information that may be relevant to this matter whether in paper or electronically stored information. Enclosed please find a Fed. R. Civ. P. 30(b)(6) deposition notice for the individual(s) most knowledgeable about the types of electronically stored information at *[name of party]* and the retention attached to that information, i.e. how far back the organization has information for each source listed. Once that deposition has been completed, we would welcome the opportunity to sit down and discuss a more narrowly tailored scope of preservation. If you would like to discuss preservation issues prior to that deposition, please contact me.

Until that time, *[party name]* is on notice that is it required to preserve all electronically stored information relating to *[describe]*, including hidden system files or metadata, presently located on or contained in a free standing computer or laptop, or on any part of a server, CPU or digital device that may contain data storage capabilities including, but not limited to hard disk drives, optical disk drives, removable media, such as floppy disk drives, CD-ROM and DVD drives, Zip drives, Jaz drives, Maxtor drives or snap drives, data processing cards, computer magnetic tapes, backup tapes, drum and disk storage devices or any other similar electronic storage media or system of whatever name or description.

Please also preserve all digital images relating to *[describe]* that may be stored on any type of hardware used to store or manipulate electronic images, including but not limited to microfilm, microfiche and their repositories and readers, or design or engineering computer systems and regardless of any digital image's format, including.jpg, .bmp, or some other advanced or proprietary form of digital image format, such as CAD layered drawings.

Please preserve all existing sources of electronically stored information relating to *[describe]* that may not presently be in use by your company or may have been deleted from your active systems, whether the source is a backup tape or disk, some other data retention system or some form of disaster recovery system.

Including the imaging of hard drives, please take all reasonable steps to preserve electronically stored information relating to *[describe]* that may have been deleted from your active files and which may not be readily recoverable from a backup medium, such as metadata.

Please also preserve electronically stored information relating to *[describe]* that is subject to your control regardless of where else it may be located on-site at your main offices, within the network infrastructure of your company or on or in one of your other computer support systems including those at your subsidiaries, predecessors, successors, assigns, joint venturers, partners, parents, agents or affiliates (in this country or throughout the world), including but not limited to the following locations:

a. Your LAN, SAN or WAN network systems, regardless of methods of connectivity (e.g., by T1, T3, or optical lines), domains, including PDCs, network OS (such as Novell, Microsoft, UNIX, Citrix, or some other similar type) or protocols, or your backup and disaster recovery hardware and media, regardless of the physical location of those electronic storage systems.

b. Your e-mail servers and any repository of your e-mail (including within the inbox, sent box, deleted box or some similar file of the computers of employees or management), any email archive, or in any backup form whatsoever, regardless of whether you use Microsoft Exchange, Outlook, Outlook Express, Lotus Notes or some combination of e-mail management software or some alternative commercial or proprietary e-mail management software.

c. Your information system administrative offices, including file servers, backup and disaster recovery restoration repositories, data retention repositories, purge repositories, training repositories, or libraries of hardcopy materials of any description (regardless of where located) and online training and operation manuals that have been scanned to disk.

d. Your offsite technical and service bureau support systems, including but not limited to application service provider support, scanning or data conversion support, offsite data storage or archive support.

e. Your web hosting and administration services, including intranet and extranet sites, regardless of whether they are now publicly posted or exist in English or some other language.

Please consider yourself under a continuing obligation to preserve electronically stored information relating to *[describe]* that may come into existence after the date of this letter, or that may exist now or in the future but of which you have no current knowledge.

Very truly yours,

[signature, etc.]

§ 9:22 Preservation letter—To client

[date]

[name 1]
[address]

Subject: *[Case Name]*
Data Preservation

Dear *[name 1]*:

Your assistance and cooperation are required with respect to preserving information in this case, including electronically stored information. Electronically stored information is an important and irreplaceable source of discovery and evidence.

This lawsuit requires that all employees preserve all information from *[organization's]* computer systems, removable electronic media, and other locations relating to *[describe]*. This includes, but is not limited to, e-mail and other electronic communication, word processing documents, spreadsheets, databases, calendars, telephone logs, contact manager information, Internet usage files, and network access information.

You must take every reasonable step to preserve this information until further notice from *[name 2]*. Failure to do so could result in extreme penalties against *[organization]* including dismissal of the case.

If you have any questions or need further information, please contact *[name 3]* at *[telephone number]*.

Sincerely,

[signature, etc.]

§ 9:23 Preservation letter—To client—Another form

[date]

[name 1]
[address]

Subject: *[Case Name]*
Preservation of Electronically
Stored Information

Dear *[name 1]*:

The purpose of this letter is to inform you that the *[organization]* is involved in a litigation proceeding known as *[case name, case no., jurisdiction]* (the Case). As a result, *[organization]* may be required to produce certain documents, including electronically stored information, relating to the case. In an effort to ensure that *[organization]* is taking all reasonable steps to preserve and safeguard evidence relating to the case, the documents in the categories listed below, whether in hard copy or electronic form, cannot be altered, destroyed or discarded for any reason.

Documents subject to this requirement may be in paper or electronic form, including e-mails, instant text messages, memorandums, and all correspondence, whether in draft or final form. Documents also refer to handwritten and typewritten documents and non-identical copies of the same documents.

Your failure to retain these documents or ignore the directive of this memorandum can result in severe consequences, including various forms of punishment imposed by a court of law.

Documents Covered:

Until further notice, please search for and then maintain any documents relating to the following topics:

Any and all documents relating to the *[describe]*, including, without limitation: *[list all potentially relevant documents]*

Any and all communications relating to, or stemming from, the *[describe]*.

Instructions:

Please instruct all personnel within the *[organization]* not to alter, destroy, discard, interfile, annotate, remove, rearrange or modify any documents identified for production in the case. Please also inform all appropriate personnel who are responsible for handling, or who have access to, the documents of the instructions conveyed in this letter. Additionally, please instruct such personnel that they must segregate and label all documents that may be produced in the *[describe]*.

Questions:

Any questions or concerns about this memorandum should be directed to *[name]* at *[telephone number]*. Thank you for your cooperation in this matter.

Very truly yours,

[signature, etc.]

§ 9:24 Preservation letter—To nonparty

[date]

[name 1]
[address]

Subject: *[Case Name]*
Data Preservation

Dear *[name 1]*:

Your assistance and cooperation are required with respect to preserving *[organization]* information in this case, including electronically stored information. Electronically stored information is an important and irreplaceable source of discovery and evidence.

You are requested to preserve all information from *[organization's]* computer systems, removable electronic media, and other locations relating to *[describe]*. This includes, but is not limited to, e-mail and other electronic communication, word processing documents, spreadsheets, databases, calendars, telephone logs, contact manager information, Internet usage files, and network access information.

You must take every reasonable step to preserve this information until further notice from *[name 2]*. Failure to do so could result in extreme penalties against *[organization]*.

If you have any questions or need further information, please contact *[name 3]* at *[telephone number]*.

Sincerely,

[signature, etc.]

§ 9:25 Preservation letter—To party seeking discovery of electronically stored information

Dear *[name of counsel listed on complaint]*,

I represent *[name of client]* in the matter captioned *[name of case]*. In response to my client's obligations to preserve relevant information under the Federal Rules of Civil Procedure and case law, my client has taken steps to identify the following custodians and sources of electronically stored information relevant to this matter. Information for these custodians will be preserved for the time period *[insert date range]*.

If I do not hear from you within seven days after receipt of this letter, I will assume you agree to the scope of preservation my client proposes. If you would like to discuss the scope, please contact me at your earliest convenience so my client can proceed with running its business while meeting its obligations for this matter to preserve information.

§ 9:26 Interim preservation order

[Caption]

Interim Order Regarding Preservation

1. Order to Meet and Confer To further the just, speedy, and economical management of discovery, the parties are ORDERED to confer as soon as practicable, no later than 30 days

after the date of this order, to develop a plan for the preservation of documents, data, and tangible things reasonably anticipated to be subject to discovery in this action. The parties may conduct this conference as part of the discovery conference if it is scheduled to take place within 30 days of the date of this order. The resulting preservation plan may be submitted to this Court as a proposed order under *[rule]*.

2. Subjects for Consideration The parties should attempt to reach agreement on all issues regarding the preservation of documents, data, and tangible things. These issues include, but are not necessarily limited to:
   (a) the extent of the preservation obligation, identifying the types of material to be preserved, the subject matter, time frame, the authors and addressees, and key words to be used in identifying responsive materials;
   (b) the identification of persons responsible for carrying out preservation obligations on behalf of each party;
   (c) the form and method of providing notice of the duty to preserve to persons identified as custodians of documents, data, and tangible things;
   (d) mechanisms for monitoring, certifying, or auditing custodian compliance with preservation obligations;
   (e) whether preservation will require suspending or modifying any routine business processes or procedures, with special attention to document-management programs and the recycling of computer data storage media;
   (f) the methods to preserve any volatile but potentially discoverable material, such as voicemail, active data in databases, or electronic messages;
   (g) the anticipated costs of preservation and ways to reduce or share these costs; and
   (h) a mechanism to review and modify the preservation obligation as discovery proceeds, eliminating or adding particular categories of documents, data, and tangible things.
3. Duty to Preserve
   (a) Until the parties reach agreement on a preservation plan, all parties and their counsel are reminded of their duty to preserve evidence that may be relevant to this action. The duty extends to documents, data, and tangible things in the possession, custody and control of the parties to this action, and any employees, agents, contractors, carriers, bailees, or other nonparties who possess materials reasonably anticipated to be subject to discovery in this action. Counsel is under an obligation to exercise reasonable efforts to identify

and notify such nonparties, including employees of corporate or institutional parties.

(b) "Documents, data, and tangible things" is to be interpreted broadly to include writings; records; files; correspondence; reports; memoranda; calendars; diaries; minutes; electronic messages; voicemail; e-mail; telephone message records or logs; computer and network activity logs; hard drives; backup data; removable computer storage media such as tapes, disks, and cards; printouts; document image files; Web pages; databases; spreadsheets; software; books; ledgers; journals; orders; invoices; bills; vouchers; checks; statements; worksheets; summaries; compilations; computations; charts; diagrams; graphic presentations; drawings; films; charts; digital or chemical process photographs; video, phonographic, tape, or digital recordings or transcripts thereof; drafts; jottings; and notes. Information that serves to identify, locate, or link such material, such as file inventories, file folders, indices, and metadata, is also included in this definition.

(c) "Preservation" is to be interpreted broadly to accomplish the goal of maintaining the integrity of all documents, data, and tangible things reasonably anticipated to be subject to discovery under *[rules]* in this action. Preservation includes taking reasonable steps to prevent the partial or full destruction, alteration, testing, deletion, shredding, incineration, wiping, relocation, migration, theft, or mutation of such material, as well as negligent or intentional handling that would make material incomplete or inaccessible.

(d) If the business practices of any party involve the routine destruction, recycling, relocation, or mutation of such materials, the party must, to the extent practicable for the pendency of this order, either

  (1) halt such business processes;
  (2) sequester or remove such material from the business process; or
  (3) arrange for the preservation of complete and accurate duplicates or copies of such material, suitable for later discovery if requested.

(e) Before the conference to develop a preservation plan, a party may apply to the court for further instructions regarding the duty to preserve specific categories of documents, data, or tangible things. A party may seek permission to resume routine business processes relating to the storage or destruction of specific categories of documents, data, or tangible things, upon a showing of undue cost, burden, or overbreadth.

4. Procedure in the Event No Agreement Is Reached If, after conferring to develop a preservation plan, counsel do not reach agreement on the subjects listed under paragraph 2 of this order or on other material aspects of preservation, the parties are to submit to the court within three days of the conference a statement of the unresolved issues together with each party's proposal for their resolution of the issues. In framing an order regarding the preservation of documents, data, and tangible things, the court will consider those statements as well as any statements made in any applications under paragraph 3(e) of this order.

Entered this date: __

____

Judge

NOTES TO FORM

Commentary

The purpose of this order is requiring the parties to confer and develop their own preservation plan. If the court determines such a conference is unnecessary or undesirable, the order may be modified to serve as a stand-alone preservation order.

§ 9:27 Preservation order halting routine destruction

[Caption]

ORDER

[Party] has moved for an order prohibiting the alteration or destruction of evidence during the pendency of this action. *[Party]* has filed papers opposing the motion.

Upon careful review of the papers submitted in support of and in opposition to the motion, the court has determined that (1) no hearing on the motion is necessary; (2) an order requiring the preservation of evidence is appropriate; and (3) an interim order shall forthwith enter requiring the parties to take steps to prevent the alteration or destruction of evidence as follows:

1. Until the issues in these proceedings can be further refined, the court reminds all parties of their duty to preserve evidence that may be relevant to this action. The duty extends to documents, data and tangible things in the possession, custody and control of the parties to this action, and any employees, agents, contractors, carriers, bailees or other nonparties who possess materials reasonably anticipated to be subject to discovery in this action. Counsel are under an obligation to exercise efforts

to identify and notify such nonparties, including employees of corporate or institutional parties.

2. "Documents, data and tangible things" is to be interpreted broadly to include writings, records, files, correspondence, reports, memoranda, calendars, diaries, minutes, electronic messages, voicemail, e-mail, telephone message records or logs, computer and network activity logs, hard drives, backup data, removable computer storage media such as tapes, disks and cards, printouts, document image files, web pages, databases, spreadsheets, software, books, ledgers, journals, orders, invoices, bills, vouchers, checks, statements, worksheets, summaries, compilations, computations, charts, diagrams, graphic presentations, drawings, films, digital or chemical process photographs, video, phonographic, tape or digital recordings or transcripts thereof, drafts, jottings and notes. Information that serves to identify, locate, or link such material, such as file inventories, file folders, indices and metadata, is also included in this definition.
3. "Preservation" is to be interpreted broadly to accomplish the goal of maintaining the integrity of all documents, data and tangible things reasonably anticipated to be subject to discovery under Fed. R. Civ. P. 45 and 56(e) in this action. Preservation includes taking reasonable steps to prevent the partial or full destruction, alteration, testing, deletion, shredding, incineration, wiping, relocation, migration, theft, or mutation of such material, as well as negligent or intentional handling that would make material incomplete or inaccessible.
4. Counsel are directed to inquire of their respective clients if the business practices of any party involve the routine destruction, recycling, relocation, or mutation on such materials and, if so, direct the party, to the extent practicable for the pendency of this order, either to
   a. halt such business processes;
   b. sequester or remove such material from the business process; or
   c. arrange for the preservation of complete and accurate duplicates or copies of such material, suitable for later discovery if requested.

The most senior lawyer or lead trial counsel representing each party shall, not later than *[date]*, submit to the court under seal and pursuant to Fed. R. Civ. P. 11, a statement that the directive in paragraph 4, above, has been carried out.

Entered this date:__

____

Judge

NOTES TO FORM

Commentary

This form is adapted from an order in In re National Security Agency Telecommunications Records Litigation, 2007 WL 3306579 (N.D. Cal. 2007).

§ 9:28 Preservation protocol for electronically stored information

[Caption]

Electronically Stored Information Preservation Protocol

1. As used in this protocol, the term "potentially discoverable electronic information" refers to Defendant's and Plaintiff's electronic "documents" that contain or potentially contain information relating to facts at issue in the litigation, where the term "documents" is used as it is defined in Fed. R. Civ. P. 34(a)
2. During the pendency of these actions, the Defendant and the Plaintiff must securely maintain, to the extent that they currently exist and may contain potentially discoverable electronic information: (1) e-mail backup tapes and (2) network backup tapes (together, the "Backup Tapes") created in the ordinary course of business during the period from *[start date]* through *[stop date]*. The Defendant and the Plaintiff are obligated to retain only one day's Backup Tapes among all Backup Tapes created in the ordinary course during a given month, provided that such day's Backup Tapes represent a complete backup of the data contained on the subject servers on that day (as opposed to merely an incremental backup of the subject servers). If only incremental backup tapes have been retained for a given month, then all such incremental tapes must be retained. All Backup Tapes other than those specifically required to be preserved pursuant to this paragraph and paragraph 3 below may be recycled, overwritten, or erased, as the case may be, pursuant to Defendant's and Plaintiff's otherwise applicable retention schedule.
3. All electronic information or data archived or backed up during the period from *[date]*, as part of a special backup, i.e., a backup made other than in the ordinary course of business by Defendant or Plaintiff, whether due to system upgrade, transition planning, system migration, disaster recovery planning, or any other reason, that potentially contains potentially

discoverable electronic information must be securely retained, to the extent they currently exist, for the remainder of the litigation.

4. All current or legacy software and hardware necessary to access, manipulate, print, etc., potentially discoverable electronic information that either is "live" or has been archived or backed up must be securely retained, to the extent that they currently exist, for the remainder of the litigation.
5. Defendants and Plaintiff must circulate retention notices designed to ensure the preservation of potentially discoverable electronic and other information to those employees potentially possessing such information. Thereafter, Defendant and Plaintiff must re-notify their employees quarterly of their continuing obligation to preserve such information.
6. Defendant and Plaintiff must take the following measures to secure and retain, to the extent that it exists, the potentially discoverable electronic information that is on the desktop and laptop hard drives of their respective employees. Either (1) hard drives containing potentially discoverable electronic data must be retained with all potentially discoverable electronic data contained therein retained intact; or, (2) employees must be instructed to copy all potentially discoverable electronic information to a secure, backed-up network storage device or backup medium for the remainder of the litigation, making all reasonable efforts to retain all metadata (file creation dates, modification dates, etc.) associated with the potentially discoverable electronic information at issue. The periodic retention notifications disseminated pursuant to paragraph 5 must advise employees potentially possessing potentially discoverable electronic information of their obligation to store discoverable electronic information on a secure, backed-up network storage device or backup medium to ensure its preservation and instruct such employees in the manner of doing so in accordance with this paragraph.
7. Within 15 days of receiving the list of business units referred to below, plaintiff must identify by name, title, or departmental category, employees of Defendant for which the Defendant is responsible for maintaining the hard drive, or a mirror-image copy (i.e., a bit-by-bit copy) of such hard drive, during the pendency of this litigation. Within 15 days of receiving the list of business units referred to below, Defendant must identify by name, title, or departmental category, employees of Plaintiff for which the Plaintiff is responsible for maintaining the hard drive, or a mirror-image copy (i.e., a bit-by-bit copy) of such hard drive, during the pendency of this litigation. In no event

will the number of computers subject to the provisions of this paragraph be greater than *[insert number]* for Defendant and Plaintiff. The hard drives or image copies of such hard drives preserved pursuant to this paragraph must be labeled to identify the employee who primarily used the computer associated with that hard drive. To facilitate the identification of the appropriate employees, the parties will provide to each other identification by business unit and positions the employees they reasonably believe could have potentially discoverable electronic information. The parties will meet and confer in good faith and exchange additional information as may be necessary to facilitate the identification, and limit the number, of employees for whom the provisions of this paragraph shall be applicable.

8. To the extent that Defendant or Plaintiff have implemented a system for the purpose of preserving external e-mails (e-mails sent to or received by Defendant's or Plaintiff's employees) in an easily accessible form, other than an e-mail server or the Backup Tapes identified in paragraph 2 or 3 above, all e-mails that were created during the period from *[date range]* that contain potentially discoverable electronic information, and that are stored on any such system as of the date hereof, must be preserved during the pendency of this litigation.
9. Within 45 days, Defendant and Plaintiff will provide written answers to the best of their ability to the questions concerning information system and electronic document retention practices set forth in attached Schedule C *[omitted]*. Should any party believe it cannot in good faith answer any of the questions as posed, the parties will confer to resolve any disputes and, if necessary, seek Court intervention.
10. By agreeing to preserve potentially discoverable electronic information in accordance with the terms hereof, Defendant and Plaintiff are not waiving any objection to the ultimate discoverability of such information at such point when discovery is authorized in these actions.
11. Nothing in this protocol shall be deemed to affect the Defendant's and Plaintiff's obligations to preserve hardcopy documents pursuant to the Court's Case Management Order. If counsel learn that potentially discoverable hardcopy documents were destroyed by a party subsequent to being named as a party in, and receiving a copy of, a complaint pertaining to that public offering, counsel for such party must notify opposing counsel in writing of such destruction within two weeks of learning so.

§ 9:29 Legal hold release notice

To: Custodians that Received Legal Hold Notice *[and any additional custodians included on matter]*

Legal Hold Release Notice

I am pleased to tell you that the *[litigation/request for information/investigation]* regarding *[insert case name/request for information/investigation or name used on legal hold notice]* has been *[resolved/satisfied/dismissed/closed]*. **The legal hold you received regarding this matter is RELEASED effective upon receipt of this notice.**

The release means that unless you have received a legal *[or tax]* hold notice in another matter requiring you to retain information or records covered by the following categories, you are no longer required to keep any records related to the areas listed below <u>for any period longer than the retention period required by the Records Retention Policy</u>:

[insert bullet pointed list of document types included in legal hold notice and those types of documents/information identified and collected during discovery]

Please resume *[following the Records Retention Policy and Retention Schedule] [your current practices]* for all records previously under legal or tax hold in this matter.

[Note—if related litigation exists, or the matter overlaps with another still active matter, use the following language: **If you are subject to a document hold for other pending matter(s) such as the ______ Litigation, those documents must remain on hold and in control to the extent they conflict with this release.**]

I *[or list another individual]* will be in touch in the next few days to discuss this release and to make sure you understand what to do.

If you have any questions or concerns about your responsibilities under this Release, please contact *[insert contact Name]*, *[title]*, at *[phone number]* or via email at *[insert email address]* or *[insert name of responsible attorney]*, *[title]*, at *[insert direct dial phone number]*, or via email at *[insert email address]*.

Thank you for your assistance with this important matter for *[insert client/organization/business name]*.

NOTES TO FORM

Commentary

This form is adapted from eDiscovery Assistant, an app for iPads.

Chapter 10

Discovery and Disclosure

I. GUIDELINES

II. CHECKLISTS

III. FORMS

Research References

Treatises and Practice Aids

Grenig & Gleisner, eDiscovery & Digital Evidence §§ 7:1 to 7:22

Trial Strategy

Recovery and Reconstruction of Electronic Mail as Evidence, 41 Am. Jur Proof of Facts 3d 1

Computer Technology in Civil Litigation, 71 Am. Jur Trials 111

Additional References

Grenig & Kinsler, Handbook of Federal Civil Discovery and Disclosure §§ 1.1 to 1.200 (3d ed.)

ABA Discovery Standards, http://www.abanet.org/litigation/discoverystandards/2005civildiscoverystandards.pdf

Electronic Discovery Reference Model Project, http://www.edrm.net

Federal Judicial Center, http://www.fjc.gov

The Sedona Conference, http://www.thesedonaconference.org

KeyCite®: Cases and other legal materials listed in KeyCite Scope can be researched through the KeyCite service on Westlaw®. Use KeyCite to check citations for form, parallel references, prior and later history, and comprehensive citator information, including citations to other decisions and secondary materials.

I. GUIDELINES

§ 10:1 Generally

For example, in tort actions, computer records of accidents may be used to support a claim that a particular product or place was dangerous. In marital dissolution cases, a home computer might show evidence of assets, such as on-line stock trading, or even evidence of infidelity. A human resources database may contain evidence of a pattern and practice of discrimination that will be helpful in an employment discrimination suit.

Basic discovery principles apply to discovery of electronically stored information.[1] Discovery is proper if the information sought is not privileged and it meets the applicable relevancy standard. Thus, like other types of information, electronically stored information is generally discoverable if it is relevant to the claim or defense of any party or appears reasonably calculated to lead to the discovery of admissible evidence.[2]

The major issue in the discovery of electronically stored infor-

---

[Section 10:1]

[1]Committee Note to 2006 amendment to Fed. R. Civ. P. 34(a): "Rule 34(a) is amended to confirm that discovery of electronically stored information stands on equal footing with discovery of paper documents"; Zubulake v. UBS Warburg LLC, 217 F.R.D. 309, 317, 91 Fair Empl. Prac. Cas. (BNA) 1574 (S.D. N.Y. 2003) ("[E]lectronic evidence is no less discoverable than paper evidence").

[2]See Fed. R. Civ. P. 26(b).

mation is not whether electronically stored information is discoverable, but the scope of preservation and production permitted or required and the cost of discovery. While discovery of electronically stored information has sometimes been equated with traditional paper-based discovery, there are important differences, including the sheer volume of digital information.

Planning for discovery of electronically stored information should begin early in the litigation. As soon as litigation is contemplated or threatens, the parties should be put on notice to preserve all sources of potentially responsive electronically stored information. This obligation is not limited to the defendants. Plaintiffs should also consider the obligations of preservation in anticipation of initiating litigation. In order to reduce the possibility of documents being deleted, parties should consider seeking a particularized preservation agreement or order ensuring that all sources, including primary, secondary or off-site computer files be preserved pending discovery.

§ 10:2 Producing and exchanging electronically stored information

There are several reasons for encouraging parties to produce and exchange electronically stored information in digital form:

- **Reducing costs.** Production of electronically stored information on disks, CD-ROMs, or by file transfers can significantly reduce the costs of copying, transporting, storing, and managing documents. Protocols may be established by the parties facilitating the handling of electronically stored information, from initial production to use in depositions, and pretrial procedures to presentation at trial.
- **Increased efficiency of search.** Depending on the ultimate form of production, electronically stored information can be more easily searched, located, and organized than paper documents. This can benefit both the responding as well as the requesting party.
- **Document depository.** Electronically stored information may form the contents for a common document depository.
- **Document review.** Current electronic document review platforms can significantly increase the speed and improve the workflow related to document review process. Categories of documents can quickly and easily be identified and ultimately marked with multiple issue or relevancy tags. The entire review process can be closely monitored, reviewed and verified.

§ 10:3 Saving time and money

Expenditures made on e-discovery, including preservation, collection and production, without proper management or oversight, can end up resulting in significant, unnecessary expenses.[1] Often increased costs related to e-discovery are the result of a general lack of understanding of the nuances of electronically stored information that impact the scope of discovery and the review process. The Manual for Complex Litigation Fourth suggests several ways to save time and money on discovery:

- *Stipulations under Federal Rule of Civil Procedure 29.* The rule gives parties authority to alter procedures, limitations, and time limits on discovery so long as they do not interfere with times set by court order. Thus, the parties can facilitate discovery by stipulating with respect to notice and manner of taking depositions and adopting various informal procedures. The court may, however, require that it be kept advised of such agreements to ensure compliance with the discovery plan and may by order preclude stipulations on particular matters.
- *Informal discovery.* The court should encourage counsel to exchange information, particularly relevant documents, without resort to formal discovery . . .. Early exchanges can make later depositions more efficient. Informal interviews with potential witnesses can help determine whether a deposition is needed, inform later discovery, and provide the basis for requests for admissions through which the results of informal discovery are made admissible at trial.
- *Automatic disclosure.* Rule 26(a)(1) and many local rules and standing orders require the parties to identify relevant witnesses and categories of documents early in the litigation, without waiting for discovery requests. By stipulation or court order, the timing and content of this disclosure may be tailored to the needs of the particular case. . . .
- *Reduction of deposition costs.* Depositions taken by telephone, videoconference, electronic recording devices, or having deponents come to central locations sometimes save money. Likewise, parties may forgo attending a deposition

[Section 10:3]

[1]A study by the Federal Judicial Center released in March 2010 found that plaintiffs who requested and produced electronically stored information reported approximately 48% higher costs. For each dispute over electronically stored information, a party had approximately 10% higher costs. See www.fjc.gov/public/pdf.nsf/lookup/costciv1.pdf/$file/costciv1.pdf.

in which they have only a minor interest if a procedure is established for supplemental questions—by telephone, videoconference, written questions, or resumption of examination in person—in the event that, after a review of the transcript, they find further inquiry necessary. . . .

- *Information from other litigation and sources.* When information is available from public records (such as government studies or reports), from other litigation, or from discovery conducted by others in the same litigation, consider requiring the parties to review those materials before undertaking additional discovery. The court may limit the parties to supplemental discovery if those materials will be usable as evidence in the present litigation. Interrogatory answers, depositions, and testimony given in another action ordinarily are admissible if made by and offered against a party in the current action. Similarly, they may be admissible for certain purposes if made by a witness in the current action. Coordination of "common" discovery in related litigation may also save costs, even if the litigation is pending in other courts. If related cases are pending in more than one court, coordinated common discovery can prevent duplication and conflicts. A joint discovery plan can be formulated for all cases, with agreement among parties that one of the cases will be treated as the lead case (with its discovery plan serving as the starting point for development of supplemental plans in the other courts), or with the use of joint deposition notices. . . . Counsel may also agree that discovery taken in one proceeding can be used in related proceedings as though taken there.
- *Joint discovery requests and responses.* In multiparty cases with no designated lead counsel, judges sometimes require parties with similar positions to submit a combined set of interrogatories, requests for production, or requests for admission. If voluminous materials are to be produced in response, the responding party may be relieved of the requirement of furnishing copies to each discovering party. . . .
- *Modified discovery responses.* When a response to a discovery request can be provided in a form somewhat different from that requested, but with substantially the same information and with less time and expense, the responding party should make that fact known and seek agreement from the requesting party. For example, information sought on a calendar year basis may be readily and inexpensively available on a fiscal year basis. Similarly, if some requested information can be produced promptly but additional time will be needed

for other items, the responding party should produce the information presently available and indicate when the remainder will be produced. Preferably, formal discovery requests should be prepared only after counsel have informally discussed what information is needed and how it can be produced most efficiently.

- *Phased or sequenced discovery of computerized data.* . . . Computerized data, however, are often not accessible by date, author, addressee, or subject matter without costly review and indexing. Therefore, it may be appropriate for the court to phase or sequence discovery of computerized data by accessibility. At the outset, allowing discovery of relevant, nonprivileged data available to the respondent in the routine course of business is appropriate and should be treated as a conventional document request. If the requesting party requests more computerized data, consider additional sources in ascending order of cost and burden to the responding party, e.g., metadata or system data, archived data, backup data, and legacy data. The judge should encourage the parties to agree to phased discovery of computerized data as part of the discovery plan. But with or without a prior agreement, the judge may engage in benefit-and-burden analysis under Rule 26(b)(2)(iii) at each stage and enter an appropriate order under Rule 26(c), which may include cost sharing between the parties or cost shifting to the requesting party. . . .
- *Computerized data produced in agreed-on formats.* Information subject to discovery increasingly exists in digital or computer-readable form. The judge should encourage counsel to produce requested data in formats and on media that reduce transport and conversion costs, maximize the ability of all parties to organize and analyze the data during pretrial preparation, and ensure usability at trial. Wholesale conversion of computerized data to paper form for production, only to be reconverted into computerized data by the receiving party, is costly and wasteful. Particularly in multiparty cases, data production on CD—ROM or by Internet-based data transfer can increase efficiency. . . .
- *Sampling of computer data.* Parties may have vast collections of computerized data, such as stored E-mail messages or backup files containing routine business information kept for disaster recovery purposes. Unlike collections of paper documents, these data are not normally organized for retrieval by date, author, addressee, or subject matter, and may be very costly and time-consuming to investigate

thoroughly. Under such circumstances, judges have ordered that random samples of data storage media be restored and analyzed to determine if further discovery is warranted under the benefit versus burden considerations of Rule 26(b)(2)(iii).

- *Combined discovery requests.* Several forms of discovery can be combined into a single request. Ordinarily, more time should be allowed for parties responding to a combined discovery request, even though such responses sometimes consume less overall time than do responses to traditional separate discovery requests. Because the rules impose no limits on requests for admission as they do on interrogatories, an order enlarging the number of permissible interrogatories may be necessary.
- *Conference depositions.* If knowledge of a subject is divided among several people and credibility is not an issue, a "conference deposition" may be feasible (see, e.g., Rule 26(b)(6)). Each witness is sworn, and the questions are then directed to the group or those having the information sought. Persons in other locations who may also be needed to provide information may be scheduled to be "on call" during the conference deposition. This procedure may be useful in obtaining background information, identifying and explaining documents, and examining reports compiled by several persons.
- *Subpoenas.* Under Rule 45, an attorney may subpoena documents or other tangibles from nonparties, avoiding unnecessary depositions. The rule also provides for subpoenas to permit inspection of premises possessed by nonparties, rendering unnecessary the commencement of an independent proceeding.[2]

§ 10:4 Cost savings through proportionality

A growing trend to address the explosion of costs associated with e-discovery encourages attention to the discovery principle of "proportionality." Fed. R. Civ. P. 26(b)(2)(C) imposes a general limitation on the scope of discovery in the form of a proportionality test, protecting against redundant or disproportionate

---

[2]MANUAL FOR COMPLEX LITIGATION FOURTH § 11.423 (Footnotes omitted).

discovery.[1] In 2010, the Sedona Conference issued *Commentary on Proportionality in Electronic Discovery* suggesting several principles intended on controlling costs associated with e-discovery.

1. **The burdens and costs of preservation of potentially relevant information should be weighed against the potential value and uniqueness of the information when determining the appropriate scope of preservation.** ***Practitioner's Tip:*** This first principle provides a framework for the subsequent principles. It establishes the fact that both non-monetary and monetary factors should be considered when determining whether, and how, potentially relevant information sources should be preserved. It is important to note that *most* sources of potentially responsive information can be successfully preserved in a variety of ways; some more "burdensome" or costly than others. If there is any question as to the value of an information sources, counsel for the requesting party should try to establish why the sources should be preserved (only source, minimal cost, damage to their client if the information is not preserved, etc.). Actual scope of searching and producing from such source can be determined separate from the question of whether the source should be preserved.
2. **Discovery should generally be obtained from the most convenient, least burdensome, and least expensive sources.** ***Practitioner's Tip:*** A note of caution to practitioners: not all sources of information are equal. Email from a user's computer may not be the same as email from the company's email server or from a third party email

[Section 10:4]

[1]See, e.g., McNally Tunneling Corp. v. City of Evanston, Illinois, 2001 WL 1568879 (N.D. Ill. 2001) (where responding party had already provided requesting party with all the information contained in its computer files in hard copy-form, requesting party has burden of establishing that the hard copies of the computer are insufficient). But see Public Citizen v. Carlin, 2 F. Supp. 2d 1, 13 (D.D.C. 1997), rev'd on other grounds, 184 F.3d 900 (D.C. Cir. 1999) (while exact duplicate of particular record might be discardable, electronic versions of records cannot categorically be regarded as valueless "extra copies" of paper versions). See Sedona Principle 2 ("When balancing the cost, burden, and need for electronically stored information, courts and parties should apply the proportionality standard embodied in Fed. R. Civ. P. 26(b)(2)(C) and its state equivalents, which require consideration of the technological feasibility and realistic costs of preserving, retrieving, reviewing, and producing electronically stored information, as well as the nature of the litigation and the amount in controversy.").

host. Counsel must understand how the custodian creates, uses, stores and archives data to make a proper determination of the "best" source of electronically stored information.

3. **Undue burden, expense, or delay resulting from a party's action or inaction should be weighed against that party.** ***Practitioner's Tip:*** Early, informed attention by counsel to their client's sources of electronically stored information will help avoid "mistakes".
4. **Extrinsic information and sampling may assist in the analysis of whether requested discovery is sufficiently important to warrant the potential burden or expense of its production.** ***Practitioner's Tip:*** Sampling or the use of early case assessment tools can provide an excellent assessment of how to approach the production of certain forms of data. This iterative approach can help inform and direct discovery to minimize unnecessary costs.
5. **Nonmonetary factors should be considered when evaluating the burdens and benefits of discovery.** ***Practitioner's Tip:*** Attorney review time and delay are examples of additional factors that should be considered when crafting a discovery plan.
6. **Technologies to reduce cost and burden should be considered in the proportionality analysis.** ***Practitioner's Tip:*** Every day, there are new technological improvements to help facilitate the discovery process. These tools can help organize, search, analyze and identify potentially relevant information. In certain situations, the adverse parties may both benefit from utilizing shared technology to complete discovery.[2]

It is important to note that the proportionality test is not limited to sources that are claimed to be "not reasonable accessible" under Fed. R. Civ. P. 26(B)(2)(b). On the contrary, proportionality factors apply to any source of electronically stored information.[3] Increasingly local rules encourage the application of

[2]See *The Sedona Conference Commentary on Proportionality in Electronic Discovery*, 11 Sedona Conf. J. 289 (2010), at https://thesedonaconference.org/publication/The%20Sedona%20Conference%20Commentary%20on%20Proportionality.

[3]See Fed. R. Civ. P. 26, Committee Note to 2006 amendment of Fed. R. Civ. P. 26 (b)(2)(2006) ("The limitations apply to all discovery apply to all discovery of electronically stored information, including that stored on reasonably accessible electronic sources.").

proportionality principles.[4] An attorney that is well informed about the sources of potentially relevant information will be best positioned to negotiate limitations (or expansions) on the proportionality factors based on their ability to contextualize the factors. Typically, the use of a phased discovery approach may serve to utilize the principles of proportionality, and thus limit costs while balancing the need to obtain complete disclosure and discovery.

There is some question as to whether the principles of proportionality impact a party's obligation of preservation. Often times, the issue of cost burden associated with preservation of a source of data is much different than the cost burden of actually producing from such data source. It is best to err on the side of preservation and thus avoid a potential spoliation issue.

§ 10:5 Cost savings through cooperative approach to discovery

The costs associated with adversarial conduct in pretrial discovery have become a serious burden. This burden rises significantly in discovery of electronically stored information. According to the Sedona Conference, e-discovery has resulted in escalating motion practice, overreaching, obstruction, and extensive, but unproductive discovery disputes.[1]

A cooperative approach to e-discovery may save all parties time and money.[2] In response to this problem, the Sedona Conference has launched a drive to promote open and forthright information sharing, dialogue (internal and external), training, and the development of practical tools to facilitate cooperative, collaborative, transparent discovery.

In 2008, the Sedona Conference issued THE SEDONA CONFERENCE COOPERATION PROCLAMATION—statement declaring that

---

[4]See e.g. Seventh Circuit Electronic Discovery Pilot Program, Proposed Standing Order Relating to the Discovery of Electronically Stored Information, Section 1.03 ("The proportionality standard set forth in Fed. R. Civ. P. 26(b)(2)(C) should be applied in each case when formulating a discovery plan. To further the application of the proportionality standard in discovery, requests for production of ESI and related responses should be reasonably targeted, clear, and as specific as practicable.").

[Section 10:5]

[1]http://www.thesedonaconference.org/contents/tsc_cooperation_proclamation/proclamation.pdf. See also Jordan, *Zealous Advocacy Balanced Against Collaborative Discovery*, LITIGATION NEWS, Feb. 4, 2013.

[2]See Tadler & Withers, *Towards a Less Hostile Discovery Process*, Trial, Mar. 2010, at 30.

adversarial discovery represents a serious burden to the American judicial system and launching a national drive to promote the development of practical tools to facilitate cooperative, collaborative, transparent discovery.[3] Subsequent publications from the Sedona Conference offer guidelines and tools for litigators seeking to participate in a cooperative approach to discovery of electronically stored information.[4]

The Sedona Conference suggests that methods to accomplish cooperation include:

1. Utilizing internal electronically stored information discovery "point persons" to assist counsel in preparing requests and responses;
2. Exchanging information on relevant data sources, including those not being searched, or scheduling early disclosures on the topic of electronically stored information;
3. Jointly developing automated search and retrieval methodologies to cull relevant information;
4. Promoting early identification of form or forms of production;
5. Developing case long discovery budgets based on proportionality principles; and
6. Considering court appointed experts, volunteer mediators, or formal ADR programs to resolve discovery disputes.[5]

The Sedona Conference acknowledges it is unrealistic to expect an outbreak of pretrial discovery cooperation. However, the Sedona Conference suggests a three-part process to increase cooperation:

Part I: Awareness.	Promoting awareness of the need and advantages of cooperation, coupled with a call to action.

---

[3]http://www.thesedonaconference.org/contents/tsc_cooperation_proclamation/proclamation.pdf.

[4]See, e.g., http://www.thesedonaconference.org/dltForm?did=Cooperation_Guidance_for_Litigators_and_In_House_Counsel.pdf.

[5]http://www.thesedonaconference.org/contents/tsc_cooperation_proclamation/proclamation.pdf.

Part II: Commitment.	Developing a detailed understanding and full articulation of the issues and changes needed to obtain cooperative fact finding.
Part III: Tools.	Developing and distributing practical "toolkits" to train and support lawyers, judges, other professionals, and students in techniques of discovery cooperation, collaboration, and transparency.[6]

Asserting that the cooperative project is not utopian, the Sedona Conference declares it is a tailored effort to effectuate the mandate of court rules calling for a "just, speedy, and inexpensive determination of every action"[7] and the fundamental ethical principles governing our profession.

Whether advocates, such as those representing employees with limited discoverable electronically stored information, will embrace the cooperative approach remains to be seen.[8] Nonetheless, it is a significant attempt to do something about the rapidly escalating costs of civil litigation—in particular the costs of discovery of electronically stored information. The alternative to this cooperative approach could be a rapid escalation in the burdensome costs of civil discovery.

§ 10:6 Types of discoverable electronically stored information

Electronically stored information includes anything created, generated or stored in digital or electronic form. Electronically stored information readily available and accessible from computers is called "active data." Active data may exist in the form of

---

[6]http://www.thesedonaconference.org/contents/tsc_cooperation_proclamation/proclamation.pdf.

[7]Fed. R. Civ. P. 1. See http://www.thesedonaconference.org/contents/tsc_cooperation_proclamation/proclamation.pdf.

[8]See descriptions of the pitfalls of overaggressive approaches to e-discovery in Sterle v. Elizabeth Arden, Inc., 2008 WL 961216 (D. Conn. 2008); Treppel v. Biovail Corp., 249 F.R.D. 111 (S.D. N.Y. 2008); Perfect Barrier LLC v. Woodsmart Solutions Inc., 2008 WL 2230192 (N.D. Ind. 2008).

e-mail messages, word processing documents, spreadsheets, databases, or calendars. In most cases, active data is the focus of discovery requests. Unless privileged, this information is normally discoverable.

Active data is not the only electronic information that is discoverable. The following is a non-comprehensive list of various types of discoverable electronically stored information.

1. E-mail and e-mail attachments
2. Word processing documents
3. Spreadsheets
4. Structured data sources (databases)
5. Web sites
6. Voicemail
7. Surveillance systems
8. Customer support recordings
9. Computer aided design (CAD) systems
10. Social networking data (posts, tweets, etc.)
11. Deleted information
12. Metadata
13. Ephemeral data (document versions, temporary files, etc.)

If may seem counterintuitive that "deleted" information is discoverable. However, the typical deletion of information on a computer merely removes the pointer or index to the file. The location of the data is no longer reserved, and can be overwritten by subsequent files that are created. It may take some time to overwrite the space containing the deleted information. The deleted electronically stored information is invisible to the ordinary user system administrator, but a computer forensic expert may be able to recover parts of the document that have not yet been overwritten. Practitioners should understand the potential relevance of deleted information and how such information may relate to the merits of the underlying legal action. Deleted information can often support claims of possession or information theft, intent of a party or fraudulent activity.

Electronically stored information also includes information on publicly available social media and Websites. Because these sources of information are often controlled by a third party and may be difficult to preserve, a discovering party should be aware of all publicly available information at the earliest possible moment. Social networking sites such as Facebook, Twitter, MySpace, Linkedin, and YouTube, as well as blogs and chatrooms can be important sources of discoverable information. An increasing number of individuals and organizations are making use of cloud-based or software-as-a-service (SaaS) applications (e.g., gMail, Google!Apps, Dropbox).

§ 10:7 Discovery plan

There are a number of steps enhancing the probability of uncovering relevant electronically stored information and forcing its discovery without breaking the bank. The following are some suggested steps a requesting party's attorney may consider:

- **Send a preservation letter to the opposing party.** Send a letter before or immediately after a lawsuit is commenced, demanding all electronically stored information be segregated and preserved. If there is reason to believe it will not be done, seek a protective order. A preservation letter to opposing party is not required, but it is a useful tool to ensure the opposing party is on notice as to the type of information that should be preserved. The letter should be specifically tailored to the present action so as to explain the sources of electronically stored information believed to be relevant to the case. ***Practitioner's Tip:*** the goal of the preservation letter is not to simply provide a laundry list of demands. The letter should be tailored to address the preservation of sources of potentially responsive information based on the merits of the case.
- **Preserve information you can access.** Consider the sources of information for which you have access. Preserve evidence existing on any Website by downloading its contents before the lawsuit is commenced. In a shared computer setting (e.g., marital, business partner), seek to preserve the information rather than rely on the responding party.
- **Utilize interrogatories.** Early in a lawsuit, serve interrogatories seeking information about the other party's computer systems. These interrogatories should seek to identify sources of potentially relevant electronically stored information. Also inquire which software programs and operating systems are being used by the party (including all of the technical specifications). Avoid using a cookie-cutter list of interrogatories that seeks all technology information about the opposing party. The goal is to identify those sources of information that are relevant to the subject case.
- **Consider Fed. R. Civ. P. 30(b)(6) depositions.** Learn who does the computer work for a party (e.g., its chief technology officer, chief information officer, management information system or information system administrators) by

use of interrogatories or through a deposition. After discovering who did or does the computer work for a party, depose those individuals. If possible, use these people to start to assemble a map of an adversary's computing infrastructure (servers, operating systems, databases, web servers, applications). If custom software is relevant, it may be useful to identify the persons (e.g., employees or consultants) who created it and may have knowledge of data sources, flows, storage, and replicas.

- **Serve narrowly tailored interrogatories based on information gathered.** Serve a second set of interrogatories that seeks disclosure of facts and evidence, and include in that set a separate section that specifically seeks disclosure of relevant digital evidence. When seeking discovery of electronically stored information, ask that any electronically stored information be provided just as it exists in the computer systems of the responding party. This may occasion a number of battles relating to format, metadata,[1] privilege, convenience, and cost. It may be necessary to postpone insisting on productions in native format until after reviewing what the other party is willing to give without a battle. However, in the best of all worlds, insist that electronically stored information be provided in the native digital format if at all possible, instead of just accepting hardcopies, PDFs, or TIFFs.
- **Seek a common data format.** It is likely that the responding party will need to process and review data in some electronic platform. In doing so, the responding party will extract metadata and searchable text from the data and collect this data in to a database. While some practitioners encourage a "native always" approach to receiving data, the option of exchanging pre-processed data can result in a significant cost savings to both parties. Electronically stored information that is provided in PDF or TIFF format is a good start (and will provide a good deal of flexibility in dealing with digital evidence), if it is organized and labeled so that it can be imported into a text and file indexer, such as the DT-Search indexer. When electronically stored information

[Section 10:7]

[1]See Barsocchini, *Developing E-Discovery Processes that Operate Without Altering Metadata,* 78 U.S.L.W. 2135 (Sept. 18, 2009); Wiener & Celeita, *Computer Infections Are Bad Enough, but the Cure Can Kill: Anti-Virus Software Can Contaminate Evidence, Even When the Intent Is Innocent,* NAT'L L.J., Aug. 24, 2009, at 17.

is received in PDF or TIFF formats with a load file, it is necessary to review it quickly in order to determine: (1) if it is responsive to the discovery requests; and (2) necessary text and metadata has been provided that will enable meaningful indexing.

- **Consider the importance of metadata and native files.** In some cases, the production of flat image files (TIFF) is not enough, even if it contains a load file with extracted metadata and text. Certain files necessitate the exchange of native files to fully assess the relevance of a document. Spreadsheet (including Microsoft Excel) files are an example of a file that should be provided in native format. It is difficult to understand the formatting, formulas and interaction of cells and tables in a spreadsheet without looking at the native file. If the native files are not exchanged in the first instance, it is highly recommended that a protocol be established to request and produce native files. Production of native files is typically the least burdensome for the responding party because no processing is required to exchange the files.
- **Consider using an expert to review information.** If there is reason to believe that significant electronically stored information exists that is being withheld or has been deleted or manipulated, consider retaining the services of a forensic computer expert to assist in pursuing more discovery.
- **Consider inspection of systems.** It may be necessary in a complex case, or a situation that involves proprietary configurations to seek onsite inspection of the responding party's computer system and, possibly, the appointment of a special master or court-appointed expert witnesses who can independently inspect the responding party's system.

§ 10:8 Discovering who does computer work

Counsel should seek to learn who does the computer work for the responding party (e.g., its management information system or information system employees and software/systems consultants hired to develop and maintain in-house systems) by using interrogatories or depositions. It should not be assumed that the chief information officer (CIO) or department head is the most knowledgeable about the storage of electronically stored information in a company database or e-mail system; it may be a relatively low level administrator.

After discovering who did, or does, the computer work for a

responding party, the discovering party's counsel should depose those individuals. In a larger enterprise it may not be a single individual, but rather a different person for email, file servers, desktop computers, and archive systems.

One should not overlook the fact a former employee may know a great deal and may have also separated on less than amicable terms from an organization. Such person may be a willing source of valuable information concerning the electronically stored information of a producing party.

§ 10:9 Initial disclosures

In federal court, the parties are required to disclose the description and location of relevant electronically stored information before a discovery request is submitted.[1] This imposes on the parties a duty to identify all sources and locations of electronically stored information.[2] Fed. R. Civ. P. 26(a)(2) also requires the parties to disclose the identities of their e-discovery or forensic experts if they will be called at trial. After disclosure, more detailed information can be obtained by using traditional discovery tools such as interrogatories, depositions, and requests for production.

In *Kleiner v. Burns*,[3] the plaintiff moved to compel Yahoo! "to disclose all voice mail, electronic mail (email or e-mail), Websites, web pages, and other digital data relevant to the above action." Relying on Fed. R. Civ. P. 26(a)(1)(B), the court ordered Yahoo! to disclose all data compilations in its possession, custody and control relevant to disputed facts alleged with particularity in the pleadings. The court went on to say that, under Fed. R. Civ. P. 26(a)(1)(B), disclosures should

> describe and categorize to the extent identified during the initial investigation, the nature and location of potentially relevant documents and records, including computerized data and other electronically-recorded information, sufficiently to enable opposing parties (1) to make an informed decision concerning which documents might need to be examined, at least, initially, and (2) to

---

[Section 10:9]

[1]See Fed. R. Civ. P. 26(a)(1)(B), requiring initial disclosure of "a copy of, or a description by category and location of all documents, electronically stored information, and tangible things that are in the possession, custody, or control of the party . . .."

[2]See Kleiner v. Burns, 48 Fed. R. Serv. 3d 644 (D. Kan. 2000).

[3]Kleiner v. Burns, 48 Fed. R. Serv. 3d 644 (D. Kan. 2000).

frame their document requests in a manner likely to avoid squabbles resulting from the words of the requests.[4]

The court held that computerized data and other digitally-recorded information

> includes, but is not limited to: voice mail messages and files, backup voice mail files, e-mail messages and files, backup e-mail files, deleted e-mails, data files, program files, backup and archival tapes, temporary files, system history files, website information stored in textual, graphical or audio format, website log files, cache files, cookies, and other electronically-recorded information.[5]

§ 10:10 Seeking expert assistance

Parties are often forced to litigate on a limited budget, and thus are tempted to forego technical assistance unless it is absolutely necessary. Many times the focus is placed on the experts needed for trial. Parties assume they can obtain enough evidence during discovery to provide those experts the information they require. When it comes to discovery of electronically stored information, this can be a very costly mistake.[1]

The expert can participate in meetings with the responding party's information technology staff, write memoranda educating the court about technology issues, and testify at hearings as to the need for electronically stored information. Using an expert may pay dividends when the responding party resists production. The expert can save hours that would otherwise be spent in depositions and preparation to understand the technology and where to find the electronically stored information.

The ideal way to find expert assistance is to seek referrals from trusted sources. It is important to review the credentials and background of the specific individual who will work on the case. If an expert is likely to be called as a witness, consideration should be given to the expert's communication skills. The expert should be an individual who can be trusted to carefully gather, search, and analyze the data. The expert must know how to safeguard evidence and document a chain of custody.

---

[4]Kleiner v. Burns, 48 Fed. R. Serv. 3d 644 (D. Kan. 2000). See also Theofel v. Farey-Jones, 359 F.3d 1066, 1078–79 (9th Cir. 2004) (overbroad e-mail subpoena exposed lawyer and client to liability).

[5]See Kleiner v. Burns, 48 Fed. R. Serv. 3d 644 (D. Kan. 2000).

[Section 10:10]

[1]See Ball, *When Do-It-Yourself e-Discovery Isn't Enough*, TRIAL, Jan. 2009, at 24.

II. CHECKLISTS

§ 10:11 Checklist for approaching discovery of electronically stored information

☐ **Make sure the party you represent has initiated a legal hold of sources of potentially responsive information consistent with the client's retention or destruction policies.** Often overlooked, a party contemplating the initiation of litigation should ensure sources of relevant information have been preserved adequately. Ideally, such preservation should be consistent with a clear, written and transparent retention policy. Unfortunately, not all clients rely on such policies to manage their electronic resources.

☐ **Raise issues relating to the preservation and production of electronically stored information immediately with opposing counsel.** Counsel should confer early and often about the preservation and production of electronically stored information. Those conferences should begin as soon as the parties anticipate that litigation may ensue. It is becoming increasingly common to raise these issues during the first notification of dispute. For example, a notice of claim or cease and desist letter may also notice the opposing party that a records should be preserved related to the dispute. From the discovering party's standpoint, it is critical that these discussions take place to make sure that no relevant data are destroyed. From the responding party's standpoint, it is critical that these discussions take place to minimize the possibility that sanctions may later be imposed and also to facilitate a focused and proportional preservation and production.

☐ **Make sure that preservation and production issues are part of the discovery conference agenda.** The discovery conference is an appropriate time to finalize any issues relating to the preservation and production of digital materials. Practitioners are well served to have as much information as possible about their client's sources of electronically stored information at such conference. Agreeing to preservation or production protocols without full knowledge of the implications on the client can be disastrous. Parties should be prepared to disclose and discuss sources of information that will and will not be subject to discovery. Issues that cannot be resolved can then be presented to the court at the scheduling conference.

☐ **The goal should be to resolve preservation and pro-**

duction issues without the court's intervention. If the court's help is needed in resolving preservation and production issues, it should be sought immediately. As with all other types of discovery disputes, the parties should do everything that they can to resolve discovery disputes without the necessity for court intervention. This is particularly true when the issues involve discovery of electronically stored information. The parties and their counsel are in the best position to resolve issues about preservation and production. However, if they must seek court intervention, delay is fatal. If there is a problem a party should seek immediate intervention. If a problem still exists at the time of the scheduling conference, a party should make sure that the issue is raised at that time.

- ☐ **Help the court resolve preservation and production issues.** Most courts will not be as conversant with technology issues as the parties and their counsel. The parties should do everything possible to educate the court and to help the court understand the discovery of electronically stored information issues. If expert testimony is presented, it is important to make sure the testimony is in understandable and useful form.
- ☐ **Use a focused discovery approach and be ready to justify your requests.** "Fishing expeditions" in the area of electronically stored information are doomed to failure, often for all parties involved. Obtaining excessive amounts of data from opposing party is not advantageous unless there is some relevance to the information. Doing so simply raises the costs of production and review. The approach to the discovery of electronically stored information must be focused. The discovering party must also be able to support its discovery requests with more than conjecture.
- ☐ **All things being equal, documents should be requested in digital form.** No rule fits absolutely in every situation. Generally, however, it makes sense to request electronically stored information in digital form. Electronically stored information in that form will generally allow for efficient search and review, and provide more useful information than the same data in paper format.
- ☐ **Counsel must rigorously communicate with their clients, particularly with the computer systems people.** It is essential that there be good communication between in house counsel, retained counsel and the systems technology people. It is essential that the lawyer comprehend the clients' computer systems and their document destruc-

tion and retention policies and practices. Bad things will happen to the lawyer and the client if the lawyer does fully understand the sources of potentially relevant ESI and the potential volatility of such information.

- ☐ **Communicate with opposing counsel and the court.** The key to successful resolution of preservation and production issues involving electronically stored information in digital form is communication—communication with opposing counsel to resolve issues and, where court intervention is necessary, communication with the court. The communication must be candid. Far too often a "head-in-the sand" or "hide-the-ball" approach to e-discovery has resulted in unnecessary costs and delay. Sanctions have often been imposed because counsel was not candid with the court and opposing counsel until it was too late. Zealous advocacy need not be adversarial.
- ☐ **Be reasonable.** More so than with any other area of discovery, the court is looking for reasonableness on both sides. On the discovering party's side, the court wants reasonable and focused discovery requests. On the responding party's side, the court expects a reasonable approach to the preservation and production of digital documents. The court also expects the parties to create reasonable solutions.
- ☐ **Consider phased discovery**. A phased approach to e-discovery that includes testing and sampling can be helpful in eliminating nonresponsive sources of information and focusing subsequent searches for information.

§ 10:12 Checklist for subjects to be explored during discovery

Note that these issues should be addressed both for your own client and in formulating requests to opposing counsel.

1. Communications

- ☐ Is e-mail used?
- ☐ What e-mail system is used?
- ☐ Are e-mail messages stored locally (on a personal computer) or on a server?
- ☐ Is e-mail accessible via smart phone or mobile devices?
- ☐ Who has access to the specific custodial email (assistants, secretaries, IT staff, etc.)?
- ☐ How and where is e-mail archived (user archives/PSTs, backup, etc.)?
- ☐ How long are e-mail messages retained?

- ☐ Does an e-email journaling system exist?
- ☐ Is SMS/text messaging used? If so, from what devices, and how is it stored and managed?
- ☐ Are any other integrated messaging services used (fax by email, voicemail, chat logs)?

2. User Files

- ☐ What computer applications are used to create user content? (i.e. Microsoft Word)
- ☐ Is a document management system used to store/manage user created documents?
- ☐ Where do users store documents (locally, private network storage, public network shares, Sharepoint, etc.)?
- ☐ How are documents categorized, organized and saved?
- ☐ From what locations can a user access user files?
- ☐ Do any network logs monitor access to user files?

3. **Employee Use Issues**

- ☐ Do employees use computers at work?
- ☐ Do employees use computers remotely? If so, how do they access the network (via firewall, terminal services, etc.)?
- ☐ Do employees use laptops?
- ☐ Do employees use personal digital assistants?
- ☐ Is the equipment owned by the responding party and returned when employees leave the job?
- ☐ Do employees store documents on network drives or on local hard drives?
- ☐ Do employees use removable media (e.g., thumb drives or USB drives)?
- ☐ Do employees use file/system encryption?
- ☐ Aside from normal "user files" what applications do users access to create content? This may include database applications, electronic resource planning systems, time/attendance systems, customer relationship systems, content management systems, etc.
- ☐ Who manages corporate applications identified above?
- ☐ Are there any policies that govern employee computer use?

4. **Overall Information Technology Infrastructure Issues**

- ☐ What is the general network configuration (type, size, location)?
- ☐ How is the network managed and by whom?

- ☐ Are computer and server network logs maintained?
- ☐ What is the archiving procedure?
- ☐ How often does the responding party backup data?
- ☐ How is such information indexed?

5. **Record Management Issues**
   - ☐ Is there a records and information management program?
   - ☐ What are the responding party's policies for document retention and encryption?
   - ☐ How is such information indexed and maintained?
   - ☐ What record retention policies are implicated by the legal hold?
   - ☐ How is hardware deployed/replaced?
6. **Third-Party Data**
   - ☐ What third-party services are used?
   - ☐ Who maintains web content/web logs?
   - ☐ What social media services are used (formally and informally)?
   - ☐ Have third-party providers been put on notice?

§ 10:13 Discovery checklist

- ☐ Request that the electronically stored information be submitted in computer-readable form, allowing for complete key word searches to locate relevant information and to reformat the information in a preferred form, such as a table or list.
- ☐ Determine how the costs for obtaining and handling the electronically stored information will be borne.
- ☐ Discuss with opposing counsel the sharing of costs.
- ☐ Identify potentially relevant electronically stored information and in what format it might be stored, such as e-mail, graphics files, or word processing files.
- ☐ Determine the discovery methods to use to discover electronically stored information, such as interrogatories, depositions, and requests for documents.
- ☐ Discuss with a computer expert technology issues such as the framing of discovery questions, the specific computer systems involved in the litigation, and the potential need for computer forensics assistance to recover electronically stored information.
- ☐ Consult with another computer expert who may act as a witness at trial.
- ☐ Consider obtaining a protective order for certain electroni-

cally stored information, such as information that contains trade secrets or is computer source code.

☐ Use discovery to obtain information on the computer system used by the opposing party, including the type of hardware, operating systems, and applications used.

☐ Determine how counsel will process and use the electronically stored information that is discovered. Processing may involve searching through the information; use of the information may involve the production of trial exhibits

NOTES

Commentary

This is a checklist of considerations to be addressed by the practitioner planning the discovery of electronically stored information. These items are useful in the formulation of discovery requests, such as interrogatories.

§ 10:14 Checklist for drafting discovery requests

☐ **Correct Names.** Make sure that to identify correctly every named entity in discovery requests and responses. Include full formal names of companies, as well as subsidiary and parent companies and d.b.a. identities, agent for process of service, company logos and brand names and locations of business activity. Computer on-line database searches are excellent for researching this type of information.

☐ **Definitions.** Use definitions for precise identification. Define the first reference of a party, location or other often repeated item as you would in drafting a contract. Check local rules on using definitions.

☐ **Precision Wording.** Be precise in defining an item or witness or conversation in a discovery request. Identify the item precisely or frame the question in such a way that the opposition will be forced to answer in a precise and focused manner.

☐ **Include Time Element.** Pinpoint specifics by including a time element if appropriate. Business records may be from a certain span of years before and after the alleged actions occurred. Organization policies should be those in effect at the time of the actionable event; and requesting previous and later policies may reveal important information about how the organization reacted to the situation that gave rise to the action. Identify meetings and events by date.

☐ **Location.** Attempt to establish the location and current possessor of any documents, including electronically stored information, or other items of evidence.

☐ **Request Additional Discovery Target Information.** If

you are following up on an interrogatory, take particular care to request the names of individuals who helped opposing counsel respond to an interrogatory as well as the reference materials used in drafting the interrogatory responses. This will often expose the existence of unsuspected discovery targets.

- ☐ **Number of Questions.** Do not ask too many questions. The number of interrogatories is limited in many jurisdictions.
- ☐ **Eliminate Vague Wording.** Eliminate vagueness from questions.

III. FORMS

§ 10:15 Guidelines for discovery of electronically stored information

General Principles

Principle 1.01 (Purpose)

The purpose of these Principles is to assist courts in the administration of Fed. R. Civ. P. 1, to secure the just, speedy, and inexpensive determination of every civil case, and to promote, whenever possible, the early resolution of disputes regarding the discovery of electronically stored information ("ESI") without court intervention. Understanding of the feasibility, reasonableness, costs, and benefits of various aspects of e-discovery will inevitably evolve as judges, attorneys and parties to litigation gain more experience with ESI and as technology advances.

Principle 1.02 (Cooperation)

An attorney's zealous representation of a client is not compromised by conducting discovery in a cooperative manner. The failure of counsel or the parties to litigation to cooperate in facilitating and reasonably limiting discovery requests and responses raises litigation costs and contributes to the risk of sanctions.

Principle 1.03 (Discovery Proportionality)

The proportionality standard set forth in Fed. R. Civ. P. 26(b)(2)(C) should be applied in each case when formulating a discovery plan. To further the application of the proportionality standard in discovery, requests for production of ESI and related responses should be reasonably targeted, clear, and as specific as practicable.

Early Case Assessment Principles

Principle 2.01 (Duty to Meet and Confer on Discovery and to Identify Disputes for Early Resolution)

(a) Prior to the initial status conference with the court, counsel shall meet and discuss the application of the discovery process set forth in the Federal Rules of Civil Procedure and these Principles to their specific case. Among the issues to be discussed are:

(1) the identification of relevant and discoverable ESI and documents, including methods for identifying an initial subset of sources of ESI and documents that are most likely to contain the relevant and discoverable information as well as methodologies for culling the relevant and discoverable ESI and documents from that initial subset (see Principle 2.05);

(2) the scope of discoverable ESI and documents to be preserved by the parties;

(3) the formats for preservation and production of ESI and documents;

(4) the potential for conducting discovery in phases or stages as a method for reducing costs and burden; and

(5) the potential need for a protective order and any procedures to which the parties might agree for handling inadvertent production of privileged information and other privilege waiver issues pursuant to Rule 502(d) or (e) of the Federal Rules of Evidence.

(b) Disputes regarding ESI that counsel for the parties are unable to resolve shall be presented to the court at the initial status conference, Fed. R. Civ. P. Rule 16(b) Scheduling Conference, or as soon as possible thereafter.

(c) The attorneys for each party shall review and understand how their client's data is stored and retrieved before the meet and confer discussions in order to determine what issues must be addressed during the meet and confer discussions.

(d) If the court determines that any counsel or party in a case has failed to cooperate and participate in good faith in the meet and confer process or is impeding the purpose of these Principles, the court may require additional discussions prior to the commencement of discovery, and may impose sanctions, if appropriate.

Principle 2.02 (E-Discovery Liaison(s))

In most cases, the meet and confer process will be aided by participation of an e-discovery liaison(s) as defined in this Principle. In the event of a dispute concerning the preservation or production of ESI, each party shall designate an individual(s) to act as e-discovery liaison(s) for purposes of meeting, conferring, and attending court hearings on the subject. Regardless of whether the e-discovery liaison(s) is an attorney (in-house or outside counsel), a third party consultant, or an employee of the party, the e-discovery liaison(s) must:

(a) be prepared to participate in e-discovery dispute resolution;
(b) be knowledgeable about the party's e-discovery efforts;
(c) be, or have reasonable access to those who are, familiar with the party's electronic systems and capabilities in order to explain those systems and answer relevant questions; and
(d) be, or have reasonable access to those who are, knowledgeable about the technical aspects of e-discovery, including electronic document storage, organization, and format issues, and relevant information retrieval technology, including search methodology.

Principle 2.03 (Preservation Requests and Orders)

(a) Appropriate preservation requests and preservation orders further the goals of these Principles. Vague and overly broad preservation requests do not further the goals of these Principles and are therefore disfavored. Vague and overly broad preservation orders should not be sought or entered. The information sought to be preserved through the use of a preservation letter request or order should be reasonable in scope and mindful of the factors set forth in Fed. R. Civ. P. 26(b)(2)(C).
(b) To the extent counsel or a party requests preservation of ESI through the use of a preservation letter, such requests should attempt to ensure the preservation of relevant and discoverable information and to facilitate cooperation between requesting and receiving counsel and parties by transmitting specific and useful information. Examples of such specific and useful information include, but are not limited to:
  (1) names of the parties;
  (2) factual background of the potential legal claim(s) and identification of potential cause(s) of action;
  (3) names of potential witnesses and other people reasonably anticipated to have relevant evidence;
  (4) relevant time period; and
  (5) other information that may assist the responding party in assessing what information to preserve.
(c) If the recipient of a preservation request chooses to respond, that response should provide the requesting counsel or party with useful information regarding the preservation efforts undertaken by the responding party. Examples of such useful

and specific information include, but are not limited to, information that:

(1) identifies what information the responding party is willing to preserve and the steps being taken in response to the preservation letter;

(2) identifies any disagreement(s) with the request to preserve; and

(3) identifies any further preservation issues that were not raised.

(d) Nothing in these Principles shall be construed as requiring the sending of a preservation request or requiring the sending of a response to such a request.

Principle 2.04 (Scope of Preservation)

(a) Every party to litigation and its counsel are responsible for taking reasonable and proportionate steps to preserve relevant and discoverable ESI within its possession, custody or control. Determining which steps are reasonable and proportionate in particular litigation is a fact specific inquiry that will vary from case to case. The parties and counsel should address preservation issues at the outset of a case, and should continue to address them as the case progresses and their understanding of the issues and the facts improves.

(b) Discovery concerning the preservation and collection efforts of another party may be appropriate but, if used unadvisedly, can also contribute to the unnecessary expense and delay and may inappropriately implicate work product and attorney-client privileged matter. Accordingly, prior to initiating such discovery a party shall confer with the party from whom the information is sought concerning: (i) the specific need for such discovery, including its relevance to issues likely to arise in the litigation; and (ii) the suitability of alternative means for obtaining the information. Nothing herein exempts deponents on merits issues from answering questions concerning the preservation and collection of their documents, ESI, and tangible things.

(c) The parties and counsel should come to the meet and confer conference prepared to discuss the claims and defenses in the case including specific issues, time frame, potential damages, and targeted discovery that each anticipates requesting. In addition, the parties and counsel should be prepared to discuss reasonably foreseeable preservation issues that relate directly to the information that the other party is seeking. The parties and counsel need not raise every conceivable issue that may arise concerning their preservation efforts; however, the identification of any such preservation issues should be specific.

(d) The following categories of ESI generally are not discoverable in most cases, and if any party intends to request the preservation or production of these categories, then that intention should be discussed at the meet and confer or as soon thereafter as practicable:
  (1) deleted slack, and fragmented, or unallocated data on hard drives;
  (2) random access memory (RAM) or other ephemeral data;
  (3) on-line access data such as temporary Internet files, history, cache, cookies;
  (4) data in metadata fields that are frequently updated automatically, such as last-opened dates;
  (5) backup data that is substantially duplicative of data that is more accessible elsewhere; and
  (6) other forms of ESI whose preservation requires extraordinary affirmative measures that are not utilized in the ordinary course of business.

(e) If there is a dispute concerning the scope of a party's preservation efforts, the parties or their counsel must meet and confer and fully explain their reasons for believing that additional efforts are, or are not, reasonable and proportionate, pursuant to Fed. R. Civ. P. 26(b)(2)(C). If the parties are unable to resolve a preservation issue, then the issue should be raised promptly with the court.

Principle 2.05 (Identification of Electronically Stored Information)

(a) At the Fed. R. Civ. P. 26(f) conference or as soon thereafter as possible, counsel or the parties shall discuss potential methodologies for identifying ESI for production.

(b) Topics for discussion may include, but are not limited to, any plans to:
  (1) eliminate duplicative ESI and whether such elimination will occur only within each particular custodian's data set or whether it will occur across all custodians;
  (2) filter data based on file type, date ranges, sender, receiver, custodian, search terms, or other similar parameters; and
  (3) use keyword searching, mathematical or thesaurus-based topic or concept clustering, or other advanced culling technologies.

Principle 2.06 (Production Format)

(a) At the Fed. R. Civ. P. 26(f) conference, counsel and the parties should make a good faith effort to agree on the format(s) for production of ESI (whether native or some other reasonably usable form). If counsel or the parties are unable to resolve a production format issue, then the issue should be raised promptly with the court.

(b) The parties should confer on whether ESI stored in a database or a database management system can be produced by querying the database for discoverable information, resulting in a report or a reasonably usable and exportable electronic file for review by the requesting counsel or party.

(c) ESI and other tangible or hard copy documents that are not text-searchable need not be made text-searchable.

(d) Generally, the requesting party is responsible for the incremental cost of creating its copy of requested information. Counsel or the parties are encouraged to discuss cost sharing for optical character recognition (OCR) or other upgrades of paper documents or nontext-searchable electronic images that may be contemplated by each party.

Education Provisions

Principle 3.01 (Judicial Expectations of Counsel)

Because discovery of ESI is being sought more frequently in civil litigation and the production and review of ESI can involve greater expense than discovery of paper documents, it is in the interest of justice that all judges, counsel and parties to litigation become familiar with the fundamentals of discovery of ESI. It is expected by the judges adopting these Principles that all counsel will have done the following in connection with each litigation matter in which they file an appearance:

(1) Familiarize themselves with the e-discovery provisions of Federal Rules of Civil Procedure, including Fed. R. Civ. P. 26, 33, 34, 37, and 45, as well as any applicable state rules of procedure;

(2) Familiarize themselves with the Advisory Committee Report on the 2006 Amendments to the Federal Rules of Civil Procedure, available at http://www.uscourts.gov/uscourts/RulesAndPolicies/rules/EDiscovery_w_Notes.pdf; and

(3) Familiarize themselves with these Principles.

Principle 3.02 (Duty of Continuing Education)

Judges, attorneys and parties to litigation should continue to educate themselves on e-discovery by consulting applicable case law, pertinent statutes, the Federal Rules of Civil Procedure, the Federal Rules of Evidence, The Sedona Conference® publications relating to e-discovery,[1] additional materials available on Web sites of the courts, and of other organizations[2] providing educational information regarding the discovery of electronically stored information.

NOTES TO FORM

Commentary

This form is adapted from Guidelines established by the Seventh Circuit Electronic Discovery Pilot Program.

§ 10:16 Default standard for discovery of electronically stored information

DEFAULT STANDARD FOR DISCOVERY OF ELECTRONICALLY STORED INFORMATION

1. Introduction. It is expected that parties to an action will cooperatively reach agreement on how to conduct e-discovery. In the event that such agreement has not been reached by the scheduling conference, however, the following default standards shall apply until such time, if ever, the parties conduct electronic discovery on a consensual basis.
2. Discovery conference. Parties must discuss the parameters of their anticipated electronic discovery at the discovery conference, as well as at the scheduling conference with the court, consistent with the concerns outlined below. More specifically, before the discovery conference, the parties must exchange the following information:
   a. A list of the most likely custodians of relevant electronically stored information, including a brief description of each person's title and responsibilities.
   b. A list of each relevant electronic system that has been in place at all relevant times and a general description of each system, including but not limited to the nature, scope, character, organization, and formats employed in each system. The parties should also discuss whether their electronically stored information is reasonably accessible. Electronically stored information that is not reasonably ac-

[Section 10:15]

[1]http://www.thesedonaconference.org/content/miscFiles/publicationshtml?grp=wgs110.

[2]E.g. http://www.discoverypilot.com, www.fjc.gov (under Educational Programs and Materials)

cessible may include information created or used by electronic media no longer in use, maintained in redundant electronic storage media, or for which retrieval involves undue burden or substantial cost.

c. The name of the individual responsible for retention and management of that party's electronically stored information ("the retention coordinator"), as well as a general description of that party's retention policies for the systems and information identified above.

d. The name of the individual who shall serve as that party's electronic discovery liaison.

e. Provide notice of any problems reasonably anticipated to arise in connection with e-discovery, e.g., email duplication.

To the extent that the state of the pleadings does not permit a meaningful discussion of the above by the time of the discovery conference, the parties must either agree on a date by which this information will be mutually exchanged or submit the issue for resolution by the court at the scheduling conference.

3. Electronic discovery liaison. In order to promote communication and cooperation between the parties, each party to a case must designate an e-discovery liaison through which all electronic discovery requests and responses shall be made ("e-discovery liaison"). Regardless of whether the electronic discovery liaison is an attorney (in-house or outside counsel), a third party consultant, or an employee of the party, the liaison must be:

a. Familiar with the party's electronic systems and capabilities in order to explain these systems and answer relevant questions.

b. Knowledgeable about the technical aspects of electronic discovery, including the storage, organization, and format issues relating to electronically stored information.

c. Prepared to participate in electronic discovery dispute resolution.

At all times, the attorneys of record are responsible for compliance with electronic discovery requests. However, the electronic discovery liaisons are responsible for organizing each party's e-discovery efforts to insure consistency and thoroughness and, generally, to facilitate the electronic discovery process.

4. Timing of electronic discovery. Discovery of electronically stored information shall proceed in a sequenced fashion.

a. After receiving requests for production, the parties must search their sources of electronically stored information, other than those identified as not reasonably accessible due to undue burden and/or substantial cost, and produce responsive electronic documents in accordance with *[rule]*.

b. Electronic searches of information identified as not reasonably accessible must not be conducted until the initial search has been completed. Requests for electronically stored information expected to be found in sources of limited accessibility must be narrowly focused with some basis in fact supporting the request.

c. Requests for on-site inspections of electronic media under *[rule]* shall be reviewed to determine where good cause and specific need have been demonstrated.

5. Search methodology. If the parties intend to employ an electronic search to locate relevant electronically stored information, the parties shall disclose any restrictions as to the scope and method which might affect their ability to conduct a complete electronic search of such information. The parties shall reach agreement as to the method of searching, and the words, terms, and phrases to be searched with the assistance of the respective e-discovery liaisons, who are charged with familiarity with the parties' respective systems. The parties also must reach agreement as to the timing and conditions of any additional searches that may become necessary in the normal course of discovery. To minimize the expense, the parties may consider limiting the scope of the electronic search (e.g., time frames, fields, document types).

6. Format. If, during the course of the discovery conference, the parties cannot agree to the format for production of their electronically stored information, such information must be produced to the requesting party as text searchable image files (e.g., PDF or TIFF), unless unduly burdensome or cost-prohibitive to do so. When text searchable image file is produced, the producing party must preserve the integrity of the electronically stored information, i.e., the original formatting, its metadata and, where applicable, the revision history. After initial production in text searchable image file format is complete, a party must demonstrate particularized need for production of electronically stored information in their native format.

7. Retention. Within the first 30 days of discovery, the parties should work towards an agreement outlining the steps each party will take to segregate and preserve the integrity of all relevant electronically stored information. In order to avoid later accusations of spoliation, a deposition of each party's retention coordinator may be appropriate.

The retention coordinators shall:

a. Take steps to ensure that e-mail of identified custodians is not permanently deleted in the ordinary course of business and that all other electronically stored information maintained by the individual custodians must not be altered.
b. Provide notice as to the criteria used for spam and/or virus filtering of e-mail and attachments; e-mails and attachments filtered out by such systems are deemed non-responsive so long as the criteria underlying the filtering are reasonable.

Within seven days of identifying the relevant custodians, the retention coordinators shall implement the above procedures and each party's counsel shall file a statement of compliance as such with the court.

8. Privilege. Electronically stored information containing privileged information or attorney work product must be immediately returned if the information appears on its face to have been inadvertently produced or if there is notice of the inadvertent production within 30 days of such notice.
9. Costs. Generally, the costs of discovery are borne by each party. However, the court may apportion the costs of electronic discovery upon a showing of good cause.
10. Discovery disputes and trial presentation. At this time, discovery disputes must be resolved and trial presentations conducted consistent with each individual judge's guidelines.

NOTES TO FORM

Commentary

This form is adapted from Guidelines used by the U.S. District Court for the District of Delaware.

§ 10:17 Protocol for discovery of electronically stored information

SUGGESTED PROTOCOL FOR DISCOVERY OF ELECTRONICALLY STORED INFORMATION

1. On December 1, 2006, amendments to Fed. R. Civ. P. 16, 26, 33, 34, 37, and 45, and Form 35, became effective, creating a comprehensive set of rules governing discovery of electronically stored information.

Given these rule changes, it is advisable to establish a suggested protocol regarding, and a basic format implementing, only those portions of the amendments that refer to electronically stored information. The purpose of this Suggested Protocol for Discovery of Electronically Stored Information ("Protocol") is to facilitate the just, speedy, and inexpensive conduct of discovery involving electronically stored information in civil cases, am to promote, whenever possible, the resolution of disputes regarding the discovery of electronically stored information without court intervention.

While this Protocol is intended to provide the parties with a comprehensive framework to address and resolve a wide range of electronically stored information, it is not intended to be an inflexible checklist. The court expects the parties will consider the nature of the claim, the amount in controversy agreements of the parties, the relative ability of the parties to conduct discovery of electronically stored information, and such other factors as may be relevant under the circumstances. Therefore not all aspects of this Protocol may be applicable or practical for a particular matter, and indeed, if the parties to do not intend to seek discovery of electronically stored information it may be entirely inapplicable to a particular case. The court encourages the parties to use this Protocol in cases in which there will be discovery of electronically stored information, and to resolve electronically stored information issues informally and without court supervision whenever possible. In this regard, compliance with this Protocol may be considered by the court in resolving discovery disputes, including whether sanctions should be awarded.

SCOPE

2. This Protocol applies to the electronically stored information provisions of Fed. R. Civ. P. 16, 26, 33, 34, or 37, and, insofar as it relates to electronically stored information, this Protocol applies to Fed. R. Civ. P. 45 in all instances where the provisions of Fed. R. Civ. P. 45 are the same as, or substantially similar to, Fed. R. Civ. P. 16, 26, 33, 34, or 37. In such circumstances, if a Conference pursuant to Fed. R. Civ. P. 26(f) is held, it may include all parties, as well as the person or entity served with the subpoena, if the Conference has not yet been conducted. If the Conference has been conducted, upon written request of any party or the person or entity served with the subpoena, a similar conference may be conducted regarding production of ESI pursuant to the subpoena. As used herein, the words "party" or "parties" include any person or entity that is served with a subpoena pursuant to Fed. R. Civ. P. 45. Nothing contained herein modifies Fed. R. Civ. P. 45 and, specifically, the provision of Rule 45(c)(2)(B) regarding the effect of a written objection to inspection or copying of any or all of the designated materials or premises.
3. In this Protocol, the following terms have the following meanings:

A. "Metadata" means: (i) information embedded in a native file that is not by the operation of a computer or other information technology system whet a native file is created, modified, transmitted, deleted or otherwise manipulated by a user of such system. Metadata are a subset of electronically stored information.

B. "Native file(s)" means electronically stored information in the electronic format of the application it which such electronically stored information is normally created, viewed and/or modified. Native files are a subset of electronically stored information.

C. "Static image(s)" means a representation of electronically stored information produced by converting native file into a standard image format capable of being viewed and printed on standard computer systems. In the absence of agreement of the parties or order of court, a static image should be provided in either Tagged Image File Format (TIFF, or.TIF files) or Portable Document Format (PDF). I load files were created in the process of converting native files to static images, or if load files may be created without undue burden or cost, load files should be produced together with Static Images.

CONFERENCE OF PARTIES AND REPORT

4. The parties are encouraged to consider conducting a Conference of Parties to discuss discovery of electronically stored information regardless of whether such a Conference is ordered by the court. The Conference of Parties should be conducted in person whenever practicable. Within 10 calendar days thereafter the parties may wish to file, or the court may order them to file, a joint report regarding the results of the conference. This process is also encouraged if applicable in connection with a subpoena for electronically stored information under Fed. R. Civ. P. 45. The report may state that the parties do not desire discovery of electronically stored information in which event Paragraphs 4A and B are inapplicable.

A. The report should, without limitation, state in the section captioned "Disclosure or Discovery of Electronically Stored Information Should Be Handled as Follows" the following:

(1) Any areas on which the parties have reached agreement and, if any, on which the parties request court approval of that agreement;

(2) Any areas on which the parties are in disagreement and request intervention of the court.

B. The report should, without limitation, if it proposes a "clawback" agreement, "quick peek," or testing or sampling, specify the proposed treatment of privileged information and work product. On-site inspections of electronically stored information under Fed. R. Civ. P. 34(b) should only be permitted in circumstances where good cause and specific need have been demonstrated by the party seeking disclosure of electronically stored information ("Requesting Party"), or by agreement of the parties. In appropriate circumstances the court may condition on-site inspections of electronically stored information to be performed by independent third-party experts, or set such other conditions as are agreed by the parties or deemed appropriate by the court.

C. Unless otherwise agreed by the parties, the report described by this provision should be filed with the court prior to the commencement of discovery of electronically stored information.

NEED FOR PRIOR PLANNING

5. Insofar as it relates to electronically stored information, before planning and preparation is essential for a Conference of Parties pursuant to Fed. R. Civ. P. 16, 26(f), and this Protocol. Counsel for the Requesting Party and counsel for the party producing, opposing, or seeking to limit disclosure of electronically stored information ("Producing Party") bear the primary responsibility for taking the planning actions. Failure to reasonably comply with the planning requirements in good faith may be a factor considered by the court in imposing sanctions.

EXCHANGE OF INFORMATION BEFORE RULE 26(f) CONFERENCE

6. Insofar as it relates to electronically stored information, in order to have a meaningful Conference of Parties, it may be necessary for parties to exchange information prior to the Fed. R. Civ. P. 26(f) Conference of Parties. Parties are encouraged to take the steps described in ¶ 7 of this Protocol and agree on a date that is prior to the Fed. R. Civ. P. 26(f) Conference of Parties, on which agreed date they will discuss by telephone whether it is necessary or convenient to exchange information about electronically stored information before the conference.

A. A reasonable request for prior exchange of information may include information relating to network design, the types of databases, database dictionaries, the access control list and security access logs and rights of individuals to access the system and specific files and applications, the electronically stored information document retention policy, organizational chart for information system personnel, or the backup and systems recovery routines, including, but not limited to, tape rotation and destruction/overwrite policy.

B. An unreasonable request for a prior exchange of information should not be made.

C. A reasonable request for a prior exchange of information should not be denied.

D. To the extent practicable, the parties should, prior to the Fed. R. Civ. P. 26(f) Conference of Parties, discuss the scope of discovery of electronically stored information, including whether the time parameters of discoverable electronically stored information, or for subsets of electronically stored information, be narrower than the parameters for other discovery.

E. Prior to the Fed. R. Civ. P. 26(f) Conference of Parties, counsel should discuss with their clients and each other who will participate in the Fed. R. Civ. P 26(f) Conference of Parties. This discussion should specifically include whether one or more participants should have an electronically stored information coordinator (see Paragraph 7.B) participate in the conference. If one participant believes the other should have an electronically stored information coordinator participate, and the other disagrees, the Requesting Party should state its reasons in a writing sent to all other parties within a reasonable time before the Rule 26(f) Conference. If the court subsequently determines the conference was not productive due to the absence of an electronically stored information coordinator, it may consider the letter in conjunction with any request for sanctions under Fed. R. Civ. P. 37.

PREPARATION FOR RULE 26(f) CONFERENCE

7. Before the Fed. R. Civ. P. 26(f) Conference of Parties, counsel for the parties should:

A. Take such steps as are necessary to advise their respective clients, including, but not limited to, key persons with respect to the facts underlying the litigation, and information systems personnel, of the substantive principles governing the preservation of relevant or discoverable electronically stored information while the lawsuit is pending. As a general principle to guide the discussion regarding legal hold policies, counsel should consider the following criteria:

(1) Scope of the legal hold, including:
  (a) A determination of the categories of potentially discoverable information to be segregated and preserved;
  (b) Discussion of the nature of issues in the case, as per Fed. R. Civ. P. 26(b)(1);
    (i) Whether electronically stored information is relevant to only some or all claims and defenses in the litigation;
    (ii) Whether electronically stored information is relevant to the subject matter involved in the action;
  (c) Identification of key persons and likely witnesses and persons with knowledge regarding relevant events;
  (d) The relevant time period for the legal hold;
(2) Analysis of what needs to be preserved, including:
  (a) The nature of specific types of electronically stored information, including, e-mail and attachments, word processing documents, spreadsheets graphics and presentation documents, images, text files, hart drives, databases, instant messages, transaction logs, audit and video files, voicemail, Internet data, computer logs, text messages, or backup materials, and native files, and how it should be preserved;
  (b) the extent to which metadata, deleted data, or fragmented data, will be subject to legal hold;
  (c) paper documents that are exact duplicates of electronically stored information;
  (d) any preservation of electronically stored information that has been deleted but not purged;
(3) Determination of where electronically stored information subject to the legal hold is maintained, including:
  (a) format, location, structure, and accessibility of active storage backup, and archives;
    (i) servers;
    (ii) computer systems, including legacy systems;
    (iii) remote and third-party locations;
    (iv) backup media (for disasters) vs. backup media for archival purposes or record retention laws;
  (b) network, intranet, and shared areas (public folders, discussion databases, departmental drives, and shared network folders)
  (c) desktop computers and workstations;
  (d) portable media; laptops; personal computers; PDAs; paging devices; mobile telephones; and flash drives;

(e) tapes, discs, drives, cartridges and other storage media;
(f) home computers (to the extent, if any, they are used for business purposes);
(g) paper documents that represent electronically stored information.

(4) Distribution of the notification of the legal hold:
(a) to parties and potential witnesses;
(b) to persons with records that are potentially discoverable;
(c) to persons with control over discoverable information including:
(i) information technology personnel/director of network services;
(ii) custodian of records;
(iii) key administrative assistants:
(d) third parties (contractors and vendors who provide information technology services)

(5) Instructions to be contained in a legal hold notice, including that:
(a) there will be no deletion, modification, alteration of electronically stored information subject to the legal hold;
(b) the recipient should advise whether specific categories of electronically stored information subject to the legal hold require particular actions (e.g., printing paper copies of e-mail and attachments) or transfer into read only media;
(c) loading of new software that materially impacts electronically stored information subject to the hold may occur only upon prior written approval from designated personnel;
(d) where metadata, or data that has been deleted but not purged, is to be preserved, either a method to preserve such data before running compression, disk defragmentation or other computer optimization or automated maintenance programs or scripts of any kind (File and System Maintenance Procedures), or the termination of all File and System Maintenance Procedures during the pendency of the legal hold in respect of Native Files subject to preservation;
(e) reasonably safeguarding and preserving all portable or removable electronic storage media containing potentially relevant electronically stored information;
(f) maintaining hardware that has been removed from ac-

tive production, if such hardware contains legacy systems with relevant electronically stored information and there is no reasonably available alternative that preserves access to the native files on such hardware.

(6) Monitoring compliance with the notification of legal hold, including:

(a) identifying contact person who will address questions regarding preservation duties;

(b) identifying personnel with responsibility to confirm that compliance requirements are met;

(c) determining whether data of key persons requires special handling (e.g., imaging/cloning hard drives);

(d) periodic checks of logs or memoranda detailing compliance;

(e) issuance of periodic reminders that the legal hold is still in effect.

B. Notify one or more information technology or information systems personnel to act as the electronically stored information coordinator and discuss electronically stored information with that person;

C. Identify those personnel who may be considered key persons by the events placed in issue by the lawsuit and determine their electronically stored information practices, including those matters set forth in Paragraph 7.D. The term key persons is intended to refer to both the natural person or persons who is/are a key person(s) with regard to the facts that underlie the litigation, and any applicable clerical or support personnel who directly prepare, store, or modify electronically stored information for that key person or persons, including, but not limited to, the network administrator, custodian of records or records management personnel, and an administrative assistant or personal secretary;

D. Become reasonably familiar with their respective clients' current and relevant past electronically stored information, if any, or alternatively, identify a person who can participate in the Fed. R. Civ. P. 26(f) Conference of Parties and who is familiar with at least the following:

(1) E-mail systems; blogs; instant messaging; Short Message Service (SMS) systems; word processing systems; spreadsheet and database systems; system history files, cache files, and cookies; graphics, animation, or document presentation systems; calendar systems; voice mail systems, including specifically, whether such systems include electronically stored information; data files; program files;

internet systems; and, internet systems. This Protocol may include information concerning the specific version of software programs and may include information stored on electronic bulletin boards, regardless of whether they are maintained by the party, authorized by the party, or officially sponsored by the party; provided, however, this Protocol extends only to the information to the extent such information is in the possession, custody, or control of such party. To the extent reasonably possible, this includes the database program used over the relevant time, its database dictionary, and the manner in which such program records transactional history in respect to deleted records.

(2) Storage systems, including whether electronically stored information is stored on servers, individual hard drives, home computers, laptop or notebook computers, personal digital assistants, pagers, mobile telephones, or removable/portable storage devices, such as CD-Roms, DVDs, floppy disks, zip drives, tape drives, external hard drives, flash, thumb or key drives, or external service providers.

(3) Backup and archival systems, including those that are onsite, offsite, or maintained using one or more third-party vendors. This Protocol may include a reasonable inquiry into the backup routine, application, and process and location of storage media, and requires inquiry into whether electronically stored information is reasonably accessible without undue burden or cost, whether it is compressed, encrypted, and the type of device on which it is recorded (e.g., whether it uses sequential or random access), and whether software that is capable of rendering it into usable form without undue expense is within the client's possession, custody, or control.

(4) Obsolete or legacy systems containing electronically stored information and the extent, if any, to which such electronically stored information was copied or transferred to new or replacement systems.

(5) Current and historical Website information, including any potentially relevant or discoverable statements contained on that or those site(s), as well as systems to backup, archive, store, or retain superseded, deleted, or removed web pages, and policies regarding allowing third parties' sites to archive client Website data.

(6) Event data records automatically created by the operation, usage, or polling of software or hardware (such as

recorded by a motor vehicle's GPS or other internal computer prior to an occurrence), if any and if applicable, in automobiles, trucks, aircraft, vessels, or vehicles or equipment.

(7) Communication systems, if any and if applicable, such as electronically stored information records of radio transmissions, telephones, personal digital assistants, or GPS systems.

(8) Electronically stored information erasure, modification, or recovery mechanisms, such as metadata scrubbers or programs that repeatedly overwrite portions of storage media in order to preclude data recovery, and policies regarding the use of such processes and software, as well as recovery programs that can defeat scrubbing, thereby recovering deleted, but inadvertently produced electronically stored information, that, in some cases, may even include privileged information.

(9) Policies regarding records management, including the retention or destruction of electronically stored information prior to the client receiving knowledge that a claim is reasonably anticipated.

(10) Legal hold policies that are instituted when a claim is reasonably anticipated, including all such policies that have been instituted, and the date on which they were instituted.

(11) The identity of custodians of key electronically stored information, including key persons and related staff members, and the information technology or information systems personnel, vendors, or subcontractors who are best able to describe the client's information technology system.

(12) The identity of vendors or subcontractors who store electronically stored information for, or provide services or applications to, the client or a key person; the nature, amount, and a description of the electronically stored information stored by those vendors or subcontractors; contractual or other agreements that permit the client to impose a legal hold on such electronically stored information, and, if not, why not

E. Negotiation of an agreement that outlines what steps each party will take to segregate and preserve the integrity of relevant or discoverable electronically stored information. This agreement may provide for depositions of information system personnel on issues related to preservation, steps taken to ensure that electronically stored information is not deleted in the ordinary course of business, steps taken to avoid alteration of discoverable electronically stored information, and criteria regarding the operation of spam or virus filters and the destruction of filtered electronically stored information.

TOPICS TO DISCUSS AT RULE 26(f) CONFERENCE

8. The following topics, if applicable, should be discussed at the Fed. R. Civ. P. 26(f) Conference of Parties:

   A. The anticipated scope of requests for, and objections to, production of electronically stored information, as well as the form of production of electronically stored information and, specifically, but without limitation, whether production will be of the native file, static image, or other searchable or non-searchable formats.

      (1) If the parties are unable to reach agreement on the format for production, electronically stored information should be produced to the Requesting Party as static images. When the static image is produced, the Producing Party should maintain a separate file as a native file and, in that separate file, it should not modify the native File in a manner that materially changes the file and the metadata. After initial production in static images is complete, a party seeking production of native file electronically stored information should demonstrate particularized need for that production.

      (2) The parties should discuss whether production of some or all electronically stored information in paper format is agreeable in lieu of production in electronic format. When parties have agreed or the court has ordered the parties to exchange all or some documents as electronic files in native file format in connection with discovery, the parties should collect and produce said relevant files in native file formats in a manner that preserves the integrity of the files, including, but not limited to, the contents of the file, the metadata (including system metadata, substantive metadata, and embedded metadata, as more fully described in Paragraph 11 of this Protocol) related to the file, and the file's creation date and time. The general process to preserve the data integrity of a file may include one or more of the following procedures: (a) duplication of responsive files in the file system (i.e., creating a forensic copy, including a bit image copy, of the file system or pertinent portion), (b) performing a

routine copy of the files while preserving metadata (including, but not limited to, creation date and time), and/or (c) using reasonable measures to prevent a file from being, or indicate that a file has been, modified, either intentionally or unintentionally, since the collection or production date of the files. If any party desires to redact contents of a native file for privilege, trade secret, or other purposes (including, but not limited to, metadata), then the Producing Party should indicate that the file has been redacted, and an original, unmodified file should be retained at least during the pendency of the case.

B. Whether metadata are requested for some or all electronically stored information and, if so, the volume and costs of producing and reviewing the electronically stored information.

C. Preservation of electronically stored information during the pendency of the lawsuit, specifically, but without limitation, applicability of the safe harbor provision of Fed. R. Civ. P. 37, preservation of metadata, preservation of deleted electronically stored information electronically stored information backup or archival electronically stored information, electronically stored information contained in dynamic systems, electronically stored information destroyed or overwritten by the routine operation of systems, and, offsite and offline electronically stored information (including electronically stored information stored on home or personal computers). A dynamic system is a system remaining in use during the pendency of the litigation and in which the electronically stored information changes on a routine and regular basis, including the automatic deletion or overwriting of such electronically stored information. This discussion should include whether the parties can agree on methods of review of electronically stored information by the responding party in a manner that does not unacceptably change metadata.

(1) If Counsel are able to agree, the terms of an agreed-upon preservation order may be submitted to the court;

(2) If Counsel are unable to agree, they should attempt to reach agreement on the manner in which each party should submit a narrowly tailored, proposed preservation order to the court for its consideration.

D. Post-production assertion, and preservation or waiver of, the attorney-client privilege, work product doctrine, and/or other privileges in light of clawback, quick peek, or testing or sampling procedures, and submission of a proposed order. If metadata are to be produced, Counsel may agree, and should discuss any agreement, that metadata not be reviewed by the recipient and the terms of submission of a proposed order encompassing that agreement to the court. Counsel should also discuss procedures under which electronically stored information that contains privileged information or attorney work product should be immediately returned to the Producing Party if the electronically stored information appears on its face to have been inadvertently produced or if there is prompt written notice of inadvertent production by the Producing Party. The Producing Party should maintain unaltered copies of all such returned materials under the control of counsel of record. This provision is procedural and return of materials pursuant to this Protocol is without prejudice to any substantive right to assert, or oppose, waiver of any protection against disclosure.

E. Identification of electronically stored information that is or is not reasonably accessible without undue burden or cost, specifically, and without limitation, the identity of such sources and the reasons for a contention that the electronically stored information is or is not reasonably accessible without undue burden or cost, the methods of storing and retrieving that electronically stored information, and the anticipated costs and efforts involved in retrieving that electronically stored information. The party asserting that electronically stored information is not reasonably accessible without undue burden or cost should be prepared to discuss in reasonable detail, the information described in Paragraph 10 of this Protocol.

F. Because identifying information may not be placed on electronically stored information as easily as bates-stamping paper documents, methods of identifying pages or segments of electronically stored information produced in discovery should be discussed, and, specifically, and without limitation, the following alternatives may be considered by the parties electronically paginating native file electronically stored information pursuant to a stipulated agreement that the alteration does not affect admissibility; renaming native files using bates-type numbering systems, e.g., ABC0001, ABC0002, ABC0003, with some method of referring to unnumbered pages within each file, using software that produces "hash marks" or "hash values" for each native file; placing pagination on static images; or any other practicable method. The parties are encouraged to discuss the use of a digital notary for producing native files.

G. The method and manner of redacting information from electronically stored information if only part of the electronically stored information is discoverable. As set forth in Paragraph 11.D, if metadata are redacted from a file, written notice of such redaction, and the scope of that redaction, should be provided.

H. The nature of information systems used by the party or person or entity served with a subpoena requesting electronically stored information, including those systems described in Paragraph 7.D. This Protocol may suggest that Counsel be prepared to list the types of information systems used by the client and the varying accessibility, if any, of each system. It may suggest that Counsel be prepared to identify the electronically stored information custodians, for example, by name, title, and job responsibility. It also may suggest that, unless impracticable, Counsel be able to identify the software (including the version) used in the ordinary course of business to access the electronically stored information, and the file formats of such electronically stored information.

I. Specific facts related to the costs and burdens of preservation, retrieval, and use of electronically stored information.

J. Cost sharing for the preservation, retrieval and/or production of electronically stored information, including any discovery database, differentiating between electronically stored information that is reasonably accessible and electronically stored information that is not reasonably accessible; provided however that absent a contrary showing of good cause, e.g., Fed. R. Civ. P. 26(b)(2)(C), the parties should generally presume that the Producing Party bears all costs as to reasonably accessible electronically stored information and, provided further, the parties should generally presume that there will be cost sharing or cost shifting as to electronically stored information that is not reasonably accessible. The parties may choose to discuss the use of an Application Service Provider that is capable of establishing a central repository of electronically stored information for all parties.

K. Search methodologies for retrieving or reviewing electronically stored information such as identification of the systems to be searched; identification of systems that will not be searched; restrictions or limitations on the search; factors that limit the ability to search; the use of key word searches, with an agreement on the words or terms to be searched; using sampling to search rather than searching all of the records; limitations on the time frame of electronically stored information to be searched; limitations on the fields or document types to be searched; limitations regarding whether backup, archival, legacy or deleted electronically stored information is to be searched; the number of hours that must be expended by the searching party or person in conducting the search and compiling and reviewing electronically stored information; and the amount of pre-production review that is reasonable for the Producing Party to undertake in light of the considerations set forth in Fed. R. Civ. P. 26(b)(2)(C).

L. Preliminary depositions of information systems personnel, and limits on the scope of such depositions. Counsel should specifically consider whether limitations on the scope of such depositions should be submitted to the court with a proposed order that, if entered, would permit Counsel to instruct a witness not to answer questions beyond the scope of the limitation, pursuant to Fed. R. Civ. P. 30(d)(1).

M. The need for two-tier or staged discovery of electronically stored information, considering whether electronically stored information initially can be produced in a manner that is more cost-effective, while reserving the right to request or to oppose additional more comprehensive production in a later stage or stages. Absent agreement or good cause shown, discovery of electronically stored information should proceed in the following sequence: 1) after receiving requests for production of electronically stored information, the parties should search their electronically stored information other than that identified as not reasonably accessible without undue burden or cost, and produce responsive electronically stored information within the parameters of Fed. R. Civ. P 26(b)(2)(C); 2) searches of or for electronically stored information identified as not reasonably accessible should not be conducted until the prior step has been completed; and, 3 requests for information expected to be found in or among electronically stored information that was identified as not reasonably accessible should be narrowly focused, with factual basis supporting each request.

N. The need for any protective orders or confidentiality orders, in conformance with the Local Rules and substantive principles governing such orders.

O. Any request for sampling or testing of electronically stored information; the parameters of such requests; the time, manner, scope, and place limitations that will voluntarily or by court order be placed on such processes; the persons to be involved; and the dispute resolution mechanism, if any, agreed-upon by the parties.

P. Any agreement concerning retention of an agreed-upon court expert, retained at the cost of the parties, to assist in the resolution of technical issues presented by electronically stored information.

PARTICIPANTS

9. The following people:
   A. Should, absent good cause, participate in the Fed. R. Civ. P. 26(f) Conference of Parties: lead counsel and at least one representative of each party.
   B. May participate in the Fed. R. Civ. P. 26(f) Conference of Parties: clients or representatives of clients or the entity served with a subpoena; the designated electronically stored information coordinator for the party; forensic experts; and in-house information system personnel. Identification of an expert for use in a Fed. R. Civ. P. 26(f) Conference of Parties does not, in and of itself, identify that person as an expert whose opinions may be presented at trial within the meaning of Fed. R. Civ. P. 26(b)(4)(A), (B).
   C. If a party is not reasonably prepared for the Fed. R. Civ. P. 26(f) Conference used to support a motion for sanctions by the opposing party for the costs incurred in connection with that conference.

REASONABLY ACCESSIBLE

10. No party should object to the discovery of electronically stored information pursuant to Fed. R. Civ. P. 26(b)(2)(B) on the basis that it is not reasonably accessible because of undue burden or cost unless the objection has been stated with particularity, and not in conclusory or boilerplate language. Wherever the term "reasonably accessible" is used in this Protocol, the party asserting that electronically stored information is not reasonably accessible should be prepared to specify facts that support its contention.

PRINCIPLES RE METADATA

11. The production of metadata apart from its native file may impose substantial costs, either in the extraction of such metadata from the native files, or in its review for purposes of redacting non-discoverable information contained in such

metadata. The persons involved in the discovery process are expected to be cognizant of those costs in light of the various factors established in Fed. R. Civ. P. 26(b)(2)(C). The following principles should be utilized in determining whether metadata may be discovered:

A. Metadata are part of electronically stored information. Such metadata, however, may not be relevant to the issues presented or, if relevant, not be reasonably subject to discovery given the Fed. R. Civ. P. 26(b)(2)(C) cost-benefit factors. Therefore, it may be subject to cost-shifting under Fed. R. Civ. P. 26(b)(2)(C).

B. Metadata may generally be viewed as either system metadata, substantive metadata, or embedded metadata. System metadata are data that are automatically generated by a computer system. For example, system metadata often include information such as the author, date and time of creation, and the date a document was modified. Substantive metadata are data that reflects the substantive changes made to the document by the user. For example, it may include the text of actual changes to a document. While no generalization is universally applicable, system metadata are less likely to involve issues of work product and/or privilege.

C. Except as otherwise provided in sub-paragraph E, metadata, especially substantive metadata, need not be routinely produced, except upon agreement of the requesting and producing litigants, or upon a showing of good cause in a motion filed by the Requesting Party in accordance with the procedures set forth in the Local Rules of this court. Consideration should be given to the production of system metadata and its production is encouraged in instances where it will not unnecessarily or unreasonably increase costs or burdens. As set forth above, upon agreement of the parties the court will consider entry of an order approving an agreement that a part: may produce metadata in native files upon the representation of the recipient that the recipient will neither access nor review such data. This Protocol does not address the substantive issue of the duty to preserve such metadata, or its admissibility into evidence or use in the course of depositions or other discovery.

D. If a Producing Party produces electronically stored information without some or all of the metadata was contained in the electronically stored information, the Producing Party should inform all other of this fact, in writing, at or before the time of production.

E. Some native files contain, in addition to substantive metadata, system metadata, embedded metadata, which for purposes of this Protocol, means the text, numbers, content, data, or other information directly or indirectly inputted into a native file by a user and which typically visible to the user viewing the output display of the native file screen or as a print out. Examples of embedded metadata include, but are not limited to, spreadsheet formulas (which display as the result formula operation), hidden columns, externally or internally linked file: sound files in PowerPoint presentations), references to external file content (e.g., hyperlinks to HTML files or URLs), references and fields the field codes for an auto-numbered document), and certain database information if the data is part of a database (e.g., a date field in a database will display as a formatted date, but its actual value is typically a long integer). Subject to the other provisions of this Protocol related to the and benefits of preserving and producing metadata (see generally Paragraph 8), subject to potential redaction of substantive metadata, and substantive metadata and subject to reducing the scope of production of embedded metadata, embedded metadata is generally discoverable and in appropriate cases, see Fed. R. Civ. P. 26(b)(2)(C), should be produced as a matter of course. If the parties determine to produce embedded metadata, either in connection wit a native file production or in connection with static image production in lieu of native file production, the parties should normally discuss and agree on use of appropriate tools and methods to remove other metadata, but preserve the embedded metadata, prior to such production.

NOTES TO FORM

Commentary

This form is adapted from a protocol developed by the U.S. District Court for the District of Maryland. It can be adapted for use in other courts, including state courts, and also adapted to fit the circumstances of a particular case.

§ 10:18 Initial disclosure

[Caption]

In accordance with Fed. R. Civ. P. 26(a)(1), *[plaintiff] [defendant]* makes its mandatory disclosure as follows:

A. Witnesses

1. *[Name]* at *[address]* is likely to have discoverable informa-

tion relevant to disputed facts alleged with particularity in the pleadings including *[describe].*

2. *[Name]* at *[address]* is likely to have discoverable information relevant to disputed facts alleged with particularity in the pleadings including *[describe].*
3. *[Name]* at *[address]* is likely to have discoverable information relevant to disputed facts alleged with particularity in the pleadings including *[describe].*

B. Documents and Electronically Stored Information

1. Contract between *[name]* and *[name]* dated *[date].*
2. Correspondence between *[name]* and *[name]* dated *[date].*
3. Memorandum from *[name]* to *[name]* dated *[date].*
4. *[Description by category and location of electronically stored information]*

C. Computation of Damages

1. Explanation

[Explain how any category of claimed damages has been calculated.]

2. Documents Upon Which Computation Based
   a. Medical bill from *[name]* dated *[date].*
   b. Automobile repair invoice from *[name]* dated *[date].*

D. Insurance Agreements

1. Insurance Policy No. issued by *[name of insurer]* on *[date].*
2. Insurance Policy No. issued by *[name of insurer]* on *[date].*

Dated: ____

[signature etc.]

§ 10:19 Order for appointment of special master

[Caption]

ORDER FOR APPOINTMENT OF SPECIAL MASTER

The stipulation of the parties for the appointment of a special master for discovery is approved, and

IT IS HEREBY ORDERED that *[name]* is appointed special master for discovery in this action to serve at the pleasure of the court and in accordance with the terms of the parties' stipulation for appointment of a special master; and

IT IS FURTHER ORDERED that the parties shall abide by the terms and conditions of the stipulation for the duration of the pendency of this action or until further order of the court.

Dated: ____

____

Judge

Chapter 11

Discovery Conferences

I. GUIDELINES

II. CHECKLISTS

III. FORMS

Research References

Treatises and Practice Aids

Grenig and Gleisner, eDiscovery & Digital Evidence §§ 6:1 to 6:19

Trial Strategy

Recovery and Reconstruction of Electronic Mail as Evidence, 41 Am. Jur Proof of Facts 3d 1

Computer Technology in Civil Litigation, 71 Am. Jur. Trials 111

Additional References

Grenig and Kinsler, Handbook of Federal Civil Discovery and Disclosure §§ 1.186 to 1.189 (3d ed.)

ABA Discovery Standards, http://www.abanet.org/litigation/discoverystandards/2005civildiscoverystandards.pdf

Electronic Discovery Reference Model Project, http://www.edrm.net

Federal Judicial Center, http://www.fjc.gov

The Sedona Conference, http://www.thesedonaconference.org

KeyCite®: Cases and other legal materials listed in KeyCite Scope can be researched through the KeyCite service on Westlaw®. Use KeyCite to check citations for form, parallel references, prior and later history, and comprehensive citator information, including citations to other decisions and secondary materials.

I. GUIDELINES

§ 11:1 Discovery Conferences—Generally

Parties should confer early in discovery with respect to preserving and producing electronically stored information.[1] The parties should seek to agree on the scope of each party's rights and responsibilities.[2]

Under Fed. R. Civ. P. 26(f), in federal court, parties must confer and develop a discovery plan at least 21 days before the Fed. R. Civ. P. 16(b) scheduling and planning conference to plan for discovery.[3] This discovery conference and resulting plan should address "disclosure or discovery of electronically stored informa-

---

[Section 11:1]

[1]See Sedona Principal 3.

[2]See Sedona Principal 3.

[3]The Manual for Complex Litigation Fourth § 11.446 emphasizes the importance of a conference as follows:

> The judge should encourage the parties to discuss the scope of proposed computer-based discovery early in the case, particularly any discovery of data beyond that available to the responding parties in the ordinary course of business. The requesting parties should identify the information they require as narrowly and precisely as possible, and the responding parties should be forthcoming and explicit in identifying what data are available from what sources, to allow formulation of a realistic computer-based discovery plan.

By local rule, a court may provide a different time frame. The attorneys of record and all unrepresented parties that have appeared in the case are jointly responsible for arranging the conference, for attempting in good faith to agree on the proposed discovery plan, and for submitting to the court within 14 days after the conference a written report outlining the plan.

tion, including the form or forms in which it would be produced"[4] and "any issues about preserving discoverable information."[5]

The duty to confer under Fed R. Civ. P. 26 is mandatory and the substantive communications between counsel may later be considered by a court in deciding issues regarding a particular side's good faith.[6] Even in states without a similar requirement, a conference to plan for discovery can be helpful to both sides and can significantly reduce costs associated with subsequent discovery.

The conference is an excellent opportunity for the parties to identify and address discovery scope issues including the most likely sources of relevant electronically stored information, what electronically stored information is at risk of deletion through normal operation of computer systems, what data systems are no longer being used, what sources may be inaccessible due to undue burden and cost, and what electronically stored information is in a remote or third-party location. Identification of these issues early in the litigation process will undoubtedly have a financial, if not a strategic, impact on the subsequent motion practice and litigation.

§ 11:2 Cooperation

A successful Rule 26(f) conference depends upon cooperation and candor. This is consistent with the fundamental principle of Fed. R. Civ. P. 1 providing that the Federal Rules of Civil Procedure "should be construed and administered to secure the just, speedy, and inexpensive determination of" every civil case.[1] There can be benefits from collaborating with the opposing party regarding criteria to be used in identifying information to be retained. On the other hand, the traditional adversarial approach may result in inefficiencies with resultant delays and increased costs.

---

[4]Rule 26(f)(3)(C).

[5]Rule 26(f)(2).

[6]See S.E.C. v. Collins & Aikman Corp., 256 F.R.D. 403, Fed. Sec. L. Rep. (CCH) ¶ 95045 (S.D. N.Y. 2009) (with few exceptions, Rule 26(f) requires the parties to hold a conference and prepare a discovery plan).

[Section 11:2]

[1]See, e.g., Board of Regents of University of Nebraska v. BASF Corp., 2007 WL 3342423, *5 (D. Neb. 2007) ("The overriding theme of recent amendments to the discovery rules has been open and forthright sharing of information by all parties to a case with the aim of expediting case progress, minimizing burden and expense, and removing contentiousness as much as practicable.").

§ 11:3 Preparing for the conference

Counsel's thorough preparation for the conference will usually have a productive and beneficial result. Counsel should be familiar with all the components of a client's information technology infrastructure.[1] Proper preparation means that routine business processes, including archiving, and destruction, will not be hampered and the day-to-day processes and procedures will remain.[2]

It is advisable to consult with specialized e-discovery counsel, discovery vendors and information technology person from the company to make certain all sources of potentially responsive information are considered prior to engaging in the conference. These individuals are also helpful in providing guidance on how to best capture or preserve such potentially relevant information, and identifying any potential hurdles that will need to be addressed with opposing counsel. An affidavit or statement from these individuals may help support a position that certain electronically stored information need not be preserved or searched. Those systems not containing electronically stored information relevant to the proceeding should be excluded from a preservation order.

This knowledge will inform counsel about the impact of any discovery protocol agreement. Parties that are forthcoming in exchanging the rationale, structure, and format of their information sources are in a much better position to receive narrowly tailored requests that minimize disruption and cost. They are also much better placed to rebut the position of requesting parties that persist with specious or overbroad requests.

§ 11:4 Attendance at the conference

Fed. R. Civ. P. 26(f) does not require that the conference be conducted in person. The conference can be conducted by

---

[Section 11:3]

[1]See Hopson v. Mayor and City Council of Baltimore, 232 F.R.D. 228, 97 Fair Empl. Prac. Cas. (BNA) 617, 63 Fed. R. Serv. 3d 582 (D. Md. 2005) (federal e-discovery amendments explicitly anticipate parties entering Rule 26(f) conference processes possessed with clear knowledge of data sources, usage, content and accessibility considerations and that these conferences were to be sufficiently informative to provide sufficient information to enable the requesting party to challenge any assertions of duplicative requests, relevance or inaccessibility).

[2]See Herr, ANNOTATED MANUAL FOR COMPLEX LITIGATION 4TH § 11.422 ("A blanket preservation order may be prohibitively expensive and unduly burdensome for parties.").

telephone. The Advisory Committee's Note to the 2006 Amendment of Fed. R. Civ. P. 26(f) expresses a preference for an in-person meeting, but recognizes the distances some counsel would have to travel and that the resulting expenses may outweigh the benefits of an in person meeting. The court may order that the parties or attorneys attend the conference in person.

§ 11:5 Topics for the conference—Generally

Fed. R. Civ. P. 26(f) provides for the following topics of discussion during the conference:

- **Sources of electronically stored information.** The parties should be prepared to discuss in some detail all sources of potentially relevant electronically stored information. Prior to the conference, counsel should learn enough about each "bucket" of information to clearly articulate why certain sources will or will not be produced. This may the need to identify information that is irrelevant, duplicative, not reasonably accessible, privileged. Counsel should consider other limiting factors such as custodial or date limitations. It is important to articulate why a source of information should or should not be considered in the applicable action.
- **Preservation of information.** Counsel must recognize that the burdens of preservation in the electronic world are not consistent with those in the world of paper. A preservation plan that dictates a client "preserve everything" can have serious economic and business impact. Therefore, it is imperative that counsel be prepared to identify those sources that have been preserved and those that will not be preserved and the basis for Disclosure of electronically stored information and preservation of that information.
- **Searches.** Counsel should discuss what electronically stored information will be included in the search for relevant documents. They should also discuss. what electronically stored information the clients have will not be searched.
- **Form of Production.** Counsel should address the form of production to opposing counsel (e.g., native file vs. another format and the load file specifications for eventual use).
- **Privilege.** The conference should discuss iIssues dealing with privilege, such as the prospect of including a clawback agreement in a court order.
- **Proportionality.** The type of case and the amount at risk should be discussed.
- **Plan for Discovery.** The parties should attempt to negotiate a plan for discovery

The parties must determine precisely what the requesting party is actually seeking, what responsive documents or information the discovering party is reasonably capable of producing, and what specific, genuine objections or other issues, if any, cannot be resolved without judicial intervention.[1] Increasingly, "[c]ourts expect parties to reach practical agreement on search terms, date ranges, key players, and the like."[2]

§ 11:6 Topics for the conference—Form of production

It is important to discuss the form for production of electronically stored information. Unlike paper records, electronically stored information can be produced in many different forms. While it is possible to simply print all electronically stored information, doing so will likely exclude metadata or conceal other potentially relevant data (e.g. spreadsheet formulas). Furthermore, production in certain formats may severely limit the ability of receiving party to search and review such information.

Similarly, the production of electronically stored information purely in native form has its challenges. Unique or proprietary data formats may be unreadable, electronic records may be difficult to identify with traditional Bates numbering, and structured data sources may be difficult to produce.

Often the issue of how data will be reviewed dictates the form of production. It is very common for parties to exchange information that has been produced in a static form with a corresponding load file containing extracted metadata and searchable text. This will often satisfy the interests of both parties by ensuring the produced data will be unaltered, searchable and highly organized.

The source of the data may also dictate the ultimate form of production. This is especially true when dealing with structured data (e.g. databases). Typically these structured data sources contain a series of highly relational data tables. The parties will often choose to extract and produce data from these sources by running targeted queries and reports.

§ 11:7 Topics for the conference—Privilege

Problems of privilege waiver can be addressed at the conference.

[Section 11:5]

[1]Williams v. Sprint/United Management Co., 245 F.R.D. 660 (D. Kan. 2007). Cf. Verigy US, Inc. v. Mayder, 2007 WL 3144577 (N.D. Cal. 2007) (plaintiff's previous request for a search of all documents containing the letter "V" strikes this court as being patently overbroad).

[2]Allman, *Conducting E-discovery After the Amendments: The Second Wave*, 10 SEDONA CONF. J. 215, 216–17 (2009).

Traditional concepts of privilege apply equally to electronically stored information. However, sheer volume of electronically stored information creates challenges in identifying and excluding privileged information. Potential disclosure of privileged information can also be problematic where the parties agree to a full exchange of electronically stored information or in quick peek situations where the produced data is not first reviewed by the producing party. Fed. R. Civ. P. 26(b)(5)(B) provides a procedure for addressing accidental production of privileged information. In these situations, clawback agreements should be given serious consideration.

Clawbacks can be used in those circumstances where information that is actually privileged is produced. A clawback agreement would include a mechanism returning, sequestering, and destroying the privileged information. In the event that the receiving party has disclosed the information before receiving notice from the producing party, the receiving party must take reasonable steps to retrieve the disclosure. It is prudent to incorporate a clawback agreement in a court order to mitigate the risk of waiver.[1] Any clawback agreement should be drafted consistent with Fed. R. Evid. 502 to ensure full protection of privilege across state and federal judicial proceedings for inadvertent disclosure.

§ 11:8 Topics for the conference—Accessibility

The question of accessibility of electronically stored information should be discussed at the conference. Under Fed. R. Civ. P. 26(b)(2)(B), electronically stored information identified by the producing party as not reasonably accessible because of cost and undue burden does not normally have to be produced. Electronically stored information that is not reasonably accessible may involve dated or obsolete hardware or software where restoration of the electronically stored information would entail undue burden or cost. Any party making a claim that a source of electronically stored information is inaccessible should clearly identify all factors that impact such burden and cost including cost to restore, identify, search, review and produce such information.

If, at the end of the discovery conference and after good faith efforts are undertaken by counsel on both sides, the parties cannot within a reasonable time resolve the issues around electroni-

[Section 11:7]

[1]See Hopson v. Mayor and City Council of Baltimore, 232 F.R.D. 228, 240, 97 Fair Empl. Prac. Cas. (BNA) 617, 63 Fed. R. Serv. 3d 582 (D. Md. 2005).

cally stored information claimed not to be reasonably accessible, the party resisting production can seek a protective order barring production. The burden is then on the movant to prove the information is not reasonably accessible. The party seeking the information, despite the fact that the information is inaccessible, may then show good cause that the evidence should be produced considering the limitations of Fed. R. Civ. P. 26(b)(2)(C).

§ 11:9 Failing to participate in framing discovery plan

Under Fed. R. Civ. P. 37(f), if a party or a party's attorney fails to participate in good faith in the development and submission of a discovery plan, the court may require the party or attorney to pay to any other party the reasonable expenses, including attorney fees caused by the failure. The court must give the party or attorney an opportunity for a hearing.

§ 11:10 Scheduling conferences

In federal court, after receiving the discovery report required under Fed. R. Civ. P. 26(f) or after conducting a scheduling conference under Fed. R. Civ. P. 16(a), the court issues a scheduling order setting timetables for pretrial matters.[1] The scheduling order must be issued within 90 days after the appearance of a defendant and within 120 days of the service of the complaint.

Fed. R. Civ. P. 16(b) requires the court's order to include time limits for completing discovery. At the court's discretion the scheduling order may include provisions governing the disclosure or discovery of electronically stored information and provisions for recalling privileged documents after production.

II. CHECKLISTS

§ 11:11 Checklist for preparing for conference

- ☐ If client has received a preservation letter from opposing party, review with client to determine whether scope is consistent with claims and applicable defenses. Determine how notice will impact legal hold. Be prepared to discuss and narrow scope during discovery conference.
- ☐ If client has received a preservation order, confirm its dissemination with legal hold, monitoring and fulfillment. Follow up to ensure its compliance.

[Section 11:10]

[1]Fed.R.Civ.P. 16(b).

- ☐ If client has not received a preservation order, draft and disseminate a legal hold letter to client and identified data and subject matter custodians. Follow up to assure its compliance.
- ☐ Identify persons knowledgeable about the client's electronically stored information with the ability to facilitate reasonably anticipated discovery.
- ☐ Contact and involve the organization's information technology personnel early in the process.
- ☐ Identify the personnel in the information technology department; specifically, which personnel control which sources of electronically stored information—including the information management program.
- ☐ Investigate how client's electronically stored information is stored and how and in what form it can be retrieved.
- ☐ Identify sources of potentially responsive electronically stored information including desktops, laptops, removable media, file and e-mail servers, databases, systems for document and enterprise resource management, and cloud-based or third-party hosted data. This requires talking with key players and support staff, including IT personnel.
- ☐ Identify any archive, backup or disaster recovery systems. Review associated retention and rotation schedules.
- ☐ Ascertain the accessibility of the sources and the reasons why a client deems certain sources of electronically stored information not reasonably accessible.
- ☐ Determine whether any challenges exist that impact the ability to preserve any source of electronically stored information.
- ☐ Review client's sources of electronically stored information to determine what sources may be used to support claims or defenses.
- ☐ Produce accurate inventories of sources of potentially relevant electronically stored information to the opposing side.
- ☐ Discuss scope and cost with the client. This includes discussing the volume of electronically stored information, approaches to discovery, use of vendors and consultants, and costs associated with preservation, collection, processing, searching, reviewing and producing the information.
- ☐ Prepare a negotiation strategy. In preparing the negotiation strategy, it is essential to determine the time and cost of implications of the process. This may include a list of custodians of electronically stored information, date ranges, potentially inaccessible sources, search technology, form of production, and timing.

☐ Prepare a disclosure strategy This may include a list of custodians, a list of preserved sources of electronically stored information, sources that have been evaluated and not preserved (including reasons why it was determined the sources did not include potentially responsive information), search and review considerations, and timing. Consider using a phased approach that allows for adjustment and modification to ensure efficiency.

☐ Prepare a request strategy. This may include a description of what you want from the opposing party and the form of production desired. It may also be appropriate to consider scheduling future conferences.

§ 11:12 Checklist for discovery conference

☐ If there are concerns about the loss or destruction of electronically stored information by the opposing party, consider sending a Send preservation letter to opposing party as soon as possible.

☐ Let the opposing side know what you will and will not be preserving.

☐ Let the opposing side know what you will and will not be searching.

☐ Determine production schedule.

☐ Draft an agreement regarding the inadvertent production of privileged documents including electronically stored information.

☐ Determine whether restoration of deleted electronically stored information is necessary

☐ Determine whether back-up or archived electronically stored information is within the scope of discovery

☐ Determine media format.

☐ Determine procedures for production.

☐ Determine who will bear costs of preservation, production, and restoration of electronically stored information, if necessary.

☐ Come to an agreement that will be incorporated into an updated discovery plan requiring a description of the process of production for electronically stored information.

☐ Document efforts to reach an accord regarding discovery and efforts to work out an agreement when disputes arise.

§ 11:13 Questions for conference

☐ What is the case about?

- ☐ Who are the key players?
- ☐ What period of time are pertinent?
- ☐ When does the duty to preserve electronically stored information begin and end?
- ☐ What electronically stored information is at greatest risk of alteration or destruction?
- ☐ What nonparties have information that must be preserved?
- ☐ What data requires forensically sound preservation?
- ☐ What metadata are relevant?
- ☐ If metadata are relevant, how will it be preserved, extracted, and produced?
- ☐ What are the other party's data retention policies and practices?
- ☐ Are legacy systems involved?
- ☐ What are the current e-mail applications?
- ☐ Are there any earlier e-mail applications? If so, what are they?
- ☐ How will voice mail be handled?
- ☐ How will instant messaging be handled?
- ☐ Are there relevant databases? If so, how will their contents be produced?
- ☐ Are there attorney-client or work product issues unique to the electronically stored information?
- ☐ What search techniques will be used to identify responsive electronically stored information?
- ☐ What search techniques will be used to identify privileged electronically stored information?
- ☐ What keywords should be used for searching?
- ☐ How will duplicate documents be handled?
- ☐ In what form or forms will electronically stored information be produced?
- ☐ Who will the redaction of privileged, irrelevant, or confidential content be handled?
- ☐ What sources of electronically stored information are claimed not to be reasonably accessible?

NOTES

Commentary

This form is adapted from Ball, *Piecing Together the E-Discovery Plan*, TRIAL, June 2008.

III. FORMS

§ 11:14 Report of parties planning meeting

[Caption]

Report of Parties' Planning Meeting

1. Pursuant to *[rule]*, a meeting was held on *[date]*, at *[place]* and was attended by:

[name] for plaintiff(s)

[name] for defendant(s) *[party name]*

[name] for defendant(s) *[party name]*

2. Pre-Discovery Disclosures. The parties *[have exchanged] [will exchange by [date]]* the information required by *[rule]*.

3. Discovery Plan. The parties jointly propose to the court the following discovery plan: *[Use separate paragraphs or subparagraphs as necessary if parties disagree.]*

Discovery will be needed on the following subjects: *[brief description of subjects on which discovery will be needed]*.

Disclosure or discovery of electronically stored information should be handled as follows: *[brief description of parties' proposals]*.

The parties have agreed to an order regarding claims of privilege or of protection as trial-preparation material asserted after production, as follows: *[brief description of provisions of proposed order]*.

All discovery commenced in time to be completed by *[date]*. *[Discovery on [issue for early discovery] to be completed by [date].]*

Maximum of interrogatories by each party to any other party. *[Responses due days after service.]*

Maximum of requests for admission by each party to any other party. *[Responses due days after service.]*

Maximum of depositions by plaintiff(s) and by defendant(s).

Each deposition *[other than of]* limited to maximum of hours unless extended by agreement of parties.

Reports from retained experts under *[rule]* due:

from plaintiff(s) by *[date]*

from defendant(s) by *[date]*

4. Other Items. *[Use separate paragraphs or subparagraphs as necessary if parties disagree.]*

Supplementations under *[rule] due [time(s) or interval(s)]*.

The parties *[request]/[do not request]* a conference with the court before entry of the scheduling order.

The parties request a pretrial conference in *[month and year]*.

Plaintiff(s) should be allowed until *[date]* to join additional parties and until *[date]* to amend the pleadings.

Defendant(s) should be allowed until *[date]* to join additional parties and until *[date]* to amend the pleadings.

All potentially dispositive motions should be filed by *[date].*
Settlement *[is likely] [is unlikely] [cannot be evaluated prior to [date]] [may be enhanced by use of the following alternative dispute resolution procedure: [date].*
Final lists of witnesses and exhibits under *[rule]* should be due
from plaintiff(s) by *[date]*
from defendant(s) by *[date]*
Parties should have __ days after service of final lists of witnesses and exhibits to list objections under *[rule].*
The case should be ready for trial by *[date] [and at this time is expected to take approximately [length of time]].*
[Other matters.]

Dated: ________

[signature, etc.]

Dated: ________

[signature, etc.]

NOTES TO FORM

Commentary

This form is adapted from Official Form 35 approved by the U.S. Supreme Court.

§ 11:15 Stipulation and order regarding discovery conference discussions

[Caption]

STIPULATION AND ORDER REGARDING DISCOVERY CONFERENCE DISCUSSIONS

WHEREAS, the parties have reached agreement on a date for their first discovery conference discussions regarding the production of digital or electronic documents as well as certain ground rules for such discussions generally;

NOW THEREFORE, the parties, through their respective counsel of record, hereby stipulate as follows:

A. On *[date]*, the parties shall engage in discussions regarding the production of electronic documents in this case. The discussions will be attended by an electronic document consultant retained by *[party]* who will have sufficient knowledge of *[party]*'s electronic documents to enable *[party]* to participate in a good faith effort to resolve all issues regarding the production of electronic documents without court action. The discussions also will be attended by an electronic document consultant retained by the *[opposing party]* who will have sufficient knowledge of the *[opposing party]*'s electronic documents to enable the *[opposing party]* to participate in a good faith effort to resolve all issues regarding the production of electronic documents without court action.

B. Except as set forth in the next sentence, any electronic document consultant who personally attends any conference regarding the production of electronic documents in this case shall not be subject to discovery requests, including requests for depositions, until such time as the parties otherwise agree or this Court orders that such discovery may be taken. If any such digital or electronic document consultant provides testimony on an issue or issues in this case, whether by affidavit, declaration, deposition, or otherwise, the consultant may be subject to discovery requests, including requests for depositions, limited to the issue or issues that are the subject of the consultant's testimony.

Dated: ____

[signature, etc.]

Dated: ____

[signature, etc.]

PURSUANT TO STIPULATION, IT IS SO ORDERED.

Dated: ________

____

Judge

§ 11:16 Interim order to confer and to preserve electronically stored information

[Caption]

Interim Order Regarding Preservation

1. Order to Confer In order to further the just, speedy, efficient, and economical management of discovery, the parties are ORDERED to confer as soon as practicable, no later than 30 days after the date of this order, to develop a plan for the preservation of documents, data, and tangible things reasonably anticipated to be subject to discovery in this action.

The parties may conduct this conference as part of the Federal Rules of Civil Procedure Rule 26(f) conference if the conference is scheduled to take place within 30 days of the date of this order. The resulting preservation plan may be submitted to this Court as a proposed order under Federal Rules of Civil Procedure Rule 16(e).

2. Subjects for Consideration The parties should attempt to reach agreement on all issues regarding the preservation of documents data, and tangible things. These issues include, but are not necessarily limited to:
   (a) the extent of the preservation obligation, identifying the types of material to be preserved, the subject matter, time frame, the authors and addressees, and key words to be used in identifying responsive materials;
   (b) the identification of persons responsible for carrying out preservation obligations on behalf of each party;
   (c) the form and method of providing notice of the duty to preserve to persons identified as custodian: of documents, data, and tangible things;
   (d) mechanisms for monitoring, certifying, or auditing custodian compliance with preservation obligations;
   (e) whether preservation will require suspending or modifying any routine business processes of procedures, with special attention to document-management programs and the recycling of computer data storage media;
   (f) the methods to preserve any volatile but potentially discoverable material, such as voicemail active data in databases, or electronic messages;
   (g) the anticipated costs of preservation and ways to reduce or share these costs; and
   (h) a mechanism to review and modify the preservation obligation as discovery proceeds, eliminating or adding particular categories of documents, data, and tangible things.
3. Duty to Preserve
   (a) Until the parties reach agreement on a preservation plan, all parties and their counsel are reminded of their duty to preserve evidence that may be relevant to this action. The

duty extends to documents, data, and tangible things in the possession, custody and control of the parties to this action, and any employees, agents, contractors, carriers, bailees, or other nonparties possessing materials reasonably anticipated to be subject to discovery in this action. Counsel is under an obligation to exercise reasonable efforts to identify and notify such nonparties, including employees of corporate or institutional parties.

(b) The term "documents, data, and tangible things" is to be interpreted broadly to include writings, records, files, correspondence, reports, memoranda, calendars, diaries, minutes, electronic messages, voicemail, e-mail; telephone message records or logs, computer and network activity logs, hard drives; backup data, removable computer storage media such as tapes, disks, and cards, printouts document image files, Web pages, databases, spreadsheets, software, books, ledgers, journals, orders, invoices, bills, vouchers, checks, statements, worksheets, summaries, compilations, computations, charts, diagrams, graphic presentations, drawings, films, charts, digital or chemical process photographs, video, phonographic, tape, or digital recordings or transcripts, drafts, jottings, and notes. Information serving to identify, locate, or link such material, such as file inventories, file folders, indices, and metadata, is also included in this definition.

(c) "Preservation" is to be interpreted broadly to accomplish the goal of maintaining the integrity of all documents, data, and tangible things reasonably anticipated to be subject to discovery under Rules 26, 45, and 56(e) of the Federal Rules of Civil Procedure in this action. Preservation includes taking reasonable steps to prevent the partial or full destruction, alteration, testing, deletion, shredding, incineration, wiping relocation, migration, theft, or mutation of such material, as well as negligent or intentional handling that would make material incomplete or inaccessible.

(d) If the business practices of any party involve the routine destruction, recycling, relocation, of mutation of such materials, the party must, to the extent practicable for the pendency of this order either

(1) halt such business processes;

(2) sequester or remove such material from the business process; or

(3) arrange for the preservation of complete and accurate duplicates or copies of such material suitable for later discovery if requested.

(e) A party may apply to the court for further instructions regarding the duty to preserve specific categories of documents, data, or tangible things before the conference to develop a preservation plan. A party may seek permission to resume routine business processes relating to the storage or destruction of specific categories of documents, data, or tangible things, upon a showing c undue cost, burden, or overbreadth.

4. Procedure in the Event No Agreement Is Reached If, after conferring to develop a preservation plan, counsel do not reach agreement on the subjects listed under paragraph 2 of this order or on other material aspects of preservation, the parties are to submit to the Court within three days of the conference a statement of the unresolved issues together with each party's proposal for their resolution of the issues. In framing an order regarding the preservation of documents, data, and tangible things, the court will consider those statements as well as any statements made in an applications under paragraph 3(e) of this order.

Dated: ________

____

Judge

NOTES TO FORM

Commentary

The primary purpose of this order is to encourage the parties to confer in order to develop their own preservation plan. The form may be modified to serve as a stand-alone preservation order. The rule references in the form are to the Federal Rules of Civil Procedure. If the action is in a state court, the rule references should be modified accordingly.

This form is adapted from Form 40.25 in THE MANUAL FOR COMPLEX LITIGATION FOURTH. When adapting for use in state court, the references to Federal Rules of Civil Procedure should be replaced by reference to applicable state rules.

§ 11:17 Case management report

[Caption]

Case Management Report

The parties have agreed on the following dates and discovery plan pursuant to *[rule]*:

DEADLINE OR EVENT	AGREED DATE

DEADLINE OR EVENT		AGREED DATE
Mandatory Initial Disclosures (pursuant to *[rule]*)		*[date]*
Certificate of Interested Persons and Corporate Disclosure Statement		
Motions to Add Parties or to Amend Pleadings		*[date]*
Disclosure of Expert Reports	Plaintiff:	**Plaintiff's deadline to disclose expert—*[date]***
		Plaintiff's deadline to disclose expert report—*[date]*
	Defendant:	**Defendant's deadline to disclose expert—*[date]***
		Defendant's deadline to disclose expert report—*[date]*
Dispositive Motions		*[date]*
Meeting *In Person* to Prepare Joint Final Pretrial		*[date]*
Statement		
Joint Final Pretrial Statement (Including a Single Set of Jointly-Proposed Jury Instructions and Verdict Form (with diskette), Voir Dire Questions, Witness Lists, Exhibit Lists with Objections on Approved Form)		*[date]*
All Other Motions Including Motions in Limine, Trial Brief		*[date]*
Final Pretrial Conference		*[date]*
Trial Term Begins		*[date]*
Estimated Length of Trial		__ days
Jury/Non-Jury		
Mediation Deadline:		*[date]*
Mediator:		*[name]*
Address:		*[address]*
Telephone:		______

DEADLINE OR EVENT	AGREED DATE
All Parties Consent to Proceed Before Magistrate Judge	———

I. Meeting of Parties in Person

Pursuant to *[rule]*, a meeting was held in person on *[date]*, at *[place]* and was attended by

Name	*Trial Counsel for:*
[name]	Plaintiff
[name]	Defendant

II. Pre-Discovery Initial Disclosures of Core Information *[rule]* Disclosures

The parties
- ☐ have exchanged
- ☐ agree to exchange information described in *[rule]* by *[date]*.

III. Agreed Discovery Plan for Plaintiff and Defendant

A. Certificate of Interested Persons and Corporate Disclosure Statement. Every party that has appeared in this action to date has filed and served or will file and serve a Certificate of Interested Persons and Corporate Disclosure Statement, which remains current:

Plaintiff filed a Certificate of Interested Persons and Corporate Disclosure Statement on *[date]*.

Defendant filed a Certificate of Interested Persons and Corporate Disclosure Statement on *[date]*.

B. Discovery Not Filed. The parties shall not file discovery materials with the Clerk except as provided in *[rule]*. The Court encourages the exchange of discovery requests on diskette. See *[rule]*. The parties further agree as follows:

i. The parties will try to furnish all discovery requests on diskette using Microsoft Word.

ii. Responses to interrogatories will include both the question posed followed by the response.

iii. Service of discovery requests by facsimile is sufficient.

iv. Documents, including electronic discovery will be produced in PDF format or by printing the electronic documents. Electronic discovery does not have to be produced in its natural form, unless the authenticity of a particular document becomes an issue in the case.

C. Limits on Discovery. Absent leave of Court, the parties may take no more than __ depositions per side (not per party). *[rule]*. Absent leave of Court, the parties may serve no more than __ interrogatories, including sub-parts. *[rule]*. Absent leave of Court or stipulation of the parties each deposition is limited to __ day(s) of __ hours. The parties may agree by stipulation on other limits on discovery. The Court will consider the parties' agreed dates, deadlines, and other limits in entering the scheduling order. In addition to the deadlines in the above table, the parties have agreed to further limit discovery as follows:
   1. Depositions: no additional agreements, but they are not waiving any rights to request additional time consistent with *[rule]*.
   2. Interrogatories: parties agree to a limit of __ interrogatories
   3. Document Requests:
   4. Request to Admit:
   5. Supplementation of Discovery:

D. Discovery Deadline. Each party shall timely serve discovery requests so that the rules allow for a response prior to the discovery deadline. The Court may deny as untimely all motions to compel filed after the discovery deadline, hi addition, the parties agree as follows:

E. Disclosure of Expert Testimony. On or before the dates set forth in the above table for the disclosure of expert reports, the parties agree to fully comply with *[rules]*. Expert testimony on direct examination at trial will be limited to the opinions, basis, reasons, data and other information disclosed in the written expert report disclosed pursuant to this order. Failure to disclose such information may result in the exclusion of all or part of the testimony of the expert witness. The parties agree on the following additional matters pertaining to the disclosure of expert testimony: The parties may agree to submission of videotaped expert testimony.

F. Confidentiality Agreements. Whether documents filed in a case may be filed under seal is a separate issue from whether the parties may agree that produced documents are confidential. The Court is a public forum, and disfavors motions to file under seal. The Court will permit the parties to file documents under seal only upon a finding of extraordinary circumstances and particularized need. A party seeking to file a document under seal must file a motion to file under seal requesting such Court action, together with memorandum of law in support. The motion, whether granted or denied, will remain in the public record.

The parties may reach their own agreement regarding the designation of materials as "confidential." There is no need for the Court to endorse the confidentiality agreement. The Court discourages unnecessary stipulated motions for a protective order. The Court will enforce appropriate stipulated and signed confidentiality agreements. Each confidentiality agreement or order shall provide, or shall be deemed to provide, that "no party shall file a document under seal without first having obtained an order granting leave to file under seal on showing of particularized need." With respect to confidentiality agreements the parties agree as follows: The parties agree that they will seek to protect confidential documents and information through confidentiality agreements entered into between counsel, as necessary.

G. Other Matters Regarding Discovery. Counsel for either party may appear telephonically for depositions and depositions may be videotaped.

Unless otherwise agreed, depositions will occur at *[place]*.

IV. Settlement and Alternative Dispute Resolution

A. Settlement The parties agree that settlement is

☐ Likely
☐ Unlikely

The parties request a settlement conference before a United States Magistrate Judge.

☐ Likely
☐ Unlikely

B. Arbitration *[Rule]* defines those civil actions that will be referred to arbitration automatically. Does this case fall within the scope of Local Rule 8.02(a)?

☐ Yes
☐ No

For cases not falling within the scope of Local Rule 8.02(a), the parties consent to arbitration pursuant to *[rule]*:

☐ Yes
☐ No

☐ Likely to agree in future

In any civil case subject to arbitration, the Court may substitute mediation for arbitration upon a determination that the case is susceptible to resolution through mediation. The parties agree that the case is susceptible to resolution through mediation, and therefore jointly request mediation in place of arbitration.

☐ Yes

☐ No

☐ Likely to agree in future

C. Mediation The parties have agreed to select a mediator from the Court's approved list of mediators as provided by the Clerk of Court or will seek approval of another mediator, and have agreed to the date stated in the table above as the last date for mediation.

D. Other Alternative Dispute Resolution The parties intend to pursue the following other methods of alternative dispute resolution:

Dated: ___

[signature, etc.]

Dated: ___

[signature, etc.]

§ 11:18 Joint case management statement and proposed case scheduling order

[Caption]

Joint Case Management Statement and Proposed Case Scheduling Order

I. INTRODUCTION

Pursuant to *[rule]*, a conference was held on *[date]*, in Case No. __, and was attended by *[names]*. The parties attended the Initial Case Management Conference for this matter on *[date]*, but since the parties could not agree as to the form of production of electronically stored information, the Court declined to issue a Scheduling Order, rather, it referred the parties to a discovery conference with Magistrate Judge *[name]* on *[date]*. The parties now appear for this Continued Case Management Conference to set the Scheduling Order in this matter.

A. Jurisdiction and Service

This case is brought under the *[statute]*. The Court has subject matter jurisdiction under *[statute]*.

Service has been effected on all named parties. Plaintiff may add additional individual defendants after the completion of initial discovery; Plaintiff will do so no later than *[date]*.

B. Facts

Plaintiff alleges that Defendant violated *[statute]* when Plaintiff *[describe]*.

C. Legal Issues

D. Motions

The parties have filed no motions and there are no motions pending before this Court. Defendant intends to file a motion for summary judgment once discovery is completed.

E. Amendment of Pleadings

The parties may amend their pleadings. A party needing to amend must do so on or before *[date]*.

F. Evidence Preservation

Defendant suspended the routine destruction of electronically stored information to preserve evidence relevant to the issues reasonably evident in this action and has preserved the information for production to Plaintiff, if necessary.

G. Disclosures

Pre-discovery Disclosures: The parties have exchanged initial disclosures required by *[rule]* on *[date]*.

H. Discovery

Defendant served its first set of Special Interrogatories and Request for Production of Documents on Plaintiff on *[date]*.

The parties propose to the court the following discovery plan:

1. Plaintiff's Discovery Plan. Plaintiff believes that discovery will be needed on the following subjects:
   a. Defendant's motivation for the selection of Plaintiffs reemployment position and its relationship to eventual termination.

b. Discovery of electronically stored documents.
c. Willful nature of Defendant's termination of Plaintiff.
d. Defendant's financials.
e. Reemployment of Plaintiff following military service.
f. Relocation of Defendant's District managerial staff.
g. Retraining schedule of Plaintiff following his reemployment.

2. Defendant's Discovery Plan. Defendant believes that discovery will be needed on the following subjects:
   a. Plaintiff's performance.
   b. Plaintiff's mitigation efforts.
   c. All issues raised in Defendant's answer and affirmative defenses.
3. Plaintiff requests a maximum of __ interrogatories by each party to any other party. Defendant objects to the propounding of any interrogatories over the limits imposed by *[rule]*.
4. No limitation on requests for admission by each party to any other party.
5. Maximum of 10 depositions by Plaintiff and by Defendant.
6. Each deposition shall be limited to a maximum of 7 hours within one day unless extended by agreement of the parties. Defendant anticipates that it may need more than seven (7) hours to complete the deposition of Plaintiff, and requests that the Court grant additional time.
7. Electronic Discovery: Defendant has agreed to provide Plaintiff with electronically stored information in its native format. Defendant will also provide a separate production in.TIP or.PDF format with *[Bates] [hash]* numbers allowing the parties to track the documents. Defendant will produce any partially privileged documents, and documents that contain confidential or proprietary information in native format and in.TIP or.PDF form along with any associated non-privileged metadata. Plaintiff does not agree to the production of any electronically stored information in any format other than the native format of the information.

Although the parties cannot agree on the form of production of privileged, confidential, or proprietary information, Magistrate Judge *[name]* deferred ruling or issuing a discovery order until an issue actually arose. Plaintiff has stated plaintiff will not intentionally seek discovery of privileged information from Defendant. The parties have filed a stipulated protective order that will govern the use of Defendant's designated confidential information.

I. Related Cases

There are no related cases.

J. Relief

In any action under *[statute]*, the court may award relief as follows: *[describe]*.

K. Settlement Alternative Dispute Resolution

The parties have filed a Stipulation and Proposed Order Selecting an ADR process: Settlement Conference with a Magistrate Judge to occur after initial discovery has been completed.

L. Consent to Magistrate Judge for All Purposes

The parties do not consent to the assignment of this case to a Magistrate Judge for trial.

M. Other References

This case is not suitable for reference to binding arbitration, a special master, or the Judicial Panel on Multidistrict Litigation.

N. Narrowing of Issues

The issues in this case cannot be narrowed by agreement. The parties will confer prior to trial to attempt to expedite the admission of evidence through stipulation. Defendant intends to file a motion to bifurcate the liability phase of trial from any trial on the issue of liquidated damages.

O. Expedited Schedule

Due to the inevitable issues surrounding the production of electronically stored information, the parties do not believe this case is suitable for an expedited schedule.

P. Scheduling

(1) All non-expert discovery shall cut off on *[date]*.
(2) Disclosure of and production of initial report from retained experts for the parties under *[rule]* are to be served on or before *[date]*.
(3) Supplementary expert disclosure and expert reports are to be served by *[date]*. Expert discovery shall cut-off on *[date]*.
(4) All dispositive motions shall be filed on or before *[date]*.
(5) The parties request a trial date of *[date]*.

Q. Trial

The parties estimate the length of trial at __ days. Plaintiff has requested a jury.

R. Disclosure of Non-Party Interested Entities or Persons

Defendant has filed its "Certification of Interested Entities or Persons" as required by *[rule]*. Defendant restates that the following entities have either: (i) a financial interest in the subject matter in controversy or in a party to the proceeding; or (ii) any other kind of interest that could be substantially affected by the outcome of the proceeding: *[names]*.

Dated: ____

[signature, etc.]

Dated: ____

[signature, etc.]

§ 11:19 Scheduling order

[Caption]

Joint Scheduling Report

Plaintiffs, *[names]*, and Defendants, *[names]*, through respective undersigned counsel, submit their Joint Scheduling Report as follows:

1. Description of the Case
   a. Attorneys:
   For the Plaintiffs:
   [names, addresses, and telephone numbers]
   For the Defendants:
   [names, addresses, and telephone numbers]
   b. Plaintiffs allege Federal jurisdiction is based on *[statute]*.
   c. Plaintiffs are *[describe]* who seek *[describe]*.
   d. Major legal and factual issues:
   Plaintiffs contend that *[describe]*. Plaintiff see damages in the amount of $____, plus interest and costs.
   Defendants contend that *[describe]*.
2. Proposed case management plan
   a) Pending motions: ____
   b) Deadline for joinder of additional parties: *[date]*

c) Deadline for amendments to pleadings: *[date]*

d)

(i) Rule 26 (a) (1) Disclosure shall be served by *[date]* (assuming confidentiality stipulation is in place).

(ii) Factual discovery shall be completed by November 1, 2007

(iii) Plaintiffs Expert Disclosure (including reports) shall be made by *[date]*. Defendants Expert Disclosure (including reports) shall be made by *[date]*.

(iv) Expert discovery shall be completed by *[date]*.

e) Final pretrial order shall be filled by *[date]*.

f) The parties estimate that a jury trial will last two weeks. The case will be trial ready on *[date]*.

g) Motions related to limitations of liability shall be filed by *[date]*.

h) The last filing date for dispositive motions is *[date]*.

i) The parties agree that service of papers can also be made by e-mail or fax.

3. **The parties do not unanimously consent to trial before magistrate.**

4. Status of settlement discussions The parties agree to discuss settlement and request a settlement conference in *[date]*.

5. Privilege

a) The parties shall agree on a date to exchange privilege logs.

b) Assertions of privilege and work product shall be permitted for documents produced for a period of up to 60 days after production.

6. Electronic Discovery

a) Counsel shall request that their clients place a litigation hold on documents related to *[describe]*.

b) E-mails and other electronic data shall be produced either on disks or printed out as if they were hard copy documents. E-mails shall be searched under terms identifying *[describe]* in question or as otherwise reasonably demanded. Data contained in backup logs or tapes need not be produced unless shown by circumstances to be necessary. No party shall intentionally erase any relevant data or intentionally move any relevant data to backup logs.

Dated: ____

____

Judge

Chapter 12

Depositions

I. GUIDELINES

II. CHECKLISTS

III. FORMS

Research References

Treatises and Practice Aids

Grenig & Gleisner, eDiscovery & Digital Evidence § 7:13

Trial Strategy

Recovery and Reconstruction of Electronic Mail as Evidence, 41 Am. Jur Proof of Facts 3d 1

Computer Technology in Civil Litigation, 71 Am. Jur Trials 111

Additional References

Grenig & Kinsler, Handbook of Federal Civil Discovery and Disclosure §§ 5.1 to 7.44 (3d ed.)

ABA Discovery Standards, http://www.abanet.org/litigation/discoverystandards/2005civildiscoverystandards.pdf

Federal Judicial Center, http://www.fjc.gov

The Sedona Conference, http://www.thesedonaconference.org

KeyCite®: Cases and other legal materials listed in KeyCite Scope can be researched through the KeyCite service on Westlaw®. Use KeyCite to check citations for form, parallel references, prior and later history, and comprehensive citator information, including citations to other decisions and secondary materials.

I. GUIDELINES

§ 12:1 Generally

Depositions, especially a deposition of information technology custodians pursuant to Fed R. Civ. P. 30(b)(6), can be an extremely useful tool to identify sources of potentially relevant electronically stored information. A deposition is testimony taken prior to trial before an officer authorized to administer oaths, subject to cross-examination, and preserved in writing. Under certain circumstances, deposition testimony may be admissible at trial. Depositions may be taken either upon oral examination or upon written questions. Depositions are almost always taken orally rather than in writing.

§ 12:2 Advantages and disadvantages of depositions upon oral examination

The major advantage of a deposition upon oral examination over any other discovery device is that oral examination permits more effective questioning. If the deponent's answers are evasive, incomplete, or non-responsive, the examiner can follow up with additional questions. In addition, the deponent's credibility and memory can be tested by questions about related matters that tend to confirm or disprove earlier answers. There is also a much better possibility of obtaining spontaneous admissions in depositions upon oral examination than with other discovery devices, such as interrogatories where the answers are usually prepared by opposing counsel. A deposition upon oral examination allows the examiner to determine the impression that a witness is likely to make on the jury if the case goes to trial.

A deposition upon oral examination may be more efficient than other discovery devices because a deposition usually can be set on just a few days' notice to the opposing party. In addition, documents can be inspected and answers can be obtained to oral questions at the time of the deposition. Depositions can be extremely useful in the context of e-discovery by allowing for the examination of individuals with knowledge of information records systems and potentially responsive sources of electronically stored information.

§ 12:3 Whose deposition may be taken—Generally

A party may take the deposition of any person, including a party or non-party witness.[1] A party may even take its own deposition. The person deposed may be a natural person, an organization such as a public or private corporation,[2] a partnership, an association, or a governmental agency. Party deponents are not entitled to witness fees. However, a nonparty deponent may be entitled to witness fees.[3]

§ 12:4 Deposition of expert witness

Under Fed. R. Civ. P. 26(b)(4)(A), a party may depose any person who has been identified as an expert and whose opinions may be presented at trial.[1] Unless manifest injustice would result, the court must require the party seeking discovery to pay the

---

[Section 12:3]

[1]See Fed. R. Civ. P. 30(a)(1).

[2]See Fed. R. Civ. P. 30(b)(6).

[3]See Fed. R. Civ. P. 45(b)(1).

[Section 12:4]

[1]Cf. Roberts v. Canadian Pacific Ry. Ltd., 2007 WL 118901 (D. Minn. 2007) (plaintiff could take deposition of defendant's computer forensics expert after an e-mail was discovered indicating a policy of destroying electronically stored information).

expert a reasonable fee for the time spent in responding to discovery.[2]

It is more common for counsel to employ e-discovery or forensic experts to assist with the discovery process or in analyzing electronically stored information. Because of the potential for these experts to be deposed or called as a witness, it may be advisable to engage both testifying and non-testifying experts in certain situations. An expert witness who is not expected to testify at trial may not be deposed except as provided by Fed. R. Civ. P. 35(b) upon a motion showing that exceptional circumstances exist under which it is impracticable for the party seeking discovery to obtain facts or opinions on the same subject by other means.

§ 12:5 Deposition of corporate representatives

Because it is not literally possible to take the deposition of a corporation or other organization, the information must be obtained from a natural person who can speak for the organization.[1] Since the deposition of any person can be taken, the deposition of any person associated with the organization and acquainted with the facts can be taken.[2] A Fed. R. Civ. P. 36(b)(6) deposition can be an effective way of deposing the person in an organization responsible for computer systems or electronically stored information.

Fed. R. Civ. P. 30(b)(6) permits the discovering party to name in the notice of deposition a public or private corporation, a partnership, an association, or a governmental agency. The notice must describe with reasonable particularity the matters on which the examination is requested. It is then the duty of the corporation to name one or more officer, director, or managing agent, or other person who consents to testify on its behalf, and these persons must testify. A corporate party is not absolutely bound to its deposition designee's recollection.

The corporation's duty to name persons who will testify on its behalf relieves the party seeking discovery of the burden of ascertaining the appropriate individual to depose while relieving the other party of the inconvenience of having an unnecessarily large number of its officers deposed. Fed. R. Civ. P. 30(b)(6) also assists organizations that find an unnecessarily large number of

---

[2]Fed. R. Civ. P. 26(b)(4)(C).

[Section 12:5]

[1]Fed. R. Civ. P. 36(b)(6).

[2]See Wright and Miller, FEDERAL PRACTICE AND PROCEDURE: Civil § 2103.

their officers and agents are being deposed by a party uncertain of who in the organization has knowledge. When a witness is designated by a corporation to speak on its behalf, producing an unprepared witness is tantamount to a failure to appear that is sanctionable.

Fed. R. Civ. P. 30(b)(6) does not preclude a party from taking the deposition of a specific individual associated with a corporation or organization. But when a party utilizes Fed. R. Civ. P. 30(b)(6), it has no right to insist that the organization choose a specific person, unless the person designated is an officer, director, or managing agent whom the corporation may be required to produce under Fed. R. Civ. P. 30(b)(1).

In the context of e-discovery, a Fed. R. Civ. P. 30(b)(6) deposition of an information technology or records manager is increasingly common. Such deposition, if well executed, can help identify and put the requesting party in a position to generate narrowly tailored interrogatories and requests for production. This is especially true in situations where the opposing party is not cooperative or forthcoming with information about potential sources of discoverable electronically stored information. It is also common to use such a deposition to explore opposing party's compliance with preservation obligations.

§ 12:6 Organization employees

Except where the employee of an organization has been designated by the organization under Fed. R. Civ. P. 30(b)(6) or the employee is an officer, director, or managing agent of the organization, the employee is treated the same as any other witness and the employee's presence must be obtained by subpoena rather than by notice. The deposition is not considered to be that of the organization and is usable only under the same circumstances as that of any other non-party witness.

§ 12:7 Specific individuals associated with organization—Officers and managing agents

If the deponent is an officer, director, or managing agent of an organization that is a party to the suit, the corporation is responsible for producing that person for the taking of the person's deposition after being served with a proper notice; a subpoena for their attendance is unnecessary. The question of whether a particular person is a managing agent is determined pragmatically on a case-by-case basis.

An adverse party "may use for any purpose the deposition of a party or anyone who, when deposed, was the party's an officer, director, or managing agent, or designee under Rule 30(b)(6) or Rule 31(a)(4)."[1] The determination of whether a particular person is an officer, director, or managing agent is made by the trial court when the deposition is sought to be introduced or when sanctions are asked for the individual's failure to appear for the taking of his or her deposition.

In determining whether an individual is an officer, director, or managing agent of an organization, courts consider the following:

- Whether the individual involved is invested by the organization with general powers to exercise his or her discretion and judgment in dealing with organization.
- Whether the individual can be depended upon to carry out the organization's direction to give testimony at the demand of a party engaged in litigation with the employer.
- Whether the individual can be expected to identify with the interests of the corporation rather than with those of the other parties.

§ 12:8 When depositions may be taken—Generally

Except when authorized by the Federal Rules of Civil Procedure, by local rule or order, or the agreement of the parties, the taking of a deposition under Fed. R. Civ. P. 30 normally cannot be noticed until the parties have conferred as required by Fed. R. Civ. P. 26(f). A showing of good cause is necessary to justify an expedited discovery order before the Fed. R. Civ. P. 26(f) discovery conference.

For an ex parte motion for expedited discovery to be justified, the evidence must show: (1) that the moving party's cause will be irreparably prejudiced if the underlying motion is heard according to the regular noticed motion procedures, and (2) the moving party is without fault in creating the crisis that requires ex parte relief or that the crisis is the result of excusable neglect. A deposition may be taken before the commencement of an action in accordance with the procedures set forth in Fed. R. Civ. P. 27.

If the time for the deposition is inconvenient, the court has the power under Fed. R. Civ. P. 26(c) to issue a protective order specifying the time or place on which discovery can be had. If the court changes the time, a second notice of taking the deposition is not necessary.

[Section 12:7]

[1]Fed. R. Civ. P. 32(a)(3).

§ 12:9 When depositions may be taken—Sequence

Depositions may be taken in any sequence, unless the court upon motion, for the convenience of the parties and witnesses and in the interests of justice, orders otherwise.[1] The fact one party is conducting discovery, by deposition or otherwise, does not delay another party's right to discovery. It is appropriate to discuss the sequence of discovery, including depositions, at the discovery conference and the scheduling conference.

§ 12:10 Notice of deposition—Generally

A party desiring to take the deposition of any person must give reasonable written notice to every other party to the action. Service of the notice must be made upon all parties. The notice must be filed either before service or within a reasonable time afterwards.

The notice must be in writing and it must state the time and place of the taking of the deposition. Additionally, the notice must state the name and address of each person to be examined, if known. If the name is not known, a general description is sufficient to identify the person or the particular class or group to which the person belongs. A list of any materials the deponent is compelled to produce at the deposition must also be attached to or included in the notice. Any subpoena directing a witness to appear at the deposition should be attached to the notice.

§ 12:11 Notice of deposition—Time of notice

Under Fed. R. Civ. P. 30(b)(1), notice of the deposition must be given within a reasonable time before the deposition. Courts have upheld notice of six days and eight days. Fed. R. Civ. P. 32(a)(5)(A) provides that a deposition cannot used against a party that has received less than 14 days' notice of the deposition, has promptly filed a motion for a protective order requesting that the deposition not be held or be held at a different time, and the motion is pending at the time the deposition is held.

[Section 12:9]

[1]Fed. R. Civ. P. 26(d).

§ 12:12 Notice of deposition—Party deponent

The deposition of a party may be taken by notice; a subpoena is not required.[1] The notice to a party deponent may be accompanied by a request made in compliance with Fed. R. Civ. P. 34 for the production of documents and tangible things at the taking of the deposition. The attendance of an officer, director, or managing agent of an entity that is a party may be compelled by notice addressed to the named person. On the other hand, an individual employee of a party-entity who is not an officer, director, or managing agent of the party-entity may be compelled to attend a deposition only by subpoena.[2]

§ 12:13 Notice of deposition—Organizational parties

A party may name as a party-deponent in the notice a public or private corporation, a partnership, an association, or a governmental agency.[1] The notice must designate with reasonable particularity the matters on which the examination is requested. An organization cannot be expected to designate an appropriate representative at a deposition if it does not know the subject matter of the testimony.

Once the deponent has satisfied his or her minimum obligation by responding to questions on matters set forth in the notice of deposition, then the scope of the deposition is determined solely by relevance. If the organization has objections to either questions outside the scope of the Fed. R. Civ. P. 30(b)(6) designation, counsel for the organization should state the objection on the record and the witness should answer the question, to the best of the witness' ability.

§ 12:14 Notice of deposition—Objection to notice

Objections to the notice of deposition are waived unless a written objection is promptly served upon the party giving notice. Possible errors or irregularities include the wrong name, an incorrect date, incorrect location, improper service, lack of timely notice, or failure to include a list of compelled materials. Whenever possible, the objection should be made before the deposition.

[Section 12:12]

[1]See Fed. R. Civ. P. 30(b)(1).

[2]See Wright and Miller, FEDERAL PRACTICE AND PROCEDURE: Civil § 2103.

[Section 12:13]

[1]See Fed. R. Civ. P. 30(b)(6).

§ 12:15 Compelling production of documents at deposition

The procedure for compelling production of documents at a deposition depends on whether the deponent is or is not a party. If a party seeks to compel another party deponent to bring with it documents and other tangible things, the notice of taking of the deposition must be accompanied with a request for the production of documents and things in compliance with the procedural requirements of for a request for production. If the deponent is not a party, production of the documents can be compelled only by a subpoena duces tecum. Witnesses may be compelled to produce documents that they control even though they do not have possession of them.

§ 12:16 Place of examination

Fed. R. Civ. P. 45(d)(2) and 26(c)(2) control the taking of a deposition. Generally, the examining party may set the place for the deposition of another party wherever the examining party wishes, subject to the court's power to grant a protective order under Fed. R. Civ. P. 26(c)(2) designating a different place. In the alternative, the parties may agree to a deposition location.

Courts usually permit an individual defendant to be deposed in the district of the defendant's residence, or, if an organizational party, at its principal place of business. However, corporate defendants are frequently deposed in places other than the location of the principal place of business, especially in the forum, for the convenience of all parties and in the general interests of judicial economy.

Factors that serve to dissipate the presumption that a corporate party's deposition should be held at its principal place of business and may persuade the court to require the deposition be conducted in the forum district or in some other place include:

- Location of counsel for the parties.
- Number of corporate representatives a party is seeking to depose.
- Likelihood of significant discovery disputes arising that would necessitate resolution by the forum court.
- Whether persons sought to be deposed often engage in travel for business purposes.
- Equities with regard to the nature of the claim and the parties' relationship.

If the deponent is an officer, director or managing agent of a corporate party, or other person designated under Fed. R. Civ. P.

30(b)(6), the place of examination is determined as if the deponent's place of residence, employment, or transacting business in person were that of the party.

An individual plaintiff must usually submit to deposition in the district where the plaintiff commenced the litigation. A plaintiff should not be able to complain of his or her chosen forum, while defendants have no similar choice.

Unless otherwise ordered by a court, party deponents are normally required to pay their own transportation costs. These rules are subject to modification based on certain factors, such as:

- Which party is better able to absorb the deponent's transportation costs.
- The location of documents necessary at the deposition.
- The convenience of the deponent, parties, and counsel.
- The location of documents or physical evidence.
- Which court is best suited to supervise the deposition.
- The deponent's physical well-being.
- The counsels' location.
- The location of prior depositions.

II. CHECKLISTS

§ 12:17 Checklist of matters to consider in selecting deponent

The deponent should be the person most knowledgeable about:

- ☐ Number, types, and locations of computers in use and no longer in use
- ☐ Network structure, volume, location and configuration
- ☐ Email or other communication system structure, volume, location and configuration
- ☐ Existence of a company data map
- ☐ Operating systems and application software in use
- ☐ File-naming and location-saving conventions
- ☐ Disk- or tape-labeling conventions
- ☐ Backup and archival system configuration, including schedule, volume, software and data sources
- ☐ Most likely locations of electronically stored information relevant to the subject matter of the case
- ☐ Creation, use and storage of information by users
- ☐ Digital records and information management policies, procedures and practices
- ☐ Corporate policies regarding employee use of company computers and data

☐ Identities of all current and former employees who have or had access to network administration, backup, archiving, or other system operations during the relevant period

☐ Use of third-party computer systems or technology, including communication systems, social media or other services

☐ Efforts taken to preserve electronically stored information in connection with the present case

§ 12:18 Checklist for deponent's attorney

Before the deposition, the deponent's attorney should:

☐ Instruct the deponent not to answer questions they do not understand.

☐ Advise the deponent not speculate or guess. The deponent should be told that if the deponent speculates in favor of the deponent, it will be disregarded; if the deponent speculates with unfavorable results for the deponent it will be used against the deponent.

☐ Tell the deponent not to volunteer information.

§ 12:19 Checklist for commencing deposition

The examining attorney may begin the deposition by stating a series of rules, establishing the framework for the deposition. These rules may include the following:

☐ I'm going to ask you a series of questions regarding the incident that is the subject of the lawsuit and which happened on *[date]*.

☐ If at any time you do not understand one of my questions, please say so and I will repeat or restate the question.

☐ All of your answers must be made in words, since the court reporter cannot take down gestures.

☐ If you do not know the answer to a question, simply state that you do not know. I do not want you to guess or to speculate as to your answers.

☐ Please state your answers clearly for the record so that the court reporter can accurately transcribe each of your words.

☐ Please wait until I finish each of my questions before answering and I will wait until you finish each of your answers before asking another questions.

☐ We will take a break about every hour to give the court reporter and all of us a chance to refresh ourselves. If you need a break before then, please ask and we will take one.

☐ Do you understand that the deposition will be transcribed by the court reporter and that everything said here today will be recorded?

- ☐ Do you understand that, at the trial, all the testimony given here today will be available in written form and if I ask you a question at trial that I ask you today, you may be asked to explain any differences that may occur in your answers?
- ☐ Do you understand that your testimony today is being given under oath, as if you were in a court of law?

§ 12:20 Checklist of objections

- ☐ Oath or affirmation
- ☐ Conduct of the parties
- ☐ Manner of taking the deposition
- ☐ Form of the questions or answers
- ☐ Leading or suggestive question
- ☐ Ambiguous or uncertain question
- ☐ Compound questions
- ☐ Question assumes a fact not in evidence
- ☐ Question calls for narrative answer
- ☐ Question calls for speculation or conjecture
- ☐ Question is argumentative
- ☐ Any kind of error that might have been corrected had a timely objection been made

§ 12:21 Witness interview checklist

- ☐ Name
- ☐ Department or Business unit
- ☐ Address
- ☐ Telephone
- ☐ Cell Phone
- ☐ Administrative Assistant if any
- ☐ E-mail address/es
- ☐ Best way to reach witness
- ☐ Record Retention
- ☐ Knowledge of litigation hold (when and what)
- ☐ Knowledge of organization's retention program
- ☐ Knowledge of backup procedures
- ☐ Employment History
- ☐ Tenure with company
- ☐ Brief description of current duties and responsibilities
- ☐ Changes over time
- ☐ Brief description of prior duties and responsibilities
- ☐ Reporting chain
- ☐ Who do you report to?

- ☐ Who reports to you?
- ☐ Computer use
- ☐ What computers do you have access to?
- ☐ Laptop
- ☐ Desktop
- ☐ Network
- ☐ PDAs
- ☐ Home
- ☐ Other
- ☐ Preservations steps
- ☐ Did you receive the litigation hold for this matter?
- ☐ What steps did you take to comply?
- ☐ Have you destroyed any data called for in the hold?
- ☐ Where do you maintain data that relates to the issues in this matter?
- ☐ Hard copy
- ☐ Computer
- ☐ Where do you store your data?
- ☐ Active files on computer
- ☐ Estimated volume of relevant data (Note: 1 GB = approximately 75,000 pages)
- ☐ Software programs used in connection with duties
- ☐ Back-ups
- ☐ Official
- ☐ Unofficial—diskettes, other portable media
- ☐ Media used
- ☐ CDs, DVDs
- ☐ Internet based backups
- ☐ Thumb drives
- ☐ Zip Drives
- ☐ Replaced or removed drives
- ☐ Any other archiving techniques/media
- ☐ Location of backups
- ☐ Any materials associated with the issues that you keep off-site?
- ☐ At home
- ☐ Elsewhere
- ☐ Any password protected files
- ☐ Which files?
- ☐ Passwords
- ☐ Any encrypted files?
- ☐ If encrypted, why?

- ☐ E-mail accounts
- ☐ Company
- ☐ Which e-mail software in use?
- ☐ Changes over time
- ☐ Particular folders associated with issues
- ☐ Any use of personal accounts such as Gmail or Yahoo in connection with duties for company?
- ☐ Hard copy files
- ☐ Where located?
- ☐ Who can provide access?
- ☐ Any desk files or informal files related to the issues?
- ☐ Estimated volume in pages (Note: Average bankers box contains approximately 2,500 pages)
- ☐ Location of other data
- ☐ Any sources of data that we have not discussed?
- ☐ Elaborate
- ☐ Other knowledgeable witnesses
- ☐ Who else might have knowledge of the issues?
- ☐ Who do you think knows the most about the issues?
- ☐ Did you have any contact with any representative of the other side?
- ☐ Details
- ☐ Interviewer Input
- ☐ Key witness
- ☐ Significant witness
- ☐ Peripheral
- ☐ Any reason to do forensic work regarding this interviewee?

☐ Yes ☐ No

NOTES

Commentary

The checklist can be used for interviewing a client's information technology personnel, preparing for trial, and for conducting a deposition.

III. FORMS

§ 12:22 Notice of deposition upon oral examination

[Caption]

To: *[name]*
Attorney for *[name]*

[Address]

PLEASE TAKE NOTICE that *[defendant] [plaintiff] [name]* will take the deposition upon oral examination of *[defendant] [plaintiff]*, *[name and address of deponent]*, before a person authorized by law to administer oaths at *[place]*, on *[date]*, at *[time]*.

[Defendant] [Plaintiff] hereby requests *[name of deponent]* to appear before this oral examination at the above time and place.

The deposition will continue from day to day until completed. You are at liberty to appear and examine the witness.

Dated: ____

[signature etc.]

§ 12:23 Notice of deposition upon oral examination—Organization

[Caption]

To: *[name]*
[address]

PLEASE TAKE NOTICE that the deposition of *[plaintiff name 1 corporation] [defendant name 2 corporation]*, will be taken upon oral examination by *[defendant name 2] [plaintiff name 1]* on *[date]*, at *[time]*, before a qualified notary public. The deposition will continue thereafter until adjournment. Pursuant to *[rule]*, *[plaintiff name 1] [defendant name 2 corporation]* shall designate one or more officers, directors, or managing agents, or other persons who consent to testify on its behalf regarding the following subjects:

1. The number, types, and locations of computers, including but not limited to desktops, laptops, handheld computers and cellular telephones, currently in use and no longer in use.
2. Past and present operating system and application software, including dates of use and number of users.
3. Type, name and version of network servers currently in use and in use at any relevant time, including server applications (e.g. file server, email server, application server), size in terms

of storage capacity, number of users supported, and dates and descriptions of system upgrades.
4. File-naming and location-saving conventions.
5. Disk and tape labeling conventions.
6. Backup and archival disk or tape inventories and schedules/logs.
7. Most likely locations of electronic records relevant to the subject matter of the action.
8. Backup, archive and disaster recovery rotation schedules procedures, including any automatic data recycling programs in use at any relevant time.
9. Electronic records and information management policies, procedures and practices.
10. Corporate policies regarding employee use of company computers, data, and other technology.
11. Identities of all current and former personnel who have or had access to network administration, backup, archiving, or other system operations during any relevant time period.

Dated: ____

[signature]

§ 12:24 Notice of deposition upon oral examination—Organization—Another Form

[Caption]

To: All Parties and to Their Attorneys of Record:

NOTICE OF DEPOSITION OF *[NAME OF ORGANIZATION]* PERSON MOST KNOWLEDGEABLE CONCERNING ELECTRONICALLY STORED INFORMATION SYSTEMS AND STORAGE

TO: ALL PARTIES AND TO THEIR ATTORNEYS OF RECORD

PLEASE TAKE NOTICE that *[name of party]* will take the deposition upon oral examination of *[name of organization]* on *[date]*, commencing at *[time]* at *[place]*, which deposition shall continue thereafter, Saturdays, Sundays and holidays excepted, until completed. The deposition will be taken before a certified court reporter authorized to administer oaths

Pursuant to *[rule]*, *[name of organization]* shall designate and produce at the deposition or more of its officers, directors, managing agents, employees, or agents most qualified to testify on its behalf as to the matters described in Exhibit 1.

Dated: ____

[signature, etc.]

EXHIBIT 1

I. GENERAL DEFINITIONS

1. The terms "document" and "documents" mean and refer to a writing and/or recording as defined in *[rule]*, including, without limitation, any printed, written, recorded (in any audio, video, digital or any other electronic or electromagnetic medium), graphic, or other tangible matter from whatever source, however produced or reproduced, whether sent, received, or neither, including, without limitation, the original, all drafts, and any non-identical copies (whether different from the original because of notes made on or attached to the copy or otherwise) thereof.

2. The terms "you," "your" and "*[name of organization]*" mean and refer to *[name of organization]*, and include all of its affiliates, subsidiaries, and parents, and any person acting under the control or on behalf of *[name of organization]* and/or its affiliates, subsidiaries, and/or parents, including their directors, officers, partners, employees, representatives, agents, attorneys and investigators.

3. The term "[party]" means and refers to *[name of parties]*, conjunctively or disjunctively.

4. The term "complaint" *[or "answer"]* means and refers to the complaint filed by *[party]* in this action on or about *[date]*.

5. The term "*[name of organization]*" means *[name]*.

6. The term "subject matters" refers to all allegations of the complaint *[or defenses raised in the answer]* and to all factual and legal assertions or claims made in the complaint.

II. TECHNICAL DEFINITIONS

7. The term "active file" means and refers to any file of electronically stored information that can be utilized by a computer in any manner without modification and/or re-construction. An active file is any file of electronically stored information that has not been erased or otherwise destroyed and/or damaged and which is readily visible to the operating system and/or the software with which it was created.

8. The terms "archive" and/or "backup" mean and refer to any processes for copying and storage, whether temporary or permanent, of electronically stored information in a computer or a network, other than active files in on-line storage. The term

"backup" means and refers to all processes used with the purpose of maintaining a copy of electronically stored information so that such data can be restored if the primary copies of it are lost or damaged, or with the purpose of keeping a record of electronically stored information on a computer or a network at a given point or several given points in time. The terms "archive" and "archiving" mean and refer to any process for maintaining electronically stored information off-line, whether referred to as an archive, dump, purge or any other terms, and also to any process or procedure for storage of electronic media which is not in current use on a computer or a network.

9. The term "computer" includes, but is not limited to, microcomputers (also known as personal computers), laptop computers, portable computers, notebook computers, palmtop computers, personal digital assistants, minicomputers and mainframe computers.

10. The term "configuration" means and refers to the elements and relationships which make up a computer or a network, including, but not limited to, the following information:

a. Computer type, brand, model and serial number

b. Brand, model, capacity, technical specifications and arrangement of all devices capable of storing and/or retrieving electronically stored information in magnetic and/or optical form, including, but not limited to, hard disk drives, floppy diskette drives, electronic storage devices and associated removable media.

c. Brand and version of all software, including operating system, private and custom developed applications, commercial applications, shareware and/or work-in-progress.

d. Communications capability, whether through internet or intranet connections, including, but not limited to, data download and/or upload capability to mainframe, and computer to computer connections via network modem and/or direct connect.

11. The term "data" is equivalent to the term "electronically stored information."

12. The term "deleted file" means and refers to any file of electronically stored information that has been erased, deleted or where such data storage locations have been marked for deletion from the electronic media on which it resided. A deleted file includes any file of electronically stored information that has been modified to indicate such information as being deleted and/or that is not readily visible to the operating system and/or the software with which it was created.

13. The term "documentation," when used in reference to computers, operating systems and utilities, application software

and/or hardware devices, shall mean and refer to all documents and files of electronically stored information containing written and/or on-line information provided by the manufacturer or seller of the item and/or by in-house sources, including all manuals, guides, instructions, programming notes, protocols, policies, procedures and other sources of information about technical specifications, installation, usage and functioning of the computer, operating systems and utilities, application software and/or hardware devices.

14. The term "electronically stored information" means information of all kinds created, maintained and/or utilized by computers and/or networks, including all non-identical copies of such information. Electronically stored information includes, but is not limited to, software (whether private, commercial or work-in-progress), programming notes or instructions, and input and/or output used or produced by any software or utility (including electronic mail messages and all information referencing or relating to such messages anywhere on a computer or a network, word processing documents and all information stored in connection with such documents, electronic spreadsheets, user created electronic documents, email, databases including all records and fields and structural information, charts, graphs and outlines, arrays of information and all other information used or produced by any software), operating systems, source code of all types, programming languages, linkers and compilers, peripheral drivers, batch files, any and all ASCII files, and any and all miscellaneous files and/or file fragments, regardless of the media on which they reside and regardless of whether such electronically stored information consists of an active file, deleted file or file fragment. electronically stored information includes any and all information stored on computer memories, hard disks, floppy disks, removable storage media, or on or in any other vehicle for digital data storage and/or transmittal. Electronically stored information also includes the file, folder tabs and/or containers and labels appended to, or associated with, any physical storage device associated with the information described above.

15. The terms "electronic media" and "media" mean and refer to any magnetic, optical or other storage device used to record electronically stored information. Electronic media storage devices may include, but are not limited to, computer memories, hard disk drives, floppy diskettes, CD-ROM disks, flash memory, USB drives, magnetic tape of all types, microfiche, punched cards, punched tape, computer chips, including, but not limited to, EPROM, PROM, RAM and ROM, or on or in any other vehicle for digital data storage and/or transmittal.

16. The terms "file fragment" and "fragmentary file" mean and refer to any file of electronically stored information existing as a subset of an original active file. A file fragment may be an active file or deleted file. The cause of fragmentation resulting in the fragmentary file can include, but is not limited to, automated processes, manual intervention, electronic surges, and/or physical defects on electronic media.

17. "Identify," when used in reference to any electronically stored information, means to provide information specifying the software and/or operating system under which the electronically stored information was created; the type of electronically stored information (for example, word processing document, spreadsheet, database, application program.); the location of the electronically stored information; and all other means of describing it with sufficient particularity to meet the requirements for its inclusion in a request for production of documents pursuant to the *[rules]*.

18. The term "layout" means and refers to the interconnections and relationships between computers and electronic media in a computer system. The term "layout" includes, but is not limited to:

a. The physical locations and relationships of all computers and/or their peripherals, of all sorts, whether physically attached or not to a given computer

b. The nature and type of any sort of Local Area, Wide Area or any other type of network, whether consisting of physical connections between nodes or not, including the functional and physical relationships of servers, workstations and terminals in each such network and the brand, name and version of all operating systems in use on the network as well as the brand, name and version of all application software available through the network

c. The nature, type and functions of all software and/or hardware or devices which operate in a capacity to share or exchange electronically stored information between two or more computers, especially any e-mail, database or executive information system.

19. The term "network" means and refers to any hardware and/or software combination that connects two or more computers together and which allows such computers to share and/or transfer digital signals between them. For the purposes of this definition, the connection between or among the computers need not be either physical or direct (wireless networks utilizing radio frequencies and data sharing via indirect routes utilizing modems and phone company facilities). In addition, there need not be a central file or data server nor a central network operating system

in place (i.e. peer-to-peer networks and networks utilizing a mainframe host to facility transfer of electronically stored information). The ability to share electronically stored information is the key factor.

20. The term "rotation" means and refers to any plan, policy, or scheme involving the reuse of electronic media after it has been used for backup, archive, or other electronically stored information storage purposes, particularly if such use results in the alternation and/or destruction of electronically stored information residing on such device before or in connection with its reuse.

21. The term "support" means and refers to any help or assistance provided to a user of a computer by another individual, whether as an official job function or not. Such help or assistance may take the form of, but is not limited to, answering questions, whether in person or by mechanical means, direct intervention, training, software troubleshooting, hardware troubleshooting, programming, systems consulting, maintenance, repair and/or user forums. Providers of support may be employees, contractors, and/or third-party providers.

22. The term "encryption" means and refers to any system program or device utilized to obtain, impart or maintain security to electronically stored information transmitted or stored in or by means of your computers.

III MATTERS ON WHICH EXAMINATION IS REQUESTED

23. The configuration documentation and layout of the computers and/or networks used by *[name of organization]* to create, process and/or store electronically stored information referencing or relating to the subject matters.

24. Archiving and backup systems and procedures available on computers and/or networks used by *[name or organization]* to create, process, and/or store electronically stored information referencing or relating to the subject matters, including, but not limited to:

a. The names and version number of all software used for archiving and/or backup purposes

b. Documentation of the archiving and/or backup systems and procedures, both on line and in paper form

c. The criteria used to classify and move sets of electronically stored information for archiving

d. Backup schedules and protocols

e. The manner in which archive and backup sets of electronically stored information are organized, and tracking and logging of such information

f. Storage of and access to archive and backup sets of electronically stored information, including the manner in which such information is written and retrieved and use of compression routines

g. Storage media used for archive and backup purposes, including the manufacturer, model and type of such media

h. Records of the existence, location and custodianship of archive and backup media, including inventories, databases, catalogs, logs, lists, and indexes of such media

i. Media labeling conventions and all other codes and abbreviations used for archive and backup purposes.

25. Record retention plans, policies and procedures of *[name of organization]* applicable to electronically stored information referencing or relating to the subject matters, including, but not limited to:

a. The contents of your retention plans, policies and procedures;

b. Implementation of your retention plans, policies and procedures;

c. Documentation, whether on line or in paper form, of your retention plans, policies and procedures; and

d. Whether any changes have been made in your retention fields, headings, and other subdivisions appearing in e-mail messages, including, but not limited to, message numbers, message trails and/or sequences, message titles and subject matter lines, locations of senders and recipients, dates of sending and receipt of messages;

26. All steps taken by you to preserve electronically stored information as evidence in connection with this action, including all steps taken to prevent or stop deletion, overwriting or modification of electronically stored information that may be relevant to this action.

27. Deletion, erasure and/or destruction of storage media including backup and/or archive sets of electronically stored information referencing or relating to the subject matters; damage to and/or destruction of media containing such electronically stored information, and logs and records of such activity.

28. The system utilities and application software programs available on computers and networks used by *[name of organization]* that have the capability of searching, retrieving, copying, writing, offloading, and/or exporting electronically stored information referencing or relating to the subject matters.

29. The e-mail and/or messaging systems used by *[name of or-*

ganization] to transmit or receive electronically stored information or other information referencing or relating to the subject matters, including, but not limited to, internal e-mail and external e-mail communications. (For the purpose of this item, "messaging systems" include paging systems, groupware, and other systems for which one of the primary purposes is transmission of documents or messages among users of your computers and/or network or between users of your computer and/or network and other such systems.) The deponent(s) should have knowledge regarding all aspects of your e-mail system(s), including, but not limited to, the following:

a. Hardware and software used for e-mail and messaging functions

b. Documentation for the e-mail and messaging system and its usage

c. The nature and the location of directories and/or lists of e-mail or messaging system users, and all systems, codes and numbers identifying users

d. Fields, headings and other subdivisions appearing in e-mail messages, including, but not limited to, message numbers, message trails and or sequences, message title and subject matter lines, locations of senders and recipients, dates of sending and receipt of messages

e. Technical specifications for the creation, transmission and storage of messages, including, but not limited to, specifications as to host systems, gateways and routers, and electronically stored information files or sets in which messages are stored and the location of such information on the system

f. Message logging functions

g. Electronically stored information storage, backup and archiving activity specifically relating to e-mail and other messaging systems, including retention plans, guidelines, rules, standards, protocols, policies and procedures;

h. Backup and/or archive media specifically relating to e-mail and other messaging systems, including inventories, databases, catalogs, logs, lists, indexes, and other documentation

i. Format and character sets used to write messages, and encoding, encryption, decoding and decryption of messages; and

j. Outside services for electronic mail and/or for information transmission and retrieval with which your computers and/or network is interconnected, including the name of the service, the time period during which your computers and/or network has been connected to it, the purposes for which the outside services are used, and which users of your computers and/or network are able to use such services.

30. Policies, procedures, guidelines, rules, standards, and protocols relating to the functioning and use of personal computers and local area networks which may have been used to create or process electronically stored information referencing or relating to the Subject: matters, including, but not limited to:

a. Availability and usage of particular application software to users

b. Directory organization access, and naming conventions

c. Storage of files of electronically stored information at local workstations and/or on network servers

d. Codes, abbreviations and naming conventions applicable to file and extension names

e. Diskette storage and labeling

f. Logging and recording user and file activity.

31. Systems for storing and retrieving recordings of telephone calls.

32. Any other information needed to identify, access, copy and read electronically stored information referred to in the above items.

33. Any other information needed to identify, access, copy and read electronically stored information reflecting electronically-facilitated communications (via e-mail or otherwise) among *[name of organization]* personnel concerning *[name of party]*, or any of them, or the events and transactions encompassed within the allegations of the complaint.

NOTES TO FORM

Commentary

This form can be adapted to the specific requirements of a particular case.

§ 12:25 Stipulation to take deposition upon oral examination

Stipulation to take deposition upon oral examination

[Caption]

[Plaintiff] and *[defendant]* stipulate and agree the deposition upon oral examination of *[name of deponent]* shall be taken by *[plaintiff/defendant]* at *[place]*, on *[date]*, at *[time]*. Notice of the time and place of this deposition as required by *[rule]* is waived.

Dated: ____

[signature etc.]

Dated: ____

[signature etc.]

§ 12:26 Deposition outline

A. Computer-related experience of deponent
   1. Formal training (degrees, certificate programs, continuing education)
   2. Positions held
   3. Descriptions of job functions
   4. Length of employment
   5. Reasons for leaving prior employers

B. Description of computer system
   1. General description of network topology (network operating system, type of file server, client computer operating system)
   2. Recent instances of hardware failures
   3. Existence of dial-up access to the network

C. Security of computer system
   1. Physical security measures (access control systems, such as passwords and key cards)
   2. Electronic protection (firewalls, virus software, intrusion detection software)
   3. Instances of attempted unauthorized access
   4. Prior instances of data loss
   5. Security policies

D. Backup Procedures
   1. Identify systems that are backed up
   2. Frequency of backups
   3. Location of backup tapes
   4. Instances of loss of backup data
   5. Software used to create backups
   6. Internet backups
   7. Backup policies
   8. Changes in backup procedures in the last twelve months

E. Software used to create relevant data
   1. Name of vendor and program
   2. Version number of program
   3. Service/maintenance updates
   4. Any custom modifications to the program
   5. Procedures for ensuring accurate entry of data

6. Procedures for ensuring accuracy of output
7. File format for data storage

Chapter 13

Interrogatories

I. GUIDELINES

II. CHECKLISTS

III. FORMS

Research References

Treatises and Practice Aids

Grenig and Gleisner, eDiscovery & Digital Evidence § 7:13

Trial Strategy

Recovery and Reconstruction of Electronic Mail as Evidence, 41 Am. Jur Proof of Facts 3d 1

Computer Technology in Civil Litigation, 71 Am. Jur Trials 111

Additional References

Grenig & Kinsler, Handbook of Federal Civil Discovery and Disclosure §§ 8.1 to 8.31 (3d ed.)

ABA Discovery Standards, http://www.abanet.org/litigation/discoverystandards/2005civildiscoverystandards.pdf

Federal Judicial Center, http://www.fjc.gov

The Sedona Conference, http://www.thesedonaconference.org

KeyCite®: Cases and other legal materials listed in KeyCite Scope can be researched through the KeyCite service on Westlaw®. Use KeyCite to check citations for form, parallel references, prior and later history, and comprehensive citator information, including citations to other decisions and secondary materials.

I. GUIDELINES

§ 13:1 Generally

In the context of e-discovery, interrogatories provide a framework for gathering information about how an adverse party utilizes technology to create, manage, transmit, store and archive electronically stored information. This provides a framework to propound subsequent specific interrogatories or production requests. Interrogatories are not available for nonparty discovery. Interrogatories must be answered in writing and under oath by the respondent within a specified time. Fed. R. Civ. P. 33(d) allows parties to produce electronically stored information in response to interrogatories.

Interrogatories may be helpful in obtaining the names and addresses of witnesses, officers, or employees. Interrogatories, document production requests, and requests for admission may all be contained in a single document.

§ 13:2 Service of interrogatories

Interrogatories may be served by delivering a copy to the party or mailing the interrogatories to the party's last known address.[1] Once a party has appeared by counsel, the interrogatories are served upon the attorney. A copy of the interrogatories should also be served on all other parties to the action.

Fed. R. Civ. P. 33(a) precludes the service of interrogatories before the time specified in Fed. R. Civ. P. 26(d), absent a court order or written stipulation. Fed. R. Civ. P. 26(d) provides that,

---

[Section 13:2]

[1]See Fed. R. Civ. P. 5.

except when authorized by local rule, order or stipulation, a party may not seek discovery from any source before the parties have conferred as required by Fed. R. Civ. P. 26(f). State rules and local rules should be consulted with respect to when interrogatories may be served.[2]

§ 13:3 Number of interrogatories

Fed. R. Civ. P. 33(a) limits the number of interrogatories one party may serve upon another party to 25, including discrete subparts, absent leave of court or written stipulation. State rules or local rules may also limit the number of interrogatories. Written stipulation to serve more than 25 interrogatories should be employed when all parties to the stipulation wish to serve excess interrogatories.

Subparts are those questions that are logically or factually subsumed within and necessarily related to the primary question. Subparts are secondary to the primary question and cannot stand alone. Subparts do not have to be separately numbered to count as separate interrogatories. An interrogatory that asks about multiple projects or events does not necessarily constitute multiple interrogatories.[1]

Leave to serve additional interrogatories should be allowed when the additional interrogatories would not cause undue burden or expense to the responding party. In many cases, it may be appropriate for the court to permit a larger number of interrogatories in the scheduling order.

§ 13:4 Propounding interrogatories

Interrogatories may relate to any matter that can be inquired into under the applicable scope of discovery. This includes the existence and location of tangible things and the identity and location of persons having knowledge of any discoverable matter. It also includes the names and addresses of persons interviewed by or on behalf of the responding party.

An interrogatory may not inquire into privileged matters or matters protected by the work product doctrine. The burden of proving the existence and application of a privilege rests with the

---

[2]See e.g. Wis. Stat. § 804.01(2)(e), which requires a conference of the parties to discuss issues of electronically stored information prior to serving any request for production or responding to an interrogatory with electronically stored information).

[Section 13:3]

[1]Banks v. Office of Senate Sergeant-at-Arms, 222 F.R.D. 7 (D.D.C. 2004).

party asserting it. When a party withholds information on the ground of privilege or work product protection, it must make the claim expressly and describe the nature of the information withheld in such a manner that, without revealing the information itself privileged or protected, will enable other parties to assess the applicability of the privilege or protection. A mere claim of privilege or work product protection, unaccompanied by factual support, is insufficient. In appropriate cases, the responding party may obtain a protective order to limit the scope of discovery.

II. CHECKLISTS

§ 13:5 Checklist of topics for interrogatories

- ☐ Identity of party's agents, and employees
- ☐ Identity of witnesses
- ☐ Identity of documents and tangible things
- ☐ Identify personnel, employees, and consultants or contractors who work on or manage party's computer system or part of system
- ☐ Identify the computer systems including any personal computers, networked computers, file servers or application servers
- ☐ Identify core business applications used to operate the business including e-mail system, word processing application, accounting package, calendaring system, document management system, etc.
- ☐ Identify any source of potentially relevant electronically stored information that is managed by a remote or third-party
- ☐ Specific databases party maintains on various subjects
- ☐ With respect to computer archive and backup systems, the schedule for making copies, the type of software used, the method of archive/backup (incremental or full), the quantity of data and location of storage of backup copies
- ☐ Identity of experts, facts, and opinions
- ☐ Details and sequences of events and transactions
- ☐ Damages information and insurance coverage
- ☐ Identity of persons who prepared answers and sources used
- ☐ Positions on issues and opinions of fact

§ 13:6 Checklist for drafting interrogatories

- ☐ **Begin with Form Interrogatories.** Use official form interrogatories initially, and then follow up with your own specially prepared interrogatories.

- [ ] **Use Your Discovery Plan.** Constantly refer to discovery plan.
- [ ] What are the elements of proof issues?
- [ ] How do the facts that must be gathered go to those elements?
- [ ] **Establish a List of Targets.** From discovery plan, develop a list of targets for interrogatories.
- [ ] **Create an Outline.** Develop a structured outline before drafting. Generally, a case-history structure works best. Consider using an issue-based or document-based structure. Build the interrogatory questions around the case chronology.
- [ ] **Chart the Outline.** Consider making a chart showing a flow-chart outline of anticipated responses. Each question will have alternative responses that may then generate new questions.
- [ ] **Draft the Questions.** Once this structure is in place, fill in the blanks with interrogatory questions.
- [ ] **Check the Number of Questions.** Rules may limit the number of questions that may be asked. Consult local rules.
- [ ] **Check Drafting.** Questions and responses are open to interpretation by opposing counsel. The jury may see the interrogatory as well. For these two reasons, questions must be concise and precise. Avoid conflicts of verb tense. Avoid questions containing negatives ("no," "not," or "never").
- [ ] **Seek the Discovery Source.** Be sure question requires the indication of a source.
- [ ] Is the reply referring to a document that should be part of your discovery?
- [ ] Is there a potential witness who should be deposed?

III. FORMS

§ 13:7 Definitions for use in interrogatories seeking information about responding party's computer system

1. "Computer or computer equipment" means all data processing equipment, including but not limited to, central processing units (CPUs), whether contained in a server or free standing computer or laptop, and all parts of a server, computer or laptop that may contain data storage capabilities including, but not limited to hard disk drives, optical disk drives, removable media, such as floppy disk drives, CD-ROM and DVD drives, Zip drives, Jaz drives, Maxtor drives or snap drives. "Computer or computer equipment" also refers to any data processing cards or computer magnetic tapes, backup tapes,

drum and disk storage devices or any other electronic storage media or system of whatever description. "Computer or computer equipment" also refers to any type of hardware used to store or manipulate electronic images, including but not limited to microfilm, microfiche and their repositories and readers.

2. "Computer system" refers to free standing servers, computers and laptops, and also refers to the network infrastructure and computer support systems of the *[responding party]*, its subsidiaries (in this country or throughout the world), predecessors, successors, assigns, joint venturers, partners, parents, agents or affiliates, including but not limited to the following:
   a. *[Responding party]*'s LAN and WAN network systems, including methods of connectivity (e.g., by T1, T3 or optical lines), domains (including PDCs, network OS and protocols), backup and disaster recovery hardware and media and the physical location of all electronic storage systems.
   b. *[Responding party]*'s IS system of administration, including, backup and disaster recovery restoration plans, electronically stored information retention plans, purge plans, training plans, and libraries of hardcopy and online training and operation manuals.
   c. All offsite technical and service bureau support, including but not limited to application service provider (ASP) support, scanning or data conversion support, offsite data storage or archive support.
   d. Web hosting and administration services, including intranet and extranet sites, regardless of whether they exist in English, or some other language.
3. "Database" refers to any software program application (such as Microsoft Access, Lotus Approach, Borland's Paradox, Summation 5.21 or Summation's Iblaze, Concordance, or some other proprietary software) used to accumulate, manage, search and retrieve large amounts of electronic data. "Database" also refers to any collection of electronic data that is the subject of such a software application. When used to refer to such a collection of electronic data, "database" means any and all electronic information, or metadata, that has been saved to the database, regardless of format. When used in these interrogatories or requests to admit, a request related to a "Database" includes by definition the following implicit requests:
   a. A full description of the method by which electronically stored information was retrieved, including the search terms and search methodology (e.g., word search or Boolean

search) employed, the search engine settings used and the data set searched to retrieve the information;

b. The name of the operator(s) who conducted the search of the database;

c. The configuration and settings of the database at the time of the search;

d. The precise physical location of the database at *[responding party]*'s facility or facilities; and

e. A complete copy of the operating manual used in connection with the database.

4. "Data Collections not included in a database" refers to any raw accumulation of data in a computer system, such as Word or PDF documents stored only in a Windows directory. "Data Collections not included in a database" also refers to any electronic text that is not identified with a particular computer program, such as for example "ASCII." Whenever a request in these interrogatories and requests to produce elicit by necessity the identification of "Data Collections not included in a database" that request by definition implicitly requires the identification of where the "Data Collections not included in a database" is physically located on *[responding party]*'s computer system.

5. "Database field" refers to a specific area of a record in a database used for a particular category of electronically stored information. For example, all data relating to the phone numbers of customers might be stored in a field called "phone##." Whenever a request for a search of a database is made in these interrogatories and requests to produce, that request includes by definition

a) the identification of the number of fields that can be searched in a database and

b) the identification of the fields that were actually searched in supplying an answer.

6. "Database record" refers to the smallest convenient block of data in a database, and usually consists of information that relates a single person, incident or document. For the purposes of these interrogatories and requests to produce, "database record" includes both the information directly saved to that record as metadata and any scanned image attached to the record (as is done in Summation).

7. "Data set" refers to the number of records that are initially the subject of a database query. "Data set" also refers to any "subset" of data that is accumulated in response to a search.

NOTES TO FORM

Commentary

These definitions are intended to be used in initial discovery seeking information about a responding party's computer system. The definitions must be modified to fit each individual circumstance.

§ 13:8 Definitions for use in interrogatories and requests to produce

"Computer or computer equipment" means all data processing equipment, including but not limited to, central processing units (CPUs), whether contained in a server or free standing computer or laptop or PDA or similar device that may contain data storage capabilities, and also including any equipment where computer files, hidden system files or metadata presently reside such as hard disk drives, optical disk drives, removable media, such as floppy disk drives, CD-ROM and DVD drives, Zip drives, Jaz drives, Maxtor drives or snap drives, data processing cards, computer magnetic tapes, backup tapes, drum and disk storage devices or any other similar electronic storage media or system of whatever name or description.

"Computer or computer equipment" also means all digital image evidence that may be stored on any type of hardware used to store or manipulate electronic images, including but not limited to microfilm, microfiche and their repositories and readers, or design or engineering computer systems and regardless of any digital image's format, including.jpg, .bmp, or some other advanced or proprietary form of digital image format, such as CAD layered drawings.

"Computer or computer equipment" also refers to sources of digital evidence that may not presently be in use by your company or may have been deleted from your active systems, whether the source is a backup tape or disk, some other data retention system or some form of disaster recovery system.

"Computer or computer equipment" also refers to places where digital evidence may reside that may have been deleted from your active files and which may not be readily recoverable from a backup medium, such as metadata.

"Computer system" refers to free standing servers, computers and laptops, and also refers to the network infrastructure and computer support systems of the defendant or subject to the defendant's control, such as its subsidiaries, predecessors, successors, assigns, joint venturers, partners, parents, agents or affiliates (in this country or throughout the world), including but not limited to the following:

1. Defendant's LAN, WAN or other network systems, regardless of methods of connectivity (e.g., by T1, T3 or optical lines), domains, including PDCs, network OS (such as Novell, Microsoft, UNIX, Citrix or some other similar type) or protocols, backup and disaster recovery hardware and media, regardless of the physical location of those electronic storage systems.
2. Defendant's e-mail servers and any repository of e-mail (including within the inbox, sent box, deleted box or some similar file of the computers of employees or management), or in any backup form whatsoever, regardless of whether you use Microsoft Exchange, Outlook, Outlook Express, Lotus Notes or some combination of e-mail management software or some alternative commercial or proprietary e-mail management software.
3. Defendant's IS administrative offices, including backup and disaster recovery restoration plans and repositories, data retention plans and repositories, purge plans and repositories, training plans and repositories, and libraries of hardcopy materials of any description (regardless of where located) and online training and operation manuals that have been scanned to disk.
4. All offsite technical and service bureau support systems, including but not limited to application service provider (ASP) support, scanning or data conversion support, offsite data storage or archive support.
5. Web hosting and administration services, including intranet and extranet sites, regardless of whether they are now publicly posted or exist in English, or some other language.

"Database" refers to any software program application (such as Microsoft Access, Lotus Approach, Borland's Paradox, Summation or Summation's Iblaze, Concordance, or some other proprietary software) used to accumulate, manage, search and retrieve large amounts of electronic data. "Database" also refers to any collection of electronic data that is the subject of such a software application. When used to refer to such a collection of electronic data, "database" means any and all electronic information, or metadata, that has been saved to the database, regardless of format. When used in these interrogatories or requests to admit, a request related to a "Database" includes by definition the following implicit requests:

1. A full description of the method by which data was retrieved, including the search terms and search methodology (e.g., word search or Boolean search) that was employed, the search engine settings that were used and the data set that was searched to retrieve the information.

2. The name of the operator(s) who conducted the search of the database.
3. The configuration and settings of the database at the time of the search.
4. The precise physical location of the database at Defendant's facility or facilities.
5. A complete copy of the operating manual that is used in connection with the database.

"Data Collections not included in a database" refers to any raw accumulation of data in a computer system, such as Word or PDF documents stored only in a Windows directory. "Data Collections not included in a database" also refers to any electronic text that is not identified with a particular computer program, such as for example ASCII. Whenever a request in these interrogatories and requests to produce elicit by necessity the identification of "Data Collections not included in a database," that request, by definition, implicitly requires the identification of where the "Data Collections not included in a database" is physically located on Defendant's computer system.

"Database field" refers to a specific area of a record in a database used for a particular category of data; for example, all data relating to the phone numbers of customers might be stored in a field called "phone##." Whenever a request for a search of a database is made in these interrogatories and requests to produce, that request includes by definition a) the identification of the number of fields that can be searched in a database and b) the identification of the fields that were actually searched in supplying an answer.

"Database record" refers to the smallest convenient block of data in a database, and usually consists of information that relates a single person, incident or document. For the purposes of these interrogatories and requests to produce, "database record" includes both the information directly saved to that record as metadata and any scanned image attached to the record (as is done in Summation).

"Data set" refers to the number of records that are initially the subject of a database query. "Data set" also refers to any "subset" of data that is accumulated in response to a search.

CD or DVD production of discovery is acceptable however the following is required when discovery production is thus produced. Each image on the CD or DVD must be Bates stamped with a unique alpha-numeric identifier (taking care not to obscure in any way any of the information contained in the image).

A. Clearly Marked and Easily Identifiable File. This index must contain the following information as to each document contained on the CD or DVD in columnar display as follows:

i. In column one, the Bates stamp number of each electronic document on the CD or DVD;

ii. In column two, a brief but reasonably descriptive word description of the contents of each electronic document on the CD or DVD that clearly identifies what that electronic document contains;

iii. In column three, a clear reference to just what interrogatory or request is satisfied by the production of each electronic document on the CD or DVD;

iv. In column four, the format of each electronic document on the CD or DVD, and how and where the original or best copy of each such document is stored on the defendant's computer system, or if located elsewhere then on the defendant's primary computer system, its location on the computer system of subsidiaries (in this country or throughout the world), predecessors, successors, assigns, joint venturers, partners, parents, agents or affiliates; and

v. In column five, a statement as to whether each electronic document contained on the CD or DVD is a first, second, third or a later generation copy of the original document located on the defendant's computer system.

B. If the images on a CD or DVD exist in an off the shelve metadata environment, then the images must be produced with all accompanying metadata, unless privileged, and the database management system used to produce and house that metadata must be identified by application name and version type.

C. If the images on a CD or DVD exist in a proprietary metadata environment, then it is required that a working copy of the proprietary software, together with any user manuals or help files and the search engine used to search for and retrieve the data, must be provided that will work with each CD or DVD.

D. All data on a CD or DVD that is in text (regardless of format), must be OCRed before production.

NOTES TO FORM

Commentary

These definitions can be used in interrogatories and requests for production. Not all definitions will be appropriate in all cases; it is necessary to select the definitions that are appropriate under the circumstances.

§ 13:9 Interrogatories

[Caption]

INTERROGATORIES TO *[NAME]*

To: *[name of party]*

You are notified to answer under oath the following interrogatories within __ days of the time service is made on you.

1. Identify all e-mail systems in use, including but not limited to the following:
   (a) List all e-mail software and versions presently and previously used by you and the dates of use.
   (b) Identify all hardware that has been used or is currently in use as a server for the e-mail system, including its name;
   (c) Identify the specific type of hardware used as terminals into the e-mail system, including but not limited to home PCs, laptops, desktops, cellular telephones, personal digital assistants (PDAs) and its current location.
   (d) State how many users have been on each e-mail system, distinguishing between past and current users.
   (e) State whether the e-mail is encrypted in any way and list the passwords for all users.
   (f) Identify all users you know of who have generated e-mail related to the subject matter of this litigation.
   (g) Identify all e-mail you know of, including the creation date, the recipient, and the sender, relating to, referencing or relevant to the subject matter of this litigation.
2. Identify and describe each computer that has been or is currently in use by you or your employees, including but not limited to desktop computers, PDAs, portable computers, laptop computers, notebook computers, and cellular telephones, including but not limited to the following:
   (a) Computer type, brand and model number.
   (b) Computers that have been re-formatted, had the operating system reinstalled or been overwritten, identifying the date of each event.
   (c) The present location of each identified computer in your response to this interrogatory.
   (d) The brand and version of all software, including operating systems, private and custom-developed applications, commercial applications and shareware for each identified computer.
   (e) The communications and connectivity for each computer, including but not limited to terminal-to-mainframe emulation, data download and/or upload capability to mainframe, and computer-to-computer connections via network, modem and/or direct connection.

(f) All computers that have been used to store, receive or generate data related to the subject matter of this litigation.

3. As to each computer network, identify the following:
   (a) Brand and version number of the network operating system currently or previously in use, including dates of all upgrades.
   (b) Quantity and configuration of all network servers and workstations.
   (c) Past and present persons, listing dates, responsible for the ongoing operations, maintenance, expansion, archiving and upkeep of the network.
   (d) Brand name and version number of all applications and other software residing on each network in use, including but not limited to electronic mail and applications.
4. Describe in detail all inter-connectivity between the computer system at *[place 1]* the computer system at *[place 2]*, including a description of the following:
   (a) All possible ways in which electronic data is shared between locations.
   (b) The method of transmission.
   (c) The type(s) of data transferred.
   (d) The names of all individuals possessing the capability for such transfer, including list and names of authorized outside users of *[name's]* electronic mail system.
   (e) The individual responsible for supervising inter-connectivity.
5. With respect to data backups performed on all computer systems currently or previously in use, identify the following:
   (a) All procedures and devices used to back up the software and the data, including but not limited to names of backup software used, the frequency of the backup process, and type of tape backup drives, including name and version number, type of media. State the capacity (bytes) and total amount of information (gigabytes) stored on each tape.
   (b) Describe the tape or backup rotation and explain how backup data is maintained and state whether the backups are full or incremental, attaching a copy of all rotation schedules.
   (c) State whether backup storage media is kept off-site or on-site. Include the location of such backup and a description of the process for archiving and retrieving on-site media.
   (d) The individuals who conduct the backup and the individual who supervises this process.
   (e) Provide a detailed list of all backup sets, regardless of the

magnetic media on which they reside, showing current location, custodian, date of backup, a description of backup content and a full inventory of all archives.

6. Identify all extra-routine backups applicable for any servers identified in response to these interrogatories, such as quarterly archival backup, and yearly backup, and identify the current location of any such backups.
7. For any server, workstation, laptop, or home PC that has been "wiped clean" or reformatted so that you claim that the information on the hard drive is permanently destroyed, identify the following:
   (a) The date on which each drive was wiped.
   (b) The method or program used.
8. Identify and attach any and all versions of document or data retention policies used by *[name]* and identify documents or classes of documents that were subject to scheduled destruction. Attach copies of document destruction inventories, logs, or schedules containing documents relevant to this action. Attach a copy of any disaster recovery plan. Also state:
   (a) The date, if any, of the suspension of this policy in total or any aspect of the policy in response to this litigation.
   (b) A description by topic, creation date, user or bytes of any and all data deleted or in any way destroyed after the commencement of this litigation. State whether the deletion or destruction of any data pursuant to the data retention policy occurred through automation or by user action.
   (c) Whether any company-wide instruction regarding the suspension of the data retention or destruction policy occurred after or related to the commencement of this litigation and if so, identify the individual responsible for enforcing said suspension.
9. Identify any users who had backup systems in their PCs and describe the nature of the backup.
10. Identify the persons responsible for maintaining any schedule of redeployment or circulation of existing equipment and describe the system or process for redeployment.
11. Identify any data deleted, physically destroyed, discarded, damaged, physically or logically, or overwritten, whether pursuant to a document retention policy or otherwise, since the commencement of this litigation. Specifically identify those documents that relate to or reference the subject matter of this litigation.
12. Identify any user who has downloaded any files in excess of ten megabytes on any computer identified above since the commencement of this litigation.

13. Identify and describe all backup tapes in your possession including:
   (a) Types and number of tapes in your possession.
   (b) Capacity (bytes) and total amount of information (gigabytes) stored on each tape.
   (c) All tapes re-initialized or overwritten since commencement of this litigation and state the date of the occurrence.

Dated: ____

[signature, etc.]

NOTES TO FORM

Commentary

This form is adapted from Paroff et al., *Electronic Discovery in Technology Litigation*, 734 PLI/Pat 297 (2003).

§ 13:10 Interrogatories—Another form

[Caption]

INTERROGATORIES TO *[NAME OF PARTY]*

To: *[name of party]*

You are notified to answer under oath the following interrogatories within __ days of the time service is made on you.

DEFINITIONS

A. The word "person" means all entities and, without limiting the generality of the foregoing, includes natural persons, joint owners, associations, companies, partnerships, joint ventures, corporations, trusts, and estates.

B. The word "document" means all written, printed, recorded, graphic, or photographic matter or sound reproductions, however produced or reproduced, pertaining to the subject matter indicated.

C. The words "identify," "identity," or "identification," when used with respect to a person or persons, require a statement of the full name and present or last known residence and business address of such person or persons and, if a natural person, his or her present or last known job title, and the name and address of his or her present or last known employer.

D. The words "identify," "identity," or "identification," when used with respect to a document or documents, requires a description of the document or documents by date, subject matter, name of the addressee, and the name and address of each person or persons having possession, custody, or control of such document or documents. If any such document was, but is no longer, in your possession, custody, or control, or in existence, state the date and manner of its disposition.

E. The word "identify," when used with respect to an act (including an alleged offense), occurrence, statement, or conduct (hereinafter collectively called "act"), means:
   (1) to describe the substance of the event or events constituting such acts, and state the date when such act occurred;
   (2) to identify each and every person or persons participating in such act;
   (3) to identify all other persons (if any) present when such act occurred;
   (4) to state whether any minutes, notes, memorandum, or other record of such act was made;
   (5) to state whether such record now exists; and
   (6) to identify the person or persons presently having possession, custody, or control of each such record.

F. The word "blocking" means either "logical blocking" or "physical blocking." "Logical blocking" means the location of fields within one record, sometimes referred to as record format. "Physical blocking" means the number of logical records written together on a storage device. In the case of unformatted records, "physical blocking" is the largest physical record that can be applied to the logical blocking factor to give the physical blocking factor.

G. The phrase "data set," although it may have a slightly different meaning as to different computer installations, means "file" in reference to any collection of data.

H. The word "equipment" means all data processing equipment, including, but not limited to, central processing units, tape drives, drum and disk storage devices, control units, and printers; all unit record equipment, including, but not limited to, accumulators, calculators, and sorters; all record storage and retrieval equipment, including, but not limited to, microfilm storage and retrieval apparatus, and audio/visual storage and retrieval apparatus.

I. The word "field" means a specific area of a record used for a particular category of data; for example, a group of card columns used to represent a wage rate, or a set of locations used to express the address of the operand.

J. The word "file" means a collection of related records treated as a unit and, in a general sense, any collection of informational items similar to one another in purpose, form, and content.
K. The word "information" means data presented in various forms related to various topics, herein used to describe one topic's data.
L. The phrase "operating system" means an organized collection of techniques and procedures for operating a computer, usually part of a software package defined to simplify housekeeping, such as input/output procedures, sort/merge generators, and the like.
M. The word "program" means a set of instructions or steps, usually in symbolic form, that generates machine instructions and tells the computer how to handle a problem.
N. The word "record" means a group of related facts or fields of information treated as a unit. A record need not be a block in length.
O. The word "system" means an assembly of operations and procedures, men, and machines united by some form of regulated interaction to form an organized whole.
P. The words "used," "use," and "uses," when used with respect to files or programs, mean access, retrieved from, changed, updated, referenced, or in any other way referred to by name, directly or indirectly.
Q. The word "output" means information that is generated by a computer to an outside source, such as a printer.

INTERROGATORIES

1. Identify by unit all equipment used in creating, processing, retrieving, or updating information relating to *[specify]*. Identify all such equipment associated with any unit, and designate with which units such equipment is associated.
2. State the location of each unit of equipment identified in your answer to Interrogatory No. 1.
3. Describe fully the operating system used for all programmable equipment identified by your answer to Interrogatory No. 1.
4. Identify all files used by any system that creates, produces, or uses any information concerning *[describe]*. Identify each such file by name so that each file is uniquely defined and can be so referred to in subsequent discovery.
5. Identify the storage media used for each file identified in your answer to Interrogatory No. 4. If more than one medium is used for any one file, state the type of each such medium.
6. State the amount of storage media used (allocation) and the

number of records for each file identified in your answer to Interrogatory No. 4.

7. Identify the organization (for example, sequential, indexed sequential, direct access) for each file identified in your answer to Interrogatory No. 4.
8. State whether each file identified in your answer to Interrogatory No. 4 is blocked or unblocked, and its physical blocking factor.
9. Identify the logical blocking for every unique record layout for each file identified in your answer to Interrogatory No. 4 that has a nonsequential organization. Identify the field or fields used as keys.
10. State the retention time for each file identified in your answer to Interrogatory No. 4.
11. If the retention period stated in your answer to Interrogatory No. 10 has changed since *[date]*, state the date or dates of each such change or changes and the previous retention period or periods.
12. State the earliest available date for each file identified in your answer to Interrogatory No. 4.
13. Identify any safe storage (off-premises storage) used by *[party]*.
14. Identify all files that are kept in safe storage. State the retention period or periods for each such file.
15. Identify all programs that use the files identified in your answer to Interrogatory No. 4. Identify each such program by name so that all programs are uniquely defined and can be so referred to in later discovery.
16. Identify which equipment units identified in your answer to Interrogatory No. 1 are used for each program identified in your answer to Interrogatory No. 15.
17. For each program identified in your answer to Interrogatory No. 15, identify the language used. If more than one language is used, identify which modules or subroutines utilize which language, and the function of each such module or subroutine.
18. For each program identified in your answer to Interrogatory No. 15, identify the schedule for running. If there is no predetermined calendar schedule, state the frequency of running during *[time frame]*.
19. For each program identified in your answer to Interrogatory No. 15, state the frequency of running during *[year]*.
20. For each program identified in your answer to Interrogatory No. 15, describe fully or identify all other output produced, but not limited to, permanent files, work files, description files, and the like.

21. Identify all output described or identified in your answer to Interrogatory No. 20 that is presently available, and the age of such output (this applies to hardcopy produced less frequently than monthly, or hardcopy not produced on a calendar schedule).
22. For each program identified in your answer to Interrogatory No. 15, describe fully or identify what variations of the standard production can be accomplished with changes in parameter cards.
23. Identify each program that can produce, as output in any form or media, the *[describe particular information desired]*.
24. State the number of hours required to write a program that would produce the output described in Interrogatory No. 23, if such a program is not available.
25. Identify each program that is now, or has since *[date]* been used to calculate *[describe information required]*.
26. As to each program identified in your answer to Interrogatory No. 25, identify the period of time during which each such program was in use in a production mode.
27. Identify each person who is now, or was, a programmer, analyst, or supervisor of the programs identified in your answer to Interrogatory No. 25, and the period of time during which each such person was associated with each such program.

Dated: ____

[signature, etc.]

NOTES TO FORM

Commentary

One judge has suggested that in conducting discovery with interrogatories, the parties' counsel should exchange computer disks on which the questions are written. Vincent v. Seaman, 142 Misc. 2d 196, 536 N.Y.S.2d 677 (County Ct. 1989). The recipient of a disk would upload it into the recipient's computer, write the answers to the disk following their respective questions, copy the disk for file storage, and then return the original disk to the proponent of the interrogatories.

§ 13:11 Interrogatories—Another form

[Caption]

INTERROGATORIES TO *[PARTY]*

To: *[name of party]*

You are notified to answer under oath the following interrogatories within __ days of the time service is made on you.

DEFINITIONS

For purposes of these Interrogatories, certain terms have the following definitions:

A. The term "computer system" refers to all file servers, stand alone computers, workstations, and laptops owned or leased by *[name of party]* or physically located at *[place]*.

B. The term "your" refers to *[name of party]*.

C. The term "e-mail" refers to the exchange of text messages and computer files over a communications network, such as a local area network, intranet, extranet, or public network like the Internet or other online service provider.

INTERROGATORIES

1. Identify each authorized user of your computer system.
2. Describe all hardware modifications to the computer system in the past twelve months.

Software Applications

3. Describe the software (e.g., version, manufacturer, any custom modifications) used to create *[describe]*.
4. Describe each of the software applications (e.g., version, manufacturer, any custom modifications) installed on *[specify computer]*.
5. Describe any and all utility programs (e.g., disk maintenance programs, file recovery programs, network maintenance programs) used to maintain the following computer(s): *[identify computer]*.
6. Describe the software (e.g., version, manufacturer, any custom modifications) used to remotely access the computer system.
7. Describe all upgrades made to any software on the computer system during *[specify period]*.
8. Describe any software that has been installed on the computer system during *[specify period]*.
9. Describe any document management software used by *[name of party]* during *[specify period]*.
10. Identify all escrow agents/services who may have copies of the source code for *[specify software]*.
11. Identify all customers who self-escrowed the source code for *[specify software]*.

12. Describe the file format used to store information created by *[specify software].*

Security

13. Describe each instance during the last five years in which an unauthorized party gained access to the computer system.
14. Describe each instance during the last five years in which a virus or other destructive program caused any data loss on the computer system.
15. Describe any disaster recovery plans for the computer system, which were in effect during *[specify time period].*
16. Describe all security measures relating to employee desktop computers.
17. Describe any methods used during *[specify period]* to monitor employee use of the computer system.
18. Describe any methods used during *[specify period]* to monitor employee use of the Internet.
19. Describe any methods used during *[specify period]* to monitor employee use of the e-mail.
20. Describe your procedures, if any, for deleting files from the computer system.
21. Describe all methods of accessing the computer system from outside *[name of organization]* (i.e., remote access procedures).
22. Describe all methods used to restrict access to the *[specify name of database]* database.

Computer Backups

23. Identify each computer in the computer system that is backed up.
24. Describe the backup schedule, if any, for each computer in the computer system.
25. Describe the backup procedures, if any, for each computer in the computer system.
26. Identify the backup software (e.g., version, manufacturer, any custom modifications) used, if any, for each computer in the computer system.
27. Identify the storage location for your archival backups.
28. Describe the types of files routinely backed up from the computer system.
29. Describe the procedures followed by *[name or party]* during *[specify time period]* for backing up information stored on its computer system(s), including, but not limited to, the

frequency of backups, the software used to accomplish the backups, the type of media backups are stored on, and the location where backups are stored.

30. Describe any and all changes to your backup procedures in the last twelve months.

Miscellaneous

31. Describe the computer system(s) used by *[specify individual]*.
32. Describe any methods used to verify the accuracy of information input into the *[identify software application]*.
33. Identify all e-mail addresses used by *[specify individual's name or business name]*, including the complete address and the dates during which the address was used.
34. Identify any computers on which a disk maintenance program (e.g., de-fragment, optimize, or compression software) has been run in the last six months.
35. Identify the person(s) responsible for the ongoing operation and maintenance of the computer system.
36. Identify each employee in your Information Systems Department.

Dated: ____

[signature, etc.]

§ 13:12 Interrogatories—Sex discrimination

[Caption]

INTERROGATORIES TO *[NAME OF PARTY]*

To: *[name of party]*

You are notified to answer under oath the following interrogatories within __ days of the time service is made on you.

DEFINITIONS

A. PLAINTIFF means *[name]*.
B. DEFENDANT means *[name]*.
C. USER means a person who has access to a computer or in any manner uses or directs another to use any information stored in or generated by a computer.
D. COMPUTER OR COMPUTER EQUIPMENT means all data

processing equipment, including but not limited to, central processing units, tape drives, drum and disk storage devices, control units, input devices, and output devices; all unit record equipment, including but not limited to, accumulators, calculators, and sorters; all record storage and retrieval equipment, including but not limited to, microfilm storage and retrieval apparatus, and audio/visual storage and retrieval apparatus.

E. COMPUTER SYSTEM means an assembly of computer operations and procedures, persons, equipment, and hardware and software, united by some form of regulated interaction to form an organized whole.

F. COMPUTER OR ELECTRONIC INFORMATION OR DATA OR DATABASE means all written or numerical information or data that is inputted, processed, or contained in the COMPUTER SYSTEM for any purpose.

G. IDENTIFY a document means to describe briefly the form of the document; describe generally the subject of its contents; state the date and place of preparation or mailing; and identify the person or firm who prepared the document, the person or firm who received it, and the person, or firm who had possession or control of the original of the document.

H. IDENTIFY an act, occurrence, statement, or conduct (hereinafter collectively referred to as "act") means to describe the substance of the event or events constituting such acts, and state the date when such act occurred; to identify each person participating in such act; to identify all other persons present when such act occurred; to state whether any minutes, notes, memoranda or other record of such act was made; to state whether such record now exists; and to identify the person presently having possession, custody, or control of each such record.

I. DOCUMENT means all written, printed, recorded, electronic, or graphic matter, photographic matter, sound reproductions, or electronically stored information however produced or reproduced, pertaining in any manner to the subject matter indicated.

J. YOU AND YOUR refer to DEFENDANT. The words YOU and YOUR shall be taken to include all officers, directors, agents, employees, attorneys, investigators, consultants, and anyone else acting on your or their behalf.

K. COMPUTER PROGRAM means a set of instructions or steps, usually in symbolic form, that generates machine instructions and tells the computer how to handle a problem or sort information.

L. COMPUTER APPLICATION means a program that performs a specific task or function including, e-mail messaging, word processing, or spread sheets.

M. DEFENDANT'S COMPUTER SYSTEM means any and all COMPUTER EQUIPMENT or COMPUTER SYSTEMS located at the defendant's premises or accessible for use by defendant.

N. E-MAIL means an electronic messaging application that provides for the receipt and sending of messages among users of a computer system and possibly to and from remote users.

O. OPERATING SYSTEM means an organized collection of programs for operating a computer, usually part of a software package defined to simplify housekeeping such as input/output procedures, sort merge generators, and so on.

P. BACK-UP TAPES means magnetic tape storage or archiving of ELECTRONIC INFORMATION originally contained on a COMPUTER SYSTEM.

Q. COMPUTER LOG means COMPUTER SYSTEM usage records such as a listing of electronically stored information, and may include title, subject matter, or first line of the document information and the date of the document.

R. COMPUTER SYSTEM MEDIA means the type of material used for storage of electronic information and includes floppy disks, hard drives, and magnetic tapes.

S. PURGE means to periodically or randomly delete or take off of the COMPUTER SYSTEM E-MAIL messages and transfer this information to BACK-UP TAPES to restore or make usable computer memory.

INTERROGATORIES

1. IDENTIFY yourself.
2. IDENTIFY all persons who assisted in preparing responses to these interrogatories.
3. Identify by name, manufacturer's model number, or serial number and unit type all COMPUTER EQUIPMENT defendant uses as part of its COMPUTER SYSTEM, and include a listing of all peripheral EQUIPMENT associated with any unit and designating with which units such EQUIPMENT is associated.
4. State the location of each unit of EQUIPMENT identified in your answer to Interrogatory 3.
5. Describe fully or identify the OPERATING SYSTEM used for all programmable EQUIPMENT identified in your answer to Interrogatories 3 and 4.

6. During the period *[date]* to *[date]*, did you discuss or engage in communications concerning the consequences to PLAINTIFF of PLAINTIFF'S departure from the company, including oral, written, or electronic discussions and communications?
7. If your answer to Interrogatory 6 is yes, describe fully the substance of each non-privileged discussion or communication.
8. If your answer to Interrogatory 6 is yes, state the date, time, place, and form of each such discussion or communication.
9. If your answer to Interrogatory 6 is yes, IDENTIFY every person who was present at each such discussion or communication, including the recipients and sender of the communication and any person to whom the communication was directed.
10. If your answer to Interrogatory 6 is yes, IDENTIFY all DOCUMENTS, including electronically stored information, that contain the discussions or communications.
11. For the period *[date]* to *[date]*, state whether BACK-UP TAPES were made of any COMPUTER SYSTEM E-MAIL messages, electronically stored information, word processing documents, or correspondence.
12. If YOUR answer to Interrogatory 11 is yes, state:
    (a) The custodian of those tapes;
    (b) Identification numbers or the system for identification for those tapes;
    (c) The location of those tapes; and
    (d) For what period of time those tapes are stored before being reused or discarded.
13. For the period *[date]* to *[date]*, state whether a periodic or random PURGE of E-MAIL messaging was performed.
14. If YOUR answer to Interrogatory 13 is yes, state when that PURGE occurred and identify the BACK-UP TAPE the electronic information was transferred to.
15. State how YOUR COMPUTER SYSTEM handles the deletion or "trash" disposal of E-MAIL messages by a computer user.
16. State whether a COMPUTER LOG is maintained listing E-MAIL messages that have been deleted or "trashed" from the COMPUTER SYSTEM.
17. If YOUR answer to Interrogatory 16 is yes, state the computer location of the COMPUTER LOG for deleted or "trashed" E-MAIL.
18. State whether YOU deleted or "trashed" E-MAIL messages regarding PLAINTIFF'S firing during the period *[date]* to *[date]*.
19. If YOUR answer to Interrogatory 18 is yes, state:
    (a) The substance of those deleted or "trashed" E-MAIL messages;

(b) The sender and recipients of those messages, and
(c) The date and time of those messages.

20. State whether similar lawsuits have been commenced or filed against YOU regarding sex discrimination.
21. If YOUR answer to Interrogatory 20 is yes, state when and in which jurisdiction those lawsuits were commenced or filed.
22. If YOUR answer to Interrogatory 20 is yes, IDENTIFY the plaintiff in those lawsuits.
23. List all persons who participated in the decision to fire the PLAINTIFF.
24. State all explanations for the YOUR firing of the PLAINTIFF.
25. Do you contend that you did not discriminate, on the basis of PLAINTIFF'S gender, against the PLAINTIFF?
26. If your answer to Interrogatory 25 is yes, please state every fact that supports your contention.
27. If your answer to Interrogatory 25 is yes, please identify every document that supports your contention.
28. If your answer to Interrogatory 25 is yes, describe every tangible item of evidence and every document, including electronically stored information, that support your contention.
29. Do you contend there is no other electronically stored information that evinces discussions or communications concerning:
    (a) The PLAINTIFF'S work performance;
    (b) *[Name]*'s departure from the company, and
    (c) The firing of the PLAINTIFF?
30. Do you contend the PLAINTIFF was fired for good cause?
31. Do you contend that no officer or director of the company insisted the PLAINTIFF be fired because the PLAINTIFF is a *[woman] [man]*?
32. Do you contend *[name]* did not send E-MAIL to officers and directors of the company stating the PLAINTIFF should be fired?
33. Do you contend that no officer or director of the company received an E-MAIL message stating the PLAINTIFF should be fired?
34. Do you contend that *[name]* did not intentionally delete or "trash"an E-MAIL message stating the PLAINTIFF should be fired?
35. Do you contend that there is another reason the PLAINTIFF was fired?
36. Do you contend the PLAINTIFF was fired for performance reasons?

Dated: ____

[signature, etc.]

NOTES TO FORM

Commentary

These interrogatories are based on a hypothetical case involving a claim of sex discrimination in employment evidenced by an e-mail message. The interrogatories are designed to elicit information the plaintiff will need to know for preparation of the case, including the circumstances of the plaintiff's firing and the defenses that will be argued. The interrogatories emphasize questions seeking information about data within or exchanged through the defendant's computer system. Accordingly, they do not represent a complete set of questions regarding a claim of sex discrimination.

§ 13:13 Interrogatories combined with requests to produce information about computer system

[Caption]

Interrogatories

To: *[name of party]*

You are notified to answer under oath the following interrogatories within __ days of the time service is made on you.

Each of the following interrogatories in this section refers ONLY to the *[name of party]*'s computer system, and not to the computer system of any of *[name of party]*'s counsel. In particular, the following interrogatories DO NOT inquire of the computer system maintained or managed by the *[name of party]*'s law firm, or any of that firm's personnel or agents.

1. Please identify the person or persons who have contributed to answering the interrogatories in this section.
2. Please identify by name, physical location, manufacturer's model number or serial number all of the computer equipment containing an installed copy of the database program.
3. Please state if there is any other location where hardcopy or electronic information regarding customer complaints resides other than within the database.
4. Is the database available in other languages besides English and, if so, what are those languages?
5. If the database is available in other languages, is there a master or main database that contains all records, regardless of language?

6. Please identify by name, physical location, manufacturer's model number or serial number all of the computer equipment physically containing actual copies of records.
7. Please identify by name, physical location, manufacturer's model number or serial number all of the computer equipment containing copies of any of the scanned electronic documents referred to in some of the records.
8. Please identify the location on your computer system where the master or main copy of the database resides.
9. Please provide the "version number" of the program currently being used at *[name of party]*, and state whether the program has been specially modified in any way by *[name of party]* computer system personnel to accommodate a) the database or b) the company's e-mail system.
10. Do any engineers or members of engineer departments at *[name of party]* use an e-mail system other than that provided by the program and, if so, what are the names of the other e-mail systems?
11. How do users of *[name of party]*'s e-mail system in the United States communicate with e-mail users in other parts of the world?
12. If there is a translation module or program used for automatically effecting a translation of e-mail from, for example, German to English, what is the name of that module or the program that effects translations?
13. Please identify by name, physical location, manufacturer's model number or serial number all of the computer equipment that is used to back up a) generally the files located on *[name of party]*'s computer system and b) specifically the e-mail system or systems used by the engineers and engineering departments at *[defendant] [plaintiff]*, its subsidiaries (in this country or throughout the world), predecessors, successors, assigns, joint venturers, partners, parents, agents and affiliates.
14. Regardless of whether it is for security purposes or for some other purpose, is e-mail use at *[name of party]*'s monitored in any way?
15. If e-mail used at *[name of party]* is monitored, where are the monitoring logs or other information concerning such monitoring information stored?
16. Regardless of the date or where in the world they may be located, please state the location or locations where all archived copies of *[name of party]* computer system files are kept, housed or stored.

17. What purchase, merger or related documents exist concerning the acquisition of *[describe]* by *[name of party]*, whether in hardcopy or in electronic format and regardless of who possesses or controls them?
18. What engineering documents originally belonging to exist, regardless of type and whether in hardcopy or in electronic format and regardless of who possesses or controls them?
19. Regardless of the date or where in the world they may be located, please state the location or locations where archived copies of engineering documents originally belonging to *[specify]* are kept, housed or stored.

Requests to Produce

20. Please provide us with unabridged copies of the *[specify]* user's manuals for each version of that program that is currently running anywhere on your computer system.
21. Please provide us with copies of all manuals, electronic or hardcopy, a) furnished to any users of the database, or b) used by the administrators or intranet Web masters responsible for the maintenance and management of the database anywhere in the world and regardless of whether those manuals are written in English or some other language.
22. Please provide us with copies of all manuals, electronic or hardcopy, a) furnished to any users of *[name of party]*'s e-mail system, or b) used by the administrators or intranet Web masters responsible for the maintenance and management of *[name of party]*'s e-mail system anywhere in the world and regardless of whether those manuals are written in English or in some other language.
23. Please provide us with copies of all manuals, electronic or hardcopy, used by the information systems personnel responsible for maintaining, backing up, restoring or purging generally the computer files located on the computer system of *[name of party]* anywhere in the world and regardless of whether those manuals are written in English or some other language.
24. Please provide us with copies of all manuals, electronic or hardcopy, used by the information systems personnel responsible for maintaining, backing up, restoring or purging the e-mail systems of *[name of party]* anywhere in the world and regardless of whether those manuals are written in English or some other language.
25. Please provide us with all policies or policy statements issued to engineer or engineer department users of *[name of party]*'s e-mail system, regardless of the date of same.

26. Please provide us with copies of any purchase, merger or related documents, whether in hardcopy or in electronic format, concerning the acquisition of by *[name of party]*.

Dated: ____

[signature, etc.]

NOTES TO FORM

Commentary

These interrogatories and requests to produce can be adapted for use after information is discovered regarding the responding party's computer system.

§ 13:14 Order granting party leave to serve additional interrogatories

[Caption]

This cause comes before the Court on the plaintiff's motion for leave of the Court to serve additional interrogatories on defendant and on defendant's response.

Having considered the motion and the tendered interrogatories, this Court determines that, while relevant, the number of interrogatories tendered for a case of this nature is burdensome. This is particularly so in light of the fact that plaintiff intends to depose the defendant.

Accordingly, the Court now grants plaintiff leave to serve an additional __ interrogatories on defendant. Plaintiff may designate __ interrogatories from those tendered. Plaintiff may delay its designation until after plaintiff has completed defendant's depositions. In the alternative, plaintiff may compose a new set of __ or fewer interrogatories consistent with this order.

Dated: ____

Judge

NOTES TO FORM

Commentary

Some court rules (including Fed. R. Civ. P. 33) limit the number of interrogatories. In such cases, the court may give permission for more interrogatories than the number permitted in the rule. In this form, the judge allows more interrogatories than the number permitted by rule, but refuses to give permission for the plaintiff to ask as many as requested. The form can be modified if the court grants the entire request.

§ 13:15 Motion to compel answers to interrogatories

[Caption]

MOTION TO COMPEL ANSWERS TO INTERROGATORIES

[Party 1] moves the Court as follows:

1. On *[date]*, *[party 1]*, after commencement of the above-entitled action, served on the *[party 2]* __ interrogatories in writing pursuant to *[rule]*, which interrogatories are attached to this motion.
2. *[Party 2]* answered interrogatories *[numbers of interrogatories]*, but did not answer such interrogatories under oath as required by *[rule]*.
3. *[Party 2]* failed to answer interrogatories *[numbers of unanswered interrogatories]*.
4. The undersigned certifies that the undersigned has in good faith attempted to confer with the attorney for *[party 2]* in an unsuccessful effort to secure the requested information without court action.

Wherefore, *[party 1]* moves that this Court enter an order directing and requiring *[party 2]* to answer all of these interrogatories under oath.

[Party 1] further moves the court for an order awarding *[party 1]* the reasonable expenses, including attorney fees incurred on this motion.

Dated: ____

[signature etc.]

§ 13:16 Order to compel answers to interrogatories

[Caption]

ORDER TO COMPEL ANSWERS TO INTERROGATORIES

This cause was heard on *[plaintiff's] [defendant's]* motion to compel *[defendant] [plaintiff]* to answer interrogatories served by *[plaintiff] [defendant]*, and upon due consideration it is

ORDERED that *[defendant] [plaintiff]* shall answer interrogatories numbers *[specify]*, and under oath, and it is

FURTHER ORDERED that the *[defendant] [plaintiff]* shall

answer under oath interrogatory number except insofar as this interrogatory asks *[defendant] [plaintiff]* to state *[describe]*.

IT IS FURTHER ORDERED that *[defendant] [plaintiff]* pay *[plaintiff] [defendant]* the sum of $____ as reasonable expenses in obtaining this order and $____ as reasonable attorney fees.

Dated: ____

Judge

Chapter 14

Requests for Production and Inspection

I. GUIDELINES

II. CHECKLISTS

III. FORMS

Research References

Treatises and Practice Aids

Grenig and Gleisner, eDiscovery & Digital Evidence § 7:14
Danner and Varn, Pattern Deposition Checklists §§ 10:01 to 10:231

Trial Strategy

Recovery and Reconstruction of Electronic Mail as Evidence, 41 Am. Jur. Proof of Facts 3d 1
Computer Technology in Civil Litigation, 71 Am. Jur. Trials 111

Additional References

Grenig and Kinsler, Federal Civil Discovery and Disclosure §§ 11.1 to 11.73 (3d ed.)
ABA Discovery Standards, http://www.abanet.org/litigation/discoverystandards/2005civildiscoverystandards.pdf
Electronic Discovery Reference Model Project, http://www.edrm.net

Federal Judicial Center, http://www.fjc.gov
The Sedona Conference, http://www.thesedonaconference.org

KeyCite®: Cases and other legal materials listed in KeyCite Scope can be researched through the KeyCite service on Westlaw®. Use KeyCite to check citations for form, parallel references, prior and later history, and comprehensive citator information, including citations to other decisions and secondary materials.

I. GUIDELINES

§ 14:1 Generally

Once information is obtained regarding the responding party's electronically stored information, discovery requests can be refined to obtain relevant electronically stored information from the locations and systems identified in the interrogatories and depositions. If the discovering party believes that there is relevant electronically stored information, the discovering party should not hesitate to seek its production just because the discovering party has already been provided with hardcopy versions.

Procedural rules, such as Fed. R. Civ. P. 34, set forth the procedures for making and responding to requests for the production of documents and tangible things and entry upon land for inspection and other purposes. The rules are normally designed to operate extrajudicially, and may be used only against parties.

Under Fed. R. Civ. P. 34, the party wishing to inspect documents or tangible things or to enter upon the property of another merely serves on the other party a request that this be permitted, setting forth what it is the party wishes to see and when, where, and how the party wishes to examine it. The opponent serves a response, either saying that the request will be granted or stating objections to the request.

If the request is granted, the inspection takes place without court involvement. If the request is objected to, the discovering party decides whether to pursue the matter further. If the discovering party decides to pursue the matter further, the party makes a motion to compel, and the court may compel the requested inspection.

§ 14:2 Actions in which production is available

Requests for production may be used in most civil actions. Although Fed. R. Civ. P. 34 applies only to pending actions, in a proceeding to perpetuate testimony under Fed. R. Civ. P. 27, the court may make orders of the nature provided for in Fed. R. Civ. P. 34.

§ 14:3 Persons to whom production requests may be directed—Generally

Fed. R. Civ. P. 34 and similar state rules may be used only against parties to the action. Document production requests may not be directed to the attorney for a party or to a witness who is not a party. Although production requests may not be directed to a party's attorney, requests directed to represented parties should be served on their attorneys.

Because Fed. R. Civ. P. 34 covers all documents and electronically stored information that are in the possession, custody or control of a party, a party must produce documents in the possession of its agents. As a result, a party cannot immunize a document from inspection by turning it over to a nonparty so long as it remains in the party's control. A document does not become privileged merely because a party gives it to the party's attorney. One exception to this rule is statements prepared by a client at the behest of their attorneys.

If an entity, typically a parent corporation, has been found to be the alter ego of a party, that entity may be subject to Fed. R. Civ. P. 34. This issue arises most frequently when the alleged alter ego is a foreign corporation outside the jurisdictional limitations of Fed. R. Civ. P. 45.

§ 14:4 Persons to whom production requests may be directed—Custody or control

Fed. R. Civ. P. 34(a) permits any party to serve on any other party a request to produce and allow the party making the request, or someone acting on the party's behalf, to inspect and copy any designated electronically stored information, documents, or things that contain matters within the scope of discovery in the possession, custody, or control of the party upon whom the request is served. Legal ownership or actual possession is not determinative.

The test is whether the party has the legal right to control or obtain the items requested. The responding party cannot provide only those electronically stored information, documents, and things within its immediate possession; it must provide all electronically stored information, documents, and things to which it has a legal right to control or may obtain upon demand.

Whether electronically stored information and documents in

the possession of a party's attorney are under the control of the party is resolved by discerning their origin.[1] If the items were originally produced by the party or its agents and then turned over to the attorney, they are considered under the party's control.

Documents and electronically stored information that the responding party may obtain from a third party by written request are within the responding party's control. If documents and electronically stored information in the possession of a third party are controlled by the responding party, the responding party may not object to a production request on the ground that the requesting party may obtain the information directly from the third party with a subpoena.

A party may be required to produce electronically stored information, documents, and things in the party's possession, although they belong to a third person who is not a party to the action. If a party has possession, custody, or control, it must produce the information even though the items themselves are beyond the jurisdiction of the court. And, even if a party lacks possession, custody or control, it may be compelled to produce such information if it fails to interpose this objection in a timely fashion.

§ 14:5 Making production requests—Generally

To inspect electronically stored information, documents, or tangible things or to enter upon the property of another party, a party merely must serve on the other party a request that this be permitted. A request may be served on a party without first obtaining an admission from that party that the documents or things exist. The written request must:

- Designate what items the requesting party wishes to see.
- Specify a reasonable time, place and manner for the inspection and related acts.[1]

What constitutes a reasonable time, place and manner is within the court's discretion.

[Section 14:4]

[1]See Phillips v. Netblue, Inc., 2007 WL 174459 (N.D. Cal. 2007) (party producing e-mails containing hyperlinks to other third-party servers was not under duty to download and preserve hyperlinked images, as such images were not within producing party's possession, custody, or control).

[Section 14:5]

[1]See Fed. R. Civ. P. 34(b).

§ 14:6 Making production requests—Timing

Fed. R. Civ. P. 34(b) precludes the service of production requests before the time specified in Fed. R. Civ. P. 26(d) absent a court order or written stipulation. Fed. R. Civ. P. 26(d) provides that, except when authorized by local rule, order or stipulation, a party may not seek discovery from any source before the parties have met and conferred as required by Fed. R. Civ. P. 26(f). Fed. R. Civ. P. 26(f) requires that the parties meet to develop, among other things, a discovery plan.

This meeting must take place as soon as practicable in the litigation process but, in any event, at least 14 days before a scheduling conference is held or a scheduling order is due under Fed. R. Civ. P. 16(b). Fed. R. Civ. P. 16(b) requires that a scheduling order be entered within 90 days after the first appearance of a defendant or 120 days after the complaint has been served on any defendant, whichever occurs earlier.

Fed. R. Civ. P. 34(b) is silent on how late in the litigation process a party may serve production requests. Trial courts have considerable discretion in determining the timeliness of discovery. Some courts have local rules governing discovery cut-off dates. Where no such rules exist, scheduling orders and pretrial orders may set a time limit for the completion of discovery, including service of or response to production requests.

Production requests should be served to allow sufficient time to complete the process before the discovery cut-off or trial deadline. Ideally, the discovery order should specify whether the discovery deadline is the deadline for service of electronically stored information and document production requests or for responses to such requests. If it is the latter, then requests must be served no less than 30 days before the discovery cut-off date.

The request must specify a reasonable time for making the inspection and performing the related acts. It must provide at least 30 days to allow for the written response. The court has the authority to shorten or lengthen the time to respond. The parties also may stipulate in writing to an extension. The request may simply call for inspection "at a time and place convenient to" the party to whom it is directed, allowing that party to designate the time and place. The actual time, place and manner of inspection is usually arranged by an informal agreement between the attorneys.

§ 14:7 Making production requests—Number of requests

There is no limit on the frequency of use of production requests, unless the court orders otherwise. There is also no required sequence of discovery. Typically, parties start the discovery process with interrogatories and production requests, followed by depositions and requests for admission, but no particular sequence is mandated. A request for production by one party does not prevent any other party from making its own request for production.

§ 14:8 Making production requests—Form and contents

Fed. R. Civ. P. 34(b) requires that each production request designate, either by individual item or by category, the item to be inspected and describe each with reasonable particularity.[1] Particularity in designation, of course, is a matter of degree, and depends on the circumstances of each case. If temporary information not routinely retained is desired, the requesting party must take effective affirmative action, including, when necessary, seeking a preservation order requiring a producing party to place transitory information into a form from which production can later be made.[2]

The request may specify the form or forms in which electronically stored information is to be produced. In making the discovery request, it is essential that the requesting party has an understanding of the responding party's digital information systems and how people interact with the system. The requesting party must determine which format will be best for the requesting party's case.

Native format files are original computer files in their original application or software forms.[3] Accordingly, it is necessary for the requesting party to understand fully what the native format is

---

[Section 14:8]

[1]See Sedona Principle 4 ("Discovery requests for electronically stored information should he as clear as possible, while responses and objections to discovery should disclose the scope and limits of the production.").

[2]See Healthcare Advocates, Inc. v. Harding, Earley, Follmer & Frailey, 497 F. Supp. 2d 627 (E.D. Pa. 2007) (no duty to preserve images automatically retained in and later deleted from temporary cache files where producing party was not aware of duty to do so); Columbia Pictures, Inc. v. Bunnell, 245 F.R.D. 443, 69 Fed. R. Serv. 3d 173 (C.D. Cal. 2007) (server log data was discoverable although it had existed only temporarily in computer's random access memory (RAM).

[3]See Wyeth v. Impax Laboratories, Inc., 248 F.R.D. 169 (D. Del. 2006) (plaintiff not required to produce electronic documents in their native format, complete with metadata, where plaintiff produced documents as image files and defendant failed to demonstrate particularized need for metadata).

for the particular discovery sought in the case. This includes how the documents were kept, what software programs were used, how files were named, and whether there was any electronic backup or overwriting of the documents.[4]

In deciding which format to request, the following factors should be considered:

- **Alterability and Spoliation.** Files converted to TIFF images cannot be altered. On the other hand, native files can normally be changed easily.
- **Bates Numbering.** It can be costly to track document in native format. Native file productions may make it impossible to Bates number the documents, prevent an effective audit trail of the documents produced. (Bates numbers can be added to the header or footer of a native document, but this modifies the document.) In contrast, a TIFF production allows for Bates number and accurate tracking of produced documents.
- **Redactions.** A TIFF review and production allows parties to redact confidential or privileged information. When documents are produced in native format, there is no effective way to place a redaction on the native file. Native file production can undermine a defendant's efforts to protect proprietary or privileged information.

"Metadata" are information that can show who created the document, when it may have been modified, and who may have altered it. Requests for the production of metadata have increased in recent years.[5] Generally, the computer creates the metadata automatically with time, date, and user stamps. Users can add layers of metadata. Metadata can show the relations documents have with other portions of documents, showing what has been cut, copied, and pasted into other materials.

"System metadata" are data that a computer's operating system compiles about a file's name, size, and location, as well as its last modified, accessed, and created dates and time stamps. "Application metadata" are information embedded in documents, includ-

---

[4]Gonzalez & Montoya, *Ten Tips Leading to Efficient and Effective eDiscovery for the Small Law Firm*, GP/SOLO, Apr. 2007.

[5]See Baldas, *Metadata Grows in Legal Import,* Nat'l L.J., Jan. 26, 2009, at 4; Wiener & Celeita, *Computer Infections Are Bad Enough, But the Cure Can Kill: Anti-Virus Software Can Contaminate Evidence, Even When the Intent Is Innocent*, Nat'l L. J., Aug. 24, 2009, at 17; Barsocchini, *Developing E-Discovery Processes that Operate Without Altering Metadata*, 78 U.S.L.W. 2135. (Sept. 15, 2009); Gable, *Examining Metadata: Its Role in E-Discovery and the Future of Records Managers*, INFORMATIONMANAGEMENT, Sept./Oct. 2009, at 28.

ing user comments and tracked changes. System metadata can facilitate searching and sorting data chronologically, and suggesting whether the data can be trusted. System metadata present little potential for disclosure of privileged or confidential information and should be routinely preserved and produced. Robocopy, a free download from Microsoft, can preserve system metadata, but it cannot restore data already corrupted. Robocopy can also be difficult to use.

Metadata may show:

- Who may have opened the file
- On what dates and times persons accessed the file
- When modifications, including additions, deletions, or revisions, were made to the file
- To whom files were distributed or forwarded
- Who made additions, deletions, or revisions to the file

Descriptive metadata describe a resource for purposes such as discovery and identification. They can include such elements as author, title, and abstract. Structural metadata indicate how compound objects are put together. They identify data format, media format, or the type of data representation and file types, hardware and software needed to render the data, and the compression method and encryption algorithms used, if any. Administrative metadata provide information to help manage a resource, such as when and how it was created, file type and other technical information, and who can access it.

If native files are produced, all associated metadata, embedded data, and hidden information will be included. Production of TIFF and PDF files with selected metadata fields allows a producing party greater control over what it is giving.[6] Metadata may be especially relevant in cases where the integrity of dates entered facially on documents.[7]

A responding party is not required to reproduce electronically stored information in more than one form.[8] Accordingly, it is important for a requesting party to consider carefully the form in

---

[6]Gonzalez & Montoya, *Ten Tips Leading to Efficient and Effective eDiscovery for the Small Law Firm*, GP/Solo, Apr. 2007.

[7]See, e.g., Ryan v. Gifford, 2007 WL 4259557 (Del. Ch. 2007) (award of stock options). See also Wyeth v. Impax Laboratories, Inc., 248 F.R.D. 169 (D. Del. 2006) (most metadata is of limited evidentiary value, and reviewing it can waste litigation resources); Kentucky Speedway, LLC v. National Ass'n. of Stock Car Auto Racing, 2006 WL 5097354 (E.D. Ky. 2006) (in most cases and for most documents, metadata does not provide relevant information).

[8]See Aguilar v. Immigration and Customs Enforcement Div. of U.S. Dept. of Homeland Sec., 255 F.R.D. 350 (S.D. N.Y. 2008) (civil rights plaintiffs who

which it wishes to receive the information before requesting that it be produced.[9]

When seeking electronically stored information, the discovering party should:

- Provide a very specific and detailed request that includes a statement of why it is important to the discovering party's case. In the case of electronically stored information, failure to do so can have serious consequences.
- Not be too specific. If the request is too specific, certain critical information may not be provided; if the request is too broad, the producing party may object to the request.
- Expressly request digital documents by type.
- Specify the production format sought. Despite the fact that one should seek electronically stored information in its native format, counsel may wish to obtain it in PDF or TIFF format for a number of reasons. For example, if counsel is using Summation it may make sense to obtain TIFF images because it will be easier to load into older versions of that program. However, the convenience of receiving electronically stored information in PDF or TIFF format is probably at the expense of receiving the total picture provided by receiving electronically stored information in its native format. Evidence provided in its native format can always be converted to PDF or TIFF.

It is prudent to seek to obtain electronically stored information in its native format. The discovering party can expect resistance when seeking to obtain electronically stored information in its native format (as opposed to PDF or TIFF format). Responding parties will frequently claim that it is burdensome for them to review all productions for privileged information or metadata, even claiming that they have an ethical duty not to disclose information in native format. That is why the discovering party's counsel must go to considerable pains to review the information

---

did not make formal request for discovery of metadata when they initially sought discovery of responsive electronic mail messages and delayed making such request until agency's process of harvesting e-mails was largely complete, were not entitled to compelled transmittal of responsive e-mails in form that preserved original metadata); Williams v. Sprint/United Management Co., 99 Fair Empl. Prac. Cas. (BNA) 1502, 2006 WL 3691604 (D. Kan. 2006).

[9]See, e.g., D'Onofrio v. SFX Sports Group, Inc., 247 F.R.D. 43, 102 Fair Empl. Prac. Cas. (BNA) 1499 (D.D.C. 2008) (plaintiff's instruction in request for production directing that document be produced in such manner as to preserve and identify file from which they were taken did not constitute request that defendant produce electronic data in their original form with metadata, and defendant could not be compelled to do so).

furnished in hardcopy, PDF, or TIFF formats before seeking a native format production.

It is not always possible to obtain electronically stored information evidence in its native format in the first instance. However, after carefully reviewing the electronically stored information by the responding party, if it appears suspicious or incomplete, it is time for the discovering party to demand that the evidence be produced in its native format just as it exists in the responding party's computer systems.

Counsel should consider requesting production of the printout of a database (remembering that metadata may not be disclosed), the programs used to produce it, and the data from which the printout was derived. Counsel should also ask for the source listing with any explanatory documentation, and give consideration to obtaining source codes in order to perform tests on the program. Counsel should ask for an intelligible listing of the data the program used to generate the printout and a machine-readable copy of the data, together with an explanation of the format in which the data is recorded.

Counsel should not overlook relevant data that live outside documents and databases (e.g., system access logs, server logs). Because most corporate information technology departments overwrite logs very frequently, timeliness will be important in preserving these logs.

CD or DVD productions are likely to be a responding party's preferred method of production, but such productions can be problematic. They will certainly contain less interesting information than a mirrored drive because slack space and deleted files will not show up on data copied to an optical drive. The digital age will not change the tendency of responding parties to make matters difficult for a discovering party. This is especially the case when it comes to the production of digital evidence on CD or DVD. It is prudent to specify in the definitional section of interrogatories seeking the production of digital evidence what a discovering party will accept when that evidence is produced on CD or DVD. If the images do not exist in a database, then a detailed index of the contents of each CD or DVD should be provided on each CD or DVD.

If the producing party maintains the electronically stored information in a searchable format, it is helpful to get an agreement or court order requiring that the information be produced in that format. If the electronically stored information is produced in a format that is not readable, searchable, or usable, the requesting party should meet with the producing party before filing a motion to compel. If agreement cannot be reached, then the requesting party should seek an order compelling production of the electronically stored information in a searchable format.

§ 14:9 Making production requests—Service

In federal court, service of production requests is governed by Fed. R. Civ. P. 5. Requests may be served by delivering a copy to the party or mailing the request to the party's last known address. Once a party has appeared by counsel, the requests are served upon the attorney. A copy of the requests should also be served on all other parties to the action. Fed. R. Civ. P. 5(d) provides that requests and responses must not be filed until they are used in the proceeding or the court orders filing.

§ 14:10 Production requests—E-mail

E-mail has become one of the most popular means of communication in the workplace.[1] Frequently, e-mail users fail to exercise care and use common sense when creating e-mail messages. Many e-mail users do not realize e-mail messages are more permanent than paper letters. E-mail is also very easy to duplicate and forward with the result that it can easily end up in the possession of an unintended recipient. In addition, if an organization runs periodic backups of its network, e-mail messages are backed up and stored on backup tapes.

An important difference between the discovery of e-mail and the discovery of paper documents is the sheer volume of e-mail. Additionally, computers have the ability to capture several copies (or drafts) of the same e-mail, multiplying the volume of documents. All of these e-mails must be scanned for both relevance and privilege.[2]

Archived e-mails typically lack a coherent filing system. Dated archival systems commonly store information on magnetic tapes

---

[Section 14:10]

[1]See, e.g., S.E.C. v. Collins & Aikman Corp., 256 F.R.D. 403, Fed. Sec. L. Rep. (CCH) ¶ 95045 (S.D. N.Y. 2009) (e-mails are inherently searchable).

[2]Compare Zakre v. Norddeutsche Landesbank Girozentrale, 2004 WL 764895 (S.D. N.Y. 2004) (providing over 200,000 e-mails on two CD-ROMs in a text-searchable format was responsive to discovery request), with Hagemeyer North America, Inc. v. Gateway Data Sciences Corp., 222 F.R.D. 594 (E.D. Wis. 2004) (when producing documents in response to discovery request, responding party may not mingle responsive documents with large numbers of nonresponsive documents; however, responding party has no duty to organize and label documents if it has produced them as they are kept in usual course of business).

that may be obsolete. Thus, parties incur additional costs in translating the data from the tapes into useable form.

E-mail does not appear as a set of files as one might see in a Windows directory. E-mail lives within an environment rich with metadata that cannot easily be split into small parts.[3] In many computers, e-mail will be contained in Microsoft Outlook. To obtain and search all of the e-mails of a responding party using Outlook, it is necessary to seek production of what is called a PST file. A PST file is a Microsoft proprietary file containing the entire Outlook e-mail database. When viewed from Windows Explorer, it can appear as a single file or a grouping of a small number of files. A PST file cannot be opened correctly except with Outlook. A single PST file can house tens of thousands of e-mails in numerous directories, together with address books, and can grow very large (a two gigabyte PST is not uncommon).

After the discovering party has reviewed the e-mails furnished in hardcopy or in PDF format, and has found several that are particularly interesting, the discovering party may wish to consider asking to see just those e-mails in their native format so counsel can inspect their metadata. With the help of a forensic computer expert, the discovering party can instruct the responding party to segregate selected e-mail into separate folders and then export them to removable media.

§ 14:11 Production requests—Videoconferencing and voicemail

Voicemail and videoconferencing systems can preserve data about who participated in an exchange, and the date, time and length of the exchange. Videoconferencing and voicemail systems may archive copies of incoming and outgoing messages. Some videoconferencing equipment makes digital records of each conference.

Many voicemail systems archive copies of incoming and outgoing messages. Although voicemail has always been subject to discovery, discovery respondents have, for the most part, successfully resisted turning over voicemails, citing expense and burden. However, the use of Unified Messaging Systems (UMS) may be changing this. UMS do not distinguish between e-mail, voicemail, and other forms of messaging. Because of the nature of UMS technology, the arguments of cost and burden will probably be less persuasive.

---

[3]See Berman and Zerkier, *Recognizing Import of E-Mail Headers in Discovery: Litigators May Use Embedded Data to Follow an "Information Trail"*, NAT'L L.J., Apr. 24, 2006, at S8.

§ 14:12 Requests to produce—Databases

While discovery frequently centers on e-mail messages and digital versions of documents, in many cases e-discovery requests include databases. A digital database is a collection of data in computers organized for rapid search and retrieval. A database program stores and organizes information on a variety of subjects in a variety of ways and provides access to information in all of its files quickly and easily. The organization of the data facilitates the rapid search and retrieval of data.

A database can include a table in a word processing program or a spreadsheet. A database also includes litigation support databases such as Summation and Concordance. These latter types of databases are sometimes referred to as "flat-file" databases—they have a single layer of data in which every record is equal in form to every other record. A table in a flat-file database cannot be related to other database tables.

A "relational" database is more complex than a flat file database. A relational database uses multiple tables to form a single database. Tables in a relational database can be related for business or information purposes. When a relational database is searched, the database matches information from a field in one table with information in a corresponding field of another table to produce a third table combining requested data from both tables. A relational database may be created using software such as Microsoft Access, Paradox, or FoxPro.

"Enterprise" databases are the most complex databases. An enterprise database can be created using Oracle, Informix, or Microsoft SQL server software. These databases are used by organizations to manage large volumes of data across large distributed networks.

Discovery of databases may be necessary to uncover all of the pieces of data that can be vital evidence in a trial. However, database discovery raises difficult issues, as databases are not made up of discrete documents, but are constantly changing, being updated, and being linked together from multiple sources. It is not a simple matter for the responding party to produce a database, especially a relational or enterprise database.

It is not possible to import all databases into a single system for review. Issues can arise involving such matters as to how the database is configured, its size, functionality, reporting forms, and search methodology. However, because databases are considered documents, they must be produced if a proper discovery request is made.

Because the field properties of a database are considered

metadata, a database discovery request should include a request for copies of operating instructions, user manuals, database design manual, and other information that may disclose the database field properties. In Dunn v. Midwestern Indemnity,[1] the court acknowledged that in many instances it will be essential for the discovering party to know the underlying theory and the procedures employed in preparing and storing machine-readable records. When this is true, the court said litigants should be allowed to discover any materials relating to the record holder's computer hardware, the programming techniques employed, the principles governing structure of the stored data, and the operation of the data processing system. The court went on to say that, when statistical analyses have been developed from more traditional records with the assistance of computer techniques, the underlying data used to compose the statistical computer input, the methods used to select, categorize, and evaluate the data for analysis, and all the computer outputs are normally proper subjects for discovery.

When making a request for production of a database, the requesting party should attempt do the following:

- Seek to determine the nature of the database requested.
- Determine the size of the database.
- Seek to determine the content of the database.

Courts have limited or denied requests for direct access to databases. For example, In re Ford Motor Co.[2] involved a plaintiff's claim that, because of defective design, her seat belt

[Section 14:12]

[1]Dunn v. Midwestern Indem., 88 F.R.D. 191 (S.D. Ohio 1980).

[2]See, e.g., Adhi Parasakthi Charitable, Medical, Educational, and Cultural Society of North America v. Township of West Pikeland, 2010 WL 1047894, *8 (E.D. Pa. 2010) (court ordered plaintiff to allow defendant's e-discovery expert to inspect plaintiff's computers where plaintiff failed to deny that responsive e-mail may have existed at one time); Bank of Mongolia v. M & P Global Financial Services, Inc., 258 F.R.D. 514, 520 (S.D. Fla. 2009); Covad Communications Co. v. Revonet, Inc., 258 F.R.D. 5 (D.D.C. 2009) (plaintiff entitled to make forensic images of drives and computers of defendant even though information was confidential, where expense associated with taking forensic image was small compared with cost of forensic search itself and provided both parties and court with best possible present depository of crucial information in database); White v. Graceland College Center for Professional Development & Lifelong Learning, Inc., 2009 WL 722056 (D. Kan. 2009), subsequent determination, 2009 WL 4571848 (D. Kan. 2009) (employee who brought Family Medical Leave Act claim against her employer was entitled to compel employer to re-produce in native format e-mails and attachments at issue; employee showed extenuating circumstances to justify compelling employer to re-produce in native format e-mails and attachments from both e-mail recipients' inbox folders and senders'

had come unbuckled during an accident. Arguing that Ford had not been forthcoming with information, the plaintiff requested direct access to Ford's database to determine what complaints Ford had received regarding seat belts. Recognizing that direct access to a database may be permissible in some circumstances, the Eleventh Circuit denied the plaintiff access because it found she had not shown discovery abuses by Ford. The court also noted that the district court had given the plaintiff unlimited, direct access to Ford's databases without establishing protocols for the search. The Eleventh Circuit pointed out that trial the court did not even designate search terms to restrict the search.

When dealing with a simple database, a database viewer can alleviate concerns about direct access to databases. A database viewer is software that allows a person to look at data and manipulate it in limited ways, but without the full functionality of the database. Relatively uncomplicated database files can also be presented in a format maintaining as much metadata and original formatting as possible. A third option is the appointment of a special master appointed by the court.

§ 14:13 Requests to inspect—Generally

There are many types of evidence that can only be recovered if one has access to a computer system. If there is a concern that the responding party's search of its computer was not thorough, and that the documents or information produced represents only a portion of the electronically stored information that actually exists, or if there is a reasonable basis to believe electronically stored information has been deleted, the requesting party should request that it be allowed to physically examine the responding party's computer system.[1]

The discovering party must be in a position to make a credible argument to the court that there may be hidden information or

---

sent folders; creation date of e-mails and attachments was disputed by parties, employee's computer expert noted discrepancies in the metadata as to creation dates, and employer did not adequately explain discrepancies); John B. v. Goetz, 531 F.3d 448 (6th Cir. 2008) (overturning court order requiring imaging of personal and state-owned computers where imaging would likely produce confidential and private data unrelated to the litigation); Bro-Tech Corp. v. Thermax, Inc., 2008 WL 724627 (E.D. Pa. 2008) (no evidence of intentional violation of order by producers as would warrant full disclosure of forensic copies of hard drives).

[Section 14:13]

[1]See, e.g., G.D. v. Monarch Plastic Surgery, P.A., 239 F.R.D. 641, 67 Fed. R. Serv. 3d 352 (D. Kan. 2007) (patients who sued health care providers for wrongful disclosure of their confidential medical information stored on com-

other metadata that can only be discovered by seeing the data in its native format. A very high threshold will have to be cleared in order to conduct such discovery.[2]

If requested access is sought to obtain information that is central to the matters at issue, courts are more likely to grant some form of access or review.[3] In Hedenburg v. Aramark Food Services,[4] the court was asked whether the defendant could make an image of the plaintiff's computer "[i]n an effort to probe the veracity of Plaintiff's claims." In denying access to the computer, the court commented that a thorough search of an adversary's

puter hard drive in discarded computer permitted to inspect, test, and evaluate computer itself).

[2]See, e.g., Carolina Bedding Direct, LLC v. Downen, 2013 WL 2431972 (M.D. Fla. 2013) (denying access to computer, phones and e-mail account absent finding of improper conduct or noncompliance with discovery rules); Bro-Tech Corp. v. Thermax, Inc., 2008 WL 724627 (E.D. Pa. 2008) (no evidence of intentional violation of order by producers as would warrant full disclosure of forensic copies of hard drives); Scotts Co. LLC v. Liberty Mut. Ins. Co., 2007 WL 1723509 (S.D. Ohio 2007) (Federal Rules of Civil Procedure do not require forensic computer search as a matter of course); Orrell v. Motorcarparts of America, Inc., 2007 WL 4287750 (W.D. N.C. 2007) (former employer entitled to inspect plaintiff's home computer where plaintiff claimed she had forwarded offensive e-mails from co-workers to her home computer); Benton v. Dlorah, Inc., 2007 WL 2225946 (D. Kan. 2007) (finding that defendants did not sustain burden of showing that plaintiff had failed to comply with requests for production, plaintiff's hard drive contained any additional information subject to discovery, or that plaintiff had spoliated evidence and denying motion that plaintiff produce hard drive); Balfour Beatty Rail, Inc. v. Vaccarello, 2007 WL 169628 (M.D. Fla. 2007) (plaintiff's request for defendants' computer hard drives denied, where plaintiff did not provide any information regarding what it sought to discover from the hard drives or make any contention that defendants had failed to provide requested information contained on hard drives).

[3]See, e.g., Frees, Inc. v. McMillian, 2007 WL 184889 (W.D. La. 2007), aff'd, 2007 WL 1308388 (W.D. La. 2007) (plaintiff allowed to inspect defendant's computer in action under Computer Fraud and Abuse Act, where plaintiff sought to show that alleged proprietary electronically stored information that was removed from plaintiff's laptop may have been downloaded to defendant's); Thielen v. Buongiorno USA, Inc., 2007 WL 465680 (W.D. Mich. 2007) (in suit under Telephone Consumer Protection Act of 1991 for allegedly sending text message to plaintiff's cellphone without plaintiff's permission, court allowed defendant to conduct a forensic examination of an image of plaintiff's computer with restrictions on scope of examination).

[4]Hedenburg v. Aramark American Food Services, 2007 WL 162716 (W.D. Wash. 2007). See also Balfour Beatty Rail, Inc. v. Vaccarello, 2007 WL 169628 (M.D. Fla. 2007) (in trade secrets case, access to computers denied because plaintiff's requests simply sought computer hard drives, and plaintiff did not provide any information regarding what it sought to discover from hard drives or make any content that defendants failed to provide requested information contained on hard drives).

computer is sometimes permitted where the contents of the computer go to the heart of the case. However, the court denied the defendant's requests, finding that the claims at issue were wholly unrelated to the contents of the plaintiff's computer.

A discovering party should not ignore alternatives to actually going on site to search a responding party's system, such as acquiring mirror images of hard drives[5] or having the computer system searched by a neutral court-appointed experts (usually at the requesting party's expense).[6]

§ 14:14 Requests to inspect—Requirement of expert assistance

Lawyers are not capable of conducting forensic computer investigations alone, or even making a case for forensic investigations.[1] First, lawyers do not want to become their own experts. Second, most lawyers cannot begin to articulate the reasons for conducting a forensic investigation without the assistance of qualified experts.

Whether counsel represents the discovering or producing party in a lawsuit, marshaling and discovering electronically stored information will very probably require the assistance of competent forensic experts. Because electronically stored information is changed every time it is viewed, in order to avoid a claim of tampering of spoliation, it may be prudent to request that a court-appointed computer expert or technical employee of the opposing party participate in the inspection.[2]

---

[5]See, e.g., Equity Analytics, LLC v. Lundin, 248 F.R.D. 331 (D.D.C. 2008) (mirror image is perfect duplication of hard drive and it is physically impossible for mirror image to contain anything the hard drive does not and for there to be anything on the mirror image that is not on the hard drive).

[6]See Eugene J. Strasser, M.D., P.A. v. Bose Yalamanchi, M.D., P.A., 669 So. 2d 1142, 1145 (Fla. 4th DCA 1996) (where there has been no evidence to establish any likelihood that purged documents can be retrieved, one alternative might be for producing party's representative to physically access the computer system in the presence of requesting party's representative under an agreed-upon set of procedures to test plaintiff's theory that it is possible to retrieve the purged data).

[Section 14:14]

[1]See Ball, *When Do-It-Yourself e-Discovery Isn't Enough*, Trial, Jan. 2009, at 24.

[2]See Scheindlin & Redgrave, *Special Masters and E-Discovery: The Intersection of Two Recent Revisions to the Federal Rules of Civil Procedure*, 30 Cardozo L. Rev. 347 (2008). Cf. Equity Analytics, LLC v. Lundin, 248 F.R.D. 331 (D.D.C. 2008) (computer forensic specialist authorized to search for evi-

§ 14:15 Responding to requests for production—Keyword terms

A traditional approach to discovery involves the review of all potentially relevant data to determine whether any particular document is relevant to the request for production. The increasing size of data sources has made this approach impossible in most cases. Fortunately, the electronic form of most documents today allows the data to be indexed, searched and analyzed in various ways that can assist in the identification of responsive documents in an automated fashion.

A simple boolean, keyword search is the most used method of identifying relevant and responsive documents. Attorneys will often negotiate a set of search terms during the meet and confer, and these search terms will be used to identify presumptively relevant documents. A simple keyword is a "word" (or string of characters) or combination of words used in a search of electronic data to identify any information that contains that word. Keyword searches often use combinations of words to make the search more focused. For example, if one wants to find all correspondence from John A. Doe sent on January 1, 2013, you may execute for the combined terms of "January 1, 2013," and "John A. Doe".

In most cases, however, the application of keywords is absolute. In the example above, the search would only locate those documents that contained the exact name "John A. Doe" and the date format of "January 1, 2013." It would not identify a document with the name "John Doe" or "Mr. Doe." Furthermore, the use of search terms is completely ineffective for identifying documents that have no searchable text. Flat image files that have not been OCRd, photographs, drawings, voice recordings and video files are all examples of data that is not typically identified through standard search terms. For this reason, effective search-term formulation requires careful formulation, even in simple circumstances, to obtain a reasonably complete yet not overbroad result.

◆ **Practice Note:** There is no requirement that the parties agree on search terms at the outset of a meet and confer. In fact, in is the obligation of the responding party to ensure they

---

dence of any e-mail contact between employee's clients and any of his former employer's current and prospective clients in examination of employee's computer, pursuant to discovery protective order). But see D'Onofrio v. SFX Sports Group, Inc., 254 F.R.D. 129 (D.D.C. 2008) (producing party not entitled to have computer forensic expert present during electronic searches of employer's servers conducted by requesting party's expert, absent evidence that requesting party party's expert was anything other than an unbiased professional).

> have performed a "good faith" production in response to the request—however they decide to apply search terms. Often it is more prudent to have your eDiscovery vendor provide you with early case assessment (ECA) statistics that identify the recall rate of certain key words before you commit to use the terms. Furthermore, a secondary, "hands-on" review of documents will necessarily educate the reviewer to additional or modified terms that may identify responsive information.[1]

U.S. Magistrate Judge Grimm, acknowledged the inherent limitations of keyword searching in *Victor Stanley,*[2] placing the focus on whether the search methodology used would prove reasonable and reliable: "[W]hile it is universally acknowledged that keyword searches are useful tools . . . all keyword searches are not created equal; and there is a growing body of literature that highlights the risks associated with conducting an unreliable or inadequate keyword search. . . ."[3] The opinion concluded that, "In this case, the Defendants have failed to demonstrate that the keyword search they performed on the text-searchable ESI was reasonable."[4]

[Section 14:15]

[1]See Sedona Conference Working Grp., The Sedona Conference Best Practices Commentary on the Use of Search and Information Retrieval Methods in E-Discovery, 8 Sedona Conf. J. 189, 194 (2007) ("The use of search and information retrieval tools does not guarantee that all responsive documents will be identified in large data collections, due to characteristics of human language. Moreover, differing search methods may produce differing results subject to a measure of statistical variation inhered in the science of information.").

[2]Victor Stanley, Inc. v. Creative Pipe, Inc., 250 F.R.D. 251, 70 Fed. R. Serv. 3d 1052 (D. Md. 2008).

[3]Victor Stanley, Inc. v. Creative Pipe, Inc., 250 F.R.D. 251, 256–57, 70 Fed. R. Serv. 3d 1052 (D. Md. 2008).

[4]Victor Stanley, Inc. v. Creative Pipe, Inc., 250 F.R.D. 251, 262, 70 Fed. R. Serv. 3d 1052 (D. Md. 2008). See also U.S. v. O'Keefe, 537 F. Supp. 2d 14, 24, 69 Fed. R. Serv. 3d 1598 (D.D.C. 2008) ("[I]f defendants are going to contend that the search terms used by the government were insufficient, they will have to specifically so contend in a motion to compel and their contention must be based on evidence that meets the requirements of Rule 702 of the Federal Rules of Evidence."); In re Seroquel Products Liability Litigation, 244 F.R.D. 650, 661 n.7, 662 (M.D. Fla. 2007) (criticizing defendants' use of keyword search in selecting ESI for production, and explaining that "while key word searching is a recognized method to winnow relevant documents from large repositories, . . . [c]ommon sense dictates that sampling and other quality assurance techniques must be employed to meet requirements of completeness"); Sedona Conference Working Grp., The Sedona Conference Best Practices Commentary on the Use of Search and Information Retrieval Methods in E-Discovery, 8 Sedona Conf. J. 189, 201 (2007) ("[A]lthough basic keyword searching techniques have been

§ 14:16 Responding to requests for production—Technolgy assisted review (TAR) and predictive coding

Technology Assisted Review (TAR), including such techniques as "predictive coding," involves the use of computers and algorithms to identify relevant and responsive documents in an automated manner. TAR has been lauded by many as a way to reduce the enormous costs associated with a sequential review of massive sets of potentially responsive ESI.[1]

Predictive coding generally involves the review of a random "seed" set of data. During this initial review process, the user will indicate whether the particular document is highly responsive, responsive or not responsive. This process does not generally involve "issue" driven coding, only relevancy. The predictive coding system will they apply algorithms to the set of reviewed data to identify additional potentially relevant documents. It is possible to continue this process in an iterative fashion in an effort to further "educate" the system and increase the relevance.

It is important to note that predictive coding does not reduce the need to understand search design procedure. Like any software, the effectiveness of the predictive coding application is entirely dependent on the adequacy of set of data used as a starting point, the quality of the human review of each iteration, how well that review is reflected in the information entered into the software prior to the next run, and, importantly the underlying proprietary logic of the particular software product employed. As with keyword searching, predictive coding will ultimately rely on the information available for analysis in the underlying documents. If this data is skewed or absent, it will not be identified.

One challenge to predictive coding is that it the method of analytical identification may not be transparent to the parties, thus raising the issue of whether evidence produced through a predictive coding process will be subject to challenge under Federal

---

widely accepted both by courts and parties as sufficient to define the scope of their obligation to perform a search for responsive documents, the experience of many litigators is that simple keyword searching alone is inadequate in at least some discovery contexts. This is because simple keyword searches end up being both over- and under-inclusive in light of the inherent malleability and ambiguity of spoken and written English (as well as all other languages).")

[Section 14:16]

[1]Moore v. Publicis Groupe, 287 F.R.D. 182, 184, 18 Wage & Hour Cas. 2d (BNA) 1479 (S.D. N.Y. 2012), adopted, 2012 WL 1446534 (S.D. N.Y. 2012) (extolling the merits of predictive coding).

Rule of Evidence 702, under which a district court is responsible for determining the relevancy and reliability of "testimony."[2] In *Moore,* one of the first cases to discuss predictive coding, Magistrate Judge Peck discusses acknowledges that a 702 may be necessary, however, analysis was ". . . premature . . . under the circumstances of this particular case" because there was opportunity for an evidentiary hearing problems emerge after actual production has taken place.[3]

In reality, predictive coding is just another method for identifying potentially relevant ESI. It is not an "easy button" for producing all relevant data, but necessarily relies on a comprehensive understanding of the underlying data coordinated with the application of sound search techniques to properly "educate" the predictive coding engine.

Even where predictive coding is used, it is highly recommended that other techniques, including sampling, be used to verify the set of data identified as non-responsive. The best advice, in the event of uncertainty, is to seek expert assistance in determining the appropriate methodology and how it should be applied. An effective search will minimize the respondents' burden and therefore opportunities for respondents to assert burden. Requesting parties should also be aware that the use of an expert will also make their evidentiary review much more efficient. These advantages can often more than offset the cost of external assistance.

II. CHECKLISTS

§ 14:17 Electronically stored information

- ☐ E-mails, including those sent, received, or drafted
- ☐ PowerPoint or similar presentations
- ☐ Tables
- ☐ Charts
- ☐ Graphs, and
- ☐ Database files
- ☐ Digital calendars
- ☐ Proprietary software files
- ☐ Internet browsing applications, including bookmarks, cookies, and history log

---

[2]Fed. R. Evid. 702. See Daubert v. Merrell Dow Pharmaceuticals, Inc., 509 U.S. 579, 113 S. Ct. 2786, 125 L. Ed. 2d 469, 27 U.S.P.Q.2d 1200, Prod. Liab. Rep. (CCH) ¶ 13494, 37 Fed. R. Evid. Serv. 1, 23 Envtl. L. Rep. 20979 (1993).

[3]Moore v. Publicis Groupe SA, 2012 WL 1446534 (S.D. N.Y. 2012).

- ☐ Cellular telephone logs

§ 14:18 Electronic media checklist

- ☐ E-mail transmitted through company networks.
- ☐ Messages transmitted through external networks (e.g., Yahoo, Google, AOL)
- ☐ Hand-held electronic personal organizers.
- ☐ Databases of personal-information from computer-based contact managers.
- ☐ Databases used by the sales staff (e.g., contact-manager software, telemarketing data).
- ☐ Computer vendors (e.g., repair shop may have hard drive).
- ☐ All previous versions of word processing and spreadsheet documents, in addition to the current version. This should include data backups.
- ☐ Complete copy of all data on a hard drive. (Note that application software is protected from duplication by copyright.)
- ☐ Central computer or server data.
- ☐ Consider requesting paper file copies of electronic information, if they exist. Penciled margin notes often yield good information.
- ☐ Request electronic media in a form that can be read by your equipment or software, or make arrangements for the material to be converted.

§ 14:19 Document production checklist

- ☐ **Coordinate with Opposing Counsel.** Before noticing the document production request, confer with opposing counsel regarding the volume of documents, including electronically stored information, and their accessibility. This will dictate the location of the production, which must be listed in the notice. From this response, determine how many people will be required to attend the production to review the documents, or if you are doing it yourself, how much time to budget.
- ☐ **Key Document Request.** Make sure key documents in the discovery plan have been included in the document request.
- ☐ **Agree on Document Numbering Approach.** Discuss a standardized document numbering conventions with all counsel.
- ☐ **Alpha-Numeric Numbering.** Documents should be numbered before copying in an alpha-numeric configuration, with the alpha portion indicating the source of the document. The

documents should be numbered prior to the production for effective document control.

- ☐ **Number Everything.** All documents, including sticky notes on top of pages, should be numbered separately. In addition, if there is information on both sides of a page, give each side its own number.
- ☐ **Review All Case Background.** Prior to the production of documents review all case background material including the actual request for documents or subpoena to be certain you know what items to expect at the document production site. Know the parameters of privilege that specifically apply to your case.
- ☐ **Check For Numbering Gaps.** If the documents produced are numbered sequentially, make certain there are no gaps in the numbering. If there are gaps, determine if the gaps are due to missing documents or documents removed for privilege.
- ☐ **Document Privilege Log.** Opposing counsel must provide an item-by-item specific description of documents being withheld for privilege. This should be in the form of a privileged document log.
- ☐ **Document Inventory Log.** Make a document inventory log of all documents by file-folder title, document number range, if possible, and a brief description of the contents of each folder. This initial log or index can be done by hand, with a tape recorder or by using a laptop computer.
- ☐ **Document Production Record/Cover Sheet.** In addition to the inventory log, create a cover sheet that gives general information about the production, including location and those attending.
- ☐ **Guard Against Disclosures About Your Case.** Do not get chatty. At the production do not offer any information about your case to those producing the documents.
- ☐ **Quality Control For Legibility.** Check for document legibility, size and double-sided sheets.
- ☐ **Copy Everything.** Instruct the copying vendor to copy everything. That includes both sides of two-sided documents, sticky notes or any other notes stapled or otherwise attached to documents. Always make sure there is a quality control check for number and legibility.
- ☐ **Index Documents.** after receiving the documents you chose at the inspection, or after getting the documents back to your office from the production, they must be indexed. A Paralegal should index each document by document number

(or number range), date, author, recipient, people or companies mentioned. The index should also include a short description. Include remarks concerning handwritten or special notations on the documents.

§ 14:20 Checklist for searching for electronically stored information

- ☐ Search each key person's:
- ☐ office computer hard drive
- ☐ home computer (if used for business purposes)
- ☐ personal digital assistants
- ☐ network files
- ☐ Search each key person's assistant's or staff member's:
- ☐ office computer hard drive
- ☐ home computer (if used for business purposes)
- ☐ personal digital assistants
- ☐ network files
- ☐ Intranet, extranet, or e-mail depositories
- ☐ Search any individual easily accessible backup data, such as floppy disks, thumb drives, CD-ROMs or DVDs
- ☐ Understand the technical architecture of the organization's computer infrastructure and be prepared to discuss all locations where digital data may reside
- ☐ Search any backup repositories that are not maintained for the purpose of disaster recovery (such as remote servers designed to make data available across an enterprise, ASPs, data warehouses, offsite storage sites, intranet, or extranet servers)
- ☐ Consider searching for metadata and relevant deleted data and be prepared to justify why such searches are burdensome or technically infeasible

§ 14:21 Business function checklist

- ☐ What records do the employees in the department or business produce in the course of business?
- ☐ What records do the employees in the department or business generate or maintain for accounting, regulatory or legal reasons?
- ☐ Which types of records are prepared, even in draft form, using computers?
- ☐ What records are stored on computer?
- ☐ What are your backup and retention policies and are they in writing?

- ☐ What type of backup repositories exist that are not maintained for the purpose of disaster recovery (such as remote server designed to make data available across an enterprise)?
- ☐ Does the organization use ASPs, data warehouses, offsite storage sites, intranet or extranet servers?
- ☐ What computer programs exist that create records without any or regular intervention of human operators (such as automatic audit or monitoring software)?

§ 14:22 Technology checklist

- ☐ Whether the backup uses media that is reused
- ☐ Identification of what electronically stored information is typically backed up
- ☐ Whether any backups are maintained for long periods of time for archival purposes
- ☐ What the backup schedule is
- ☐ What type of backup repositories exist that are not maintained for the purpose of disaster recovery (such as remote servers designed to make electronically stored information available across an enterprise)

§ 14:23 Database checklist

- ☐ Ask that the production request be specific, providing information regarding field definitions, query forms, and reports to help refine the request.
- ☐ Produce the requested information in a form usable to the requesting party, although it may vary from database to database.
- ☐ Where no existing single report gives a full view of the data, advise the requesting party whether it is possible to create such a report and what it would cost to develop a custom report.
- ☐ Only allow onsite access to databases for purposes of defining queries where no other alternative information regarding structure is available.

§ 14:24 Checklist for quality check

QUALITY CHECK

- ☐ **Redacted text are not produced.** An image can be redacted, but unless the corresponding text file and metadata are redacted, the client's privileged information will be disclosed.

- ☐ **Privileged documents are not produced.** Privileged documents must not be produced. Using red labels for DVDs containing a client's privileged documents make it less likely that the wrong disk will be given to opposing counsel.
- ☐ **Text is extracted rather than OCRed.** Many vendors OCR text without anyone else knowing it. While extracting the text of a document for use in keyword filters is 100% accurate, OCR is at best only 70% to 80% accurate, meaning that this process overlooks 20% to 30% of the documents.
- ☐ **Metadata are not altered by opening difficult documents instead of simply viewing them**. Many documents are TIFFed by using QuickView Plus, which does not actually open the document, it simply views it. QuickView Plus cannot TIFF all documents. For these problem documents, vendors sometimes load them onto one of their computers to open before TIFFing it. In so doing, they change the metadata so it reflects information from the e-discovery vendor's computer—including the file path, custodian, and last accessed date—not the true custodian's computer.
- ☐ **All file types are collected.** Some people create their own file extension names for their own unique naming convention. Instead of using ".doc" for a word processing document, they may use ".ltr" to denote a letter, or ".mem" for a memo. If the vendor only processes the main file extension types, the vendor may be missing many documents. There are software programs that do not rely on the file extension alone to identify file types.
- ☐ **Spreadsheets columns are opened to widest cell and show hidden cells.** When an image of a spreadsheet is created, it is very easy to miss data if each column is not expanded to the width of the widest cell in the column. While data in the native file can still be seen, it will be missing in the TIFF if every column is not expanded.
- ☐ **Spreadsheet formulas are produced.** Typically the numbers in a spreadsheet are not nearly as important as how the numbers are calculated. Simply printing out a spreadsheet to PDF loses the formulas.
- ☐ **"Current dates" are not altered.** Sometimes memoranda, letters, or other documents will have fields that will automatically display the current date. This practice can be good to make sure a one does not misdate a letter one intends to write, but bad if one later wants to determine when the letter was written. If care is not taken in the discovery process, these dates may display the date the document was processed by the e-discovery vendor, the true date intended by the document's author.

- ☐ **Dates are not altered by mishandling the documents.** The last modified date for each document may reflect the date the documents were processed for discovery, as opposed to their true date. This mistake happens all the time.
- ☐ **Documents are not produced out of order.** Some vendors order documents in the order they get processed, which means that the order may get mixed up if larger files take longer to process than smaller ones.
- ☐ **Incorrect time is not stamped.** If a vendor in California processes documents received from a custodian in Florida, the documents' creation date, could be different than the original files due to the time zone the documents are processed in. Let the vendor know if the files being processed are from a different time zone or have them default to Greenwich Mean Time (GMT).
- ☐ **File sizes are not limited.** Some e-discovery processing programs will not process files that are over a specified size. The result is that these files are simply left out of the production. It is much better to learn about such limitations before the e-discovery vendor is deposed by the other side.

NOTES

Commentary

This checklist is adapted from a list compiled by Attorney Kenton Hutcherson of Dallas, Texas.

§ 14:25 Checklist for logging electronically stored information

- ☐ E-discovery identification and inventory number (we strongly recommend using a barcode labeling system)
- ☐ Date received
- ☐ Matter name
- ☐ Client name
- ☐ Client/matter number
- ☐ Name of person/company/shipper delivering evidence
- ☐ Description of items, including manufacturer name, model number and unique identifier/serial number whenever possible
- ☐ MD5 Hash of each piece of media where possible (electronic fingerprint)
- ☐ Name of person receiving evidence (Logged by)
- ☐ Check Out
- ☐ If Yes
- ☐ Date

- ☐ Reason
- ☐ Custodian name
- ☐ Name of recipient (when evidence shipped from e-discovery provider to anyone)
- ☐ Name of shipper
- ☐ Shipper's tracking number
- ☐ Date of shipment
- ☐ Date of receipt
- ☐ Check-in date

III. FORMS

§ 14:26 Requests to produce

[Caption]

[PARTY'S] REQUESTS FOR PRODUCTION

In accordance with *[rule]*, *[plaintiff] [defendant] [name 1]* request *[defendant] [plaintiff] [name 2]* to produce the documents specified below, within thirty days of service, or at such other time and place, or in such other manner, as may be mutually agreed upon by the parties. *[Name 2's]* production of documents must be in accordance with the Instructions and Definitions set forth below and *[rule]*.

INSTRUCTIONS AND DEFINITIONS

A. Whenever reference is made to a person, it includes any and all of that person's principals, employees, agents, attorneys, consultants and other representatives.

B. When production of any document in *[name 2's]* possession is requested, the request includes documents subject to the *[name 2's]* possession, custody or control. In the event that *[name 2]* is able to provide only part of the document or documents called for in any particular Request for Production, *[name 2]* must provide all document or documents that *[name 2]* is able to provide and state the reason, if any, for the inability to provide the remainder.

C. "Document" or "documents" means all materials within the full scope of *[rule]*, including but not limited to all writings and recordings, including the originals and all non-identical copies, whether different from the original by reason of any notation made on such copies or otherwise (including but without limitation to, e-mail and attachments, correspondence, memoranda, notes, diaries, minutes, statistics, letters, telegrams, minutes, contracts, reports, studies, checks, statements, tags, labels, invoices, brochures, periodicals, telegrams, receipts, returns, summaries, pamphlets, books, interoffice and intraoffice communications, offers, notations of any sort of conversations, working papers, applications, permits, file wrappers, indices, telephone calls, meetings or printouts, teletypes, telefax, invoices, worksheets, and all drafts, alterations, modifications, changes and amendments of any of the foregoing), graphic or aural representations of any kind (including without limitation, photographs, charts, microfiche, microfilm, videotape, recordings, motion pictures, plans, drawings, surveys), and electronic, mechanical, magnetic, optical or electric records or representations of any kind (including without limitation, computer files and programs, tapes, cassettes, discs, recordings), including metadata.

D. If any document is withheld from production under a claim of privilege or other exemption from discovery, state the title and nature of the document, and furnish a list signed by the attorney of record giving the following information with respect to each document withheld:
   (1) the name and title of the author or sender, or both, and the name and title of the recipient;
   (2) the date of the document's origination;
   (3) the name of each person or persons, other than stenographic or clerical assistants, participating in the preparation of the document;
   (4) the name and position, if any, of each person to whom the contents of the documents have previously been communicated by copy, exhibition, reading or substantial summarization;
   (5) a statement of the specific basis on which privilege is claimed and whether or not the subject matter or the contents of the document is limited to legal advice or information provided for the purpose of securing legal advice; and
   (6) the identity and position, if any, of the person or persons supplying the attorney signing the list with the information requested in subparagraphs above.

E. "Relate(s) to," "related to" or "relating to" means to refer to, reflect, concern, pertain to or in any manner be connected with the matter discussed.

F. Every Request for Production herein must be deemed a continuing Request for Production and Defendant is to supplement its answers promptly if and when Defendant obtains responsive documents which add to or are in any way inconsistent with *[name 2's]* initial production.

G. These discovery requests are not intended to be duplicative. All requests should be responded to fully and to the extent not covered by other requests. If there are documents that are responsive to more than one request, then please so note and produce each such document first in response to the request that is more specifically directed to the subject matter of the particular document.

H. Any word written in the singular must be construed as plural or vice versa when necessary to facilitate the response to any request.

I. "And" as well as "or" must be construed disjunctively or conjunctively as necessary in order to bring within the scope of the request all responses which otherwise might be construed to be outside its scope.

DOCUMENT REQUESTS

1. All documents with reference to or written policies, procedures and guidelines related to Defendant's computers, computer systems, electronic data and electronic media including, but not limited to, the following:
   a. Backup tape rotation schedules;
   b. Electronic data retention, preservation and destruction schedules;
   c. Employee use policies of company computers, data, and other technology;
   d. File naming conventions and standards,
   e. Password, encryption, and other security protocols;
   f. Diskette, CD, DVD, and other removable media labeling standards;
   g. E-mail storage conventions (such as limitations on mailbox sizes/storage locations; schedule and logs for storage);
   h. Electronic media deployment, allocation, and maintenance procedures for new employees, current employees, or departed employees;
   i. Software and hardware upgrades (including patches) for *[time]*, indicating who and what organization conducted such upgrades; and
   j. Personal or home computer usage for work-related activities.
2. Organization charts for all Information Technology or Information Services departments or divisions from *[relevant time period]*.

3. Backup tapes containing e-mail and other electronic data related to this action from *[date]*.
4. Exact copies (i.e., bit-by-bit copies) of all hard drives on the desktop computers, laptop computers, notebook computers, personal digital assistant computers, servers, and other electronic media related to this action from *[date]*.
5. Exact copies of all relevant disks, CDs, DVDs and other removable media related to this action from *[date]*.
6. For each interrogatory set forth in *[name 1's]* First Interrogatories, produce all documents that *[name 2]* referred to, relied upon, consulted or used in any way in answering such interrogatory.
7. All documents that contain or otherwise relate to the facts or information that *[name 2]* contends refute, in any way, the allegations contained in the *[Complaint] [Answer]* in this action.
8. All reports, including drafts, submitted by any expert witness or potential expert witness retained or consulted by any *[name 2]* with respect to the issues raised in this case.

Dated: ____

[signature, etc.]

§ 14:27 Requests to produce and to inspect

[Caption]

The *[requesting party]* requests that the *[producing party]* respond within __ days to the following requests:

1. To produce and permit the plaintiff to inspect and copy and to test or sample the following documents, including electronically stored information:

[Describe each document and the electronically stored information, either individually or by category.]

[State the time, place, and manner of the inspection and any related acts.]

2. To produce and permit the plaintiff to inspect and copy, and to test or sample, the following tangible things:

[Describe each thing, either individually or by category.]

[State the time, place, and manner of the inspection and any related acts.]

3. To permit the plaintiff to enter onto the following land to inspect, photograph, test, or sample the property or an object or operation on the property.

[Describe the property and each object or operation.]

[State the time and manner of the inspection and any related acts.]

Dated: ____

[signature, etc.]

NOTES TO FORM

Commentary

This form is adapted from Official Form 50 approved by the U.S. Supreme Court.

§ 14:28 Plaintiff's request for production of documents

[Caption]

PLAINTIFF'S REQUEST FOR PRODUCTION OF DOCUMENTS

Pursuant to *[rule]*, the Defendant *[name]* is requested to identify the documents set forth below in its possession, custody, or control or in the possession, custody, or control of the Defendant's agents, attorneys, employees, and/or representatives.

The documents are to be produced for inspection on the date and time and at the location specified above. The Defendant may satisfy this Demand for Production of Documents by mailing copies of the documents requested to the Plaintiff's attorney and making the originals available on reasonable notice.

INSTRUCTIONS

A. Copies of writings.

If there are several copies of a writing, and if any of the copies are not identical or are no longer identical because they have been written on or modified in any way, front or back, then each of the nonidentical copies is considered a separate writing and must be produced.

B. Withholding documents under a claim of privilege.

If any document is withheld under a claim of privilege, please identify the writing by providing the following information: the basis for the claim of privilege, the date of the document, the subject of the document, the author, the addressee(s) and all other persons who received the writing or copies of the document, as well as all those to whom the document or copies became available at any time, together with each person's job title and address. A privilege log must be included with your written response.

C. Documents no longer in the Responding Party's possession or control.

If any writing to be produced is no longer in the Defendant's possession or control or is no longer in existence, please state whether the writing is missing or lost, destroyed, transferred voluntarily or involuntarily to others (and if so, to whom), or otherwise disposed of. In each instance, explain the circumstances surrounding the authorization for the disposition and the date of the disposition.

D. Documents stored electronically.

Pursuant to *[rule]*, electronically stored information shall be reduced to hardcopy form.

DEFINITIONS

For purposes of this Request certain terms are defined as follows:

1. The term "writing" is defined as in *[rule]* and includes, but is not limited to, all originals and duplicates of correspondence, memoranda, records, data sheets, purchase orders, tabulations, reports, evaluations, work papers, summaries, opinions, journals, calendars, diaries, statistical records, checks, notes, transcriptions, telegrams, teletypes, telex messages, telefaxes, recordings of telephone calls, electronically stored information, and other communications, including but not limited to notes, notations, memoranda, and other writings of or relating to telephone conversations and conferences, minutes and notes of transcriptions of all meetings and other communications of any type, microfiche, microfilms, tapes or other records, logs and any other information stored or carried electronically, by means of computer equipment or otherwise, and which can be retrieved in printed, graphic, or audio form, including, but not limited to, information stored in the memory of a computer, data stored on removable magnetic or optical media (for example, magnetic tape, floppy disks, removable cartridge

disks, and optical disks), e-mail, data used for electronic data interchange, audit trails, digitized pictures and audio (for example, data stored in MPEG, JPEG, and GIF), digitized audio, and voice mail.

2. The term "original" is defined as in *[rule]* and includes the writing itself or any counterpart intended to have the same effect by a person executing or issuing it. An original of a photograph includes the negative or any print therefrom. If data are stored in a computer or similar device, any printout or other output readable by sight, shown to reflect the data accurately, is an original.
2. The term "duplicate" is defined as in *[rule]* and includes a counterpart produced by the same impression as the original, or from the same matrix, or by means of photography, including enlargements and miniatures, or by mechanical or electronic rerecording, or by chemical reproduction, or by equivalent technique accurately reproducing the original.
3. The term "person" is defined as in *[rule]* and includes a natural person, firm, association, organization, partnership, business trust, corporation, limited liability company, or public entity.
4. The term "relating to" includes referring to, embodying, in connection with, referencing, evidencing, commenting on, corresponding to, sharing, describing, concerning, analyzing, reflecting, or constituting.
5. The terms "you" or "your" refer to Defendant and its agents, employees, representatives, and attorneys.
6. The term "computer" includes, but is not limited to, personal computers, microcomputers, laptop computers, portable computers, notebook computers, palmtop computers, personal digital assistants, file servers, application servers, workstations, network computers (sometimes called "thin clients"), minicomputers, and mainframes.
7. The term "computer system" refers to all file servers, stand alone computers, workstations, laptops, and personal digital assistants owned or leased by Defendant or physically located at *[place]*.
8. The term "network" refers to the local area network located at *[place]*, including, but not limited to, all files servers, client computers, workstations, firewalls, routers, proxy servers, Internet servers, mail servers, application servers.
9. The term "log file" refers to the information automatically collected by Websites on the Internet. Such information includes, but is not limited to, the Internet address of each visitor, the date and time of the visit to the Website, the particular pages

of the site viewed, prior Websites visited, and whether the visit was successful or whether a failure resulted (that is, an error occurred on the Website).

10. The term "Website" refers to the World Wide Website located at *[address]*, the hypertext markup language (HTML) pages making up the site, and all information collected and stored by the site, including all log files relating to the usage of the site.
11. The term "e-mail" refers to the exchange of text messages and computer files over a communications network, such as a local area network, intranet, extranet, or public network like the Internet or other online service provider.

DOCUMENTS REQUESTED

The documents or writings to be identified and produced pursuant to this Demand are as follows:

Requests Relating to Corporate Policies and Guidelines

12. All writings relating to guidelines and policies governing employee use of the computer system prepared or adopted within the last five years, including, but not limited to, drafts of all such guidelines and policies.
13. All writings relating to guidelines and policies governing maintenance of hard disks on the computer system, including, but not limited to, guidelines and policies regarding the use of utility software to scan the disks for errors, to optimize disks, and to conduct low and high level formatting of disks.
14. All writings relating to guidelines and policies governing employee use of e-mail prepared or adopted within the last five years, including, but not limited to, drafts of all such guidelines and policies.
15. All writings relating to guidelines and policies governing employee use of the Internet prepared or adopted within the last five years, including, but not limited to, drafts of all such guidelines and policies.
16. All writings relating to guidelines and policies governing when files are deleted from the computer system.

Requests Relating to Use of the Computer System

17. All writings relating to instances in which an employee has been disciplined in any way for misusing or abusing the computer system.
18. All writings relating to instances in which an employee has

been disciplined in any way during the past five years for sending harassing, offensive, or sexually explicit e-mail to another employee.

19. Copies of all e-mail sent or received by *[specify individual]* relating to *[describe]*.
20. Copies of all e-mail during *[specify period]* sent or received by *[specify first individual]* in which *[specify second individual]* was also a recipient, including e-mail in which *[specify second individual]* was copied or blind-copied.
21. Copies of all e-mail sent or received by account name *[specify account name]*.

Requests Relating to Security

22. All writings relating to procedures and policies you followed during *[specify period]* for backing up files and other data from your computer.
23. All writings relating to procedures and policies you followed during *[specify period]* concerning the security of the computer system, including, but not limited to, all training materials for employees.
23. All writings relating to any security reviews or analyses of the computer system prepared within the last five years, including, but not limited to, reports, memoranda, and correspondence prepared by or sent to third party security consultants.
24. All writings relating to any instances in the last five years in which an unauthorized party gained access to the computer system.
25. All writings relating to any instances in the last five years in which a virus or other destructive program caused any data loss on the computer system.
26. All writings relating to any instances in the last five years in which an equipment or software malfunction caused data loss on the computer system.
27. All writings relating to any instances in the last five years in which a hard disk has been replaced in any computer on the network.
28. All writings relating to any disaster recovery plans established during *[specify period]* for the network.
29. All writings relating to methods of accessing the network from outside Defendant (that is, remote access procedures).

Employee Monitoring

30. All writings relating to your efforts to monitor employee use of the network.

31. All writings relating to your efforts to monitor employee use of the Internet.
32. All writings relating to your efforts to monitor employee use of e-mail.

Requests Relating to the Website

33. All writings relating to the design and development of the Website, including, but not limited to, copies of the executed development agreement and all drafts of the agreement with *[specify developer]*.
34. All writings relating to orders for merchandise made through the Website during *[specify period]*.
35. All writings relating to instances in which an unauthorized party attempted to gain access to the Website during *[specify period]*.
36. All writings relating to any instances in the last five years in which an equipment or software malfunction caused data loss on the Website.
37. Copies of all log files generated by the Website from *[specify beginning date]* to *[specify ending date]*, including, but not limited to, log files generated by duplicate or mirror Websites.
38. All e-mail relating to *[describe]*, including, but not limited to, e-mail stored on desktop computer hard disks, floppy disks and other removable electronic storage media, file servers, workstations, laptops, handheld organizers, backup tapes, and Internet e-mail servers.

Requests Relating to Trading Partner Agreements

39. A copy of the trading partner agreement between Defendant and *[trading partner]*, dated *[specify date]*.
40. All writings relating to the negotiation of the trading partner agreement between Defendant and *[trading partner]*, including, but not limited to, drafts of the agreement, negotiation notes, and correspondence.
41. All writings relating to the trading partner agreement between *[trading partner]* and Defendant, dated *[date]*, including, but not limited to, confirmations of orders, acknowledgements of receipt, and tracking information.
42. All writings relating to communications with *[specify value added network]* regarding electronic data interchange transactions with *[specify trading partner]*.

Miscellaneous Requests

43. An organizational chart for your Information Systems Department.

44. A list of all authorized users of the computer system.
45. A copy of the network map.
46. All writings relating to source code escrow agreements for *[specify software]*.
47. Copies of any and all source code escrow agreements for *[specify software]*, including, but not limited to, copies of all drafts of such agreements.

Dated: ____

[signature, etc.]

§ 14:29 Request to produce information from databases

[Caption]

REQUESTS TO PRODUCE

To: *[name]*

In accordance with *[rule]*, *[discovering party] [name 1]* requests *[responding party] [name 2]* to produce the documents specified below, within thirty days of service, or at such other time and place, or in such other manner, as may be mutually agreed upon by the parties. *[Name 2's]* production of documents must be in accordance with the Instructions and Definitions set forth below and *[rule]*.

INSTRUCTIONS AND DEFINITIONS

A. Whenever reference is made to a person, it includes any and all of that person's principals, employees, agents, attorneys, consultants and other representatives.
B. When production of any document in *[name 2's]* possession is requested, the request includes documents subject to the *[name 2's]* possession, custody or control. In the event that *[name 2]* is able to provide only part of the document or documents called for in any particular Request for Production, *[name 2]* must provide all document or documents that *[name 2]* is able to provide and state the reason, if any, for the inability to provide the remainder.
C. "Document" or "documents" means all materials within the full scope of *[rule]*, including but not limited to all electronically stored information, writings and recordings, including the originals and all non-identical copies, whether different from the original by reason of any notation made on such copies or otherwise (including but without limitation to, e-mail and attachments, correspondence, memoranda, notes, diaries,

minutes, statistics, letters, telegrams, minutes, contracts, reports, studies, checks, statements, tags, labels, invoices, brochures, periodicals, telegrams, receipts, returns, summaries, pamphlets, books, interoffice and intraoffice communications, offers, notations of any sort of conversations, working papers, applications, permits, file wrappers, indices, telephone calls, meetings or printouts, teletypes, telefax, invoices, worksheets, and all drafts, alterations, modifications, changes and amendments of any of the foregoing), graphic or aural representations of any kind (including without limitation, photographs, charts, microfiche, microfilm, videotape, recordings, motion pictures, plans, drawings, surveys), and electronic, mechanical, magnetic, optical or electric records or representations of any kind (including without limitation, computer files and programs, tapes, cassettes, discs, recordings), including metadata.

D. If any document is withheld from production under a claim of privilege or other exemption from discovery, state the title and nature of the document, and furnish a list signed by the attorney of record giving the following information with respect to each document withheld:
   (1) the name and title of the author or sender, or both, and the name and title of the recipient;
   (2) the date of the document's origination;
   (3) the name of each person or persons, other than stenographic or clerical assistants, participating in the preparation of the document;
   (4) the name and position, if any, of each person to whom the contents of the documents have previously been communicated by copy, exhibition, reading or substantial summarization;
   (5) a statement of the specific basis on which privilege is claimed and whether or not the subject matter or the contents of the document is limited to legal advice or information provided for the purpose of securing legal advice; and
   (6) the identity and position, if any, of the person or persons supplying the attorney signing the list with the information requested in subparagraphs above.

E. "Relate(s) to," "related to" or "relating to" means to refer to, reflect, concern, pertain to or in any manner be connected with the matter discussed.

F. Every Request for Production herein must be deemed a continuing Request for Production and *[name 2]* is to supplement its answers promptly if and when *[name 2]* obtains responsive documents which add to or are in any way inconsistent with *[name 2's]* initial production.

G. These discovery requests are not intended to be duplicative. All requests should be responded to fully and to the extent not covered by other requests. If there are documents that are responsive to more than one request, then please so note and produce each such document first in response to the request that is more specifically directed to the subject matter of the particular document.

H. Any word written in the singular must be construed as plural or vice versa when necessary to facilitate the response to any request.

I. "And" as well as "or" must be construed disjunctively or conjunctively as necessary in order to bring within the scope of the request all responses which otherwise might be construed to be outside its scope.

REQUEST

Each of the following requests to produce in this section are directed toward eliciting database searches of actual *[name 2]* databases or other electronic data collections located at *[name 2]*. in particular, the following interrogatories ARE NOT to be answered from any data collections maintained or managed by the law firm, or any of that firm's personnel or agents.

1. Please search the master or main database residing on the *[defendant] [plaintiff]* computer system and produce search results based on the following requests for information:
   a. Any records, of whatever date or from whatever region of the world, containing complaints about *[describe]*.
   b. Any records, of whatever date or from whatever region of the world, containing complaints about any *[describe]*, regardless of *[specify]*.
   c. Any records, of whatever date or from whatever region of the world, containing complaints about *[describe]*.
2. Please search the master or main database residing on the *[defendant's] [plaintiff's]* computer system and produce search results based on the following requests for information:
   a. Any records, of whatever date or from whatever region of the world, discussing or referring to *[describe]*.
   b. Any records, of whatever date or from whatever region of the world, discussing or referring to *[describe]*, regardless of *[specify]*.
   c. Any records, of whatever date or from whatever region of

the world, discussing or referring to *[describe]*, as that term is defined above, of any *[defendant] [plaintiff] [describe]*.

d. Any records, of whatever date or from whatever region of the world, discussing or referring to possible, recommended, planned or actual design improvements, as that term is defined above, of any *[describe]*, regardless of *[specify]*.

e. Any records, of whatever date or from whatever region of the world, discussing or referring to possible, recommended, planned or actual design improvements, as that term is defined above, of *[describe]* manufactured at any time.

3. With regard to each and all of the preceding search results, and recalling that the definition of above includes every database that is referred to in any record, please produce any database records from any other *[defendant] [plaintiff]* databases referred to in the records that comprise the preceding search results.

4. Please search the main or master database residing on the *[defendant's] [plaintiff's]* computer system, and any data collections not included in a database (as that term is defined above) but residing on the *[defendant] [plaintiff]* computer system, and produce database search results or other documents based on the following requests for information:

a. Any records, or other documents from any data collections not included in a database (as that term is defined above), of whatever date or from whatever region of the world, discussing or referring to possible, recommended, planned or actual design improvements, as that term is defined above, of any *[describe]* manufactured at any time based on studies conducted by any *[defendant] [plaintiff]* committee charged with the responsibility of conducting competitive tear down, as that latter term is defined above.

b. Any records, or other documents from any data collections not included in a database (as that term is defined above), of whatever date or from whatever region of the world, discussing or referring to possible, recommended, planned or actual design improvements, as that term is defined above, of any *[defendant] [plaintiff] [describe]* manufactured at any time, regardless of who authored the record or document.

c. Any records, or other documents from any data collections not included in a database (as that term is defined above), of whatever date or from whatever region of the world, discussing or referring to the advisability of making design improvements (as that term is defined above) to *[defendant's] [plaintiff's] [describe]* manufactured at any time, regardless of who authored the record or document.

5. With regard to each and all of the preceding search results that include *[describe]* records, and recalling that the definition of *[specify]* includes every database referred to in any *[describe]* record, please produce any database records from any other *[defendant] [plaintiff]* databases referred to in the *[describe]* records that comprise the preceding search results.
6. Please search the e-mail databases, whether active databases or stored or archived databases, residing on the *[defendant] [plaintiff]* computer system and produce search results based on the following requests for information:
   a. Any e-mail, of whatever date or from whatever region of the world, discussing or referring to possible, recommended, planned or actual design improvements, as that term is defined above, of any *[defendant] [plaintiff] [describe]* manufactured at any time, regardless of who authored the e-mail.
   b. Any e-mail, of whatever date or from whatever region of the world, discussing or referring to the advisability of making design improvements, as that term is defined above, to *[defendant] [plaintiff] [describe]* manufactured at any time, regardless of who authored the e-mail.

   Dated: ____

[signature, etc.]

§ 14:30 Instructions where production on CDs or DVDs is anticipated

CD or DVD production of discovery is acceptable however the following is required when discovery production is thus produced:

(1) Each image on the CD or DVD must be Bates stamped with a unique alpha-numeric identifier (taking care not to obscure in any way any of the information contained in the image).

(2) If the images do not exist in a metadata database, then a detailed index of the contents of each CD or DVD must be provided on each CD or DVD in a clearly marked and easily identifiable file.

(3) This index must contain the following information as to each document contained on a CD or DVD in columnar display as follows:

   a) In column one, the Bates stamp number of each electronic document on a CD or DVD;
   b) In column two, a word description of the contents of each electronic document on a CD or DVD clearly identifying what that electronic document contains;

c) In column three, a clear reference to just what interrogatory or request is satisfied by the production of each electronic document on a CD or DVD;

d) In column four, the format of each electronic document on a CD or DVD, and how and where the original or best copy of each such document is stored on the defendant's computer system, or if located elsewhere then on the *[responding party's]* primary computer system, its location on the computer system of subsidiaries (in this country or throughout the world), predecessors, successors, assigns, joint venturers, partners, parents, agents or affiliates; and

e) In column five, a statement as to whether each electronic document contained on a CD or DVD is a first, second, third or a later generation copy of the original document located on the *[responding party's]* computer system.

(4) If the images on a CD or DVD exist in an off the shelve metadata environment, then the images must be produced with all accompanying metadata, unless privileged, and the database management system used to produce and house that metadata must be identified by application name and version type. If the images on a CD or DVD exist in a proprietary metadata environment, then it is required that a working copy of proprietary software, together with any user manuals or help files and the search engine used to search for and retrieve the data, must be provided on each CD. In addition, When the data on a CD or DVD is in text (regardless of format), it is required that the documents be OCRed before production.

NOTES TO FORM

Commentary

This form can be used with a request to produce or even with interrogatories where it is anticipated that the information requested may be provided on a CD or DVD.

§ 14:31 General definitions and instructions

Definitions

1. For the purposes of these document requests, the term "document" means a writing of any kind, whether produced manually or by mechanical, chemical, electrical, or other artificial process, or by any combination of these methods, and whether visible to the unaided human eye or only with the aid of some devise, machine, or process. The term "document" includes but is not limited to:

(a) the original (or identical copy when the original is not available) of all:

(1) letters, notes, and all other correspondence, including but not limited to:
  (aa) handwritten notes,
  (bb) electronic or other transcriptions or taping of telephone or personal conversations or conferences,
  (cc) taped correspondence,
  (dd) electronic mail,
  (ee) all original telephone logs, memoranda, telephone bills reflecting calls between the parties at issue during the relevant time period,
  (ff) internal memoranda;
(2) reports, tabulations, analyses, opinions, summaries, and studies;
(3) financial documents;
(4) telegrams, cables, and teletype messages;
(5) messages, including reports, summaries, and minutes of telephone conversations, meetings, speeches, and all other oral communications;
(6) meeting minutes;
(7) transcripts and their digests, summaries, and analyses;
(8) purchase orders, bills, contracts, agreements, invoices, records of purchase or sale, purchase orders, leases, estimates, appraisals, valuations, releases, and other similar commercial documents;
(9) questionnaires and surveys;
(10) information stored in a computer, floppy disk, CD-ROM, or other storage device;
(11) diaries;
(12) computer printouts, printout summaries, and programs;
(13) audio recordings;
(14) still photographs and their negatives;
(15) motion picture film and its negative;
(16) audio and video tapes;
(17) graphs, charts, maps, plans, instructions, blueprints, diagrams, sketches, and drawings;
(18) tabulations, tallies, and other data compilations;
(19) books, pamphlets, periodicals, magazines, circulars, and bulletins;

(b) non-identical copies of original documents, whether different from their originals by reason of notations made on such copies, or otherwise;
(c) all attachments and enclosures to any requested item which are not separated;

(d) drafts and all revisions of any documents that are in the possession, custody, or control of, or known to the party answering these document requests. This definition applies to any document:
   (1) prepared by the answering party for its own use,
   (2) prepared by the answering party for transmittal to any other person, including a wholly or partially owned subsidiary, whether or not the document was actually transmitted,
   (3) prepared by another person, including a wholly or partially owned subsidiary of the answering party, for transmittal to or reception by the answering party, whether or not the document was actually transmitted or received;

(e) all documents must be sequential, organized in file folders, and identified by department and location.

2. For the purposes of these document requests, "financial documents" include but are not limited to:
   (a) documents related to all of *[name's]* assets;
   (b) documents related to all of *[name's]* expenditures, including but not limited to those for business, travel, entertainment, and other expense accounts;
   (c) canceled checks, bank statements, and checkbooks for all checking accounts in which *[name]* has or has had an interest;
   (d) federal and state individual income tax returns, with all schedules;
   (e) books, records, financial statements, profit and loss statements, journal ledgers, and annual reports;
   (f) vouchers or statements submitted by all of *[name's]* credit card companies;
   (g) correspondence with bookkeepers, accountants, or auditors regarding *[name's]* operations and financial condition;
   (h) documents evidencing gifts or inheritances;
   (i) appraisals, insurance policies, pension plans, veteran's benefit plans, profit sharing, or retirement plans, in which *[name]* has a present, future, or potential future interest of any kind;
   (j) financial or personal statements of financial condition given to any bank, savings and loan, mortgage company, credit union, credit bureau, financial company, business, or financial institution of any kind;
   (k) all available budgets or projections;
   (l) employment contracts, which are pertinent to *[name's]* assets, debts and liabilities, and income;

(m) deeds, mortgages, agreements of sale, and other documents pertaining to the assets owned by *[name]*;
(n) documents related to any financial loss, debts, and liabilities, including but not limited to
  (1) documents related to unsatisfactory past loans,
  (2) any filing for bankruptcy or any document discussing or considering it,
  (3) documents related to any cessation of *[name's]* work or business.

3. For the purposes of these document requests, the term "person" means:
  (a) natural persons,
  (b) non-natural persons, including but not limited to:
    (1) associations,
    (2) bid depositories,
    (3) clubs,
    (4) companies,
    (5) cooperatives,
    (6) corporations,
    (7) estates,
    (8) foundations,
    (9) institutes,
    (10) joint owners,
    (11) joint ventures,
    (12) limited partnerships,
    (13) nonprofit organizations,
    (14) partnerships,
    (15) professional corporations,
    (16) service corporations,
    (17) sole proprietorships,
    (18) societies,
    (19) syndicates,
    (20) trade associations,
    (21) unions, whether or not formally incorporated under the laws of any political jurisdiction,
    (22) domestic and foreign federal, state, departmental, regional, and local governments and their divisions, departments, agencies, and other governmental subdivisions.

4. For the purposes of these document requests, the term "personnel files" refers to any documents pertaining to an individual's employment history. Personnel files include but are not limited to:

(a) resumes and curriculum vitae,
(b) certificates or licenses,
(c) job applications,
(d) job descriptions,
(e) job duties and responsibilities,
(f) contracts and terms and conditions of employment,
(g) length of employment,
(h) performance evaluations, including reprimands,
(i) any investigations regarding complaints about job performance,
(j) prior occupations,
(k) attendance records,
(l) agreements with any labor union,
(m) collective bargaining agreements,
(n) physical or mental examinations, including drug tests,
(o) qualifications,
(p) termination notices,
(q) all other correspondence.

5. For the purposes of these document requests, the term "policy" means any rule, regulation, standard operating procedure, or other principle formally or informally adopted for the purpose of guiding or otherwise conducting the business operations of the answering party. The term "policy" also means any normal, frequent, or habitual course of conduct in which the answering party actually engages or has actually engaged during the relevant time period.
6. For the purposes of these document requests, the terms "you" and "your" mean:
   (a) the party producing the documents from this request,
   (b) its wholly or partially owned domestic and foreign subsidiaries,
   (c) its merged or acquired predecessors,
   (d) its successors by merger or acquisition,
   (e) its present and foreign directors, trustees, officers, partners, consultants, agents and representatives,
   (f) all other persons acting or purporting to act on behalf of those persons in paragraphs (a) through (e) above,
   (g) all past and present employees exercising non-clerical or discretionary decision-making or policy-making authority on behalf of the answering party,
   (h) divisions, departments, profit centers, and other corporate subdivisions of the answering party.
7. For the purposes of these document requests, the terms "defendant" and "plaintiff" mean:

(a) the party producing the documents from this request,
(b) its wholly or partially owned domestic and foreign subsidiaries,
(c) its merged or acquired predecessors,
(d) its successors by merger or acquisition,
(e) its present and foreign directors, trustees, officers, partners, consultants, agents and representatives,
(f) all other persons acting or purporting to act on behalf of those persons in paragraphs (a) through (e) above,
(g) all past and present employees exercising non-clerical or discretionary decision-making or policy-making authority on behalf of the answering party,
(h) divisions, departments, profit centers, and other corporate subdivisions of the answering party.

8. For the purposes of these document requests, the words "corporate documents" refer to all documents describing the structure, function, and maintenance of a business or corporation. "Corporate documents" include but are not limited to all documents consisting of or pertaining to:
(a) documents filed with any state or other governmental agency related to the incorporation of any entity,
(b) articles of incorporation,
(c) by-laws,
(d) each department and division and their functions,
(e) lists of each branch office,
(f) the list of directors and shareholders,
(g) stock registers,
(h) personnel files for all employees,
(i) annual reports,
(j) partnership agreements,
(k) minute books,
(l) stock tender offers,
(m) poison pills adopted,
(n) merger agreements,
(o) any takeover documents,
(p) company sales information, including but not limited to:
(1) receivables and payables lists,
(2) lists of the largest customers with the amount of sales to each, and
(3) lists of the largest suppliers with the amount of purchases from each.

9. For the purposes of these documents requests, words in the masculine gender shall be construed to include the feminine

and the neuter; words in the feminine gender shall be construed to include the masculine and the neuter; and neutral words shall be construed to include the masculine and the feminine.

10. For the purposes of these document requests, words importing the singular shall be construed to include the plural, and words importing the plural shall be construed to include the singular.
11. For the purposes of these document requests, anything that is "related to" the subject matter requested is meant to include but is not limited to anything that constitutes, contains, embodies, reflects, identifies, states, refers to, alludes to, responds to, deals with, comments on, is in any way pertinent to, in connection with, in response to, about, regarding, announcing, explaining, discussing, showing, describing, studying, reflecting, analyzing, or constituting.
12. For the purposes of these document requests, the word "and" also means "and/or."
13. For the purposes of these document requests, the word "all" also means "any and all."
14. For the purposes of these document requests, the word "any" also means "any and all."
15. For the purposes of these document requests, the word "between" also means "between and among."
16. For the purposes of these document requests, the word "including" also means "including but not limited to."
17. For the purposes of these document requests, the term "relevant time period" shall mean the period of time (choose only one):
   (a) from a date five years before the alleged occurrence until the date of the filing of the complaint in this action,
   (b) beginning with *[date]* and ending with the filing of the complaint in this action,
   (c) beginning with the first date of the occurrence as alleged in the complaint and ending with the filing of the complaint in this action.
18. For the purposes of these document requests, the term "identify" means when used in reference to:
   (a) a document, to state separately:
      (1) its description (e.g., letter, report, memorandum, etc.),
      (2) its date,
      (3) its subject matter,
      (4) the identity of each author or signer,
      (5) its present location and the identity of its custodian,

(b) an oral statement, communication, conference or conversation, to state separately:
 (1) its date and the place where it occurred,
 (2) its substance,
 (3) the identity of each person participating in the communication or conversation,
 (4) the identity of all notes, memoranda or other documents memorializing, referring to or relating to the subject matter of the statement,

(c) a natural person or persons, to state separately:
 (1) the full name of each such person,
 (2) his or her present or last known business address and his or her present or last known residential address,
 (3) the employer of the person at the time to which the request is directed and the person's title or position at that time,

(d) an organization or entity other than a natural person (e.g., a company, corporation, firm, association, or partnership), to state separately:
 (1) the full name and type of organization or entity,
 (2) the date and state of organization or incorporation,
 (3) the address of each of its principal places of businesses,
 (4) the nature of the business conducted.

19. For the purpose of these document requests, the term "communication" shall mean any transmission of information, the information transmitted, and any process by which information is transmitted, and shall include written communications and oral communications.
20. For the purposes of these document requests, the term "claim" means a demand or assertion, whether oral or written, formal or informal, by any person for monetary payment, the undertaking of action, or the cessation of action.
21. For the purposes of these document requests, the terms "consulted" or "contracted" means any form of communication, e.g., oral statements, telephone conversations or other mechanical communications or any other type of communication including written letters or documents.
22. For the purposes of these document requests, the terms "management" and "manage" includes any act of directing, conducting, administering, controlling, or handling an identified function or duty.

Instructions for Answering

1. You are required, in responding to this request to obtain and furnish all information available to you and any of your representatives, employees, agents, brokers, servants, or attorneys and to obtain and furnish all information, that is in your possession or under your control, or in the possession or under the control of any of your representatives, employees, agents, servants, or attorneys.
2. Each request which seeks information relating in any way to communications, to, from, or within a business and/or corporate entity, is hereby designated to demand, and should be construed to include, all communications by and between representatives, employees, agents of the business and/or corporate entity.
3. Each request should be responded to separately. However, a document which is the response to more than one request may, if the relevant portion is marked or indexed, be produced and referred to in a later response.
4. All documents produced shall be segregated and identified by the paragraphs to which they are primarily responsive. Where required by a particular paragraph of this Request, documents produced shall be further segregated and identified as indicated in this paragraph. For any documents that are stored or maintained in files for the normal course of business, such documents shall be procured in such files, or in such a manner as to preserve and identify the file from which such documents were taken.
5. If you object to part of any request, please furnish documents responsive to the remainder of the request.
6. Each request refers to all documents that are either known by the party to exist or that can be located or discovered by reasonably diligent efforts of the party.
7. The documents produced in response to this Request shall include all attachments and enclosures.
8. The documents requested for production include those in the possession, custody, or control of the party and the party's agents, representatives, or attorneys.
9. References to the singular include the plural.
10. The use of any tense of any verb shall be considered also to include within its meaning all other tenses of the verb so used.
11. *[If under Federal Rules of Civil Procedure]* Please note that the party, pursuant to Fed. R. Civ. P. 26(e), is under a continuing duty to seasonably supplement the production with documents obtained after the preparation and filing of a response to each request.

12. All documents called for by this request or related to this request, for which the party claims a privilege or statutory authority as a ground for nonproduction shall be listed chronologically as follows:
   (a) the place, date, and manner of recording or otherwise preparing the document,
   (b) the name and title of the sender,
   (c) the identity of each person or persons (other than stenographic or clerical assistants) participating in the preparation of the document,
   (d) the identity and title with the party, if any, of the person or persons supplying the party's attorneys with the information requested above,
   (e) the identity of each person to whom the contents of the document have heretofore been communicated by copy, exhibition, sketch, reading or substantial summarization, the date of said communication, and the employer and title of said person at the time of said communication,
   (f) type of document,
   (g) subject matter (without revealing the relevant information for which privilege or statutory authority is claimed), and
   (h) factual and legal basis for claim, privilege or specific statutory or regulatory authority which provides the claimed ground for nonproduction.
13. Each request to produce a document or documents shall be deemed to call for the production of the original document or documents to the extent that they are in, or subject to, directly or indirectly, the control of the party to whom this request is addressed. In addition, each request should be considered as including a request for separate production of all copies and, to the extent applicable, preliminary drafts of documents that differ in any respect from the original or final draft, or from each other (e.g., by reason of differences in form, or content, or by reason of handwritten notes, or comments having been added to one copy of a document, but not to the original or other copies thereof).
14. All documents produced in response to this Request shall be produced *in toto* notwithstanding the fact that portions thereof may contain information not requested.
15. If any documents requested herein have been lost or destroyed, the documents so lost or destroyed shall be identified by author, date, and subject matter.
16. Where exact information cannot be furnished, estimated information is to be supplied to the extent possible. Where

estimation is used, it should be so indicated, and an explanation should be given as to the basis on which the statement was made and the reason exact information cannot be furnished.

17. With respect to any document requested which was once in the party's possession, custody or control, but no longer is, please indicate the date and the manner in which the document ceased to be in the party's possession, custody, or control and the name and address of its present custodian.
18. Unless otherwise indicated, each request is to be construed as encompassing all documents which pertain to the stated subject matter and to events which transpired between *[date]* up to the present.

NOTES TO FORM

Commentary

This form contains many more definitions than will be needed in any single case. It can be adapted to the specific requests for production.

§ 14:32 Request for physical inspection of computer

[Caption]

To: Defendant and its attorneys of record

Pursuant to *[rule]*, Plaintiff requests that Defendant permit Plaintiff, Plaintiff's attorneys, and consultants to enter onto the premises located at *[specify address]* and inspect the computer described as: *[specify computer to be examined, e.g., serial number, type and model]*.

Such entry and inspection shall include, but will not necessarily be limited to, the following activities: photographing, physical inspection of network topography, preparation of a network map, and creation of a mirror copy of the hard disk(s).

Dated: ____

[signature, etc.]

NOTES TO FORM

Commentary

Courts have become less inclined in recent years to grant inspection rights of a party's computers based merely on a suspicion the systems contain relevant evidence. See, e.g., Bethea v. Comcast, 218 F.R.D. 328, 57 Fed. R. Serv. 3d 428 (D.D.C. 2003) (former employee's request for an inspection order for her employer's computer systems based only on a mere suspicion the former employer had failed to produce all relevant documents rejected by court).

§ 14:33 Procedure for reviewing computer's hardware, software, and operating system

[Caption]

Procedure for Reviewing Computer Hardware, Software, and Operating System

A. This procedure shall apply to the following stated purposes of *[requesting party]* as outlined in the Motion to Compel:
  (1) Inspect the computer to determine its operating system and applicable software applications
  (2) Inspect the computer to explore how the files are kept on the computer and how they are identified
  (3) Determine what actions *[producing party]* took to protect confidential information on the computer
  (4) Determine the actions that were taken to allow confidential information to be accessed by the *[name]*
  (5) Determine how the software that opens images functions
  (6) Review registries and logs in the computer's operating system to determine, if possible, the people who have logged on to the computer as well as what files were opened after *[date]*

B. Procedure
  (1) The court hereby appoints *[name]* as an expert to conduct an examination of defendants' computer.
  (2) The parties shall submit a Protective Order for the court's approval, which will subsequently be entered, and signed by the Expert.
  (3) Once a Protective Order is entered, *[producing party]* shall make available to the Expert, at *[producing party's]* place of business, and at a mutually agreeable time, the computer at issue in this litigation.
  (4) The Expert will use its best efforts to avoid unnecessarily disrupting the normal business activities or business operations of the *[producing party]* while inspecting *[producing party's]* computer
  (5) The computer at all times shall be maintained on *[producing party's]* premises.
  (6) The only persons authorized to inspect or otherwise handle the computer are the Expert and employees of the Expert assigned to this project.
  (7) No employee of *[requesting party]*, *[requesting party's]*, or *[requesting party]*, will inspect or otherwise handle the computer produced.

(8) The Expert will maintain all information in the strictest confidence;

(9) Once the computer is produced, the Expert shall attempt to recover a "mirror image," or forensic image, of the hard drive, in the presence of only the *[producing party]* or *[producing party's]* counsel, and at the *[producing party's]* convenience. after a forensic copy is made, one copy shall be transmitted to the court and one copy shall be transmitted to the *[producing party].*

(10) On the forensic copy, the Expert shall identify the computer's operating system and software applications related to the creation, storage, and viewing of files—Including images—on the computer;

(11) The Expert shall identify the internal hardware components of the computer, including the existing RAM card in the computer, and any other matters that the Expert deems relevant.

(12) The Expert shall then inspect the computer to determine its operating system and all software applications installed on the computer.

(13) The Expert shall inspect the computer and identify how individual files are organized on the computer and how files may be identified;

(14) The Expert shall inspect the computer to determine what actions defendants took to protect confidential information on the computer.

(15) The Expert shall inspect the computer to determine what, if any, actions were taken that specifically allowed *[name]* to access confidential information on the computer;

(16) The Expert shall inspect the computer to determine how the software that opens image files functions.

(17) If the file system permits, the Expert shall review the computer's registries and logs in the computer's operating system to determine the people who have logged on to the computer after it was discarded as well as what files were opened after the computer had been discarded; and

(18) The Expert shall provide a summary of the above information to plaintiffs and defendants.

Dated: ____

Judge

NOTES TO FORM

Commentary

This form is adapted from the record in G.D. v. Monarch Plastic Surgery, P.A., 239 F.R.D. 641, 67 Fed. R. Serv. 3d 352 (D. Kan. 2007). The case involved the claim that the defendant health care providers wrongfully disclosed plaintiffs' medical information stored on a computer hard drive by placing the computer on the curb for trash disposal. after the computer was placed on the curb, plaintiffs allege a collector removed the computer and took it to a computer repair shop. Plaintiffs claim the repair shop employees were able to make the computer operable, and the collector was then able to view the confidential medical files.

§ 14:34 Procedure for reviewing information stored on producing party's computer

[Caption]

Procedure for Reviewing Information Stored on Computer

A. This procedure shall apply to the following stated purposes of *[requesting party]*:

(1) Search for all documents that concern the *[requesting party]* in this case

(2) Review the metadata concerning each file that concerns the *[requesting party]*

(3) Search the computer for deleted documents concerning the *[requesting party]*.

B. Procedure

(1) The court hereby appoints *[name]* as an expert to conduct an examination of defendants' computer.

(2) The parties shall submit a Protective Order for the court's approval, which will subsequently be entered, and signed by the Expert.

(3) Once a Protective Order is entered, *[producing party]* shall make available to the Expert, at *[producing party's]* place of business, and at a mutually agreeable time, the computer at issue in this litigation.

(4) The Expert will use its best efforts to avoid unnecessarily disrupting the normal business activities or business operations of the *[producing party]* while inspecting *[producing party's]* computer

(5) The computer at all times shall be maintained on *[producing party's]* premises.

(6) The only persons authorized to inspect or otherwise handle the computer are the Expert and employees of the Expert assigned to this project.

(7) No employee of *[requesting party]*, *[requesting party's]*, or

[requesting party], will inspect or otherwise handle the computer produced.

(8) The Expert will maintain all information in the strictest confidence;

(9) Once the computer is produced, the Expert shall attempt to recover a "mirror image," or forensic image, of the hard drive, in the presence of only the *[producing party]* or *[producing party's]* counsel, and at the *[producing party's]* convenience. after a forensic copy is made, one copy shall be transmitted to the court and one copy shall be transmitted to the *[producing party]*.

(10) *[Producing party]* shall review such mirror image copy in collaboration with the Expert, and shall produce to *[requesting party]* all responsive documents *[requesting party]* seek in their Motion to Compel for which the court has granted production Specifically, *[producing party]* shall provide to *[requesting party]* in hard-copy format:

a. All documents that concern *[requesting party]* in this case;
b. All metadata related to the documents that concern *[requesting party]* in this case; and
c. All recovered deleted documents concerning the *[requesting party]* in this case.

(11) In addition to the aforementioned responsive documents, *[producing party]* shall also provide a privilege log to *[requesting party]*, describing the nature of any privileged documents or communications in a manner that, without revealing information that is privileged or protected, will enable *[requesting party]* to assess the applicability of the privilege or protection claimed;

(12) *[Producing party]* shall forward a copy of the privilege log to the court for potential in camera review;

(13) Once *[requesting party]* has reviewed the documents produced by *[producing party]*, as well as the privilege log, if the *[requesting party]* raises a dispute as to any of the documents, by providing a cogent basis for doubting the claim of privilege, or for believing that there are further relevant documents, the court will conduct an in camera review, limited to the issues raised.

NOTES TO FORM

Commentary

This form is adapted from the record in G.D. v. Monarch Plastic Surgery, P.A., 239 F.R.D. 641, 67 Fed. R. Serv. 3d 352 (D. Kan. 2007). The case involved the claim that the defendant health care providers wrongfully disclosed plaintiffs' medical information stored on a computer hard drive by placing the computer on the curb for trash disposal. After the computer was placed on the curb, plaintiffs allege a collector removed the computer and took it to a computer repair shop. Plaintiffs claim the repair shop employees were able to make the computer operable, and the collector was then able to view the confidential medical files.

§ 14:35 Motion for default judgment against defendant for failure to comply with order for production of documents

[Caption]

Plaintiff moves the Court that judgment be rendered in favor of plaintiff and against defendant by default, as provided for by *[rule]*, for failure of defendant to comply with the order of this Court entered on *[date]*, requiring defendant to produce certain enumerated books and writings for inspection by plaintiff.

The undersigned certifies that the undersigned has in good faith attempted to confer with the *[defendant's]* attorney in an unsuccessful effort to secure the requested information without court action.

The attached *[affidavit] [declaration]* of *[name]* will be relied upon in support of this motion.

Dated: ____

[signature etc.]

§ 14:36 Motion for dismissal of action for plaintiff's failure to comply with order for production of documents

[Caption]

MOTION FOR DISMISSAL OF ACTION

Defendant moves the Court that the above-entitled action against defendant be dismissed as provided for by *[rule]*, for failure of plaintiff to comply with the order of this court entered on *[date]*, requiring plaintiff to produce certain enumerated books and writings for inspection by defendant.

The undersigned certifies that the undersigned has in good faith attempted to confer with the *[party's]* attorney in an unsuccessful effort to secure the requested information without court action.

The attached *[affidavit] [declaration]* of *[name]* will be relied upon in support of this motion.

Dated: ____

[signature etc.]

§ 14:37 Order for default judgment or dismissal of action for failure to comply with order for production of documents

[Caption]

ORDER

On the motion of *[plaintiff for a default judgment] [defendant for an order dismissing the action]*, for failure of *[defendant] [plaintiff]* to comply with the order of *[date]*, granting *[plaintiff] [defendant]* leave to examine certain documents pertinent to the issues in this action and in the possession of *[defendant] [plaintiff]*, it is

ORDERED that pursuant to *[rule] [judgment be entered for the plaintiff for such damages as plaintiff has sustained as alleged in the complaint] [the action be dismissed]*, and *[[plaintiff]* be forbidden to support plaintiff's claim] *[[defendant]* be forbidden to oppose the plaintiff's claim] *[[defendant's]* defense is stricken] *[[defendant is forbidden to introduce in evidence the following documents: [specify]]*.

Dated: ____

Judge

§ 14:38 Plaintiff's emergency motion to prevent the further destruction of evidence and for sanctions for spoliation of evidence

[Caption]

Plaintiff's Emergency Motion to Prevent the Further Destruction of Evidence and for Sanctions for Spoliation of Evidence

Plaintiff, for the reasons more fully set forth in the accompanying memorandum, respectfully requests this Court to enter an Order:

1. Requiring defendant to retain all electronic evidence, including e-mails, and cease deleting e-mails immediately;
2. Sanctioning defendant for spoliation of evidence, including but not limited to the entry of a default or, at a minimum, an adverse jury instruction at trial and an order barring defen-

dant from claiming that its male employees did not circulate or show pornographic, lewd and inappropriate e-mail to members of the putative class;
3. Requiring defendant to cooperate with and provide access to plaintiff's forensic data recovery experts to perform data recovery and to pay the costs of these services; and
4. For such other and further relief as this Court deems appropriate.

Dated: ____

[signature, etc.]

NOTES TO FORM

Commentary

This motion is adapted from the record in Wiginton v. Ellis, 2003 WL 22439865 (N.D. Ill. 2003).

§ 14:39 Chain-of-custody log

Chain-of-Custody Log

Name of Individual Receiving Information: ________

Date of collection or receipt: ________

Time of collection or receipt: ________

Place of collection or receipt: ________

Name of custodian: ________

Electronically stored information obtained, including media:
Media Type:________
Media Standard: ________
Media Manufacturer: ________
Media Serial Numbers and/or Volume Names: ________
____
Writing on Labels: ________
Characterization of data: ________
Amount of data: ________
Type of data: ________
Write-Protection Status: ________

Data Collection Procedures
Tools Used for Each Procedure: ________

____

Name of Individual Conducting Each Procedure: ________

____

Outcome of Procedures: ________
Problems Encountered: ________

Additional Documentation
Movement of Evidence: ________
Purpose of Movement: ________
Date of Media Check In: ________
Time of Media Check In: ________
Date of Media Check Out from Secured Storage: ________
Time of Media Check Out from Secure Storage: ________
Physical Inspection of Information: ________
Description of Analysis: ________

____

NOTES TO FORM

Commentary

A chain-of-custody log is intended to prove the integrity of the information produced has been maintained from its production through introduction court. A chain-of-custody log should document how the information was gathered, analyzed, and preserved. Because electronically stored information can be easily altered if proper precautions are not taken, a chain-of-custody log for electronically stored information must demonstrate the following: (1) the information has been properly copied, transported, and stored; (2) the information has not been altered in any way; and (3) all media has been secured throughout the process.

Documentation must be maintained throughout the life of the information and should be ready for review at any time. Every of contact with the information must be documented during the discovery process. A complete and accurate logging procedure will help assure that electronically stored information can be authenticated in court.

§ 14:40 Response to request for production of documents

[Caption]

REQUEST NUMBER ONE:

[Set forth terms of response.]

RESPONSE TO REQUEST NUMBER ONE:

[Set forth any objections, then indicate whether such documents will be produced.]

Dated: ______________________

[signature etc.]

§ 14:41 Quick peek agreement

1. *[Name of responding party]* agrees to make relevant information requested by *[name of requesting party]* available for inspection.
2. *[Name of requesting]* shall review the information and designate the information it believes is responsive to its requests.
3. *[Name of responding party]* shall then review the designated information for privilege and work-product protection.
4. Following the review *[name of responding party]* shall produce the information it believes is relevant and not protected by privilege or the work-product doctrine.

NOTES TO FORM

Commentary

This is an excerpt from a quick peek agreement, containing the essentials. The agreement could also provide for such things as who will be allowed to see the documents. In order to prevent a claim of waiver of privilege made by a third-party, it is appropriate to have the agreement incorporated into a court order.

§ 14:42 Order requiring production

[Caption]

ORDER

This is a *[describe]* action involving *[describe]*. *[Name 1]* has moved the Court for an order compelling *[name 2]* to produce the documents listed in a document entitled *[specify]* *[and otherwise to produce the initial disclosures required under [rule]]*. *[Name 2]* has responded and moved for a protective order.

The scheduling order of *[date]*, required the parties to make all disclosures required by *[rule]* on or before the discovery meeting, which took place on *[date]*. *[Name 1]* made its disclosures on *[date]*. *[Name 2]* made no disclosures under *[rule]* until *[date]*, when a document entitled *[specify]* was faxed to *[name 2]*'s counsel. Section of this disclosure statement consisted of a listing of the documents identified by *[name 2]* as being relevant under *[rule]*. *[Name 2]* indicated the documents would be produced "after entry of an appropriate protective order." No *[name 2]* documents were produced at that time or subsequently. Further, *[name 2]* indicated in the "disclosure statement" that it was self-insured and also carried "aggregate excess liability insurance coverage" but did not identify the insurer(s) or produce copies of the insurance agreements, as required by *[rule]*.

At the hearing held in this matter on *[date]*, the parties advised the Court that they had agreed upon a protective order. From a review of the record, it appears the protective order was entered on *[date]*. Thus, that request by *[name 2]* is considered moot. *[Name 2]* is otherwise ORDERED to produce by *[date]*, any outstanding documentation mandated by *[rule]*. *[Name 1]*'s request for sanctions, expenses and attorney fees will be taken under further advisement at this time. Thus, *[name 1]*'s motion to compel is GRANTED IN PART AS MODIFIED. *[Name 2]* is forewarned that a failure to cooperate fully in discovery will lead to sanctions.

[Name 1] has moved for sanctions under Fed. R. Civ. P. 37(d) for *[name 2]*'s failure to respond to both interrogatories and requests to produce. *[Name 2]* has responded.

[Name 1] asserts that *[name 2]* has engaged in a clear, discernable pattern of conduct that, taken as a whole, constitutes a calculated, deliberate, systematic and flagrant abuse of discovery. Pursuant to Fed. R. Civ. P. 37(d), plaintiffs request an order entering sanctions against *[name 2]*, including the sanction of Fed. R. Civ. P. 37(b)(2) (B) of striking DCC's affirmative defenses, on the grounds that *[name 2]* has without cause or justification refused to produce witnesses in response to timely and appropriate *[rule]* notices of examination. *[Name 1]* also seeks an order entering sanctions on the grounds that *[name 2]* has provided only partial and incomplete responses to *[name 1]*'s first set of requests to produce, which responses consist of tens of thousands of unindexed, incomplete or illegible written materials in violation of *[rule]*.

[Name 1] contends those responses, contained mainly on CDs, constitute sham responses to *[name 1]*'s requests to produce and have been provided in an attempt to inundate the *[name 1]* without providing any substantive factual material responsive to *[name 1]*'s requests to produce. *[Name 1]* argues the CD responses occasioned considerable unnecessary effort and expense on the part of *[name 1]*'s counsel.

[Name 2] states the CDs it produced contained files that were clearly a listing of the documents being provided. Each file name included the word and most contained the word "list." Upon opening these files, lists are found, setting forth the contents of the remainder of the folder. *[Name 2]* claims it has gone to obvious

lengths to satisfy what are, in many cases, overly broad and unduly burdensome requests.

In addition to other orders of this court, *[name 2]* is ORDERED to produce the following by *[date]*: legible and properly scanned documents to replace the illegible ones previously provided on the CDs; the 5,000 graphical images claimed to be undecipherable by *[name 1]*; all documents requested concerning *[describe]*; unredacted versions of all documents requested unless privilege is claimed; and any appendices it may have neglected to produce; any cross-referenced documents concerning *[describe]*.

Within the relevant time frame, *[name 2]* is also ORDERED to allow *[name 1]* access to any available searchable databases that may contain relevant discovery material. *[Name 1]* shall have unrestricted right to use and examine the databases subject to the protective order currently in place in this case. *[Name 2]* must also provide information as to how documents are organized on *[name 2]*'s main database and further explain the information divulged on the CDs.

[Name 1]'s motion for sanctions is taken under further advisement at this time. *[Name 2]* is again forewarned that failure to fully and completely cooperate in discovery will lead to sanctions.

Dated: ____

____

Judge

§ 14:43 Order for production—Another form

[Caption]

ORDER CONCERNING E-DISCOVERY HEARING Purpose and Areas of Discussion

My responsibilities as the discovery Judge in this case are to insure that all significantly relevant and discoverable materials are preserved and produced, to expedite the discovery process, to minimize costs, and to achieve a reasonable balance between the legitimate discovery needs of the parties and the corresponding burden on the producing party. Because of the nature of the litigation, it is probable that the most significant discovery problems will arise in connection with Plaintiffs' discovery of Defendant's materials.

To carry out these responsibilities, a hearing on e-discovery has been scheduled for *[date]*. The parties and I will make every attempt to tie down issues now, in an effort to head off problems and to facilitate discovery.

Defendant acknowledges the existence of a significant amount of discoverable electronic data. As the parties know, preservation, discovery, and production of electronic materials presents special problems.

I am interested in learning about the following:

1. Defendant's electronic document depository. A presentation and demonstration will be welcome.
2. Defendant's corporate structure and operations, including which departments or divisions would be involved in research and development, government approval, marketing, and monitoring the involved product.
3. The identities of the key individuals within each of the above areas of responsibility that would have been involved with the product.
4. The time frame during which relevant electronic or other discoverable information may have been created.
5. Basic information about the process of obtaining government approval for the product in question, including citations to regulations covering retention of research and other materials involved in the approval process.
6. Basic information about necessary record-keeping and reporting to the government during the time the product is marketed.
7. Defendant's computer systems, including servers, networks, e-mail systems, voice mail systems, data bases, desktop or laptop computers, PDAs, and backup or archival tapes or other similar storage media.
8. Changes made in Defendant's systems during the relevant period and any information as to the existence of any relevant and discoverable electronic data which is not located on currently used electronic devices (legacy data).
9. Whether relevant and discoverable electronic data may exist in third party storage or processing entities, such as internet storage or servicing facilities.
10. Any steps taken to insure preservation of relevant and discoverable materials—in addition to in-house counsel's memorandum to employees dated *[date]*, directing the preservation of hard copy and electronic documents. Whether any individuals have been given the responsibility of monitoring the process, and, if so, their names and positions.
11. Whether the parties anticipate special problems with discovery by Defendant of the various Plaintiffs' medical and other relevant and discoverable information.

No later than *[date]*, Defendant must submit information about its basic corporate structure, as listed in items 2 and 3 above, and information about the government approval and monitoring process as mentioned in paragraph 5 above. The Court needs somewhat more detailed information than that listing "management, medical affairs, regulatory affairs and labeling, and marketing," which appeared in *[name's]* Statement Regarding Document Preservation, Collection and Production filed *[date]*. Perhaps the organizational charts listed in the proposed order, if not too extensive, would be helpful.

Defendant must also have present for the hearing the individual or individuals most knowledgeable about its computer system. Any additional information bearing on the above categories that the parties could submit prior to the hearing would be welcome.

Preservation of Data

One concern I have with the proposed document depository is that the documents are being produced in Tagged Image File Format (.tif). Thus, although the documents would be in electronic form, it appears the production is the functional equivalent of a "hard copy" production and no "metadata" such as document history, earlier or deleted versions, electronic marginal comments, etc., would be available. Of further concern is 'Defendant's statement that after a document is scanned and the ".tiff" image created, Wyeth is "returning the original documents needed for ongoing business to the files."' As to electronic documents, this may result in destruction or alteration of relevant data. Therefore, all parties and their counsel are reminded of their duty to preserve evidence that may be relevant to this action. The duty extends to documents, data, and tangible things in the possession, custody, and control of the parties to this action, and any employees, agents, contractors, carriers, bailees, or other non-parties who possess materials reasonably anticipated to be subject to discovery in this action. Counsel is under an obligation to exercise reasonable efforts to identify and notify such non-parties, including employees of corporate or institutional parties.

"Documents, data, and tangible things" are to be interpreted broadly to include writings; records; files; correspondence; reports; memoranda; calendars; diaries; minutes; electronic messages; voicemail; e-mail; telephone message records or logs; computer and network activity logs; hard drives; backup data; removable computer storage media such as tapes, disks, and cards; printouts; document image files; Web pages; databases; spreadsheets; software; books; ledgers; journals; orders; invoices; bills; vouchers; checks; statements; worksheets; summaries; compilations;

computations; charts; diagrams; graphic presentations; drawings; films; charts; digital or chemical process photographs; video, phonographic, tape, or digital recordings or transcripts thereof; drafts; jottings; and notes. Information that serves to identify, locate, or link such material, such as file inventories, file folders, indices, and metadata, is also included in this definition.

"Preservation" is to be interpreted broadly to accomplish the goal of maintaining the integrity of all documents, data, and tangible things reasonably anticipated to be subject to discovery under *[rule]* in this action. Preservation includes taking reasonable steps to prevent the partial or full destruction, alteration, testing, deletion, shredding, incineration, wiping, relocation, migration, theft, or mutation of such material, as well as negligent or intentional handling that would make material incomplete or inaccessible.

If Defendant's business practices involve the routine destruction, recycling, relocation, or mutation of such materials, Defendant must, to the extent practicable for the pendency of this order, either (1) halt such business processes; (2) sequester or remove such material from the business process; or (3) arrange for the preservation of complete and accurate duplicates or copies of such material, suitable for later discovery if requested.

Before or after the hearing, Defendant may apply to the court for further instructions regarding the duty to preserve specific categories of documents, data, or tangible things. Defendant may seek permission to resume routine business processes relating to the storage or destruction of specific categories of documents, data, or tangible things, upon a showing of undue cost, burden, or overbreadth.

IT IS SO ORDERED this *[date]*.

Judge

NOTES TO FORM

Commentary

This form is adapted from an order in a case involving a consumer action against a manufacturer of prescription drugs.

§ 14:44 Order for expedited forensic imaging

[Caption]

ORDER

1. The Forensic Examiner's costs shall be borne by the *[party]*.

2. Computer forensic analysis will be performed by *[specify]*.
3. All Forensic Examiners utilized must agree in writing to be bound by the terms of this Order prior to the commencement of their services.
4. Within two days of this Order or at such other time agreed to by the parties, *[party]* shall make its Computer(s), Server(s), and any other electronic storage devices located at *[party's]* place of business at *[address]*, *[including but not limited to [name's]* laptop, which may be located at a different location,] available to the Forensic Examiner to make mirror images of those devices as set out below:
   a. Imaging of the Computer(s), Server(s), any other electronic storage devices in *[party's]* possession, custody, or control, *[and [name's]* laptop] shall be created using Encase or a similar hardware or software tool that creates a forensically sound, bit-for-bit, mirror image of the original hard drives. A bit-stream mirror image copy of the media item(s) will be captured and will include all file slack and unallocated space.
   b. *[Party's]* Computers may include, but are not limited to, computers named *[describe]*. This Order does not limit imaging to one server if *[party]* possesses or has custody or control of additional servers, each of which shall be imaged pursuant to this Order.
   c. All images and copies of images shall be authenticated by generating an MD5 hash value verification for comparison to the original hard drive.
   d. The forensic images shall be copied and retained by the Forensic Examiner until such time the court or both parties request the destruction of the forensic image files.
5. The Forensic Examiner will maintain all mirrored images and do so in the strictest confidence, and not disclose any information obtained to unauthorized persons.
6. The Forensic Examiner will use its best efforts to avoid unnecessarily disrupting the normal activities or business operations of the defendants while inspecting, copying, and imaging the computers and storage devices.

IT IS SO ORDERED this *[date]*.

Judge

NOTES TO FORM

Commentary

This form is adapted from an order in Xpel Technologies Corp. v. American Filter Film Distributors, 2008 WL 744837 (W.D. Tex. 2008).

§ 14:45 Order for forensic search of party's computer systems

[Caption]

ORDER

1. Within seven days of the date of this Opinion and Order, *[producing party's]* forensic computer expert shall mirror image both of *[producing party's]* computer systems' hard drives and *[producing party]* shall preserve this mirror image.
2. *[Producing party's]* forensic computer expert shall then remove only *[producing party's]* confidential personal information from the mirror image of *[producing party's]* computer systems' hard drives. *[Producing party's]* expert shall provide *[receiving party]* with the protocol he utilized to remove the confidential information.
3. *[Producing party]* shall then provide *[receiving party's]* computer forensic expert access to *[producing party's]* computer systems' hard drives.
4. *[Receiving party's]* forensic computer expert shall mirror image *[producing party's]* computer systems' hard drives in approximately four to eight hours for each system. If the expert finds that this is not enough time, *[producing party]* is expected to be reasonable in allowing some additional time. *[Receiving party]* is expected to be considerate with regard to scheduling times that are less intrusive to *[producing party]* and *[producing party's]* business.
5. *[Receiving party's]* expert shall review the expert's findings in confidence with *[producing party]* prior to making any findings available to *[receiving party]*.
6. *[Producing party]* shall identify for deletion any information that is irrelevant and create a specific privilege log of any relevant information for which *[producing party]* claims privilege. The computer forensic expert shall remove the information claimed as privileged and provide all other information to *[receiving party]*.
7. *[Receiving party's]* expert shall provide *[producing party]* with the protocol the expert utilized to remove the privileged information.
8. Forensic computer experts *[names]* shall act as officers of this Court. *[Receiving party]* shall be responsible for remunerating *[name]* and *[producing party]* shall be responsible for remunerating *[name]*.

IT IS SO ORDERED this *[date]*.

Judge

NOTES TO FORM

Commentary

This form is adapted from an order in Ferron v. Search Cactus, L.L.C., 2008 WL 1902499 (S.D. Ohio 2008).

§ 14:46 Order for forensic search with clawback provision

[Caption]

ORDER

1. *[Producing party]* will conduct, at a minimum, searches of its e-mail database using following terms: *[specify]*
2. These searches will create a universe of presumptively responsive documents. From those presumptively responsive documents, *[producing party]* may search for and preliminarily withhold as presumptively privileged any communications between counsel and corporate principals or upper management, provided however that the presumption of privilege shall not apply to any communications also disclosed to opposing counsel in any litigation, or where any other action has been taken with respect to those communications which would result in the waiver of any claim of attorney-client privilege or work product protection. The Court will leave it to *[producing party]* to design the protocol it wishes to use to identify presumptively privileged documents. However, *[producing party]* shall provide *[receiving party]* with a complete description of the protocol utilized.
3. *[Producing party]* shall produce to party all presumptively responsive documents, less any presumptively privileged documents, not later than thirty days from the entry of this Order. *[Producing party]* may, however, review for privilege any presumptively responsive documents prior to their production. If, after conducting that review, *[producing party]* should believe that the attorney-client privilege or work product protection applies to any document, then *[producing party]* may withhold that document subject to *[producing party's]* obligation to provide a privilege log complying fully with the requirements of Fed. R. Civ. P. 26(b)(5)(A).
4. *[Producing party]* shall review all presumptively privileged documents and produce, on a rolling basis, any documents within this category to which the attorney-client privilege or work product protection does not apply. For any presumptively

privileged documents not so produced, *[producing party]* shall provide a privilege log complying fully with the requirements of Fed. R. Civ. P. 26(b)(5)(A). *[Producing party's]* production of such documents shall be completed no later than 45 days from the entry of this Order.

5. Any documents produced pursuant to this Order shall be considered confidential and subject to the Protective Order __ governing this case. Paragraph __ of that Order is hereby modified to apply to any documents or communications produced pursuant to this Order.
6. Any documents produced pursuant to this Order shall be subject to the "clawback provision" set forth in this Order.
7. *[Producing party]* shall not refuse to produce any document returned by the searches stated above on the basis of relevancy, undue burden, or any other ground not specifically provided herein without first obtaining a protective order from this Court.
8. All documents produced pursuant to this Order shall be made available to *[receiving party]* in a searchable, electronic form.
9. The parties may, by mutual agreement, develop and employ search protocols which vary from those set forth above. In the absence of such agreement, however, production shall proceed in the manner described above.
10. If, upon completion of the production described above, *[receiving party]* believes that an additional search of *[producing party's]* e-mail database is warranted, *[receiving party]* may raise that issue with the Court at the appropriate time.

Inadvertent Production of Documents Clawback Provision

1. The inadvertent production of any document or other information during discovery in this action shall be without prejudice to any claim that such material is protected by any legally cognizable privilege or evidentiary protection including, but not limited to, the attorney-client privilege or the work product doctrine, and no party shall be held to have waived any rights by such inadvertent production.
2. Upon written notice of an unintentional production by the producing party or oral notice if notice must be delivered at a deposition, the receiving party must promptly return or destroy the specified document and any hard copies the receiving party has and may not use or disclose the information until the privilege claim has been resolved. To the extent that the producing party insists on the return or destruction of electronic cop-

ies, rather than disabling the documents from further use or otherwise rendering them inaccessible to the receiving party, the producing party shall bear the costs of the return or destruction of such electronic copies.

3. To the extent that the information contained in a document subject to a claim has already been used in or described in other documents generated or maintained by the receiving party, then the receiving party will sequester such documents until the claim has been resolved. If the receiving party disclosed the specified information before being notified of its inadvertent production, it must take reasonable steps to retrieve it. The producing party shall preserve the specified information until the claim is resolved.
4. The receiving party shall have ten days from receipt of notification of the inadvertent production to determine in good faith whether to contest such claim and to notify the producing party in writing of an objection to the claim of privilege and the grounds for that objection.
5. The producing party will then have ten days from the receipt of the objection notice to submit the specified information to the Court under seal for a determination of the claim and will provide the Court with the grounds for the asserted privilege or protection. Any party may request expedited treatment of any request for the Court's determination of the claim.
6. Upon a determination by the Court that the specified information is protected by the applicable privilege, and if the specified information has been sequestered rather than returned or destroyed, the specified information shall be returned or destroyed.
7. Upon a determination by the Court that the specified information is not protected by the applicable privilege, the producing party shall bear the costs of placing the information into any programs or databases from which it was removed or destroyed and render accessible any documents that were disabled or rendered inaccessible, unless otherwise ordered by the Court.

IT IS SO ORDERED this *[date]*.

Judge

NOTES TO FORM

Commentary

This form is adapted from an order in Williams v. Taser Intern., Inc., 2007 WL 1630875 (N.D. Ga. 2007).

Part IV

MISCELLANEOUS

Chapter 15

Requests for Admissions

I. GUIDELINES

II. CHECKLISTS

III. FORMS

Research References

Treatises and Practice Aids

Grenig and Gleisner, eDiscovery & Digital Evidence § 7:14

Trial Strategy

Recovery and Reconstruction of Electronic Mail as Evidence, 41 Am. Jur Proof of Facts 3d 1

Computer Technology in Civil Litigation, 71 Am. Jur. Trials 111

Additional References

Grenig and Kinsler, Handbook of Federal Civil Discovery and Disclosure §§ 11.1 to 11.73 (3d ed.)

ABA Discovery Standards, http://www.abanet.org/litigation/discoverystandards/2005civildiscoverystandards.pdf

Federal Judicial Center, http://www.fjc.gov

The Sedona Conference, http://www.thesedonaconference.org

> **KeyCite®:** Cases and other legal materials listed in KeyCite Scope can be researched through the KeyCite service on Westlaw®. Use KeyCite to check citations for form, parallel references, prior and later history, and comprehensive citator information, including citations to other decisions and secondary materials.

I. GUIDELINES

§ 15:1 Generally

A request for admission is a device by which a litigant may request that an adversary admit, for the purposes of the pending action only, the truth of any matters relevant to the action, including statements of fact, opinions of fact, the application of law to fact, or the genuineness of documents.[1] Requests for admissions may be useful in establishing the following types of facts:

- The creator of a particular document.
- The owner of an e-mail address or domain name.
- The date a specified file was created or deleted.

A party served with a request for admission has several options:

- Admit the matter in full.
- Deny the matter in full setting forth in detail the reasons for such denial.
- Admit part and deny part.
- Object to the request setting for the reasons therefor.
- State that after making a reasonable inquiry the information known or readily obtainable by the answering party is insufficient to enable the party to admit or deny.

[Section 15:1]

[1]See Fed. R. Civ. P. 36.

- Seek a protective order.
- Move the court for an extension of time to answer.
- Seek a stipulation from the requesting party extending the time to answer.

Once the time period prescribed for answering expires (including any authorized extensions), the requesting party has several options:

- Accept the answer or objection.
- Move the court to determine the sufficiency of the answer or objection; if the court finds that the answer or objection is incomplete or insufficient, it may order that the request be re-answered.
- If the answering party denies the request and the proposition is proved during trial, and if the court in a post-trial hearing finds that the refusal was improper, the costs of proof may be imposed on the answering party.
- If the answering party fails to answer or object within the time specified in the applicable rule, the request will be deemed admitted.

§ 15:2 Role of requests for admissions

Unlike other discovery devices, requests for admission are not designed to discover facts. Because of the form in which requests for admission are submitted, it is assumed that the requesting party knows the facts before asking an adverse party to admit that the statement is true. Requests for admission ask the answering party to "admit that so-and-so" is true. Requests for admission are not substitutes for interrogatories. As a result, requests for admission may not be used to "gather" information after a party has exhausted the numerical limit on interrogatories.

Requests for admission serve two vital purposes. Admissions are sought, first, to facilitate proof with respect to issues that cannot be eliminated from the case, and secondly, to narrow the issues by eliminating those that can be. Thus, requests for admission can be used to define the issues involved in the case and to resolve some or all of the conflicts prior to trial.

§ 15:3 Disadvantages of requests for admissions

There are few disadvantages to using requests for admission. Answers to requests are only binding on the party who made them. Neither the requests nor the answers are binding on the party who propounded the requests for admission. A litigant does not bind itself to the truth of an admission by another party by submitting the request for admission. The requesting party may disregard an answer, even though it chooses to offer other answers from the same request into evidence.

There are, however, some minor disadvantages in propounding requests for admission. First, if requests are drawn too narrowly, they may reveal the drafting attorney's trial strategy. Second, unless drafted carefully and precisely, a denial will probably be upheld by the court, resulting in wasted time and money.

The ease with which answering parties effectively dodge requests for admission may be their greatest disadvantage. Often the answering party will respond to a request by stating that further discovery and investigation is necessary before it can give an intelligent response. In all likelihood, this response will be acceptable to the courts, especially early in the litigation. Another disadvantage of utilizing requests for admission is that the process of drafting requests may take substantially more time than the process of answering them. This is particularly true if the answering party can simply deny the requests.

§ 15:4 Actions in which requests for admissions may be used

Requests for admission may be made by any party upon any other party in an action. Information required from a non-party may be obtained by oral deposition or by a deposition upon written questions. In addition, documents and tangible things may be obtained from non-parties by subpoena.

§ 15:5 Timing

Fed. R. Civ. P. 26(f) requires that the parties meet to develop, among other things, a discovery plan. This meeting must take place as soon as practicable in the litigation process but, in any event, at least 21 days before a scheduling conference is held or a scheduling order is due under Rule 16(b). Fed. R. Civ. P. 16(b) requires that a scheduling order be entered within 90 days after the first appearance of a defendant or 120 days after the complaint has been served on any defendant, whichever occurs earlier. Together, Fed. R. Civ. P. 26 and 36 preclude the service of requests for admission until after the parties meet to develop a discovery plan, which may occur two or three months after the complaint is filed.

Fed. R. Civ. P. 36(a) is silent on how late in the litigation process a party may serve requests for admission. Trial courts have considerable discretion in determining the timeliness of discovery.

Some courts have local rules governing discovery cut-off dates. Where no such rules exist, scheduling orders and pretrial orders may set a time limit for the completion of discovery, including service of or response to requests for admission.

Requests should be served to allow sufficient time to complete the process before the discovery cut-off or trial deadline. Ideally, the discovery order should specify whether the discovery deadline is the deadline for service of requests for admission or for responses to such requests. If it is the latter, then requests must be served no less than 30 days before the discovery cut-off date.

Discovery requests served on the eve of trial may be stricken by the court, but the fact that a party has waited a considerable time before making a discovery request is no bar in itself to the discovery. Of course, the parties can stipulate to extend the time in which requests for admission may be served, provided they do not extend it beyond any discovery cut-off date imposed by the court. The fact that a motion for summary judgment has been filed, or that an evidentiary hearing has been conducted does not preclude the service of requests for admission.

§ 15:6 Number of requests

Fed. R. Civ. P. 33 limits the number of interrogatories a party may serve on an adversary without leave of court. No similar limits are placed on requests for admission. There is no limit on the number of times a party may serve requests for admission on an adversary. A party may serve multiple requests for admission as it learns more about the case.

Once the answers to the interrogatories are received, requests to produce electronically stored information and documents should be served on all parties. The requests to produce should seek all relevant documents, records, photographs and other tangible evidence, including any such evidence identified in the answer to interrogatories. The requesting party may also demand access to an adversary's computer to inspect and analyze electronically stored information. This would also be the time to serve document subpoenas on non-parties.

After the requesting party has received the electronically stored information, documents, and other tangible items, depositions should be taken of the opposing party and all essential witnesses. Depositions are designed to obtain detailed information from parties and non-parties, and to tie down each of them to a particular account of the relevant events. Depositions are also useful for obtaining admissions and other impeachment material. In cases where a party's physical or mental condition is at issue, a physical or mental examination of the party may be warranted at this point in the discovery process. In such cases, the requesting party must seek an order from the court requiring an adversary to appear for examination. After all other discovery has been completed, requests for admission should be served on the answering party.

§ 15:7 Service of requests

Requests may be served by delivering a copy to the party or mailing the requests to the party's last known address.[1] Once a party has appeared by counsel, the requests are served upon the attorney. A copy of the requests should also be served on all other parties to the action. Under Fed. R. Civ. P. 5(d), requests for admission must not be filed with the court until they are used in the proceeding or the court orders the filing.

§ 15:8 Form of requests

Each matter for which an admission is requested must be separately set forth in short, numbered paragraphs. Requests should be simple and direct statements containing a single proposition. A request should be phrased so it can be admitted or denied without explanation. A request should not be argumentative in tone.

Except when documents are sought to be authenticated, requests for admission should not incorporate outside material, such as pleadings, motions or deposition transcripts. Incorporation by reference is improper because it unjustly casts upon the answering party the burden of determining at its peril what portions of the incorporated material contain relevant matters of fact that must be either admitted or denied. Facts admitted in response to a request for admission should be ascertainable merely by examination of the request and of the answer. The requests for admission and the answers should be in such a form so as to be read to the jury, without reference to extraneous materials. Incorporation by reference also gives the answering party too much room to evade the admission. In complex cases, drafting attorneys should also consider defining terms that will be used in more than one request. An instruction section may also be appropriate in complicated cases.

[Section 15:7]

[1]See Fed. R. Civ. P. 5.

§ 15:9 Scope of requests

According to Fed. R. Civ. P. 36(a), a party may serve upon any other party a written request for admission of the truth of any matters within the scope of Fed. R. Civ. P. 26(b)(1). Essentially, Fed. R. Civ. P. 36(a) entitles a party to require any other party to admit or deny the truthfulness of opinions or facts; the application of law to fact; or the genuineness of documents. Requests for admission, in other words, may pertain to any fact or fact-based issue in the litigation.

Fed. R. Civ. P. 36 is not limited to matters known to the responding party. Fed. R. Civ. P. 36 requests may be directed to undisputed facts or to facts crucial to the case. The Advisory Committee explained the scope of Rule 36 as follows:

> [Rule 36] provides that a request may be made to admit any matters within the scope of Rule 26(b) that relate to statements or opinions of fact or of the application of law to fact. It thereby eliminates the requirement that the matter be "of fact." This change resolves conflicts in the court decisions as to whether a request to admit matters of "opinion" and matters involving "mixed law and fact" is proper under the rule.

§ 15:10 Effect of admission

Any matter admitted is conclusively established unless the court on motion permits withdrawal or amendment of the admission. Such admissions may be used only in the pending action.

§ 15:11 Authentication of documents and electronically stored information

Requests for admission are best suited for establishing the necessary foundation for real and documentary evidence at trial. Admissions may be used to obviate the need for authenticating a document or electronically stored information at trial. Being able to authenticate electronic documents by means of a request for admission is particularly useful. Using admissions for this purpose is common practice in state and federal courts.

It is not enough to ask the answering party to admit that a document or electronically stored information is genuine; rather, the requesting party must ensure that all foundational questions are included in the requests for admission. If a request asks the respondent to admit the genuineness of a document or electronically stored information, the document or a copy of the electronically stored information should be attached to the request and incorporated by reference.

The proper foundation for documents or electronically stored information can be established well in advance of trial, saving both time and money. In addition, a request may ask the answering party to admit the genuineness of documents belonging to someone other than the answering party, as long as the answering party has reasonable access to such documents or electronically stored information.

Fed. R. Civ. P. 36 does not require that the document or electronically stored information be attached to a request for admission. Rather it provides that "[c]opies of the documents shall be served with the request unless they have been or are otherwise furnished or made available for inspection and copying." If a document has already been identified in discovery, such as an exhibit in a prior deposition, it need not be attached to the requests for admission, so long as there is no question about which document the requesting party is referring to.

Because questions may arise as to how a party may admit the authenticity of electronically stored information, it may be helpful to print a hardcopy version of the file in question along with information relating to its creation date, author, etc. For example, when an e-mail is printed, the printout usually contains the original sender's name, the recipient, date of transmission, and other relevant information. All of this can be included on the document for which authentication is being requested.

If the proponent of the discovery desires to have an electronic file, itself, authenticated, this can be done by copying the file to WORM (write-once, read many) media. Certain types of writeable CDs are WORM. The party desiring authentication need only copy the relevant files to the CD. Thereafter, the files cannot be modified or changed in any way. The responding party can then be requested to admit the authenticity of the files indelibly stored on the CD.

II. CHECKLISTS

§ 15:12 Requests for admissions drafting checklist

- ☐ Review any interrogatories or depositions for damaging testimony and draft requests for admissions based on that information.
- ☐ When drafting, use an evolving discovery plan to focus firmly on proving your case (or disproving that of your opponent).
- ☐ Since requests for admissions are generally based on issues raised by the pleadings, they work best when they are constructed on a framework using the language of that pleading. Use the pleading as a form, adding or demanding

specifics as needed, depending on the level of disputed information.

- ☐ Draft with an extremely narrow focus. Any vagueness will provide grounds for denial.
- ☐ Keep requests for admissions simple. Complex or ambiguous requests will probably be objected to and not admitted.
- ☐ Stick to factual areas only. Avoid attempting to draw conclusions on issues of law.

III. FORMS

§ 15:13 Requests for admissions

[Caption]

The *[requesting party]* asks the *[responding party]* to respond within 30 days to these requests by admitting, for purposes of this action only and subject to objections to admissibility at trial:

1. The genuineness of the following documents, copies of which *[are attached] [are or have been furnished or made available for inspection and copying]*.

[List each document.]

The truth of each of the following statements: *[List each statement.]*

Dated: ________

[signature, etc.]

NOTES TO FORM

Commentary

This form is adapted from Official Form 51 approved by the U.S. Supreme Court.

§ 15:14 Requests for admissions—Another form

[Caption]

To: *[name]*

[Party 1], by counsel, pursuant to *[rule]*, hereby submits the following request for admissions.

You must file and serve a written response to this request within 30 days following service these requests. Your response to each matter may be in the form of an admission, a specific denial, an objection (with reasons clearly stated), or a statement that the matter cannot be admitted or denied. You may not give lack of information or knowledge as a reason for failure to admit or deny unless you state that you have made reasonable inquiry and the information known or readily available to you is insufficient to enable you to admit or deny.

TRUTHFULNESS OF FACTS

1. Each of the following documents exhibited with this request is genuine.

[List the documents, including electronically stored information, and describe each document.]

2. Each of the following statements is true.

[List the statements.]

Dated: ________

[signature etc.]

§ 15:15 Requests for admissions—Alternate form

[Caption]

To: *[name]*

[Party 1], by counsel, pursuant to *[rule]*, hereby submits the following request for admissions.

You must file and serve a written response to this request within 30 days following service these requests. Your response to each matter may be in the form of an admission, a specific denial, an objection (with reasons clearly stated), or a statement that the matter cannot be admitted or denied. You may not give lack of information or knowledge as a reason for failure to admit or deny unless you state that you have made reasonable inquiry and the information known or readily available to you is insufficient to enable you to admit or deny.

TRUTHFULNESS OF FACTS

Please admit the truthfulness of each of the facts set forth below.

REQUEST FOR ADMISSION NO. 1:

Admit that *[specify employee name]* was assigned the following e-mail address: *[specify e-mail address]*.

REQUEST FOR ADMISSION NO. 2:

Admit that *[specify company name]* is the registered owner of the following domain name: *[specify domain name]*.

REQUEST FOR ADMISSION NO. 3:

Admit that on or about *[specify date]* the following files were deleted from *[specify user name]*'s desktop computer.

REQUEST FOR ADMISSION NO. 4:

Admit that *[name]* had no disaster recovery plan in effect for the network as of *[date]*. For purposes of these Requests for Admissions, certain terms have the following definitions: The term "network" refers to the local area network located at, including, but not limited to, all files servers, client computers, workstations, firewalls, routers, proxy servers, Internet servers, mail servers, and application servers.

GENUINENESS OF DOCUMENTS

Please admit the genuineness of each of the documents described below; copies of the documents are attached to this Request.

REQUEST FOR ADMISSION RE GENUINENESS OF DOCUMENT NO. 1:

Admit that the e-mail dated *[specify date]* from *[specify sender]* to *[specify recipient]* is genuine. A copy of the e-mail is attached as Exhibit A.

REQUEST FOR ADMISSION RE GENUINENESS OF DOCUMENT NO. 2:

Admit that the audit trail, with a printout date of *[date]*, is genuine. A copy of the audit trail is attached as Exhibit B.

REQUEST FOR ADMISSION RE GENUINENESS OF DOCUMENT NO. 3:

Admit that the printout, dated *[date]*, of the files and directories residing on the hard disk of *[name's]* computer is genuine. A copy of the file and directory printout is attached as Exhibit C.

REQUEST FOR ADMISSION RE GENUINENESS OF DOCUMENT NO. 4:

Admit that the Employee Computer Use Policy, dated *[date]*, is genuine. A copy of the Policy is attached as Exhibit D.

REQUEST FOR ADMISSION RE GENUINENESS OF DOCUMENT NO. 5:

Admit that the Disaster Recovery Plan, dated *[date]*, is genuine. A copy of the Disaster Recovery Plan is attached as Exhibit E.

Dated: ________

[signature, etc.]

§ 15:16 Requests for admissions—Genuineness of documents

[Caption]

To: *[name]*

[Party 1], by counsel, pursuant to *[rule]*, hereby submits the following requests for admissions.

You must file and serve a written response to this request within 30 days following service these requests. Your response to each matter may be in the form of an admission, a specific denial, an objection (with reasons clearly stated), or a statement that the matter cannot be admitted or denied. You may not give lack of information or knowledge as a reason for failure to admit or deny unless you state that you have made reasonable inquiry and the information known or readily available to you is insufficient to enable you to admit or deny.

You are hereby requested to admit the genuineness of the following described documents:

1. The printout, dated *[date]*, of the files and directories residing on the hard disk of *[name's]* computer is genuine. A copy of the file and directory printout is attached as Exhibit D.

[Describe additional documents with specificity.]

Dated: ________

[signature, etc.]

§ 15:17 Motion for order that matter is admitted on grounds of insufficiency of answer or objection

[Caption]

MOTION FOR ORDER THAT MATTER IS ADMITTED

[Requesting party] moves the Court for an order that the answer of *[responding party]* to [requesting party's requests for admissions, as set forth below, does not comply with the requirements of *[rule]*, and that the facts as set forth below in *[responding party's]* requests for admissions be deemed admitted, and for an award of expenses in this matter pursuant to *[rule]*.

The grounds for this motion are as follows:

1. *[Requesting party]* served on *[responding party]* on *[date]*, requests for admissions of the following facts: *[include specific requests for admissions]*.

2. *[Responding party]* served on *[requesting party]* on *[date]*, a response to the requests for admissions as follows: *[include responding party's response verbatim]*.

3. *[Responding party's]* response does not contain a specific answer to *[requesting party's]* requests for admissions and does not comply with the requirements of *[rule]*, nor does it state any objection to *[requesting party's]* requests for admissions.

Dated: ________

[signature etc.]

§ 15:18 Motion for award of expenses incurred to prove matter opponent failed to admit

[Caption]

MOTION FOR AWARD OF EXPENSES

[Requesting party] moves the Court for an order requiring *[responding party]* to pay *[requesting party's]* reasonable expenses incurred in making proof, at the trial of the above-entitled action, of the matters of substantial importance listed below on the following grounds:

1. On *[date]*, *[requesting party]* served upon *[responding party]* and filed a request *[for the admission of the following facts: [number and list requests] [for the admission of the genuineness of the following documents: [number and list requests]*.

2. In response to *[requesting party's]* request for admissions, *[responding party]* served a response upon *[requesting party]* on *[date]*, *[in which [responding party] denied the following facts [list the fact statements denied] [in which plaintiff denied the genuineness of the following documents and here list the documents as in the request]*.

3. At the trial of the above-entitled action, *[requesting party]*t proved the truth of the facts so denied by *[responding party]* by prove of the genuineness of the documents by the following evidence *[describe]*, which evidence was not controverted by *[responding party]*.

The reasonable expenses incurred in the proof of the above-described facts were $____, as more fully appears by the attached *[affidavit] [declaration]*.

Dated: ________

[signature etc.]

Chapter 16

Discovery from Non-Parties of Electronically Stored Information

I. GUIDELINES

II. CHECKLISTS

III. FORMS

Research References

Treatises and Practice Aids

Grenig and Gleisner, eDiscovery & Digital Evidence §§ 7:10, 10:2 to 10:7

Trial Strategy

Recovery and Reconstruction of Electronic Mail as Evidence, 41 Am. Jur Proof of Facts 3d 1

Computer Technology in Civil Litigation, 71 Am. Jur. Trials 111

Additional References

Grenig & Kinsler, Handbook of Federal Civil Discovery and Disclosure § 5.10 (3d ed.)

Grenig, West's Federal Forms: District Court (4th ed.)

ABA Discovery Standards, http://www.abanet.org/litigation/discoverystandards/2005civildiscoverystandards.pdf

Federal Judicial Center, http://www.fjc.gov

The Sedona Conference, http://www.thesedonaconference.org

I. GUIDELINES

§ 16:1 Generally

Rules of civil procedure, including the Federal Rules of Civil Procedure, authorize the following formal methods for obtaining discovery:

- Depositions upon oral examination or written questions
- Written interrogatories
- Production of documents or things or permission to enter upon land or other property for inspection
- Physical or mental examination
- Requests for admission

Of these methods, only depositions can be used with respect to non-parties. In order to obtain documents or permission to inspect with respect to a non-party, the subpoena process must be used. Even the taking of a deposition of a non-party requires use of a subpoena.

Under the Federal Rules of Civil Procedure, Fed. R. Civ. P. 45(a) and (b) apply to the issuance of subpoenas for the attendance of witnesses and for the production of documents at the trial or hearing. Fed. R. Civ. P. 45(c) provides for the service of a subpoena. Fed. R. Civ. P. 45(d) contains provisions relating to deposition subpoenas. Fed. R. Civ. P. 45(e) contains provisions relating to the issuance and service of subpoenas.

§ 16:2 Subpoenas—Generally

There are two types of subpoenas:

- A subpoena ad testificandum compels the attendance of a witness.
- A subpoena duces tecum calls for the production of documents and things.

§ 16:3 Subpoenas—Issuance

In many state jurisdictions, the clerk of the court may issue the subpoena in blank to a party requesting it. Local rules may require a written request for subpoena. Fed. R. Civ. P. 45(a)(3) empowers an attorney to issue a subpoena, so long as the attorney is admitted in the district in which the action is pending. The attorney must sign the subpoena, but the seal of the court is no longer required. The attorney must specify the district court "from" which the subpoena is issued. The clerk will still issue the subpoena when a party itself applies for it.

In federal proceedings, a subpoena for attendance at a deposition is issued by the court for the district in which the deposition is to occur and bears the same case name and number as the case in the court where the trial is to occur. If a separate subpoena is issued commanding the production of documents or an inspection, the subpoena issues from the court for the district in which the production or inspection is to occur.

§ 16:4 Subpoenas—Service

Fed. R. Civ. P. 45(b) sets forth the requirements for serving a subpoena in federal cases. State and local rules should be consulted for other jurisdictions. Fed. R. Civ. P. 45(b)(2) permits a pretrial subpoena (e.g., a deposition subpoena or a subpoena seeking the pretrial production of documents) to be served in any of the following areas:

- Anywhere within the district of the court "by which" it is issued
- Anywhere within a 100-mile radius of the site selected for the deposition, production, or inspection
- Anywhere within the state containing that site.

It is necessary to issue the subpoena in the name of a district court whenever the witness from whom testimony or a document or other tangible is sought cannot be reached within any of the three enumerated areas as measured from the trial court. In seeking the proper district from which to issue a pretrial subpoena when the witness is not amenable to service within the stated areas measured from the trial court, the attorney should be careful to choose a district whose geography fully satisfies not only Fed. R. Civ. P. 45(b)(2), but also Fed. R. Civ. P. 45(c)(3)(A)(ii) and 45(e), if that is possible.

Fed. R. Civ. P. 45(e)(1) also allows service "at a place within the state where a state statute or rule of court permits service of a subpoena issued by a state court of general jurisdiction sitting in the place where the district court is held." When a statute of the United States so provides and upon proper application and cause, a court may authorize a subpoena for trial to be served outside the district or beyond 100 miles from the place of hearing or trial.

Service of the subpoena must be accompanied by tendering to the witness the fees for one day's attendance and the mileage allowed by law. Fees and mileage need not be tendered if the subpoena is issued on behalf of the United States or an officer or agency of the United States.

Whenever a subpoena under Fed. R. Civ. P. 45 is served on a person and sets up a deposition, Fed. R. Civ. P. 45(b)(1) requires that notice of the subpoena be given to parties before the subpoena is served on the person commanded to produce or permit inspection. Notice should be served in accordance with Fed. R. Civ. P. 5.

§ 16:5 Depositions

A non-party witness can be compelled to give deposition testimony only by service of a subpoena and the payment or tendering of a witness fee. An individual employee of a party who is not an officer, director, or managing agent of the party-entity may only be compelled to attend a deposition by subpoena.

In federal court, subpoenas for the attendance of a witness at a deposition are issued pursuant to Fed. R. Civ. P. 45(a)(2). These subpoenas must be issued from the court for the district in which the deposition is to be taken. Fed. R. Civ. P. 45(a)(2) and 45(c) limit the places at which a deposition may be taken. Fed. R. Civ. P. 45(a)(2) provides that a deposition subpoena must state the method of recording the testimony.

If a corporation, partnership, association, or governmental unit is a non-party, the subpoena must notify the entity of its duty to designate the person or persons to testify for it. If a subpoena is issued to a person not a party calling upon that person to produce documents but not to appear for the taking of a deposition or to testify, there is authority that the subpoena is irregular and must be quashed.

§ 16:6 Production of documents and electronically stored information—Generally

Document and electronically stored information requests under Fed. R. Civ. P. 34 may be used only against parties to the action. There are several ways to circumvent Fed. R. Civ. P. 34's party-only restriction, for the courts have shown a tendency to liberally construe the term "parties" for purposes of production. First, federal courts have permitted document production requests to be directed to persons who, though not technically parties to the action, are sufficiently similar to parties to allow the request.

Second, because Fed. R. Civ. P. 34 covers all documents and electronically stored information in the possession, custody, or control of a party, a party must produce documents and electronically stored information in the possession of its agents. As a result, a party cannot immunize documents and electronically stored information from inspection by turning it over to a non-party so long as it remains in the party's control.

Third, although Fed. R. Civ. P. 34 may not be used to discover materials from a non-party, Fed. R. Civ. P. 34(c) expressly provides that a person not a party to the action may be compelled to produce documents and things or to submit to an inspection as provided in Fed. R. Civ. P. 45. Fed. R. Civ. P. 45 authorizes a party to inspect the documents of non-parties by a subpoena duces tecum. Fourth, if an entity, typically a parent corporation, has been found to be the alter ego of a party, that entity may be subject to Fed. R. Civ. P. 34.

A subpoena duces tecum compels the production of documents and electronically stored information or things possessed or controlled by a non-party. If a subpoena duces tecum is served on one who has custody of records that belong to another person, formal notice should be served on the owner of the records before production will be required. A subpoena duces tecum may not be used to obtain privileged documents.

The form of a subpoena duces tecum is the same as a subpoena for the attendance of witnesses with the addition of language commanding the person to whom it is directed to produce the documents or things designated in the subpoena. The subpoena should designate with reasonable particularity the documents and electronically stored information to be produced. If a party does not know exactly what documents and electronically stored information it wishes produced, the party may require the production of all documents and electronically stored information relating to a certain specified matter or issue. If the documents and electronically stored information are to be produced at the taking of a deposition, the scope of the documents electronically stored information sought may be the same as the scope of discovery under the applicable rule of civil procedure

A subpoena duces tecum seeking production of electronically stored information or documents from a non-party may be used independently of the regular testimonial subpoena. A subpoena duces tecum may be used to obtain electronically stored information or documents from a non-party without any scheduling of a deposition of the non-party.

The party who seeks a pretrial production of electronically stored information or documents from a non-party through use of a subpoena duces tecum must serve notice on all the other parties, including the time and place of the examination and all related particulars. If testimony is also sought from the custodian of the electronically stored information or documents, the subpoena served on the custodian can include both testimonial and document production clauses. The scope of a subpoena duces tecum is as broad against a non-party as against a party.

Under Fed. R. Civ. P. 45(c)(1)(A), a person commanded to produce documents, electronically stored information, or tangible things, or to permit the inspection of premises, need not appear in person at the place of production or inspection unless also commanded to appear for a deposition, hearing, or trial.

Fed. R. Civ. P. 45(a)(1)(B) provides that a subpoena is available to permit testing and sampling as well as inspection and copying. Courts must vigilantly protect non-parties under Fed. R. Civ. P. 45(c) when testing and sampling are requested.

§ 16:7 Production of documents and electronically stored information—Form of production

Fed. R. Civ. P. 45(a)(1) provides that a subpoena can designate a form or forms for production of electronically stored information. Fed. R. Civ. P. 45(c)(2) authorizes the person served with a subpoena to object to the requested form or forms. Fed. R. Civ. P. 45(d)(1)(B) provides that, if the subpoena does not specify the form or forms for electronically stored information, the person served with the subpoena must produce electronically stored information in a form or forms in which it is usually maintained or in a form that is reasonably usable.[1]

One court has concluded that production of native format in re-

[Section 16:7]

[1]See Auto Club Family Ins. Co. v. Ahner, 2007 WL 2480322 (E.D. La. 2007) (third-party producer ordered to produce information in electronic format).

sponse to a subpoena was the least burdensome form for production.[2] However, because electronically stored information is frequently voluminous and setting up the necessary security protocols to protect the information may be time consuming, disruptive, and expensive, native format should not be considered presumptively the least burdensome form.

§ 16:8 Challenging a subpoena

The proper procedure for challenging a subpoena requiring personal attendance is by motion to quash. The court can modify or quash the subpoena if it is unreasonable or oppressive. When a nonparty seeks protection from discovery by means of a motion for a protective order or a motion to quash a subpoena, the district court must apply the balancing standards of relevance, need, confidentiality, and harm.[1]

Fed. R. Civ. P. 45(c)(2)(B) provides that a person commanded to produce documents or tangible things or to permit inspection may serve on the party or attorney designated in the subpoena a written objection to inspecting, copying, testing or sampling any or all of the materials or to inspecting the premises—or to producing electronically stored information in the form or forms requested. The objection must be served before the earlier of the time specified for compliance or 14 days after the subpoena is served.

If an objection is made, at any time, on notice to the commanded person, the serving party may move the issuing court for an order compelling production or inspection.[2] These acts may be required only as directed in the order, and the order must protect a person who is neither a party nor a party's officer from significant expense resulting from compliance.[3] An order requiring compliance must protect a person who is neither a party nor a party's officer from significant expense resulting from compliance.[4]

---

[2]In re Honeywell Intern., Inc. Securities Litigation, 230 F.R.D. 293 (S.D. N.Y. 2003).

[Section 16:8]

[1]Fed. R. Civ. P. 26(c) and 45. See, e.g., Snoznik v. Jeld-Wen, Inc., 259 F.R.D. 217 (W.D. N.C. 2009).

[2]See Cohen v. City of New York, 255 F.R.D. 110 (S.D. N.Y. 2008) (subpoena for videotapes of plaintiff's arrest upheld).

[3]Fed. R. Civ. P. 45(c)(1)(A).

[4]Fed. R. Civ. P. 45(c)(2)(B).

Under the Electronic Communications Privacy Act[5] an Internet service provider cannot be required to produce witness e-mails.[6] The Privacy Act does not provide an exception for civil discovery subpoenas from non-governmental parties.

§ 16:9 Protecting privileges or work product

The recipient of a subpoena duces tecum may refuse to produce privileged documents. If the issuing party contests the asserted privilege, a party can request the court to conduct an in camera inspection of the documents.

Fed. R. Civ. P. 45(d)(2) adds a procedure for asserting a privilege or protecting trial-preparation materials after production. If a non-party produces electronically stored information subject to a claim of privilege, Fed. R. Civ. P. 45(d)(2) require that, once notified, the receiving party promptly return, sequester, or destroy the specified information and not make any use of it until the privilege issue is resolved.

Media entities, such as newspapers, Internet service providers, and Website hosts, and may have standing to assert the First Amendment rights of users of its Website hosts may, under the principle of "jus tertii standing," assert First Amendment rights of their readers and subscribers.[1] The terms of service for an online blog may create a reasonable expectation of privacy for registered users, for First Amendment purposes, where the blog's privacy policy reflects that the media company would disclose user's personally identifiable information only in very limited situations.[2]

§ 16:10 Protection from undue burden or expenses

Fed. R. Civ. P. 45(c)(1) requires a party or attorney responsible for issuing and serving a subpoena to take reasonable steps to

---

[5]18 U.S.C.A. §§ 2510 to 2521, 18 U.S.C.A. §§ 2701 to 2710.

[6]In re Subpoena Duces Tecum to AOL, LLC, 550 F. Supp. 2d 606 (E.D. Va. 2008).

[Section 16:9]

[1]McVicker v. King, 266 F.R.D. 92, 108 Fair Empl. Prac. Cas. (BNA) 1462, 38 Media L. Rep. (BNA) 1650 (W.D. Pa. 2010).

[2]McVicker v. King, 266 F.R.D. 92, 108 Fair Empl. Prac. Cas. (BNA) 1462, 38 Media L. Rep. (BNA) 1650 (W.D. Pa. 2010) (need for discovery did not outweigh First Amendment rights of bloggers). But see Arista Records, LLC v. Doe 3, 604 F.3d 110, 94 U.S.P.Q.2d 1587 (2d Cir. 2010) (defendant's First Amendment right to anonymity did not warrant quashing of recording companies' subpoena).

avoid imposing undue burden or expense on a person subject to the subpoena. The issuing court must enforce this duty and impose an appropriate sanction—which may include lost earnings and reasonable attorney fees—on a party or attorney who fails to comply.

Under Fed. R. Civ. P. 45(c), third parties enjoy more protection from burdensome and costly discovery than parties. Fed. R. Civ. P. 45(d)(1)(D) permits the responding person to refuse to provide discovery of electronically stored information from sources the party identifies as not reasonably accessible, unless the court orders such discovery for good cause.[1] A third-party seeking a protective order must make a particular and specific demonstration of fact in support of its motion.[2]

In *Apple, Inc. v. Samsung Electronics Co.*,[3] the court granted Apple's motion to compel Google, a non-party, to produce the search terms and list of custodian Google used when responding to Apple's subpoena. The court concluded the production of Google's search terms and custodians to Apple will aid in uncovering the sufficiency of Google's production and served the greater purposes of transparency in discovery.[4]

II. CHECKLISTS

§ 16:11 Deposition subpoena checklist

☐ Check local rules of the applicable jurisdiction regarding subpoenas.

[Section 16:10]

[1]Auto Club Family Ins. Co. v. Ahner, 2007 WL 2480322 (E.D. La. 2007) (lawyer's statement in memorandum in support of motion for protective order that electronically stored information is not reasonably accessible or that it would be unduly burdensome to comply with request was not evidence). See, e.g., Bank of America Corp. v. SR Intern. Business Ins. Co., Ltd., 2006 NCBC 15, 2006 WL 3093174 (N.C. Super. Ct. 2006) (subpoena requesting production of e-mails from eight persons over a two-year period from 350 to 400 backup tapes was found to be undue burden on a non-party); U.S. v. Amerigroup Illinois, Inc., 2005 WL 3111972 (N.D. Ill. 2005) (subpoena seeking production was undue burden where it was difficult and time consuming for non-party to restore deleted e-mails, and backup tapes were by their very nature highly inaccessible)

[2]Auto Club Family Ins. Co. v. Ahner, 2007 WL 2480322 (E.D. La. 2007) (rejecting motion for protective order permitting movant to provide hard copy of files rather than electronic version).

[3]Apple, Inc. v. Samsung Electronics Co. Ltd., 2013 WL 1942163 (N.D. Cal. 2013).

[4]See also DeGeer v. Gillis, 755 F. Supp. 2d 909 (N.D. Ill. 2010).

- ☐ Use the jurisdiction's form for a deposition subpoena, or use that form as a model for your own form.
- ☐ If you are requesting documents at the deposition, draft a subpoena duces tecum.
- ☐ Serve the notice of deposition on all parties.
- ☐ In many jurisdictions you will need to have the court issue the subpoena. You will need proof of service of the notice of deposition, along with the notice and the subpoena itself. In some jurisdictions, California for example, any attorney of record may issue a subpoena. Submit duplicate copies of all items so they may be file-stamped and returned to you for your files.
- ☐ after checking jurisdiction rules for witness fees, attach a check for the witness fee to a photocopy of the subpoena. A copy is left with the deponent, and the original is simply displayed at the time of service.
- ☐ Hire a process server to complete service and provide the server with the witness fee check, the original and a copy of the subpoena and any information that will help locate the deponent for efficient and accurate service.

III. FORMS

§ 16:12 Deposition subpoena

[Caption]

To: *[name]*

Greeting:

We command you, that all business and excuses being laid aside, you and each of you attend before an officer authorized by law to take deposition at *[address]*, on *[date]*, at *[time]*, to testify and give evidence on behalf of the *[party]* in a case pending and undetermined in the *[court]* in which *[name 1]* is plaintiff and *[name 2]* is one of the defendants, No. __.

And this you shall in no way omit, under the penalty of the law in that case made and provided, and you also are to diligently and carefully search for and bring with you and produce at the time and place stated above the documents described in Attachment A.

The testimony shall be recorded by *[sound] [sound and visual] [videotape] [stenographic means]*.

Dated __

[signature etc.]

ATTACHMENT A TO SUBPOENA

Instructions

Documents to be produced include all documents in the possession, custody or control of *[organization]*, wherever located, including documents in the possession, custody or control of its directors, officers, employees, representatives or agents. As used in this subpoena, the term "document" means any written, recorded, or graphic material of any kind, whether prepared by a director, officer, employee, representative, or agent of *[organization]* or by any other person, that is in *[organization's]* possession, custody, or control. Without limitation on the term "control," a document is deemed to be in *[organization's]* control if you have the right to secure that document or a copy thereof from another person.

The terms "documents" and "records," as used in this subpoena include any relevant electronic files, stored on file servers, e-mail servers, hard drives, or other electronic storage media within *[organization's]* control. The terms "documents" and "records" refer to and include every document, report, summary, bulletin, manual, purchase order, purchase contract, release, map, policy statement, notation, worksheet, memorandum, letter or other written record reflecting the indicated information. Any such electronic documents or records are to be produced in usable form, along with instructions for reading such data.

Documents to Be Produced

[List of documents]

§ 16:13 Deposition subpoena—Another form

[Caption]

To: *[name]*

YOU ARE HEREBY COMMANDED to appear in the office of *[attorney's office and address]* to give testimony in the above-entitled cause on *[date]*, at *[time]*, to bring with you the documents described in the attached Addendum, and not to depart without leave.

The testimony shall be recorded by *[sound] [sound and visual] [videotape] [stenographic means]*.

Dated: ____

[signature etc.]

ADDENDUM TO CIVIL SUBPOENA TO __

(a) all documents, upon which you intend to rely in your testimony;

(b) all documents referring in any way, either directly or indirectly, to communications between you *[or anyone else associated with [describe]]* and *[describe]* relating to: *[describe with particularity subject matter of deposition]*.

§ 16:14 Deposition subpoena—Corporate officer

[Caption]

To: *[name]*

Greeting:

We Command You, that all business and excuses being laid aside, you and each of you attend at *[address]*, on *[date]*, at *[time]*, to testify and give evidence in a certain cause now pending and undetermined in the Court, in which *[name 1]* is plaintiff and *[name 2]*, on the part of *[defendant] [name 2]*.

And you also are to diligently and carefully search for, examine, and inquire after and bring with you, and produce at the above time and place, the documents described in the attached schedule and made a part of this subpoena which are in the possession, custody or control of *[name 1]*, or any of its subsidiaries or controlled companies, or the officers, directors, agents, representatives, employees or counsel of any of them.

The testimony shall be recorded by *[sound] [sound and visual] [videotape] [stenographic means]*.

Definitions

The term "documents" includes all writings, or records of any kind, including, but not limited to, the originals and all copies and drafts of contracts, agreements, and amendments to them, correspondence, e-mail, text messages, memoranda, reports, recordings and other transcription of telephone or other conversations, conferences or meetings, affidavits, books of account, transcripts of testimony in judicial or administrative proceedings, minutes of meetings, including directors' meetings and committee meetings, diaries, intra-office communications, logs, advertisements, scrap-books, press and publicity releases, reports to stockholders or to governmental bodies, records, reports, or summaries of negotiations and all other writings of every kind, including documents passing from or to or between *[name 1]* or its domestic or foreign subsidiaries or affiliated or controlled companies, or the officers, or representatives or any of them, and any documents passing from or to or between those companies and foreign companies, or the officers, directors, agents, representatives, employees or counsel of any of them.

The term "*[name 1]*" as used here includes *[specify]* and any and all domestic or foreign subsidiaries and affiliated companies under the control of *[name 1]*.

The term "patent" as used here means any patent usable in the manufacture or sale of radio and television apparatus or any constituent part.

Subpoena Duces Tecum

1. All documents referring or relating to foreign patents or foreign patent licenses or rights of any kind covering any invention which is the subject of any United States patent licensed under the standard license agreements issued or proffered by *[name 1]* to any licensee or prospective licensee in the United States at any time during the life of the patent in suit.
2. All communications between *[name 1]* and any company or person having licensing rights under foreign patents of *[name 1]*, referring to or relating to the actual or proposed licensing of any foreign patent on inventions which are the subject of any United States patent licensed under any *[name 1]* standard license agreement issued or proffered in the United States at any time during the life of the patent in suit.
3. All documents referring or relating to the following foreign patent licensing organizations or any of their patent pooling or licensing activities: *[list]* Any other foreign patent pool or company or organization having licensing rights under any of the patents of *[name 1]* and any other patentee and all communications between *[name 1]* or any of its officers, agents, representatives or counsel and any of the foreign patent licensing organizations, or any of the officers, agents, representatives or counsel of any of the organizations.
4. All documents concerning the creation, administration, operation, purposes or policies of any and all patent pools or licensing organizations having rights in respect of patents of *[name 1]* or foreign patents covering inventions of *[name 1]*, including without limiting the generality of the foregoing, *[list]*.

5. All documents referring or relating to the issuance or denial of any license to import or export under any foreign patent of *[name 1]*.
6. All documents relating to the assertion against *[name 2]* or others engaged in the manufacture or sale of *[describe]* in the United States of America, Canada or any other country of any foreign or domestic patents or patent rights owned or licensed by *[name 1]*.
7. All documents relating or referring to policies or practices of *[name 1]* or of any person having a right to extend licenses under any patent rights of *[name 1]* in the United States of America or any foreign country in respect of any actual or proposed license of the export or import of *[describe]*.
8. All documents relating or referring to any request or inquiry, by any person or company manufacturing or selling *[describe]*, for a license under some but less than all of the patent rights owned by *[name 1]* or in which *[name 1]* has, or at any time during the life of the patent in suit has had, a beneficial interest.
9. All documents relating or referring to package licensing of *[name 1]* patent rights, together with all copies, drafts, and vouchers relating to the documents, and all other documents, letters, and paper writings whatsoever, that can or may afford any information or evidence in this cause. And this you shall not omit, under the penalty of the law in that case made and provided.

Dated: ____

[signature etc.]

§ 16:15 Request for subpoena

[Caption]

To: Clerk of the Court:

Please issue a Subpoena for *[name 1]* to appear as witness on behalf of *[name of party] [at a deposition scheduled for [time]* on *[date]*.

Dated: ____

[signature etc.]

NOTES TO FORM

Commentary

Local rules may require a request for a subpoena. This form may be modified to conform to local requirements. Rule 45 permits the attorney for a party to issue a subpoena.

§ 16:16 Notice of taking deposition upon oral examination—Naming and describing person not a party

[Caption]

To: *[names]*

Please take notice that at *[time]* on *[date]*, at *[address]*, *[defendant] [plaintiff] [name 1]* will take the deposition upon oral examination of *[name 2]* before *[name 3]*, a notary public, or before some other officer authorized by law to take depositions. The oral examination will continue from day-to-day until completed. You are invited to attend and cross-examine.

The testimony will be recorded by *[sound] [sound and visual] [videotape] [stenographic means]*.

Dated: __

[signature etc.]

§ 16:17 Notice of taking of deposition of witness—Including designation of materials in related subpoena duces tecum

[Caption]

To: *[names]*

Please take notice that at *[time]* on *[date]*, at *[address]*, *[defendant] [plaintiff] [name 1]* will take the deposition of *[name 2]*, of *[address]*, upon oral examination before *[name 3]*, a notary public, or before some other officer authorized by law to take depositions. The oral examination will continue from day-to-day until completed. You are invited to attend and cross-examine.

Attached is a designation of the materials to be produced upon the oral examination of *[name 2]*, pursuant to a subpoena duces tecum to be served upon that person.

The testimony will be recorded by *[sound] [sound and visual] [videotape] [stenographic means]*.

Dated: ____

[signature etc.]

§ 16:18 Notice of taking deposition of witness—Including reference to materials designated in attached subpoena

[Caption]

To: *[names]*

PLEASE TAKE NOTICE that pursuant to Rule 30 of the Federal Rules of Civil Procedure, *[defendant] [plaintiff] [name 1]* will take the deposition upon oral examination of *[name 2]* before a notary public on *[date]*, at *[time]*, and thereafter from day-to-day until completed, at *[address]*.

[Defendant] [Plaintiff] [name 1] requests that deponent bring to this deposition all documents described in the attached Addendum to Civil Subpoena.

The testimony will be recorded by *[sound] [sound and visual] [videotape] [stenographic means]*.

Dated: ____

[signature etc.]

Chapter 17

Privilege and Privacy

I. GUIDELINES

A. INTRODUCTION

B. STATUTES PROTECTING ELECTRONICALLY STORED INFORMATION

C. WORK PRODUCT

D. PRIVILEGES

E. LEGAL HOLD NOTICES

F. FIFTH AMENDMENT

G. INADVERTENT PRODUCTION

II. CHECKLISTS

III. FORMS

Research References

Treatises and Practice Aids

Grenig and Gleisner, eDiscovery & Digital Evidence §§ 10:8 to 10:19

Trial Strategy

Recovery and Reconstruction of Electronic Mail as Evidence, 41 Am. Jur Proof of Facts 3d 1

Computer Technology in Civil Litigation, 71 Am. Jur Trials 111

Additional References

ABA Discovery Standards, www.abanet.org/litigation/discoverystandards/2005civildiscoverystandards.pdf

Electronic Discovery Reference Model Project, http://www.edrm.net

Federal Judicial Center, http://www.fjc.gov

The Sedona Conference, http://www.thesedonaconference.org

> **KeyCite®:** Cases and other legal materials listed in KeyCite Scope can be researched through the KeyCite service on Westlaw®. Use KeyCite to check citations for form, parallel references, prior and later history, and comprehensive citator information, including citations to other decisions and secondary materials.

I. GUIDELINES

A. INTRODUCTION

§ 17:1 Generally

Although confidential information of a person or an organization may become subject to discovery once litigation commences, some confidential information may be protected by federal or state statutes, common law privileges, or the attorney work-product doctrine. In addition, parties frequently agree at the beginning of litigation on appropriate restrictions regarding the discovering party's right to use or disseminate confidential discovery material.

It is important to protect confidential or private information from formal and informal discovery.[1] Even during the most contentious litigation, serious consideration must be given to implementing appropriate procedures to protect digital information from inadvertent disclosure as well as intentional interception or tampering.

[Section 17:1]

[1]See Sedona Principle 10 ("A responding party should follow reasonable procedures to protect privileges and objections in connection with the production of electronically stored information."); Barkett, *The Challenge of Electronic Communications: Privilege, Privacy, and Other Myths*, Litig., Fall 2011, at 17; Jaeger and Smith, *Computer and Electronic Snooping: Opportunities to Violate State and Federal Law*, 34 Am. J. Trial Advoc. 473 (2011); Dietrich, *Preserve Confidentiality When Using Technology*, Wis. L., Feb. 2012, at 24.

§ 17:2 First Amendment Protection

An author's decision to remain anonymous is an aspect of the freedom of speech protected by the First Amendment.[1] This First Amendment protection extends to speech via the Internet.[2] Anonymous speech on the Internet, like speech from identifiable sources, does not have absolute protection.[3] Courts have ordered disclosure of identifying subscriber information in circumstances involving copyright infringement,[4] and where the anonymous

---

[Section 17:2]

[1]McIntyre v. Ohio Elections Com'n, 514 U.S. 334, 342, 115 S. Ct. 1511, 131 L. Ed. 2d 426, 23 Media L. Rep. (BNA) 1577 (1995) (ban on distributing anonymous campaign literature violates First Amendment; anonymity is a shield from tyranny of majority). See also Buckley v. American Constitutional Law Foundation, Inc., 525 U.S. 182, 200, 119 S. Ct. 636, 142 L. Ed. 2d 599 (1999) (Colorado law requiring initiative-petition circulators wear name badge violated First Amendment).

[2]See Reno v. American Civil Liberties Union, 521 U.S. 844, 870, 117 S. Ct. 2329, 138 L. Ed. 2d 874, 25 Media L. Rep. (BNA) 1833 (1997) (Supreme Court precedent provides no basis for qualifying level of First Amendment scrutiny that should be applied to Internet); McVicker v. King, 266 F.R.D. 92, 108 Fair Empl. Prac. Cas. (BNA) 1462, 38 Media L. Rep. (BNA) 1650 (W.D. Pa. 2010) (need for discovery did not outweigh First Amendment rights of anonymous bloggers).

[3]See Patrick Collins, Inc. v. Does 1-26, 843 F. Supp. 2d 565 (E.D. Pa. 2011) (factors court considers when weighing party's need to discover identity of Internet service provider subscriber against subscriber's First Amendment interest in maintaining anonymity include: (1) party's concrete showing of prima facie claim of actionable harm; (2) specificity of party's discovery request; (3) absence of alternative means to obtain subpoenaed information; (4) central need for subpoenaed information to advance party's claim; and (5) subscriber's expectation of privacy).

[4]See First Time Videos, LLC v. Does 1-500, 276 F.R.D. 241, 80 Fed. R. Serv. 3d 106 (N.D. Ill. 2011) (alleged infringers' First Amendment right to anonymous speech on Internet could not overcome right of owner of adult videos and photographs to use judicial process to pursue its prima facie copyright infringement claims by serving subpoenas on alleged infringers' Internet service providers seeking their names, addresses, telephone numbers, e-mail addresses, and Media Access Control addresses); Call of the Wild Movie, LLC v. Does 1-1,062, 770 F. Supp. 2d 332, 79 Fed. R. Serv. 3d 203 (D.D.C. 2011) (although Internet file-sharers engage in expressive activity when they interact with other users via file-sharing protocol, First Amendment interest implicated is minimal, since file-sharers' ultimate aim is not to communicate a thought or convey an idea, but to obtain copyrighted movies and music for free, and even if expression is ancillary aim, underlying method of communication is illegal, and therefore file-sharer's First Amendment right to anonymity is exceedingly small); London-Sire Records, Inc. v. Doe 1, 542 F. Supp. 2d 153, 231 Ed. Law Rep. 750 (D. Mass. 2008) (copyright infringement, per se, is clearly not speech entitled to First Amendment protection).

speaker allegedly made defamatory statements and disclosed confidential insider information online.[5]

Federal and state trial courts have developed a range of standards that plaintiffs must satisfy in order to obtain information related to the anonymous speaker's identity.[6] A party seeking disclosure must clear a higher hurdle where the anonymous poster is a non-party.[7]

---

[5]See McVicker v. King, 266 F.R.D. 92, 108 Fair Empl. Prac. Cas. (BNA) 1462, 38 Media L. Rep. (BNA) 1650 (W.D. Pa. 2010) (need for discovery in defamation act did not outweigh First Amendment rights of anonymous bloggers).

[6]See Patrick Collins, Inc. v. Does 1-26, 843 F. Supp. 2d 565 (E.D. Pa. 2011) (factors court considers when weighing party's need to discover identity of Internet service provider subscriber against subscriber's First Amendment interest in maintaining anonymity include: (1) party's concrete showing of prima facie claim of actionable harm; (2) specificity of party's discovery request; (3) absence of alternative means to obtain subpoenaed information; (4) central need for subpoenaed information to advance party's claim; and (5) subscriber's expectation of privacy); Enterline v. Pocono Medical Center, 751 F. Supp. 2d 782, 37 Media L. Rep. (BNA) 1057 (M.D. Pa. 2008) (applying four-part test); Doe I v. Individuals, 561 F. Supp. 2d 249, 254–55 (D. Conn. 2008) (setting forth a seven-factor test); Krinsky v. Doe 6, 159 Cal. App. 4th 1154, 72 Cal. Rptr. 3d 231, 245, 36 Media L. Rep. (BNA) 1321 (6th Dist. 2008) (collecting and analyzing cases); Doe v. Cahill, 884 A.2d 451, 460, 33 Media L. Rep. (BNA) 2441 (Del. 2005) (holding disclosure may only be obtained if plaintiff comes forward with "facts sufficient to defeat a summary judgment motion"); Dendrite Intern., Inc. v. Doe No. 3, 342 N.J. Super. 134, 775 A.2d 756, 17 I.E.R. Cas. (BNA) 1336, 29 Media L. Rep. (BNA) 2265 (App. Div. 2001) (requiring plaintiff to set forth a prima facie cause of action).

[7]See McVicker v. King, 266 F.R.D. 92, 108 Fair Empl. Prac. Cas. (BNA) 1462, 38 Media L. Rep. (BNA) 1650 (W.D. Pa. 2010) (need for discovery sought in former employee's action against borough and council members did not outweigh First Amendment rights of anonymous bloggers, for purposes of subpoena directed to non-party media company; even though subpoena was issued in good faith and information sought was relevant to employee's core claims, information for impeaching individual defendants was available from other sources); Doe v. 2TheMart.com Inc., 140 F. Supp. 2d 1088, 1095, 29 Media L. Rep. (BNA) 1970, 49 Fed. R. Serv. 3d 404, 120 A.L.R.5th 725 (W.D. Wash. 2001) (to enforce civil subpoena seeking identifying information of non-party individual who has communicated anonymously over Internet, party seeking information must demonstrate, by clear showing on record, that: (1) subpoena seeking information was issued in good faith and not for any improper purpose, (2) information sought relates to core claim or defense, (3) identifying information is directly and materially relevant to claim or defense, and (4) information sufficient to establish or to disprove claim or defense is unavailable from any other source); Mobilisa, Inc. v. Doe, 217 Ariz. 103, 170 P.3d 712, 720, 36 Media L. Rep. (BNA) 2007 (Ct. App. Div. 1 2007) (where anonymous poster is nonparty witness "along with a number of known witnesses with the same information," the "potential for chilling speech by unmasking identity of anonymous or pseud-

The trend among courts that have been presented with the question of whether an Internet provider has standing to assert an anonymous poster's rights is to hold that entities such as newspapers, Internet service providers, and Website hosts may, under the principle of jus tertii standing, assert the rights of their readers and subscribers.[8]

In *Enterline v. Pocono Medical Center*,[9] the court held that a newspaper had standing to assert the constitutional rights of anonymous posters to its Website. The *Enterline* court concluded that "the relationship between [the newspaper] and readers posting in the [n]ewspaper's online forums is the type of relationship that allows [the newspaper] to assert the First Amendment rights of the anonymous commentators."[10] The court further held that (1) the anonymous commentators to the newspaper Website faced practical obstacles to asserting their own First Amendment rights because doing so would require revelation of their identities; (2) the newspaper itself displays the adequate injury-in-fact to satisfy Article III's case or controversy requirements; and (3) the newspaper will zealously argue and frame the issues before the court.

In *McVicker v. King*,[11] the court that the terms service agreement provided that the identity of the user will be protected. According to the court, the provider's privacy policy clearly reflected that the provider would disclose its users personally identifiable information only in very limited situations. The court found the terms of service of a blog created an expectation of privacy for any registered user.

The *McVicker* court rejected the argument that the personally identifiable information of the bloggers should be disclosed because "the identity of the bloggers would be relevant to impeach" the testimony of the four individual defendants. The court considered whether (1) the subpoena seeking the information was issued in good faith and not for any improper purpose, (2) the information sought relates to a core claim or defense, (3)

---

onymous IInternet speaker" weighs against disclosure when balancing test is performed).

[8]McVicker v. King, 266 F.R.D. 92, 108 Fair Empl. Prac. Cas. (BNA) 1462, 38 Media L. Rep. (BNA) 1650 (W.D. Pa. 2010).

[9]Enterline v. Pocono Medical Center, 751 F. Supp. 2d 782, 37 Media L. Rep. (BNA) 1057 (M.D. Pa. 2008).

[10]Enterline v. Pocono Medical Center, 751 F. Supp. 2d 782, 37 Media L. Rep. (BNA) 1057 (M.D. Pa. 2008).

[11]McVicker v. King, 266 F.R.D. 92, 108 Fair Empl. Prac. Cas. (BNA) 1462, 38 Media L. Rep. (BNA) 1650 (W.D. Pa. 2010).

the identifying information is directly and materially relevant to that claim or defense, and (4) information sufficient to establish or to disprove that claim or defense is unavailable from any other source.

Applying the first of the four factors the court found the subpoena was issued in good faith and not for any improper purpose. Turning to the second factor, the court found the information sought related to a core claim in the plaintiff's case. As to the third factor, the court found the plaintiff had not demonstrated the identifying information was directly and materially relevant to that claim or defense. With respect to the fourth and final factor, the court found that plaintiff had not demonstrated that the information requested was not available from other sources.

B. STATUTES PROTECTING ELECTRONICALLY STORED INFORMATION

§ 17:3 Health Insurance Portability and Accountability Act—Generally

The Health Insurance Portability and Accountability Act[1] ("HIPAA") was enacted in 1996 to address various issues related to health insurance and medical care. One of the purposes of HIPAA is to provide uniform privacy protection for health care records. Title II of HIPAA provides extensive rules regarding the secure storage and exchange of electronic data transactions and requirements promoting the confidentiality and privacy of individually identifiable health information. The Secretary of Health and Human Services has issued HIPAA regulations limiting disclosure of protected healthcare information.[2]

HIPAA generally applies only to:[3]

- health plans,
- health care clearinghouses, and
- health care providers ("providers").

HIPAA also obligates providers to enter into contracts with "business associates"—a term including any person or entity having access to the provider's medical records or information—requiring the business associates to comply with HIPAA.

HIPAA applies only to "protected health information," broadly

---

[Section 17:3]

[1]Pub. L. No. 104-191.

[2]45 C.F.R. § 164.512.

[3]45 C.F.R. § 160.102.

defined to include any individually identifiable health information. This includes any records or information that identifies an individual or could reasonably be used to identify an individual.[4]

HIPAA regulates the methods by which a health care provider may release a patient's health information, including oral medical records. An attorney must comply with HIPAA before communicating (whether informally or through discovery) with a patient's treating physician. HIPAA provides three mechanisms for discovery of health care information in civil litigation. These are:

- Patient authorization
- Court order
- Certain types of subpoenas or discovery requests

§ 17:4 Health Insurance Portability and Accountability Act—Obtaining patient's health care records or information

Probably the easiest and least expensive method of obtaining a patient's health care records or information is to have the patient execute a HIPAA authorization. A health care provider may release a patient's protected health information to an attorney or litigant upon receipt of a HIPAA authorization executed by the patient. To be effective, a HIPAA authorization must include a long list of criteria spelled out in 45 C.F.R. § 164.508. These criteria must be tailored to each case. It is also advisable to attach a cover letter to any patient authorization explaining that the authorization complies with HIPAA.

The second method for discovering protected health care records and information is by order of a court or administrative tribunal.[1] The health care provider may only disclose the health care information expressly authorized by the order. Thus, the parties and the court must ensure that the order is prepared with precision. The order may result from a contested motion or by agreement of the parties. A court may also order a party to sign a HIPAA patient authorization. A subpoena signed by a judge should suffice as a HIPAA order.

Protected health information may be discovered by subpoena,

---

[4] 45 C.F.R. § 160.103.

[Section 17:4]

[1] 45 C.F.R. § 164.512(e). See, e.g., A Helping Hand, LLC v. Baltimore County, Md., 295 F. Supp. 2d 585, 592 (D. Md. 2003) (courts may order disclosure of protected health information).

discovery request, or other lawful process if the health care provider receives satisfactory assurance, as described below, from the discovering party that reasonable efforts have been made by the discovering party to:

- Ensure that the individual who is the subject of the protected health information that has been requested (i.e., the patient) has been given notice of the request; or
- Secure a qualified protective order that meets the requirements set forth below.[2]

Satisfactory assurance that the discovering party has given notice to the patient exists where the health care provider receives from the discovering party a written statement and accompanying documentation demonstrating that:

- The discovering party has made a good faith attempt to provide written notice to the patient (or, if the patient's location is unknown, to mail notice to the patient's last known address);
- The notice includes sufficient information about the litigation or proceeding in which the protected health information is requested to permit the patient to raise an objection to the court or administrative tribunal; and
- The time (probably a minimum of 10 days) for the patient to raise objections has elapsed and no objections were filed or all objections were resolved in favor of the discovering party.

The subpoena should not be served on the health care provider until the time for objections has expired.

Satisfactory assurance that the discovering party has made reasonable efforts to secure a qualified protective order exists where the health care provider receives from the discovering party a written statement and accompanying documentation demonstrating that:

- The parties to the dispute giving rise to the request for information have agreed to a qualified protective order and have presented it to the court or administrative tribunal with jurisdiction over the dispute;[3] or
- The discovering party has requested a qualified protective

[2]45 C.F.R. § 164.512(e)(1)(ii).

[3]45 C.F.R. § 164.512(e)(1)(iii) to (iv). See, e.g., Hutton v. City of Martinez, 219 F.R.D. 164, 57 Fed. R. Serv. 3d 850 (N.D. Cal. 2003) (health care provider ordered to release records where the parties had agreed to qualified protective order).

order from such court or administrative tribunal.[4] HIPAA does not require the entry of a protective order; it merely requires the discovering party to make reasonable efforts to secure a qualified protective order.

A "qualified protective order" is an order of a court or of an administrative tribunal or a stipulation by the parties that: (1) prohibits the parties from using or disclosing the protected health information for any purpose other than the litigation or proceeding for which such information was requested; and (2) requires the return to the covered entity or destruction of the protected health information (including all copies made) at the end of the litigation or proceeding.[5]

§ 17:5 Federal Wiretap Act

The Federal Wiretap Act[1] prohibits the unauthorized interception and disclosure of wire, oral or electronic communications.[2] "Electronic communication" includes e-mail, voice mail, cellular telephones, and satellite communications.[3] Online communications are covered by the Act.[4]

Federal courts have consistently held that, in order to be intercepted, electronic communications must be acquired contemporaneously with transmission and that electronic communications are not intercepted within the meaning of the Act if they are retrieved from storage.[5]

Producing counsel normally will not be justified under the Act

---

[4] 45 C.F.R. § 164.512(e)(1)(iv).

[5] 45 C.F.R. § 164.512(e)(1)(iii) and (vi).

[Section 17:5]

[1] 18 U.S.C.A. §§ 2510 et seq. The Act is Title III of the Omnibus Crime Control and Safe Streets Act of 1968.

[2] 18 U.S.C.A. § 2511.

[3] 18 U.S.C.A. § 2510(12).

[4] 18 U.S.C.A. § 2510(1). See, e.g., In re Pharmatrak, Inc., 329 F.3d 9, 18 (1st Cir. 2003) (transmissions of completed online forms constitute electronic communications under Act); U.S. v. Kennedy, 81 F. Supp. 2d 1103 (D. Kan. 2000) (applying Act to collection and disclosure of Internet subscriber information); U.S. v. Hambrick, 225 F.3d 656 (4th Cir. 2000) (analyzing Internet service's providing customer information under Act).

[5] See Theofel v. Farey-Jones, 359 F.3d 1066, 1077 (9th Cir. 2004) (no "interception" occurred in violation of Wiretap Act when defendant allegedly gained unauthorized access to plaintiff's e-mails that were already delivered to recipients and stored electronically by plaintiff's Internet service provider); In re Pharmatrak, Inc., 329 F.3d 9, 22 (1st Cir. 2003) (contemporaneous aspect of interception clearly present where Web traffic monitoring service's computer

in refusing to produce e-mail or other digital evidence contained on a discovery target's computer system on the theory it is protected from disclosure as a form of communication. In almost every instance, e-mail sought during discovery will be on some type of storage media, and thus "interception" within the meaning of the Act will not be a valid concern.

§ 17:6 Electronic Communications Privacy Act

The Electronic Communications Privacy Act[1] ("ECPA") extensively amended the Federal Wiretap Act.[2] It prohibits the interception of wire, oral, or electronic communications, or the use of electronic means to intercept oral communications, or the use of electronic means to intercept oral communications or to disclose or use any communications that were illegally intercepted.[3]

The ECPA provides a broad, functional definition of electronic communications, including any transfer of signs, signals, writing, images, sounds, data, or intelligence of any nature transmitted in whole or in part by a wire, radio, electromagnetic, photoelectric, or photo-optical system that affects interstate or foreign commerce, with certain exceptions. Title II of the ECPA limits access to stored electronic communications.[4]

ECPA restrictions regarding disclosure of stored e-mail information facially apply only to public systems and e-mails stored

---

code was effectively an automatic routing program because it automatically duplicated part of communication between user and pharmaceutical site employing service, and set this information to third-party service); U.S. v. Steiger, 318 F.3d 1039, 1050 (11th Cir. 2003) (there is only narrow window during which e-mail interception may occur—the seconds or mili-seconds before which newly composed message is saved to any temporary location following send command; unless some type of automatic routing software is used (for example, duplicate of all of employee's messages are automatically sent to employee's boss), interception of e-mail within prohibition of Wiretap Act is virtually impossible).

[Section 17:6]

[1]Pub. L. No. 99-508, 100 Stat. 1848 (1986), codified as 18 U.S.C.A. §§ 2510 to 2521, 2701 to 2710.

[2]18 U.S.C.A. §§ 2510 et seq.

[3]18 U.S.C.A. § 2701(a).

[4]See First Time Videos, LLC v. Does 1-500, 276 F.R.D. 241, 80 Fed. R. Serv. 3d 106 (N.D. Ill. 2011) (ECPA permitted Internet service providers to disclose to copyright owner the names, addresses, telephone numbers, e-mail addresses, and Media Access Control addresses of alleged infringers of owner's adult videos and photographs in response to subpoenas served on ISPs by owner in its infringement action, where owner was not a government entity.).

within such systems. In *Anderson Consulting LLP v. UOP*,[5] the court held a proprietary system operated by an employer was not a public system, although during a project an accounting firm was allowed to use the system.[6]

In *Pure Power Boot Camp Inc v. Warrior Fitness Boot Camp*,[7] the court held the ECPA was violated when a company accessed, without proper authorization, its former employee's Hotmail account e-mails from the company computer the employee had purportedly used to view the employee's e-mails. The court observed that an employee's implied consent based on clear statements in an employee handbook may provide sufficient authorization under the Act to permit an employer's access to a personal e-mail account.

Online commerce uses various methods to collect information about system users and their online behavior patterns, in order to tailor advertising or other responses to mesh with those patterns. This frequently involves the use of "cookies." Cookies are computer programs commonly used by Websites to store useful information such as usernames, passwords, and preferences, making it easier for users to access Web pages in an efficient manner.

The use of cookies, their ability to capture and retain data about individual users without necessarily requiring the system user's assent raises a number of privacy issues. The ECPA was the basis for privacy claims in *In re DoubleClick, Inc. Privacy Litigation*.[8] The court rejected three federal statutory bases for objecting to the use of cookies to track the use of computers. However, in *In re Intuit Privacy Litigation*,[9] the court refused to dismiss a claim under the ECPA dealing with cookies.

Producing counsel will want to consider whether the rights of individuals in information or e-mails stored on a computer system are protected under the ECPA because the system is in effect

[5]Andersen Consulting LLP v. UOP, 991 F. Supp. 1041 (N.D. Ill. 1998).

[6]See Freeman v. DirecTV, Inc., 457 F.3d 1001 (9th Cir. 2006) (provisions of ECPA imposing civil liability on providers of electronic communication services that knowingly divulged contents of those communications while being stored by provider did not create secondary liability for aiding and abetting or conspiracy to violate those provisions).

[7]Pure Power Boot Camp v. Warrior Fitness Boot Camp, 587 F. Supp. 2d 548 (S.D. N.Y. 2008).

[8]In re DoubleClick Inc. Privacy Litigation, 154 F. Supp. 2d 497 (S.D. N.Y. 2001).

[9]In re Intuit Privacy Litigation, 138 F. Supp. 2d 1272 (C.D. Cal. 2001).

public. In light of *Anderson Consulting LLP v. UOP*,[10] it is unlikely that any but the most clearly public system will be subject to the ECPA, but caution is definitely appropriate.

§ 17:7 Stored Communications and Transactional Records Act

The Stored Communications and Transactional Records Act,[1] created as part of the Electronic Communications Privacy Act of 1986, prohibits certain access to electronic communications service facilities, as well as disclosure by such services of information contained on those facilities. It permits private plaintiffs to bring a private civil action against those who knowingly or intentionally violate the Act.[2] The Act is useful for protecting the privacy of e-mail and other Internet communications.

The Act prohibits service providers from knowingly disclosing the contents of a communication to any person or entity while in electronic storage by that service.[3] It also prohibits the service provider from knowingly disclosing to any governmental agency any record or other information pertaining to a subscriber of the service.[4] Accordingly, most service providers will not disclose such information without a subpoena. However, the Ninth Circuit has found that disclosure by an Internet service provider of a customer's e-mail messages pursuant to an invalid and overly broad civil subpoena did not constitute an "authorized" disclosure by the provider, as would allow the defendant to avoid liability under the Act.[5]

In *Jessup-Morgan v. America Online, Inc.*,[6] a subscriber sued AOL, alleging a violation of the Act, invasion of privacy, and other claims arising out of the provider's disclosure of her identity

---

[10]Andersen Consulting LLP v. UOP, 991 F. Supp. 1041 (N.D. Ill. 1998).

[Section 17:7]

[1]18 U.S.C.A. §§ 2701 to 2711. See generally, Note, *Exploring Challenges with the Discovery of Text Messages in Federal Cases Through the Lens of the Federal Rules of Civil Procedure and the Stored Communications Act, 18 U.S.C. §§ 2701–11*, 15 SUFFOLK J. TRIAL & APP. ADVOC. 143 (2010).

[2]18 U.S.C.A. § 2707(a).

[3]18 U.S.C.A. § 2701(a). But see KLA-Tencor Corp. v. Murphy, 717 F. Supp. 2d 895 (N.D. Cal. 2010) (fact employee e-mails were deleted from corporate servers at same time deleted on employee computers weighed against finding messages were "backups" protected under the Stored Communications Act).

[4]18 U.S.C.A. § 2701(a).

[5]Theofel v. Farey-Jones, 359 F.3d 1066, 1073 (9th Cir. 2004).

[6]Jessup-Morgan v. America Online, Inc., 20 F. Supp. 2d 1105, 26 Media L. Rep. (BNA) 2426 (E.D. Mich. 1998).

pursuant to a subpoena. The plaintiff had posted messages inviting users to engage in sexual liaisons with her husband's prior wife. The court held that disclosure of the subscriber's identity did not violate the Act because the Act specifically authorizes such disclosures of subscriber information to private parties.[7]

§ 17:8 Computer Fraud and Abuse Act

The Computer Fraud and Abuse Act[1] makes it illegal to access a "protected" computer under certain circumstances, including computers operated by or on behalf of financial institutions.[2] The Act also makes it a crime to intentionally access a computer without authorization or to exceed authorized access, and obtain information from any "protected computer" if the conduct involved an interstate or foreign communication.[3] A "protected computer" is a computer:

- Used exclusively for the use of a financial institution; or
- Used by or for a financial institution, and the conduct constituting the offense affects that use by or for the financial institution; or
- Used in interstate or foreign commerce or communication.[4]

§ 17:9 Judicial privacy policy

Unless sealed or otherwise subject to restricted access by stat-

---

[7]But see O'Grady v. Superior Court, 139 Cal. App. 4th 1423, 44 Cal. Rptr. 3d 72, 34 Media L. Rep. (BNA) 2089, 79 U.S.P.Q.2d 1398 (6th Dist. 2006), (disclosure of identity of author of stored message not permitted by Act, but Act authorizes disclosure of a record or other information pertaining to a subscriber to or customer of the service, not including the contents of communications). See also 18 U.S.C.A. § 2703(c)(1)(A).

[Section 17:8]

[1]18 U.S.C.A. §§ 1030 et seq.

[2]See 18 U.S.C.A. § 1030(a)(2)(A). See, e.g., International Airport Centers, L.L.C. v. Citrin, 440 F.3d 418, 24 I.E.R. Cas. (BNA) 129 (7th Cir. 2006) (former employee's installation and use of a secure-erasure program to delete files on his employer-issued laptop prior to leaving that job was sufficient for employer to state a claim under CFAA). See also Samuels and Villanueva, *The Computer Fraud and Abuse Act: "Authorization" in Flux and the Ninth Circuit Dilemma*, 80 U.S.L.W. 1193 (March 6, 2012).

[3]18 U.S.C.A. § 1030(a)(2)(C). See LVRC Holdings LLC v. Brekka, 581 F.3d 1127, 29 I.E.R. Cas. (BNA) 1153 (9th Cir. 2009) (employee did not access computer "without authorization" nor "exceed authorized access" in violation of CFAA when employee e-mailed documents from his work computer to himself and to his wife while he was still employed).

[4]18 U.S.C.A. § 1030(e)(2)(A) and (B).

ute, rule or regulation, or policy, judicial records are presumed available for public inspection and copying.[1] The privacy policy of the Judicial Conference of the United States sets forth requirements relating to privacy and public access to electronic case files.[2] The policy recognizes that certain types of cases, categories of information, and specific documents may require special protection from unlimited public access.[3] The policy observes that the federal courts are not required to provide electronic access to case files, assuming a paper file is maintained.

§ 17:10 European Data Protection Directive

In 1998 the European Union enacted the European Data Protection Directive.[1] The Directive prohibits transferring "personal data" to countries where private protection is inadequate. It also can have an impact on Websites utilizing cookies to collect data about customers.

On February 6, 2012, the American Bar Association House of Delegates adopted a resolution seeking to reconcile U.S. civil discovery obligations with international privacy and blocking laws.[2] The resolution urges U.S. courts to "consider and respect, as appropriate, the data protection and privacy laws of any applicable foreign sovereign, and the interests of any person who is subject to or benefits from such laws, with regard to data sought in discovery in civil litigation."

[Section 17:9]

[1]See, e.g., Richmond Newspapers, Inc. v. Virginia, 448 U.S. 555, 575–78, 100 S. Ct. 2814, 65 L. Ed. 2d 973, 6 Media L. Rep. (BNA) 1833 (1980) (tradition of public access to case files is also rooted in constitutional principles); Nixon v. Warner Communications, Inc., 435 U.S. 589, 597, 98 S. Ct. 1306, 1312, 55 L. Ed. 2d 570, 3 Media L. Rep. (BNA) 2074 (1978) (there is a common law right to inspect and copy public records and documents, including judicial records and documents).

[2]See http://www.privacy.uscourts.gov/b4amend.htm.

[3]See, e.g., U.S. Dept. of Justice v. Reporters Committee For Freedom of Press, 489 U.S. 749, 761, 109 S. Ct. 1468, 1476, 103 L. Ed. 2d 774, 16 Media L. Rep. (BNA) 1545 (1989) (technology may affect the balance between access rights and privacy and security interests).

[Section 17:10]

[1]Council Directive 97/66/EC at http://www.bioheathmatics.com/heathinformatics/eudir.aspx.

[2]See Resolution 103 of the ABA House of Delegates at http://www.abanow.org/wordpress/wp-content/files_flutter/13285610062012mm103.pdf. See Raul, ABA Resolution Urges U.S. Courts to Respect Foreign Data Laws, 80 U.S.L.W. 1161 (Feb. 29, 2012).

§ 17:11 Trade secrets and proprietary information

Fed. R. Civ. P. 26(c)(7) provides protection for trade secrets. The owner of a trade secret generally may keep the information confidential so long as there is no attempt to conceal fraud or otherwise work an injustice.

"Trade secret" is defined as information including a formula, pattern, compilation, program, device, method, technique or process that:

1. Derives independent economic value, actual or potential from not being generally known to, and not being readily ascertainable by proper means by, other persons who can obtain economic benefit from its disclosure or use, and
2. Is the subject of efforts to maintain its secrecy that are reasonable under the circumstances.[1]

In order to obtain a protective order, the moving party must demonstrate that disclosure of the allegedly confidential information will work a clearly defined and very serious injury to the movant's business and put the holder of the trade secret at a competitive disadvantage.[2] If the information is not currently confidential or difficult to acquire, or if it was obtained before litigation, it will not constitute a trade secret under Fed. R. Civ. P. 26(c)(7).

C. WORK PRODUCT

§ 17:12 Generally

In *Hickman v. Taylor*,[1] the U.S. Supreme Court recognized that certain trial preparation materials are protected from discovery under the work product doctrine. *Hickman* established three important principles. First, items gathered by counsel when

---

[Section 17:11]

[1]Unif.Trade Secrets Act § 1(4).

[2]See, e.g., Chembio Diagnostic Systems, Inc. v. Saliva Diagnostic Systems, Inc., 236 F.R.D. 129 (E.D. N.Y. 2006) (in determining whether information warrants protection from discovery as trade secret, courts should consider: (1) extent to which information is known outside business; (2) extent to which it is known by employees and others involved in business; (3) measures taken to guard information's secrecy; (4) value of information to business or to its competitors; (5) amount of time, money, and effort expended in development of information; and (6) ease or difficulty or duplicating or properly acquiring information).

[Section 17:12]

[1]Hickman v. Taylor, 329 U.S. 495, 67 S. Ct. 385, 91 L. Ed. 451, 1947 A.M.C. 1 (1947).

preparing for trial are protected from disclosure. Second, this protection is not absolute and opposing counsel may obtain materials by showing a need for them. Third, protection from discovery is greatest for materials that demonstrate the attorney's thought process.

The work product doctrine is not a "privilege" within the meaning of the Federal Rules of Evidence; it is a tool of judicial administration to safeguard the adversarial process. The work product doctrine protects trial preparation materials that reveal an attorney's strategy, intended lines of proof, evaluation of strengths and weaknesses, and inferences drawn from interviews. The work product doctrine is designed to preserve the privacy of attorneys' thought processes and to prevent parties from "borrowing the wits of their adversaries."

The holding of *Hickman* can be summarized as follows:

- Information as to facts and witnesses' statements obtained by the adverse party's attorney is not within the common law attorney-client privilege.
- The broader policy against invasion of a lawyer's files does not make them absolutely immune from discovery.
- The party asking for disclosure of information protected by the work product doctrine must show special circumstances in order to obtain it.
- When the proponent of discovery can obtain the desired information elsewhere, the proponent has not met the burden of showing such special circumstances.

In 1970, Fed. R. Civ. P. 26 was amended to provide express protection of work product. The work product doctrine, as a federal right derived from the Federal Rules of Civil Procedure, is resolved according to federal law in a diversity suit. Fed. R. Civ. P. 26(b)(3) provides work product with qualified protection from discovery. Fed. R. Civ. P. 26(b)(3) does the following:

- It defines the class of materials protected as work product.
- It describes the showing required to obtain discovery of work product material.
- It protects an attorney's mental impressions, conclusions, opinions, or legal theories concerning the litigation.

Fed. R. Civ. P. 26(b)(3) provides a qualified protection for documents and tangible things otherwise discoverable and prepared in anticipation of litigation or for trial by or for another party. In order to come within the qualified immunity from discovery created by Fed. R. Civ. P. 26(b)(3), three tests must be satisfied. The material must be:

- Documents and tangible things
- Prepared in anticipation of litigation or for trial
- By or for another party or by or for that other party's representative

A party asserting work product protection has the burden of establishing that the protection applies. To carry that burden, the party must make a clear showing that the asserted protection applies. The party must describe in detail the documents or information sought to be protected and provide precise reasons for the objection to discovery. The information provided must be sufficient to enable the court to determine whether each element of the asserted protection is satisfied. A blanket claim as to the applicability of work product protection does not satisfy the burden of proof.

D. PRIVILEGES

§ 17:13 Generally

If a party claims privilege, Fed. R. Civ. P. 26(b)(5) provides that the party must "make the claim expressly and shall describe the nature of the documents, communications, or things not produced or disclosed in a manner that, without revealing information itself privileged or protected, will enable other parties to assess the applicability of the privilege or protection." This provision does not attempt to define for each case what information must be provided when a party asserts a claim of privilege.

A party invoking the attorney-client privilege must show:

- a communication between a client and the client's attorney that
- was intended to be and was in fact kept confidential, and
- was made for the purpose of obtaining or providing legal advice.

Confidential communication between client and attorney are protected only if the predominant purpose of the communication was to render or solicit legal advice. Once established, the attorney-client privilege can be waived if the communication is shared with corporate employees who are not directly concerned with or did not have primary responsibility for the subject matter of the communication.

When information is withheld on the basis of a privilege, the party claiming the privilege should:

- Expressly claim the privilege; and
- Describe the nature of the documents, communications or things not produced or disclosed in a manner that will en-

able other parties to assess the applicability of the privilege or protection.

Failure to claim a privilege in a timely manner may constitute waiver of the privilege.

§ 17:14 Metadata

Unless the creator of an electronic document removes the metadata or sends an image file, such as a PDF, when sharing electronic documents with others, recipients of the document will be able to access this information. Because of the potential of metadata to reveal confidential client information, confidences, and strategies, ethics opinions have emphasized the sending attorney's responsibility to ensure that metadata are not transmitted inadvertently.

Lawyers frequently prepare documents and electronically circulate drafts among other lawyers in the firm for their review and comment. The other lawyers may insert their suggested revisions and comments; some may address the strengths and weaknesses of the client's position. If the final version of such a document is electronically transmitted to opposing counsel, it may be possible for opposing counsel to discover the comments and revisions. The sender of the document may not be aware of the metadata embedded within the document, or that the metadata remain in the electronic document despite the sender's good faith belief that it was "deleted."

All the state bars that have addressed the issue of metadata have agreed that a sending lawyer has a duty to protect confidential or privileged information from being disclosed, but they split on the duty of an opposing party. With respect to the ethical obligations of a lawyer who receives inadvertently disclosed confidential information, one of the more thoughtful ethics opinions is that of the D.C. Bar Association. The opinion states, in pertinent part, as follows:

> Where a lawyer has inadvertently included documents containing client secrets or confidences in material delivered to an adversary lawyer, and the receiving lawyer in good faith reviews the documents before the inadvertence of the disclosure is brought to that lawyer's attention, the receiving lawyer engages in no ethical violation by retaining and using those documents. Where, on the other hand, the receiving lawyer knows of the inadvertence of the disclosure before the documents are examined, Rule 1.15(a) requires the receiving lawyer to return the documents to the sending lawyer; the receiving lawyer also violates Rule 8.4(c) if the lawyer reads and/or uses the material. Depending on the facts, the lawyer making the inadvertent disclosure may, by so doing, violate Rule 1.1, requiring a lawyer to use diligence and care in a representation.

The D.C. Committee stated that where the underlying law holds that inadvertently disclosed information is no longer protected, there would appear to be no justification for requiring the receiving lawyer to accord it special treatment. The Committee explained that, once read, the inadvertently disclosed information becomes part of the body of knowledge residing in the mind of the receiving lawyer, who may wish to use it to further the interests of that lawyer's client. Should those lawyers take action, such as directing discovery to the claimant, the Committee explained that seeking to develop evidence of that party's prior knowledge of allegedly fraudulent representations, the lawyers would be courting an ethical violation unless they could establish that their litigation strategy derived from some source other than the inadvertently disclosed information. According to the D.C. Committee, an interpretation of the ethical rules that required the receiving lawyer to protect the confidentiality of these materials would, we believe, place too much of a burden on the exercise of a lawyer's obligation to represent his client zealously and diligently.

Where the receiving lawyer has not examined the misdirected material before gaining knowledge of the inadvertence of the disclosure, it was the D.C. Committee's opinion that the lawyer should, at a minimum, seek guidance from the sending lawyer and, if that lawyer confirms the inadvertence of the disclosure and requests return of the material, unread, the receiving lawyer should do so. The Committee said that, in its view, a failure to do so would be a dishonest act.

The D.C. Committee disagreed with the discussion in the ABA Opinion that its conclusion would also apply even where the receiving lawyer did not become aware of the inadvertence until after the lawyer read the documents. According to the D.C. Committee, the ABA Opinion overlooks the other important considerations that apply in such a circumstance (i.e., the fact that the information cannot be purged from the mind of the receiving lawyer, the lawyer's obligation to his client of zealous representation, and the potential conflict of interest, and may have been mistaken in its view that most courts do not treat inadvertent disclosure as a waiver of the privilege.

The Ethics Panel of the New Hampshire Bar Association has concluded the New Hampshire disciplinary rules prohibit attorneys from searching for, reviewing, or using secrets hidden in metadata within electronic materials received from opposing counsel. Recognizing a split of opinion on the issue across the country, the committee rejected the American Bar Association's view that lawyers have no professional obligation to refrain from reviewing and using metadata. According to the panel, plundering metadata is much like eavesdropping. As for attorneys who create electronic materials that include metadata, the panel endorsed the prevailing view that such lawyers must use reasonable care to prevent disclosure of confidential information in metadata to opposing counsel. In reaching these conclusions, the panel emphasized that New Hampshire Rule of Professional Conduct 4.4(b) is not the same as the corresponding standard in the ABA Model Rules of Professional Conduct.

According to the New Hampshire panel, metadata must always be viewed as "inadvertently sent" unless counsel have mutually agreed otherwise. Moreover, the receiving lawyer necessarily "knows" under New Hampshire Rule 4.4(b) that the confidential information was transmitted inadvertently, the committee said.

The New Hampshire panel said that attorneys who transmit electronic materials to opposing counsel are required to take reasonable care to avoid improper disclosure of confidential information contained in metadata, the panel said. It found a general consensus to this effect in other jurisdictions. According to the opinion, attorneys need not necessarily purchase expensive computer software to scrub metadata from all documents. The panel said that simply substituting a scanned version of sensitive documents may be adequate in most circumstances.

§ 17:15 Privilege log

Under Fed. R. Civ. P. 26(b)(5), a party asserting a privilege must specifically identify each document or communication and the type of privilege or protection being asserted in a privilege log. To properly demonstrate that a privilege exists, the privilege log should contain a brief description or summary of the contents of the document, the date the document was prepared, the person or persons who prepared the document, the person to whom the document was directed, or for whom the document was prepared, the purpose in preparing the document, the privilege or privileges asserted with respect to the document, and how each element of the privilege is met as to that document. The summary should be specific enough to permit the court or opposing counsel to determine whether the privilege asserted applies to that document.

The summary should be specific enough to permit the court or opposing counsel to determine whether the privilege asserted applies to that document. In a privilege log concerning a string of e-mail communications, only the privileged communication identified by the date, time, and participants in the communication may be withheld; every other part of the string not so-identified must be produced.

While a party claiming a privilege should provide reasonable specifics, the party should not be required to expend undue effort in preparing privilege logs or similar listings of withheld materials. In some cases, the burden of specifying the withheld materials may justify a protective order. Where the number of documents is extremely voluminous, the court may permit the preparation of a privilege log on a categorical basis. The validity of a privilege log can be tested by using statistical sampling.

Generally, a party may not file a privilege log under seal absent court order. Even when stipulated to by adverse parties, the court must weigh any interests in confidentiality against that of the public to open records. Moreover, by not providing a copy to the opposing party, a party negates the very purpose of a privilege log, which is to enable other parties to assess the applicability of the privilege log or protection.

§ 17:16 Reviewing documents

The costs of reviewing electronically stored information for privilege and confidentiality can be enormous. However, it may be possible to protect a producing party's documents at much lower cost by enforcement of a confidentiality order and a protocol requiring that documents be reviewed on an attorneys' eyes-only basis and that review of privileged documents not be deemed a waiver of the privilege.

Even with such protections, disclosure of privileged documents cannot be compelled. Accordingly, it may still be necessary to determine who should bear the costs if, notwithstanding the implementation of precautions, the producing party chooses to conduct a complete review before production.

E. LEGAL HOLD NOTICES

§ 17:17 Generally

Courts generally have held that legal hold notices from attorneys to their clients are protected attorney work product or are protected by the attorney-client privilege. In *Gibson v. Ford Motor Co.*, the plaintiffs requested the document sent to defendant's employees instructing them not to destroy certain kinds of documents required to be maintained as a result of the litigation. Specifically, the plaintiffs wanted the list of material employees were required to maintain. Denying the request, the court said the information was not reasonably calculated to lead to the discovery of admissible evidence. The court explained:

> In the Court's experience, these instructions are often, if not always, drafted by counsel, involve their work product, are often overly inclusive, and the documents they list do not necessarily bear a reasonable relationship to the issues in litigation. This is not a document relating to the Defendant's business. Rather, the document relates exclusively to this litigation, was apparently created after this dispute arose, and exists for the sole purpose of assuring compliance with discovery that may be required in this litigation. Not only is the document likely to constitute attorney work-product, but its compelled production could dissuade other businesses from issuing such instructions in the event of litigation. Instructions like the one that appears to have been issued here insure the availability of information during litigation. Parties should be encouraged, not discouraged, to issue such directives. Defendants are not required to produce these materials.

In *Munro v. Target Corp.*, the defendant argued that its legal hold notices were subject to the attorney-client privilege and were also entitled to work product protection. Agreeing with the defendant, the court said that the notices seemed to be communications of legal advice from corporate counsel to corporate employees regarding document preservation.

F. FIFTH AMENDMENT

§ 17:18 Generally

The U.S. Court of Appeals for the Eleventh Circuit has held the government cannot compel a suspect to decrypt the suspect's computer hard drives without grating the suspect full immunity from prosecution where the act of unlocking the drives would itself be testimonial. The court explained that an individual's act of production can be "testimonial" for Fifth Amendment purposes when that act conveys some explicit or implicit statement of fact that certain materials exist, are in the subpoenaed individual's possession or control, or are authentic.

The court noted that any files contained in hidden portions of a laptop and external hard drives possess by an individual are not, themselves, testimonial for purposes of an individual's assertion of the individual's Fifth Amendment protection against self-incrimination.

G. INADVERTENT PRODUCTION

§ 17:19 Generally

Because of the volume of digital materials that may be produced, a privilege review of the materials may be incredibly expensive and time consuming. Additionally, there is always the possibility that some privileged documents may be missed during an extensive privilege review.[1]

Model Rule of Professional Conduct 4.4(b) was adopted by the American Bar Association in August 2002. The rule provides that a "lawyer who receives a document relating to the representation of the lawyer's client and knows or reasonably should know that the document was inadvertently sent shall promptly notify the sender." The rule requires only that the receiving attorney notify the sender; it does not require return of the document. Although a lawyer is not obligated to return a document unread if the lawyer notices that it was sent inadvertently, the decision to do so voluntarily is a "matter of professional judgment ordinarily reserved to the lawyer."[2] after notification, the comments to Fed. R. Civ. P. 4.4(b) indicate that the next step is to determine whether the disclosure has waived the privileged status of the document.[3]

§ 17:20 Recovery of produced material

Fed. R. Civ. P. 26(b)(5)(B) provides a procedure for a party to assert a claim of privilege or work-product protection after information is produced in discovery. If the claim is contested, the rule permits any party that received the information to present the matter to the court for resolution. Fed. R. Civ. P. 26(b)(5) does not address whether the privilege or protection that is asserted after production was waived by the production.

Problems of recovery can be ameliorated if the parties discuss the privilege issues during the discovery conference. Fed. R. Civ. P. 26(f) directs the parties to discuss privilege issues in preparing their discovery plan. A court may incorporate any party agreement concerning privileged matters into a scheduling order.[1]

§ 17:21 Rule 502 of the Federal Rules of Evidence

The 2006 amendments to the Federal Rules of Civil Procedure did not address whether a privilege is waived when privileged

---

[Section 17:19]

[1]See Allen, *The Recipient's Dilemma: Inadvertent Disclosure of Privileged Information*, THE BRIEF, Winter 2012, at 38.

[2]Model Rule of Prof. Conduct 4.4(b), comment [3].

[3]Model Rule of Prof. Conduct 4.4(b), comment [2].

[Section 17:20]

[1]Fed. R. Civ. P. 16(b)(4).

material is inadvertently produced during discovery.[1] Fed. R. Evid. 502 attempts to address this question and to provide some certainty and restraint on costs associated with inadvertent disclosure.[2] Rule 502 provides:

> The following provisions apply, in the circumstances set out, to disclosure of a communication or information covered by the attorney-client privilege or work-product protection.
>
> **(a) Disclosure made in a Federal proceeding or to a Federal office or agency; scope of a waiver.** When the disclosure is made in a Federal proceeding or to a Federal office or agency and waives the attorney-client privilege or work-product protection, the waiver extends to an undisclosed communication or information in a Federal or State proceeding only if:
>
> **(1)** the waiver is intentional;
>
> **(2)** the disclosed and undisclosed communications or information concern the same subject matter; and
>
> **(3)** they ought in fairness to be considered together.
>
> **(b) Inadvertent disclosure.** When made in a Federal proceeding or to a Federal office or agency, the disclosure does not operate as a waiver in a Federal or State proceeding if:
>
> **(1)** the disclosure is inadvertent;
>
> **(2)** the holder of the privilege or protection took reasonable steps to prevent disclosure; and
>
> **(3)** the holder promptly took reasonable steps to rectify the error, including (if applicable) following Fed. R. Civ. P. 26(b)(5)(B).
>
> **(c) Disclosure made in a State proceeding.** When the disclosure is made in a State proceeding and is not the subject of a State-court order concerning waiver, the disclosure does not operate as a waiver in a Federal proceeding if the disclosure:
>
> **(1)** would not be a waiver under this rule if it had been made in a Federal proceeding; or
>
> **(2)** is not a waiver under the law of the State where the disclosure occurred.

[Section 17:21]

[1]See Hopson v. Mayor and City Council of Baltimore, 232 F.R.D. 228, 235, 97 Fair Empl. Prac. Cas. (BNA) 617, 63 Fed. R. Serv. 3d 582 (D. Md. 2005) (although federal amendments encourage prudent counsel to utilize "quick peek" or "clawback" agreements, they are certainly not risk free, particularly with regard to third parties).

[2]See Burg & Hunter, *A Review of How Courts Are Analyzing New Federal Rule of Evidence 502*, 78 U.S.L.W. 2499 (2010); Comment, *Nonwaiver Agreements after Federal Rule of Evidence 502: A Glance at Quick-Peek and Clawback Agreements*, 56 U.C.L.A. L. REV. 1835 (2009).

(d) Controlling effect of a court order. A Federal court may order that the privilege or protection is not waived by disclosure connected with the litigation pending before the court—in which event the disclosure is also not a waiver in any other Federal or State proceeding.

(e) Controlling effect of a party agreement. An agreement on the effect of disclosure in a Federal proceeding is binding only on the parties to the agreement, unless it is incorporated into a court order.

(f) Controlling effect of this rule. Notwithstanding Rules 101 and 1101, this rule applies to State proceedings and to Federal court-annexed and Federal court-mandated arbitration proceedings, in the circumstances set out in the rule. And notwithstanding Rule 501, this rule applies even if State law provides the rule of decision.

(g) Definitions. In this rule:

(1) "attorney-client privilege" means the protection that applicable law provides for confidential attorney-client communications; and

(2) "work-product protection" means the protection that applicable law provides for tangible material (or its intangible equivalent) prepared in anticipation of litigation or for trial.

ADVISORY COMMITTEE NOTES

Explanatory Note (Revised 11/28/2007)

This new rule has two major purposes:

1) It resolves some longstanding disputes in the courts about the effect of certain disclosures of communications or information protected by the attorney-client privilege or as work product—specifically those disputes involving inadvertent disclosure and subject matter waiver.

2) It responds to the widespread complaint that litigation costs necessary to protect against waiver of attorney-client privilege or work product have become prohibitive due to the concern that any disclosure (however innocent or minimal) will operate as a subject matter waiver of all protected communications or information. This concern is especially troubling in cases involving electronic discovery. *See, e.g.*, Hopson v. Mayor and City Council of Baltimore, 232 F.R.D. 228, 244, 97 Fair Empl. Prac. Cas. (BNA) 617, 63 Fed. R. Serv. 3d 582 (D. Md. 2005) (electronic discovery may encompass "millions of documents" and to insist upon "record-by-record pre-production privilege review, on pain of subject matter waiver, would impose upon parties costs of production that bear no proportionality to what is at stake in the litigation").

The rule seeks to provide a predictable, uniform set of standards under which parties can determine the consequences of a disclosure of a communication or information covered by the attorney-client privilege or work-product protection. Parties to litigation need to know, for example, that if they exchange privileged information pursuant to a confidentiality order, the court's order will be enforceable. Moreover, if a federal court's confidentiality order is not enforceable in a state court then the burdensome costs of privilege review and retention are unlikely to be reduced.

The rule makes no attempt to alter federal or state law on whether a communication or information is protected under the attorney-client privilege or work-product immunity as an initial matter. Moreover, while establishing some exceptions to waiver, the rule does not purport to supplant applicable waiver doctrine generally.

The rule governs only certain waivers by disclosure. Other common-law waiver doctrines may result in a finding of waiver even where there is no disclosure of privileged information or work product. *See, e.g.*, Nguyen v. Excel Corp., 197 F.3d 200, 5 Wage & Hour Cas. 2d (BNA) 1352, 45 Fed. R. Serv. 3d 1298 (5th Cir. 1999) (reliance on an advice of counsel defense waives the privilege with respect to attorney-client communications pertinent to that defense); Byers v. Burleson, 100 F.R.D. 436, 38 Fed. R. Serv. 2d 403 (D.D.C. 1983) (allegation of lawyer malpractice constituted a waiver of confidential communications under the circumstances). The rule is not intended to displace or modify federal common law concerning waiver of privilege or work product where no disclosure has been made.

Subdivision (a). The rule provides that a voluntary disclosure in a federal proceeding or to a federal office or agency, if a waiver, generally results in a waiver only of the communication or information disclosed; a subject matter waiver (of either privilege or work product) is reserved for those unusual situations in which fairness requires a further disclosure of related, protected information, in order to prevent a selective and misleading presentation of evidence to the disadvantage of the adversary. *See, e.g.*, In re United Mine Workers of America Employee Ben. Plans Litigation, 159 F.R.D. 307, 312 (D.D.C. 1994) (waiver of work product limited to materials actually disclosed, because the party did not deliberately disclose documents in an attempt to gain a tactical advantage). Thus, subject matter waiver is limited to situations in which a party intentionally puts protected information into the litigation in a selective, misleading and unfair manner. It follows that an inadvertent disclosure of protected information can never result in a subject matter waiver. See Rule 502(b). The rule rejects the result in In re Sealed Case, 877 F.2d 976, 28 Fed. R. Evid. Serv. 358 (D.C. Cir. 1989), which held that inadvertent disclosure of documents during discovery automatically constituted a subject matter waiver.

The language concerning subject matter waiver—"ought in fairness"—is taken from Rule 106, because the animating principle is the same. Under both Rules, a party that makes a selective, misleading presentation that is unfair to the adversary opens itself to a more complete and accurate presentation.

To assure protection and predictability, the rule provides that if a disclosure is made at the federal level, the federal rule on subject matter waiver governs subsequent state court determinations on the scope of the waiver by that disclosure.

Subdivision (b). Courts are in conflict over whether an inadvertent disclosure of a communication or information protected as privileged or work product constitutes a waiver. A few courts find that a disclosure must be intentional to be a waiver. Most courts find a waiver only if the disclosing party acted carelessly in disclosing the communication or information and failed to request its return in a timely manner. And a few courts hold that any inadvertent disclosure of a communication or information protected under the attorney-client privilege or as work product constitutes a waiver without regard to the protections taken to avoid such a disclosure. *See generally* Hopson v. Mayor and City Council of Baltimore, 232 F.R.D. 228, 97 Fair Empl. Prac. Cas. (BNA) 617, 63 Fed. R. Serv. 3d 582 (D. Md. 2005), for a discussion of this case law.

The rule opts for the middle ground: inadvertent disclosure of protected communications or information in connection with a federal proceeding or to a federal office or agency does not constitute a waiver if the holder took reasonable steps to prevent disclosure and also promptly took reasonable steps to rectify the error. This position is in accord with the majority view on whether inadvertent disclosure is a waiver.

Cases such as Lois Sportswear, U.S.A., Inc. v. Levi Strauss & Co., 104 F.R.D.

103, 105, 17 Fed. R. Evid. Serv. 1440 (S.D. N.Y. 1985) and Hartford Fire Ins. Co. v. Garvey, 109 F.R.D. 323, 332 (N.D. Cal. 1985), set out a multi-factor test for determining whether inadvertent disclosure is a waiver. The stated factors (none of which is dispositive) are the reasonableness of precautions taken, the time taken to rectify the error, the scope of discovery, the extent of disclosure and the overriding issue of fairness. The rule does not explicitly codify that test, because it is really a set of non-determinative guidelines that vary from case to case. The rule is flexible enough to accommodate any of those listed factors. Other considerations bearing on the reasonableness of a producing party's efforts include the number of documents to be reviewed and the time constraints for production. Depending on the circumstances, a party that uses advanced analytical software applications and linguistic tools in screening for privilege and work product may be found to have taken "reasonable steps" to prevent inadvertent disclosure. The implementation of an efficient system of records management before litigation may also be relevant.

The rule does not require the producing party to engage in a post-production review to determine whether any protected communication or information has been produced by mistake. But the rule does require the producing party to follow up on any obvious indications that a protected communication or information has been produced inadvertently.

The rule applies to inadvertent disclosures made to a federal office or agency, including but not limited to an office or agency that is acting in the course of its regulatory, investigative or enforcement authority. The consequences of waiver, and the concomitant costs of pre-production privilege review, can be as great with respect to disclosures to offices and agencies as they are in litigation.

Subdivision (c). Difficult questions can arise when 1) a disclosure of a communication or information protected by the attorney-client privilege or as work product is made in a state proceeding, 2) the communication or information is offered in a subsequent federal proceeding on the ground that the disclosure waived the privilege or protection, and 3) the state and federal laws are in conflict on the question of waiver. The Committee determined that the proper solution for the federal court is to apply the law that is most protective of privilege and work product. If the state law is more protective (such as where the state law is that an inadvertent disclosure can never be a waiver), the holder of the privilege or protection may well have relied on that law when making the disclosure in the state proceeding. Moreover, applying a more restrictive federal law of waiver could impair the state objective of preserving the privilege or work-product protection for disclosures made in state proceedings. On the other hand, if the federal law is more protective, applying the state law of waiver to determine admissibility in federal court is likely to undermine the federal objective of limiting the costs of production.

The rule does not address the enforceability of a state court confidentiality order in a federal proceeding, as that question is covered both by statutory law and principles of federalism and comity. See 28 U.S.C. § 1738 (providing that state judicial proceedings "shall have the same full faith and credit in every court within the United States . . . as they have by law or usage in the courts of such State . . . from which they are taken"). *See also* Tucker v. Ohtsu Tire & Rubber Co., Ltd., 191 F.R.D. 495, 499 (D. Md. 2000) (noting that a federal court considering the enforceability of a state confidentiality order is "constrained by principles of comity, courtesy, and . . . federalism"). Thus, a state court order finding no waiver in connection with a disclosure made in a state court proceeding is enforceable under existing law in subsequent federal proceedings.

Subdivision (d). Confidentiality orders are becoming increasingly important in limiting the costs of privilege review and retention, especially in cases involving electronic discovery. But the utility of a confidentiality order in reducing discovery costs is substantially diminished if it provides no protection outside the particular litigation in which the order is entered. Parties are unlikely to be able to reduce the costs of pre-production review for privilege and work product if the consequence of disclosure is that the communications or information could be used by non-parties to the litigation.

There is some dispute on whether a confidentiality order entered in one case is enforceable in other proceedings. *See generally* Hopson v. Mayor and City Council of Baltimore, 232 F.R.D. 228, 97 Fair Empl. Prac. Cas. (BNA) 617, 63 Fed. R. Serv. 3d 582 (D. Md. 2005), for a discussion of this case law. The rule provides that when a confidentiality order governing the consequences of disclosure in that case is entered in a federal proceeding, its terms are enforceable against non-parties in any federal or state proceeding. For example, the court order may provide for return of documents without waiver irrespective of the care taken by the disclosing party; the rule contemplates enforcement of "claw-back" and "quick peek" arrangements as a way to avoid the excessive costs of pre-production review for privilege and work product. *See* Zubulake v. UBS Warburg LLC, 216 F.R.D. 280, 290, 92 Fair Empl. Prac. Cas. (BNA) 684, 56 Fed. R. Serv. 3d 326 (S.D. N.Y. 2003) (noting that parties may enter into "so-called 'claw-back' agreements that allow the parties to forego privilege review altogether in favor of an agreement to return inadvertently produced privilege documents"). The rule provides a party with a predictable protection from a court order—predictability that is needed to allow the party to plan in advance to limit the prohibitive costs of privilege and work product review and retention.

Under the rule, a confidentiality order is enforceable whether or not it memorializes an agreement among the parties to the litigation. Party agreement should not be a condition of enforceability of a federal court's order.

Under subdivision (d), a federal court may order that disclosure of privileged or protected information "in connection with" a federal proceeding does not result in waiver. But subdivision (d) does not allow the federal court to enter an order determining the waiver effects of a separate disclosure of the same information in other proceedings, state or federal. If a disclosure has been made in a state proceeding (and is not the subject of a state-court order on waiver), then subdivision (d) is inapplicable. Subdivision (c) would govern the federal court's determination whether the state-court disclosure waived the privilege or protection in the federal proceeding.

Subdivision (e). Subdivision (e) codifies the well-established proposition that parties can enter an agreement to limit the effect of waiver by disclosure between or among them. Of course such an agreement can bind only the parties to the agreement. The rule makes clear that if parties want protection against non-parties from a finding of waiver by disclosure, the agreement must be made part of a court order.

Subdivision (f). The protections against waiver provided by Rule 502 must be applicable when protected communications or information disclosed in federal proceedings are subsequently offered in state proceedings. Otherwise the holders of protected communications and information, and their lawyers, could not rely on the protections provided by the Rule, and the goal of limiting costs in discovery would be substantially undermined. Rule 502(f) is intended to resolve any potential tension between the provisions of Rule 502 that apply to state proceedings and the possible limitations on the applicability of the Federal Rules of Evidence otherwise provided by Rules 101 and 1101.

The rule is intended to apply in all federal court proceedings, including court-annexed and court-ordered arbitrations, without regard to any possible limitations of Rules 101 and 1101. This provision is not intended to raise an inference about the applicability of any other rule of evidence in arbitration proceedings more generally.

The costs of discovery can be equally high for state and federal causes of action, and the rule seeks to limit those costs in all federal proceedings, regardless of

whether the claim arises under state or federal law. Accordingly, the rule applies to state law causes of action brought in federal court.
Subdivision (g). The rule's coverage is limited to attorney-client privilege and work product. The operation of waiver by disclosure, as applied to other evidentiary privileges, remains a question of federal common law. Nor does the rule purport to apply to the Fifth Amendment privilege against compelled self-incrimination.
The definition of work product "materials" is intended to include both tangible and intangible information. *See* In re Cendant Corp. Securities Litigation, 343 F.3d 658, 662, 62 Fed. R. Evid. Serv. 577, 56 Fed. R. Serv. 3d 710 (3d Cir. 2003) ("work product protection extends to both tangible and intangible work product").

§ 17:22 Application of Rule 502—Generally

In order to secure the protection of Rule 502(b), the part producing the documents must show:

(1) the disclosure is inadvertent;
(2) the holder of the privilege or protection took reasonable steps to prevent disclosure; and
(3) the holder promptly took reasonable steps to rectify the error, including (if applicable) following Fed. R. Civ. P. 26(b)(5)(B).

§ 17:23 Application of Rule 502—Inadvertence

The first inquiry under Rule 502(b) is whether the disclosure of the privileged material was inadvertent.[1] Normally, the party claiming inadvertent disclosure has the burden of proof regarding an alleged inadvertent disclosure of privileged documents.[2]

Some courts have indicated the inquiry focus on the behavior of counsel, rather than other agents such as discovery service vendors.[3] The Heriot analysis appears to disregard that, if a party intentionally discloses privileged material, the party waives the privilege as to that material and possibly as to the subject matter; if a party mistakenly discloses privilege material, even if it fails to take reasonable steps to prevent disclosure, the party is

---

[Section 17:23]

[1]See Coburn Group, LLC v. Whitecap Advisors LLC, 640 F. Supp. 2d 1032, 80 Fed. R. Evid. Serv. 307 (N.D. Ill. 2009).

[2]Callan v. Christian Audigier, Inc., 263 F.R.D. 564 (C.D. Cal. 2009); Amobi v. District of Columbia Dept. of Corrections, 262 F.R.D. 45, 53, 81 Fed. R. Evid. Serv. 271 (D.D.C. 2009).

[3]See e, g., Heriot v. Byrne, 257 F.R.D. 645 (N.D. Ill. 2009), subsequent determination, 2009 WL 982490 (N.D. Ill. 2009) (court considered factors such as total number of documents reviewed, procedures used to review documents before they were produced, and actions of producing party after discovering that documents had been produced).

not at risk for subject matter waiver and may avoid waiving the privilege as to the disclosed material depending on the reasonableness of the precaution and its steps to rectify the error.[4]

In *Coburn Group LLC v. Whitecap Advisors LLC*,[5] the court stated that the factors considered in Heriot are more properly considered separately from the inadvertence inquiry. The court in *Coburn* said Congress enacted Rule 502 with a view towards a simpler inadvertence analysis that essentially asks whether the party intended a privileged or work-product protected document to be produced or whether the party intended a privileged or work-product protected document to be produced or whether the production was a mistake.[6]

§ 17:24 Application of Rule 502—Precautions

After the inadvertence threshold is satisfied, a court examines "the reasonableness of the precautions taken by parties and counsel in guarding against disclosure.[1] In order to avoid a waiver, the precautions must be reasonable.[2] Rule 502(b) does not remove the parties' responsibility to take reasonable precautions against disclosure of privileged documents. The reasonableness of the precautions taken to protect a privilege is an explicit consideration in determining whether waiver occurred, no matter

---

[4]Burg & Hunter, *A Review of How Courts Are Analyzing New Federal Rule of Evidence 502*, 78 U.S.L.W. 2499, 2500 (2010).

[5]Coburn Group, LLC v. Whitecap Advisors LLC, 640 F. Supp. 2d 1032, 80 Fed. R. Evid. Serv. 307 (N.D. Ill. 2009).

[6]See Amobi v. District of Columbia Dept. of Corrections, 262 F.R.D. 45, 53, 81 Fed. R. Evid. Serv. 271 (D.D.C. 2009) (there is every reason to suppose Congress intended to define inadvertent as mistaken).

[Section 17:24]

[1]See Ceglia v. Zuckerberg, 88 Fed. R. Evid. Serv. 240 (W.D. N.Y. 2012), aff'd, 2012 WL 3527935 (W.D. N.Y. 2012) (plaintiff failed to take reasonable steps to prevent e-mail's disclosure); D'Onofrio v. Borough of Seaside Park, 88 Fed. R. Evid. Serv. 697 (D.N.J. 2012) ("privilege waived where, despite reasonableness of defendants' initial efforts to preclude production, subsequent warnings that something was profoundly awry with their document production and privilege review" failed to result in defendants' discovery that privileged information had been produced); Thorncreek Apartments III, LLC v. Village of Park Forest, 2011 WL 3489828 (N.D. Ill. 2011) (privilege waived as to inadvertently produced documents where defendants failed to take reasonable steps to prevent disclosure).

[2]See Rhoads Industries, Inc. v. Building Materials Corp. of America, 254 F.R.D. 216, 77 Fed. R. Evid. Serv. 1513 (E.D. Pa. 2008), order clarified, 254 F.R.D. 238 (E.D. Pa. 2008) (standard is one of objective reasonableness).

the inadvertency of the disclosure.[3] A party claiming inadvertent disclosure must provide details regarding precautions it took to prevent disclosure of the documents.[4]

A court should consider the following factors in determining whether the precautions were reasonable:

- The reasonableness of the precautions taken to prevent inadvertent disclosure in view of the extent of the document production.
- The number of inadvertent disclosures.
- The extent of the disclosure.
- Any delay and measures taken to rectify the disclosure.
- Whether the overriding interests of justice would or would not be served by relieving the party of its errors.[5]

A producing party should carefully document the privilege review process. A producing party's bare assertion that a privilege review was conducted without more (such as, when the review occurred, how much time the attorney took to review the documents, what documents were reviewed, and other basic details of the review process) does not satisfy the producing party's burden of proof.[6] How the disclosure is discovered and

---

[3]Amobi v. District of Columbia Dept. of Corrections, 262 F.R.D. 45, 53, 81 Fed. R. Evid. Serv. 271 (D.D.C. 2009).

[4]See Callan v. Christian Audigier, Inc., 263 F.R.D. 564 (C.D. Cal. 2009) (party did not meet burden that its disclosure of privileged documents in response to discovery request was inadvertent or that documents were actually privileged); Kumar v. Hilton Hotels Corp., 2009 WL 1683479 (W.D. Tenn. 2009) (reasonable precautions were taken by producing party where legal assistant failed to redact e-mails marked "Attorney/Client Privileged Information" prior to production as requested in notes drafted by attorney). But see Preferred Care Partners Holding Corp. v. Humana, Inc., 258 F.R.D. 684, 79 Fed. R. Evid. Serv. 437 (S.D. Fla. 2009) (if material is clearly privileged, court presumes party did not intend to produce it).

[5]Advisory Committee Note to Enactment of Rule 502. See, e.g., Edelen v. Campbell Soup Co., 265 F.R.D. 676 (N.D. Ga. 2010); Amobi v. District of Columbia Dept. of Corrections, 262 F.R.D. 45, 54, 81 Fed. R. Evid. Serv. 271 (D.D.C. 2009); Rhoads Industries, Inc. v. Building Materials Corp. of America, 254 F.R.D. 216, 77 Fed. R. Evid. Serv. 1513 (E.D. Pa. 2008), order clarified, 254 F.R.D. 238 (E.D. Pa. 2008) (the court also noted plaintiff's limitation of search terms to weed out potentially privileged documents, tasking an inexperienced attorney with the review, the limitation of the search to e-mail address lines, and the plaintiff's exclusive reliance upon keyword searches without other quality assurance measures as indicia of unreasonable precautionary measures).

[6]See, e.g., Ceglia v. Zuckerberg, 88 Fed. R. Evid. Serv. 240 (W.D. N.Y. 2012), aff'd, 2012 WL 3527935 (W.D. N.Y. 2012) (plaintiff failed to act promptly to rectify inadvertent production upon its discovery); Thorncreek Apartments

rectified is more important than when the actual discovery of the disclosure occurs.

In *American Coal Sales Co. v. Nova Scotia Power, Inc.*,[7] the court found that the producing party took reasonable precautions to avoid inadvertent disclosure by having two attorneys review documents before production. It said that the inadvertent production of one document out of over 2,000 documents did not weigh in favor of waiver.

§ 17:25 Application of Rule 502—Prompt remedial measures

A party must take prompt remedial measures when it discovers the disclosures.[1] In *American Coal Sales Co. v. Nova Scotia Power, Inc.*,[2] the court found that an inadvertently disclosed document had not worked its way into the fabric of the litigation. It concluded the plaintiff had taken prompt measures to rectify the disclosure when it immediately objected at the time the e-mail was introduced at a deposition.

A claim of inadvertent disclosure cannot be used to withhold information from opposing counsel once the information has found its way into an expert's hands—however unintentional that may be.[3]

II. CHECKLISTS

§ 17:26 Privilege log checklist

- ☐ A brief description of the document explaining whether it is a memorandum, letter, e-mail, etc.

III, LLC v. Village of Park Forest, 2011 WL 3489828 (N.D. Ill. 2011) (privilege waived as to inadvertently produced documents where defendants failed recitfy error in a timely way); Peterson v. Bernardi, 262 F.R.D. 424, 80 Fed. R. Evid. Serv. 134 (D.N.J. 2009); Amobi v. District of Columbia Dept. of Corrections, 262 F.R.D. 45, 53, 81 Fed. R. Evid. Serv. 271 (D.D.C. 2009) (denying claim that reasonable precautions were taken where proponent of privilege did not indicate what specific efforts were taken to prevent disclosure).

[7]North American Rescue Products, Inc. v. Bound Tree Medical, LLC, 82 Fed. R. Evid. Serv. 601 (S.D. Ohio 2010); American Coal Sales Co. v. Nova Scotia Power Inc., 2009 WL 467576 (S.D. Ohio 2009).

[Section 17:25]

[1]See, e.g., Laethem Equipment Co. v. Deere & Co., 261 F.R.D. 127, 80 Fed. R. Evid. Serv. 692 (E.D. Mich. 2009).

[2]American Coal Sales Co. v. Nova Scotia Power Inc., 2009 WL 467576 (S.D. Ohio 2009).

[3]MVB Mortg. Corp. v. F.D.I.C., 2010 WL 582641 (S.D. Ohio 2010).

☐ The date the document was prepared
☐ The date of the document, if different from the preparation date
☐ The identity of the person or persons who prepared the document
☐ The identity of the persons for whom the document was prepared, including a showing based on competent evidence supporting any assertion the document was created by or under the supervision of an attorney
☐ The identity of the persons to whom the document and any copies were sent
☐ The purpose for preparing the document, including an evidentiary showing supporting any assertion that the document was prepared in the course of adversarial litigation or I anticipation of a threat of adversarial litigation that was real and imminent; a similar evidentiary showing that the subject of the communications within the document relates to seeking or giving advice; and a showing that the documents do not contain or incorporate non-privileged underlying facts
☐ The number of pages in the document
☐ The privilege or privileges asserted with respect to the document
☐ How each element of the privilege is met as to that document
☐ Any other pertinent information necessary to establish the elements of each asserted privilege

NOTES

Commentary

This form is adapted from Blaser v. Mt. Carmel Regional Medical Center, Inc., 2007 WL 1452993 (D. Kan. 2007).

§ 17:27 Checklist for determining whether information is a trade secret

☐ The extent to which the information is known outside the business
☐ The extent to which it is known by employees and others involved in the business
☐ The extent of measures taken by the employer to guard the secrecy of the information
☐ The value of the information to the employer and to the employer's competitors
☐ The amount of effort or money expended by the employer in developing the information

- ☐ The ease or difficulty with which the information could be properly acquired or duplicated by others

NOTES

Commentary

See Restatement (First) of Torts § 757 comment b. See, e.g., Jet Spray Cooler, Inc. v. Crampton, 361 Mass. 835, 840, 282 N.E.2d 921, 925, 174 U.S.P.Q. 272 (1972).

§ 17:28 Checklist for determining whether conduct of business implies desire that information be kept secret

- ☐ The existence of absence of an express agreement restricting disclosure
- ☐ The nature and extent of security precautions taken by the possessor to prevent acquisition of the information by unauthorized third parties
- ☐ The circumstances under which the information was disclosed to any employee to the extent they give rise to a reasonable inference that further disclosure, without the consent of the possessor, is prohibited
- ☐ The degree to which the information has been placed in the public domain or rendered readily ascertainable by third parties through patent applications or unrestricted product marketing

NOTES

Commentary

See Trent Partners and Associates, Inc. v. Digital Equipment Corp., 120 F. Supp. 2d 84, 111 (D. Mass. 1999).

III. FORMS

§ 17:29 Privilege log

LOG NUMBER	DISCOVERY REFERENCE OR EXHIBIT NUMBER
Identity and Position of Author	
Identity and Position of Recipients	
Privilege Claimed	
Present Location	

LOG NUMBER	DISCOVERY REFERENCE OR EXHIBIT NUMBER

Identity and Position of Author
Identity and Position of Recipients
Privilege Claimed
Present Location

§ 17:30 Privilege log—Another form

Doc. Number	Type of Doc.	Date	Author	Recipient/ Addressee	Other Recipients	Descrip-tion	Applicable Privileges

§ 17:31 Written authorization by patient for release of protected health information

AUTHORIZATION BY PATIENT FOR RELEASE OF PROTECTED HEALTH INFORMATION

Patient Name: Medical Record #:
Date of Birth: Social Security #:

I hereby authorize the use or disclosure of the Protected Health Information ("PHI") described below to be provided to or obtained by the following:

Name of Individual/Facility/ Company to Receive PHI	Name of Individual/Facility to Disclose PHI
Address:	Address:

Information authorized for use or disclosure or to be obtained:

☐ All medical information concerning this patient.
☐ Medical information of this patient compiled from ____ to ____.
☐ Only: ____
Dates of Treatment, if known:

The information will be obtained, used, or disclosed for the **following purpose(s) only**:

☐ Insurance
☐ Continued treatment
☐ Legal
☐ At the request of the patient or patient's representative

☐ Other (specify)

I understand:

I may revoke this authorization at any time, in writing, except revocation will not apply to information already used or disclosed in response to this authorization. I may revoke this document by presenting my written revocation as provided in the Notice of Privacy Practices of [Name of Health Care Facility or Health Care Provider]. Unless revoked or otherwise indicated, the automatic expiration date will be one year from the date of signature or upon occurrence of the following event:

I release the entities listed above, their agents and employees from any liability in connection with the use or disclosure of the protected health information covered by this authorization. The entity authorized to disclose the information will not be compensated by the recipient for the disclosure, except for the cost of copying and mailing as authorized by law.

Information used or disclosed pursuant to this authorization may be subject to redisclosure by the recipient and no longer protected by federal law. However, the recipient may be prohibited from disclosing substance abuse information under the Federal Substance Abuse Confidentiality Requirements.

I have the right to inspect the health information to be released and I may refuse to sign this authorization.

Unless the purpose of this authorization is to determine payment of a claim for benefits, the requesting entity will not condition the provision of treatment or payment for my care on my signing this authorization.

Signature of Patient or Legal Representative	Date
Description of Legal Representative's Authority	Expiration Date of Authorization

§ 17:32 Motion to authorize disclosure of protected health information

[Caption]

MOTION TO AUTHORIZE DISCLOSURE OF PROTECTED HEALTH INFORMATION

Defendant *[name]*, moves the Court for an order authorizing disclosure of protected health information of Plaintiff *[name]* from *[health care facility or provider from whom discovery is sought]* pursuant to 45 C.F.R. § 164.512(e)(1)(i).

1. This motion is made on the grounds that Plaintiff *[name]* has sued the Defendant, *[name]*, for *[describe]* and Plaintiff *[name]* is relying on Plaintiff's *[physical] [mental] [emotional]* condition in this action as an element of Plaintiff's claim.

2. Under *[statute]*, Plaintiff has waived any privilege granted by law concerning any communication made with a physician or health care provider relevant to that *[physical] [mental] [emotional]* condition.

3. Defendant is seeking from *[health care facility or provider from whom discovery is sought]* all *[describe medical records sought]* relevant to the *[physical] [mental] [emotional]* condition of Plaintiff.

4. Plaintiff has refused to provide Defendant with a written authorization for release of protected health information.

5. This Motion is supported by the accompanying brief.

Dated: ____

[signature, etc.]

§ 17:33 Subpoena duces tecum to produce documents or other things—Attendance of witness not required

[Caption]

SUBPOENA DUCES TECUM TO HEALTH CARE PROVIDER SEEKING PROTECTED HEALTH INFORMATION

TO: [Name of Health Care Provider]

You are commanded to produce and permit inspection and copying of the following described protected health information at the offices of *[name 1]*, attorney for Defendant *[name 2]*, located at *[address]*, on *[date]*, at *[time]*. *[Describe protected health information with reasonable particularity.]*

In order to allow objections to be filed to the production of documents and things that have been requested, you should not produce any of them until the date specified in this subpoena, and if an objection is filed, until the court rules on the objection.

In addition, you may not release these records until you are provided with a written statement from the undersigned attorney of satisfactory assurance of reasonable efforts to *[provide notice to [name 3] [secure a qualified protective order]]*.

Dated: ____

[signature, etc.]

§ 17:34 Written statement of satisfactory assurance of notice to patient

WRITTEN STATEMENT OF SATISFACTORY ASSURANCE OF NOTICE TO PATIENT

TO: *[List health care facilities and providers from whom discovery of protected health information is sought.]*

PATIENT NAME:

SUBJECT: *[Identify type of records sought]*

Defendant *[name 1]* is a party in the action entitled pending before the Hon. *[name 2]* of the Court. *[Specify Court]*. Pursuant to 45 C.F.R. § 164.512(e)(1)(ii)(A), Defendant is seeking the protected health information described above of *[name 3]*. Defendant has made a good faith effort to provide written notice to *[name 3]*.

The Notice to Patient informed *[name 3]* Defendant was seeking protected health information for purposes of the above-described litigation and provided *[name 3]* with ten days to make an objection to the disclosure to the Court. Attached is a copy of the Notice to Patient and a registered mail receipt showing that the Notice to Patient was mailed to the last known address for *[name 3]* on *[date]*.

The time for *[name 3]* to make an objection to the disclosure to the Court has expired and no objection has been filed.

or

[Name 2] filed an objection to the disclosure, and the Court ruled on the objection by an Order authorizing disclosure of the protected health information. A copy of the Order is attached.
Dated: ____

[signature, etc.]

§ 17:35 Notice to patient of intent to discover protected health information

NOTICE TO PATIENT OF INTENT TO DISCOVER PROTECTED HEALTH INFORMATION

TO: *[Name of Patient]*

SUBJECT: *[Identify type of records sought]*

PLEASE TAKE NOTICE that Defendant *[name 1]* has *[prepared a subpoena for the production of records from] [issued subpoena for a deposition of] [identify health care facility or provider]* in connection with the action entitled pending before the Hon. *[name 2]* of the Court. Defendant is seeking the following protected health information concerning you pursuant to 45 C.F.R. § 164.512(e)(1)(ii)(A): *[Describe protected health information with reasonable particularity.]*

If you object to this discovery, you must file an objection in the above-described action by *[date]*. If you do not file an objection, Defendant will proceed with this discovery.

Dated: ____

[signature, etc.]

§ 17:36 Written statement of satisfactory assurance of reasonable efforts to secure a qualified protective order

WRITTEN STATEMENT OF SATISFACTORY ASSURANCE OF REASONABLE EFFORTS TO SECURE A QUALIFIED PROTECTIVE ORDER

TO: *[List Health Care Facilities and Providers From Whom Discovery of Protected Health Information Is Sought]*

PATIENT NAME: *[name 3]*

SUBJECT: *[Identify type of records sought]*

Defendant *[name 1]* is a party in the action entitled pending before the Hon. *[name 2]* of the Court. *[Defendant]* is seeking the protected health information of *[name 3]* described above pursuant to 45 C.F.R. § 164.512(e)(1)(ii)(B).

Defendant has requested a qualified protective order from the court in the litigation described above.

or

[Name 3] and Defendant have agreed to a qualified protective order and have presented it to the court in the litigation described above.

A copy of the *[Motion for a qualified Protective Order] [Agreed qualified Protective Order]* is attached.

Dated: ____

[signature, etc.]

§ 17:37 Agreed qualified protective order (HIPAA)

[Caption]

AGREED QUALIFIED PROTECTIVE ORDER

This matter is before the Court on the Agreement of Plaintiff *[name 1]* and Defendant *[name 2]* for a qualified Protective Order complying with 45 C.F.R. § 164.512(e)(1)(v)(A) and (B) and authorizing disclosure of protected health information pursuant to 45 C.F.R. § 164.512(e)(1)(iv)(A).

Based on the agreement of the parties, this Court finds that:

1. Plaintiff *[name 1]* has relied on plaintiff's *[physical] [mental] [emotional]* condition in this action as an element of Plaintiff's claim and under *[statute]* has waived any privilege granted by law concerning any communication made with a physician or health care provider relevant to that *[physical] [mental] [emotional]* condition; and

2. Defendant is seeking all *[identify type of medical records sought]* from *[identify health care facility or provider from whom discovery is sought]* that are relevant to the *[physical] [mental] [emotional]* condition of Plaintiff.

IT IS THEREFORE ORDERED that:

1. Plaintiff's protected health information may be obtained by Defendant *[name 2]* pursuant to discovery;

2. *[Identify health care facility or provider from whom discovery is sought]* is authorized to disclose, in response to any discovery request from Defendant *[name 2]* any and all protected health information relevant to the physical/mental/emotional condition of Plaintiff *[name 1]* to Counsel for Defendant *[name 2]*;

3. Defendant *[name 2]* is prohibited from using or disclosing the protected health information for any purpose other than this litigation; and

4. At the end of this litigation Defendant *[name 2]* is ordered to destroy all protected health information, including any copies made of the information.

Dated: ____

____

Judge

Approved As to Form:

Dated: ____

[signature, etc.]

§ 17:38 Confidentiality agreement

NO WAIVER OF PRIVILEGE

1. Inspection or production of documents (including physical objects) shall not constitute a waiver of the attorney-client privilege or work product immunity or any other applicable privilege if, as soon as reasonably possible after the producing party becomes aware of any inadvertent or unintentional disclosure, the producing party designates any such documents as protected from disclosure by attorney-client privilege or work product protection or any other applicable privilege and requests return of such documents to the producing party.

2. Upon request by the producing party, the receiving party immediately shall return to the producing party all copies of such inadvertently produced document(s), all copies thereof and any materials derived from or based thereon to the producing party. Notwithstanding this provision, outside litigation counsel of record are not required to delete information that may reside on their respective firm's electronic back-up systems that are overwritten in the normal course of business.

§ 17:39 Confidentiality agreement—Another form

CONFIDENTIALITY AGREEMENT

The parties have agreed to produce all documents deemed discoverable under the *[rules]*, including electronically stored information, that are responsive to the discovery requests and not privileged or otherwise exempted from discovery under the *[rules]*, or other applicable source of law.

A. Some of the electronically stored information as well as other documents produced in this matter may contain communications or other information protected by the attorney-client privilege or work-production doctrine and not subject to discovery under *[rules]*.

B. Some of the produced electronically stored information and other documents in this matter may contain protected work-product material prepared or compiled in anticipation of litigation and not subject to discovery under *[rules]*.

C. The parties acknowledge that, despite each party's best efforts to conduct a thorough pre-production review of all electronically stored information and other documents, some material protected by the work-product doctrine or attorney-client privilege may be inadvertently disclosed to the other party during the course of this litigation;

D. The volume of potentially discoverable electronically stored information may substantially increase the total volume of documents that will be produced by the parties, thereby increasing the risk of inadvertent disclosure of material protected by the attorney-client privilege or the work-product doctrine.

E. In the course of this litigation, the parties may, either inadvertently or knowingly, produce information that is of a confidential, private, personal, trade secret, or proprietary nature ("confidential information").

F. The undersigned parties desire to establish a mechanism to avoid waiver of privilege or any other applicable protective evidentiary doctrine as a result of the inadvertently disclosure of material protected by the attorney-client privilege or work-product doctrine or confidential information.

G. The parties agree that this Agreement governs the disclosure of sensitive material and material protected by the attorney-client privilege or work-product doctrine in this action.

NON-WAIVER OF PRIVILEGE OR OTHER PROTECTIVE DOCTRINE BY INADVERTENT DISCLOSURE

1. The inadvertent disclosure of any document subject to a legitimate claim that the document should have been withheld from disclosure as protected by the attorney-client privilege or-work product doctrine does not waive any protection for that document or for the subject matter of the inadvertently disclosed document if the producing party, upon becoming aware of the disclosure, promptly requests its return and takes reasonable precautions to avoid such inadvertent disclosure.

2. Unless the requesting party disputes the claim, any documents the producing party deems to contain inadvertently disclosed material protected by attorney-client privilege or work-product doctrine must be upon written request promptly returned

to the producing party or destroyed at the producing party's option. This includes all copies, electronic or otherwise, of any such documents. In the event that the producing party requests destruction, the requesting party must provide written certification of compliance within thirty (30) days of the written request. In the event that the requesting party disputes the producing party's claim as to the protected nature of the inadvertently disclosed material, a single set of copies may be sequestered and retained by and under the control of requesting party for the sole purpose of seeking court determination of the issue pursuant to Fed. R. Civ. P. 26(b)(5)(B).

3. Any such material protected by the attorney-client privilege or work-product doctrine inadvertently disclosed by the producing party to the requesting party pursuant to this Agreement, must be and remain the property of the producing property.

4. To the extent there may be inconsistency between this Agreement and *[rules]*, the *[rules]* control.

CONFIDENTIAL TREATMENT OF CONFIDENTIAL MATERIAL

5. Any material protected by the attorney-client privilege or work-product doctrine or confidential material disclosed in this litigation is to be considered confidential and proprietary to the producing party and the requesting party must hold it in confidence and must not use any such material other than for the purposes of this litigation. To that end, the parties limit the disclosure of all such material only to those persons with a need to know the information for purposes of supporting their position in this litigation. In addition, such material must not be disclosed, published or otherwise revealed to any other party in this litigation except with the specific prior written authorization of the producing party.

6. If any material protected by the attorney-client privilege or work-product doctrine or confidential material is disclosed through inadvertence or otherwise to any person not authorized under this Agreement, the party causing the disclosure must inform the person receiving such material that the information is covered by this Agreement, make its best efforts to retrieve such material, and promptly inform the producing party of the disclosure.

7. The requesting party has no confidentiality obligations with respect to any information that:

a. is already known to the requesting party without restriction;

b. is or becomes publicly known otherwise than by the requesting party's breach of this Agreement;

c. is received by the requesting party without restriction from a third-party who is not under an obligation of confidentiality;

d. is independently developed by the requesting party;

e. is approved for release by written authorization of the producing party; or

f. is disclosed by the requesting party pursuant to judicial action, provided that producing party is notified at the time such action is initiated.

8. Any material protected by the attorney-client privilege or work-product doctrine or confidential material disclosed by the producing party to the requesting party pursuant to this Agreement is and remains the property of the producing property.

GENERAL PROVISIONS

9. This Agreement terminates and supersedes all prior understandings or agreements on the subject matter hereof.

10. This Agreement is binding on the parties to the Agreement when signed regardless of whether or when the court enters its Order on it.

11. Nothing in this Agreement prevents any party from applying to the court for a modification of this Agreement should the moving party believe the Agreement, as originally agreed upon, is hampering its efforts to prepare for trial; or from applying to the court for further or additional protective Agreements; or from an Agreement between the parties to any modification of this Agreement, subject to the approval of the court.

12. This Agreement shall survive the final termination of this case regarding any retained documents or contents thereof.

13. The effective date of this Agreement is *[date]*.

Dated: ____

[signature, etc.]

Dated: ____

[signature, etc.]

§ 17:40 Stipulation for protective order

[Caption]

STIPULATED PROTECTIVE ORDER

Upon the stipulation of counsel and for good cause appearing:

IT IS HEREBY ORDERED that the following Protective Order be entered:

1. *[Rule]* Good Faith Designation. In responding to a discovery request, counsel for a party may in good faith designate any document containing "protected health information" under the Health Insurance Portability and Accountability Act of 1996 ("HIPAA") as "CONFIDENTIAL" by labeling the item with the mark "CONFIDENTIAL" or otherwise including that designation on an appropriate cover letter or document sufficient to advise the document's recipient of the designation.

2. "Document" Defined. The word "document" or "documents" as used herein means all paper and any other tangible thing, including, but not limited to, electronic files, produced in response to a formal or informal discovery request herein.

3. Inadvertence/Oversight. Inadvertent production of protected document(s) shall not constitute a waiver of the right to make an after-the-fact good faith designation. Upon the discovery of such inadvertent production, the producing party shall notify the parties in receipt of the document that it is designated "CONFIDENTIAL." An after-the-fact designation may be made orally on the record in any deposition, together with any explanation relative to inadvertence or oversight, and shall be honored by all present in the same manner as if originally designated "CONFIDENTIAL."

4. Disagreement Over Designation. In the event a recipient of a document declared "CONFIDENTIAL" disagrees with the designation, the proponent of confidentiality shall be so advised in writing by the objecting party and the producing party shall have 10 days within which to withdraw the confidential designation or move the Court to make a determination of confidentiality of any document in dispute. Pending such determination by the Court, any document in issue shall continue to be protected pursuant to the provisions of this Order.

5. General Use of CONFIDENTIAL Documents. Pursuant to 45 C.F.R. § 164.512(e)(1)(v), documents identified as "CONFIDENTIAL" and the confidential information contained therein may be used only for purposes of this litigation.

6. Disclosure to Others. "CONFIDENTIAL" information shall only be produced, revealed or disclosed to:

a. the Court, its staff, court reporters, jury and witnesses at trial;

b. attorneys in this action and employees of such counsel to whom it is necessary that the material be shown for purposes of the prosecution or defense of this action;

c. the parties to this action;

d. consultants or experts unrelated to the parties to this action and retained by them in order to assist in the prosecution or defense of this action, provided such persons are first given a copy of this Order and advised of the obligation to maintain the confidentiality of the information;

e. a deponent at the time of deposition, provided that such persons are first given a copy of this Order and advised of the obligation to maintain the confidentiality of the information; and

f. any other person by the parties' mutual written agreement or order of the Court after notice to all parties. Any such person who is given access to protected information shall be given a copy of this Order and advised of the obligation to maintain the confidentiality of the information.

7. Filing of CONFIDENTIAL Documents. In the event a party seeks to use "CONFIDENTIAL" documents as part of any court filing, the party shall comply with the procedures set forth in the *[rule]*. The Clerk of the Court is authorized, pursuant to *[rule]*, to accept materials submitted by the parties for filing under seal without further order of this Court. Documents filed under seal pursuant to the terms of this Protective Order shall be excluded, as provided by *[rule]*, from both the public case file and the electronic docket.

8. Use of CONFIDENTIAL Documents in Deposition. In the event a party seeks to use "CONFIDENTIAL" documents in a deposition, those portions of the deposition transcripts describing or incorporating any protected materials shall be deemed designated as "CONFIDENTIAL."

9. Admissibility. The provisions of this Order shall not determine whether and to what extent any document or information is admissible into evidence.

10. HIPAA. This Order is intended to comply with the HIPAA requirements of 45 C.F.R. § 164.512(e)(1)(v).

11. Return at Close of Litigation. Within 30 days of the final resolution of this litigation, a party that has received "Confidential" documents containing "protected health information" under HIPAA must either destroy or return such documents to the producing party.

IT IS SO STIPULATED:

Dated:

[signature etc.]

Dated:

[signature etc.]

IT IS SO ORDERED.
Dated: ____

____
Judge

NOTES TO FORM

Commentary

This form is adapted from the record in Abbott v. Good Shepherd Medical Center, 2005 WL 318575 (D. Or. 2005).

§ 17:41 Confidentiality order

[Caption]

CONFIDENTIALITY ORDER

To expedite the flow of discovery material, facilitate the prompt resolution of disputes over confidentiality, protect adequately material entitled to be kept confidential, and ensure that protection is afforded only to material so entitled, it is, pursuant to the court's authority under *[rule]* and with the consent of the parties, ORDERED:

1. Nondisclosure of Stamped Confidential Documents Except with the prior written consent of the party or other person originally designating a document to be stamped as a confidential document, or as hereinafter provided under this order, no stamped confidential document may be disclosed to any person.

[A "stamped confidential document" means any document that bears the legend (or that must otherwise have had the legend recorded upon it in a way that brings it to the attention of a reasonable examiner) "Confidential-Subject to Protective Order in Civil Action No. ____, [court]" to signify that it contains information believed to be subject to protection under [rule]. For purposes of this order, the term "document" means all written, recorded, or graphic material, whether produced or created by a party or an-

other person, whether produced pursuant to Rule 34, subpoena, by agreement, or otherwise. Interrogatory answers, responses to requests for admission, deposition transcripts and exhibits, pleadings, motions, affidavits, and briefs that quote, summarize, or contain materials entitled to protection may be accorded status as a stamped confidential document, but, to the extent feasible, must be prepared in such a manner that the confidential information is bound separately from that not entitled to protection.]

2. Permissible Disclosures Notwithstanding paragraph 1, stamped confidential documents may be disclosed to counsel for the parties in this action who are actively engaged in the conduct of this litigation; to the partners, associates, secretaries, Paralegal assistants, and employees of such counsel to the extent reasonably necessary to render professional services in the litigation; to persons with prior knowledge of the documents or the confidential information contained therein, and their agents; and to court officials involved in this litigation (including court reporters, persons operating video recording equipment at depositions, and any special master appointed by the court). Subject to the provisions of subparagraph (c), such documents may also be disclosed—

(a) to any person designated by the court in the interest of justice, upon such terms as the court may deem proper; and

(b) to persons noticed for depositions or designated as trial witnesses to the extent reasonably necessary in preparing to testify; to outside consultants or experts retained for the purpose of assisting counsel in the litigation; to employees of parties involved solely in one or more aspects of organizing, filing, coding, converting, storing, or retrieving data or designing programs for handling data connected with these actions, including the performance of such duties in relation to a computerized litigation support system; and to employees of third-party contractors performing one or more of these functions; provided, however, that in all such cases the individual to whom disclosure is to be made has signed and filed with the court a form containing—

(1) a recital that the signatory has read and understands this order;

(2) a recital that the signatory understands that unauthorized disclosures of the stamped confidential documents constitute contempt of court; and

(3) a statement that the signatory consents to the exercise of personal jurisdiction by this court.

(c) Before disclosing a stamped confidential document to any person listed in subparagraph (a) or (b) who is a competitor (or an employee of a competitor) of the party that so designated the document, the party wishing to make such disclosure must give at least 10 days' advance notice in writing to the counsel who designated such information as confidential, stating the names and addresses of the person(s) to whom the disclosure will be made, identifying with particularity the documents to be disclosed, and stating the purposes of such disclosure. If, within the 10-day period, a motion is filed objecting to the proposed disclosure, disclosure is not permissible until the court has denied such motion. The court will deny the motion unless the objecting party shows good cause why the proposed disclosure should not be permitted.

3. Declassification A party (or aggrieved entity permitted by the court to intervene for such purpose) may apply to the court for a ruling that a document (or category of documents) stamped as confidential is not entitled to such status and protection. The party or other person that designated the document as confidential must be given notice of the application and an opportunity to respond. To maintain confidential status, the proponent of confidentiality must show by a preponderance of the evidence that there is good cause for the document to have such protection.

4. Confidential Information in Depositions

(a) A deponent may during the deposition be shown and examined about stamped confidential documents if the deponent already knows the confidential information contained therein or if the provisions of paragraph 2(c) are complied with. Deponents must not retain or copy portions of the transcript of their depositions that contain confidential information not provided by them or the entities they represent unless they sign the form prescribed in paragraph 2(b). A deponent who is not a party or a representative of a party must be furnished a copy of this order before being examined about, or asked to produce, potentially confidential documents.

(b) Parties (and deponents) may, within 15 days after receiving a deposition, designate pages of the transcript (and exhibits thereto) as confidential. Confidential information within the deposition transcript may be designated by underlining the portions of the pages that are confidential and marking such pages with the following legend: "Confidential-Subject to Protection Pursuant to Court Order." Until expiration of the 15-day period, the entire deposition will be treated as subject to protection against disclosure under this order. If no party or deponent timely designates confidential information in a deposition, then none of the transcript or its exhibits will be treated as confidential; if a timely designation is made, the confidential portions and exhibits must be filed under seal separate from the portions and exhibits not so marked.

5. Confidential Information at Trial Subject to the *[rules]*, stamped confidential documents and other confidential information may be offered in evidence at trial or any court hearing, provided that the proponent of the evidence gives five days' advance notice to counsel for any party or other person that designated the information as confidential. Any party may move the court for an order that the evidence be received in camera or under other conditions to prevent unnecessary disclosure. The court will then determine whether the proffered evidence should continue to be treated as confidential information and, if so, what protection, if any, may be afforded to such information at the trial.

6. Subpoena by Other Courts or Agencies If another court or an administrative agency subpoenas or orders production of stamped confidential documents that a party has obtained under the terms of this order, such party must promptly notify the party or other person who designated the document as confidential of the pendency of such subpoena or order.

7. Filing Stamped confidential documents need not be filed with the clerk except when required in connection with motions under *[rules]* or other matters pending before the court. If filed, they must be filed under seal and must remain sealed while in the office of the clerk so long as they retain their status as stamped confidential documents.

8. Client Consultation Nothing in this order must prevent or otherwise restrict counsel from rendering advice to their clients and, in the course thereof, relying generally on examination of stamped confidential documents; provided, however, that in rendering such advice and otherwise communicating with such clients, counsel must not make specific disclosure of any item so designated except pursuant to the procedures of paragraphs 2(b) and (c).

9. Prohibited Copying If a document contains information so sensitive that it should not be copied by anyone, it must bear the additional legend "Copying Prohibited." Application for relief from this restriction against copying may be made to the court, with notice to counsel so designating the document.

10. Use Persons obtaining access to stamped confidential documents under this order must use the information only for preparation and trial of this litigation (including appeals and retrials), and must not use such information for any other purpose, including business, governmental, commercial, administrative, or judicial proceedings. *[For purposes of this paragraph, the term*

"this litigation" includes other related litigation in which the producing person or company is a party.]

11. Non-Termination The provisions of this order must not terminate at the conclusion of these actions. Within 120 days after final conclusion of all aspects of this litigation, stamped confidential documents and all copies of same (other than exhibits of record) must be returned to the party or person that produced such documents or, at the option of the producer (if it retains at least one copy of the same), destroyed. All counsel of record must make certification of compliance herewith and must deliver the same to counsel for the party who produced the documents and not more than 150 days after final termination of this litigation.

12. Modification Permitted Nothing in this order must prevent any party or other person from seeking modification of this order or from objecting to discovery that it believes to be otherwise improper.

13. Responsibility of Attorneys The attorneys of record are responsible for employing reasonable measures, consistent with this order, to control duplication of, access to, and distribution of copies of stamped confidential documents. Parties must not duplicate any stamped confidential document except working copies and for filing in court under seal.

14. No Waiver

(a) Review of the confidential documents and information by counsel, experts, or consultants for the litigants in the litigation must not waive the confidentiality of the documents or objections to production.

(b) The inadvertent, unintentional, or in camera disclosure of confidential document and information must not, under any circumstances, be deemed a waiver, in whole or in part, of any party's claims of confidentiality.

15. Nothing contained in this protective order and no action taken pursuant to it shall prejudice the right of any party to contest the alleged relevancy, admissibility, or discoverability of the confidential documents and information sought.

Dated: ________

____

Judge

NOTES TO FORM

Commentary

The order may indicate whether disclosure may be made to in-house counsel actively involved in the conduct of the litigation and to attorneys involved in related litigation in other courts.

Chapter 18

Spoliation

E. RULE 37 OF THE FEDERAL RULES OF CIVIL PROCEDURE

II. CHECKLISTS

III. FORMS

Research References

Treatises and Practice Aids

Grenig and Gleisner, eDiscovery & Digital Evidence §§ 11:1 to 11:19
O'Malley, Grenig, & Lee, Federal Jury Practice and Instructions (6th ed.)

Trial Strategy

Recovery and Reconstruction of Electronic Mail as Evidence, 41 Am. Jur Proof of Facts 3d 1
Computer Technology in Civil Litigation, 71 Am. Jur. Trials 111

Additional References

Grenig and Kinsler, Handbook of Federal Civil Discovery and Disclosure §§ 16.1 to 16.22 (3d ed.)
ABA Discovery Standards, http://www.abanet.org/litigation/discoverystandards/2005civildiscoverystandards.pdf
Federal Judicial Center, http://www.fjc.gov
The Sedona Conference, http://www.thesedonaconference.org

> **KeyCite®**: Cases and other legal materials listed in KeyCite Scope can be researched through the KeyCite service on Westlaw®. Use KeyCite to check citations for form, parallel references, prior and later history, and comprehensive citator information, including citations to other decisions and secondary materials.

I. GUIDELINES

A. INTRODUCTION

§ 18:1 Generally

Spoliation is the destruction, significant alteration, or the failure to preserve property for another's use as evidence in pending or reasonably foreseeable litigation.[1] Spoliation can occur as the result of actions by parties or by nonparties. It can be inadvertent or intentional. It can be the product of absolute good faith, the result of negligence[2] or the exercise of consummate."[3]

Persons and organizations are free to develop their own document retention and destruction policies so long as they are consistent with legislation, court rules, and court decisions, and they are reasonably tailored to the needs of the person or organization.[4] However, there are times when the normal document destruction policy must be suspended, and documents must be retained and

---

[Section 18:1]

[1]See Micron Technology, Inc. v. Rambus Inc., 645 F.3d 1311, 98 U.S.P. Q.2d 1693 (Fed. Cir. 2011) ("'Spoliation' refers to the destruction or material alteration of evidence or to the failure to preserve property for another's use as evidence in pending or reasonably foreseeable litigation."); Pension Committee of University of Montreal Pension Plan v. Banc of America Securities, 685 F. Supp. 2d 456 (S.D. N.Y. 2010) (abrogated on other grounds by, Chin v. Port Authority of New York & New Jersey, 685 F.3d 135, 115 Fair Empl. Prac. Cas. (BNA) 720, 95 Empl. Prac. Dec. (CCH) ¶ 44555 (2d Cir. 2012)); Rimkus Consulting Group, Inc. v. Cammarata, 688 F. Supp. 2d 598 (S.D. Tex. 2010); Sampson v. City of Cambridge, Md., 251 F.R.D. 172 (D. Md. 2008); Nucor Corp. v. Bell, 251 F.R.D. 191 (D.S.C. 2008); Zubulake v. UBS Warburg LLC, 220 F.R.D. 212, 216, 92 Fair Empl. Prac. Cas. (BNA) 1539 (S.D. N.Y. 2003).

[2]But see American Family Mut. Ins., Co. v. Roth, 2009 WL 982788, *9 (N.D. Ill. 2009) ("A party claiming spoliation by its adversary must prove that the destruction was intentional or the result of fault—generally beyond mere negligence, and that the document was relevant to an issue at trial.").

[3]See Treppel v. Biovail Corp., 249 F.R.D. 111 (S.D. N.Y. 2008); Solovy & Byman, *Discovery: Evidence Destruction*, NAT'L L.J., Nov. 16, 1998, at B12.

[4]See Gippetti v. United Parcel Service, Inc., 2008 WL 3264483 (N.D. Cal. 2008) (spoliation sanctions for destruction of ESI pursuant to document retention policy denied under Fed. R. Civ P. 37(e) safe harbor provision).

protected. The failure to take such action may have serious consequences.

Because electronically stored information is routinely deleted or altered, affirmative steps are often required to preserve it. Deletions, alterations and losses of electronically stored information cannot be spoliation unless there is a duty to preserve the information, a culpable breach of that duty, and resulting prejudice.[5] Unlike paper documents, requiring an overt act like shredding to be destroyed, electronically stored information can be and often is destroyed or modified by routine computer use. Simply turning on a personal computer can destroy slack and temporary files, cause electronically stored information to be overwritten, or alter metadata (for example, data showing when a file was created or modified). Just clicking on a file can change its last-accessed date, inviting a suggestion that it has been altered.[6]

While courts cannot expect parties to meet a standard of perfection, courts expect that litigants and counsel will take the necessary steps to ensure that relevant records are preserved when litigation is pending or is reasonably anticipated, and that such records are collected, reviewed and produced to the opposing party.[7] A failure to preserve records and to search in the right places for those records may result in spoliation of evidence.[8] Spoliation of evidence, particularly of electronically stored information, has assumed a level of importance in litigation raising grave concerns.[9]

Spoliation of electronically stored information can have very severe consequences and the act of spoliation may be easier to establish in the case of electronically stored information than it is

---

[5]Rimkus Consulting Group, Inc. v. Cammarata, 688 F. Supp. 2d 598 (S.D. Tex. 2010).

[6]Gates Rubber Co. v. Bando Chemical Industries, Ltd., 167 F.R.D. 90 (D. Colo. 1996).

[7]Pension Committee of University of Montreal Pension Plan v. Banc of America Securities, 685 F. Supp. 2d 456 (S.D. N.Y. 2010) (abrogated on other grounds by, Chin v. Port Authority of New York & New Jersey, 685 F.3d 135, 115 Fair Empl. Prac. Cas. (BNA) 720, 95 Empl. Prac. Dec. (CCH) ¶ 44555 (2d Cir. 2012)).

[8]Pension Committee of University of Montreal Pension Plan v. Banc of America Securities, 685 F. Supp. 2d 456 (S.D. N.Y. 2010) (abrogated on other grounds by, Chin v. Port Authority of New York & New Jersey, 685 F.3d 135, 115 Fair Empl. Prac. Cas. (BNA) 720, 95 Empl. Prac. Dec. (CCH) ¶ 44555 (2d Cir. 2012)).

[9]Rimkus Consulting Group, Inc. v. Cammarata, 688 F. Supp. 2d 598 (S.D. Tex. 2010).

in the case of paper documents. Courts have made it clear they take the preservation of electronically stored information very seriously. If advised of a threat in advance, a court may order the preservation of electronically stored information during the pendency of a lawsuit.[10]

Motions for spoliation sanctions are very time consuming, distracting and expensive for the parties and the court.[11] A court should give the most careful consideration before it finds a party has violated its duty to comply with discovery obligations and deserves to be sanctioned.[12] In addition, parties must anticipate and undertake document preservation with the most serious and thorough care.[13]

Determining the boundaries of the duty to preserve involves two related inquiries:

- When does the duty to preserve attach?
- What evidence must be preserved?

A court is not required to hold an evidentiary hearing to determine the validity of spoliation allegations.[14] Appellate courts will not hear spoliation claims unless the claims were raised at the district court.[15]

---

[10]See, e.g., In re Cell Pathways, Inc., Securities Litigation, II, 203 F.R.D. 189, Fed. Sec. L. Rep. (CCH) ¶ 91507 (E.D. Pa. 2001); In re Bridgestone/Firestone, Inc., ATX, ATX II, 129 F. Supp. 2d 1207 (S.D. Ind. 2001).

[11]Pension Committee of University of Montreal Pension Plan v. Banc of America Securities, 685 F. Supp. 2d 456 (S.D. N.Y. 2010) (abrogated on other grounds by, Chin v. Port Authority of New York & New Jersey, 685 F.3d 135, 115 Fair Empl. Prac. Cas. (BNA) 720, 95 Empl. Prac. Dec. (CCH) ¶ 44555 (2d Cir. 2012)). See Willoughby, Jr., et al., *Sanctions for E-Discovery Violations: By the Numbers*, 60 Duke L.J. 789 (2010); Chalmers, *Successful Spoliation Motions Are Rarer Than You May Think*, LITIG., Fall 2011, at 8.

[12]Pension Committee of University of Montreal Pension Plan v. Banc of America Securities, 685 F. Supp. 2d 456 (S.D. N.Y. 2010) (abrogated on other grounds by, Chin v. Port Authority of New York & New Jersey, 685 F.3d 135, 115 Fair Empl. Prac. Cas. (BNA) 720, 95 Empl. Prac. Dec. (CCH) ¶ 44555 (2d Cir. 2012)).

[13]Pension Committee of University of Montreal Pension Plan v. Banc of America Securities, 685 F. Supp. 2d 456 (S.D. N.Y. 2010) (abrogated on other grounds by, Chin v. Port Authority of New York & New Jersey, 685 F.3d 135, 115 Fair Empl. Prac. Cas. (BNA) 720, 95 Empl. Prac. Dec. (CCH) ¶ 44555 (2d Cir. 2012)).

[14]Busch v. Dyno Nobel, Inc., 40 Fed. Appx. 947, 48 U.C.C. Rep. Serv. 2d 874 (6th Cir. 2002).

[15]Ridgeway v. O'Bryan, 88 Fed. Appx. 259 (9th Cir. 2004).

B. DUTY TO PRESERVE

§ 18:2 Generally

The obligation to preserve electronically stored information requires reasonable and good faith efforts to retain and preserve information that may be relevant to pending or threatened litigation.[1] If litigation is pending or reasonably foreseeable, the legal standard for the retention of documents is their discoverability in the litigation.[2] The duty applies to plaintiffs and defendants.[3]

While a litigant is under no duty to keep or retain every paper or digital document in the litigant's possession once a complaint is filed, a litigant is under a duty to preserve what it knows, or reasonably should know, is relevant in the action, is reasonably calculated to lead to discovery of admissible evidence, is reasonably likely to be requested during discovery, and/or is the subject of a pending discovery request.

A person's exposure to spoliation liability in discarding records under a routine procedure depends primarily on: (1) the relevance of the documents to pending or reasonably foreseeable litigation; and (2) the nature of the person's document retention policy. Even if a person were to inadvertently dispose of documents discoverable in reasonably foreseeable litigation, pursuant to its

---

[Section 18:2]

[1]Passlogix, Inc. v. 2FA Technology, LLC, 708 F. Supp. 2d 378 (S.D. N.Y. 2010); Nucor Corp. v. Bell, 251 F.R.D. 191 (D.S.C. 2008). See Sedona Principle 5 ("The obligation to preserve electronically stored information requires reasonable and good faith efforts to retain information that may be relevant to pending or threatened litigation. However, it is unreasonable to expect parties to take every conceivable step to preserve all potentially relevant electronically stored information.").

See Chin v. Port Authority of New York & New Jersey, 685 F.3d 135, 115 Fair Empl. Prac. Cas. (BNA) 720, 95 Empl. Prac. Dec. (CCH) ¶ 44555 (2d Cir. 2012), cert. denied, 133 S. Ct. 1724, 185 L. Ed. 2d 785, 117 Fair Empl. Prac. Cas. (BNA) 1412 (2013) (failure to adopt good preservation practices is one factor in determining whether a discovery sanction should issue).

[2]Fujitsu Ltd. v. Federal Exp. Corp., 247 F.3d 423, 436 (2d Cir. 2001).

[3]See, e.g., Rimkus Consulting Group, Inc. v. Cammarata, 688 F. Supp. 2d 598 (S.D. Tex. 2010) (former employees were obligated to preserve documents information when they were about to preemptively sue employer to challenge noncompetition covenants).

formal policy, the person would not necessarily be sanctioned for spoliation.[4]

§ 18:3 Foreseeability of future litigation

Absent actual notice, all forms of spoliation liability turn on foreseeability.[1] When a complaint has not yet been filed and there is no specific statutory or other legal duty between the parties, the question is whether it is reasonably foreseeable a lawsuit will ensue and the evidence will be discoverable in connection with that suit. Once a party reasonably anticipates litigation, the party must suspend its routine document retention and destruction program and put in place a legal hold ensuring preservation of relevant documents.[2]

The duty to preserve evidence before the filing of a lawsuit typically arises when the party is on notice that the litigation is likely to be commenced. This notice usually occurs when a person is served with either a judicial or administrative complaint, but it also may occur as a result of prelitigation conduct or communication with the plaintiff.[3] A plaintiff's duty to preserve is

---

[4]See Fed. R. Civ. P. 37(e) (absent exceptional circumstances, a court may not impose sanctions under the Federal Rules of Civil Procedure for electronically stored information lost through "routine good-faith operation" of an electronic information system rather than through intentional acts intended to make evidence unavailable). See also Rimkus Consulting Group, Inc. v. Cammarata, 688 F. Supp. 2d 598 (S.D. Tex. 2010).

[Section 18:3]

[1]See, e.g., Computer Associates Intern., Inc. v. American Fundware, Inc., 133 F.R.D. 166, 169, 18 U.S.P.Q.2d 1649 (D. Colo. 1990) (prelitigation correspondence constitutes actual notice of litigation). But see Getty Properties Corp. v. Raceway Petroleum, Inc., 2005 WL 1412134 (D.N.J. 2005) (failure to retain interim or transitory information not required for business purposes is not kind of willful action that discovery sanctions are intended to redress).

[2]Pension Committee of University of Montreal Pension Plan v. Banc of America Securities, 685 F. Supp. 2d 456 (S.D. N.Y. 2010) (abrogated on other grounds by, Chin v. Port Authority of New York & New Jersey, 685 F.3d 135, 115 Fair Empl. Prac. Cas. (BNA) 720, 95 Empl. Prac. Dec. (CCH) ¶ 44555 (2d Cir. 2012)); Treppel v. Biovail Corp., 249 F.R.D. 111, 118 (S.D. N.Y. 2008); Zubulake v. UBS Warburg LLC, 220 F.R.D. 212, 218, 92 Fair Empl. Prac. Cas. (BNA) 1539 (S.D. N.Y. 2003).

[3]Nacco Materials Handling Group, Inc. v. Lilly Co., 278 F.R.D. 395 (W.D. Tenn. 2011) (defendant's duty to preserve was triggered on date dealer was served with plaintiff's complaint);

often triggered before litigation commences because a plaintiff's control the timing of litigation.[4]

In making determinations of foreseeability, courts should recognize the unique problems faced by large organizations and guard against imposing unreasonably expansive duties to preserve evidence. Courts should require only that the would-be spoliator act reasonably under the circumstances. This means that, where litigation is merely possible, but not reasonably foreseeable, routine document disposal should be highly unlikely to result in spoliation sanctions.

For example, a manufacturer should not be required to preserve all documents for decades in the absence of reasonably foreseeable litigation simply because of the possibility that some documents might be relevant to future litigation. Discovery sanctions for spoliation are warranted only if evidence was destroyed when a product liability action was contemplated, rather than merely possible.

One way in which courts have determined the existence of notice is through consideration of prior complaints or lawsuits filed against the company over similar or related matters.[5] There are very few reported cases that treat the issues of related litigation or similar products in the context of spoliation, and there is not enough detail in the available cases to define these terms for purposes of determining when additional litigation is reasonably foreseeable.

In *Lewy v. Remington Arms Co.*,[6] a products liability action relating to a rifle that fired upon the release of its safety. The manufacturer's record retention policy provided for the destruc-

---

[4]Pension Committee of University of Montreal Pension Plan v. Banc of America Securities, 685 F. Supp. 2d 456 (S.D. N.Y. 2010) (abrogated on other grounds by, Chin v. Port Authority of New York & New Jersey, 685 F.3d 135, 115 Fair Empl. Prac. Cas. (BNA) 720, 95 Empl. Prac. Dec. (CCH) ¶ 44555 (2d Cir. 2012)); Innis Arden Golf Club v. Pitney Bowes, Inc., 257 F.R.D. 334, 340, 70 Env't. Rep. Cas. (BNA) 1045 (D. Conn. 2009); Cyntegra, Inc. v. Idexx Laboratories, Inc., 2007 WL 5193736, *3 (C.D. Cal. 2007), order aff'd, 322 Fed. Appx. 569, 2009-1 Trade Cas. (CCH) ¶ 76574 (9th Cir. 2009).

[5]Cf. Stevenson v. Union Pacific R. Co., 354 F.3d 739, 63 Fed. R. Evid. Serv. 166, 57 Fed. R. Serv. 3d 617 (8th Cir. 2004) (declaring that there must be some indication of an intent to destroy the evidence for the purpose of obstructing or suppressing truth in order to impose sanction of adverse inference instruction, court upheld sanctions against defendant, because defendant had been careful to preserve a voice tape in other cases where tape proved to be beneficial to defendant and had made immediate effort to preserve other types of evidence but not voice tape in this case).

[6]Lewy v. Remington Arms Co., Inc., 836 F.2d 1104, Prod. Liab. Rep. (CCH) ¶ 11662, 24 Fed. R. Evid. Serv. 516 (8th Cir. 1988).

tion of complaints and gun examination reports after three years, absent any action concerning a particular record. Since other complaints had been filed against the manufacturer with respect to the rifle model in question, the court remanded the case for a determination regarding the propriety of destroying the plaintiff's records under the circumstances. The court suggested frequent discovery requests for a specific type of document in litigation over the same product may establish the reasonable foreseeability of the relevance and probably materiality of other documents of that type in future litigation.

Remington suggests limits on what courts will consider similar products. The *Remington* court did not rule that complaints about the defective firing pin meant that the defendant should foresee lawsuits involving all of its firing pins, let alone all of its rifles. Rather, it announced the common-sense rule that there was an issue as to whether destruction of documents involving a specific model was appropriate, where the company had received a series of complaints about that model. There is apparently no additional authority to assist in determining when products are sufficiently similar to assume that complaints about one create foreseeable litigation involving another.

Additional facts surrounding the document retention policy may also indicate the reasonable foreseeability of litigation. The *Remington* court suggested a three-year retention period might be appropriate for some types of documents but not others, including possibly customer complaints. Finally, the court thought it relevant whether lawsuits concerning the complaint or related complaints had been filed, the frequency of such complaints, and the magnitude of the complaints. In *Remington*, lawsuits concerning the complaint and related complaints would appear to refer to lawsuits or complaints pertaining to the firing controls of the specific rifle model in question.

The issue of whether a company must maintain documents prior to actual notice of litigation arose in *Scott v. IBM Corp.*[7] In that case, an employee brought an action against his former employer for discrimination. The suit arose out of IBM's decision to layoff Scott as part of a company-wide reduction-in-force. Before the suit, IBM destroyed documents related to the reduction in force. The court held the destruction warranted sanctions because the detailed nature of the destroyed documents themselves demonstrated that IBM was on notice of the sensitive nature of the layoff. Moreover, the court concluded:

---

[7]Scott v. IBM Corp., 196 F.R.D. 233, 12 A.D. Cas. (BNA) 99 (D.N.J. 2000).

> [W]hile litigation was not guaranteed, it could be viewed as reasonably foreseeable. IBM managers knew that Mr. Scott, if not others included in the [reduction in force], were protected by federal employment discrimination laws. Mr. Scott had made previous claims of race discrimination within IBM, and thus IBM had ample notice that it was discharging a litigious employee when it fired him. Common sense would dictate preserving all helpful documentation when dealing with the discharge of an employee with a litigious history.[8]

In *Sanchez v. Stanley-Bostich, Inc.*,[9] the court approved an adverse inference instruction against the plaintiff (Sanchez) based on spoliation. Sanchez claimed he was injured while using the defendant's staple gun. After the accident, Sanchez's lawyer instructed him to take photographs of the staple gun at issue, but neither Sanchez nor his lawyer did anything to preserve the staple gun itself. The court was asked to determine whether Sanchez had an obligation to preserve the gun for Stanley's use. Answering this question affirmatively, the court stated:

> The obligation to preserve evidence may arise before the filing of a complaint where a party is on notice that litigation will likely be commenced. Here, at the time the photographs were taken Sanchez had already retained counsel, and indeed was acting at his direction. Clearly, the photographs were taken in preparation of a possible lawsuit. Yet, Stanley was not informed of the anticipated claim.[10]

§ 18:4 What electronically stored information must be preserved

Once a person has notice of potential litigation, the person has a duty to act reasonably in preserving documents. Although a litigant is not under a duty to keep or retain every document in its possession once a complaint is filed, a litigant is under a duty to preserve what it knows, or reasonably should know, is relevant in the claims or defenses in action, is reasonably calculated to lead to the discovery of admissible evidence, is reasonably likely

---

[8]Scott v. IBM Corp., 196 F.R.D. 233, 249, 12 A.D. Cas. (BNA) 99 (D.N.J. 2000).

[9]Sanchez v. Stanley-Bostich, Inc., Prod. Liab. Rep. (CCH) ¶ 15635, 1999 WL 639703 (S.D. N.Y. 1999). See also Rimkus Consulting Group, Inc. v. Cammarata, 688 F. Supp. 2d 598 (S.D. Tex. 2010) (former employees were obligated to preserve documents information when they were about to preemptively sue employer to challenge noncompetition covenants).

[10]Sanchez v. Stanley-Bostich, Inc., Prod. Liab. Rep. (CCH) ¶ 15635, 1999 WL 639703 (S.D. N.Y. 1999).

to be requested during discovery, or is the subject of a pending discovery request.[1]

Zubulake v. UBS Warburg LLC[2] contains a practical summary of the scope of the duty to preserve electronically stored information:

> The scope of a party's preservation obligation can be described as follows: Once a party reasonably anticipates litigation, it must suspend its routine document retention/destruction policy and put in place a "legal hold" to ensure the preservation of relevant documents. As a general rule, that legal hold does not apply to inaccessible backup tapes (e.g., those typically maintained solely for the purpose of disaster recovery), which may continue to be recycled on the schedule set forth in the company's policy. On the other hand, if backup tapes are accessible (i.e., actively used for information retrieval), then such tapes would likely be subject to the legal hold.
>
> However, it does make sense to create one exception to this general rule. If a company can identify where particular employee documents are stored on backup tapes, then the tapes storing the documents of "key players" to the existing or threatened litigation should be preserved if the information contained on those tapes is not otherwise available. This exception applies to all backup tapes.[3]

This articulation of the duty to preserve strikes a reasonable balance between a party's right to discover relevant evidence and an organization's need to operate without undue burden or expense. It also emphasizes the necessity of having a written, reasonable, need-based, and transparent document retention and destruction policy so that a court can understand what documents are being preserved or destroyed and why that action is being taken. Without such a policy, the duty to preserve will be, by necessity, much broader than it need be.

[Section 18:4]

[1]Passlogix, Inc. v. 2FA Technology, LLC, 708 F. Supp. 2d 378 (S.D. N.Y. 2010); Rimkus Consulting Group, Inc. v. Cammarata, 688 F. Supp. 2d 598 (S.D. Tex. 2010); Zubulake v. UBS Warburg LLC, 220 F.R.D. 212, 217–18, 92 Fair Empl. Prac. Cas. (BNA) 1539 (S.D. N.Y. 2003).

[2]Zubulake v. UBS Warburg LLC, 220 F.R.D. 212, 217–18, 92 Fair Empl. Prac. Cas. (BNA) 1539 (S.D. N.Y. 2003).

[3]Zubulake v. UBS Warburg LLC, 220 F.R.D. 212, 92 Fair Empl. Prac. Cas. (BNA) 1539 (S.D. N.Y. 2003). See Consolidated Aluminum Corp. v. Alcoa, Inc., 244 F.R.D. 335 (M.D. La. 2006) (as general rule, party's duty to place a legal hold on evidence does not apply to inaccessible backup tapes for electronic evidence—those typically maintained solely for purpose of disaster recovery, which may continue to be recycled on the schedule set forth in party's policy, but if backup tapes are accessible (actively used for information retrieval), then such tapes would likely be subject to legal hold).

Counsel face a number of important considerations when it comes to deciding what to preserve and how. The *Zubulake* decision only touches on some of the issues. In deciding what electronically stored information to preserve, counsel should carefully research the subject. Counsel should not rely on counsel's own understanding of what constitutes electronically stored information or how it can be preserved. Counsel does not want to be in the position of becoming a technical witness if and when the question of digital data preservation becomes an issue in litigation. Moreover, most counsel are not in a strong position to determine:

- What metadata are and how they ought to be preserved, if at all.
- What the distinction is between backup and disaster tape systems.
- What backup or data storage sequences should be suspended.
- What steps should be taken to image hard drives.
- What steps should be taken to segregate business e-mail from personal e-mail or otherwise protect employee privacy or trade secret privileges.
- What must be done to distinguish between unique and duplicate digital data.
- What steps should be taken to preserve Web pages, intranet systems, or ASP data depositories.

Courts do not require organizations to hold onto every piece of discoverable paper in their files, even under certain circumstances when litigation is foreseeable. Nor do courts oblige frequently sued organizations to preserve all their records. Beyond this, however, not much is absolutely clear. It appears courts are least likely to impose sanctions where the following is true:

- Litigation is remote or foreseeability is otherwise attenuated
- Documents are disposed of pursuant to a routine, evenly applied, established policy
- There is no evidence of conscious effort to interfere with the litigation
- The evidence disposed of is not critical to the opponent's likelihood of success

§ 18:5 How to preserve electronically stored information

One of the biggest problems with preserving electronically stored information is finding and identifying it. Generally, data management systems are developed to satisfy daily business practices, not to accommodate discovery needs. An additional problem is created by the volatility of electronically stored information. Electronically stored information can be altered, overwritten, or destroyed simply by running conflicting software or by conducting routine maintenance.

A first look at what documents should be retained normally revolves around the persons named in the disclosures made pursuant to Fed. R. Civ. P. 26(a)(1)(a). If a person is named in those disclosures, electronically stored information made by or for that person must be preserved.[1] Other electronically stored information that should be retained is that involving persons in the organization likely to have relevant information as that term is defined by Fed. R. Civ. P. 26(b)(1).[2]

Once the persons whose electronically stored information should be retained are identified, those persons must retain all relevant electronically stored information (but not multiple identical copies) in existence at the time the duty to preserve attaches, and any relevant documents created thereafter.[3] Beyond taking these initial steps, there is no magic way to fulfill the preservation obligation. Rather, the touchstone should be reasonableness—whether the party has taken all reasonable steps necessary to preserve the relevant or potentially relevant documents.[4]

One of the most common preservation mistakes is failing to cease document destruction procedures upon notice of suit or the likelihood of suit. The Court in *Zubulake v. UBS Warburg LLC*[5] described the obligation of a party who anticipates litigation to preserve digital evidence in the following terms:

> A party or anticipated party must retain all relevant documents (but not multiple identical copies) in existence at the time the duty to preserve attaches, and any relevant documents created thereafter. In recognition of the fact that there are many ways to manage electronic data, litigants are free to choose how this task is

[Section 18:5]

[1]Zubulake v. UBS Warburg LLC, 220 F.R.D. 212, 218, 92 Fair Empl. Prac. Cas. (BNA) 1539 (S.D. N.Y. 2003).

[2]Zubulake v. UBS Warburg LLC, 220 F.R.D. 212, 218, 92 Fair Empl. Prac. Cas. (BNA) 1539 (S.D. N.Y. 2003).

[3]Zubulake v. UBS Warburg LLC, 220 F.R.D. 212, 218, 92 Fair Empl. Prac. Cas. (BNA) 1539 (S.D. N.Y. 2003).

[4]See Zubulake v. UBS Warburg LLC, 220 F.R.D. 212, 92 Fair Empl. Prac. Cas. (BNA) 1539 (S.D. N.Y. 2003).

[5]Zubulake v. UBS Warburg LLC, 220 F.R.D. 212, 92 Fair Empl. Prac. Cas. (BNA) 1539 (S.D. N.Y. 2003).

> accomplished. For example, a litigant could choose to retain all then-existing backup tapes for the relevant personnel (if such tapes store data by individual or the contents can be identified in good faith and through reasonable effort), and to catalog any later-created documents in a separate electronic file. That, along with a mirror-image of the computer system taken at the time the duty to preserve attaches (to preserve documents in the state they existed at that time), creates a complete set of relevant documents. Presumably there are a multitude of other ways to achieve the same result.
>
> The scope of a party's preservation obligation can be described as follows: Once a party reasonably anticipates litigation, it must suspend its routine document retention/destruction policy and put in place a legal hold to ensure the preservation of relevant documents. As a general rule, that legal hold does not apply to inaccessible backup tapes (e.g., those typically maintained solely for the purpose of disaster recovery), which may continue to be recycled on the schedule set forth in the company's policy. On the other hand, if backup tapes are accessible (i.e., actively used for information retrieval), then such tapes *would* likely be subject to the legal hold.[6]

§ 18:6 Written preservation plans

A written preservation plan focuses on preserving electronically stored information once litigation is foreseeable. Counsel must evaluate the extent to which retention policies must be suspended because of the impending litigation. Before adoption of a plan, evidence generally may be legitimately destroyed when done pursuant to a document retention policy that is reasonable and evenly applied.

The success of a preservation plan depends to a very large degree on an intimate knowledge on the part of producing counsel of the administrative controls and architecture of a defendant's computer system. For most attorneys, such knowledge can only be acquired by retaining technical assistance, and this is especially important when it comes to devising workable preservation plans.

Retention polices are not the same as preservation plans. It may be necessary to suspend retention policies in order to insure that relevant evidence is not destroyed in the course of the routine reuse of backup tapes. The destruction of electronically stored information pursuant to a bona fide retention policy where no litigation is anticipated will normally be acceptable.

Still, counsel should approach existing or planned retention

---

[6]Zubulake v. UBS Warburg LLC, 220 F.R.D. 212, 218, 92 Fair Empl. Prac. Cas. (BNA) 1539 (S.D. N.Y. 2003) (italics in original).

policies with a degree of skepticism. The issue often becomes whether an organization in adopting a retention policy knew or should have known that litigation was imminent. In *Lewy v. Remington Arms Co.*,[1] the Eighth Circuit ruled:

> In cases where a document retention policy is instituted in order to limit damaging evidence available to potential plaintiffs, it may be proper to give an [adverse inference] instruction similar to the one requested by the Lewys. Similarly, even if the court finds the policy to be reasonable given the nature of the documents subject to the policy, the court may find that under the particular circumstances certain documents should have been retained notwithstanding the policy. For example, if the corporation knew or should have known that the documents would become material at some point in the future then such documents should have been preserved. Thus, a corporation cannot blindly destroy documents and expect to be shielded by a seemingly innocuous document retention policy.

§ 18:7 Ethical considerations

Lawyers who aid the deliberate concealment or destruction of evidence may be disciplined under relevant ethical codes or rules of court.[1] For example, the American Bar Association's Model Code of Professional Conduct may be violated when evidence is concealed or destroyed by a lawyer. Under Model Rule 3.4(a), a lawyer must not "unlawfully obstruct another party's access to evidence or unlawfully alter, destroy or conceal a document or other material having potential evidentiary value."

The Model Code of Professional Responsibility states that a lawyer must not "conceal or knowingly fail to disclose that which he is required by law to reveal," during representation of a client. (ABA Code DR 7-102(A)(3).) DR 7-109(A) adds that "[a] lawyer shall not suppress any evidence that he or his client has a legal obligation to reveal or produce." Spoliation performed by the client at the lawyer's direction may also violate the Model Rules. (See ABA Code DR 7-102(A)(7) ("In his representation of a client, a lawyer shall not counsel or assist his client in conduct that the lawyer knows to be illegal or fraudulent."); Model Rule of Professional Conduct 3.4(a) (same).) This prohibition may embrace doc-

---

[Section 18:6]

[1]Lewy v. Remington Arms Co., Inc., 836 F.2d 1104, 1112, Prod. Liab. Rep. (CCH) ¶ 11662, 24 Fed. R. Evid. Serv. 516 (8th Cir. 1988).

[Section 18:7]

[1]See Donato v. Fitzgibbons, 172 F.R.D. 75, 79, 38 Fed. R. Serv. 3d 1086 (S.D. N.Y. 1997) (obligation to preserve evidence runs first to counsel, who has duty to advise client of type of information potentially relevant to lawsuit and of the necessity of preventing its destruction).

ument retention policies designed in bad faith at the behest of the lawyer.

Counsel should carefully monitor their clients' document production, as many clients may not appreciate the implications of hiding or destroying damaging evidence.[2] Additionally, counsel must monitor experts. Many tests require destruction of the electronically stored information itself and could lead to spoliation claims. Constant vigilance by a lawyer may avoid costly litigation or sanctions, as well as prevent ethical conflicts from arising.

§ 18:8 Consequences of preservation

Preservation does not mean a party must later agree to produce the electronically stored information. By preserving electronically stored information, a party is only assuring that the electronically stored information will be available if the electronically stored information is later determined to be relevant or discoverable. If it is later determined the party should have preserved electronically stored information but did not, the party's counsel could face charges of complicity in evidence spoliation that could subject counsel and the client to serious penalties.

C. DETERMINING WHETHER SANCTIONS SHOULD BE IMPOSED

§ 18:9 Generally

If a court determines a person or organization disposed of or failed to preserve discoverable evidence, including electronically stored information, in the face of reasonably foreseeable litigation, the court has considerable discretion in deciding whether sanctions should be imposed for the person's actions.[1] In diversity

---

[2]See, e.g., Board of Regents of University of Nebraska v. BASF Corp., 2007 WL 3342423 (D. Neb. 2007) (when responding to request for production of documents, counsel are required to direct conduct of thorough search for responsive documents with due diligence and ensure all responsive documents under the "custody or control" of the client unless protected from discovery, are produced); In re September 11th Liability Insurance Coverage Cases, 243 F.R.D. 114, 68 Fed. R. Serv. 3d 526 (S.D. N.Y. 2007) (imposition of sanctions of $500,000 against insurer and its attorneys jointly and severally in insurance coverage litigation appropriate for discovery violations).

[Section 18:9]

[1]See Fujitsu Ltd. v. Federal Exp. Corp., 247 F.3d 423, 436 (2d Cir. 2001) (determination of appropriate sanction is confined to sound discretion of trial

cases, federal courts generally apply federal rules rather than state spoliation law.[2]

The right to impose sanctions for spoliation arises from a court's inherent power to control the judicial process and litigation, but the power is limited to that necessary to redress conduct abusing the judicial process.[3] If an applicable statute or rule can adequately sanction conduct, that statue or rule should ordinarily be applied rather than a more flexible or expansive inherent power.[4] When inherent power applies, it should be interpreted

---

judge and is assessed on a case-by-case basis); United Medical Supply Co., Inc. v. U.S., 77 Fed. Cl. 257 (2007) (government's reckless disregard of preservation duty warranted spoliation sanctions). See generally, Adams, *Spoliation of Electronic Evidence: Sanctions Versus Advocacy*, 18 MICH. TELECOMM. & TECH. L. REV. 1 (2011); Willoughby, Jr., et al., *Sanctions for E-Discovery Violations: By the Numbers*, 60 DUKE L.J. 789 (2010); Chalmers, *Successful Spoliation Motions Are Rarer Than You May Think*, LITIG., Fall 2011, at 8; Owen, *Restoring the Balance: An Expanded Proposal Concerning Preservation*, 80 U.S.L.W. 707 (Nov. 29, 2011).

[2]Rimkus Consulting Group, Inc. v. Cammarata, 688 F. Supp. 2d 598 (S.D. Tex. 2010); Condrey v. SunTrust Bank of Georgia, 431 F.3d 191, 203 (5th Cir. 2005); Fakhro v. Mayo Clinic Rochester, 2004 WL 909740 (D. Minn. 2004); Silvestri v. General Motors Corp., 271 F.3d 583, 590, 51 Fed. R. Serv. 3d 694 (4th Cir. 2001); Townsend v. American Insulated Panel Co., Inc., 174 F.R.D. 1, 4, 37 Fed. R. Serv. 3d 1166 (D. Mass. 1997). But see Warden v. Cross, 94 Fed. Appx. 474 (9th Cir.2004) (applying California law); Ward v. Texas Steak Ltd., 2004 WL 1280776 (W.D. Va. 2004) (recognizing it is court of limited jurisdiction and concluding that, when spoliation of evidence does not occur during pending federal litigation, federal court exercising diversity jurisdiction in which rule of decision is supplied by state law is required to apply those spoliation principles forum state would apply); State Farm Fire & Cas. Co. v. Frigidaire, a Div. of General Motors Corp., 146 F.R.D. 160, 161–62, 26 Fed. R. Serv. 3d 95 (N.D. Ill. 1992) (spoliation sanctions are substantive rather than procedural and the relevant state's law should be applied). But see Evans v. Mobile County Health Dept., 2012 WL 206141 (S.D. Ala. 2012) (applying Alabama law where no circuit law).

[3]Passlogix, Inc. v. 2FA Technology, LLC, 708 F. Supp. 2d 378 (S.D. N.Y. 2010) (court has inherent power to impose sanctions for spoliation of evidence, even where there has been no explicit order requiring production of evidence); Pension Committee of University of Montreal Pension Plan v. Banc of America Securities, 685 F. Supp. 2d 456 (S.D. N.Y. 2010) (abrogated on other grounds by, Chin v. Port Authority of New York & New Jersey, 685 F.3d 135, 115 Fair Empl. Prac. Cas. (BNA) 720, 95 Empl. Prac. Dec. (CCH) ¶ 44555 (2d Cir. 2012)); Zubulake v. UBS Warburg LLC, 229 F.R.D. 422, 94 Fair Empl. Prac. Cas. (BNA) 1, 85 Empl. Prac. Dec. (CCH) ¶ 41728 (S.D. N.Y. 2004).

[4]Rimkus Consulting Group, Inc. v. Cammarata, 688 F. Supp. 2d 598 (S.D. Tex. 2010).

narrowly, and its reach limited by its ultimate source—the court's need to orderly and expeditiously perform its duties.[5]

Fed. R. Civ. P. 37(b)(2)(A) permits sanctions where a party's officer, director or managing agent—or a witness designated under Fed. R. Civ. P. 30(b)(6) or 31(a)(4)—fails to obey an order to provide or permit discovery, including an order under Fed R. Civ. P. 26(f), 35, or 37(a). In addition, a court has statutory authority to impose costs, expenses, and attorney fees on "any attorney . . . who so multiplies the proceedings in any case unreasonably and vexatiously.[6]

Determining whether sanctions are warranted and, if so, what they should include, requires a court to consider both the spoliating party's culpability and the level of prejudice to the party seeking discovery.[7] Whether sanctions are appropriate and the level of sanctions warranted turn on three key factors:

- the degree of fault of the party who altered or destroyed the evidence;
- the degree of prejudice suffered by the opposing party; and
- whether there is a lesser sanction that will avoid substantial unfairness to the opposing party, and, where the offending party is seriously at fault, will serve to deter such conduct in the future.[8]

A party seeking sanctions for spoliation must establish that:

---

[5]See Rimkus Consulting Group, Inc. v. Cammarata, 688 F. Supp. 2d 598 (S.D. Tex. 2010); Newby v. Enron Corp., 302 F.3d 295, 302, Blue Sky L. Rep. (CCH) ¶ 74280, Fed. Sec. L. Rep. (CCH) ¶ 91956, 2 A.L.R. Fed. 2d 593 (5th Cir. 2002); Chambers v. NASCO, Inc., 501 U.S. 32, 43–46, 111 S. Ct. 2123, 115 L. Ed. 2d 27, 19 Fed. R. Serv. 3d 817 (1991). Cf. Arista Records LLC v. Usenet.com, Inc., 633 F. Supp. 2d 124, 138, 91 U.S.P.Q.2d 1744, 79 Fed. R. Evid. Serv. 1480, 73 Fed. R. Serv. 3d 1797 (S.D. N.Y. 2009) (discovery sanctions under court's inherent power require showing of bad faith or willfulness).

[6]28 U.S.C.A. § 1927.

[7]Rimkus Consulting Group, Inc. v. Cammarata, 688 F. Supp. 2d 598 (S.D. Tex. 2010); Phillip M. Adams & Associates, L.L.C. v. Dell, Inc., 621 F. Supp. 2d 1173, 1192 (D. Utah 2009).

[8]See Micron Technology, Inc. v. Rambus Inc., 645 F.3d 1311, 98 U.S.P.Q.2d 1693 (Fed. Cir. 2011) (district court failed to adequately determine whether patentee acted with bad faith in spoliating evidence, as required to impose sanction of declaring patents unenforceable in alleged infringer's action seeking declaratory judgment of unenforceability; district court alluded to factors that could lead to bad faith determination, but did not make a clear determination that patentee implemented document-destruction policy to obtain advantage in litigation through control of information and evidence); Paramount Pictures Corp. v. Davis, 234 F.R.D. 102, 111–13, 77 U.S.P.Q.2d 1933 (E.D. Pa. 2005) (defendant's wiping his home computer's memory clean after learning of producer's suit warranted application of spoliation inference).

- the party having control over the evidence had an obligation to preserve it at the time it was destroyed,
- the records were destroyed with a culpable state of mind, and
- the destroyed evidence was relevant to the party's claim or defense such that a reasonable trier of fact could find that it would support that claim or defense.[9]

§ 18:10 Culpability

Spoliation may occur along a continuum of fault, ranging from innocent behavior to negligence[1] to willful violation of the law.[2] Courts agree that a willful or intentional destruction of evidence to prevent its use in litigation can justify severe sanctions.[3] The standard of acceptable conduct is determined through experience; in the discovery context. The standards have been set by years of judicial decisions as to what a party must do to meet its obligation.[4] Failure to conform to this standard is negligent "even if it results from a pure heart and an empty head."[5]

---

[9]Passlogix, Inc. v. 2FA Technology, LLC, 708 F. Supp. 2d 378 (S.D. N.Y. 2010).

[Section 18:10]

[1]But see American Family Mut. Ins., Co. v. Roth, 2009 WL 982788, *9 (N.D. Ill. 2009) ("A party claiming spoliation by its adversary must prove that the destruction was intentional or the result of fault—generally beyond mere negligence, and that the document was relevant to an issue at trial.").

[2]Reilly v. Natwest Markets Group Inc., 181 F.3d 253, 267, 52 Fed. R. Evid. Serv. 676, 44 Fed. R. Serv. 3d 260 (2d Cir. 1999); Beil v. Lakewood Engineering and Mfg. Co., 15 F.3d 546, 552, 27 Fed. R. Serv. 3d 1453, 1994 FED App. 0024P (6th Cir. 1994).

[3]Rimkus Consulting Group, Inc. v. Cammarata, 688 F. Supp. 2d 598 (S.D. Tex. 2010).

[4]Pension Committee of University of Montreal Pension Plan v. Banc of America Securities, 685 F. Supp. 2d 456 (S.D. N.Y. 2010) (abrogated on other grounds by, Chin v. Port Authority of New York & New Jersey, 685 F.3d 135, 115 Fair Empl. Prac. Cas. (BNA) 720, 95 Empl. Prac. Dec. (CCH) ¶ 44555 (2d Cir. 2012)).

[5]Pension Committee of University of Montreal Pension Plan v. Banc of America Securities, 685 F. Supp. 2d 456 (S.D. N.Y. 2010) (abrogated on other grounds by, Chin v. Port Authority of New York & New Jersey, 685 F.3d 135, 115 Fair Empl. Prac. Cas. (BNA) 720, 95 Empl. Prac. Dec. (CCH) ¶ 44555 (2d Cir. 2012)).

Gross negligence is a failure to exercise even that care a careless person would use.[6] After a discovery duty is well established, a party's failure to adhere to contemporary standards can be considered gross negligence.[7] The following conduct supports of finding of gross negligence when a duty to preserve has attached:

- Failure to issue a written legal hold.
- Failure to identify all the key players and to ensure that their electronic and paper records are preserved.
- Failure to cease the deletion of e-mail or to preserve the records of former employees that are in a party's possession.
- Failure to preserve backup tapes when they are the sole source of relevant information or when they related to key players, if the relevant information maintained by those players is not obtainable from readily accessible sources.[8]

Conduct is willful, wanton, and reckless if the actor intentionally did an act of an unreasonable character in disregard of a known or obvious risk that was so great as to make it highly probable that harm would follow. It is usually accompanied by a conscious indifference to the consequences.[9]

A failure to preserve evidence resulting in the lost or destruction of relevant information is "surely negligent," and, depending

---

[6]Pension Committee of University of Montreal Pension Plan v. Banc of America Securities, 685 F. Supp. 2d 456 (S.D. N.Y. 2010) (abrogated on other grounds by, Chin v. Port Authority of New York & New Jersey, 685 F.3d 135, 115 Fair Empl. Prac. Cas. (BNA) 720, 95 Empl. Prac. Dec. (CCH) ¶ 44555 (2d Cir. 2012)); Passlogix, Inc. v. 2FA Technology, LLC, 708 F. Supp. 2d 378 (S.D. N.Y. 2010).

[7]Pension Committee of University of Montreal Pension Plan v. Banc of America Securities, 685 F. Supp. 2d 456 (S.D. N.Y. 2010) (abrogated on other grounds by, Chin v. Port Authority of New York & New Jersey, 685 F.3d 135, 115 Fair Empl. Prac. Cas. (BNA) 720, 95 Empl. Prac. Dec. (CCH) ¶ 44555 (2d Cir. 2012)).

[8]Jones v. Bremen High School Dist. 228, 2010 WL 2106640 (N.D. Ill. 2010) (school officials were reckless and grossly negligent in directing three supervisors implicated in secretary's employment discrimination suit to search their own email without help from counsel and to cull relevant documents in lieu of imposing a legal hold on all employees' email); . Cf. Ortega Melendres v. Arpaio, 2010 WL 582189 (D. Ariz. 2010) (defendant's failure to communicate plaintiff's preservation request and failure to implement a legal hold resulted in adverse inference instruction); Merck Eprova AG v. Gnosis S.P.A., 2010 WL 1631519 (S.D. N.Y. 2010) (defendant's were "at least" grossly negligent for failing to issue written legal hold).

[9]Pension Committee of University of Montreal Pension Plan v. Banc of America Securities, 685 F. Supp. 2d 456 (S.D. N.Y. 2010) (abrogated on other grounds by, Chin v. Port Authority of New York & New Jersey, 685 F.3d 135, 115 Fair Empl. Prac. Cas. (BNA) 720, 95 Empl. Prac. Dec. (CCH) ¶ 44555 (2d Cir. 2012)).

on the circumstances, may be grossly negligent or willful.[10] The intentional destruction of relevant records after the duty to preserve is willful.[11] The failure to issue a written legal hold constitutes gross negligence because that failure is likely to result in the destruction of relevant information.[12]

Depending on the extent of the failure to collect evidence or the sloppiness of the review, the resulting loss or destruction of evidence is "surely negligent," and, depending on the circumstances, may be grossly negligent or willful.[13] The failure to collect records from key players constitutes gross negligence or willful as does the destruction of e-mail or certain backup tapes after the duty to preserve has attached.[14] The failure to obtain records from all employees, as opposed to key players, likely constitutes

---

[10]Pension Committee of University of Montreal Pension Plan v. Banc of America Securities, 685 F. Supp. 2d 456 (S.D. N.Y. 2010) (abrogated on other grounds by, Chin v. Port Authority of New York & New Jersey, 685 F.3d 135, 115 Fair Empl. Prac. Cas. (BNA) 720, 95 Empl. Prac. Dec. (CCH) ¶ 44555 (2d Cir. 2012)); Treppel v. Biovail Corp., 249 F.R.D. 111, 121 (S.D. N.Y. 2008).

[11]Pension Committee of University of Montreal Pension Plan v. Banc of America Securities, 685 F. Supp. 2d 456 (S.D. N.Y. 2010) (abrogated on other grounds by, Chin v. Port Authority of New York & New Jersey, 685 F.3d 135, 115 Fair Empl. Prac. Cas. (BNA) 720, 95 Empl. Prac. Dec. (CCH) ¶ 44555 (2d Cir. 2012)); Gutman v. Klein, 2008 WL 5084182 (E.D. N.Y. 2008), subsequent determination, 2009 WL 3296072 (E.D. N.Y. 2009), aff'd, 515 Fed. Appx. 8 (2d Cir. 2013).

[12]Pension Committee of University of Montreal Pension Plan v. Banc of America Securities, 685 F. Supp. 2d 456 (S.D. N.Y. 2010) (abrogated on other grounds by, Chin v. Port Authority of New York & New Jersey, 685 F.3d 135, 115 Fair Empl. Prac. Cas. (BNA) 720, 95 Empl. Prac. Dec. (CCH) ¶ 44555 (2d Cir. 2012)). Compare Adorno v. Port Authority of New York and New Jersey, 258 F.R.D. 217, 228–29, 73 Fed. R. Serv. 3d 10 (S.D. N.Y. 2009) (defendants were only negligent where they instituted form of legal hold limited in scope); with Treppel v. Biovail Corp., 249 F.R.D. 111, 121 (S.D. N.Y. 2008) (failure to preserve backup tapes after December 2003 was sufficient to constitute gross negligence or recklessness).

[13]Pension Committee of University of Montreal Pension Plan v. Banc of America Securities, 685 F. Supp. 2d 456 (S.D. N.Y. 2010) (abrogated on other grounds by, Chin v. Port Authority of New York & New Jersey, 685 F.3d 135, 115 Fair Empl. Prac. Cas. (BNA) 720, 95 Empl. Prac. Dec. (CCH) ¶ 44555 (2d Cir. 2012)).

[14]Pension Committee of University of Montreal Pension Plan v. Banc of America Securities, 685 F. Supp. 2d 456 (S.D. N.Y. 2010) (abrogated on other grounds by, Chin v. Port Authority of New York & New Jersey, 685 F.3d 135, 115 Fair Empl. Prac. Cas. (BNA) 720, 95 Empl. Prac. Dec. (CCH) ¶ 44555 (2d Cir. 2012)).

negligence.[15] The failure to take all appropriate measures to preserve electronically stored information likely is negligence.[16]

§ 18:11 Prejudice to the discovering party

No matter what level of culpability is found, the spoliating party should have the opportunity to demonstrate the innocent party has not been prejudiced by the missing information.[1] Prejudice by loss of evidence must be measured in light of other evidence available.[2] Some courts have ruled severe sanctions such as granting default judgment, striking pleadings, or giving adverse inference instructions may not be imposed unless there is evidence of bad faith.[3] Others have held that, if the evidence is highly prejudicial but there is no evidence of bad faith, negligence justifies sanctioning the spoliator.[4] The clearest conclusion that can be derived from the varying cases in the numerous jurisdictions is the fact-specific balancing approach provides courts with the necessary flexibility for results-oriented analyses.

---

[15]Pension Committee of University of Montreal Pension Plan v. Banc of America Securities, 685 F. Supp. 2d 456 (S.D. N.Y. 2010) (abrogated on other grounds by, Chin v. Port Authority of New York & New Jersey, 685 F.3d 135, 115 Fair Empl. Prac. Cas. (BNA) 720, 95 Empl. Prac. Dec. (CCH) ¶ 44555 (2d Cir. 2012)).

[16]Pension Committee of University of Montreal Pension Plan v. Banc of America Securities, 685 F. Supp. 2d 456 (S.D. N.Y. 2010) (abrogated on other grounds by, Chin v. Port Authority of New York & New Jersey, 685 F.3d 135, 115 Fair Empl. Prac. Cas. (BNA) 720, 95 Empl. Prac. Dec. (CCH) ¶ 44555 (2d Cir. 2012)); Treppel v. Biovail Corp., 249 F.R.D. 111, 121 (S.D. N.Y. 2008). See also Cache La Poudre Feeds, LLC v. Land O'Lakes, Inc., 244 F.R.D. 614, 627–28, 68 Fed. R. Serv. 3d 1181 (D. Colo. 2007) (failure to collection information from files of former employees that remained in party's possession or control after duty to preserve has attached constituted gross negligence); Victor Stanley, Inc. v. Creative Pipe, Inc., 250 F.R.D. 251, 259–62, 70 Fed. R. Serv. 3d 1052 (D. Md. 2008) (failure to assess accuracy and validity of selected search terms was negligence).

[Section 18:11]

[1]Passlogix, Inc. v. 2FA Technology, LLC, 708 F. Supp. 2d 378 (S.D. N.Y. 2010).

[2]Phillip M. Adams & Associates, L.L.C. v. Dell, Inc., 621 F. Supp. 2d 1173, 1195 (D. Utah 2009).

[3]Rimkus Consulting Group, Inc. v. Cammarata, 688 F. Supp. 2d 598 (S.D. Tex. 2010); Condrey v. SunTrust Bank of Georgia, 431 F.3d 191, 203 (5th Cir. 2005); Ratliff v. City of Gainesville, Tex., 256 F.3d 355, 363–64, 86 Fair Empl. Prac. Cas. (BNA) 472 (5th Cir. 2001).

[4]See, e.g., Collazo-Santiago v. Toyota Motor Corp., 149 F.3d 23, 29, Prod. Liab. Rep. (CCH) ¶ 15280 (1st Cir. 1998) (of particular importance when considering appropriateness of sanctions is prejudice to nonoffending party and degree of fault of offending party).

A showing the lost information is relevant and prejudicial is important. Speculative or generalized assertions that the missing information would have been favorable to the party seeking sanctions are insufficient.[5] When the evidence as a whole would allow a reasonable fact finder to conclude the missing evidence would have helped the requesting party support its claims or defenses, that may be a sufficient showing of both relevance and prejudice to make an adverse inference instruction appropriate.[6]

In *Pension Committee v. Banc of America Securities, LLC*, the court held that, even for severe sanctions, relevance and prejudice may be presumed when the spoliating party acts in a grossly negligent manner.[7] The spoliating party may rebut the presumption by showing the innocent party had access to the evidence allegedly destroyed or the evidence would not have been helpful to the innocent party.[8] When the level of culpability is mere negligence, the presumption of relevance and prejudice is not available.[9]

---

[5]See, e.g., Rimkus Consulting Group, Inc. v. Cammarata, 688 F. Supp. 2d 598 (S.D. Tex. 2010); Mintel Intern. Group, Ltd. v. Neergheen, 30 I.E.R. Cas. (BNA) 396, 2010 WL 145786 (N.D. Ill. 2010); Consolidated Aluminum Corp. v. Alcoa, Inc., 244 F.R.D. 335, 346 (M.D. La. 2006).

[6]See, e.g., Rimkus Consulting Group, Inc. v. Cammarata, 688 F. Supp. 2d 598 (S.D. Tex. 2010); Broccoli v. Echostar Communications Corp., 229 F.R.D. 506, 511–12, 62 Fed. R. Serv. 3d 817 (D. Md. 2005); Vodusek v. Bayliner Marine Corp., 71 F.3d 148, 155–57, 1996 A.M.C. 330, 43 Fed. R. Evid. Serv. 869 (4th Cir. 1995).

[7]Pension Committee of University of Montreal Pension Plan v. Banc of America Securities, 685 F. Supp. 2d 456 (S.D. N.Y. 2010) (abrogated on other grounds by, Chin v. Port Authority of New York & New Jersey, 685 F.3d 135, 115 Fair Empl. Prac. Cas. (BNA) 720, 95 Empl. Prac. Dec. (CCH) ¶ 44555 (2d Cir. 2012)). But see Condrey v. SunTrust Bank of Georgia, 431 F.3d 191, 203 n.8 (5th Cir. 2005) (adverse inference was not appropriate because there was no evidence of bad faith, but also noting that, even if bad faith had been shown, an adverse inference would have been improper because relevance was not shown).

[8]Pension Committee of University of Montreal Pension Plan v. Banc of America Securities, 685 F. Supp. 2d 456 (S.D. N.Y. 2010) (abrogated on other grounds by, Chin v. Port Authority of New York & New Jersey, 685 F.3d 135, 115 Fair Empl. Prac. Cas. (BNA) 720, 95 Empl. Prac. Dec. (CCH) ¶ 44555 (2d Cir. 2012)).

[9]Pension Committee of University of Montreal Pension Plan v. Banc of America Securities, 685 F. Supp. 2d 456 (S.D. N.Y. 2010) (abrogated on other grounds by, Chin v. Port Authority of New York & New Jersey, 685 F.3d 135, 115 Fair Empl. Prac. Cas. (BNA) 720, 95 Empl. Prac. Dec. (CCH) ¶ 44555 (2d Cir. 2012)).

D. DETERMINING WHAT SANCTIONS SHOULD BE APPLIED

§ 18:12 Generally

The trial judge has discretion to determine an appropriate penalty for sanctions.[1] Sanctions for spoliation of evidence are meant to:

- Deter parties from destroying evidence
- Place the risk of an erroneous evaluation of the content of the destroyed evidence on the party responsible for its destruction, and
- Restore the party harmed by the loss of evidence helpful to its case to where the party would have been in the absence of spoliation.[2]

A sliding scale of sanctions may be imposed depending on the degree of control the alleged spoliator had over the evidence and the spoliator's subjective intentions.[3] The severity of a sanction for failing to preserve when a duty to do so has arisen must be proportionate to the culpability involved and the prejudice that results. Such a sanction should be no harsher than necessary to respond to the need to punish or deter and to address the impact on discovery.[4]

The most important factors in determining the appropriate sanction are the culpability of the alleged spoliator and the resulting prejudice to the innocent party. Other factors include the degree of interference with the judicial process, whether a lesser sanction will remedy the harm, whether sanctions are necessary to deter similar conduct, and whether sanctions will unfairly punish an innocent party for spoliation committed by an attorney.

[Section 18:12]

[1]Passlogix, Inc. v. 2FA Technology, LLC, 708 F. Supp. 2d 378 (S.D. N.Y. 2010); Pension Committee of University of Montreal Pension Plan v. Banc of America Securities, 685 F. Supp. 2d 456 (S.D. N.Y. 2010) (abrogated on other grounds by, Chin v. Port Authority of New York & New Jersey, 685 F.3d 135, 115 Fair Empl. Prac. Cas. (BNA) 720, 95 Empl. Prac. Dec. (CCH) ¶ 44555 (2d Cir. 2012)); Residential Funding Corp. v. DeGeorge Financial Corp., 306 F.3d 99, 109, 53 Fed. R. Serv. 3d 1105 (2d Cir. 2002); Fujitsu Ltd. v. Federal Exp. Corp., 247 F.3d 423, 436 (2d Cir. 2001).

[2]Passlogix, Inc. v. 2FA Technology, LLC, 708 F. Supp. 2d 378 (S.D. N.Y. 2010).

[3]Phillip M. Adams & Associates, L.L.C. v. Dell, Inc., 621 F. Supp. 2d 1173, 1193 (D. Utah 2009).

[4]Rimkus Consulting Group, Inc. v. Cammarata, 688 F. Supp. 2d 598 (S.D. Tex. 2010). See Passlogix, Inc. v. 2FA Technology, LLC, 708 F. Supp. 2d 378 (S.D. N.Y. 2010).

Sanctions for spoliation include:

- Criminal penalties[5]
- Unfavorable evidentiary presumptions[6]
- Discovery sanctions[7]
- Dismissal of law suits[8]
- An adverse inference instruction[9]
- Other sanctions including reimbursement of attorney fees,

---

[5]See, e.g., U.S. v. Lundwall, 1 F. Supp. 2d 249 (S.D. N.Y. 1998) (withholding and subsequent destruction of documents of defendant held to be criminal obstruction of justice under 18 U.S.C.A. § 1503). But see In re E.I. DuPont De Nemours & Company-Benlate Litigation, 99 F.3d 363, 36 Fed. R. Serv. 3d 427, 27 Envtl. L. Rep. 20432 (11th Cir. 1996) ($100 million sanction ordered payable to civil court overturned as primarily criminal in nature).

[6]Dillon v. Nissan Motor Co., Ltd., 986 F.2d 263, 268, 38 Fed. R. Evid. Serv. 82, 25 Fed. R. Serv. 3d 304 (8th Cir. 1993) (expert testimony excluded as sanction for destroying evidence); BTO Logging, Inc. v. Deere & Co., 174 F.R.D. 690, 692–93, 39 Fed. R. Serv. 3d 637 (D. Or. 1997) (same).

[7]In re Prudential Ins. Co. of America Sales Practices Litigation, 169 F.R.D. 598, 36 Fed. R. Serv. 3d 767 (D.N.J. 1997); Edwards v. Louisville Ladder Co., 796 F. Supp. 966, 971 (W.D. La. 1992).

[8]See, e.g., Southern New England Telephone Co. v. Global NAPs Inc., 624 F.3d 123 (2d Cir. 2010) (district court dismissing case as sanction for spoliation must it did not explain why only dismissal would "vindicate the trifold aims of: (1) deterring future spoliation of evidence; (2) protecting the defendants' interests; and (3) remedying the prejudice defendants suffered as a result of [Rambus's] actions." Dismissal is appropriate sanction if there is showing of willfulness, bad faith or fault on part of sanctioned party); Walters ex rel. Walters v. General Motors Corp., 209 F. Supp. 2d 481, Prod. Liab. Rep. (CCH) ¶ 16408 (W.D. Pa. 2002) (summary judgment entered against spoliator); Elwell v. Conair, Inc., 145 F. Supp. 2d 79, 88 (D. Me. 2001) (dismissal is the most severe sanction and should be reserved for cases where a party has maliciously destroyed relevant evidence); Barsoum v. NYC Housing Authority, 202 F.R.D. 396, 399, 50 Fed. R. Serv. 3d 26 (S.D. N.Y. 2001) (outright dismissal is a harsh remedy to be used only in extreme cases).

[9]See Nursing Home Pension Fund v. Oracle Corp., 254 F.R.D. 559 (N.D. Cal. 2008) (sanction of adverse inference instruction was warranted due to defendants' failure to preserve materials created in connection with drafting book about corporation and one of its senior officers). Cf. McDowell v. Government of Dist. of Columbia, 233 F.R.D. 192, 202–03, 63 Fed. R. Serv. 3d 1233 (D.D.C. 2006) (proposing negative inference sanction jury instruction be given if defendants failed to produce requested database); Stevenson v. Union Pacific R. Co., 354 F.3d 739, 747, 63 Fed. R. Evid. Serv. 166, 57 Fed. R. Serv. 3d 617 (8th Cir. 2004) (there must be some indication of intent to destroy the evidence for purpose of obstructing or suppressing truth in order to impose sanction of adverse inference instruction, court upheld sanctions against defendant, because defendant had been careful to preserve a voice tape in other cases where tape proved to be beneficial to defendant and had made immediate effort to preserve other types of evidence but not voice tape in this case).

monetary penalties against the party or attorney, recovery of discovery costs, striking an answer, barring the presentation of evidence relating to the destroyed material, barring the filing of pleadings, and, in the most egregious instances, entry of default judgment or dismissal against the spoliator[10]

Most courts are careful to impose the least severe sanctions commensurate with the wrongdoing.[11] Sanctions from least harsh to harshest are:

- Further discovery
- Cost shifting
- Fines
- Special jury instructions
- Preclusion
- Termination[12]

§ 18:13 Burden of proof

The burden of proof differs depending upon the severity of the

[10]See Micron Technology, Inc. v. Rambus Inc., 645 F.3d 1311, 98 U.S.P.Q.2d 1693 (Fed. Cir. 2011) (district court failed to adequately determine whether patentee acted with bad faith in spoliating evidence, as required to impose sanction of declaring patents unenforceable in alleged infringer's action seeking declaratory judgment of unenforceability; district court alluded to factors that could lead to bad faith determination, but did not make a clear determination that patentee implemented document-destruction policy to obtain advantage in litigation through control of information and evidence); Krumwiede v. Brighton Associates, L.L.C., 2006 WL 1308629 (N.D. Ill. 2006), subsequent determination, 2006 WL 2349985 (N.D. Ill. 2006) (default judgment entered against producing party that intentionally destroyed evidence).

[11]Webb v. District of Columbia, 146 F.3d 964, 971, 104 Fair Empl. Prac. Cas. (BNA) 1366, 73 Empl. Prac. Dec. (CCH) ¶ 45480, 41 Fed. R. Serv. 3d 120 (D.C. Cir. 1998) (default judgment not appropriate where less onerous remedies would have sufficed); ABC Home Health Services, Inc. v. International Business Machines Corp., 158 F.R.D. 180 (S.D. Ga. 1994); Turner v. Hudson Transit Lines, Inc., 142 F.R.D. 68 (S.D. N.Y. 1991); E.E.O.C. v. Jacksonville Shipyards, Inc., 690 F. Supp. 995, 998, 47 Fair Empl. Prac. Cas. (BNA) 267, 47 Empl. Prac. Dec. (CCH) ¶ 38228 (M.D. Fla. 1988) (default judgment inappropriate where lesser sanctions may effectively remedy prejudice suffered by the EEOC). Courts are prepared to impose severe sanctions where spoliation is egregious. See U.S. v. Philip Morris USA, Inc., 327 F. Supp. 2d 21 (D.D.C. 2004) (spoliator ordered to pay $2,750,000 into court as sanction).

[12]Pension Committee of University of Montreal Pension Plan v. Banc of America Securities, 685 F. Supp. 2d 456 (S.D. N.Y. 2010) (abrogated on other grounds by, Chin v. Port Authority of New York & New Jersey, 685 F.3d 135, 115 Fair Empl. Prac. Cas. (BNA) 720, 95 Empl. Prac. Dec. (CCH) ¶ 44555 (2d Cir. 2012)).

sanction.[1] For less severe sanctions, such as fines and cost shifting, the inquiry focuses more on the conduct of the spoliating party rather than on whether documents were lost, and, if so, whether those documents were relevant and resulted in prejudice to the innocent party.[2] For more severe penalties, such as dismissal, preclusion, or imposition of an adverse inference instruction, the court must consider the conduct of the spoliating party, whether any missing evidence was relevant, and whether the innocent party has been prejudiced by the loss of evidence.[3]

When the spoliating party was negligent, the innocent party must prove both relevance and prejudice in order to justify the imposition of a severe sanction.[4] The innocent party must prove the following three elements:

- The spoliating party had control over the evidence and an obligation to preserve it at the time of destruction or loss.
- The spoliating party acted with a culpable state of mind upon destroying or losing the evidence.
- The missing evidence is relevant to the innocent party's claim or defense.[5]

In determining whether missing evidence was relevant, the

[Section 18:13]

[1]Pension Committee of University of Montreal Pension Plan v. Banc of America Securities, 685 F. Supp. 2d 456 (S.D. N.Y. 2010) (abrogated on other grounds by, Chin v. Port Authority of New York & New Jersey, 685 F.3d 135, 115 Fair Empl. Prac. Cas. (BNA) 720, 95 Empl. Prac. Dec. (CCH) ¶ 44555 (2d Cir. 2012)).

[2]Pension Committee of University of Montreal Pension Plan v. Banc of America Securities, 685 F. Supp. 2d 456 (S.D. N.Y. 2010) (abrogated on other grounds by, Chin v. Port Authority of New York & New Jersey, 685 F.3d 135, 115 Fair Empl. Prac. Cas. (BNA) 720, 95 Empl. Prac. Dec. (CCH) ¶ 44555 (2d Cir. 2012)).

[3]Pension Committee of University of Montreal Pension Plan v. Banc of America Securities, 685 F. Supp. 2d 456 (S.D. N.Y. 2010) (abrogated on other grounds by, Chin v. Port Authority of New York & New Jersey, 685 F.3d 135, 115 Fair Empl. Prac. Cas. (BNA) 720, 95 Empl. Prac. Dec. (CCH) ¶ 44555 (2d Cir. 2012)).

[4]Pension Committee of University of Montreal Pension Plan v. Banc of America Securities, 685 F. Supp. 2d 456 (S.D. N.Y. 2010) (abrogated on other grounds by, Chin v. Port Authority of New York & New Jersey, 685 F.3d 135, 115 Fair Empl. Prac. Cas. (BNA) 720, 95 Empl. Prac. Dec. (CCH) ¶ 44555 (2d Cir. 2012)); Byrnie v. Town of Cromwell, Bd. of Educ., 243 F.3d 93, 108, 151 Ed. Law Rep. 776, 85 Fair Empl. Prac. Cas. (BNA) 323, 82 Empl. Prac. Dec. (CCH) ¶ 40939 (2d Cir. 2001).

[5]Pension Committee of University of Montreal Pension Plan v. Banc of America Securities, 685 F. Supp. 2d 456 (S.D. N.Y. 2010) (abrogated on other grounds by, Chin v. Port Authority of New York & New Jersey, 685 F.3d 135,

party seeking sanctions must adduce sufficient evidence from which a reasonable trier of fact could infer that the destroyed or unavailable evidence would have been of the nature alleged by the innocent party.[6] The innocent party must show that the destroyed evidence would have been responsive to the document request and that the evidence would have been helpful in proving the innocent party's claims or defenses.[7]

In cases where bad faith or gross negligence is established, relevance and prejudice are presumed.[8] Regardless of the level of culpability, any presumption is rebuttable and the spoliating party should have the opportunity to demonstrate that the innocent party has not been prejudiced by the absence of the missing information.[9] When the spoliating party offers proof there has been no prejudice, the innocent party may offer evidence to counter that proof. Bad faith, for purposes of discovery sanctions,

115 Fair Empl. Prac. Cas. (BNA) 720, 95 Empl. Prac. Dec. (CCH) ¶ 44555 (2d Cir. 2012)); Residential Funding Corp. v. DeGeorge Financial Corp., 306 F.3d 99, 109, 53 Fed. R. Serv. 3d 1105 (2d Cir. 2002).

[6]Residential Funding Corp. v. DeGeorge Financial Corp., 306 F.3d 99, 108–09, 53 Fed. R. Serv. 3d 1105 (2d Cir. 2002).

[7]Pension Committee of University of Montreal Pension Plan v. Banc of America Securities, 685 F. Supp. 2d 456 (S.D. N.Y. 2010) (abrogated on other grounds by, Chin v. Port Authority of New York & New Jersey, 685 F.3d 135, 115 Fair Empl. Prac. Cas. (BNA) 720, 95 Empl. Prac. Dec. (CCH) ¶ 44555 (2d Cir. 2012)).

[8]Passlogix, Inc. v. 2FA Technology, LLC, 708 F. Supp. 2d 378 (S.D. N.Y. 2010); Pension Committee of University of Montreal Pension Plan v. Banc of America Securities, 685 F. Supp. 2d 456 (S.D. N.Y. 2010) (abrogated on other grounds by, Chin v. Port Authority of New York & New Jersey, 685 F.3d 135, 115 Fair Empl. Prac. Cas. (BNA) 720, 95 Empl. Prac. Dec. (CCH) ¶ 44555 (2d Cir. 2012)); Residential Funding Corp. v. DeGeorge Financial Corp., 306 F.3d 99, 109, 53 Fed. R. Serv. 3d 1105 (2d Cir. 2002).

But see Chin v. Port Authority of New York & New Jersey, 685 F.3d 135, 115 Fair Empl. Prac. Cas. (BNA) 720, 95 Empl. Prac. Dec. (CCH) ¶ 44555 (2d Cir. 2012), cert. denied, 133 S. Ct. 1724, 185 L. Ed. 2d 785, 117 Fair Empl. Prac. Cas. (BNA) 1412 (2013) (finding of gross negligence permits, rather than requires, a district court to give an adverse inference instruction).

[9]Pension Committee of University of Montreal Pension Plan v. Banc of America Securities, 685 F. Supp. 2d 456 (S.D. N.Y. 2010) (abrogated on other grounds by, Chin v. Port Authority of New York & New Jersey, 685 F.3d 135, 115 Fair Empl. Prac. Cas. (BNA) 720, 95 Empl. Prac. Dec. (CCH) ¶ 44555 (2d Cir. 2012)); Stevenson v. Union Pacific R. Co., 354 F.3d 739, 750, 63 Fed. R. Evid. Serv. 166, 57 Fed. R. Serv. 3d 617 (8th Cir. 2004).

can be shown by (1) clear evidence or (2) harassment or delay or other improper purposes.[10]

In *American Service Marketing Corp. v. Bushnell*,[11] the discovering party failed to demonstrate by clear and convincing evidence that the producing party had violated a preliminary injunction by deleting computer files. The defendant had been enjoined from deleting files and updating the registrant information for his allegedly infringing website, and was ordered to immediately disclose and convey all password and user names. The court said the deleted files could have been deleted before it ordered the injunction, and the discovering party did not cite any specific actions to support the claim the producing party violated the court's order.

§ 18:14 Further Discovery

A court may order additional discovery, including a forensic search of the spoliating party's computer.[1] In *A.N.S.W.E.R. Coalition v. Salazar*,[2] the court found the defendants' productions were patently inadequate and that representations by the defendants and their attorneys as to the completeness of production were false. The court concluded the plaintiffs had incurred some expense as a result of defendant's discovery behavior and that the required expenditure of funds to pursue discovery is prejudice enough to justify cost shifting. However the court refused the plaintiffs' request to shift costs related to the search of backup tapes resisted by the defendants where the plaintiffs had not proposed an e-discovery plan at the outset of litigation and the plaintiffs failed to meaningfully address Fed. R. Civ. P. 26(b)(2) in their briefing.

Where defendants' production of summaries designated "for settlement purposes only," the court held the response was an inadequate response to discovery.[3] The court ordered production of the underlying data from both hard copy and electronic sources in order to ascertain definitively whether all documents had been produced.

---

[10] Arista Records LLC v. Usenet.com, Inc., 608 F. Supp. 2d 409, 430 (S.D. N.Y. 2009).

[11] Am. Service Marketing Corp. v. Bushnell, 2009 WL 1870887 (E.D. La. 2009).

[Section 18:14]

[1] See, e.g. Treppel v. Biovail Corp., 249 F.R.D. 111, 123–24 (S.D. N.Y. 2008).

[2] A.N.S.W.E.R. Coalition v. Salazar, 258 F.R.D. 36 (D.D.C. 2009).

[3] Anthropologie, Inc. v. Forever 21, Inc., 2009 WL 690239 (S.D. N.Y. 2009).

§ 18:15 Cost shifting

A court may order cost shifting.[1] In *Fendi Adele S.R.L. v. Filene's Basement, Inc.*,[2] a handbag manufacturer accused of manufacturing counterfeit bags was subjected to monetary sanctions for discovery violations. The court found an evident pattern of non-production of documents, coupled with false assurances that the manufacturer had produced all of its documents. The initial production of a handful of documents was notably bare of some of the most basic documents that a company of the size and sophistication of the manufacturer would unquestionably maintain. The court said the production was manifestly inadequate and the representation that there were no more documents was absurd on its face. It declared that the process of extracting those records ultimately consumed a plainly unreasonable amount of time. The court ordered the plaintiffs reimbursed for their expenses.

§ 18:16 Fines and Monetary Sanctions

A court may award monetary sanctions to the innocent party.[1] Such sanctions are appropriate to punish the spoliator and to deter spoliation, sending the message that egregious conduct will not be tolerated.[2] Monetary sanctions also serve the remedial purpose of compensating the innocent party for the reasonable costs incurred in bringing a motion for sanctions.[3]

[Section 18:15]

[1]U.S. v. Philip Morris USA, Inc., 327 F. Supp. 2d 21, 25 (D.D.C. 2004) (ordering defendant to pay $2.75 million in fines).

[2]Fendi Adele v. Filene's Basement, Inc., 2009 WL 855955 (S.D. N.Y. 2009).

[Section 18:16]

[1]See, e.g., Passlogix, Inc. v. 2FA Technology, LLC, 708 F. Supp. 2d 378 (S.D. N.Y. 2010) ($10,000 sanction imposed for intentional, bad faith spoliation); Richard Green (Fine Paintings) v. McClendon, 262 F.R.D. 284, 291–92 (S.D. N.Y. 2009).

[2]Pension Committee of University of Montreal Pension Plan v. Banc of America Securities, 685 F. Supp. 2d 456 (S.D. N.Y. 2010) (abrogated on other grounds by, Chin v. Port Authority of New York & New Jersey, 685 F.3d 135, 115 Fair Empl. Prac. Cas. (BNA) 720, 95 Empl. Prac. Dec. (CCH) ¶ 44555 (2d Cir. 2012)); Richard Green (Fine Paintings) v. McClendon, 262 F.R.D. 284, 291 (S.D. N.Y. 2009).

[3]Pension Committee of University of Montreal Pension Plan v. Banc of America Securities, 685 F. Supp. 2d 456 (S.D. N.Y. 2010) (abrogated on other grounds by, Chin v. Port Authority of New York & New Jersey, 685 F.3d 135, 115 Fair Empl. Prac. Cas. (BNA) 720, 95 Empl. Prac. Dec. (CCH) ¶ 44555 (2d

In *Passlogix, Inc. v. 2FA Technology, LLC*,[4] the court ordered monetary sanctions in the amount of $10,000. The court found that the defendants had spoliated relevant information, including e-mails, Skype messages, and computer logs. The court was not persuaded by the defendants' "spoofing" defense—a claim that an employee of the plaintiff may have spoofed a defendant's IP address in an effort to impersonate him on the Internet.

In *Qualcomm, Inc. v. Broadcom, Corp.*,[5] a magistrate judge imposed sanctions of $8,568,633 against Qualcomm based on Qualcomm's intentional failure to produce over 46,000 responsive e-mails and other discovery misconduct, ordered certain in-house and former outside counsel to participate in a comprehensive "Case Review and Enforcement of Discovery Obligations" program to create a case management protocol that would serve as a model for future litigants, and referred investigation of possible ethical violations to the California State Bar. Rejecting a claim of inadvertence, the magistrate judge found that Qualcomm had failed to conduct basic searches for electronic documents.

Pointing out that Fed. R. Civ. P. 26(g) imposes a duty of good faith and reasonable inquiry on all attorneys involved in litigation who rely on discovery responses executed by another attorney, the magistrate judge faulted the outside counsel for accepting unsubstantiated assurances of the client that searches for documents had been sufficient, particularly in light of warning signs to the contrary. Because the California Rules of Professional Conduct (unlike those in many other states) do not permit lawyers to reveal client confidences and secrets even in order to protect themselves against accusations of wrongdoing, the lawyers were not permitted to reveal their side of the story regarding their dealings with Qualcomm during discovery.

The magistrate judge noted a number of warning signs that signaled Qualcomm's failure to comply with its obligation to search for and produce all responsive documents. Qualcomm did not search the computers of the corporate representatives who were selected for Fed. R. Civ. P. 30(b)(6) depositions or take reasonable steps to be sure that those representatives had Qualcomm's knowledge about the matter in dispute. Qualcomm

---

Cir. 2012)); Richard Green (Fine Paintings) v. McClendon, 262 F.R.D. 284, 291 (S.D. N.Y. 2009).

[4]Passlogix, Inc. v. 2FA Technology, LLC, 708 F. Supp. 2d 378 (S.D. N.Y. 2010).

[5]Qualcomm Inc. v. Broadcom Corp., 2008 WL 66932 (S.D. Cal. 2008), vacated in part on other grounds, 88 U.S.P.Q.2d 1169, 2008 WL 638108 (S.D. Cal. 2008).

ignored the significance of a distribution list indicating that one of its employees was a member of a group working on a key matter.

Qualcomm accepted and paid the $8,568,633.24 in sanctions ordered by the magistrate judge. A district judge vacated and remanded that portion of the magistrate judge's January 7 order imposing sanctions against Qualcomm's six outside counsel.[6] The judge instructed that, in any future hearing held by the magistrate judge, the attorneys be allowed to defend their conduct by any and all means, and not be prevented from doing so by Qualcomm's attorney-client privilege.

While *Qualcomm* presents an extreme case involving the concealment of a large quantity of electronically stored information and the implausibility of a claim that a reasonable search could have missed this much material, the case sends a message to attorneys: attorneys must exercise reasonable diligence to assure themselves that a client has searched for all relevant information; they must heed and act upon warning signs. Clients must also be made aware of the consequences of the failure to comply with discovery requests.

Qualcomm illustrates the importance of performing a thorough factual investigation before filing suit.[7] It also demonstrates the importance of having a records management and litigation protocol in place before suit is filed (or before being sued). Law firms must develop practice management systems insuring that clients are properly advised at the beginning of litigation about the scope of discovery obligations, their likely cost, and the nature of the attorneys' obligations to the court to insure compliance by the client.

Law firms may be reluctant to agree to represent a client if the client is unwilling to give the attorneys full access to the information the lawyers deem necessary to comply with discovery requests. Once litigation begins, firms should have in place oversight systems to assure that individual attorneys are comply-

[6]The magistrate judge subsequently lifted the sanctions against the outside lawyers for Qualcomm, finding insufficient evidence of bad faith. She made the finding after the lawyers were allowed to ignore attorney-client privileges and defend their actions. Qualcomm Inc. v. Broadcom Corp., 2010 WL 1336937 (S.D. Cal. 2010).

[7]See, e.g., Atmel Corp. v. Authentec Inc., 2008 WL 276393 (N.D. Cal. 2008) (plaintiff's attorney acknowledged not doing any investigation to determine how negotiations and discussions about the covenant not to sue were carried out without leaving any paper or electronic trail of responsive documents).

ing with their responsibilities to oversee the discovery process. In response to these issues, some law firms have established special units within their litigation practice groups to assist firm lawyers with e-discovery issues and to ensure compliance with obligations imposed by the courts and the Federal Rules of Civil Procedure.

In *ACORN v. County of Nassau*,[8] the defendants were found to be grossly negligent in failing to implement a timely legal hold. Because the plaintiffs could not prove the relevance of the information destroyed, the court declined to order an adverse inference instruction, but ordered the defendants to pay the plaintiffs' reasonable costs for making the motion, including attorney fees.

In *Armisted v. State Farm Mutual Insurance*,[9] the defendant's failure to produce discovery documents in a timely manner or altogether did not sufficiently prejudice the insured, as required to warrant the imposition of a default judgment upon the insurer, but rather warranted a substantial monetary sanction against the insurer. The requested documents, including the insurance policies, the claims manual, and education and training documents, while relevant, were not contested in the case.

§ 18:17 Jury instructions

An adverse inference instruction instructs the jury to draw an adverse inference based on matters probably contained within the destroyed evidence.[1] An adverse inference charge serves two purposes—remediation and punishment.[2] The remedial purpose of the sanction serves to place the prejudiced party in the same position to prove its case as it would have been if the evidence

---

[8]Acorn (New York Association of Community Organizations for Reform Now) v. County of Nassau, 2009 WL 605859 (E.D. N.Y. 2009).

[9]Armisted v. State Farm Mut. Auto. Ins. Co., 2009 WL 81103, *11 (E.D. Mich. 2009).

[Section 18:17]

[1]See Blinzler v. Marriott Intern., Inc., 81 F.3d 1148, 1159 (1st Cir. 1996) (when evidence indicates party is aware of circumstances likely to give rise to future litigation, and yet destroys potentially relevant records without particularized inquiry, fact finder may reasonably infer that party probably did so because records would harm its case).

[2]Pension Committee of University of Montreal Pension Plan v. Banc of America Securities, 685 F. Supp. 2d 456 (S.D. N.Y. 2010) (\abrogated on other grounds by, Chin v. Port Authority of New York & New Jersey, 685 F.3d 135, 115 Fair Empl. Prac. Cas. (BNA) 720, 95 Empl. Prac. Dec. (CCH) ¶ 44555 (2d Cir. 2012)); Barsoum v. NYC Housing Authority, 202 F.R.D. 396, 399, 50 Fed. R. Serv. 3d 26 (S.D. N.Y. 2001) (purpose of sanctions is to deter future spoliation of evidence, shift risk of erroneous judgment onto party responsible for loss of evidence, and remedy prejudice suffered by nonspoliating party).

had been preserved. The punitive purpose both deters parties from destroying relevant evidence and directly punishes the party responsible for spoliation.[3] In the event of a spoliation inference, the fact finder is allowed to draw an unfavorable inference against the spoliator in a lawsuit because the spoliator is presumed to have been motivated by the concern that the material hidden, destroyed, or lost would have been unfavorable to its position.[4]

Courts tend to consider the intent of the actor and the content of the missing evidence to be the two most important factors in determining whether the adverse inference is warranted.[5] Courts are split as to whether a showing of bad faith or intent necessary to merit the spoliation inference.[6]

---

[3]See Passlogix, Inc. v. 2FA Technology, LLC, 708 F. Supp. 2d 378 (S.D. N.Y. 2010); Donato v. Fitzgibbons, 172 F.R.D. 75, 81–82, 38 Fed. R. Serv. 3d 1086 (S.D. N.Y. 1997).

[4]Byrnie v. Town of Cromwell, Bd. of Educ., 243 F.3d 93, 107, 151 Ed. Law Rep. 776, 85 Fair Empl. Prac. Cas. (BNA) 323, 82 Empl. Prac. Dec. (CCH) ¶ 40939 (2d Cir. 2001). See also Zubulake v. UBS Warburg LLC, 229 F.R.D. 422, 94 Fair Empl. Prac. Cas. (BNA) 1, 85 Empl. Prac. Dec. (CCH) ¶ 41728 (S.D. N.Y. 2004) (concept of "relevance" encompasses not only the ordinary meaning of the term, but also that the destroyed evidence would have been favorable to the movant).

[5]See Select Medical Corp. v. Hardaway, 2006 WL 859741 (E.D. Pa. 2006) (denying motion for spoliation inference because producing party had legitimate reason for erasing hard drive); Advantacare Health Partners v. Access IV, 2004 WL 1837997 (N.D. Cal. 2004) ("The evidentiary rationale applies here. The record clearly indicates that Defendants destroyed evidence in response to impending litigation. This behavior suggests that the evidence would have been threatening to the defense of the case and that it is therefore relevant in an evidentiary sense."); Zubulake v. UBS Warburg LLC, 229 F.R.D. 422, 94 Fair Empl. Prac. Cas. (BNA) 1, 85 Empl. Prac. Dec. (CCH) ¶ 41728 (S.D. N.Y. 2004) (party seeking an adverse inference instruction based on spoliation must establish three elements: (1) party having control over evidence had an obligation to preserve it at the time it was destroyed, (2) records were destroyed with a "culpable state of mind," and (3) destroyed evidence was relevant to party's claim or defense such that reasonable trier of fact could find it would support that claim or defense).

[6]Intent or bad faith required: See, e.g., Evans v. Mobile County Health Dept., 2012 WL 206141 (S.D. Ala. 2012) (adverse instruction appropriate where plaintiff burned personal computer but defendant was not left unable to defend against plaintiff's allegations); Rimkus Consulting Group, Inc. v. Cammarata, 688 F. Supp. 2d 598 (S.D. Tex. 2010); Phillip M. Adams & Associates, L.L.C. v. Dell, Inc., 621 F. Supp. 2d 1173, 1192 (D. Utah 2009); Turner v. Public Service Co. of Colorado, 563 F.3d 1136, 1149, 106 Fair Empl. Prac. Cas. (BNA) 113, 92 Empl. Prac. Dec. (CCH) ¶ 43560 (10th Cir. 2009); Faas v. Sears, Roebuck & Co., 532 F.3d 633, 644, 103 Fair Empl. Prac. Cas. (BNA) 1241, 91 Empl. Prac. Dec. (CCH) ¶ 43254 (7th Cir. 2008), Great American Ins. Co. of New York v. Lowry Development, LLC, 2007 WL 4268776 (S.D. Miss. 2007) (defendant's disposal of

In *Pension Committee v. Banc of America Securities, LLC*,[7] the court stated it would give a jury charge for the grossly negligent plaintiffs that:

- Laid out the elements of spoliation.
- Instructed the jury that the plaintiffs were grossly negligent in performing discovery obligations and failed to preserve evidence after a preservation duty arose.
- Told the jury it could presume that the lost evidence was relevant and would have been favorable to the defendant.
- Told the jury that if they declined to presume that the lost evidence was relevant or favorable, the jury's inquiry into spoliation was over; (5) explained that if the jury did presume relevance or prejudice, it then had to decide if any of the six plaintiffs had rebutted the presumption; and (6) explained the consequences of a rebutted and an unrebutted presumption.

---

laptop and untruthful testimony of circumstances of disposal warranted adverse inference instruction); Greyhound Lines, Inc. v. Wade, 485 F.3d 1032 (8th Cir. 2007); Morgan v. U.S. Xpress, Inc., 2006 WL 1548029 (M.D. Ga. 2006) (mere negligence in losing or destroying evidence is not enough for adverse inference as it does not sustain an inference of consciousness of a weak case); Daimler-Chrysler Motors v. Bill Davis Racing, Inc., 2005 WL 3502172 (E.D. Mich. 2005) (court must consider reasons for destruction of evidence to determine if they support inference of bad faith); Jinks-Umstead v. England, 68 Fed. R. Evid. Serv. 1200 (D.D.C. 2005); Hodge v. Wal-Mart Stores, Inc., 360 F.3d 446, 64 Fed. R. Evid. Serv. 200 (4th Cir. 2004); Stevenson v. Union Pacific R. Co., 354 F.3d 739, 746, 63 Fed. R. Evid. Serv. 166, 57 Fed. R. Serv. 3d 617 (8th Cir. 2004); Penalty Kick Management Ltd. v. Coca Cola Co., 318 F.3d 1284, 1294, 65 U.S.P. Q.2d 1563 (11th Cir. 2003); Wyler v. Korean Air Lines Co., Ltd., 928 F.2d 1167, 1174 (D.C. Cir. 1991). Negligence sufficient if there is serious prejudice: World Courier v. Barone, 2007 WL 1119196 (N.D. Cal. 2007); Hodge v. Wal-Mart Stores, Inc., 360 F.3d 446, 450, 64 Fed. R. Evid. Serv. 200 (4th Cir. 2004); Residential Funding Corp. v. DeGeorge Financial Corp., 306 F.3d 99, 107, 53 Fed. R. Serv. 3d 1105 (2d Cir. 2002); Silvestri v. General Motors Corp., 271 F.3d 583, 593, 51 Fed. R. Serv. 3d 694 (4th Cir. 2001). In the Third Circuit, the courts balance the degree of fault and prejudice. See, e.g., Bull v. United Parcel Service, Inc., 665 F.3d 68, 25 A.D. Cas. (BNA) 1204, 95 Empl. Prac. Dec. (CCH) ¶ 44379 (3d Cir. 2012). The court in Pension Committee of University of Montreal Pension Plan v. Banc of America Securities, 685 F. Supp. 2d 456 (S.D. N.Y. 2010) (abrogated on other grounds by, Chin v. Port Authority of New York & New Jersey, 685 F.3d 135, 115 Fair Empl. Prac. Cas. (BNA) 720, 95 Empl. Prac. Dec. (CCH) ¶ 44555 (2d Cir. 2012)), imposed a form of adverse inference instruction based on a finding of gross negligence.

[7]Pension Committee of University of Montreal Pension Plan v. Banc of America Securities, 685 F. Supp. 2d 456 (S.D. N.Y. 2010) (abrogated on other grounds by, Chin v. Port Authority of New York & New Jersey, 685 F.3d 135, 115 Fair Empl. Prac. Cas. (BNA) 720, 95 Empl. Prac. Dec. (CCH) ¶ 44555 (2d Cir. 2012)).

The court noted it was important to explain that the jury is bound the court's determination that certain plaintiffs destroyed documents after the duty to preserve arose but that the jury is not instructed that the court has made any finding as to whether that evidence is relevant or whether its loss caused any prejudice to the defendants.[8] The court said the jury must make these determinations because, if the jury finds both relevance and prejudice, it then may decide to draw an adverse inference in favor of the defendants that could have an impact on the verdict, and such a finding is within the province of the jury not the court.[9]

Although adverse inference instructions can take varying forms ranging in harshness, they are among the most severe sanctions a court can administer.[10] In its strictest form, the spoliation inference establishes prima facie the elements of the injured party's claim that cannot be proven without the missing evidence.[11] When a spoliating party has acted willfully or in bad faith, a jury can be instructed that certain facts are deemed admitted and must be accepted as true.[12] At the next level, when a spoliating party has acted willfully or recklessly, a court may impose a mandatory

---

[8]Pension Committee of University of Montreal Pension Plan v. Banc of America Securities, 685 F. Supp. 2d 456 (S.D. N.Y. 2010) (abrogated on other grounds by, Chin v. Port Authority of New York & New Jersey, 685 F.3d 135, 115 Fair Empl. Prac. Cas. (BNA) 720, 95 Empl. Prac. Dec. (CCH) ¶ 44555 (2d Cir. 2012)).

[9]Pension Committee of University of Montreal Pension Plan v. Banc of America Securities, 685 F. Supp. 2d 456 (S.D. N.Y. 2010) (abrogated on other grounds by, Chin v. Port Authority of New York & New Jersey, 685 F.3d 135, 115 Fair Empl. Prac. Cas. (BNA) 720, 95 Empl. Prac. Dec. (CCH) ¶ 44555 (2d Cir. 2012)).

[10]Rimkus Consulting Group, Inc. v. Cammarata, 688 F. Supp. 2d 598 (S.D. Tex. 2010).

[11]See, e.g., Zubulake v. UBS Warburg LLC, 229 F.R.D. 422, 94 Fair Empl. Prac. Cas. (BNA) 1, 85 Empl. Prac. Dec. (CCH) ¶ 41728 (S.D. N.Y. 2004) (spoliation of evidence germane to proof of an issue at trial can support inference that evidence would have been unfavorable to party responsible for its destruction); Kelley v. United Airlines, Inc., 176 F.R.D. 422, 39 Fed. R. Serv. 3d 898 (D. Mass. 1997) (airline was negligent in failing to search for and preserve relevant documents thereby warranting adverse inference sanction); Nation-Wide Check Corp., Inc. v. Forest Hills Distributors, Inc., 692 F.2d 214, 218, 11 Fed. R. Evid. Serv. 1588 (1st Cir. 1982). Cf. Residential Funding Corp. v. DeGeorge Financial Corp., 306 F.3d 99, 107, 53 Fed. R. Serv. 3d 1105 (2d Cir. 2002) (adverse inference instruction may be warranted in some circumstances for the untimely production of evidence).

[12]Pension Committee of University of Montreal Pension Plan v. Banc of America Securities, 685 F. Supp. 2d 456 (S.D. N.Y. 2010) (abrogated on other grounds by, Chin v. Port Authority of New York & New Jersey, 685 F.3d 135,

presumption.[13] However, even where the instruction includes a mandatory presumption, the presumption is rebuttable.[14]

The least harsh instruction permits a jury to presume the lost evidence is both relevant and favorable to the innocent party.[15] If the jury makes this presumption, the spoliating party's rebuttal evidence must be considered by the jury, which must then decide whether to draw an adverse inference against the spoliating party.[16] Such an instruction benefits the innocent party by allowing the jury to consider the misconduct of the spoliating party as well as proof of prejudice to the innocent party.[17]

§ 18:18 Precluding litigating claims or defenses

A spoliator may be precluded from litigating certain claims or

---

115 Fair Empl. Prac. Cas. (BNA) 720, 95 Empl. Prac. Dec. (CCH) ¶ 44555 (2d Cir. 2012)); Smith v. Kmart Corp., 177 F.3d 19, 29 n.4 (1st Cir. 1999).

[13]Pension Committee of University of Montreal Pension Plan v. Banc of America Securities, 685 F. Supp. 2d 456 (S.D. N.Y. 2010) (abrogated on other grounds by, Chin v. Port Authority of New York & New Jersey, 685 F.3d 135, 115 Fair Empl. Prac. Cas. (BNA) 720, 95 Empl. Prac. Dec. (CCH) ¶ 44555 (2d Cir. 2012)); West v. Goodyear Tire & Rubber Co., 167 F.3d 776, 780, 42 Fed. R. Serv. 3d 1161 (2d Cir. 1999); Knowlton v. Teltrust Phones, Inc., 189 F.3d 1177, 1182, 80 Fair Empl. Prac. Cas. (BNA) 1062, 78 Empl. Prac. Dec. (CCH) ¶ 40048, 44 Fed. R. Serv. 3d 864 (10th Cir. 1999).

[14]Pension Committee of University of Montreal Pension Plan v. Banc of America Securities, 685 F. Supp. 2d 456 (S.D. N.Y. 2010) (abrogated on other grounds by, Chin v. Port Authority of New York & New Jersey, 685 F.3d 135, 115 Fair Empl. Prac. Cas. (BNA) 720, 95 Empl. Prac. Dec. (CCH) ¶ 44555 (2d Cir. 2012)).

[15]Pension Committee of University of Montreal Pension Plan v. Banc of America Securities, 685 F. Supp. 2d 456 (S.D. N.Y. 2010) (abrogated on other grounds by, Chin v. Port Authority of New York & New Jersey, 685 F.3d 135, 115 Fair Empl. Prac. Cas. (BNA) 720, 95 Empl. Prac. Dec. (CCH) ¶ 44555 (2d Cir. 2012)).

[16]Pension Committee of University of Montreal Pension Plan v. Banc of America Securities, 685 F. Supp. 2d 456 (S.D. N.Y. 2010) (abrogated on other grounds by, Chin v. Port Authority of New York & New Jersey, 685 F.3d 135, 115 Fair Empl. Prac. Cas. (BNA) 720, 95 Empl. Prac. Dec. (CCH) ¶ 44555 (2d Cir. 2012)); Nucor Corp. v. Bell, 251 F.R.D. 191, 203 (D.S.C. 2008); Zimmermann v. Associates First Capital Corp., 251 F.3d 376, 383, 85 Fair Empl. Prac. Cas. (BNA) 1505, 81 Empl. Prac. Dec. (CCH) ¶ 40835 (2d Cir. 2001); Vodusek v. Bayliner Marine Corp., 71 F.3d 148, 156, 1996 A.M.C. 330, 43 Fed. R. Evid. Serv. 869 (4th Cir. 1995).

[17]Pension Committee of University of Montreal Pension Plan v. Banc of America Securities, 685 F. Supp. 2d 456 (S.D. N.Y. 2010) (abrogated on other grounds by, Chin v. Port Authority of New York & New Jersey, 685 F.3d 135, 115 Fair Empl. Prac. Cas. (BNA) 720, 95 Empl. Prac. Dec. (CCH) ¶ 44555 (2d Cir. 2012)).

defenses.[1] This may be particularly appropriate where the evidence alleged to have been destroyed or lost in the case would have been directly relevant to the precluded claim or defense.[2]

§ 18:19 Termination

Terminating sanctions should be used only as a sanction for spoliation of evidence in extreme circumstances, such as where a party has engaged in perjury, tampering with evidence, intentionally destroying evidence by burning, shredding, or wiping computer hard drives.[1] Dismissal or default has been upheld when the spoliator's conduct was so egregious as to amount to a forfeiture of the spoliator's claim, and the effect of the spoliator's conduct was so prejudicial that it substantially denied the defendant the ability to defend the claim.[2]

[Section 18:18]

[1]Arista Records LLC v. Usenet.com, Inc., 633 F. Supp. 2d 124, 141, 91 U.S.P.Q.2d 1744, 79 Fed. R. Evid. Serv. 1480, 73 Fed. R. Serv. 3d 1797 (S.D. N.Y. 2009); Brown v. Coleman, 2009 WL 2877602 (S.D. N.Y. 2009), order aff'd, 2010 WL 882977 (S.D. N.Y. 2010); American Stock Exchange, LLC v. Mopex, Inc., 215 F.R.D. 87 (S.D. N.Y. 2002).

[2]See, e.g., Harkabi v. SanDisk Corp., 275 F.R.D. 414 (S.D. N.Y. 2010) (terminating sanctions not warranted since there was no indication that evidence had been intentionally destroyed); Passlogix, Inc. v. 2FA Technology, LLC, 708 F. Supp. 2d 378 (S.D. N.Y. 2010) (evidence reclusion is harsh action preserved for exceptional cases where party's failure to provide requested discovery results in prejudice to requesting party); Arista Records LLC v. Usenet.com, Inc., 633 F. Supp. 2d 124, 142, 91 U.S.P.Q.2d 1744, 79 Fed. R. Evid. Serv. 1480, 73 Fed. R. Serv. 3d 1797 (S.D. N.Y. 2009); Leon v. IDX Systems Corp., 464 F.3d 951, 960, 18 A.D. Cas. (BNA) 784, 25 I.E.R. Cas. (BNA) 1, 88 Empl. Prac. Dec. (CCH) ¶ 42522 (9th Cir. 2006).

[Section 18:19]

[1]Arista Records LLC v. Usenet.com, Inc., 633 F. Supp. 2d 124, 138–39, 91 U.S.P.Q.2d 1744, 79 Fed. R. Evid. Serv. 1480, 73 Fed. R. Serv. 3d 1797 (S.D. N.Y. 2009); Pension Committee of University of Montreal Pension Plan v. Banc of America Securities, 685 F. Supp. 2d 456 (S.D. N.Y. 2010) (abrogated on other grounds by, Chin v. Port Authority of New York & New Jersey, 685 F.3d 135, 115 Fair Empl. Prac. Cas. (BNA) 720, 95 Empl. Prac. Dec. (CCH) ¶ 44555 (2d Cir. 2012)); Gutman v. Klein, 2008 WL 5084182 (E.D. N.Y. 2008), subsequent determination, 2009 WL 3296072 (E.D. N.Y. 2009), aff'd, 515 Fed. Appx. 8 (2d Cir. 2013).

[2]Rimkus Consulting Group, Inc. v. Cammarata, 688 F. Supp. 2d 598 (S.D. Tex. 2010); Gutman v. Klein, 2008 WL 5084182 (E.D. N.Y. 2008), subsequent determination, 2009 WL 3296072 (E.D. N.Y. 2009), aff'd, 515 Fed. Appx. 8 (2d Cir. 2013); Sampson v. City of Cambridge, Md., 251 F.R.D. 172, 180 (D. Md. 2008); Leon v. IDX Systems Corp., 464 F.3d 951, 959, 18 A.D. Cas. (BNA) 784, 25 I.E.R. Cas. (BNA) 1, 88 Empl. Prac. Dec. (CCH) ¶ 42522 (9th Cir. 2006).

When considering whether dismissal is an appropriate sanction, the court should consider:

- The degree of actual prejudice to the opposing party.
- The degree of interference with the judicial process.
- The litigant's culpability.
- Whether the litigant was warned in advance that dismissal was a likely sanction.
- Whether a lesser sanction would be effective.[3]

§ 18:20 Contempt

To be held in civil contempt, a person must have violated an order or decree setting forth in specific detail an unequivocal command.[1] It is not necessary for a finding of contempt that a violation was willful; it is enough a party has not been reasonably diligent and energetic in attempting to accomplish what was ordered.[2] The party asserting a violation of a judicial order has the burden of proving the violation by clear and convincing evidence.[3] While a court order is a prerequisite to a finding of contempt, it is not a necessary antecedent to a finding of spoliation or to a duty to preserve evidence.[4] In *American Family Mutual Insurance Co. v. Roth*,[5] the court found a producing party to be in contempt for discarding the party's hard drive in violation of a judge's order.

§ 18:21 Independent cause of action

No independent claim for spoliation of evidence exists under

---

[3]Phillip M. Adams & Associates, L.L.C. v. Dell, Inc., 621 F. Supp. 2d 1173, 1193 (D. Utah 2009).

[Section 18:20]

[1]American Family Mut. Ins., Co. v. Roth, 2009 WL 982788, *3 (N.D. Ill. 2009); Pearle Vision, Inc. v. Romm, 541 F.3d 751, 757 (7th Cir. 2008).

[2]American Family Mut. Ins., Co. v. Roth, 2009 WL 982788, *3 (N.D. Ill. 2009); Goluba v. School Dist. of Ripon, 45 F.3d 1035, 1037 (7th Cir. 1995).

[3]American Family Mut. Ins., Co. v. Roth, 2009 WL 982788, *3 (N.D. Ill. 2009); Prima Tek II, L.L.C. v. Klerk's Plastic Industries, B.V., 525 F.3d 533, 537–538, 87 U.S.P.Q.2d 1025 (7th Cir. 2008); S.E.C. v. Homa, 514 F.3d 661, 676 (7th Cir. 2008).

[4]American Family Mut. Ins., Co. v. Roth, 2009 WL 982788, *15 (N.D. Ill. 2009); Trask-Morton v. Motel 6 Operating L.P., 534 F.3d 672, 681 (7th Cir. 2008).

[5]American Family Mut. Ins., Co. v. Roth, 2009 WL 982788, *3 (N.D. Ill. 2009).

federal law.[1] Some states, however, recognize an independent tort of spoliation of evidence, destruction of evidence or a similar cause of action.[2]

E. RULE 37 OF THE FEDERAL RULES OF CIVIL PROCEDURE

§ 18:22 Generally

Fed. R. Civ. P. 37 gives federal courts wide discretion to structure the form of sanctions.[1] Courts have generally employed this discretion to provide a sanction commensurate with the measure of bad faith exhibited by the spoliator.[2] The sanction for spoliation, like any sanction, lies within the sound discretion of the court, and should be designed to deter spoliation and restore the prejudiced party to the same position the party would have been in absent the destruction of evidence by the opposing party, as well as to shift the burden of an erroneous judgment to the spoliator.

Although federal courts routinely state that Fed. R. Civ. P. 37 sanctions may not be imposed as punishment, this is often the effect of the sanctions. The decision to impose sanctions for spolia-

---

[Section 18:21]

[1]See, e.g., Sterbenz v. Attina, 205 F. Supp. 2d 65, 54 Fed. R. Serv. 3d 348 (E.D. N.Y. 2002); Silvestri v. General Motors Corp., 271 F.3d 583, 590, 51 Fed. R. Serv. 3d 694 (4th Cir. 2001); Cloud v. ABC, Inc., 30 Media L. Rep. (BNA) 1402, 2001 WL 1622250 (S.D. N.Y. 2001); Tiano v. Jacobs, 2001 WL 225037 (S.D. N.Y. 2001); Lombard v. MCI Telecommunications Corp., 13 F. Supp. 2d 621 (N.D. Ohio 1998). See also Larison v. City of Trenton, 180 F.R.D. 261 (D.N.J. 1998) (existence of affirmative cause of action for spoliation determined by state law).

[2]Jurisdictions include Alaska (rejected Hazen v. Municipality of Anchorage, 718 P.2d 456 (Alaska 1986) ; Illinois (Rodgers v. St. Mary's Hosp. of Decatur, 149 Ill. 2d 302, 173 Ill. Dec. 642, 597 N.E.2d 616 (1992)); Indiana (Thompson ex rel. Thompson v. Owensby, 704 N.E.2d 134 (Ind. Ct. App. 1998)); Kansas (Foster v. Lawrence Memorial Hosp., 809 F. Supp. 831 (D. Kan. 1992)); New Jersey (modified Hirsch v. General Motors Corp., 266 N.J. Super. 222, 628 A.2d 1108 (Law Div. 1993) (holding modified by, Rosenblit v. Zimmerman, 166 N.J. 391, 766 A.2d 749 (2001)); North Carolina Henry v. Deen, 310 N.C. 75, 310 S.E.2d 326 (1984)); Ohio (Smith v. Howard Johnson Co., Inc., 67 Ohio St. 3d 28, 1993-Ohio-229, 615 N.E.2d 1037 (1993)).

[Section 18:22]

[1]Ellicott Mach. Corp. Intern. v. Jesco Const. Corp., 199 F. Supp. 2d 290, 52 Fed. R. Serv. 3d 1239 (D. Md. 2002) (court has broad discretion to sanction spoliators).

[2]Carlucci v. Piper Aircraft Corp., Inc., 775 F.2d 1440, 1448, 3 Fed. R. Serv. 3d 325 (11th Cir. 1985).

tion under Fed. R. Civ P. 37 requires consideration of three factors:

- the obligation of the party against whom sanctions are sought to preserve the evidence in issue;
- the spoliating party's intent; and
- the relevance of the evidence to the contested issues or the prejudice to the nonspoliating party.[3]

§ 18:23 Safe harbor

Fed. R. Civ. P. 37(e) provides what is sometimes referred to as a "safe harbor." Under Fed. R. Civ. P. 37(e), absent exceptional circumstances, a court may not impose sanctions "on a party for failing to provide electronically stored information lost as a result of the routine, good-faith operation of an electronic information system."[1] This provision applies only to electronic evidence.[2] The party invoking Fed. R. Civ. P. 37(e) has the burden of showing that the loss of electronically stored information was the result of routine, good-faith operation of an electronic information system.[3]

Fed. R. Civ. P. 37(e) recognizes a distinctive feature of computer operations—the routine alteration and deletion of information that attends ordinary use of a computer. Fed. R. Civ. P. 37(e) applies only to information lost because of the "routine operation of an electronic information system"—the ways in which such systems are generally designed, programmed, and implemented to meet the party's technical and business needs.[4]

The operation of the computer system resulting in alteration or

---

[3]Ellicott Mach. Corp. Intern. v. Jesco Const. Corp., 199 F. Supp. 2d 290, 52 Fed. R. Serv. 3d 1239 (D. Md. 2002); Barsoum v. NYC Housing Authority, 202 F.R.D. 396, 399–400, 50 Fed. R. Serv. 3d 26 (S.D. N.Y. 2001). Cf. Greyhound Lines, Inc. v. Wade, 485 F.3d 1032 (8th Cir. 2007).

[Section 18:23]

[1]Cf. Petcou v. C.H. Robinson Worldwide, Inc., 2008 WL 542684 (N.D. Ga. 2008) (sanctions denied using routine operations analysis although Rule 37(e) was not mentioned).

[2]Phillip M. Adams & Associates, L.L.C. v. Dell, Inc., 621 F. Supp. 2d 1173, 1191 (D. Utah 2009).

[3]Phillip M. Adams & Associates, L.L.C. v. Dell, Inc., 621 F. Supp. 2d 1173, 1192 (D. Utah 2009).

[4]See Doe v. Norwalk Community College, 248 F.R.D. 372, 231 Ed. Law Rep. 292 (D. Conn. 2007) (safe-harbor provision requires routine system in place and some affirmative action by party to prevent system from destroying or altering information); Disability Rights Council of Greater Washington v. Washington Metropolitan Transit Authority, 242 F.R.D. 139 (D.D.C. 2007) (safe harbor was not intended to apply to situation where defendant did not stop automatic destruction of e-mails following filing of law suit). See also Diabetes

deletion of information must have been in good faith. Good faith in the routine operation of a computer system may involve a party's intervention to modify or suspend certain features of that routine operation to prevent the loss of information, if that information is subject to a preservation obligation.[5]

According to the Advisory Committee, the good faith requirement of Fed. R. Civ. P. 37(e) means that a party is not permitted to exploit the routine operation of an information system to thwart discovery obligations by allowing that operation to continue in order to destroy specific stored information that it is required to preserve. When a party is under a duty to preserve information because of pending or reasonably anticipated litigation, intervention in the routine operation of an information system is one aspect of what is often called a "legal hold." Among the factors that bear on a party's good faith in the routine operation of an information system are the steps the party took to comply with a court order in the case or party agreement requiring preservation of specific electronically stored information.

The Advisory Committee's Notes state that, whether good faith would call for steps to prevent the loss of information on sources the party believes are not reasonably accessible under Fed. R. Civ. P. 26(b)(2), depends on the circumstances of each case. One factor is whether the party reasonably believes that the information on such sources is likely to be discoverable and not available from reasonably accessible sources.

The protection provided by Fed. R. Civ. P. 37(e) applies only to sanctions under the Federal Rules of Civil Procedure. It does not affect other sources of authority to impose sanctions or rules of professional responsibility. Fed. R. Civ. P. 37(e) does not prevent a court from making the kinds of adjustments frequently used in managing discovery if a party is unable to provide relevant responsive information. The Advisory Committee explains that, for example, a court could order the responding party to produce an additional witness for deposition, respond to additional interrogatories, or make similar attempts to provide substitutes or alternatives for some or all of the lost information.

Centers of America, Inc. v. Healthpia America, Inc., 2008 WL 336382 (S.D. Tex. 2008) (suggesting inadequate keyword searches could be basis for spoliation sanctions when defective searches cause evidence to be lost).

[5]See Arista Records, L.L.C. v. Tschirhart, 241 F.R.D. 462 (W.D. Tex. 2006) (default judgment against defendant was warranted for bad faith and willful destruction of evidence on computer in violation of discovery order).

II. CHECKLISTS

§ 18:24 Checklist of counsel's responsibilities

- ☐ **Counsel's Duty to Monitor Compliance.**
  - ☐ Once a party reasonably anticipates litigation, it must suspend its routine document retention or destruction policy and put in place a "legal hold" to ensure the preservation of relevant documents.
  - ☐ Generally, the legal hold does not apply to inaccessible backup tapes (those typically maintained solely for the purpose of disaster recovery), which may continue to be recycled on the schedule set forth in the party's policy.
  - ☐ Where back tapes are accessible (actively used for information retrieval, then such tapes likely are subject to the legal hold.
  - ☐ Counsel must oversee compliance with the legal hold, monitoring the party's efforts to retain and produce the relevant documents. Proper communications between a party and the party's counsel will ensure:
    - ☐ All relevant information or at least all sources of relevant information is discovered
    - ☐ Relevant information is retained on a continuing basis
    - ☐ Relevant non-privileged material is produced to the opposing party.
- ☐ **Counsel's Duty to Locate Relevant Information.**
  - ☐ after a "legal hold" is in place, a party and the party's counsel must make certain all sources of potentially relevant information are identified placed on hold.
  - ☐ Counsel must become fully familiar with the client's document retention policies, as well as the client's data retention architecture.
    - ☐ This invariably involves speaking with information technology personnel who can explain system-wide backup procedures and the actual implementation of the party's recycling policy.
    - ☐ It involves communicating with the key players in the litigation in order to understand how they stored information.
    - ☐ Unless counsel interviews each employee, it is impossible to determine whether all potential sources of information have been inspected.
    - ☐ To the extent it is not feasible for counsel to speak

with every key player, it may be possible to run a system-wide keyword search. Counsel should preserve a copy of each "hit."

- ☐ It is not sufficient to notify all employees of a legal hold and expect the party will retain and produce all relevant information.
- ☐ Counsel must take affirmative steps to monitor compliance so that all sources of discoverable information are identified and searched.

☐ **Counsel's Continuing Duty to Ensure Preservation.**

- ☐ Once a party and its counsel have identified all the sources of potentially relevant information, they are under a duty to retain that information and to produce information responsive to the opposing party's requests.
- ☐ The duty to supplement responses under applicable rules of civil procedure, while nominally the party's, really falls on counsel.
- ☐ The continuing duty to supplement disclosures strongly suggests that parties also have a duty to be sure discoverable information is not lost.

☐ **There are a number of steps counsel can take to ensure compliance with this preservation obligation.**

- ☐ First, counsel must issue a legal hold at the outset of litigation or whenever litigation is reasonably anticipated. Periodically the legal hold should be reissued so that new employees are aware of it, and so that the legal hold is fresh in the minds of all employees.
- ☐ Second, counsel should communicate directly with the "key players" (people identified in a party's initial disclosure and any subsequent supplementation).
  - ☐ Because these persons are employees likely to have relevant information, it is important that the preservation duty be communicated clearly to them.
  - ☐ The key players should be periodically reminded that the legal hold is still in place.
- ☐ Third, counsel should instruct all employees to produce digital copies of their relevant active files.
  - ☐ Counsel must also be sure that all backup media the party is required to retain is identified and stored in a safe place.
  - ☐ Where a small number of relevant backup tapes are

involved, it is advisable for counsel to take physical possession of backup tapes or have the backup tapes segregated and placed in storage.

NOTES

Commentary

See Zubulake v. UBS Warburg LLC, 229 F.R.D. 422, 94 Fair Empl. Prac. Cas. (BNA) 1, 85 Empl. Prac. Dec. (CCH) ¶ 41728 (S.D. N.Y. 2004).

§ 18:25 Checklist for determining whether destruction of documents pursuant to records retention policy constitutes spoliation of evidence

- ☐ Was the policy reasonable under the facts and circumstances?
- ☐ Had lawsuits concerning the current complaint or related complaints been filed?
- ☐ Was the policy instituted in bad faith (to limit damaging evidence available to plaintiffs)?
- ☐ Did the organization know, or should it have known, that the destroyed documents would become "material at some point in the future"?

NOTES

Commentary

See Lewy v. Remington Arms Co., Inc., 836 F.2d 1104, 1112, Prod. Liab. Rep. (CCH) ¶ 11662, 24 Fed. R. Evid. Serv. 516 (8th Cir. 1988).

§ 18:26 Checklist for avoiding spoliation

- ☐ Timely suspend document retention policies when litigation is reasonably foreseeable.
- ☐ Honor preservation letters.
- ☐ Turn off digital devices only by unplugging in most cases.
- ☐ Request that information be preserved in native format whenever possible to preserve metadata.
- ☐ Quarantine digital media.
- ☐ Create bit-stream backups (imaging) of digital media.
- ☐ Avoid booting up suspect machines.
- ☐ Avoid redeploying machines unless the data they contain are irrelevant to imminent or ongoing litigation.
- ☐ Forbid forensically naive network administrators or other members of the information technology department from checking out or otherwise investigating relevant devices.

§ 18:27 Checklist for detecting potential spoliation

- ☐ Scrutinize the timing and sequence of the opponent's

documents. A clear indication of potential spoliation is a gap in routinely filed documents. Missing pages are another obvious red flag.

- ☐ Track down all drafts. If a document is labeled "fourth draft," make sure you also have drafts one, two, and three.
- ☐ Spot-check "cc" recipients. Tracing the path of every document through a large organization is a waste of resources, but trailing key documents can reveal changes or undisclosed drafts.
- ☐ Dissect drafts of important letters and memoranda. Important documents are usually preceded by one or more drafts. Check your opponent's word processing archives if drafts are not produced.
- ☐ Do not forget e-mail. E-mail is routinely ignored by attorneys gathering documents responsive to requests. If the opponent uses an e-mail system, insist that you receive any relevant messages in their native format. The informal language used in e-mails is often more damaging than carefully crafted documents.

NOTES

Commentary

See Conley & Seidman, *Identifying Spoliation in the 1990s*, FED. DISC. NEWS, May 1995, at 4.

III. FORMS

§ 18:28 Preservation policy

Preservation Policy (Legal hold)

1. If an employee believes, or is informed by *[organization]* that certain records are relevant to litigation or potential litigation, the employee must preserve those records, including electronically stored information, until the *[organization's]* Legal Department determines the records are no longer needed. This duty to preserve supersedes any established destruction schedule for those records.

2. If an employee believe the duty to preserve may apply, or has any question regarding the possible applicability of the duty to preserve, the employee should contact the *[organization's]* Legal Department. An employee's failure to comply with this Document Retention Policy may result in disciplinary action, including suspension or termination. An employee should refer questions about this policy to *[name]*, at *[telephone number]* or *[e-mail address]*.

3. The duty to preserve extends to documents, data, and

tangible things in the possession, custody and control of the parties to this action, and any employees, agents, contractors, carriers, bailees, or other nonparties possessing materials reasonably anticipated to be subject to discovery in this action. Counsel is under an obligation to exercise reasonable efforts to identify and notify such nonparties, including employees of corporate or institutional parties.

4. The term "documents, data, and tangible things" is to be interpreted broadly to include writings, records, files, electronically stored information, correspondence, reports, memoranda, calendars, diaries, minutes, electronic messages, voice-mail, e-mail; telephone message records or logs, computer and network activity logs, hard drives; backup data, removable computer storage media such as tapes, disks, and cards, printouts document image files, Web pages, databases, spreadsheets, software, books, ledgers, journals, orders, invoices, bills, vouchers, checks, statements, worksheets, summaries, compilations, computations, charts, diagrams, graphic presentations, drawings, films, charts, digital or chemical process photographs, video, phonographic, tape, or digital recordings or transcripts, drafts, jottings, and notes. Information serving to identify, locate, or link such material, such as file inventories, file folders, indices, and metadata, is also included in this definition.

5. "Preservation" is to be interpreted broadly to accomplish the goal of maintaining the integrity of all documents, data, and tangible things reasonably anticipated to be subject to discovery under *[rules]* in this action. Preservation includes taking reasonable steps to prevent the partial or full destruction, alteration, testing, deletion, shredding, incineration, wiping relocation, migration, theft, or mutation of such material, as well as negligent or intentional handling that would make material incomplete or inaccessible.

6. The following categories of electronically stored information are to be segregated and preserved: *[specify]*.

7. During this legal hold there will be no deletion, modification, alteration of electronically stored information subject to the legal hold.

8. Employees should advise whether specific categories of electronically stored information subject to the legal hold require particular actions (e.g., printing paper copies of e-mail and attachments) or transfer into "read only" media.

9. Loading of new software that materially impacts electronically stored information subject to the hold may occur only upon prior written approval from *[name]*.

10. In order to preserve metadata, or data that has been

deleted but not purged, the Information Technology Department shall *[describe]*.

11. Employees must reasonably safeguard and preserve all portable or removable electronic storage media containing potentially relevant electronically stored information.

12. Employees shall maintain hardware that has been removed from active production, if such hardware contains legacy systems with relevant electronically stored information and there is no reasonably available alternative that preserves access to the native files on such hardware.

13. *[Name]* is the contact person who will address questions regarding preservation duties.

14. *[Names]* have the responsibility to confirm that compliance requirements are met.

§ 18:29 Legal hold letter—To client

[date]

[name 1]
[address]

Subject: *[Case Name]*

Data Preservation

Dear *[name 1]*:

Your assistance and cooperation are required with respect to preserving information in this case, including electronically stored information. Electronically stored information is an important and irreplaceable source of discovery and evidence.

This lawsuit requires that all employees preserve all information from *[organization's]* computer systems, removable electronic media, and other locations relating to *[describe]*. This includes, but is not limited to, e-mail and other electronic communication, word processing documents, spreadsheets, databases, calendars, telephone logs, contact manager information, Internet usage files, and network access information.

You must take every reasonable step to preserve this information until further notice from *[name 2]*. Failure to do so could result in extreme penalties against *[organization]* including dismissal of the case.

If you have any questions or need further information, please contact *[name 3]* at *[telephone number]*.

Sincerely,

[signature, etc.]

§ 18:30 Legal hold letter—To client—Another form

[date]

[name 1]
[address]

Subject: *[Case Name]*
Preservation of Electronically Stored Information

Dear *[name 1]*:

The purpose of this letter is to inform you that the *[organization]* is involved in a litigation proceeding known as *[case name, case no., jurisdiction]* (the Case). As a result, *[organization]* may be required to produce certain documents, including electronically stored information, relating to the case. In an effort to ensure that *[organization]* is taking all reasonable steps to preserve and safeguard evidence relating to the case, the documents in the categories listed below, whether in hard copy or electronic form, cannot be altered, destroyed or discarded for any reason.

Documents subject to this requirement may be in paper or electronic form, including e-mails, instant text messages, memorandums, and all correspondence, whether in draft or final form. Documents also refer to handwritten and typewritten documents and nonidentical copies of the same documents.

Your failure to retain these documents or ignore the directive of this memorandum can result in severe consequences, including various forms of punishment imposed by a court of law.

Documents Covered:

Until further notice, please search for and then maintain any documents relating to the following topics: *[specify]*.

Any and all documents relating to the *[describe]*, including, without limitation: *[list all potentially relevant documents]*

Any and all communications relating to, or stemming from, the *[describe].*

Instructions:

Please instruct all personnel within the *[organization]* not to alter, destroy, discard, interfile, annotate, remove, rearrange or modify any documents identified for production in the case. Please also inform all appropriate personnel who are responsible for handling, or who have access to, the documents of the instructions conveyed in this letter. Additionally, please instruct such personnel that they must segregate and label all documents that may be produced in the *[describe].*

Questions:

Any questions or concerns about this memorandum should be directed to *[name]* at *[telephone number].* Thank you for your cooperation in this matter.

Very truly yours,

[signature, etc.]

Please preserve all electronically stored information relating to *[describe]*, including hidden system files or metadata, presently located on or contained in a free standing computer or laptop, or on any part of a server, CPU or digital device that may contain data storage capabilities including, but not limited to hard disk drives, optical disk drives, removable media, such as floppy disk drives, CD-ROM and DVD drives, Zip drives, Jaz drives, Maxtor drives or snap drives, data processing cards, computer magnetic tapes, backup tapes, drum and disk storage devices or any other similar electronic storage media or system of whatever name or description.

Please also preserve all digital images relating to *[describe]* that may be stored on any type of hardware used to store or manipulate electronic images, including but not limited to microfilm, microfiche and their repositories and readers, or design or engineering computer systems and regardless of any digital image's format, including.jpg, .bmp, or some other advanced or proprietary form of digital image format, such as CAD layered drawings.

Please preserve all existing sources of electronically stored information relating to *[describe]* that may not presently be in use by your company or may have been deleted from your active systems, whether the source is a backup tape or disk, some other data retention system or some form of disaster recovery system.

Including the imaging of hard drives, please take all reasonable steps to preserve electronically stored information relating to *[describe]* that may have been deleted from your active files and which may not be readily recoverable from a backup medium, such as metadata.

Please also preserve electronically stored information relating to *[describe]* that is subject to your control regardless of where else it may be located on-site at your main offices, within the network infrastructure of your company or on or in one of your other computer support systems including those at your subsidiaries, predecessors, successors, assigns, joint venturers, partners, parents, agents or affiliates (in this country or throughout the world), including but not limited to the following locations:

a. Your LAN and WAN network systems, regardless of methods of connectivity (e.g., by T1, T3 or optical lines), domains, including PDCs, network OS (such as Novell, Microsoft, UNIX, Citrix or some other similar type) or protocols, or your backup and disaster recovery hardware and media, regardless of the physical location of those electronic storage systems.

b. Your e-mail servers and any repository of your e-mail (including within the inbox, sent box, deleted box or some similar file of the computers of employees or management), or in any backup form whatsoever, regardless of whether you use Microsoft Exchange, Outlook, Outlook Express, Lotus Notes or some combination of e-mail management software or some alternative commercial or proprietary e-mail management software.

c. Your IS administrative offices, including backup and disaster recovery restoration repositories, data retention repositories, purge repositories, training repositories, or libraries of hardcopy materials of any description (regardless of where located) and online training and operation manuals that have been scanned to disk.

d. Your offsite technical and service bureau support systems, including but not limited to ASP (application service provider) support, scanning or data conversion support, offsite data storage or archive support.

e. Your Web hosting and administration services, including intranet and extranet sites, regardless of whether they are now publicly posted or exist in English or some other language.

Please consider yourself under a continuing obligation to preserve electronically stored information relating to *[describe]* that may come into existence after the date of this letter, or that may exist now or in the future but of which you have no current knowledge.

Very truly yours,

[signature, etc.]

§ 18:31 Adverse inference instruction

If a party fails to produce evidence that is under that party's control and reasonably available to that party and not reasonably available to the adverse party, then you may infer that the evidence is unfavorable to the party who could have produced it and did not.

NOTES TO FORM

Commentary

Under the "adverse inference rule," when a party has relevant evidence within its control that the party fails to produce, that failure gives rise to an inference that the evidence is unfavorable to it. International Union, United Auto., Aerospace and Agr. Implement Workers of America (UAW) v. N. L. R. B., 459 F.2d 1329, 1336, 79 L.R.R.M. (BNA) 2332, 67 Lab. Cas. (CCH) ¶ 12374, 32 A.L.R. Fed. 807 (D.C. Cir. 1972); Rockingham Machine-Lunex Co. v. N.L.R.B., 665 F.2d 303, 304, 108 L.R.R.M. (BNA) 3228, 92 Lab. Cas. (CCH) ¶ 13142 (8th Cir. 1981). See also Interstate Circuit v. U.S., 306 U.S. 208, 226, 59 S. Ct. 467, 474, 83 L. Ed. 610, 40 U.S.P.Q. 299 (1939) (production of weak evidence when strong is available can lead only to conclusion that strong evidence would have been adverse).

When a party has destroyed evidence relevant to the dispute being litigated, a "spoliation inference" arises to the effect that the destroyed evidence would have been unfavorable to the position of the offending party. Schmid v. Milwaukee Elec. Tool Corp., 13 F.3d 76 (3d Cir.1994).

No inference can be drawn from the failure to produce evidence not in a party's control. Savard v. Marine Contracting Inc., 471 F.2d 536, 541–42, 1973 A.M.C. 323 (2d Cir. 1972).

The rule that an unfavorable inference shall be drawn against a party that fails to introduce evidence known to be in its control does not apply where party has good reason to believe that its opponent has failed to meet its burden of proof. N.L.R.B. v. Chester Valley, Inc., 652 F.2d 263, 271, 107 L.R.R.M. (BNA) 3148, 91 Lab. Cas. (CCH) ¶ 12861 (2d Cir. 1981). In such situations, there is a good faith belief that there is no need to offer further evidence, and therefore no inference can properly be drawn from nonproduction. The inference raised by nonproduction of material evidence in control of a party can be rebutted by adequate explanation for nonproduction. Fernandez v. Chios Shipping Co., Ltd., 542 F.2d 145, 155, 1976 A.M.C. 1780, 1 Fed. R. Evid. Serv. 355 (2d Cir. 1976); Tupman Thurlow Co., Inc. v. S. S. Cap Castillo, 490 F.2d 302, 308, 1974 A.M.C. 51, 18 Fed. R. Serv. 2d 36 (2d Cir. 1974).

In Zimmermann v. Associates First Capital Corp., 251 F.3d 376, 383, 85

Fair Empl. Prac. Cas. (BNA) 1505, 81 Empl. Prac. Dec. (CCH) ¶ 40835 (2d Cir. 2001), the Second Circuit approved the following instruction where the employer failed to produce information critical to plaintiff's attempt to demonstrate disparate treatment:

> You have heard testimony about records which have not been produced. Counsel for plaintiff has argued that this evidence was in the defendant's control and would have proven facts material to the matter in controversy.
>
> If you find that the defendant could have produced these records were within their control and would have proven facts material to the matter in controversy.
>
> If you find that the defendant could have produced these records and that the records were within their control, and that these records would have been material in deciding facts in dispute in this case, then you are permitted, but not required to, infer that this evidence would have been unfavorable to the defendant.
>
> In deciding whether to draw this inference you should consider whether the evidence not produced would merely have duplicated other evidence already before you. You may also consider whether the defendant had a reason for not producing this evidence, which was explained to your satisfaction.

In Zubulake v. UBS Warburg LLC, 229 F.R.D. 422, 94 Fair Empl. Prac. Cas. (BNA) 1, 85 Empl. Prac. Dec. (CCH) ¶ 41728 (S.D. N.Y. 2004), the court gave the following instruction regarding spoliation:

> If you find that UBS could have produced this evidence, and that the evidence was within its control, and that the evidence would have been material in deciding facts in dispute in this case, you are permitted, but not required, to infer that the evidence would have been unfavorable to UBS.

Chapter 19

Protective Orders and Costs

I. GUIDELINES

A. INTRODUCTION

C. OBJECTIONS TO SCOPE OR FREQUENCY

D. UNDUE BURDEN

E. NOT REASONABLY ACCESSIBLE ELECTRONICALLY STORED INFORMATION

F. COST SHIFTING

G. AWARDING COSTS

II. CHECKLISTS

III. FORMS

Research References

Treatises and Practice Aids

Grenig and Gleisner, eDiscovery & Digital Evidence §§ 7:1 to 7:4

Trial Strategy

Recovery and Reconstruction of Electronic Mail as Evidence, 41 Am. Jur Proof of Facts 3d 1

Computer Technology in Civil Litigation, 71 Am. Jur. Trials 111

Additional References

Grenig and Kinsler, Handbook of Federal Civil Discovery and Disclosure §§ 7.1 to 7.4 (3d ed.)

ABA Discovery Standards, http://www.abanet.org/litigation/discoverystandards/2005civildiscoverystandards.pdf

Electronic Discovery Reference Model Project, http://www.edrm.net

Federal Judicial Center, http://www.fjc.gov

The Sedona Conference, http://www.thesedonaconference.org

> **KeyCite®:** Cases and other legal materials listed in KeyCite Scope can be researched through the KeyCite service on Westlaw®. Use KeyCite to check citations for form, parallel references, prior and later history, and comprehensive citator information, including citations to other decisions and secondary materials.

I. GUIDELINES

A. INTRODUCTION

§ 19:1 Generally

With many responding parties, the first response to any e-discovery request is a demand for a protective order. Often sought as an effort by the defending party to protect claimed trade secrets or to reduce the burden and expense of the discovery request, the goal of the request is to limit the scope of discoverable information or to restrain the discovering party from sharing discovered information with other persons who have similar cases.

The purpose of a protective order normally is not to prevent full disclosure, but to minimize the disruption and inconvenience inherent in discovery. Protective orders provide a safeguard for parties and other persons in light of the otherwise broad reach of discovery. In order to further that objective, courts have broad discretionary powers to limit by protective orders the scope and manner of discovery and the procedures to be used.[1] Under extraordinary circumstances, a court may even prohibit discovery in any form at all.[2]

Fed. R. Civ. P. 26(c) empowers a court to make a wide variety of orders for the protection of parties and witnesses in the discovery process. Protective orders are a necessary corollary to

---

[Section 19:1]

[1]See, e.g., Chemical & Indus. Corp. v. Druffel, 301 F.2d 126, 129, 133 U.S.P.Q. 133 (6th Cir. 1962); Patrnogic v. U.S. Steel Corp., 43 F.R.D. 402, 403, 11 Fed. R. Serv. 2d 800 (S.D. N.Y. 1967); Textured Yarn Co. v. Burkart-Schier Chemical Co., 41 F.R.D. 158, 160, 10 Fed. R. Serv. 2d 843 (E.D. Tenn. 1966). See generally Buffmire, Enter the Order, Protect the Privilege: Considerations for Courts Entering Protective Order Under Federal Rule of Evidence 502(d), 81 Fordham L. Rev. 1621 (2013).

[2]See Salter v. Upjohn Co., 593 F.2d 649, 651, 27 Fed. R. Serv. 2d 822 (5th Cir. 1979) (very unusual for trial court to prohibit taking of deposition altogether, and, absent extraordinary circumstances, such order would likely be in error).

the scope of discovery permitted by Fed. R. Civ. P. 26(b)(1). Fed. R. Civ. P. 26(c) permits a court to issue orders protecting a party or person from annoyance, embarrassment, oppression, or undue burden or expense.

§ 19:2 Good cause

Where the discovery is relevant, the burden is on the party seeking a protective order to show good cause.[1] Authorization to enter a protective order is not a blanket authorization for the court to prohibit disclosure of information whenever it deems it advisable to do so, but is rather a grant of power to impose conditions on discovery in order to prevent injury, harassment, or abuse of the court's process. A party seeking a protective order based on the undue burden or expense of complying with a discovery request must submit affidavits or declarations or other detailed explanations as to the nature and extent of the claimed burden or expense unless the request is unduly burdensome on its face.[2]

§ 19:3 Procedure

Protective orders may be granted on motion of a party or the person from whom discovery is sought "for good cause shown" and "as justice requires."[1] A party may not ask for an order to protect the rights of another party or a witness if that party or witness does not claim protection for itself, but a party may seek an order if the party believes its own interest is jeopardized by discovery sought from a third person.[2] While a party may not seek a protective order to protect the rights of another party, but a third party may be allowed to intervene to contest the issuance of a protective order.

In federal court, a motion for a protective order must be accompanied by a certification that the movant has in good faith

---

[Section 19:2]

[1] Security Ins. Co. of Hartford v. Trustmark Ins. Co., 218 F.R.D. 24 (D. Conn. 2003).

[2] Aikens v. Deluxe Financial Services, Inc., 217 F.R.D. 533 (D. Kan. 2003).

[Section 19:3]

[1] See, e.g., Fed. R. Civ. P. 26(c).

[2] See American Rock Salt Co., LLC v. Norfolk Southern Corp., 228 F.R.D. 426, 466 (W.D. N.Y. 2004) (motion for protective order generally must be brought by individual whose interests are affected, and party may not move for protective order to protect interests of another, but may move to protect party's own interests when discovery is sought from another).

conferred or attempted to confer with other affected parties in an effort to resolve the dispute without court action. Fed. R. Civ. P. 26(c) does not state a time period within which a motion for a protective order must be sought, but the motion should be brought on or before the date the discovery in question is to take place.[3]

§ 19:4 Good cause standard

Fed. R. Civ. P. 26(c) requires the movant to show good cause why the protective order should be granted. The application of the good cause standard varies depending upon the nature of the material sought to be protected and the method of discovery. Generally, the burden of establishing good cause for a protective order is on the party seeking the order.[1] It is not enough for the party seeking a protective order to argue that no reason exists not to enter the order; the movant must show a positive reason why the order should be entered.[2]

The moving party must make a clear showing of a particular and specific need for the order.[3] Even if good cause for a protec-

---

[3]See National Independent Theatre Exhibitors, Inc. v. Buena Vista Distribution Co., 748 F.2d 602, 609, 1984-2 Trade Cas. (CCH) ¶ 66311, 40 Fed. R. Serv. 2d 954 (11th Cir. 1984) (untimely protective order granted on condition that opponent's costs be paid).

[Section 19:4]

[1]See In re Agent Orange Product Liability Litigation, 821 F.2d 139, 145, 7 Fed. R. Serv. 3d 1091 (2d Cir. 1987); Blankenship v. Hearst Corp., 519 F.2d 418, 429, 1975-2 Trade Cas. (CCH) ¶ 60384 (9th Cir. 1975); Schorr v. Briarwood Estates Ltd. Partnership, 178 F.R.D. 488, 491 (N.D. Ohio 1998).

[2]See Lohrenz v. Donnelly, 187 F.R.D. 1 (D.D.C. 1999) (party seeking protective order against discovery bears burden of making showing of good cause sufficient to overcome defendant's legitimate and important interest in trial preparation); Pro Billiards Tour Ass'n, Inc. v. R.J. Reynolds Tobacco Co., 187 F.R.D. 229, 44 Fed. R. Serv. 3d 1269 (M.D. N.C. 1999) (burden of showing good cause for protective order rests on part requesting it); Gottstein v. National Ass'n for the Self Employed, 186 F.R.D. 654 (D. Kan. 1999) (party seeking protective order carries burden of persuasion to show good cause for it by submitting particular and specific demonstration of fact, as distinguished from stereotyped and conclusory statements); G-69 v. Degnan, 130 F.R.D. 326, 331 (D.N.J. 1990).

[3]See U.S. E.E.O.C. v. Caesars Entertainment, Inc., 237 F.R.D. 428, 432, 66 Fed. R. Serv. 3d 71 (D. Nev. 2006) (mere showing that discovery may involve some inconvenience or expense does not suffice to establish good cause for a protective order); reconsider Washington v. Thurgood Marshall Academy, 230 F.R.D. 18, 21 (D.D.C. 2005), on reconsideration, 232 F.R.D. 6, 203 Ed. Law Rep. 698, 63 Fed. R. Serv. 3d 754 (D.D.C. 2005) (when moving for protective order, movant must establish good cause by demonstrating the specific evidence of the

tive order is shown, the court must still balance the interests in allowing discovery against the relative burdens to the parties and nonparties.[4]

The likelihood that discovery will be time-consuming or costly is an insufficient basis for a protective order, unless the burden outweighs any possible benefit to the party propounding the discovery.[5] The moving party has the burden to show that responding to the discovery is unduly burdensome.[6] A court may recognize the burdensome nature of discovery in considering a non-party's request for a protective order.[7]

---

harm that would result); clarified Peskoff v. Faber, 230 F.R.D. 25, 28, 62 Fed. R. Serv. 3d 503 (D.D.C. 2005), order clarified, 233 F.R.D. 207 (D.D.C. 2006) (same).

[4]See Beyer v. Medico Ins. Group, 266 F.R.D. 333 (D.S.D. 2009) (fact medical insurer would have to scan images to make them text-searchable or search manually for 5,040 documents relating to similar denied claims was not sufficient reason to find insured's request unduly burdensome); Swackhammer v. Sprint Corp. PCS, 225 F.R.D. 658, 666, 60 Fed. R. Serv. 3d 945 (D. Kan. 2004) (in ruling on undue burden objection, court must keep in mind that discovery should be allowed unless claimed hardship is unreasonable in light of benefits to be secured from discovery).

[5]Beach v. City of Olathe, Kansas, 203 F.R.D. 489, 493 (D. Kan. 2001) (discovery should be allowed unless hardship is unreasonable compared to benefits from discovery).

[6]See U.S. E.E.O.C. v. Caesars Entertainment, Inc., 237 F.R.D. 428, 432, 66 Fed. R. Serv. 3d 71 (D. Nev. 2006) (party seeking protective order must point to specific facts supporting the request, as opposed to conclusory or speculative statements about the need for a protective order and the harm that will be suffered without one); Cory v. Aztec Steel Bldg., Inc., 225 F.R.D. 667, 672 (D. Kan. 2005) (defendants statement that complying with plaintiff's request for production of documents would require "numerous man hours" did not establish that establish that request was unduly burdensome, absent sufficient details or information in terms of time, money, or procedure involved in complying with request); Culkin v. Pitney Bowes, Inc., 225 F.R.D. 69, 71 (D. Conn. 2004) (party objecting to discovery request on grounds of overbreadth or undue burden bears burden of supporting objection via affidavits or evidence); Swackhammer v. Sprint Corp. PCS, 225 F.R.D. 658, 666, 60 Fed. R. Serv. 3d 945 (D. Kan. 2004) (party objecting to interrogatory on ground of undue burden must provideaffidavit or other evidentiary proof of time or expense involved).

[7]See Anker v. G.D. Searle & Co., 126 F.R.D. 515, 519 (M.D. N.C. 1989) (burden on involuntary party expert should be mitigated by assessing costs on deposing party and by limited protective order).

C. OBJECTIONS TO SCOPE OR FREQUENCY

§ 19:5 Relevance

The Federal Rules of Civil Procedure regulate the scope of discovery.[1] Generally, any matter is discoverable, subject to the following specific limitations:

- The matter must be relevant to the claim or defense of any party.[2]
- The matter must not be privileged.
- The matter must not be protected by the work product doctrine.
- The matter is not protected information from non-testimonial experts.
- The matter is not protected by a recognized right to privacy.

Under most rules of procedure, a court can limit discovery if it determines, among other things, that discovery is:

- Unreasonably cumulative or duplicative
- Obtainable from another source that is more convenient
- Burden or expense of proposed discovery outweighs its likely benefit[3]

§ 19:6 Frequency or extent of discovery

Fed. R. Civ. P. 26(b)(2)(C) provides that, on motion or on its own, a court must limit the frequency or extent of discovery otherwise allowed by these rules or by local rule if it determines that:

- the discovery sought is unreasonably cumulative or duplica-

---

[Section 19:5]

[1]See Fed. R. Civ. P. 26(b).

[2]See Fed. R. Civ. P. 26(b)(1). The description of the scope of discovery may be different in state rules. See Bolton v. Sprint/United Management Co., 89 Empl. Prac. Dec. (CCH) ¶ 42763, 2007 WL 756644 (D. Kan. 2007) (objection to production of metadata in native files as not relevant to plaintiff's claims).

[3]See In re Priceline.com Inc. Securities Litigation, 233 F.R.D. 83, 85 (D. Conn. 2005). Cf. Favale v. Roman Catholic Diocese of Bridgeport, 233 F.R.D. 243, 245–46, 206 Ed. Law Rep. 929 (D. Conn. 2005) (court may limit discovery if it determines, among other things, that discovery is (1) unreasonably cumulative or duplicative, (2) obtainable from another source that is more convenient, less burdensome, or less expensive, or (3) that burden or expense of proposed discovery outweighs its likely benefit); Pointer v. DART, 417 F.3d 819, 821, 96 Fair Empl. Prac. Cas. (BNA) 285, 86 Empl. Prac. Dec. (CCH) ¶ 42036 (8th Cir. 2005) (appellate review of district court's relevancy determination on motion to quash a subpoena is for abuse of discretion).

tive or can be obtained from some other source that is more convenient, less burdensome, or less expensive;

- the party seeking discovery has had ample opportunity to obtain the information by discovery in the action; or
- the burden or expense of the proposed discovery outweighs its likely benefit, considering the needs of the case, the amount in controversy, the parties' resources, the importance of the issues at stake in the action, and the importance of the discovery in resolving the issues.

The Advisory Committee explained this provision enables a court to keep tighter rein on the extent of discovery. It noted that the information explosion of recent decades has greatly increased both the potential cost of wide-ranging discovery and the potential for discovery to be used as an instrument for delay or oppression.

D. UNDUE BURDEN

§ 19:7 Generally

Fed. R. Civ. P. 26(b)(2)(B) permits a court to issue a protective order where the party from whom discovery is sought shows the information is not reasonably accessible because of undue burden or cost.[1] Fed. R. Civ. P. 26(b)(2) provides a party is not required to produce electronically stored information that is not "reasonably accessible" because of "undue burden or cost." The amendment attempts to codify *Zubulake*[2] with respect to cost shifting.

Fed. R. Civ. P. 26(b)(2)(C) imposes a general limitation on the scope of discovery in the form of a proportionality test, protecting against redundant or disproportionate discovery.[3] Faced with an overly broad discovery request, a protective order can be sought

---

[Section 19:7]

[1]See Peskoff v. Faber, 240 F.R.D. 26, 67 Fed. R. Serv. 3d 760 (D.D.C. 2007), subsequent determination, 244 F.R.D. 54 (D.D.C. 2007) (accessible data must be produced at the cost of the producing party; cost shifting does not even become a possibility unless there is first a showing of inaccessibility).

[2]Zubulake v. UBS Warburg LLC, 216 F.R.D. 280, 283, 92 Fair Empl. Prac. Cas. (BNA) 684, 56 Fed. R. Serv. 3d 326 (S.D. N.Y. 2003).

[3]See, e.g., McNally Tunneling Corp. v. City of Evanston, Illinois, 2001 WL 1568879 (N.D. Ill. 2001) (where responding party had already provided requesting party with all the information contained in its computer files in hard copyform, requesting party has burden of establishing that the hard copies of the computer are insufficient). But see rev'd Public Citizen v. Carlin, 2 F. Supp. 2d 1, 13 (D.D.C. 1997), rev'd on other grounds, 184 F.3d 900 (D.C. Cir. 1999) (while exact duplicate of particular record might be discardable, electronic versions of records cannot categorically be regarded as valueless "extra copies" of paper

limiting the scope of discovery. Where the requested discovery, whether electronic or paper, is unduly burdensome or expensive, the court may order an allocation of costs.[4]

A party cannot avoid the production of electronically stored information merely by responding that the requests are unduly burdensome.[5] A party objecting on the grounds of undue burden must explain the specific and particular way in which a request is unduly burdensome.[6] Claims that discovery requests for production of documents are unduly burdensome should be supported by a statement, generally an affidavit or declaration, with specific information demonstrating how the request is overly burdensome.

In *Apsley v. Boeing Co.*,[7] an age discrimination case, the court was called upon to determine whether a request for the defendants to produce e-mail was overly broad and unduly burdensome. The plaintiffs sought to compel the production of all the defendants' e-mails meeting specified criteria. The criteria included a description of the individuals whose e-mails should be targeted for screening, the time period during which the e-mails sought would have been sent, a description of the possible subject matters of the e-mails, and nineteen search terms.

The defendants responded there were multiple servers located in different cities that could contain relevant e-mails, that the number of individuals likely to be subject to search was large, and that many of them had multiple e-mail addresses. Setting the matter for a hearing, the court directed the parties to address question regarding details of the discovery request and what responding to the request would entail.

---

versions). See Sedona Principle 2 ("When balancing the cost, burden, and need for electronically stored information, courts and parties should apply the proportionality standard embodied in Fed. R. Civ. P. 26(b)(2)(C) and its state equivalents, which require consideration of the technological feasibility and realistic costs of preserving, retrieving, reviewing, and producing electronically stored information, as well as the nature of the litigation and the amount in controversy.").

[4]See, e.g., City of Seattle v. Professional Basketball Club, LLC, 2008 WL 539809 (W.D. Wash. 2008) (bald assertions of burden insufficient to establish undue burden); Zubulake v. UBS Warburg LLC, 217 F.R.D. 309, 320–23, 91 Fair Empl. Prac. Cas. (BNA) 1574 (S.D. N.Y. 2003).

[5]See, e.g., Giardina v. Lockheed Martin Corp., 2003 WL 1338826 (E.D. La. 2003).

[6]Bank of Mongolia v. M & P Global Financial Services, Inc., 258 F.R.D. 514, 519 (S.D. Fla. 2009).

[7]Apsley v. Boeing Co., 2007 WL 163201 (D. Kan. 2007).

§ 19:8 Protection of Nonparties

Fed. R. Civ. P. 45 provides protection from undue impositions on nonparties. Fed. R. Civ. P. 45(c)(1) requires a party serving a subpoena to take reasonable steps to avoid imposing an undue burden or expense on a person subject to the subpoena. Fed. R. Civ. P. 45(c)(2)(B) permits the persons served to object to the subpoena and directs that an order requiring compliance must protect a person who is neither a party nor a party's officer from significant expense resulting from compliance.

E. NOT REASONABLY ACCESSIBLE ELECTRONICALLY STORED INFORMATION

§ 19:9 Generally

It is often easier to locate and retrieve electronically stored information than paper-based information. However, some sources of electronically stored information can be accessed only with substantial burden and cost. That burden and cost may make the information on such sources not reasonably accessible.[1]

The responding party may be able to identify difficult-to-access sources that may contain responsive information, but that the responding party is not able to retrieve the information or even to determine whether any responsive information in fact is on the sources—without incurring substantial burden or cost.[2] Fed. R. Civ. P. 26(b)(2)(B) addresses issues raised by difficulties in locating, retrieving, and providing discovery of some electronically stored information.

According to the Advisory Committee:

> The volume of—and the ability to search—much electronically stored information means that in many cases the responding party will be able to produce information from reasonably accessible sources that will fully satisfy the parties' discovery needs. In many

---

[Section 19:9]

[1]Advisory Committee Note to 2006 Amendment to Fed. R. Civ. P. 26.

[2]See Sedona Principle 8 ("The primary source of electronically stored information for production should be active data and information. Resort to disaster recovery backup tapes and other sources of electronically stored information that are not reasonably accessible requires the requesting party to demonstrate need and relevance that outweigh the costs and burdens of retrieving and processing the electronically stored information from such sources, including the disruption of business and information management activities."), and Sedona Principle 9 ("Absent a showing of special need and relevance, a responding party should not be required to preserve, review, or produce deleted, shadowed, fragmented, or residual electronically stored information.").

circumstances the requesting party should obtain and evaluate the information from such sources before insisting that the responding party search and produce information contained on sources that are not reasonably accessible. If the requesting party continues to seek discovery of information from sources identified as not reasonably accessible, the parties should discuss the burdens and costs of accessing and retrieving the information, the needs that may establish good cause for requiring all or part of the requested discovery even if the information sought is not reasonably accessible, and conditions on obtaining and producing the information that may be appropriate.[3]

Sources that might be considered not reasonably accessible sources of electronically stored information include:

- Backup tapes intended for disaster recovery purposes
- Legacy data remaining from obsolete systems that is unintelligible on successor systems
- Deleted electronically stored information that remains in a fragmented form requiring a forensics to restore and retrieve
- Electronically stored information in a database that was designed to create information in ways such that it would lose its significance when produced outside the database[4]

The Advisory Committee acknowledged that amended Fed. R. Civ. P. 26(b)(2)(B) might encourage some to "bury" information in some inaccessible format in order to keep it from being discovered in litigation, but noted that this conduct would be subject to sanctions under both the present and the proposed rules.[5]

§ 19:10 Two-tiered analysis

Fed. R. Civ. P. 26(b)(2)(B) creates what is frequently referred to as a two-tier system. Under Fed. R. Civ. P. 26(b)(2)(B), a party

---

[3]Advisory Committee Note to 2006 Amendment to Fed. R. Civ. P. 26.

[4]Report of the Civil Rules Advisory Committee (May 27, 2005). See W.E. Aubuchon Co., Inc. v. BeneFirst, LLC, 245 F.R.D. 38, 68 Fed. R. Serv. 3d 361 (D. Mass. 2007) (categories of sources of electronically stored information, from most to least accessible, are (1) active online data (e.g., hard drives), (2) near-line data (typically, robotic storage devices such as optical disks) and offline storage/archives (removable optical disks or magnetic tape media that can be labeled and stored in shelf or rack), (3) backup tapes (devices like tape records that read data from and write it onto a tape, sequential access devices that are not typically organized for retrieval of individual documents or files), and (4) erased, fragmented or damaged data, which can only be accessed after significant processing).

[5]Advisory Committee Note to Proposed Amendment to Fed. R. Civ. P. 26(b)(2) (May 27, 2005).

is not required to provide discovery of electronically stored information from sources the party identifies as not reasonably accessible because of undue burden or cost. However, a court may nonetheless order discovery from sources identified as not reasonably accessible if the requesting party shows good cause, considering the limitations of Fed. R. Civ. P. 26(b)(2)(C) applicable to all discovery.

In many circumstances, the two-tier approach will be worked out by negotiation. At the same time, more easily accessed sources—whether computer-based, paper, or human—may yield all the reasonably useful information.[1] According to the Advisory Committee: "Lawyers sophisticated in these problems are developing a two-tier practice in which they first sort through the information that can be provided from easily accessed sources and then determine whether it is necessary to search the difficult-to-access sources."[2]

§ 19:11 Responding party's claim information not reasonably accessible

Under Fed. R. Civ. P. 26(b)(2)(B), the responding party is required to identify, by category or type, the sources containing potentially responsive information that it is neither searching nor producing. The identification should provide enough detail to enable the requesting party to evaluate the burdens and costs of providing the discovery and the likelihood of finding responsive information on the identified sources.[1]

If the parties cannot agree on what terms the sources identi-

---

[Section 19:10]

[1]Advisory Committee Note to Proposed Amendment to Fed. R. Civ. P. 26(b)(2) (May 27, 2005). See, e.g., Rodriguez-Torres v. Government Development Bank of Puerto Rico, 265 F.R.D. 40 (D.P.R. 2010) (in employment discrimination case, electronically stored information requested by plaintiffs was not reasonably accessible—requests were likely to produce hundreds, if not thousands of irrelevant, confidential and potentially privileged documents and estimated cost of production was $35,000).

[2]Advisory Committee Note to Proposed Amendment to Fed. R. Civ. P. 26(b)(2) (May 27, 2005).

[Section 19:11]

[1]See, e.g., City of Seattle v. Professional Basketball Club, LLC, 2008 WL 539809 (W.D. Wash. 2008) (bald assertions of burden insufficient); Parkdale America, LLC v. Travelers Cas. and Sur. Co. of America, Inc., 2007 WL 4165247 (W.D. N.C. 2007) (plaintiffs failed to establish e-mail in LotusNotes format was not reasonably accessible because of undue burden or cost). But see Best Buy Stores, L.P. v. Developers Diversified Realty Corp., 247 F.R.D. 567, 69 Fed. R.

fied as not reasonably accessible should be searched and discoverable information produced, the issue may be raised either by a motion to compel discovery or by a motion. The responding party then has the burden to show that the identified sources are not reasonably accessible because of undue burden or cost.[2]

While Fed. R. Civ. P. 26(b)(2)(B) relieves producing parties from the initial obligation of producing potentially discoverable information from sources the party identifies as not reasonably accessible because of undue burden or cost, it does not relieve the party of its common law or statutory duties to preserve evidence.[3] Whether the party is required to preserve unsearched sources of potentially responsive information it believes are not reasonably accessible depends on the circumstances of each case.[4] A responding party is entitled to conduct a cost-benefit analysis under Fed. R. Civ. P. 26(b)(2)(C). If the burden of preservation is extraordinarily high and the potential benefit is low, there should be no need to preserve. If the cost of preservation is low and the risk of losing potentially relevant data is high, preservation is the prudent course.

A responding party may wish to resolve the issue by moving for a protective order.[5] By making a motion for a protective order, a responding party may be able to resolve whether, or the extent to which, it must preserve the information stored on the difficult-to-access sources until discoverability is resolved.[6]

§ 19:12 Order requiring discovery of information not reasonably accessible

A finding that the responding party has shown that a source of information is not reasonably accessible does not preclude

---

Serv. 3d 1035 (D. Minn. 2007) (plaintiff not required to produce database prepared in separate litigation).

[2]See Semsroth v. City of Wichita, 239 F.R.D. 630, 634, 105 Fair Empl. Prac. Cas. (BNA) 988, 27 A.L.R.6th 705 (D. Kan. 2006) (relying on the proposed 2006 amendments of Fed. R. Civ. P. 26(2)(B)).

[3]Advisory Committee Note to 2006 Amendment to Fed. R. Civ. P. 26.

[4]Advisory Committee Note to 2006 Amendment to Fed. R. Civ. P. 26. (the decision is left to the good judgment and risk tolerance of the organization's decision-maker).

[5]Advisory Committee Note to Proposed Amendment to Fed. R. Civ. P. 26(b)(2) (May 27, 2005).

[6]Advisory Committee Note to Proposed Amendment to Fed. R. Civ. P. 26(b)(2) (May 27, 2005).

discovery; the court may still order discovery for good cause.[1] In ordering discovery of information that is not reasonably accessible, the court may specify conditions for the discovery.[2] Appropriate considerations in determining whether not reasonably accessible information should be produced include:

- The specificity of the discovery request
- The quantity of information available from other and more easily accessed sources
- The failure to produce relevant information that seems likely to have existed but is no longer available on more easily accessed sources
- The likelihood of finding relevant, responsive information that cannot be obtained from other, more easily accessed sources
- Perceptions as to the importance and usefulness of the further information
- The importance of the issues at stake in the litigation
- The parties' resources[3]

In some cases a single proceeding may suffice both to find that a source is not reasonably accessible and also to determine whether good cause nonetheless justifies discovery and to set any conditions that should be imposed.[4] Conditions include limits on the amount, type, or sources of information that must be accessed and produced. In addition, the court may require the requesting party to pay part or all of the reasonable costs of obtaining the information from inaccessible costs.

The proceedings may have to be staged if focused discovery is necessary to determine the costs and burdens in obtaining information from the sources identified as not reasonably accessible, the likelihood of finding responsive information on such sources, and the value of the information to the litigation.[5] A finding that a source is not reasonably accessible may lead to further proceed-

---

[Section 19:12]

[1]Advisory Committee Note to Proposed Amendment to Fed. R. Civ. P. 26(b)(2) (May 27, 2005).

[2]Peskoff v. Faber, 244 F.R.D. 54 (D.D.C. 2007) (it was appropriate to ascertain cost of forensic testing to see if it justified forensic search for relevant e-mails).

[3]Baker v. Gerould, 2008 WL 850236 (W.D. N.Y. 2008).

[4]Advisory Committee Note to Proposed Amendment to Fed. R. Civ. P. 26(b)(2) (May 27, 2005).

[5]Advisory Committee Note to Proposed Amendment to Fed. R. Civ. P. 26(b)(2) (May 27, 2005).

ings to determine whether there is good cause to order limited or extensive searches and the production of information stored on such sources.[6]

In many cases, discovery obtained from accessible sources will be sufficient to meet the needs of the case.[7] If information from such sources does not satisfy the requesting party, Fed. R. Civ. P. 26(b)(2)(B) allows that party to obtain additional discovery from sources identified as not reasonably accessible, subject to judicial supervision, on a showing of good cause.[8] One method of showing a need for discovery is by sampling the sources to determine what they contain and how difficult it would be obtain what they contain.[9]

In determining whether the requesting party has shown good cause for obtaining discovery from a source of electronically stored information that is not reasonably accessible, consideration must be given to the limitations of Fed. R. Civ. P. 26(b)(2)(C) balancing the costs and potential benefits of discovery.[10] A determination of good cause depends not only on the burdens and cost of discovery, but also whether those burdens and costs can be justified in the circumstances of the case.[11] The test is based on the burden and cost of locating, restoring, and retrieving potentially responsive information from the sources in which it is stored.[12]

Fed. R. Civ. P. 26(b)(2)(C) permits a court to limit discovery if it determines:

---

[6]Advisory Committee Note to Proposed Amendment to Fed. R. Civ. P. 26(b)(2) (May 27, 2005).

[7]Advisory Committee Note to Proposed Amendment to Fed. R. Civ. P. 26(b)(2) (May 27, 2005).

[8]Advisory Committee Note to Proposed Amendment to Fed. R. Civ. P. 26(b)(2) (May 27, 2005).

[9]See, e.g., Hagemeyer North America, Inc. v. Gateway Data Sciences Corp., 222 F.R.D. 594 (E.D. Wis. 2004) (requiring defendant to restore sample of backup tapes and requiring parties to address whether expense of satisfying entire discovery request was proportionate to likely benefit); Zubulake v. UBS Warburg LLC, 217 F.R.D. 309, 91 Fair Empl. Prac. Cas. (BNA) 1574 (S.D. N.Y. 2003) (ordering restoration by defendant of that five backup tapes selected by plaintiff be restored by defendant and examination to determine whether they had responsive e-mail messages); McPeek v. Ashcroft, 202 F.R.D. 31, 50 Fed. R. Serv. 3d 528 (D.D.C. 2001) (ordering backup restoration of e-mails attributable to specified period).

[10]Fed. R. Civ. P. 26(b)(2)(B).

[11]Advisory Committee Note to 2006 Amendment to Fed. R. Civ. P. 26.

[12]Advisory Committee Note to Proposed Amendment to Fed. R. Civ. P. 26(b)(2) (May 27, 2005). But see Reidy & Baros, Win the Battle for Access to E-data, Trial, Dec. 2006, at 49, 52 ("because information deemed not reasonably accessible is specially protected (it need not be searched for responsive docu-

- the discovery sought is unreasonably cumulative or duplicative, or is obtainable from some other source that is more convenient, less burdensome or less expensive;
- the party seeking discovery has had ample opportunity by discovery in the action to obtain the information sought; or
- the burden or expense of the proposed discovery outweighs its likely benefit, taking into account the needs of the case, the amount in controversy, the parties' resources, the importance of the issues at stake in the litigation, and the importance of the proposed discovery in resolving the issues.

The ultimate question is whether the burden of complying with the discovery request outweighs the likely benefit of the proposed discovery.[13] The first inquiry should be to ask what the benefits to be derived from the discovery are.[14] This involves the following questions:

- What is the likelihood that the discovery will uncover relevant information?
- What is the potential value of that information in resolving the issues of the case?

Then, these benefits should be compared to the cost of burden resulting from the discovery.[15] The following questions should be asked:

- What is the total cost of production compared with the amount in controversy?
- What is the total cost of production compared to the resources available to each party?

These factors should be given such weight as may be justified by the individual case as they are all critical to the ultimate question of whether the costs outweigh the likely benefits of production.[16]

---

ments)", the "undue burden or cost test" should be more demanding than the "unduly burdensome").

[13]Zubulake v. UBS Warburg LLC, 217 F.R.D. 309, 322–23, 91 Fair Empl. Prac. Cas. (BNA) 1574 (S.D. N.Y. 2003). Accord Semsroth v. City of Wichita, 239 F.R.D. 630, 638, 105 Fair Empl. Prac. Cas. (BNA) 988, 27 A.L.R.6th 705 (D. Kan. 2006).

[14]Semsroth v. City of Wichita, 239 F.R.D. 630, 638, 105 Fair Empl. Prac. Cas. (BNA) 988, 27 A.L.R.6th 705 (D. Kan. 2006).

[15]Semsroth v. City of Wichita, 239 F.R.D. 630, 638, 105 Fair Empl. Prac. Cas. (BNA) 988, 27 A.L.R.6th 705 (D. Kan. 2006).

[16]Semsroth v. City of Wichita, 239 F.R.D. 630, 638, 105 Fair Empl. Prac. Cas. (BNA) 988, 27 A.L.R.6th 705 (D. Kan. 2006).

§ 19:13 Backup media

Backup media, including backup tapes, are a reasonable storage method for purpose of disaster recovery.[1] Backup media created as a disaster-recovery measure have been considered to be an inaccessible format because the electronically stored information is not organized for retrieval of individual documents, and it is usually more time consuming and expensive to restore the information due because the information has been compressed.[2] Because organizations are increasingly opting for Internet or disc-based backups, rather than tape drives, these newer technologies overcome the sequential-access problem associated with tape drives.

Because backup media must be restored before they can be searched for relevant electronically stored information, this suggests the process of producing such information would constitute an unreasonable burden.[3] The more likely it is the backup media contains important, relevant to the requesting party's case, the

---

[Section 19:13]

[1]Advisory Committee Note to 2006 amendment to Fed. R. Civ. P. 26. See Semsroth v. City of Wichita, 239 F.R.D. 630, 635, 105 Fair Empl. Prac. Cas. (BNA) 988, 27 A.L.R.6th 705 (D. Kan. 2006) (applying then-proposed 2006 amendments of Fed. R. Civ. P. 26(2)(B)). But see Quinby v. WestLB AG, 245 F.R.D. 94 (S.D. N.Y. 2006), subsequent determination, 2007 WL 38230 (S.D. N.Y. 2007) (party converted data into an inaccessible format at a time when it should have reasonably anticipated litigation and should have anticipated that data would be discoverable in such litigation). See generally Wescott, *Shedding Light on Backup Tape E-Discovery*, INFORMATIONMANAGEMENT, Sept./Oct. 2009, at 48.

[2]Zubulake v. UBS Warburg LLC, 217 F.R.D. 309, 319, 91 Fair Empl. Prac. Cas. (BNA) 1574 (S.D. N.Y. 2003). Accord Semsroth v. City of Wichita, 239 F.R.D. 630, 636, 105 Fair Empl. Prac. Cas. (BNA) 988, 27 A.L.R.6th 705 (D. Kan. 2006). But see Treppel v. Biovail Corp., 249 F.R.D. 111 (S.D. N.Y. 2008) (inadequate preservation efforts necessitated restoration and production of e-mail from backup tapes).

[3]Petcou v. C.H. Robinson Worldwide, Inc., 2008 WL 542684 (N.D. Ga. 2008) (no duty to search backup tapes for e-mails of sexual nature); Zubulake v. UBS Warburg LLC, 217 F.R.D. 309, 318, 91 Fair Empl. Prac. Cas. (BNA) 1574 (S.D. N.Y. 2003). Accord Semsroth v. City of Wichita, 239 F.R.D. 630, 637, 105 Fair Empl. Prac. Cas. (BNA) 988, 27 A.L.R.6th 705 (D. Kan. 2006). But see Reidy and Baros, Win the Battle for Access to E-data, TRIAL, Dec. 2006, at 49, 54 ("restoration is not necessarily burdensome or costly").

fairer it is to require the responding party to search at its own expense.[4]

Generally, backups are viewed as short-term retention copies of a file or record in case the original is lost or damaged. An archive is thought of as the means to meet a requirement to retain a record for future reference.

Archival data is information an organization maintains for long-term storage and record keeping purposes, but which is not immediately accessible to the computer system users. It may be written to removable media, tape, or other electronic storage devices. Some systems allow users to retrieve archival data directly while others require the intervention of a professional. Electronic archives preserve the content, prevent or track alterations, and control access to electronic records. Most archival data is reasonably accessible.

§ 19:14 Legacy systems

Many cases involve legacy databases that using outdated or obsolete technology, including outdated operating systems and hardware. Customized solutions are often required to collect potentially relevant data from legacy databases. The Advisory Committee has indicated legacy data remaining from obsolete systems that is unintelligible on successor systems is considered information no reasonably accessible.[1]

Even when legacy data can be read and used, a database contains a large quantity of unformatted electronically stored information that becomes useful only when it is put into a report. Databases contain entries and complex table structures appear nonsensical if just providing the raw data. Many databases do not permit the creation of customized reports containing the information in the form that is deemed potentially relevant in the litigation. Therefore, a third party is frequently required to write customized software to extract electronically stored information from various locations in the database and to create a formatted document that can be reviewed.

Because of the costs, an organization may be tempted to make portions of a database available to the requesting party, forcing requesting party to pay the costs of securing the electronically

---

[4]Zubulake v. UBS Warburg LLC, 217 F.R.D. 309, 333, 91 Fair Empl. Prac. Cas. (BNA) 1574 (S.D. N.Y. 2003), citing McPeek v. Ashcroft, 202 F.R.D. 31, 34, 50 Fed. R. Serv. 3d 528 (D.D.C. 2001).

[Section 19:14]

[1]Advisory Committee Note to 2006 Amendment to Fed. R. Civ. P. 26.

stored information from the database. Great caution should be taken in agreeing to turn over unreviewed databases to opposing counsel. The courts are split over whether to grant access to the responding party's databases for the requesting party to run searches.[2]

When dealing with older technology, legacy systems or databases, it is important to describe the complexity of the collection and production of that information as early as possible. It may be necessary to use outside experts who can provide testimony regarding the complexity, time involved, and cost of obtaining legacy information. If the parties to the case cannot agree on a reasonable approach to this problem, a court may need to issue an order specifying the appropriateness and limits of collecting and producing the legacy data.

§ 19:15 Deleted information

While deleted electronically stored information is often retrievable, it may require considerable effort. While this does not put the information beyond discovery, the difficulty of accessing the information usually means the information is not reasonably accessible.

§ 19:16 Databases

A database contains large quantities of electronically stored information that is typically unformatted and becomes useful only when it is put into a report. Databases appear nonsensical if they just provide the raw data. Many database systems do not permit the creation of customized reports containing the information in the form that is deemed potentially relevant in the litigation. A third party is often needed to write customized software to extract data from various locations in the database and create a formatted document that can be reviewed.

Thus, according to the Advisory Committee, databases that "cannot readily create very different kinds or forms of information from the kind or form from which they were designed are a problem in discovery".[1] It may be possible to avoid this problem if the requesting party formulates the request to fit the design of the database.

---

[2]Compare In re Honeywell Intern., Inc. Securities Litigation, 230 F.R.D. 293 (S.D. N.Y. 2003) (providing access), with In re Ford Motor Co., 345 F.3d 1315, 56 Fed. R. Serv. 3d 438 (11th Cir. 2003) (not providing access).

[Section 19:16]

[1]Advisory Committee Note to 2006 Amendment to Fed. R. Civ. P. 26.

§ 19:17 Sampling

"Sampling" backup tapes and other media that are difficult to access may provide an effective means for determining whether the records contain relevant information.[1] Requesting parties should attempt to identify which of their opponent's inaccessible data would most likely yield the largest amount of, and the most useful, evidence, and they should target the most promising subset for sampling. Once samples are identified, the parties should make convincing presentations as to why production should or should not be required, and, if required, why in fairness the other side should pay for it.[2]

F. COST SHIFTING

§ 19:18 Generally

It is typically presumed that a responding party bears its own costs of complying with discovery requests.[1] However, where producing the information is "unduly burdensome or expensive," a

---

[Section 19:17]

[1]S.E.C. v. Collins & Aikman Corp., 256 F.R.D. 403, Fed. Sec. L. Rep. (CCH) ¶ 95045 (S.D. N.Y. 2009); Zubulake v. UBS Warburg LLC, 217 F.R.D. 309, 324, 91 Fair Empl. Prac. Cas. (BNA) 1574 (S.D. N.Y. 2003). Cf. Peskoff v. Faber, 244 F.R.D. 54 (D.D.C. 2007) (appropriate to ascertain cost of forensic testing of computers and server to see if it justified forensic search for relevant e-mails).

[2]See, e.g., Hagemeyer North America, Inc. v. Gateway Data Sciences Corp., 222 F.R.D. 594 (E.D. Wis. 2004) (defendant required to restore sample of backup tapes in question).

[Section 19:18]

[1]Oppenheimer Fund, Inc. v. Sanders, 437 U.S. 340, 358, 98 S. Ct. 2380, 2393, 57 L. Ed. 2d 253, Fed. Sec. L. Rep. (CCH) ¶ 96470, 25 Fed. R. Serv. 2d 541 (1978); D'Onofrio v. SFX Sports Group, Inc., 254 F.R.D. 129 (D.D.C. 2008). See Peskoff v. Faber, 251 F.R.D. 59 (D.D.C. 2008) (cost of search properly allocated to producing party where cost did not represent burden or expense so undue as to justify shift to requesting party); Cason-Merenda v. Detroit Medical Center, 2008 WL 2714239 (E.D. Mich. 2008) (where producing party elected to suffer expense of discovery and only then seek contribution from requesting party, court denied request for contribution). See Sedona Principle 13 ("Absent a specific objection, party agreement or court order, the reasonable costs of retrieving and reviewing electronically stored information should be borne by the responding party, unless the information sought is not reasonably available to the responding party in the ordinary course of business. If the information sought is not reasonably available to the responding party in the ordinary course of business, then, absent special circumstances, the costs of retrieving and reviewing such electronic information may be shared by or shifted to the requesting party."). See generally Fax, A Trend Toward Cost Shifting in Discovery?, Litigation News, Spring 2013, at 18; Duker & Zemel, *E-discovery:*

court may condition "discovery on the requesting party's payment of the costs of discovery."[2]

In considering requests for cost shifting with respect to expensive and burdensome discovery, the most important consideration is the extent to which the request is specifically tailored to discovery relevant information.[3] The normal and reasonable translation of electronically stored information into a form usable by the discovering party should be the ordinary and foreseeable burden of a respondent in the absence of a showing of extraordinary hardship.[4]

§ 19:19 Determining when cost shifting may be appropriate

A court will order a cost shifting protective order only upon motion of the responding party to a discovery request and for good cause shown.[1] The responding party has the burden of proof on a motion for cost shifting.[2] In determining whether cost shifting may be appropriate it is necessary to thoroughly understand

---

Are Prevailing Party Costs for e-Discovery Vendors Recoverable Under 28 U.S.C. § 1920?, INSIDECOUNSEL, April 23, 2013; Altman & Lewis, *Cost shifting in ESI Discovery Disputes: A Five-Factor Test to Promote Consistency and Set Party Expectations*, 36 N. Ky. L. Rev. 569 (2009).

[2]Universal Del., Inc. v. Comdata Corp., 2010 WL 1381225 (E.D. Pa. 2010) (plaintiff and nonparty ordered to split costs of creating searchable database of electronically stored information from backup tapes and other databases in the possession of the nonparty).

[3]S.E.C. v. Collins & Aikman Corp., 256 F.R.D. 403, Fed. Sec. L. Rep. (CCH) ¶ 95045 (S.D. N.Y. 2009) (because requesting party's request was not specifically tailored and must be revised, parties were directed to negotiate reasonable search protocol).

[4]See OpenTV v. Liberate Technologies, 219 F.R.D. 474, 57 Fed. R. Serv. 3d 539 (N.D. Cal. 2003) (cost shifting warranted where digital data in the form of source code was stored in an inaccessible format for purposes of discover, where process of extracting search code from its database took between 1.25 and 1.5 hours per source code, amounting to between 125–150 hours of work to complete extraction process for approximately 100 versions of source code requested by requesting party); Daewoo Electronics Co., Ltd. v. U.S., 10 Ct. Int'l Trade 754, 650 F. Supp. 1003, 1006, 8 Int'l Trade Rep. (BNA) 1627 (1986). Cf. One River Place Condominium Ass'n, Inc. v. Axis Surplus Ins. Co., 2010 WL 235028 (E.D. La. 2010) (document imaging costs were not recoverable; no indication that electronic product was more expensive or duplicative of hard copy costs).

[Section 19:19]

[1]Zubulake v. UBS Warburg LLC, 216 F.R.D. 280, 283, 92 Fair Empl. Prac. Cas. (BNA) 684, 56 Fed. R. Serv. 3d 326 (S.D. N.Y. 2003).

[2]Zubulake v. UBS Warburg LLC, 216 F.R.D. 280, 283, 92 Fair Empl. Prac. Cas. (BNA) 684, 56 Fed. R. Serv. 3d 326 (S.D. N.Y. 2003). See Mikron Industries,

the responding party's computer system, both with respect to active and stored data.

Accessibility turns largely on the expense of production.[3] Electronically stored information is not exempt from cost shifting merely because it is in an accessible rather than an inaccessible format.[4]

For electronically stored information kept in an accessible format, the usual rules of discovery apply: the responding party should pay the costs of producing responsive electronically stored information. A court should consider cost shifting only when electronically stored information is relatively inaccessible, such as in backup media.[5]

A court should carefully consider the following in determining whether costs of discovery should be shifted:

- The extent to which the request is specifically tailored to discover relevant information.
- The availability of such information from other sources.
- The total cost of production, compared to the amount in controversy.
- The total cost of production, compared to the resources available to each party.
- The relative ability of each party to control costs and its incentive to do so.
- The importance of the issues at stake in the litigation.

Inc. v. Hurd Windows & Doors, Inc., 2008 WL 1805727 (W.D. Wash. 2008) (cost shifting rejected where moving party failed to meet and confer in good faith and conclusory characterization of ESI as "inaccessible" were insufficient).

[3]See OpenTV v. Liberate Technologies, 219 F.R.D. 474, 476–77, 57 Fed. R. Serv. 3d 539 (N.D. Cal. 2003) ("While the source code at issue in this case is not 'backed up' . . ., it is similarly expensive and time consuming to make it available in a usable form for discovery.").

[4]Couch v. Wan, 2011 WL 2971118 (E.D. Cal. 2011) (court explained that cost of search for information in question—$54,000—was "a significant burdensome amount"). See also OpenTV v. Liberate Technologies, 219 F.R.D. 474, 57 Fed. R. Serv. 3d 539 (N.D. Cal. 2003).

[5]See, e.g., Peskoff v. Faber, 240 F.R.D. 26, 67 Fed. R. Serv. 3d 760 (D.D.C. 2007), subsequent determination, 244 F.R.D. 54 (D.D.C. 2007) (accessible data must be produced at cost of producing party; cost shifting does not become possibility unless there is first showing of inaccessibility). See Boehning & Toal, Courts *Consider When Cost shifting Is Appropriate: A Ruling Suggests It Is Called for only When Data Are Inaccessible*, NAT'L L.J., Aug. 20, 2007, at S3.

- The relative benefits to the parties of obtaining the information.[6]

The seven factors should not be weighted equally. When evaluating cost shifting, the central question must be, does the request impose an "undue burden or expense" on the responding party?[7] Weighing the factors in descending order of importance may solve the problem and avoid a mechanistic application of the test.[8]

The first two factors comprise the "marginal utility" test, the next four as addressing cost issues, and the last factor is "the least important because it is fair to presume that the response to a discovery request generally benefits the requesting party."[9] In the unusual case where production will provide a tangible or strategic benefit to the responding party, that factor may weigh against shifting costs.[10]

Requiring the responding party to restore and produce backup tapes or other electronically stored information that is not reasonably accessible may inform the cost shifting analysis. When based on an actual sample, the marginal utility test will not be an exercise in speculation—there will be tangible evidence of what the backup tapes may have to offer.[11] There will also be tangible evidence of the time and cost required to restore the backup tapes, which in turn will inform the second group of cost shifting factors.[12]

---

[6] Zubulake v. UBS Warburg LLC, 217 F.R.D. 309, 324, 91 Fair Empl. Prac. Cas. (BNA) 1574 (S.D. N.Y. 2003).

[7] Zubulake v. UBS Warburg LLC, 217 F.R.D. 309, 322–23, 91 Fair Empl. Prac. Cas. (BNA) 1574 (S.D. N.Y. 2003) ("Put another way, 'how important is the sought-after evidence in comparison to the cost of production?' ").

[8] Zubulake v. UBS Warburg LLC, 217 F.R.D. 309, 323, 91 Fair Empl. Prac. Cas. (BNA) 1574 (S.D. N.Y. 2003). See also McPeek v. Ashcroft, 202 F.R.D. 31, 34, 50 Fed. R. Serv. 3d 528 (D.D.C. 2001) ("The more likely it is that the backup tape contains information that is relevant to a claim or defense, the fairer it is that the [responding party] search at its own expense. The less likely it is, the more unjust it would be to make the [responding party] search at its own expense. The difference is 'at the margin.' ").

[9] Zubulake v. UBS Warburg LLC, 217 F.R.D. 309, 323, 91 Fair Empl. Prac. Cas. (BNA) 1574 (S.D. N.Y. 2003).

[10] Zubulake v. UBS Warburg LLC, 217 F.R.D. 309, 323, 91 Fair Empl. Prac. Cas. (BNA) 1574 (S.D. N.Y. 2003).

[11] Zubulake v. UBS Warburg LLC, 217 F.R.D. 309, 324, 91 Fair Empl. Prac. Cas. (BNA) 1574 (S.D. N.Y. 2003).

[12] Zubulake v. UBS Warburg LLC, 217 F.R.D. 309, 324 n.77, 91 Fair Empl. Prac. Cas. (BNA) 1574 (S.D. N.Y. 2003) ("Of course, where the cost of a sample

§ 19:20 Resisting and avoiding cost sharing

The groundwork for resisting a motion to shift costs can be established by the discovering party's insisting on conferences, constructing reasonable and focused requests, seeking court assistance when the responding party resists discovery, and educating the court from the beginning about why the electronically stored information sought will expedite the litigation.[1] When seeking to avoid cost shifting, a requesting party should consider the following arguments:[2]

- The requesting party's need for the discovery
- The inability of the requesting party to pay the costs related to the discovery in comparison with the producing party's ability to pay
- The likelihood that the requested information will lead to the discovery of admissible evidence
- The difficulty the requesting party will encounter in finding information from any other source
- The ease with which the responding party can find and produce the information requested
- The specificity of the discovery request
- The quantity of information available from other and more easily accessed sources
- The failure of the responding party to produce relevant information that seems likely to have existed, but is no longer available on more easily accessible sources
- Predictions as to the importance and usefulness of the further information
- The importance of the issues at stake in the litigation
- The parties respective sources

A discovering party needs to be very aware of the risk that sloppy, imprecise, or overly broad discovery can result in substantial cost shifting expenses, and possibly sanctions. There was a time when a discovering party could issue broad discovery requests and then it became the obligation of the responding

---

restoration is significant compared to the value of the suit, or where the suit itself is patently frivolous, even this minor effort may be inappropriate.") (italics in original).

[Section 19:20]

[1]See, e.g., In re Livent, Inc. Noteholders Securities Litigation, 2003 WL 23254 (S.D. N.Y. 2003) (ordering parties to review Rowe and confer to reach an agreement on issues such as cost shifting).

[2]Fed. R. Civ. P. 26(b)(2). See Gonzalez & Montoya, *Ten Tips Leading to Efficient and Effective eDiscovery for the Small Law Firm*, GPS/SOLO, Apr. 2007.

party to decide whether a particular request mandated the production of certain evidence. Those days are past. A solid understanding of an adversary's computing infrastructure will aid a targeted and well-considered discovery effort. Doing due diligence with the experts will help to formulate specific, justifiable requests.

Discovery requests not drafted with thoughtful specificity may carry a significant price tag for a careless counsel. In the words of the court in *Rowe Entertainment, Inc. v. William Morris Agency, Inc.*:[3]

> The less specific the requesting party's discovery demands, the more appropriate it is to shift the costs of production to that party. Where a party multiplies litigation costs by seeking expansive rather than targeted discovery, that party should bear the expense.

Rowe teaches that a discovering party conducts fishing expeditions very much at that party's peril. Before searches of large amounts of electronically stored information will be permitted, a discovering party may be required to demonstrate that such searches are likely to result in the production of relevant evidence.[4] One way to do this is to require a discovering party to produce evidence from witnesses that there is important relevant electronically stored information on a responding party's computer system.[5]

In the case of large amounts of unindexed electronically stored information, such as might be found on disaster recovery backup tapes, one might allow the discovering party to have searches conducted on a limited number of tapes, by means of a test run, looking for certain evidence. The more hits there are, the less likely costs of discovery will be shifted to the discovering party.[6]

Rowe also makes allowance for the fact that a discovering party who has received documents in one format may have the right to request them in a different format, but only if the plaintiff is prepared to pay the costs:

---

[3]Rowe Entertainment, Inc. v. William Morris Agency, Inc., 205 F.R.D. 421, 429–30, 2002-1 Trade Cas. (CCH) ¶ 73567, 51 Fed. R. Serv. 3d 1106 (S.D. N.Y. 2002).

[4]Rowe Entertainment, Inc. v. William Morris Agency, Inc., 205 F.R.D. 421, 430, 2002-1 Trade Cas. (CCH) ¶ 73567, 51 Fed. R. Serv. 3d 1106 (S.D. N.Y. 2002).

[5]Rowe Entertainment, Inc. v. William Morris Agency, Inc., 205 F.R.D. 421, 430, 2002-1 Trade Cas. (CCH) ¶ 73567, 51 Fed. R. Serv. 3d 1106 (S.D. N.Y. 2002).

[6]McPeek v. Ashcroft, 202 F.R.D. 31, 34, 50 Fed. R. Serv. 3d 528 (D.D.C. 2001).

Some cases that have denied discovery of electronic evidence or have shifted costs to the requesting party have done so because equivalent information either has already been made available or is accessible in a different format at less expense. In *Anti-Monopoly, Inc. v. Hasbro, Inc.*, 1996 WL 22976 *1 (S.D.N.Y. 1996). the defendant had already produced the requested data in hard copy. However, the plaintiff sought the same information in electronic form, presumably to facilitate computerized analysis. While recognizing that prior production in one form did not foreclose the plaintiff's demand, the court held that "[if] plaintiff wants the computerized information, it will have to pay defendants' reasonable costs of creating computer programs to extract the requested data from defendants' computers."[7]

Rowe makes an important distinction between electronically stored information retained for the purposes of accessing it in the ordinary course of business and data that has been retained just for the purpose of disaster or emergency recovery. According to *Rowe*, no cost shifting is allowed where data that has been retained with an intention that it can be retrieved in the ordinary course of business, whereas the cost of retrieving data from emergency backup tapes may be shifted to the requesting party.[8]

G. AWARDING COSTS

§ 19:21 Generally

The courts are divided on the question of whether the costs of e-discovery are recoverable under Fed. R. Civ. P. 54(d) as either "exemplification" or the cost of making copies.[1] Some courts have held that fees associated with creating.TIFF files and the corresponding OCR files are recoverable costs, while expenses associated with data extraction and storage are not recoverable.[2]

Some courts have made a distinction between "creating" electronically searchable documents and "producing" electronic

---

[7]Rowe Entertainment, Inc. v. William Morris Agency, Inc., 205 F.R.D. 421, 430, 2002-1 Trade Cas. (CCH) ¶ 73567, 51 Fed. R. Serv. 3d 1106 (S.D. N.Y. 2002).

[8]Rowe Entertainment, Inc. v. William Morris Agency, Inc., 205 F.R.D. 421, 430, 2002-1 Trade Cas. (CCH) ¶ 73567, 51 Fed. R. Serv. 3d 1106 (S.D. N.Y. 2002).

[Section 19:21]

[1]See Costello, LOSER PAYS—AT LEAST THE COSTS OF E-DISCOVERY?, 80 U.S.L.W. 431 (Oct. 4, 2011).

[2]See, e.g., Fast Memory Erase, LLC v. Spansion, Inc., 2010 WL 5093945 (N.D. Tex. 2010), report and recommendation adopted, 2010 WL 5093944 (N.D. Tex. 2010), aff'd, 423 Fed. Appx. 991 (Fed. Cir. 2011).

documents.[3] Other cases have held that e-discovery costs associated with preservation, collection, processing, and production are the equivalent of the activities listed in 28 U.S.C.A. § 1920.[4]

In *Race Tires America, Inc. v. Hoosier Racing Tire Corp.*,[5] the court held charges for an e-discovery vendors' work in an antitrust action, which did not produce illustrative evidence or the authentication of public records, did not qualify as fees for "exemplification" within meaning of the federal statute governing taxation of costs. The court explained, of the numerous services the e-discovery vendor performed in an antitrust action, only the scanning of hard copy documents, the conversion of native files to the agreed-upon default format for production of electronically stored information, and the transfer of VHS tapes to DVD involved "copying," and the costs attributable to only those activities were recoverable as "costs of making copies of any materials" under the statute.

In *In re Aspartame Antitrust Litigation*,[6] the court held the defendant producers were entitled to costs for creation of litigation database, storage of data, imaging hard drives, keyword searches, deduplication, data extraction and processing, and privilege screen, following summary judgment in producers' favor in class action alleging that producers engaged in worldwide horizontal antitrust conspiracy in violation of Sherman Act; producers' use of third party vendors to conduct keyword searches and remove duplicate documents allowed producers to reduce their pool of potentially responsive documents by 87% and 38.5% respectively, at significant cost savings.

The Virginia Supreme Court has upheld a judgment allowing a plaintiff to recover as damages fees totaling $371,002 the plaintiff paid a computer forensics firm to conduct a forensics investigation because the fees were "costs *[the plaintiff]* incurred litigating

---

[3]See, e.g., Mann v. Heckler & Koch Defense, Inc., 2011 WL 1599580 (E.D. Va. 2011); Gabriel Technologies Corp. v. Qualcomm Inc., 2010 WL 3718848 (S.D. Cal. 2010).

[4]See, e.g., CBT Flint Partners, LLC v. Return Path, Inc., 654 F.3d 1353, 99 U.S.P.Q.2d 1610 (Fed. Cir. 2011).

[5]Race Tires America, Inc. v. Hoosier Racing Tire Corp., 674 F.3d 158, 2012-1 Trade Cas. (CCH) ¶ 77837 (3d Cir. 2012), cert. denied, 133 S. Ct. 233, 184 L. Ed. 2d 43 (2012).

[6]In re Aspartame Antitrust Litigation, 817 F. Supp. 2d 608 (E.D. Pa. 2011).

this case."[7] The court explained the evidence at trial was sufficient to demonstrate that the defendants' actions caused the plaintiff to initiate the computer forensics investigation to determine whether the defendants had copied files containing trade secrets on the plaintiff's computers and downloaded the files on their computers.

II. CHECKLISTS

§ 19:22 Checklist of cost shifting factors

- ☐ The extent to which the request is specifically tailored to discover relevant information.
- ☐ The availability of such information from other sources.
- ☐ The total cost of production, compared to the amount in controversy.
- ☐ The total cost of production, compared to the resources available to each party.
- ☐ The relative ability of each party to control costs and its incentive to do so.
- ☐ The importance of the issues at stake in the litigation.
- ☐ The relative benefits to the parties of obtaining the information.

NOTES

Commentary

See Zubulake v. UBS Warburg LLC, 217 F.R.D. 309, 322, 91 Fair Empl. Prac. Cas. (BNA) 1574 (S.D. N.Y. 2003).

§ 19:23 Checklist of factors to consider in compelling disclosure of e-mail

- ☐ How many persons are covered by the requesting party's e-mail request?
- ☐ What is the estimate cost of complying with the request?
- ☐ What are the benefits of discovery that the requesting party is requesting?
- ☐ Do the search terms and their quantity materially increase the cost of discovery?
- ☐ Should the costs of discovery be shifted?
- ☐ What computer resources or expertise did the requesting party rely on in formulating a search protocol?
- ☐ If the information is produced, how will the requesting party process the information?

---

[7]21st Century Systems, Inc. v. Perot Systems Government Services, Inc., 284 Va. 32, 726 S.E.2d 236, 2012-1 Trade Cas. (CCH) ¶ 77933 (2012).

☐ Is there a more efficient method for discovering the information requested?

NOTES

Commentary

This form is adapted from the record in Apsley v. Boeing Co., 2007 WL 163201 (D. Kan. 2007).

§ 19:24 Checklist of considerations for determining whether to require discovery of electronically stored information that is not reasonably accessible

☐ The specificity of the discovery request
☐ The quantity of information available from other and more easily accessed sources
☐ The failure to produce relevant information that seems likely to have existed but is no longer available on more easily accessed sources
☐ The likelihood of finding relevant, responsive information that cannot be obtained from other, more easily accessed sources
☐ Predictions as to the importance and usefulness of the further information
☐ The importance of the issues at stake in the litigation
☐ The parties' resources

NOTES

Commentary

Adapted from Advisory Committee Note to 2006 Amendment to Rule 26.

III. FORMS

§ 19:25 Notice and motion for protective order

[Caption]

NOTICE AND MOTION FOR PROTECTIVE ORDER

To: *[name]*

Attorney for *[party]*

[Address]

Please take notice that on *[date]* at *[time]*, or as soon thereafter as counsel can be heard, the undersigned will move this court at *[location]* for an order forbidding the taking of the deposition of *[name]*, on the ground that the examination is sought for the sole purpose of annoying and embarrassing the defendant *[name]*.

At the hearing, the undersigned will rely upon the affidavit of *[name]*, a copy of which is attached as Exhibit A.

The undersigned will further move for the reasonable expenses incurred in obtaining the order sought by this motion, including reasonable attorney fees.

Dated: ____

[signature etc.]

§ 19:26 Motion to stay all discovery pending resolution of certain motions submitted pursuant to stipulation

[Caption]

MOTION TO STAY DISCOVERY

Pursuant to an agreement with plaintiff *[name]*, defendant *[name]* moves for entry of an order staying all discovery in this matter pending resolution by the Court of defendant's Motion for *[specify]* pursuant to *[rule]*. In support of this motion, defendant submits the attached stipulation of the parties.

Dated: ____

[signature etc.]

STIPULATION

The parties, by their counsel, hereby stipulated that all discovery in this cause should be stayed pending a resolution of the defendant's Motion for *[specify]*.

Dated: ____

[signature etc.]

Dated: ____

[signature etc.]

§ 19:27 Motion for return of computer backup tapes

[Caption]

Defendant's Motion for Return of Computer Backup Tapes

To: *[name]*
[address]

Defendant *[name 1]*, by its attorneys, respectfully moves this Court for an order requiring Plaintiffs to return to *[name 1]* a set of improperly-obtained computer backup tapes from *[name 1's]* office. In support of its motion, Defendant *[name 1]* states as follows:

1. Counsel for the parties held a case management conference on *[date]*. At that meeting, Plaintiffs' counsel advised Defendant's counsel for the first time that, on *[date]*, Plaintiffs' counsel had received an anonymous box of approximately backup tapes that appeared to belong to defendant *[name 1]*. Plaintiffs' counsel advised further that they sent the box of tapes to *[name 2]* (Plaintiffs' computer forensic vendor), along with another backup tape they had received from Plaintiff *[name 3]* (who had been the Defendant's information technology employee working with the tapes during *[name 3]*'s employment with Defendant).

2. At the request of Defendant's counsel, Plaintiffs' counsel subsequently provided an inventory of those tapes, which appear to be total tapes from Defendant's office.

3. On *[date]*, Defendant's counsel faxed a letter to Plaintiffs' counsel asking for immediate return of the tapes, along with the box and any packing materials in which they were received. See Exhibit A. In that letter, Defendant's counsel asked Plaintiffs' counsel to provide the following information regarding the delivery of these tapes, including: (a) the disposition of the box and any packing materials in which they were received; (b) the date and location identified on the postmark; (c) the approximate time they were received; (d) who at the law firm representing plaintiffs received and opened the box; (e) whether anything was removed from the box; (f) when the box was transferred to *[name 2]* and to whom at *[name 2]*; (g) the chain of custody for the transfer of the tapes from the law firm representing Plaintiffs to *[name 2]*; and (h) whether any tapes were reviewed or analyzed by anyone on Plaintiffs' legal team, any of the Plaintiffs, or anyone at *[name 2]*).

4. As of the time of this motion, Plaintiffs' counsel has not responded to Defendant's counsel's *[date]* letter. On *[date]*, Defendant's counsel telephoned Plaintiffs' counsel to follow up on the *[date]* letter. Plaintiffs' counsel represented that Plaintiffs would not turn over the tapes without a court order.

5. Defendant *[name 1]* keeps and uses the data on its computer backup tapes in the ordinary course of business. They are regularly used to restore lost data, e.g., when an employee's computer crashes. That is why Defendant *[name 1]* created the backup tapes in the first place.

6. The backup tapes received by Plaintiffs contain stolen data, and may even be stolen originals. Defendant *[name 1]* is attempting to ascertain whether Plaintiffs received the original backup tapes, but it may take months to make this determination.

7. Regardless of whether Plaintiffs received original or copied backup tapes, Plaintiffs have a duty to return the tapes to defendant.

8. Moreover, it is illegal for Plaintiffs to refuse to return the tapes to Defendant. *[Statute]* states that a person commits theft when the person knowingly obtains control over stolen property knowing the property to have been stolen or under such circumstances as would reasonably induce the person to believe the property was stolen. If it were not already apparent to Plaintiffs' counsel by their mysterious receipt of an anonymous box of tapes, Defendant's counsel's *[date]*, letter to Plaintiffs' counsel, and the *[date]*, conversation with Plaintiffs' counsel put Plaintiffs on notice that the data on the tapes, and perhaps the very tapes themselves, were stolen.

WHEREFORE, for the foregoing reasons, Defendant *[name 1]* respectfully moves this Court for an order requiring Plaintiffs to return to Defendant the improperly-obtained computer backup tapes from Defendant's office.

Dated: ____

[signature, etc.]

NOTES TO FORM

Commentary

This form is adapted from a motion in Wiginton v. CB Richard Ellis, Inc., 229 F.R.D. 568, 94 Fair Empl. Prac. Cas. (BNA) 627 (N.D. Ill. 2004). While the motion involves the return of backup tapes, it can be adapted for use in seeking the return any electronic media.

§ 19:28 Motion to shift costs

[Caption]

Defendant's Memorandum in Support of Motion for Fair Apportionment of Electronic Discovery Costs

INTRODUCTION

Over the course of a few months, Defendants reviewed a total of 1,082,807 pages of e-mails and attachments based on Plaintiffs' requests for: (i) the restoration of 108 backup tapes from four different timeframes; and (ii) the search of those tapes with 39 different search terms and numerous variations thereof. The cost of this massive project exceeded several hundred thousand dollars. Nineteen people worked on the e-mail review, many on an almost full-time basis.

The size and complexity of this undertaking was staggering. Plaintiffs knew that their requests would require extraordinary time and effort, yet they took the position that they should contribute none of the costs, let alone a fair share, caused by their own overly broad document requests. Defendants undertook their review and production subject to their right to seek such a fair allocation, which is the purpose of this Motion.

Courts recognize that electronic discovery is qualitatively and quantitatively different than traditional paper discovery due to the ability of modern technology to store vast amounts of information. E-discovery can, and often does, impose substantial burdens and expenses on the responding party. Accordingly, many courts (including this Court) allocate an equitable distribution of the costs of e-discovery between the requesting and the producing parties in appropriate circumstances.

As discussed below, these circumstances clearly are present in this case. The first and most important factor applied by the courts—the extent to which the requests are specifically tailored to discover relevant information—clearly mandates an allocation of costs to Plaintiffs. Plaintiffs have requested broad and expansive restorations, searches, reviews and productions of e-mails from Defendants' backup tapes. On their face, Plaintiffs' search terms are vague, ambiguous, and disconnected to the specific issues raised in this litigation. For example, Plaintiffs' search terms include such common words as "cherry*," "pregnan*," "cancer," and "marketing," with the asterisks representing any prefix or suffix associated with those terms. Plaintiffs' demanded terms snag everything in their path, and catch e-mails about such irrelevant topics as recipes or baby showers. The proof, however, is in the tangible impacts of Plaintiffs' requests, which have required Defendants to review 151,315 e-mails and attachments, comprising a total of 1,082,807 pages. Out of this massive amount of documents, Defendants identified and produced only 26,324 responsive documents. The breadth and expansiveness of Plaintiffs' requests are demonstrated by this extraordinary disparity between the searches demanded by Plaintiffs and the e-mails that are even potentially relevant in this case.

Plaintiffs already have represented to the court that they intend to avoid shouldering their fair share of the costs by making baseless accusations about the production process, many of which contradict their own prior accusations. Plaintiffs even have asserted that Defendants, not Plaintiffs, are somehow responsible for the breadth and scope of Plaintiffs' own requests encompassing over 300 individuals, 39 search terms (and multiple variations thereof) and 108 backup tapes. Plaintiffs' mudslinging, however, fails to counter the facts that: (1) Plaintiffs requested and are responsible for the production, and instead of narrowing or focusing the review, actually expanded the process to include additional persons, search terms and dates; and (2) the production methods employed by Defendants, through their consultant (Consultant), are the most efficient and cost-effective methods available, especially considering the breadth and scope of Plaintiffs' requested searches and the tight deadlines under which the parties were operating.

For those reasons and others set forth below, Defendants hereby request that this Court apportion to Plaintiffs 50% of the costs caused by Plaintiffs' requests concerning the restoration, search, review, and production of e-mails from backup tapes.

BACKGROUND

A. Plaintiffs' Initial Requests Required A Relatively Focused Production of E-mails In Their Native Format.

When Plaintiffs initially requested electronic versions of e-mails from Defendants, it was in connection with document requests to Defendant served on *[date]*, and a subpoena served on *[name]* on or about *[date]*. Prior to this time, Plaintiffs had not issued a formal request for the electronic production of e-mails. Defendants expended considerable time and effort in negotiating and reaching agreement with Plaintiffs concerning the search terms to be used and the scope of backup tapes to be reviewed. When all was said and done, very little time remained before the *[date]* fact discovery cut-off for Defendants to restore and produce the documents.

Because only two timeframes of backup tapes were implicated by Plaintiffs' requests, Defendants undertook the restoration process in-house and produced the documents in their native format (as they were stored on the Outlook system). Because the documents existed in their native format, they could not be bates-labeled without alteration, and Plaintiffs complained on a number of occasions about that inherent deficiency of a native production. The native format documents also could not be redacted electronically. Instead, documents requiring redaction had to printed, redacted, and produced in hard copy form. Once again, Plaintiffs complained. Plaintiffs even went so far as to seek an order from the Court compelling the production of these redacted documents electronically.

B. Plaintiffs Requested An Additional Restoration of A Multitude Of Backup Tapes and Demanded Searches With Overbroad Criteria.

One day after the Court entered an order on *[date]*, extending the fact-discovery deadline, Plaintiffs demanded a new restoration, search, review and production of backup e-mails. Plaintiffs then informed Defendants that Plaintiffs also demanded the production to be bates-labeled, that Plaintiffs demanded Boolean searches performed on the e-mails, and that Plaintiffs demanded additional persons to be added to the search list.

As Plaintiffs' demands accumulated, it became clear that Plaintiffs were insisting on the restoration and search of 108 backup tapes and the search of 327 individuals' e-mail accounts using 39 search terms (and multiple variations thereof). Subsequently, Plaintiffs insisted on the search of the e-mail accounts of several more individuals. Defendants, fully cognizant of *[date]*, Order and the need to avoid any delay in the production process, discussed and memorialized their "concerns . . . based on *[the]* burden" of Plaintiffs' requests, but agreed to proceed subject to all "rights and remedies with regard to the costs incurred in performing additional restorations and searches and undertaking the production." As Defendants made clear: "We are proceeding with the work so that we avoid any delay based on the parties' failure to agree regarding the allocation of costs. However, we intend to seek reimbursement for a fair portion of the costs associated with the extensive and expensive tasks necessitated by the backup e-mail production that Plaintiffs have requested."

C. Defendants Needed To Retain A Consultant To Restore and Search the Backup Tapes and Enable Defendants To Review The E-mails.

Defendants could not avoid incurring substantial costs in connection with this production in light of Plaintiffs' broad search demand, including the number of backup tapes requiring restoration and the nature and scope of the demanded search terms. Nevertheless, Defendants did select the most efficient and least costly method available to them. Defendants employed Consultant, one of the nation's leading providers of e-discovery services, to assist with the production. Defendants simply could not undertake a restoration, search and review of the size and complexity demanded by Plaintiffs without the assistance of a consultant like Consultant. Furthermore, after Consultant began the restoration process, it discovered that five of the 108 backups tapes contained corrupted information. It is unlikely that Amerigroup Illinois would have been able to restore these corrupted tapes without Consultant's technical expertise.

Specifically, Consultant performed the following work on the backup tapes:

a) *Restoration of media*—Consultant extracted all data on every tape (unless corrupt) onto a hard drive for further analysis;

b) *Header Scan*—Consultant included header information on all tapes to allow backup tapes to be properly ordered;

c) *Restoration of Exchange Databases*—Consultant attempted to locate and extract case-specific custodians as instructed by Defendants;

d) *Tape Copy and Recovery*—Consultant copied corrupt tapes in an attempt to recover corrupt data;

e) *Exchange Database Analysis*—Consultant analyzed the database to determine user names located on corrupt tapes;

f) *Exchange Database Repair*—Consultant attempted to obtain relevant data from the corrupt tape after users were located on corrupt media;

g) *Exchange Database Repair*—Level 2—Consultant employed repair processes for cases of more serious corruption; and

h) *Expedite Fees*—Consultant rescheduled other work in order to make this job a priority.

As part of the restoration procedure, Consultant processed the documents from their native application into PDF format, with text and metadata preserved and indexed for search accuracy. Consultant then uploaded the PDF documents onto its Online Review Application, which is an Internet-based system. This enabled multiple reviewers to examine the restored e-mails for responsiveness, another critical capability necessitated by the breadth of Plaintiffs' requests and the number of e-mails resulting therefrom. This is a standard method for conducting such a large volume e-mail production. *See* Wiginton v. CB Richard Ellis, Inc., 229 F.R.D. 568, 570, 94 Fair Empl. Prac. Cas. (BNA) 627 (N.D. Ill. 2004) (shifting 75% of e-discovery costs where outside vendor was hired to "restore and extract the user e-mails from the tapes, perform searches for keywords and file attachment types, and load the results of the searches onto *[vendor's]* Internet-based system, for review").

PDF processing was critical to this process for a number of reasons. First, native file review quickly becomes extremely complicated and expensive due to the variety of software programs, including outdated versions of the same program, that are often encountered. In this case, Consultant processed over 90 distinct file types. If this data were reviewed natively, each computer employed in the review process would require software compatible with all 90 of these file types.

Furthermore, Consultant's PDF processing made it feasible to review, search, categorize, redact, and produce e-mails on the scale necessitated by Plaintiffs' requests. If the documents remained in a native application, such as Microsoft Outlook, each attachment would have to be opened manually to check for relevant or privileged information. Duplicative e-mails and attachments would need to be reviewed separately, increasing the number of e-mails to be reviewed by tens of thousands and raising serious risks of inconsistent responsiveness and privilege determinations by different reviewers. Additionally, no redactions could electronically be made to documents in their native format. Nor could the documents be bates-labeled or marked "confidential."

Moreover, processing the documents into a PDF format avoids the potential for inadvertent changes to the native files. For example, a document created in a word-processing program typically stores a "date last modified" field in the document's metadata. The simple act of opening a file for review, even when no changes are made, can alter the document's modification history. Other changes, such as modifying the "create" date, can occur when native files are copied for review, before reviewers even begin their work. Without proper precautions, relevant and material information can be forever altered. These changes to the metadata can occur during the review process and/or after documents are produced to opposing counsel.

D. Plaintiffs' Overly Broad Requests Resulted in Substantial Costs to Defendants.

The total cost of work performed by Consultant in restoring the backup tapes, performing the specified searches, and uploading the data to the Online Review Application, which includes project management, software maintenance, software upgrades, hosting, database security and all functionality provided by the Online Review application, and performing additional necessary work is $238,508.66. This figure does not include the costs associated with the time spent by personnel in the course of the review and production, which far exceeds the total for the work performed by Consultant.

Since Defendants are seeking a fair allocation of the costs of the electronic discovery, Defendants are not seeking reimbursement for, and have redacted from the attached invoices, costs (i) that relate solely to the Defendants' production needs; and (ii) that relate to duplicate production resulting from the need to insure family groups of e-mails and their attachments remained together.

The bottom line is that the total costs incurred in connection with responding to Plaintiffs' e-discovery requests have exceeded several hundred thousands of dollars. Defendants therefore request a fair apportionment of these costs.

ARGUMENT

Courts agree that shifting the costs of e-discovery is appropriate under the *[rules]*, but they disagree about the standard to be used in determining when such cost-shifting should take place. Cost-shifting is implicit in the protective order provisions of *[rule]*, which authorizes "any order which justice requires to protect a party or person from . . . undue burden or expense." *See also* Advisory Committee Notes to 1970 Amendments to Rule 34 ("The courts have ample power under Rule 26(c) to protect respondent against undue burden or expense, either by restricting discovery or requiring that the discovering party pay costs."). Furthermore, as one court has noted, "the maturation of Rule 26(b)(2) over several decades allows judges to use the limitations of Rule 26(b)(2) with increasing frequency and with an eye toward equity . . . *[which]* undeniably, includes cost-shifting in discovery." United Parcel Service of America, Inc. v. The Net, Inc., 222 F.R.D. 69, 71 (E.D. N.Y. 2004).

The Northern District of Illinois, in particular, has embraced cost-shifting of electronic discovery expenses. *See, e.g.*, Portis v. City of Chicago, 2004 WL 2812084 (N.D. Ill. 2004) ("cost-shifting is not that unusual, particularly in cases involving discovery of electronic evidence"); *Wiginton*, 229 F.R.D. at 577 (shifting 75% of e-discovery costs to the requesting party); Byers v. Illinois State Police, 53 Fed. R. Serv. 3d 740 (N.D. Ill. 2002).

Of the three tests devised by the courts for determining the appropriateness of cost-shifting, the most recent test, announced in

Zubulake v. UBS Warburg LLC, 217 F.R.D. 309, 91 Fair Empl. Prac. Cas. (BNA) 1574 (S.D. N.Y. 2003) ("*Zubulake I*"), now predominates. The Zubulake I court concluded that the following seven factors should be considered, in descending order of importance:

1. the extent to which the requested information is specifically tailored to discover relevant information;
2. the availability of such information from other sources;
3. the total cost of production, compared with the amount in controversy;
4. the total cost of production compared to the resources available to each party;
5. the relative ability of each party to control costs and its incentive to do so;
6. the importance of the issues at stake in the litigation; and
7. the relative benefits to the parties of obtaining the information.

217 F.R.D. at 322. As the *Zubulake I* test has been applied by this Court, Defendants focus on those factors for purposes of this Motion. *See Wiginton*, 229 F.R.D. at 573.

A. COST-SHIFTING IS NECESSARY AND APPROPRIATE BECAUSE THE E-MAILS ARE STORED ON BACKUP TAPES.

Under *Zubulake I*, the threshold test for determining whether cost-shifting may prove appropriate in any particular case is whether the data sought is "inaccessible." *Zubulake I*, 217 F.R.D. at 323 ("[a] court should consider cost-shifting *only* when electronic data is relatively inaccessible, such as in backup tapes") (emphasis in original). *Zubulake I* identifies two categories of electronic data that are considered "inaccessible" and thus appropriate for cost-shifting: (1) backup tapes, and (2) erased, fragmented or damaged data. *Id.* All of the e-mails at issue here are stored on 108 backup tapes. Furthermore, five of the 108 backup tapes contained corrupted data that had to be recovered and restored. Accordingly, the threshold test is met in this case, permitting this Court to allocate a portion of the e-discovery costs to Plaintiffs.

B. THE FACTORS WEIGH HEAVILY IN FAVOR OF COST-SHIFTING.

Taken together, Factors 1 and 2 restate what is better known as the "marginal utility" test, which weighs the relative costs and benefits of the e-discovery requests. *See McPeek*, 202 F.R.D. at

34. These factors are the most important of the seven *Zubulake I* factors, and carry the greatest weight in determining whether e-discovery costs should be shifted. *Zubulake I*, 217 F.R.D. at 322. Here, the "marginal utility" test strongly weighs in favor of cost-shifting due to the overbroad and unduly burdensome nature of Plaintiffs' requests.

In Zubulake v. UBS Warburg LLC, 216 F.R.D. 280, 287, 92 Fair Empl. Prac. Cas. (BNA) 684, 56 Fed. R. Serv. 3d 326 (S.D. N.Y. 2003) ("*Zubulake III*"), the court found that cost-shifting was appropriate even though "the discovery request was narrowly tailored to discover relevant information." In sharp contrast to the present case, the Zubulake plaintiff *narrowed* her original request from communications with all employees to e-mails that were sent to or from only five specified employees. *Id.* at 285. This resulted in a mere 1,075 e-mails after duplicates were eliminated, 600 of which were responsive and were produced. *Id.* at 282.

Here, Plaintiffs expanded their initial e-discovery requests to encompass 108 backup tapes. Plaintiffs also expanded the scope of the search to include 327 persons and 39 different search terms and variations thereof. Compounding the breadth of their requests, Plaintiffs demanded that various search terms beginning or ending with asterisks must be searched for "all forms of a word that have characters where *[each]* asterisk is located." Plaintiffs' search terms included such common words as "cherry*," "pregnan*," "marketing," and "cancer." As an inevitable result of Plaintiffs' choice of these terms, Defendants were forced to review a multitude of irrelevant and unresponsive documents. The search terms, which would ordinarily serve to narrow and focus the documents to be reviewed, instead required Defendants to review everything from resumes and interview schedules to chain e-mails circulating among Defendants' employees.

The numbers demonstrate the overbreadth and impropriety of Plaintiffs' requests including the search terms and methodology. Unlike the approximately 1,000 potentially responsive e-mails in *Zubulake III*, Plaintiffs' overly-broad requests flagged over 151,315 e-mails and attachments to be reviewed for potential production. Only 26,324 of the reviewed e-mails were produced, which amounts to a paltry 17.39%. By contrast, 55.8% of documents were responsive in *Zubulake III*, yet the court still held that 25% of the e-discovery costs should be shifted to the plaintiffs. In *Wiginton*, where the response rate was only 4.5 to 6.5%, the court shifted 75% of the costs of the discovery. 229 F.R.D. at 577. Here, where the response rate falls between these extremes, the marginal utility test weighs in favor of cost-shifting, and it would be both fair and equitable to shift 50% of the e-discovery costs to Plaintiffs.

The fact that the e-mails on the backup tapes were not readily available from other sources does not change this analysis. In *Wiginton*, for example, responsive and relevant documents were "only available through restoring and searching the backup tapes." 229 F.R.D. at 574. Nevertheless, the Court held that "because the search also revealed a significant number of unresponsive documents . . . the marginal utility test weigh[ed] slightly in favor of cost-shifting." *Id.* Here, similarly, the significant number of unresponsive documents resulting from Plaintiffs selection of broad search terms means the marginal utility test weighs in favor of cost shifting.

The third *Zubulake I* factor—the total cost of the production compared with the amount in controversy—also weighs in favor of cost shifting. As set forth above, the costs incurred in responding to Plaintiffs' e-discovery requests exceeded several hundred thousands of dollars. The amount in controversy, however, is entirely speculative at this point. While Plaintiffs will no doubt claim that there is the potential for a multi-million dollar recovery, a similar argument was unavailing in *Wiginton*. In *Wiginton*, the court found that this factor weighed in favor of cost-shifting despite Plaintiffs' claim that that their recovery could potentially be in the "tens of millions:"

Plaintiffs claim that should a class be certified, their class recovery could extend into the tens of millions of dollars. While the Court cannot completely accept Plaintiffs' speculative estimate of its potential damage award, neither can it accept that their claims are worthless . . . . Nevertheless, several hundred thousand dollars for one limited part of discovery is a substantial amount of actual dollars to pay for such a search. Therefore, this factor weighs in favor of cost-shifting. 229 F.R.D. at 575. The total cost of production in this case will meet or even exceed the total in *Wiginton*. Plaintiffs here should similarly bear their fair share of the e-discovery costs.

With respect to the fourth factor—the total cost of production compared to the resources available to each party—the *Zubulake* case recognizes that "it is not unheard of for plaintiff's firms to front huge expenses when multi-million dollar recoveries are in sight." *Zubulake III*, 216 F.R.D. at 288. Furthermore, Tyson is not the only plaintiff in this case. The State of Illinois elected to intervene, and in so doing brought with it all of the State's vast resources. The Illinois State Budget for fiscal year 2006, for example, provides for a total budget in excess of $70 million for the Office of the Attorney General. And the United States government also intervened in this case, providing even deeper pockets to fund the litigation. Plaintiffs' resources also show the need for cost-shifting.

The fifth factor—the relative ability of each party to control costs and its incentive to do so—also weighs in favor of allocating costs to Plaintiffs. The *Wiginton* court held that the scope of the search that a plaintiff requires is an important element in the costs of the production, because "[a] smaller search term list would result in less hits, and less documents that must be transferred to an electronic viewer." *Wiginton*, 229 F.R.D. at 576. *See also* Byers v. Illinois State Police, 53 Fed. R. Serv. 3d 740 (N.D. Ill. 2002) (noting that shifting a portion of the costs to a plaintiff provides an incentive for more focused requests). Here, Plaintiffs' demands encompassed over 300 individuals and 39 search terms, with multiple variations thereof.

In contrast, Defendants have done what they can to control the substantial costs caused by Plaintiffs' requests. The magnitude and complexity of the restoration process required the services of a large consultant, such as Consultant, with the resources and manpower to handle the task in a timely manner. Defendants, in conjunction with Consultant, then selected the most efficient and least costly restoration process available. As discussed above, converting the native files to PDF format, and then uploading them to Consultant's Online Review Application, resulted in substantial savings of both time and money. Indeed, this Court has recognized the need for such Internet-based systems in large-scale electronic discovery. *Wiginton*, 229 F.R.D. at 570. It was simply not feasible for Defendants to handle this document production in a less expensive manner.

The final two factors also support the need to allocate costs to Plaintiffs. Plaintiffs have demanded these restorations, searches, reviews and production in order to benefit their case. Indeed, Plaintiffs are touting and citing certain produced e-mails as supposedly supporting their allegations in this matter. Defendants undertook these processes at the requests of Plaintiffs, who should pay a fair proportion of the resulting costs.

CONCLUSION

For the reasons set forth above and in the Motion, this Court should allocate 50% of the $238,508.66 costs of the backup e-mail production process to Plaintiffs.

Dated: ____

[signature, etc.]

NOTES TO FORM

Commentary

This form is adapted from a motion in The United States of America, ex rel. Cleveland A. Tyson, the State of Illinois, ex rel. Cleveland A. Tyson, the State of Illinois, and the United States of America, Plaintiffs, v. Amerigroup Illinois, Inc. and Amerigroup Corporation, Defendants., 2006 WL 1782970 (N.D. Ill. 2006). Because the fact-intense nature of a cost-shifting motion, the basic facts have been left in the form to illustrate the amount of detail that may be necessary.

§ 19:29 Defendant's opposition to plaintiffs' motion to compel defendant to produce electronic documents in native format with metadata

[Caption]

Defendant's Opposition to Plaintiffs' Motion to Compel Defendant to Produce Electronic Documents in Native Format with Metadata

Defendant respectfully opposes Plaintiff's Motion to Compel Defendant to Produce Electronic Documents in Native Format with Metadata. Defendant respectfully requests that Plaintiffs' motion be denied. To the extent that Plaintiffs' motion is granted, Defendant respectfully requests that the associated costs be shifted to Plaintiffs.

INTRODUCTION

This is a patent case involving United States Patent No. 6,685,941 ("the '941 patent"). As Plaintiffs identified, this case involves a number of issues—invalidity of the '941 patent, unenforceability of the '941 patent due to inequitable conduct, a license granted by Plaintiffs to Defendant to practice the '941 patent, Bristol's ownership rights of the '941 patent pursuant to an agreement with UM, and alleged infringement of the '941 patent.

Plaintiffs have requested Defendant to produce paper and electronic documents. They are amendable to Defendant producing the paper documents converted to TIFF format with search capability. Yet, this same format is not acceptable to Plaintiffs for electronic files. They allege there may be hidden data or data about the documents that is relevant that will not be available in TIFF format (TIFF file images are similar to what an electronic document would look like if printed). Instead, Plaintiffs insist that native files and metadata be produced for every electronic document. However, information associated with native files and metadata for the vast majority of the documents will have marginal, if any, relevance to the claims and the defenses of this litigation. And, insisting upon the wholesale production of native files and metadata for every document is an unreasonable request that would result in an undue burden and undue expense on Defendant, without any likelihood of benefit to Plaintiffs. In fact, courts have held that a requesting party needs to make a showing of *a particularized need* before a motion to compel native files and metadata will be granted. In the spirit of compromise, Defendant proposed to provide Plaintiffs with native files and metadata for specific documents, following Plaintiffs review of the files in TIFF format, within reason. Not happy with this compromise, Plaintiffs filed the present motion, before even reviewing the TIFF versions of the electronic documents.

Plaintiffs state that Defendant "steadfastly has maintained that it will not produce native documents together with their metadata." This is simply not true, as is evidenced by Defendant's letters:

ARGUMENT

I. The Production of Native Files and/or Metadata Upon a Showing of a Particularized Need Is Consistent with Recent Case Law

Plaintiffs insist that native files and metadata be produced for each and every electronic document Defendant intends to produce. Defendant proposed to provide Plaintiffs with native files and metadata for specific documents following Plaintiffs review of the files in TIFF format, within reason. In practice, courts have not been as kind—requiring requesting parties to show *a particularized need* for the native files and/or metadata before ordering them produced.

The Sedona Conference, as one of its fourteen principles for electronic document production, states that "[u]nless it is material to resolving the dispute, there is no obligation to preserve or produce metadata absent agreement of the parties or order of the court." THE SEDONA PRINCIPLES: BEST PRACTICES RECOMMENDATIONS & PRINCIPLES FOR ADDRESSING ELECTRONIC DOCUMENT PRODUCTION (The Sedona Conference Working Group Series, July 2005 Version). The Sedona Conference recognizes that information associated with native files and metadata is sometimes inaccurate, and that in most cases it need not be produced (*Id.* at 46–47).

II. The Information Contained in Native Files and/or Metadata Is Not Relevant in Most Cases

The fact that the information contained in native files and/or metadata is not relevant in most cases (and in fact is incorrect in many cases) militates against a wholesale production of native files and metadata. Plaintiffs argue that "whenever a document is relevant, it is almost certainty that the identity of the document's author and editors, the date of its creation and modification, the title of the document, and the directory location of the document would also be relevant or reasonably calculated to lead to the discovery of admissible evidence" (P. Br. at 5). This is contrary to what courts and The Sedona Conference have concluded. For example, the fact that a letter dated February 10, 1999 was actually created on February 8, 1999 or that a secretary was the typist is not relevant. However, should Plaintiffs identify a particular document where the creation date, author, or other issues of authenticity are legitimately subject to question, Defendant's proposal provides a remedy to this concern. Therefore, just because Defendant is producing a document in TIFF format does not make the native files or metadata of the document relevant to the claims or defenses of the litigation.

III. The Burden and Expense of Plaintiffs' Request Outweigh Its Likely Benefit

Plaintiffs' motion should be denied as the burden and expense that would be incurred by Defendant would be undue, particularly in light of the minimal, if any, benefit that would be conferred upon Plaintiffs by the production of native files and metadata for every electronic file produced.

Defendant is currently reviewing the electronic files in imaged (TIFF) format. This allows the attorneys to review the documents without opening a software application other than the image viewer. Based on the document review performed thus far, Defendant estimates that the review of the documents in imaged format will take approximately one to two minutes per document (that is, to determine whether or not the document is relevant, privileged, confidential, or highly confidential).

If documents are to be reviewed in their native format (the format requested by Plaintiffs), it is necessary to first open the appropriate software application (e.g., to review a Microsoft Word document, the reviewer first has to open the document in the Microsoft Word application). Then, if the next document happens to be a Microsoft Excel document, the reviewer would need to open the Microsoft Excel application. This alone would add a significant quantity of time to the document review process, as the review is expected to encompass approximately 6,500,000 pages (approximately 650,000 documents). After the correct software application is opened, then the reviewer needs to determine if there is information present that would not otherwise be printed. For example, with respect to a Microsoft Word application, the reviewer needs to turn on the feature that allows tracked changes to be viewed before being able review this information. Then, the reviewer would need to review the metadata associated with the document. Defendant expects the impact of reviewing the files in their native format along with the information available from the native files and metadata will increase the time to review each document from one to two minutes to two to three minutes. While this may seem insignificant, as Defendant expects to review approximately 650,000 documents, this equates to an estimated increase of 5,400 man-hours to the review process.

Defendant's outside counsel is attempting to minimize the cost of the review, but the additional man-hours are expected to yield an increase of at least approximately $500,000 to the document review process This does not include the additional costs associated with Defendant's counsel obtaining the native files and producing them to Plaintiffs, which is expected to exceed $100,000. It would be far less burdensome for the requesting party to identify the files for which it needs metadata or native files.

Plaintiffs argue that the production of native files and metadata for select documents "would not aid in searching and understanding the montage of Defendant's production." But, Plaintiffs have not identified a tangible benefit that understanding the montage of the production would provide them nor how the montage is relevant to the claims or defenses. They state that they would need to "attempt to divine—by complete guesswork those documents for which the original electronic file might contain relevant metadata or other printed information." But, Defendant is not suggesting divining or guesswork; rather, Defendant is suggesting that the Plaintiffs identify specific documents for which they would like to review the native files and metadata. To the extent that native files and metadata do exist, Defendant will provide it, within reason.

Plaintiffs also state that the identification of specific files for which they need the native files or metadata "reveals attorney work product about which documents plaintiffs are focusing on, which they may intend to use for deposition, and the like." But, this is nothing new—it is necessary to reveal such information throughout litigation. For example, the parties exchanged keyword search terms that they view as important for the case for the purpose of filtering electronic documents, and Plaintiffs have identified documents that they are focusing on for their infringement contentions.

In light of the fact that most of the information associated with the native files and metadata for the electronic documents is of limited evidentiary value and reviewing it can waste litigation resources, and in light of the fact that most of the information available from native files or metadata is not relevant, the burden and expense is undue. Moreover, as Defendant has agreed to provide Plaintiffs with the native files and metadata to the extent that they make a reasonably request after Plaintiffs review of the documents in imaged format, this undue expense is also unnecessary.

IV. Bristol Requests that Plaintiffs Be Asked to Bear the Cost Burden to the Extent that Bristol Is Compelled to Review and Produce the Native Files and Metadata

As illustrated above, it is Defendant's position that the burden and expense of producing native files and metadata for every electronic document outweighs the small, if any, benefit received by Plaintiffs. Therefore, to the extent that the Court grants Plaintiffs' motion, Bristol respectfully requests that Plaintiffs be asked to bear the financial burden associated with the Bristol's review and production of the information.

While this Court is not limited to performing the cost-shifting analysis based on a particular set of factors, the Southern District of New York has set forth a commonly-cited seven factor test to determining whether cost-shifting is appropriate, weighed more-or-less in the following order:

1. The extent to which the request is specifically tailored to discover relevant information;
2. The availability of such information from other sources;
3. The total cost of production, compared to the amount in controversy;
4. The total cost of production, compared to the resources available to each party;
5. The relative ability of each party to control costs and its incentive to do so;
6. The importance of the issues at stake in the litigation; and
7. The relative benefits to the parties of obtaining the information.

Zubulake v. UBS Warburg LLC, 217 F.R.D. 309, 322–24, 91

Fair Empl. Prac. Cas. (BNA) 1574 (S.D. N.Y. 2003). While *Zubulake* addressed the situation where the electronic data is not accessible, cost-shifting is not limited to situations where the electronic data is not accessible.

Regarding the first factor, Plaintiffs request is not specifically tailored to discover relevant information. The information associated with native files and metadata is rarely relevant (see above). And, Plaintiffs are requesting the information for every electronic file produced. This factor weighs in favor of cost-shifting.

Regarding the second factor, the relevant information will likely be available from other sources. For example, the author of a letter, date of the letter, and recipients are likely to be on the letter itself (which will be provided in TIFF format). This factor weighs in favor of cost shifting.

Regarding the third factor, while the Plaintiffs have not identified an amount in controversy, the cost for the review and production of this information is not insignificant—expected to be at least approaching $500,000; with at least another $100,000 to obtain and produce the native files. Regarding the fourth factor, while Defendant has significant resources, these resources should not be wasted. These factors weigh in favor of cost shifting.

Regarding the fifth factor, Plaintiffs can control the cost by requesting native files or metadata for specified files, but they have no incentive to do so unless they bear the financial burden. To the contrary, during its document review, Defendant will be reviewing all of the information simultaneously and therefore has an incentive to control cost. This factor weighs in favor of cost shifting.

Regarding the sixth factor, while the issues of this litigation are important, the production of native files and metadata is not expected to have any effect on the outcome of the litigation. Regarding the seventh factor, the benefit expected to be conferred upon either party by producing all of the native files and metadata is expected to be minimal. Therefore, these factors are neutral.

Looking at these factors as a whole, cost shifting is appropriate.

CONCLUSION

Based on the foregoing, Defendant respectfully requests that Plaintiffs' motion be denied. In the alternative, Defendant respectfully requests that the cost associated with obtaining, reviewing, and producing the native files and metadata be shifted to the Plaintiffs.

Dated: ____

[signature, etc.]

NOTES TO FORM

Commentary

This form is adapted from a motion in Repligen Corporation and the Regents of the University of Michigan, Plaintiffs, v. Bristol-Myers Squibb Company, Defendant., 2007 WL 684265 (E.D. Tex. 2007).

§ 19:30 Order to quash notice to take depositions and subpoenas

[Caption]

This matter is pending on a motion by the *[party]* to quash certain of *[party's]* notice to take depositions. A memorandum filed this date is incorporated in and made a part of this order. Accordingly,

IT IS HEREBY ORDERED that the motion of the defendant is granted and the notice to take the deposition of *[name]* is quashed on the condition that *[for example]* an officer or managing agent of the *[party]* who has knowledge of the issues in controversy be directed to appear and have his/her deposition taken at the place indicated in *[party's]* motion within ten days from this date.

IT IS FURTHER ORDERED that the subpoena directed to *[name]* directing him/her to produce *[describe]* is also quashed.

Dated: ____

____

Judge

§ 19:31 Order extending time within which to answer requests for admissions

[Caption]

This cause was heard on the motion of the *[plaintiff] [defendant]* for additional time, through *[date]*, within which to answer the *[defendant's] [plaintiff's]* Requests for Admissions and the motion having been considered by the Court,

IT IS ORDERED that *[plaintiff's] [defendant's]* motion be and is hereby granted and *[plaintiff] [defendant]* is hereby allowed through *[date]*, within which to answer the [defendant's *[plaintiff's]* Requests for Admissions.

Dated: ____

____

Judge

[signature etc.]

§ 19:32 Order sealing answers to interrogatories

[Caption]

The answers to the interrogatories filed in this matter by *[plaintiff] [defendant]* on *[date]* are hereby sealed and the parties and parties' counsel are admonished not to disclose their contents to anyone.

Dated: ____

____

Judge

§ 19:33 Defendant's motion for protective order regarding re-creation of backup server tapes

[Caption]

Defendant *[Name's]* Motion for Protective Order Regarding Re-Creation of Backup Server Tapes

Defendant *[name]*, through its undersigned counsel and pursuant to *[rules]*, hereby moves the Court for the entry of a Protective Order with regard to the recreation of __ backup server tapes. Defendant is filing the present motion in the abundance of caution in light of the impending close of discovery.

As required to do by *[rules]*, prior to filing the instant motion, Defendant disclosed to Plaintiff the issues addressed herein and since that time, the parties have been attempting to arrive at a resolution of the present dispute. Defendant will advise the Court immediately should the parties resolve the issues addressed in this motion.

Factual Background

1. On *[date]*, Plaintiff served Defendant with its First Request for Production of Documents ("First Request"). Defendant responded to the First Request on *[date]*, and in connection with the First Request has produced over ____ pages of documents.

2. Prior to the *[date]*, pursuant to *[rule]*, both parties

exchanged additional documents. As a result of such supplemental productions and in light of the forthcoming holiday, on *[date]*, Defendant filed a Motion for a Two-Week Enlargement of the Discovery Deadline of *[date]*, in order to confirm that all responsive documents, electronic or otherwise, had been produced in response to the First Request.

3. On *[date]*, the Court granted Defendant's Motion for a Two-Week Enlargement of the Discovery Deadline. Accordingly, the discovery period is now set to close on *[date]*.

4. In connection with the confirmation process that all responsive documents to the First Request had been produced, Defendant has recently learned of the existence of __ backup server tapes which, after a reconstruction process, may possibly have responsive documents that may not have been previously produced in the instant action.

5. By way of background, shortly after being served with the lawsuit, Defendant's Law Department identified close to __ individuals who were involved with Plaintiff's account. The Law Department sent each of the identified individuals who were still employed with the Defendant, a Notice to Preserve explicitly instructing them to preserve any documentation, including electronic documents, that had anything to do with *[name]* Medical Center. Thereafter, the Law Department obtained responsive documents that have been produced to Plaintiff.

6. As part of its standard operating procedure, Defendant backs up approximately ____ servers on a weekly basis. The backup server tapes contain not just e-mails, but Defendant's entire computer network. Thus, each backup tape contains a possible mixture of e-mails and other data maintained on Defendant's computer network. The backed-up e-mails include the non-deleted e-mails for its current employees as well as the non-deleted e-mails for its former employees. If a user has deleted an e-mail prior to the end of the week backup date, such an e-mail will not be on the backup tape. (If person A sends an e-mail to person B and both users delete the exchange of e-mails prior to the weekly backup date, the e-mails will not be on the backup tapes regardless of whether the persons were still employed by the company at the time the Notice to Preserve was issued.) Thus, by the time the Notice to Preserve was issued, the e-mails for the former employees were already on the Defendant's backup server tapes.

7. Accordingly, along with the Notice to Preserve, the Law Department sent a simultaneous request to Defendant's IT Department that it extract from the backup server tapes any e-mail data related to Plaintiff generated by the close to thirty individuals previously identified as having had some involvement

with Plaintiff's account. Unfortunately, Defendant has just recently confirmed to counsel that the IT Department inadvertently failed to undertake this step.

8. Defendant's IT Department still has the backup server tapes in its possession. The total number of backup tapes dating back to *[date]*, is ____. In order to determine which tape contains backup e-mails, the library for each tape must first be examined. Once a tape has been identified as having backup e-mails, the e-mails need to be restored and then reviewed for responsiveness to the discovery requests served in the underlying lawsuit. Moreover, without reviewing all of the tapes and then reconstructing those containing backups of the e-mail server, Defendant cannot determine which users' e-mails are on a particular tape. Thus, there is no manner by which to limit the recreation process to just those users who were no longer employed by the company at the time the lawsuit was filed.

9. After the possible responsive documents, if any, are identified and reconstructed, any previously produced e-mails would have to be removed in order to avoid duplicate production. Lastly, any responsive, but previously not produced, e-mails would have to be reviewed for privilege. At this juncture, Defendant cannot determine whether in fact there are any responsive documents on the backup server tapes and, if there are any such e-mails, whether they are merely duplicates of what has already been produced in the litigation. Only by examining, re-creating and reviewing the backup server tapes can this possibility be explored and laid to rest.

10. The processes described in the foregoing paragraphs are extremely expensive and time-consuming. The preliminary estimates that Defendant has received from outside data reconstruction vendors to review each of the backup server tapes to determine which of the tapes contain backup e-mails, and thereafter re-create the e-mails, review the e-mails for possible responsiveness, and eliminate all previously produced e-mails all exceed $________, not including attorney and Paralegal review time. Additionally, with the use of the outside vendors, completion of the foregoing processes would take between three to six weeks.

11. As soon as undersigned counsel received all of the foregoing information, the same was provided to Plaintiff's counsel. Indeed, on *[date]*, Defendant's counsel provided Plaintiff's counsel with detailed correspondence explaining the Notice to Preserve process, the IT Department's inadvertent oversight, and the costs involved with recreating the backup server tapes in the search for possible additional documents. On *[date]*, Plaintiff's counsel

requested additional follow-up information from Defendant as to the identity of the approximately __ individuals identified as having some involvement with Plaintiff's account. Such information was provided to Plaintiff's counsel on the same date. Plaintiff has not yet advised whether it wishes to have the backup server tapes recreated and, if so, the exact scope of such a recreation. In light of the undue burden and extraordinary costs involved with such an undertaking, Defendant respectfully submits that, if Plaintiff does elect to insist on such a course of action, the costs involved with such a procedure should be borne by the Plaintiff, and not the Defendant.

Argument and Citation of Authority

I. Re-Creation of the Data on the Backup Sever Tapes Is Not Reasonably Accessible and, Therefore, an Undue Burden

Rule 26(b)(2)(B) of the Federal Rules of Civil Procedure provides that:

> A party need not provide discovery of electronically stored information from sources that the party identifies as not reasonably accessible because of undue burden or cost. On motion to compel discovery or for a protective order, the party from whom discovery is sought must show that the information is not reasonably accessible because of undue burden or cost. If that showing is made, the court may nonetheless order discovery from such sources if the requesting party shows good cause, considering the limitations of Rule 26(b)(2)(C). The court may specify conditions for the discovery.

The facts of the present situation are similar to those addressed by the court in *Cognex Corp. v. Electro Scientific Industries, Inc.*, 2002 WL 32309413 (D. Mass. 2002). At issue in *Cognex*, were 820 of the defendant's electronic backup tapes, covering a period from 1992 through 2001, which had not been searched yet by the defendant for relevant documents. *Cognex Corp. v. Electro Scientific Industries, Inc.*, 2002 WL 32309413, *1 (D. Mass. 2002). The plaintiff not only sought to compel the recreation and search of the backup tapes but offered to bear the "full burden and costs of such a search." *Cognex Corp. v. Electro Scientific Industries, Inc.*, 2002 WL 32309413, *3 (D. Mass. 2002). Nevertheless, the Court denied the Motion to Compel. In deciding not to compel the defendant to search the 820 backup tapes, the *Cognex* Court emphasized the following factors:

- The defendant had already conducted an extensive search for relevant documents.
- There was no evidence that the defendant had consciously destructed documents or that there were serious discrepancies in the discovery.

• The fact that the defendant disclosed the backup tapes during this late stage of the case was not indicative of bad faith.

• The case was not one where one would expect the most relevant e-mails to be deleted and transferred to backup tapes.

• There was nothing inherently wrong with the defendant, which was a big corporation, adopting a backup policy; there was no suggestion of any improper action by the defendant in either the adoption or practice of such a policy.

Cognex Corp. v. Electro Scientific Industries, Inc., 2002 WL 32309413, *5 (D. Mass. 2002).

All of the above factors are present in the instant case. First, as described above, Defendant identified the individuals who were involved with Plaintiff's account and sent a Notice to Preserve to those individuals who were still employed by the company. It then had its Law Department gather responsive documents. Subsequent to this process, as further individuals have been identified as having been involved with the case, the documents and e-mails of such individuals have been produced through supplemental productions. In this regard, to date, Defendant has produced over __ pages of documents in connection with a single-count breach of contract claim.

Second, there is no evidence that Defendant has consciously destroyed documents. To the contrary, the backup server tapes are still in the Defendant's possession and the Defendant has voluntarily disclosed the existence of the same.

Third, although Defendant voluntarily disclosed the existence of the backup tapes at the close of the discovery period; the timing of such a disclosure does not, in and of itself, indicate any bad faith by the Defendant. Moreover, the issue is not one that was created by virtue of the timing of the self-disclosure. Due to the costly and cumbersome process involved with examining and re-creating the backup tapes and the existence of the former employees' e-mails on the backup tapes since the inception of the lawsuit, the issue, by necessity, is one that would have had to be addressed at some point during the course of this litigation.

Fourth, this is not the type of case were one would expect the most relevant e-mails to be deleted and transferred to backup tapes. The sheer volume of e-mails and documents already produced vitiate any such possible inference.

Fifth, there is nothing inherently wrong with Defendant's policy with regard to its backup server tapes and, specifically, with regard to its policy of having its former employees' e-mails saved on backup server tapes. Indeed, most companies recycle backup tapes after a certain period of time; Defendant does not.

Therefore, this is not the case where Defendant consciously set out to devise a process to conceal or frustrate Plaintiff's ability to obtain responsive documents in connection with its lawsuit. Rather, this is a case where possible additional responsive documents are, and from the inception of the case have been, inaccessible due to the undue burden and costs of recreating data from backup server tapes. As noted by the court in *Cognex*, "[t]here is certainly no controlling authority for the proposition that restoring all backup tapes is necessary in every case." *Cognex Corp. v. Electro Scientific Industries, Inc.*, 2002 WL 32309413, *4 (D. Mass. 2002). Here, Defendant has turned over data that was reasonably accessible at the time the lawsuit was filed and throughout the course of the litigation. It should not, however, be required to re-create and turn over data which was never in an accessible format in order to ensure that every possible relevant document has been disclosed. *Cognex,* 2002 WL at *5 ("[a]t some point, the adversary system needs to say 'enough is enough' and recognize that the costs of seeking every relevant piece of discovery is not reasonable"). Accordingly, Defendant respectfully submits that it should not be required to examine the __ backup server tapes and recreate the e-mail date contained within such tapes.

II. If the Court Orders the Re-Creation of the Backup Server Tapes, the Costs Should Be Shifted to the Plaintiff

In the event that the Court concludes that the backup server tapes do have to be reexamined and re-created, Defendant respectfully submits that the costs of such an endeavor should be shifted to the Plaintiff. The factors to be considered by a court in a cost-shifting analysis were set forth by Judge Scheindlin in *Zubulake v. UBS Warburg LLC*, 217 F.R.D. 309, 91 Fair Empl. Prac. Cas. (BNA) 1574 (S.D. N.Y. 2003). They are as follows:

(1) The extent to which the request is specifically tailored to discover relevant information;

(2) The availability of such information from other sources;

(3) The total cost of production, compared to the amount in controversy;

(4) The total cost of production, compared to the resources available to each party;

(5) The relative ability of each party to control costs and its incentive to do so;

(6) The importance of the issues at stake in the litigation; and

(7) The relative benefits to the parties of obtaining the information.

217 F.R.D. at 322.

According to the court in *Zubulake*, the first two factors, known as the "marginal utility test," are the most important. The marginal utility test provides: "The more likely it is that the backup tape contains information that is relevant to a claim or defense, the fairer it is that the *[responding party]* search at its own expense. The less likely it is, the more unjust it would be to make the *[responding party]* search at its own expense. The difference is 'at the margin.' " *Zubulake v. UBS Warburg LLC*, 217 F.R.D. 309, 91 Fair Empl. Prac. Cas. (BNA) 1574 (S.D. N.Y. 2003). The second group of factors addresses the cost issues." These factors include the total cost of production compared to the amount in controversy, the total cost of production compared to the resources available to each party, and the relative ability of each party to control costs and its incentive to do so. *Zubulake v. UBS Warburg LLC*, 217 F.R.D. at 323. The next factor is the importance of the litigation, which rarely comes into play. *Zubulake v. UBS Warburg LLC*, 217 F.R.D. at 323. The last, and least important, factor is the "relative benefits of production as between the requesting and producing parties . . . because it is fair to presume that the response to a discovery request generally benefits the requesting party." *Zubulake v. UBS Warburg LLC*, 217 F.R.D. at 323.

With regard to the first two factors, Defendant submits that a request for e-mails regarding all possible individuals involved with Plaintiff's account is not specifically tailored to the discovery of relevant information. Moreover, given the duplicative and repetitive nature of e-mail communications, it is highly likely that an e-mail from a former employee that that was sent to a current employee but presently resides in one of the backup servers has already been produced as part of the e-mails retrieved and disclosed from the current employees. Therefore, the cost of re-creating the possible former employee to former employee e-mails in comparison to the amount in controversy becomes of utmost importance. As set forth above, the costs of reviewing the backup tapes and re-creating the stored e-mails, not including any attorney and paralegal time, exceeds $____. The amount in controversy in this matter, according to Plaintiff's own Initial Disclosures and Interrogatory responses is in excess of $____, of which only approximately $____ constitute non-consequential, compensatory damages. Thus the backup server recreation costs could actually equal or exceed Plaintiff's claim for compensatory damages. Defendant therefore respectfully submits that the possible recreation costs are completely out of proportion with Plaintiff's possible recovery in the case. Accordingly, if Plaintiff wishes to have the backup server tapes recreated, this Court should require it to bear the cost of such a process.

That Defendant might have the financial resources to bear the recreation costs of more than $____ should be of minimal importance. No company, regardless of size, should be required to recreate inaccessible data when the cost of such an undertaking bears no resemblance to the compensatory damages in the case.

Defendant recognizes that the Court in *Zublake* emphasized the importance of an extensive factual analysis to support a cost-shifting conclusion and, in this regard, first ordered a sample recreation of a certain number of backup server tapes in order to make a factual-based determination as to all of the factors. Although Plaintiff has not, to date, offered such a suggestion, depending on the parameters of such a sample, Defendant might not be opposed to such a course of action.

Conclusion

For the reasons set forth above, Defendant submits that it should not be required to undertake the extraordinary costs of recreating backup server tapes to eliminate the possibility of additionally relevant e-mails that may have not been previously produced in the litigation. To the extent the Court concludes otherwise, Defendant respectfully requests that, in light of the lack of proportionality between the recreation costs and the amount in controversy, the costs of the recreation process be borne by the Plaintiff.

Dated: __

[signature, etc.]

NOTES TO FORM

Commentary

This form is adapted from a motion in Mount Sinai Medical Center of Florida, INC., a Florida not-for-profit corporation, Plaintiff, v. McKesson Medication Management, LLC, a foreign limited liability company, Defendant., 2006 WL 4034460 (S.D. Fla. 2006).

§ 19:34 Order governing discovery of deleted data

[Caption]

Order Governing Discovery of Deleted Data

The following is a protocol for allowing discovery of deleted files and documents in computer memories. In general, the Court previously ordered *[plaintiff]* to select and to pay an expert in recovery of such information, and to have that expert serve as an officer of the court and to turn over the recovered information to *[defendant's]* counsel for appropriate review to supplement *[plaintiff's]* discovery responses. The court also set a further hearing on the matter for resolution of further details. *[Plaintiff]* has identified an appropriate expert to carry out the inspection of the relevant computers; *[defendant]* has identified the computer in question; and counsel for the parties conferred and drafted a proposed order. The court heard argument on several disputed details on *[date]*. Pursuant to the parties' draft and the arguments presented, the court now orders as follows:

1. This inspection process applies to the following computers: *[specify]*.

2. Pursuant to the *[plaintiff's]* designation and *[defendant's]* statement that it has no objections, *[expert]* is hereby appointed as an officer of the court to carry out the inspection and copying of data from *[defendant's]* designated computers. From the date of this order, all communications between *[expert]* and *[plaintiff's]* counsel shall take place either in the presence of *[defendant's]* counsel or through written or electronic communication with a copy to *[defendant's]* counsel.

3. Before carrying out any inspections pursuant to this order, *[expert]* shall sign a protective order in the form adopted previously by the court in this action. Execution of such order shall be deemed acceptance of appointment pursuant to this entry.

4. On or before *[date]*, *[expert]* shall inspect *[defendant's]* designated computers and create an exact copy or bit stream image of the hard drives of those computers. The court intends that the inspection be carried out to minimize disruption of and interference with *[defendant's]* business, and that *[defendant]* and its counsel shall cooperate in providing access to the designated computers.

5. On or before *[date]*, *[expert]* shall recover from the designated computers all available word-processing documents, incoming and outgoing electronic mail messages, PowerPoint or similar presentations, spreadsheets, and other files, including but not limited to those files that were deleted. Files making up operating systems and higher-level systems are not to be duplicated. The copying is to be limited to the types of files reasonably likely to contain material potentially relevant to this case.

6. On or before *[date]*, *[expert]* shall provide such documents in a reasonably convenient form to *[defendant's]* counsel, along with, to the extent possible, (a) information showing when any recovered deleted files were deleted, and (b) information about the deletion and the contents of deleted files that could not be

recovered. The court shall also be provided with a copy of the information in (a) and (b).

7. On or before *[date]*, *[expert]* shall file a report with the court setting forth the scope of the work performed and describing in general terms (without disclosing the contents) the volume and types of records provided to *[defendant's]* counsel.

8. On or before *[date]*, *[defendant's]* counsel shall review the records for privilege and responsiveness, shall appropriately supplement *[defendant's]* response to discovery requests, and shall send by overnight delivery to *[plaintiff's]* counsel all responsive and non-privileged documents and a privilege log reflecting which documents were withheld pursuant to the attorney-client privilege or work product immunity.

9. On or before 30 days after either a judgment becomes final and non-appealable or a settlement agreement has been executed by both parties, *[expert]* shall destroy the records copied from the designated computers and shall confirm such destruction to the satisfaction of defendant.

10. In accepting appointment as officers of the court for purposes of this assignment, *[expert]* agrees that it shall be compensated for its time and expenses only by *[plaintiff]*, and that it shall have no right to seek reimbursement or compensation from *[defendant]* or the United States.

Dated: ________

____
Judge

Index